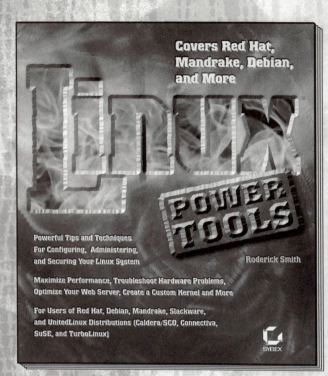

What's on the CD?

This book includes a copy of the Publisher's Edition of Red Hat® Linux® from Red Hat, Inc., which you may use in accordance with the license agreement found at: http://www.redhat.com/licenses. Official Red Hat® Linux®, which you may purchase from Red Hat, includes the complete Red Hat® Linux® distribution, Red Hat's documentation, and may include technical support for Red Hat® Linux®. You also may purchase or download technical support from Red Hat. You may purchase Red Hat® Linux® and technical support from Red Hat through the company's web site (www.redhat.com) or its toll-free number 1.888.REDHAT1.

System Requirements

- ◆ Pentium CPU or higher—Pentium 200MHz for text mode, Pentium II 400MHz for graphical mode

- ◆ 64MB of RAM for text mode, 128MB of RAM minimum for a graphical workstation—192MB is recommended

- ◆ 475MB of hard disk space—2GB or more will greatly enhance your freedom to experiment with Linux

- ◆ Bootable CD-ROM Drive or Floppy

- ◆ A backup of your current system in case of emergency

- ◆ A supported video card and monitor

- ◆ A keyboard and mouse

- ◆ Red Hat Linux supports most modern Intel-compatible PC hardware. If you have questions about hardware compatibility with Red Hat Linux 9, check the hardware compatibility list at http://hardware.redhat.com/hcl.

Software Support

Components of the supplemental Software and any offers associated with them may be supported by the specific Owner(s) of that material but they are not supported by SYBEX. Information regarding any available support may be obtained from the Owner(s) using the information provided in the appropriate README files or listed elsewhere on the media.

Should the manufacturer(s) or other Owner(s) cease to offer support or decline to honor any offer, SYBEX bears no responsibility. This notice concerning support for the Software is provided for your information only. SYBEX is not the agent or principal of the Owner(s), and SYBEX is in no way responsible for providing any support for the Software, nor is it liable or responsible for any support provided, or not provided, by the Owner(s).

Contents

Bonus Chapters on the Web

Web Chapter 1: Generic Linux Certifications

Web Chapter 2: Red Hat Certifications

Web Chapter 3: More Information Online

Web Chapter 4: GNU General Public License

Web Chapter 5: Red Hat Linux Packages By Group

NOTE *The web chapters are bonus material provided on the Sybex website (www.sybex.com). They can be found and downloaded by navigating to the Sybex website and doing a search for Mastering Red Hat Linux 9, then clicking the Downloads link.*

Introduction

ACCORDING TO *Business Week* (March 3, 2003), Linux is "one of the few technology products that's booming in the midst of the lengthy and distressing tech malaise."

Red Hat Linux is the leading Linux distribution. In this book, we give you the help you need to use Red Hat Linux 9 productively in business and in life—as a server or as a desktop operating system.

Linux is inexpensive. Linux is reliable. Linux is secure. With Linux, you can get the computing applications that you need—for a fraction of the cost of other operating systems. You need not worry about licensing fees. You can build a custom solution with the tools at hand.

In this time of stagnant budgets in information technology, the corporate world is getting more bang for the buck by moving toward Linux. Leading names in the financial sector, such as Goldman Sachs, Merrill Lynch, and Morgan Stanley, are moving toward Linux. Big online companies such as Amazon and Google use Linux to power their systems. IBM and Hewlett-Packard are generating billions of dollars of revenue from Linux. The list goes on.

While the heart of Linux is the command-line interface, Red Hat has developed a series of excellent graphical tools to help the administrators of other operating systems make the transition. Linux is built for networking. It is customized for TCP/IP, the language of the Internet.

Red Hat Linux is the most popular Linux distribution. It includes applications such as office suites and specialized services that can easily cost hundreds of dollars per computer.

Linux is about freedom of choice. You can download Red Hat Linux 9 for free. You can get it for a nominal fee from third parties. You can purchase it, with support and documentation from Red Hat. We explain each of these options at the end of this introduction. But no matter which version you are working with, this book will help you get the most from Red Hat Linux.

What's in This Book

I've divided this book into eight parts, each addressing a different set of skills that can help you become productive in Red Hat Linux. You can read this book from cover to cover, or use it as a resource when you need to know more about a specific skill.

Installing Red Hat Linux   In Chapter 1 we explain the roles that Linux can play as a desktop, as a small business server, and as a server for the enterprise. If you're planning to install Linux on multiple computers, you'll want to read Chapter 2 carefully, because you need to be sure that your hardware is ready for Linux. While Chapter 3 focuses on installing Red Hat Linux locally using the graphical user interface, Chapter 4 shows you how you can install

Linux over a network. In Chapter 5, we show you how to automate the installation process, which can be a great help if you're going to install Red Hat Linux on a group of computers.

Linux Fundamentals   To learn Linux in-depth, you need to know how to use the command-line interface. Once you learn how to navigate the file system in Chapter 6, the command-line interface can be your friend. In Chapter 7, we guide you through the skills you need to organize Linux filesystems. Once you've read Chapter 8, you'll know how to make the command-line shell work for you.

Basic Linux Administration   Because Linux is built for networking, it is also built with a number of administrative tools. Administrators of this multiuser system need to know how to create, organize, and manage users and groups (Chapter 9). We show you how to use the Red Hat Package Manager and up2date to install, upgrade, and manage applications securely (Chapter 10).

As an administrator, you'll need to go "under the hood" with the boot process (Chapter 11) and the Linux kernel (Chapter 12). You'll also want to know how to automate, manage, and troubleshoot basic services (Chapter 13), as well as back up your system (Chapter 14).

X Window Management   Desktop users need the graphical user interface (GUI). While ordinary users should never have to tinker with the basic X Window configuration (Chapter 15), administrators must know how to make it sing. This is the foundation for the two major Linux GUI desktop environments: GNOME (Chapter 16) and KDE (Chapter 17). You can install a number of useful applications, including multiple office suites on either desktop environment (Chapter 18). Administrators who are less comfortable with the command-line interface may appreciate the graphical Red Hat administration tools discussed in Chapter 19.

Basic Linux Networking   Linux is built on TCP/IP, the language of the Internet. We guide you through the basics of TCP/IP as it applies to Linux. You can learn about basic TCP/IP protocols in Chapter 20, and the commands you need to apply them to your local area network (LAN) in Chapter 21. And we guide you through the fundamentals of network security in Chapter 22.

Linux Network Services   Linux is built to serve all of the computers on a network. As an administrator, you need to know how to configure remote access (Chapter 23). TCP/IP networks require domain names and IP addresses, which are organized in DNS and DHCP servers (Chapter 24). Users on a network will want to print (Chapter 25) and use e-mail (Chapter 26).

Linux File Sharing Services   Users share files between their computers. There are a number of ways to share files in Red Hat Linux. You can set up an FTP server just for files (Chapter 27). If you're administering a network of computers that are running Linux and other Unix-style operating systems, you can share directories and configuration files with NFS and NIS servers (Chapter 28). If your network includes Microsoft Windows computers, you can make your Linux computer look like a client or a server on that network (Chapter 29). Finally, Apache is the most popular web server on the Internet and is optimized for Linux (Chapter 30).

A Bonus Certification Primer   On the Sybex website (www.sybex.com), you'll find bonus materials on the variety of Linux certifications. Many readers learn Linux to improve their job prospects. Today, that goes hand in hand with Linux certification. The three major distribution-neutral Linux certification programs are CompTIA's Linux+ exams, SAIR's Linux Certified Professional and Administrator exams, and LPI's Level I exams. Web Chapter 1 provides an overview of these exams targeted at Linux users with six months to two years of experience. Web Chapter 2 focuses on the requirements for the Red Hat certifications: the Red Hat Certified Technician and the Red Hat Certified Engineer.

Appendicies   This book may be just one part of your journey into the world of Linux. The Appendix in the book details a few of the commands that every administrator should know at the command-line interface. On the Sybex website (`www.sybex.com`), you'll find three appendices of additional bonus material: Web Chapter 3, More Information Online, is a very brief list of available online resources; Web Chapter 4, GNU General Public License, is a copy of the GNU General Public License; and finally, Web Chapter 5, Red Hat Linux Packages By Group, is a detailed look at the `comps.xml` file, which provides the foundation for Red Hat Linux installations.

Conventions Used in This Book

If you're new to the world of Sybex books, you need to know about a number of conventions that we use.

- Linux commands such as `ls` and files such as `/etc/passwd` within the main body of a paragraph are offset as `inline code`.

- Longer lists of commands and code are organized in separate lines. The command prompt is shown as a hash mark (#).

  ```
  # mkbootdisk 2.4.20-8
  ```

- Hash marks are also commonly used in a program file to indicate a comment; I've done my best to make the context clear.

  ```
  # System initialization
  ```

- Sometimes the code you enter depends on a variable such as the version number, in which case the code is italicized:

  ```
  # mkbootdisk kernel_version
  ```

- Due to publishing constraints, continuation arrows (➡) break a single command line such as

  ```
  passwd chat = *New*password* %n\n *Retype*new*password* %n\n *passwd:
  ➡*all*authentication*tokens*updated*successfully*
  ```

  into two different lines in the book. It still is a command that you enter on one line.

- *Italics* generally represent new terms.

- If an item is in bold in code, it represents what you might type in at the command-line interface to get the given output:

  ```
  # /usr/lib/yp/ypinit -m
  ```

  ```
  At this point, we have to construct a list of the hosts which will run NIS servers.
  RH9 is in the list of NIS server hosts. Please continue to add the names for the
  other hosts, one per line. When you are done with the list, type a <control D>.
  ```

◆ + signs indicate key combinations. For example, Ctrl+Alt+F2 means that you should press these keys simultaneously.

◆ With URLs, I've omitted the `http://` and the trailing slash for brevity (and to prevent bad line breaks). For example, the home page of the Linux Documentation Project appears as `www.tldp.org`, where it technically should be `http://www.tldp.org/`. Fortunately, with the defaults in web browsers and server software such as Apache, this generally makes no difference.

◆ When we discuss the Linux GUI, the menu arrow, ➤, points you to a choice from a menu or submenu. For example, Main Menu ➤ Graphics ➤ The Gimp tells you to click on the Main Menu button, navigate to the Graphics menu, and then click The Gimp.

NOTE   *Notes, in general, provide additional information outside the flow of a topic.*

TIP   *Tips, on the other hand, are intended to help you in everyday use, such as configuring an application.*

WARNING   *Warnings may highlight dangers to an application, the operating system, your hardware, and more.*

Getting Red Hat Linux 9

For you convenience, we include the Publisher's Edition of Red Hat Linux 9. It is a two-CD set. Due to space constraints, 162 packages available for Red Hat Linux 9 are not available in the CDs included with this book. Some of these packages are important for Linux administrators, such as the *kernel-source-** RPM described in Chapter 12. In addition, another 25 packages in the Publisher's Edition, including the Linux kernel, either include less information or are out of date.

If you install Red Hat Linux 9 from the Publisher's Edition CDs, the process skips a number of steps shown in Chapters 3 and 4. We therefore recommend that you get the full version of Red Hat Linux 9, which requires three CDs for installation. You can do this in one of three ways:

◆ You can download the three Red Hat Linux 9 installation CDs for free. If you have a CD-writer, you can then write the data onto blank CDs. As strange as it sounds, the downloaded CDs actually include packages that are (slightly) more up to date than the Red Hat boxed sets.

◆ You can purchase the three Red Hat Linux 9 installation CDs from a number of third-party sources.

◆ You can purchase an official Red Hat Linux 9 Personal or Professional boxed set. Once you've installed Red Hat Linux 9, consider using the `up2date` utility described in Chapter 10 to make sure that you have the latest packages installed on your computer. In addition, if you intend to install Red Hat Linux 9 over a network using an FTP connection as described in Chapter 4, we recommend that you use the vsFTP server described in Chapter 27.

Downloading Red Hat Linux 9

If you have a high-speed Internet connection such as a cable modem or DSL adapter, you can download the Red Hat Linux installation CDs. I recommend that you use an FTP client such as gFTP.

Microsoft Windows users may use clients such as WS FTP or Cute FTP. The steps in any GUI FTP client should be similar.

NOTE *I tried downloading Red Hat Linux over a telephone modem once—it took nearly two full days to download the first installation CD. Once downloaded, the data was corrupt. If you connect to the Internet through a telephone modem, I strongly suggest that you get Red Hat Linux from a third party or Red Hat itself.*

To download the Red Hat Linux 9 CDs, you'll need an FTP client, sufficient room on your hard drive (at least 2.1GB of free space for the three installation CDs), and the information described below:

FTP Site While the standard FTP site is `ftp.redhat.com`, it's often quite busy. There are a number of alternative sites worldwide available at `www.redhat.com/download/mirror.html`. You may get a faster response, especially if you're downloading from outside the U.S. Just be aware that there is often a delay between the release of a Red Hat Linux version and its availability on a mirror FTP site.

Username and Password Normal FTP sites for downloading Red Hat Linux 9 CDs (including `ftp.redhat.com`) allow anonymous access. On such sites, the username is **anonymous**, and the password should be your e-mail address (though it isn't required).

Directory on the FTP Server The actual directory on the FTP Server varies with the site that you're using. While the Red Hat Linux CD files should be in some subdirectory of `/pub/redhat/linux`, some browsing may be required.

The Right CDs You'll probably find six Red Hat Linux 9 CDs, code name Shrike, in an undifferentiated list that will look similar to:

```
shrike-i386-disc1.iso
shrike-i386-disc2.iso
shrike-i386-disc3.iso
shrike-i386-SRPMS-disc1.iso
shrike-i386-SRPMS-disc2.iso
shrike-i386-SRPMS-disc3.iso
```

The first three Shrike CDs are the binary installation CDs that you need to install Red Hat Linux on your computer. The last three Shrike CDs contain the associated source code.

Depending on the FTP site, you may also see other CDs of interest, which include Red Hat Linux documentation and an extended rescue disk.

A CD Writer The Red Hat Linux 9 CDs are on huge files. You'll need CD writing software and a CD drive that is capable of writing data to writable compact disks. Linux includes a number of good CD writing applications described in Chapters 14 and 16.

Alternate instructions are available from Red Hat at `www.redhat.com/download/howto_download.html`.

Third-Party CDs with the Red Hat Linux 9 Installation Files

Not everyone has a high-speed Internet connection. In that case, it may be more practical to purchase the downloaded CDs from a third-party reseller. The cost of all three CDs is typically around $10 U.S. (or less).

A directory of these resellers is available online at `directory.google.com`; click on Computers ➤ Software ➤ Operating Systems ➤ Linux ➤ Companies ➤ Resellers for a list.

NOTE   *The General Public License (see Web Chapter 4 on the Sybex website or* `www.gnu.org/copyleft/gpl.html`*) allows you to download and distribute Red Hat Linux 9 for free. You can sell the CDs that you download. The content of the CDs can be identical to Red Hat Linux 9. However, if you're not Red Hat and you resell the CDs, you cannot call it Red Hat Linux.*

Getting the Red Hat Linux 9 Boxed Set

You can purchase a full version of Red Hat Linux from `www.redhat.com` and many major computer retailers. The two entry-level options include:

◆   Red Hat Linux 9 Personal Edition includes seven CDs: the installation packages are on three CDs, the source code for each package is included in three more CDs; the final CD includes documentation in HTML and PDF formats. This edition comes with 30 days of web-based installation support and a 30-day basic one-computer subscription to the Red Hat Network.

◆   Red Hat Linux 9 Professional Edition includes nine CDs: the installation packages are on three CDs, and the source code for each package is included in three more CDs. Additional CDs with documentation, office and multimedia applications, and system administration tools are also included. All this information is also available on DVD. This edition comes with 60 days of web and telephone-based installation support and a 60-day basic one-computer subscription to the Red Hat Network.

There are other versions available with support, which I briefly describe in Chapter 1. For a full list, see `www.redhat.com/software`.

Tell Us What You Think

We wrote this book to meet your needs, and only you can tell us if we've succeeded. If there are topics you expected to find here that we haven't covered, or if you find any errors, let us know by going to the page for this book at `www.sybex.com`, and choosing the Submit a Review link. Of course, if this book has helped you to work better and faster with Red Hat Linux or if there are features we've included that you particularly like, we'd like to hear about that too. Good or bad, we'll use your feedback to build an even better book next time.

Part 1

Installing Red Hat Linux

In this Part, you will learn how to:
- ◆ Take full advantage of Red Hat Linux
- ◆ Prepare your hardware
- ◆ Install Linux on a stand-alone system
- ◆ Install Linux over a network
- ◆ Kickstart Linux on multiple computers

Chapter 1

Introducing Red Hat Linux

LINUX IS A BETTER way to run your computers. It is reliable, secure, and flexible. It's surprisingly easy to install. It's easier to use than most people think. It's highly customizable. It's built for networking. And because you can download the latest complete Linux operating system for free, the price is right.

For many people, Red Hat Linux is Linux. That isn't quite right. Linux is based on software developed by a worldwide community of volunteers. Much of the initial work was spearheaded by the Free Software Foundation (`www.fsf.org`). Originally it was developed as a clone of the Unix operating system. Today, it is so much more. It's evolving to meet the needs of a wide variety of people, such as aerospace engineers, movie makers, theoretical physicists, and consumers. Yes, consumers. Even Wal-Mart is selling computers with a version of Linux.

Strictly speaking, Linux is just the kernel, the part of the operating system that allows your software and hardware to communicate. But oh, what a kernel! You can customize it in thousands of ways and update it for new features. Properly configured, it can optimize the effective speeds on your computer.

Red Hat Linux is a distribution, which includes the basic Linux operating system with a number of free applications. These include a fully featured office suite, as well as graphics and multimedia programs that can satisfy most users. Comparable Microsoft programs cost many hundreds of dollars—for each computer.

Linux is fast becoming the major alternative to Microsoft Windows. As a server, it includes all the tools that you might need to configure and administer a wide variety of networks. It has the backing of some major companies, which as of this writing includes Oracle, Dell, and Hewlett-Packard. IBM has invested over a billion dollars in Linux. More and more companies are adopting Linux: as a server, and as a desktop operating system.

NOTE *For those who are dedicated to the Apple Macintosh, remember that the latest Mac OS X was developed from an operating system closely related to Linux, the Berkeley Standard Distribution (BSD).*

There is no one company behind Linux, but you can get support. Red Hat offers a good support system; other companies do as well. If you participate in the give and take of the Linux community, there are thousands of developers who will bend over backwards to help you. This chapter covers the following topics:

◆ Introducing Red Hat Linux 9

◆ A short history of Unix and Linux

◆ Exploring the kernel

◆ Why choose Linux?

◆ The role of a Linux computer

Introducing Red Hat Linux 9

Red Hat Linux 9 is more than just an operating system: It is a complete distribution. It includes a wide variety of commands, utilities, and applications. Installing additional software in packages from the CDs is easy. With the right downloads from the Internet, you can always keep your version of Red Hat Linux up-to-date.

OTHER RED HAT LINUX PRODUCTS

Several versions of Red Hat Linux are available as of this writing. All include the same basic software that you'll find in Red Hat Linux 9, and you can download them using the directions you'll find in the introduction. Each version includes additional features, such as CDs and support, for a price. The features I cite were available at the time of this writing. They include:

RED HAT LINUX 9.0 PERSONAL EDITION

As described in the introduction, Red Hat Linux 9.0 Personal Edition includes three installation CDs, three source CDs, and a documentation CD. It includes the software that you need to install Red Hat Linux in Personal Desktop, Workstation, Server, or Custom configurations. It also includes 30 days of web-based installation support and a 30-day subscription to the Red Hat network for the latest updates.

RED HAT LINUX 9.0 PROFESSIONAL EDITION

Red Hat Linux 9.0 Professional Edition includes the components in Red Hat Linux 9.0 Personal, plus an eighth CD with office and multimedia applications and a ninth CD with system administration tools. It also includes 60 days of web-based and telephone support as well as a 60-day subscription to the Red Hat network for the latest updates.

While you can install any version of Red Hat Linux as a server, the followoing versions of Red Hat Linux are explicitly designed for servers with more than one CPU. Their subscriptions include free updates during the subscription period.

Continued on next page

OTHER RED HAT LINUX PRODUCTS *(continued)*

RED HAT ENTERPRISE LINUX WS (WORKSTATION)

Red Hat Enterprise Linux Workstation includes the components in Red Hat Linux 9.0, with features customized to work with Red Hat Enterprise Linux Servers. You can get this operating system bundled with 64-bit Itanium 2-based workstations.

RED HAT ENTERPRISE LINUX ES (ENTRY-LEVEL SERVER) BASIC EDITION

This version of Red Hat Linux supports basic servers, limited to 2 CPUs and 4GB of RAM. The Basic Edition includes downloads, basic installation and configuration support for 90 days, and support through the Red Hat Enterprise network for one year.

RED HAT ENTERPRISE LINUX ES (ENTRY-LEVEL SERVER) STANDARD EDITION

This version of Red Hat Linux supports basic servers, limited to 2 CPUs and 4GB of RAM. The Standard Edition includes downloads, basic installation and configuration support as well as support through the Red Hat Enterprise network for one year.

RED HAT ENTERPRISE LINUX AS (ADVANCED SERVER) STANDARD EDITION

Red Hat Enterprise Linux AS Standard Edition includes the components and support associated with the Red Hat Enterprise Linux ES Server, plus one year of installation support, configuration support, advanced configuration support, and systems administration support.

RED HAT ENTERPRISE LINUX AS (ADVANCED SERVER) PREMIUM EDITION

Red Hat Enterprise Linux AS Premium Edition includes the components and support associated with Red Hat Enterprise Linux AS Standard Edition, plus high availability clustering support and 24x7 emergency support for Severity 1 Issues, as defined in the associated license.

OTHER RED HAT PRODUCTS

Red Hat has other specialty operating systems. These include the high-security Stronghold Enterprise Apache Server, and versions specifically designed for IBM's eServer platforms.

Basic Hardware Requirements

Table 1.1 shows the minimum hardware requirements associated with Red Hat Linux 9. These requirements are not absolute; for example, I've run Red Hat Linux 9 with just the command-line interface with as little as 16MB of RAM. Other hardware requirements are described in Chapter 2.

These minimums assume a stand-alone Linux computer with a minimum of services. Earlier versions of even Red Hat Linux can be installed on less RAM and Intel 386 CPUs. If you want to install additional software, configure a graphical user interface (GUI), or set up a server, the requirements go up accordingly.

TABLE 1.1: BASIC HARDWARE REQUIREMENTS

TYPE	MINIMUM
CPU	Pentium-class
	Recommended for text-mode: 200MHz Pentium class or better
	Recommended for graphical-mode: 400MHz Pentium II class or better
RAM	For a text-mode workstation, 64MB; for a graphical workstation, 128MB (192MB recommended)
Hard disk	475MB (not including swap space or other files); more for other types of installations, as described in Chapter 3

New Features

Red Hat is constantly incorporating new features and updating software. Most important are updates to the latest kernel and services. The following list includes some of the major improvements that Red Hat has incorporated recently:

◆ Linux kernel version 2.4.20, which includes proven changes to the Linux 2.5 beta series kernels, as well as a number of updated drivers.

◆ The Common Unix Print System (CUPS), now the default print server, replacing LPD. For more information, see Chapter 25.

◆ Apache 2.0.40, now the standard Red Hat Linux web server. For more information, see Chapter 30.

◆ `iptables`, now the default firewall tool (described in Chapter 22).

◆ OpenOffice, a fully featured suite of Microsoft Office–style applications. For more information, see Chapter 18.

◆ XFree86 Version 4.3 includes support for additional graphics adapters. It also has experimental support for RandR, the X Resize, Rotate, and Reflect extension (`www.xfree86.org/~keithp/talks/randr/protocol.txt`)

Red Hat has also configured several tools not found in other Linux distributions. You can start these tools from a command-line interface inside a GUI such as GNOME or KDE, using a `redhat-config-*` command. For example, `redhat-config-samba` lets you configure Samba, the service that allows Linux to work on a Microsoft Windows network. Samba is discussed in detail in Chapter 29.

Basic Components

Linux can be broken down into a number of modules. The modular nature of Linux allows developers to work independently and more efficiently. They can reuse and reconfigure these modules to achieve different results. At least six categories of modules are associated with Linux: kernel, network, `init`, daemons, shells and utilities, and the X Window.

KERNEL

The kernel is the most important part of any operating system. It allows Linux and any software that you install to communicate with computer hardware. The kernel communicates with your hardware through dedicated device drivers. For example, when you mount a floppy drive, a specific kernel driver sends and receives messages to and from the floppy drive.

If you install new hardware and it isn't detected when you start Linux, you can add a driver module to your kernel, as described in Chapter 11. If you have to download a driver for your new hardware, you should also add that driver module to the kernel.

Other parts of the kernel manage the Linux filesystem as well as any data stored in such areas as your disk cache. The kernel is loaded into protected-mode memory when you start Linux. You can learn how to configure and compile the kernel in Chapter 12.

NETWORK

Linux computers are most commonly organized in a client/server network. Some computers act as workstations, or clients, for users; others are servers, which control resources shared by multiple users on different workstations. In this type of network, clients ask servers for items they need, like files or applications. In a Linux network, clients can even ask for X Window information. In other words, you can set up terminals on Linux clients that access their GUI data from a Linux server.

The network modules of the Linux operating system are designed to keep client/server communication running as smoothly as possible. Ideally, the connection between client and server is seamless. If your network is fast enough, your users won't be able to tell the difference between local and network services.

Because network modules are loaded in the same area as the kernel, their failure may mean that you have to reboot Linux. We cover the basics of Linux networking in Chapters 20–22.

INIT

In general, the only way to start a Linux program is with another Linux program. For example, you log into the Linux terminal program, known as `mingetty`. But something has to start the terminal program. When you boot Linux on your computer, the kernel loads and starts `init`. The `init` program then mounts your drives, and starts your terminal programs. When you log in, the terminal program starts your command-line interface shell.

After Linux boots on your computer, `init` watches for anything that might shut down your computer, such as a power failure signal from an uninterruptible power supply (UPS) or a reboot command. Details of `init` and the governing `/etc/inittab` file are discussed in Chapter 11.

DAEMONS

Linux includes a series of services. These are programs that can run in the background and start as needed. Many Linux services are known as *daemons*. In Linux, several dozen daemons can run simultaneously, standing at the ready to start your network, serve web pages, print your files, or connect you to other Linux or Windows computers. Typical daemons include:

- Apache, the most popular web server on the Internet, also known as `httpd`. Apache is covered in Chapter 30.

◆ Samba (also known as `smbd`), the network service that allows Linux to talk to Microsoft Windows computers.

◆ A printer daemon that manages communication with your printers. The CUPS daemon is `cupsd`; it's covered in more detail in Chapter 25.

We discuss various Linux daemons in detail throughout this book.

TIP   *Case matters in Linux. For example, the acronym for the Common Unix Print System is CUPS; the associated daemon is* `cupsd`.

SHELLS AND UTILITIES

Any Linux program or utility that talks to the kernel is a user-mode program, which consists of shells and utilities. User-mode programs don't communicate directly with your hardware (that's a job for the kernel). In other words, these programs can crash without affecting the basic operation of the Linux operating system. There are three basic types of user-mode programs:

◆ *Login* programs associate a user ID with a user's shell and other personalized settings, such as with the X Window and web browsers.

◆ *Shell* programs act as Linux command interpreters. The most common Linux shell is known as bash, short for the Bourne Again Shell.

◆ *Utilities* are small-scale commands used inside a shell.

The basics of the bash shell and associated commands are covered in Chapters 6–8.

X WINDOW

Linux builds the GUI from different program modules. GUI window managers, such as GNOME and KDE, as well as all GUI applications are built on the foundation of the X Window. The basics of the X Window and associated applications are covered in Chapters 15–19.

A Short History of Unix and Linux

Linux was developed as a clone of Unix. In other words, the developers of Linux built their system without using the programming instructions, also known as the source code, used to build Unix. Because Linux is a Unix clone, you can use most of the same command-line commands on either operating system.

Although it would have been easier to adapt Unix for the personal computer, important historical reasons lie behind the development of Linux. And the way Linux was developed drives the way Linux developers, companies, and users work today.

Unix and the Coming Internet

Computers were once quite expensive. They were the domain of universities and larger corporations. There was a lot of demand for these early computers; to support this demand, a number of computer scientists developed the concept of *time-sharing*, where multiple users are connected to the same computer simultaneously.

Even though computers have become more powerful and less expensive, we have returned to this notion of time-sharing. Today, administrators are quite familiar with the concept of the time-sharing system: it is now known as the multiuser server. One network often includes multiple servers; your username may be the same across all of these servers. In fact, it's fair to say that we're all time-sharing users on the biggest network of all—the Internet.

Let's take a look at some of the developments that occurred along the road to Linux.

MULTICS

One of the early time-sharing projects was Multics (Multiplexed Information and Computing Service), a joint project between MIT, AT&T's Bell Labs (now Lucent Technologies), and General Electric. Although Bell Labs withdrew from the project in 1969, two of their developers, Ken Thompson and Dennis Ritchie, still had an itch for what would become the multiuser operating systems we know today.

UNIX

Thompson and Ritchie continued development work through the early 1970s. Perhaps the key to their success was their development of the C programming language for writing the kernel and a number of basic commands, including those in the Bourne shell.

When Unix was developed in 1969, AT&T was a regulated monopoly in the United States. Various court and regulatory rulings and agreements kept AT&T out of the computer business.

In 1974, AT&T distributed Unix to the University of California for the cost of the manuals and tapes. It quickly became popular at a number of universities. Nevertheless, AT&T was not allowed to make money from it.

A COOPERATIVE ENVIRONMENT

Bell Labs has a history of groundbreaking research. The company had some of the best minds in the world working on fundamental problems. Bell Labs wanted the goodwill of the academic community. Since AT&T wasn't allowed to make money from software, it kept the license for Unix and distributed the operating system with source code to universities for a nominal fee. In exchange, AT&T's lawyers insisted that the license explicitly state that Unix came with no warranty. This release technique became known as *open source*.

The timing was good. Various universities adapted the Unix source code to work with three different kinds of computers available at the time: mainframes, minicomputers, and microcomputers.

At about the same time, the U.S. Department of Defense's Advanced Research Project Agency (ARPA) wanted to set up a nationwide communications network that could survive a nuclear war. Most universities on this ARPA network used Unix. TCP/IP was built on Unix and eventually became the communication protocol for the ARPANET. The ARPANET eventually developed into the Internet that you know today. Unix and derivative clones, like Linux, are critical parts of the Internet.

THE AT&T CONSENT DECREE

AT&T retained the license to Unix through the 1980s. When the U.S. government settled the AT&T antitrust suit in 1982, one of the provisions allowed AT&T to go into the computer business. This became known as the AT&T consent decree. At that point, AT&T was able to sell the Unix operating system and source code with all the protections associated with a copyright.

The programmers who used Unix wanted to keep the advantages of an open-source operating system. Unix programmers wanted the ability to customize the software. As academics, they wanted to share the results. The Unix users of the time had the high level of knowledge that made open-source software worthwhile.

Ironically, AT&T was never very successful at selling Unix and eventually sold the rights to the operating system. The direct successor is now owned by the SCO Group, which also owns the rival SCO (formerly Caldera) Linux distribution.

NOTE   *The SCO Group has recently filed suit against IBM over Unix. This is controversial as there are many in the Linux community who see this as a threat.*

Unix Alternatives

At the time, with their limited budgets, universities did not have the money to purchase the now proprietary Unix, and they did not want to have their academic freedoms limited by copyrights. Generally, academics are most comfortable when they can share all of their data. To this end, Douglas Comer developed Xinu (Unix, spelled backwards) in 1983 to illustrate operating system structures in a classroom setting. In 1986, Andrew Tannenbaum developed Minix as a Unix clone and free alternative. Like Linux, Minix does not use Unix's source code, and therefore does not infringe on any of AT&T's Unix copyrights.

Even before the consent decree, Bill Joy of the University of California worked on Unix. He also started work on the Berkeley Standard Distribution (BSD), which, like Unix, was released under an open-source style license. A number of BSD utilities were incorporated into later versions of Unix. In 1982, Joy became a cofounder of Sun Microsystems.

Several other operating systems are closely related to Unix, as shown in Table 1.2.

TABLE 1.2: UNIX-STYLE OPERATING SYSTEMS

OPERATING SYSTEM	DESCRIPTION
AIX	The Advanced Interactive eXecutive operating system, developed by IBM; used with high-end CPUs such as Power4 and RS64 IV (64-bit PowerPC chips).
BSD	The Berkeley Standard Distribution, an open-source alternative to Linux.
HP-UX	Developed by Hewlett-Packard; version 11i is developed for 64-bit RISC and Itanium CPUs.
IRIX	Developed by Silicon Graphics for 64-bit CPUs.
Linux	The free operating system clone of Unix.
Solaris	Developed by Sun Microsystems for its UltraSPARC CPUs.
Tru64	Formerly known as Digital Unix, optimized for 64-bit CPUs.
UnixWare	The successor to AT&T's version of Unix, now owned by the SCO Group.

One telling trend is that a number of these companies are moving toward using Linux on many of their servers. While this book is based on the 32-bit Red Hat Linux kernel, a 64-bit Red Hat kernel is available.

The Free Software Foundation

Some of the work of the academic community eventually became something of a rebellion. In its early stages, it was led by Richard Stallman and his Free Software Foundation (FSF). (For more information, see the website at `www.fsf.org`.)

Stallman started work on the GNU's Not Unix (GNU) project in 1984. He summarized the focus of the FSF in his introductory Usenet message: "I consider that the golden rule requires that if I like a program I must share it with other people who like it." Stallman's purpose was to set up a group where the free sharing of software would be strongly encouraged. To realize his dream, Stallman needed an operating system, free of the code that was then copyrighted by AT&T.

The FSF developed the General Public License (GPL) to build a body of free software protected from those who would use it to create proprietary closed-source systems. This same license still protects Linux today; you can read it in Web Chapter 4, which can be found on the Sybex website at `www.sybex.com`.

By 1991, the FSF had cloned all of the major components of a Unix-style operating system, except the kernel.

THE GENERAL PUBLIC LICENSE

Richard Stallman developed the GPL to bring the advantages previously available with Unix to the general software community. He wanted to develop a license that would protect software from anyone who would hide its source code. GNU software is licensed under the GPL. While you can read the GPL in Web Chapter 4, you can also read about three basic principles behind the GPL:

◆ All GPL software must be distributed with a complete copy of the source code. The source code must include clear documentation.

◆ Any software added to GPL software must also be clearly documented. If the new software interacts with the GPL software, the package as a whole must be distributed as GPL software.

◆ Any GPL software comes without a warranty.

Linus Develops a Kernel

In 1991, Linus Torvalds was a graduate student in Finland. He was not happy with the operating systems available for his new computer with a 386 CPU. So he put together a kernel to allow some operating system components to communicate with computer hardware. By 1995, several companies assembled Linus's kernel with the GNU software of the FSF to produce the first Linux distributions.

NOTE   Richard Stallman and the people of the FSF believe that the Linux operating system is more properly known as GNU/Linux because it combines a large number of GNU-licensed programs, commands, and utilities with one Linux kernel.

Exploring the Kernel

Life in any operating system begins and ends with the kernel. When properly configured, any operating system can work like a wonderful ballet where hardware is ready just when you need it. When problems crop up, the kernel can slow or stop your computer.

With the Linux kernel, you can configure hardware, filesystems, networking support, and more. Hardware drivers can be configured within the kernel or as separate modules.

Configuring the Kernel

If you ever need to reconfigure your kernel, you'll become familiar with the Linux Kernel Configuration menu shown in Figure 1.1. As you can see, there are a number of different hardware components, such as SCSI and USB devices, that you can configure through the kernel. Each of the buttons shown in the menu opens individual submenus.

FIGURE 1.1

Linux Kernel
Configuration

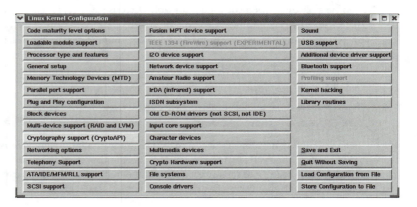

You can also see some kernel options not directly associated with hardware, such as Networking Options and Code Maturity Level Options. For example, in the Networking Options menu, you can set up Linux to work with different network protocols. You'll find detailed information on this process in Chapter 12.

The */proc* Filesystem

The /proc directory is a virtual filesystem stored in your RAM. It documents the way the Linux kernel interacts with your computer. A number of these files document how the Linux kernel reads your hardware. When you read the right file, you can find hardware settings for different components. You can find more information on /proc in Chapter 11.

Modular or Monolithic

You can set up every hardware driver within the main part of the Linux kernel. This would be a *monolithic* kernel. But for most configurations, there are many hundreds of hardware drivers. If you put them together into one kernel file, the sheer size of the hardware drivers can overload your system.

It is usually more efficient to configure a modular kernel. Various kernel modules, normally associated with various hardware components, are loaded after Linux starts on your computer. Figure 1.2 shows an example from my desktop computer.

FIGURE 1.2

Linux modules

```
Module           Size  Used by    Not tainted
smbfs            44400  1  (autoclean)
sr_mod           18168  0  (autoclean)
agpgart          47296  4  (autoclean)
parport_pc       19076  1  (autoclean)
lp                8996  0  (autoclean)
parport          37056  1  (autoclean) [parport_pc lp]
autofs           13268  0  (autoclean) (unused)
8139too          18088  1
mii               3912  0  [8139too]
ipt_REJECT        3736  6  (autoclean)
iptable_filter    2412  1  (autoclean)
ip_tables        14968  2  [ipt_REJECT iptable_filter]
ide-scsi         12240  0
scsi_mod        107128  2  [sr_mod ide-scsi]
ide-cd           35772  0
cdrom            33696  0  [sr_mod ide-cd]
loop             12152  0  (autoclean)
keybdev           2976  0  (unused)
mousedev          5492  1
hid              22148  0  (unused)
input             5888  0  [keybdev mousedev hid]
usb-uhci         26412  0  (unused)
usbcore          78432  1  [hid usb-uhci]
ext3             84960  7
jbd              52020  7  [ext3]
raid5            18888  1
xor               9020  0  [raid5]
lvm-mod          62176  3
[root@RH9Desk root]#
```

As you can see, there are hardware modules, such as usbcore, to support USB hardware. There are also software modules, such as smbfs, to support the Samba filesystem. For more information on managing kernel modules, see Chapter 11. If you want to make sure that your kernel is modular, see Chapter 12.

Why Choose Linux?

Linux is most often compared to Microsoft Windows. Linux is also replacing other Unix-style operating systems described earlier in Table 1.2. Four factors make Linux a better choice for many users and organizations: cost, reliability, flexibility, and support.

Cost

You can download Red Hat Linux for free from the Internet. This cost difference can be significant when compared to the thousands of dollars associated with many other Unix-style operating systems. It's still a significant advantage when compared to the continuing licensing costs of Microsoft operating systems.

It isn't enough just to consider the price of the operating system. You should take into account the other costs, generally associated with the time for installation, configuration, and support.

Red Hat Linux 9 includes installation options suitable for everything from a home desktop to a network server. For more information, see Chapter 3. This is one operating system distribution that you can use to install Linux on a wide variety of computers.

NOTE   *Red Hat also offers several heavy-duty server products based on what was originally Red Hat Advanced Server. It includes much of the same software that's available in Red Hat 9. One variation is Red Hat's Stronghold Enterprise Secure web server. For more information, see* www.redhat.com.

Red Hat Linux has one additional cost advantage: The CDs are loaded with a number of fully featured applications. For example, OpenOffice is a fully featured office suite, with all of the features that most users could ever want. Red Hat includes several other free applications that can save you hundreds of dollars.

INSTALLATION

As you install Linux over the next few chapters, you'll learn that the process is not difficult. If you're installing Red Hat Linux on a group of computers, you can use the kickstart techniques described in Chapter 5 to automate the installation process.

Since Red Hat Linux 9 can be installed on most PCs without a problem, the discussion of hardware in Chapter 2 might seem extreme. However, if you're an administrator responsible for installing Linux on several computers, mistakes can quickly get expensive.

CONFIGURATION

To make any operating system useful, you need to install and configure it. Whether you're configuring a desktop computer at home, a workstation for your users, or a server for your corporate network, the basic configuration process is the same. Linux has always had the command-line tools with the flexibility to satisfy most Linux gurus.

With the redhat-config-* tools described in Chapter 19, Red Hat Linux now offers the graphical tools that can help administrators of other operating systems make the transition.

Reliability

Linux is reliable. There are reports of Linux servers that run for several months at a time without reboots. Imagine never having to reboot your computer after installing new software. Imagine being able to stop a runaway program without rebooting your computer. That is the power of Linux.

Linux is not perfect. Mistakes happen. We describe troubleshooting techniques throughout this book. If you ever have a problem booting Linux, you can rescue most systems with your Red Hat Linux installation CD (without reinstalling Linux).

Flexibility

Linux is a flexible operating system. The Red Hat Package Management (RPM) system makes it easy to add more software as needed. For more information on RPM packages and the rpm command, see Chapter 10. The redhat-config-packages tool described in Chapter 19 makes this process of software management even easier.

You can optimize the Linux kernel using the techniques discussed in Chapter 12. An optimized kernel makes everything faster in Linux, from the boot process to networking. With the right techniques, you should always have an easily accessible working kernel; in contrast, small errors when changing the Microsoft Windows Registry can be disastrous.

Linux is easily upgradeable. You can keep an older version of Linux up-to-date with the latest in kernels, applications, and other software. The `rpm` and `up2date` tools described in Chapter 10 help you with this process.

Support

Very good support is available for Linux. Unfortunately, many administrators and IT managers are intimidated by the "lack" of a single source of corporate support, like Microsoft. But remember, Microsoft support is not free.

If you purchase an official Red Hat Linux boxed set, you qualify for a limited amount of support. You can purchase additional support from Red Hat or from a third-party vendor such as Linuxcare (`www.linuxcare.com`). Some of the large companies behind Linux, such as IBM, also provide support for Red Hat Linux as installed on their systems.

There are two bonus sources of support for Linux. Because Linux is open source, administrators can often fix many problems. If you're working with a closed-source system, you can't even "look under the hood."

Since Linux is developed by a community, there are many in that community who are anxious to make their name by solving new problems. Their insights are available online. It's quite possible that the answer to your problem is already available in the Internet newsgroup database, accessible through `groups.google.com`.

The Role of a Linux Computer

You can configure Linux as a server or as a desktop computer. Linux is flexible; you can install it on many older computers that you might otherwise have to scrap.

Red Hat includes a number of additional programs and applications that enhance what Linux can do on the desktop, for small organizations, and for the enterprise.

Linux as a Server

Linux is built for networking. You can set it up as a server to manage many different kinds of resources for your network. Table 1.3 lists just a few of the Linux services that you can configure. Many of these services have their own individual daemons. Others are associated with the Extended Internet Services Daemon (`xinetd`) described in Chapter 23.

TABLE 1.3: LINUX SERVER SERVICES

SERVICE	DESCRIPTION	CHAPTER
crond	Runs scripts on a schedule	13
cups	Manages the Common Unix Print System	25
httpd	The Apache Web Server	30
named	The Domain Name Service	24

Continued on next page

TABLE 1.3: LINUX SERVER SERVICES *(continued)*

SERVICE	DESCRIPTION	CHAPTER
nfs	A Network File System server	28
sendmail	A common e-mail transport agent	26
smb	Samba, which makes Linux computers members of Microsoft Windows networks	29
sshd	Secure Shell	23
vsftpd	The Very Secure FTP Daemon	27
xinetd	The Extended Internet Services Daemon	23
ypserv	A Network Information Service server	28

It's common to install Linux on older computers. You can set up a Linux computer as a server with limited functionality. In many cases, this does not require a great deal of RAM or hard disk space. For example, you could set up a Linux computer as a modern print server or a firewall. You would not have to purchase dedicated hardware for these purposes.

Linux on the Desktop

Linux is a serious alternative on the desktop. As you'll see in Chapters 15–17, Linux provides essentially the same basic GUI applications and configuration tools that you can find in any version of Microsoft Windows.

In addition, three major office suites are available that you can use in place of Microsoft Office. Mozilla and Konqueror are fully featured web browsers; alternatively, you can still install Netscape or Opera on Linux. Evolution provides an alternative to Microsoft Outlook.

People are taking a serious look at Linux on the desktop. As of this writing, Wal-Mart is selling five different computers with Lindows (`www.lindows.com`), a version of Linux that is customized to run a number of Microsoft Windows applications. Linux is getting a serious look as a desktop alternative outside the United States.

Game manufacturers are creating ways to play on Linux. Tux Games is an online store (`www.tuxgames.com`) with a warehouse of interesting games. There's even a version of The Sims for Linux, courtesy of TransGaming Technologies (`www.transgaming.com`).

Applications available for Linux may not meet everyone's needs. In the personal finance area, GNUcash, in my opinion, does not compare well with the latest versions of Quicken. Other Linux personal finance programs are listed at `www.linuxlinks.com/Software/Financial/Personal_Finance/`.

If you need a few Microsoft Windows programs, multiple solutions are available. CrossOver Office (`www.codeweavers.com`) allows you to run Microsoft Office 97/2000, Quicken, Lotus Notes, and more. You can set up Microsoft Windows inside a virtual computer inside Linux, courtesy of VMWare (`www.vmware.com`) or Win4Lin (`www.trelos.com`).

Red Hat Linux for Desktops

Red Hat started a recent push toward the desktop market with version 8.0. According to Erik Troan, senior director of product marketing for Red Hat, the company is targeting the Red Hat Linux desktop for both the personal and corporate markets. At least for now, Red Hat's focus is on markets such as financial institutions and call centers. It is also looking toward high-end users who want heavy-duty software, such as computer-aided design (CAD) and applications on the same computer.

To this end, Red Hat is moving toward configuring both GNOME and KDE with a similar look and feel. The changes that Red Hat has made to GNOME and KDE is known as Bluecurve.

GNOME, the GNU Network Object Model Environment, is described in Chapter 16. KDE, the K Desktop Environment, is covered in Chapter 17. These are the two most popular GUI desktops in use for Linux today. They've also enhanced available GUI tools for both desktops, as described in Chapter 18.

Desktop users may be pleased with the wide array of applications that come with Red Hat Linux 9. They include:

- OpenOffice, a fully featured office software suite.

- Mozilla and Konqueror, web browsers as fully featured as Microsoft Internet Explorer.

- Internet utilities such as Instant Messenger, news clients, remote desktops, and more.

- Multimedia applications that allow you to write CDs and even DVDs at full speed.

While the Red Hat desktop graphics utilities don't yet have the CMYK (cyan, magenta, yellow, and black) graphics software such as Paint Shop Pro, a number of movie studios do create animation and special effects on Linux computers.

NOTE *CMYK is a color model more popular in high-end graphics applications than the original RGB (red-green-black) standard.*

Red Hat Linux for Small Businesses

Red Hat Linux can be a fantastic option for a small businesses or organizations. You can install it on all desktops and servers. You save the cost of the operating systems and applications that you would otherwise have to install.

Red Hat Linux is fairly easy to configure in a network, even if you have Microsoft Windows computers. You can even configure Red Hat Linux as a primary domain controller (PDC) in a Microsoft Windows–style network. Once Samba is properly configured (see Chapter 29), other Microsoft computers won't be able to tell the difference.

With the right configuration, you can easily connect your network to the Internet. You can also protect your network from many of the ravages of the Internet with appropriate settings on your firewall and other network tools.

Red Hat Linux for the Enterprise

Many corporations use enhanced versions of Red Hat Linux, such as Red Hat's Enterprise Server line. When configured with other tools, such as Oracle databases and the Stronghold web server, Red Hat Linux can be a powerful tool for the enterprise.

Amazon.com has saved millions by converting to Red Hat. Google runs its search engine databases on a cluster of over 8000 servers running Red Hat Linux. Red Hat is becoming more popular for other large organizations as well, such as BP, Kenwood, and MIT. In a Red Hat case study, Toyota actually found slightly *lower* support costs after converting their computers to Red Hat Linux.

REPORTING PROBLEMS

Linux is a work in progress. Developers are constantly adding and revising features for new software and hardware. It's possible that in your journey with Linux, you'll run into a problem or two. There are four ways to look for a solution:

Newsgroups As described earlier, many users bring up problems that they have in different newsgroups. Google collected recent newsgroup messages into a searchable database through groups.google.com. If you want to post on a newsgroup, it's best to use a newsgroup reader such as those described in Chapters 16 and 17. Alternatively, you can post messages using Google's interface (registration is required).

Mailing lists Red Hat has a series of mailing lists on different topics and versions; you can sign up at www.redhat.com/mailing-lists/. The developers of a number of different applications maintain their own mailing lists, which you can find on their websites.

Red Hat support If you've paid for an official copy of Red Hat Linux, you can get some amount of support for your issue. The support may be limited by the version that you've purchased.

Bugzilla If you're certain that the problem is with Red Hat Linux, you can submit a bug report to Red Hat. Navigate to bugzilla.redhat.com and click Login Now. Create an account if you don't already have one. You can then search through the Bugzilla database to see if someone else has already raised the issue with Red Hat. If not, and if you've exhausted the other resources, submit a bug report through the Red Hat Bugzilla system.

Summary

Linux was developed as a clone of Unix. Much of it was engineered by the Free Software Foundation; critical was Linus Torvalds's creation of the Linux kernel. Most of it is protected through the General Public License.

As Red Hat Linux 9 is being released, businesses and governments are focused on reducing costs. Linux has at least an initial cost advantage over other operating systems such as Microsoft Windows. And Red Hat Linux, as the most popular Linux distribution, is in the forefront of this change.

Red Hat Linux 9 includes the same basic components as all other Linux distributions: the kernel, init, daemons, user mode shells and utilities, network, and the X Window. It incorporates the latest changes to the Linux kernel, as well as new improvements in printing, web services, and more. The `redhat-config-*` graphical tools make it easier for administrators of other operating systems to make the transition.

If there is a key to Linux, it is in the kernel. It is highly configurable; when modular, it is also quite flexible.

When looking at Linux, you should consider four factors: cost, reliability, flexibility, and support. I believe that Linux has advantages in all four areas when compared to other operating systems.

Red Hat Linux can play many roles in computing. Traditionally, it's used as a server, and functions well even on many older computers. Red Hat is adding tools that make it suitable as a desktop operating system. Such flexibility makes Red Hat a viable alternative for small businesses. Red Hat is also being used in the enterprise, on clusters of computers to meet the heaviest demands.

In the next chapter, we'll start looking at getting your computers ready for Red Hat Linux. Installation often does proceed easily on most modern computers. However, if you're installing Red Hat Linux on two or more computers on a network, mistakes can be painful. If you're responsible for installing Linux on a network, you need to know more about the hardware in your computers.

Chapter 2

Preparing Your Hardware

IN MOST CASES, INSTALLING Red Hat Linux is a trouble-free process. If you're installing Red Hat Linux on a new computer, all you *probably* need to do is insert the installation CD in the correct drive, set your computer's BIOS to boot from the CD, restart your computer, and you're ready to go. The Red Hat Linux installation program should start and detect most hardware automatically.

If you have a relatively new PC with at least a Pentium-level CPU, and if you don't have the absolute latest in computer hardware, you may never have to worry about Linux drivers. While you should at least read the first sections on disk partitions, you may be able to skim much of this chapter.

However, suppose your PC includes proprietary hardware without Linux drivers. Perhaps your PC has hardware that is too new to have Linux drivers. Or you have a slightly older PC that is prone to hardware conflicts.Perhaps you're responsible for installing Linux on a network of computers where hardware problems can get expensive.

In that case, it pays to have a detailed list of hardware on your PCs. Then you can review available lists of compatible hardware. With a little work, a perfect match isn't even required. With the right resources, even configuring the dreaded "Winmodem" is easier than you might expect.

Many Linux users set their computers up in a "dual-boot" configuration, where they can start either Red Hat Linux or Microsoft Windows (or even another operating system) during the boot process. Preparing a computer that currently has only Microsoft Windows for Linux does take some work. This chapter covers the following topics:

- ◆ Creating hard disk partitions

- ◆ Configuring Microsoft and Linux on the same computer

- ◆ Why worry about hardware?

- ◆ Finding compatible hardware

- ◆ Preparing a hardware checklist

- ◆ BIOS tips

Creating Hard Disk Partitions

The latest hard disks are now quite large. Partitions help you configure hard disks in manageable chunks. When configured correctly, partitions can help protect your system. For example, if someone overloads your FTP server with files, the right partitions ensure that your system still has room to run.

Alternatively, if you have a smaller hard disk (less than 4GB), you'll need to be efficient. If you over-partition a drive, you may not have enough space for certain types of additional files.

You can organize each physical hard disk into *primary*, *extended*, and *logical* partitions. The details depend on whether you're configuring a regular IDE (Integrated Drive Electronics) hard disk or a SCSI (Small Computer Systems Interface) hard disk.

Linux is organized into directories. You can mount different directories onto partitions according to the Filesystem Hierarchy Standard. We cover the FHS and typical partition configurations for Red Hat Linux in Chapter 7.

Partition Styles

You can even configure different operating systems on the same hard disk, using different partitions. Each filesystem can be formatted to different filesystems, such as the default Red Hat Third Extended Filesystem (ext3) or Microsoft's FAT32. In this vein, there are four ways to partition a hard drive:

Primary partition   You can have up to four different primary partitions on a hard drive. One primary partition must be marked as "active" and can include a bootloader, such as the Grand Unified Bootloader (GRUB). If you mount a Linux directory on a primary partition, it is also known as a *volume*.

Extended partition   If four partitions are not enough, you can convert one of the primary partitions into an extended partition. You can then subdivide the extended partition into as many logical partitions as you need. But you can't mount a directory on an extended partition.

Logical partition   You can subdivide an extended partition into as many logical partitions as you need. Although you can't set up a Linux directory in an extended partition, you can set up Linux directories on logical partitions. Therefore, logical partitions are also "volumes." In the Microsoft world, these would be "logical drives."

Swap partition   In Linux, it is common to set up a swap partition as an exclusive area for the virtual memory on your hard drive. Swap partitions aren't a different kind of partition per se; they can be mounted on a primary or logical partition. While the appropriate size of a swap partition is highly debatable, Red Hat recommends that you set up a swap partition with twice the amount of memory in your RAM.

Partition Names

The Linux naming convention for hard disk partitions is straightforward. The naming system also applies to any CD that doesn't require a direct connection to a sound card. The first two letters of the name reflect the kind of disk you have. If you have a regular IDE hard disk, the letters are hd. If you have a SCSI hard disk, the letters are sd.

The third letter depends on your hard disk's position. The first hard disk is designated as a, the second disk is designated as b, and so on. In other words, if you have two different physical IDE hard disks attached to the primary controller, the second (slave) disk is known as hdb. In contrast, SCSI hard disk letters correspond to their designated ID numbers. For example, if you have two SCSI drives with IDs of 0 and 1, the SCSI drive with an ID of 0 is known as sda; the SCSI drive with an ID of 1 is known as sdb. For naming purposes, CD and DVD drives are also categorized as hard disks.

The character in the fourth position reflects how you've partitioned that disk. Because you can have up to four primary partitions, they are designated as 1, 2, 3, and 4. The first logical drive that you create is in position number 5, even if you have only one primary partition.

Every partition is associated with a Linux device file in the /dev directory. When you mount a directory on a partition, you're associating it with the device file. Some examples of different partition device files are shown in Table 2.1.

TABLE 2.1: TYPICAL PARTITION DEVICE NAMES

NAME	DESCRIPTION
/dev/hda3	The third primary partition on the master hard disk on the primary IDE controller; depending on your configuration, it may also be an extended partition.
/dev/sdc8	The fourth logical partition on the third SCSI hard disk.
/dev/hdb7	The third logical partition on the slave hard disk on the primary IDE controller.
/dev/sda1	The first primary partition on the first SCSI hard disk.
/dev/hdb	Since there is no number, this refers to a CD or DVD drive attached as the slave on the primary IDE controller.
/dev/sdc	Since there is no number, this refers to a CD or DVD drive attached to the third position on a SCSI interface.

On an IDE drive, you can have up to 16 partitions. On a SCSI drive, you can have up to 15 partitions.

Configuring Microsoft and Linux on the Same Computer

Installing Microsoft Windows and Linux on the same computer can be a good idea for many reasons. Good software is available that, as of this writing, works only on Microsoft Windows. The software that runs many businesses was written to work only on Microsoft Windows. Users who are making the transition to Linux are more comfortable when the old familiar Microsoft operating system is there, just in case.

You have alternatives. Using two separate computers is one option. You could try the software created as part of the WINE (Wine Is Not an Emulator) project, which allows you to use some Microsoft software on Linux. You could try related software, such as that offered by Xandros, Lindows, or CodeWeavers (CrossOver Office). You could even install Microsoft Windows inside a Linux third-party proprietary virtual machine application, such as VMWare or Win4Lin.

However, the most commonly used option is still a dual-boot configuration. In other words, you can set up two different operating systems on the same computer. For example, Figure 2.1 shows the standard GRUB menu, configured to start either Red Hat Linux or a Microsoft Windows server operating system.

You can set up a dual-boot with operating systems on separate physical hard drives. Alternatively, you can reconfigure the available free space on an existing hard drive. In this case, follow the procedures described in the Step-by-Step section later in this chapter carefully.

Whatever you do, start by backing up your data. Mistakes happen, and you want to be able to recover from a disaster.

The Easy Way: A New Hard Drive

In this section, we describe the easiest way to install Linux on an existing computer. Your BIOS should detect the second hard drive automatically. When it does, you know that the Red Hat installation program, Anaconda, should also detect that drive automatically.

As long as you limit the changes to the new empty drive, the risks are minimal. You can configure and format partitions with fewer risks to your Microsoft Windows data on the existing hard drive.

WARNING   *The default settings for a Red Hat Linux server installation will remove all data on all hard drives, even if it includes Microsoft Windows.*

As of this writing, Red Hat Linux can be installed directly only on a regular IDE or SCSI hard drive. While you can use hard drives connected through USB, IEEE 1394, or parallel ports to store Linux directories, Anaconda may not support the installation of Red Hat Linux on these drives.

NOTE   *IEEE 1394 systems are also known by their proprietary names, FireWire (Apple's trademark) and iLink (Sony's trademark).*

WARNING   *One more reason to add a new hard drive: Anaconda will not install Red Hat Linux 9 on hard drives with bad blocks.*

The Cheaper Way: An Existing Hard Drive

Not everyone can get a second hard drive. Even if you do, you may not have room inside your computer for that drive. Many people who want to set up Linux and Microsoft Windows in a dual-boot configuration will need to use the free space on an existing hard drive.

If you want to install Red Hat Linux on the available free space on your hard drive, follow this basic procedure. Keep in mind that deviations can put your current data at risk. These are basic steps; the next section describes the dual-boot configuration process in detail.

1. Make room on your Microsoft Windows physical hard drive. In most cases, you can use Microsoft's Disk Defragmenter program for this purpose. To learn about the space you need for Linux, see Chapter 3.

2. Split the partition with your Microsoft Windows data. This is possible with FIPS.EXE, available on the first Red Hat Linux installation CD. If you prefer, third-party tools are also available. Be sure to leave enough room for Microsoft Windows virtual memory.

NOTE   *FIPS, the First Interactive Partition Splitter, can split only primary partitions. And as of this writing, it cannot split partitions formatted to Microsoft's NTFS filesystem.*

3. If desired, use fdisk to organize the new partitions. You can also do this when you run Anaconda. If you use Microsoft's FDISK.EXE program, you'll be able to create only one primary partition.

If you want to use the free space on an existing hard drive, some planning is required. Make sure that the free space is sufficient for all the Red Hat Linux programs and packages that you want to install. Remember to include additional free space for your data and for any applications that you might install at a later date. We discuss space requirements in more detail in Chapter 3. And make sure that there is sufficient space for your Microsoft Windows operating system and its virtual memory requirements.

As an example, look at Figure 2.2. This is a view of a 20GB hard disk. You have 5GB of files for Microsoft Windows. You could easily split this hard drive into two partitions of 10GB each. The first partition would include enough free space for the Microsoft Windows files and virtual memory. The second partition would include enough room for installing everything from the Red Hat Linux installation CDs.

TIP   *Microsoft Windows requires significant free space for virtual memory. Linux does not require this kind of free space, because Linux virtual memory is normally contained in a separate swap partition. In my experience, a Microsoft Windows partition doesn't work well if it's more than 60 percent full of files. But this is just a guideline; this is not a book on optimizing Microsoft Windows. If you want more information on this topic, Sybex has some excellent books in this series, including* Mastering Windows 98, Mastering Windows 2000 Professional *(Second Edition),* Mastering Windows XP Home *(Second Edition), and* Mastering Windows XP Professional *(Second Edition).*

NOTE   *Some Linux users prefer a different utility,* parted. *You can use this GNU program to add, delete, resize, and format partitions. I'm hopeful that eventually it will incorporate the functionality of* mkfs, fips, *and* fdisk. *As of this writing, it makes changes to disk immediately, and therefore I consider it a riskier tool than* fdisk. *The one advantage is that, like Partition Magic or System Commander, it can resize existing partitions. More information on* parted *is available from the GNU project at* **www.gnu.org/software/parted**.

FIGURE 2.2

Hard disk dual-boot
scenario

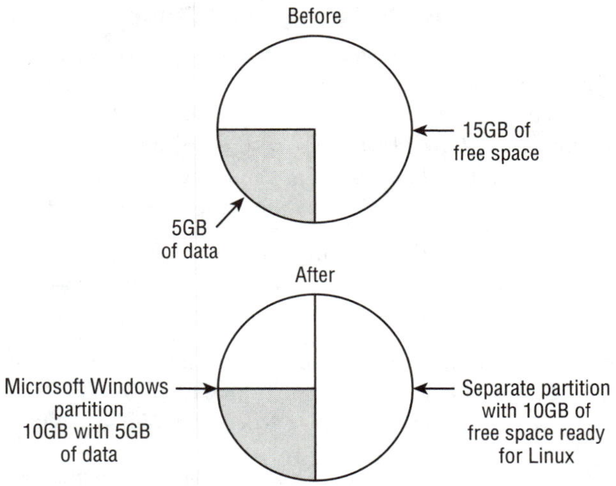

Before

← 15GB of
free space

5GB ↗
of data

After

Microsoft Windows →
partition
10GB with 5GB
of data

← Separate partition
with 10GB of
free space ready
for Linux

Step-by-Step Procedure

With the "big picture" in mind, you're ready to go through the step-by-step procedure of preparing your hard drive for Linux. We've assumed that you want to install Linux on the same physical hard drive where you already have Microsoft Windows installed.

WARNING   *This section uses FIPS. Use it at your own risk. FIPS explicitly comes with "ABSOLUTELY NO WARRANTY." I've used it frequently without problems; however, it is fairly easy to accidentally destroy your data with FIPS.*

We've assumed that your hard drive is organized as only one partition, with all space allocated to the Windows C: drive. Alternatively, you could use these steps if the other drives don't provide enough room.

If you already have a hard disk with two or more partitions, you'll probably see this in Microsoft Windows as at least a C: and a D: drive. If you can move all of your files to the C: drive and still have enough room for Windows virtual memory, you can skip this process. Just make a note of the size of each of these drives, to help you identify them during the Linux installation process.

To prepare your hard disk for Linux, follow these steps:

1. Find the capacity of your hard disk and the amount of space occupied by existing files. Determine the amount of room that you want to allocate to Microsoft Windows and Red Hat Linux.

2. Defragment your hard disk. Use the Disk Defragmenter, which is typically available from the Windows Start menu in the Programs ➢ Accessories ➢ System Tools folder. The exact steps and location vary depending on your version of Microsoft Windows.

3. Prepare a partition splitter. If you want to use `FIPS.EXE`, copy it, along with `RESTORRB.EXE` and `ERRORS.TXT`, to a Microsoft Windows or MS-DOS boot disk. Alternatively, you can use the boot disk that comes with a third-party partition splitter such as Partition Magic or System Commander. In the remaining steps, we assume that you're using FIPS.

NOTE *You can create MS-DOS boot disks from downloads available from* **www.bootdisk.com**. *I prefer the Microsoft Windows 98 boot disk.*

4. Reboot your computer with the boot floppy. When you see the DOS A:\ prompt, run the FIPS command.

5. After you see the warning about not using FIPS in a multitasking environment, you see directions to "Press any key" to continue.

   If you have more than one hard drive, you are asked to choose; they're listed in boot order, similar to what is shown here. Drive 1 should be either the first IDE or SCSI hard drive on your computer. Select a drive.

   ```
   Which Drive (1=0x80/2=0x81)
   ```

6. Next, you see a partition table (see Figure 2.3), listing the four primary partitions. If all four primary partitions are used, FIPS will fail, because it can split only primary partitions. If you have more than one partition that you can split, you are asked to select it, by number.

FIGURE 2.3

The FIPS partition table

```
     | bootable|Head Cyl. Sector|System|Head Cyl. Sector| Sector |Sectors |   MB
Part.|        |             |      |             |        |        |
1    |    yes|   1   0        1|  83h| 127  24      63|      63|  201537|   98
2    |     no|   0  25        1|  83h| 127 476      63|  201600| 3644928|1779
3    |     no|   0 477        1|  82h| 127 524      63| 2846528|  387072| 189
4    |     no|   0   0        0|  00h|   0   0       0|       0|       0|   0
~
~
~
~
~
~
~
~
~
~
~
~
~
~
```

7. If you see the following message, this means you have to select from among the available primary partitions. Make your selection and continue. (If you select an extended partition, FIPS won't be able to handle it and will abort.)

   ```
   Which Partition do you want to split (1/2/3)?
   ```

8. Your selected partition is scanned. You're shown basic information about the partition, and then you're asked whether you want to write backup copies of the boot and root sectors to a bootable floppy disk. This is an excellent idea. Answer *YES* to both questions. You see a message similar to Writing file a:\rootboot.000. Make a note of this file. If you have a problem, you can restore the original partition table by using the RESTORRB.EXE command.

9. Now you can define how you're going to split the partition. Using the arrow keys, you can change the size of the existing and new partitions. Make a note of the size of the new partition.

```
Old partition            Cylinder            New Partition
  2075.3 MB                 280                 932.8 MB
```

10. When you're ready, press Enter to confirm the two new partitions. The old partition should contain the existing data. Next, FIPS tests the space to be occupied by the new partition. If it's empty, FIPS presents you with a new partition table similar to Figure 2.3. Next you must decide whether you want "...to continue or re-edit the partition table (c/r)?" If you press r, return to step 6. If you like your changes, press c to continue.

11. Finally, you're asked whether "...you want to proceed (y/n)?" to write the new partition scheme to disk.

12. Once the new partition scheme is written, you're ready to install Linux. The new partition should show up during the Red Hat Linux installation process. If all goes well, it should show up as empty, and it should be the size you created with FIPS.

More information is available on FIPS from its website at www.igd.fhg.de/~aschaefe/fips.

Why Worry about Hardware?

The community of developers who support Linux has done an excellent job creating drivers for an overwhelming majority of PC hardware. Many—perhaps even most—new components get Linux drivers within months of their release. Many hardware manufacturers, in fact, include Linux drivers with their hardware or make them available for download from their website. With the advances in Linux plug and play, most hardware is now detected and configured automatically. So in many cases, you don't have to worry about hardware when you install Red Hat Linux on your computer.

However, there can be problems. If you're planning to install Linux on a group of computers, hardware problems can be expensive. Not all hardware is built for Linux—or for Microsoft Windows XP, for that matter. And not all hardware has Linux drivers.

Hardware Problems Can Be Expensive

It's true that the cost of hardware tends to fall over time. However, when you're planning for a group of computers, the cost of replacing every network card quickly adds up, not only in hardware, but in the labor required for each computer.

Some components are more expensive than others. If you make a mistake with your video configuration, you could easily blow the circuits associated with your monitor. And if that monitor is your laptop display, the cost can be frightening. Therefore, you should at least record the specifications for your video card and monitor.

If you make a mistake while configuring a video adapter, you could make it send signals that exceed the capability of your monitor. This is true on Linux as well as Microsoft Windows computers.

NOTE *In most cases, modern monitors just tell you that you've made a mistake.*

When video adapters send signals to monitors, they send them at specific frequencies and refresh rates. Monitors have limits on the frequencies and refresh rates that they can handle. The results could burn out circuits on your monitor. While some monitors have protective circuits built in, why take the risk?

Not All Hardware Is Built for Linux

Some manufacturers release the source code for their hardware. Some of this code is even released under the General Public License (GPL). That makes it easy for a Linux developer to design a driver for that hardware component.

However, not all hardware is built for Linux. For example, a group of modems and printers, Winmodems and Winprinters, were explicitly designed for Microsoft Windows. They explicitly use Microsoft Windows driver libraries to function. Since Microsoft does not release the source code for its driver libraries, that makes it difficult for Linux developers to create drivers. Strangely enough, because of the changes in Microsoft Windows XP many Winmodems and Winprinters may also not work on these latest Microsoft operating systems.

TIP   A number of Linux books suggest that you avoid Winmodems at all costs. That may no longer be necessary. I have Winmodems that Linux recognizes on both my laptop and desktop computers.

Sometimes Linux developers haven't had the time to create drivers for the latest components. As of this writing, Linux drivers are incomplete for three types of components: USB, IEEE 1394, and IEEE 802.11 wireless systems. While Linux support for USB 1.x components is fairly good, USB 2.0 requires a kernel that supports the Enhanced Host Controller Interface (EHCI), which is still experimental for the kernel that is supplied with Red Hat Linux 9.

Linux support for some IEEE 1394 equipment is available as experimental drivers. Linux support for regular wireless networking (IEEE 802.11b) is good; drivers for IEEE 802.11a–11g are currently in the works. Later in this chapter, in the "Questionable Hardware" section, you can find the home pages for those who are developing these cutting-edge drivers.

TIP   Starting with version 8.0, Red Hat Linux can no longer be installed on computers with 386- and 486-level CPUs.

Finding Compatible Hardware

On its website, Red Hat includes the latest available information on compatible hardware. Visit the hardware compatibility section of its site, currently available at `http://hardware.redhat.com/hcl`, as shown in Figure 2.4. Linux-compatible hardware is often organized in what is known as a Hardware Compatibility List (HCL).

Red Hat has tested hardware on a number of different PCs. However, the company also relies on the work of other Linux developers. Red Hat classifies hardware in one of the four categories described in Table 2.2.

FIGURE 2.4

Red Hat Hardware
Compatibility List

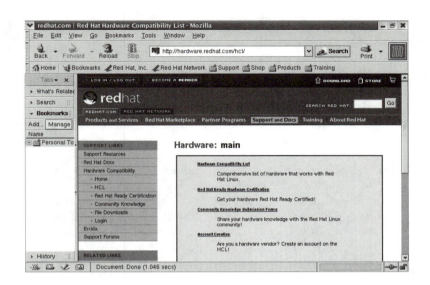

FIGURE 2.4

Red Hat Hardware
Compatibility List

TABLE 2.2: RED HAT HARDWARE COMPATIBILITY CATEGORIES

CATEGORY	DESCRIPTION
Certified	Hardware that has been officially tested by Red Hat through its official certification program, and is known to work with Linux.
Compatible	Hardware that has been reviewed by Red Hat personnel, outside the official certification program.
Community knowledge	Hardware that has been found by others to be compatible with Linux. While Red Hat may include drivers for such hardware as part of the installation CDs, it is not supported by Red Hat, Inc.
Not supported	Hardware that has been officially tested by Red Hat through its official certification program, and is known to *not* work with Linux.

Examples of each category of hardware are discussed in the following sections.

Certified Hardware

Certified hardware has been officially tested by Red Hat Linux. Generally, you'll find entire systems, such as IBM branded servers, listed as Red Hat–certified hardware, but not single components. There are exceptions.

On the Red Hat HCL web page, you can click the Hardware Compatibility List link to navigate to a search engine for the Red Hat HCL. It's a straightforward search engine. Once you've found hardware, you can find Red Hat's review of the component. For example, Figure 2.5 shows Red Hat's review of a network card from D-Link.

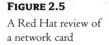

FIGURE 2.5

A Red Hat review of
a network card

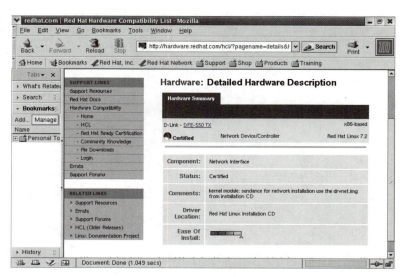

From this web page, you can see that the D-Link DFE-550 TX network card is certified using the
`sundance.o` driver, which is available on the Red Hat Linux installation CD. If you're installing Linux
over a network, you can enable the network card through the `drvnet.img` installation driver floppy,
and it's very easy to install. In other words, you can install Red Hat Linux through this network card.
You just need to make your computer read the driver disk, as described in Chapter 3. Finally, note that
this card was tested for Red Hat Linux 7.2. While this network card should work in later versions of
Red Hat Linux, there is no guarantee.

Compatible Hardware

There is a subtle difference between certified and compatible hardware. Certified hardware generally
consists of entire systems; compatible hardware includes individual components such as CPUs, hard
drives, graphics adapters, and network cards. It's difficult to test every possible combination of components; unknown interactions can affect compatibility with any operating system.

Red Hat provides limited support to licensed users of Red Hat Linux for "compatible hardware."
It's easy to find a list of compatible hardware on the Red Hat HCL. Navigate to `http://hardware`
`.redhat.com/hcl`, and under the support links, click HCL. At the bottom of the page, you'll see four
tabs that can help you search through the Red Hat HCL.

I've performed an "Advanced Search" for Video Devices that are known to be compatible with
Red Hat 8.0; the results are shown in Figure 2.6.

NOTE *Web links may change by the time you read this book. If the link does not work, you'll have to use your own
insight on the Internet to find the data that you need. In this case, I believe that Red Hat will always maintain an HCL,
even if it's just up to Red Hat Linux 9. You should be able to find it in a support area of the site.*

FIGURE 2.6

Compatible video
hardware

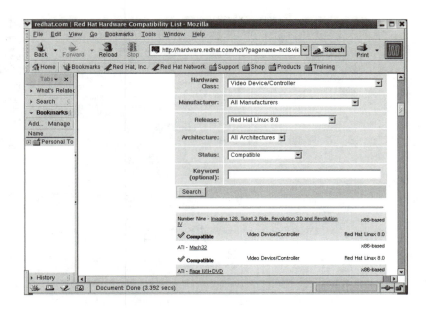

Questionable Hardware

There are several categories of hardware where Linux support is less than ideal. Yet Linux developers have made progress in a number of areas. For example, it is no longer necessary to avoid all Winmodems. If you have questions about your hardware, a good place to start is the Hardware Compatibility HOWTO of the Linux Documentation Project, currently available at `www.tldp.org/HOWTO/`
`Hardware-HOWTO`.

We've listed several different categories of questionable hardware, along with resources that can help. If you can't find a driver for some component on your PC, look through the associated websites. An enterprising Linux developer may have the driver or solution for you.

TIP   When you look for drivers, you may not need a perfect match. For example, you may be able to configure a video card using an older driver from the same manufacturer.

Cameras   Digital camera manufacturers generally use proprietary programs and interfaces. Despite these limits, the gPhoto developers have developed software that works with hundreds of digital cameras (see `www.gphoto.net`).

FireWire/iLink/IEEE 1394   FireWire and iLink are tradenames for the IEEE 1394 standard. It supports high-speed data transfer for external devices such as hard disks and video cameras. While kernel support for these devices is still "experimental," help is available through `www.linux1394.org`. You may need to recompile your kernel (as discussed in Chapter 12) to enable IEEE 1394 support.

Graphics cards   Red Hat Linux works fine with almost all graphics cards, at least in VESA (Video Electronics Standards Association) mode, as described in Chapter 3. But developers are improving drivers all the time. Assuming you use the default Red Hat Linux XFree86 Server, you may be able to find a driver update for your card through the XFree86 project at `www.xfree86.org`.

Laptops Red Hat Linux works fine on most laptop computers. However, there are risks, because laptop manufacturers use a considerable amount of proprietary software. The Linux on Laptops web page at `www.linux-laptop.net` offers the experience of a number of users on different laptop computers. The Linux-Mobile-Guide provides detailed information on configuring laptop computers and other mobile devices at `http://tuxmobil.org/howtos.html`.

Network cards Red Hat Linux works well with most standard network cards. But as network speeds increase, new network cards are under development; you may not find the latest driver for various Gigabit or 10 Gigabit Ethernet network card on the Red Hat Linux 9 CDs. Development work on the latest Linux network card drivers is sponsored by Scyld Computing, at `www.scyld.com/network`.

Printers The so-called Winprinter can be as difficult to configure as the Winmodem, and new printers with more features are released at an astonishing rate. The developers at `www.linuxprinting.org` have done astonishing work developing new print drivers and configuration files.

Scanners The Scanner Access Now Easy (SANE) home page provides tips and tricks for configuring regular and USB scanners for Linux. Currently, the home page for SANE development is at `www.mostang.com/sane`.

Sound cards Sound cards can be difficult to configure in Linux. For example, some cards need multiple DMA channels; others can be configured to emulate one of the Sound Blaster cards. The latest information in Linux sound card support is available from the Advanced Linux Sound Architecture (ALSA) project at `www.alsa-project.org`.

USB While Red Hat Linux can detect the basic USB keyboard and mouse during the installation process, Linux support for USB devices is currently less than ideal. But as PCs move toward converting external devices to USB and IEEE 1394 standards, Linux developers will be creating new drivers for every type of external hardware. As of this writing, support for IEEE 1394 and USB 2.0 standard high-speed equipment is still experimental. The latest information on Linux support for USB is available from the Linux USB Project at `www.linux-usb.org`.

Winmodems As described earlier, Winmodems depend on Microsoft Windows driver libraries to support their functionality. However, the people behind the Linmodem project have developed Linux drivers that work seamlessly with many Winmodems. Many of their drivers are incorporated into Red Hat Linux 9. Many Winmodems are now detected automatically through the Linux plug-and-play system. But not all Winmodems work in Linux. For the latest status, see `www.linmodems.org`.

Community Knowledge Hardware

The Linux operating system is based on a collective effort of developers from around the world. People in the Linux community have organized themselves into a number of groups. As described earlier, many of these groups are dedicated to creating and updating drivers for specific types of hardware. Their progress is documented at their websites and in mailing lists.

When you want the latest community knowledge about Linux hardware, there are four ways to direct your research. The Linux Hardware HOWTO provides an overall view of Linux hardware compatibility. However, it may not include the latest hardware information. More data is available at the websites for many hardware-specific Linux support groups, as described in the previous section. Many of these groups have open mailing lists, where developers exchange information on their latest work. Finally, users ask questions about hardware all the time on the Internet newsgroups. A searchable newsgroup database is available at `http://groups.google.com`.

NOTE *Before asking a question on a mailing list or newsgroup, do your research first. Many Linux developers have jobs and don't have time to give you answers that can already be found in documentation, such as the LDP HOWTOs at* `www.tldp.org`*. In fact, many will show their annoyance if you waste their time. Before you ask a question on a newsgroup or mailing list, check the documentation available on the subject. Search the newsgroups or mailing list database to see if your question has been answered before.*

Creating a Hardware Checklist

Ideally, you should collect information on every hardware component in your computer. This section provides a checklist on the information that you need. Once you've identified your hardware, you can check the Red Hat and other websites for the drivers and configuration tips that you may need.

At a minimum, you should get the specifications for your graphics card and monitor before installing Red Hat Linux. Once Linux is installed, test each hardware component. Make a list of those components that are hard to configure or that do not work to your satisfaction. Detected components are normally configured in the /proc directory, as described in Chapter 11. The next time you install Red Hat Linux, you'll be ready with the drivers and configuration commands that you need. This is a good approach if you're installing Red Hat Linux on a group of computers.

In the following sections, you'll learn about the information that you should collect on each hardware component. Then, you'll find how to associate each component with a specific driver. Finally, we provide a table where you can fill in the blanks with the data you need.

Collecting Information

Before starting to install Red Hat Linux on your computer, you should keep in mind a few basic things. You don't absolutely need to know everything about every hardware component; most are automatically detected during the installation process. Review the list of priority hardware in Table 2.3.

TABLE 2.3: PRIORITY HARDWARE

COMPONENT	REQUIRED INFORMATION
CPU	Red Hat Linux 9 requires at least a 200MHz Pentium-level CPU. If you want a GUI, you'll need at least a 400MHz Pentium II-level CPU. In addition, if you have a non-Intel (or compatible) CPU, you will need a different set of installation packages.
RAM	The amount of RAM you need depends on whether you're using the computer with a GUI, and/or for multiple users. While 64MB of RAM may be enough for a command-line interface, you should have at least 128MB (and preferably 192MB) of RAM to install Red Hat Linux with a GUI interface.

Continued on next page

TABLE 2.3: PRIORITY HARDWARE *(continued)*

COMPONENT	REQUIRED INFORMATION
Graphics card	You need to know a few things about your video card. The Linux XFree86 server packages include a database that can configure your card based on the make and model. If Linux does not recognize the card, you should be able to configure it separately knowing the video RAM and available vertical and horizontal refresh rates.
Monitor	You should know the capabilities of the monitor: its resolution, as well as its vertical and horizontal refresh rates. If the graphics card can put out refresh signals above the monitor's capacity, be careful; the wrong settings can burn out your monitor.

In other words, you should know the make, the model, and the specifications of at least the priority hardware components on your computer.

Collecting Drivers

Drivers for most hardware components are already included with the Red Hat Linux installation CDs. Most drivers are automatically configured during the Linux installation process.

But Red Hat Linux does not include drivers for all hardware. No Microsoft operating system includes drivers for all hardware. There are two basic ways to collect additional drivers. One is based on community knowledge, as discussed earlier. The other is based on drivers created by hardware manufacturers.

Many hardware manufacturers are friendly to Linux. Remember, IBM has invested over a billion U.S. dollars in Linux development. A lot of manufacturers have followed their lead and provided Linux drivers for their hardware. Many Linux drivers are downloadable from manufacturer websites. Typically, documentation and instructions are available from the same sites.

Once drivers are available, they can be installed with commands such as `insmod`. You can make sure that the drivers are installed the next time Linux starts with the right commands in `/etc/modules .conf`. More information on this process is available in Chapter 11.

Hardware Checklist

For your convenience, this section includes a table of hardware information that you should collect for your PC. This is more important if you have a group of PCs with similar configurations, to help you avoid potentially costly errors. The hardware you need to detail is listed in Table 2.4.

You should make special note of any devices that don't conform to plug-and-play standards. You may need to reserve IRQ ports or I/O addresses in your BIOS for any such hardware.

TABLE 2.4: HARDWARE CHECKLIST

COMPONENT	DETAIL
CPU type, speed	
RAM Memory, in MB	

Continued on next page

TABLE 2.4: HARDWARE CHECKLIST *(continued)*

COMPONENT	DETAIL
Keyboard, make, model	
Mouse, protocol, make, model, buttons	
Hard drive 1 size	
Partitions and mount points, such as /home and /dev/sda1	
Hard drive 2 size	
Partitions and mount points, such as /var and /dev/sdb1	
Hard drive 3 size	
Partitions and mount points, such as /usr and /dev/sdc1	
Hard drive 4 size	
Partitions and mount points, such as /boot and /dev/hda1	
CD-ROM, type	
CD-writer, type	
DVD-ROM, type	
SCSI adapter, make, model	
Network card, make, type, model, speed	
Network card 2, make, type, model, speed	
Telephone modem, make, model, speed	
Graphics card, memory, make, model, vertical and horizontal refresh	
Monitor, make, model, vertical and horizontal refresh	
Monitor 2, make, model, vertical and horizontal refresh	
Sound card, make, model, chipset	
USB device 1, make, model	
USB device 2, make, model	
USB device 3, make, model	
USB device 4, make, model	
IEEE 1394 device 1, make, model	
IEEE 1394 device 2, make, model	

BIOS Tips

There are three things that you may be able to configure in your computer's BIOS. One is the boot order of your hard drives. Next is the boot sequence; for example, you can configure your BIOS to boot the Red Hat Linux installation program from the appropriate CD. Finally, you may be able to reserve key communications channels, such as IRQ ports and I/O addresses.

A wide variety of BIOS menus are available. It is therefore not possible to provide specific directions on how to configure a BIOS. What you can configure depends on the BIOS menu and any upgrades that you may have installed.

Normally, you can review your BIOS menu by pressing a key such as F1, F2, or Del on your keyboard just after the initial beeps on your computer. Sometimes, you'll see a menu such as Figure 2.7 during the boot process.

FIGURE 2.7

PC Startup menu

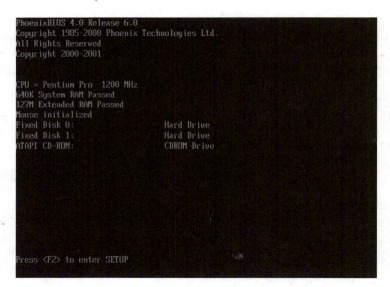

Sometimes the menu is hidden, perhaps by a screen associated with your computer or motherboard manufacturer. Press F1, F2, or Del. If one of these commands does not start your BIOS menu, consult the documentation for your PC or motherboard. In the BIOS menu, you should see detected IDE drives.

NOTE *With some Compaq and Acer computers, you'll need to press Ctrl+Alt+Esc to access the BIOS menu.*

IDE Hard Drives

On a standard PC, you may have up to four IDE drives. They may be hard drives or CD/DVD drives, and should be detected as such in the BIOS menu.

If you have installed IDE drives and they're not detected in your BIOS, you may have a hardware problem. For more information on troubleshooting PC hardware installation, please refer to *Complete PC Upgrade and Maintenance Guide, 2003 Edition* (Sybex, 2002).

Standard PCs have two IDE adapters: a primary and a secondary. Each adapter can be connected to two different IDE drives: a master and a slave. Linux associates very specific device files with these drives, as shown in Table 2.5.

TABLE 2.5: LINUX IDE DEVICE DRIVER DRIVE DEVICE FILES

DRIVE	DEVICE FILE
Primary master	/dev/hda
Primary slave	/dev/hdb
Secondary master	/dev/hdc
Secondary slave	/dev/hdd

SCSI Hard Drives

There are several different types of SCSI standards. SCSI-1, SCSI-2, and SCSI-3 standards are associated with a maximum of 8 or 16 devices, with data transfer speeds of up to 80MBps. Each SCSI device has an ID, which specifies its priority on your PC.

SCSI hard drives can be installed internally or externally. Most newer BIOSes can detect SCSI drives at least as part of its boot sequence menu. On older PCs, you may need a SCSI BIOS.

NOTE   IEEE 1394 drives are technically SCSI drives without LUN numbers. As of this writing, you can't boot Linux from an IEEE 1394 drive.

Boot Sequence

In your BIOS menu, you should see a Boot Sequence option, which allows you to specify the boot order. Your PC's BIOS looks at these drives in order for the **/boot** directory for the Linux startup files and kernel. You can configure your PC to look to any detected drive first. However, you need to set up your BIOS to look to a specific drive for the **/boot** directory.

If you have IDE drives connected to both the primary master and primary slave attach points, **/boot** must be installed on one of these drives (**/dev/hda** or **/dev/hdb**). This applies even if a CD/DVD is connected to one of these attach points. If you have two primary IDE drives, the Red Hat Linux installation program in fact forces you to configure **/boot** on one of these drives.

If you have one primary IDE drive and one SCSI drive, **/boot** must be installed on one of these drives. The SCSI drive must have an ID of 0.

If you have no primary IDE drives and two or more SCSI drives, **/boot** must be installed on one of the first two SCSI drives, with an ID of 0 or 1.

Non–Plug-and-Play Hardware

While Linux can now detect most plug-and-play hardware, there are legacy devices that don't conform to plug-and-play standards. In many newer BIOS menus, you can reserve IRQ ports and I/O addresses for such hardware. For example, an older network card may require a standard port, such as IRQ 10, and a standard I/O address, such as 0x300. If you can reserve these locations, you can configure that network card appropriately after Linux is installed.

Summary

Before you can install Red Hat Linux, you need to prepare your hardware. You may have to prepare hard disk partitions on IDE and/or SCSI drives for Linux. Special preparations are required if you want to configure Linux and another operating system, such as Microsoft Windows, on the same computer.

If you already have Microsoft Windows installed, it's easiest to install Linux on a second empty hard drive. The Red Hat Linux installation program, Anaconda, should detect the new empty hard drive and configure partitions on this drive. If you don't have a second hard drive, all you need is sufficient room on the first drive. With the Microsoft Windows Disk Defragmenter, you can make room. Using the FIPS utility, you can split an existing partition into two. You can then install Linux in the free space of the newly created partition.

Red Hat Linux detects most current PC hardware. Usually, there are no hardware concerns when installing Red Hat Linux. But if you're planning to install Linux on a group of computers, problems can be expensive. Not all hardware is built for Linux. And some hardware, specifically related to the graphics system, can be put at risk during the installation process.

Red Hat can help you find compatible hardware. Red Hat classifies hardware in four categories: certified, compatible, community knowledge, and not compatible. Community knowledge hardware may require additional work; drivers, directions, and advice are available from a number of sources.

You should collect basic information at least on the CPU, RAM, and graphics system. Drivers are available from a number of sources, including those discussed as community knowledge, as well as from the websites of a number of hardware manufacturers. We provided a hardware checklist and table to help you collect data on the other components in your PC.

To prepare your PC, you should also at least review the settings in your BIOS. The BIOS can help you configure IDE and SCSI hard drives. The Linux /boot directory should be installed on very specific drives. The boot sequence should work with these drives. You can also reserve specific channels in many BIOS menus for non–plug-and-play legacy hardware.

In the next chapter, you'll install Red Hat Linux, using various boot methods, from files on local Red Hat Linux installation CDs. Once Linux is installed, you'll see how easy it is to register your computer for updates on the Red Hat Network.

Chapter 3

Installing Linux Locally

IN THIS CHAPTER, WE'LL look at the graphical Red Hat Linux installation process, from the installation CDs, step by step. In most cases, all you need to do is set your PC to boot from the first Red Hat Linux installation CD, restart your computer, and follow the prompts. You can also customize Red Hat Linux to your specifications.

The Red Hat Linux installation program is known as Anaconda. A very flexible program, it can accommodate separate boot disks or, as you'll see in Chapter 4, network sources. If you're installing from CD, Anaconda includes a `mediacheck` option that inspects the integrity of your installation CDs. If it recognizes a previous installation of Red Hat Linux, it supports upgrades.

This chapter focuses on the graphical Anaconda installation process from a CD, which per spec requires 128MB of RAM on your computer. If you want to install Red Hat Linux over a network or use the Anaconda text-mode installation process, read Chapter 4.

Once the installation is complete, we will look at how you can diagnose typical installation problems. We'll then proceed with the first graphical and text login screens.

If you set Red Hat Linux to log in graphically by default, you'll see the `firstboot` process the first time you restart your computer. It lets you synchronize your date and time with a network time server, search for a sound card, register your computer with the Red Hat Network, and install additional software.

Due to space constraints, certain components available in Red Hat Linux are not available in the Publisher's Edition (two CDs) of Red Hat Linux included with this book. The complete version is available for free download (see the introduction to this book for instructions) or for purchase from Red Hat or a third-party retailer. While the Publisher's Edition should work for most installations, in this chapter we demonstrate the installation of Red Hat Linux using the standard three-CD set.

This chapter covers the following topics:

◆ Starting with a boot disk

◆ Checking the installation CDs

◆ Installing Red Hat Linux, step by step

◆ Running the Red Hat Setup Agent

◆ Troubleshooting the installation

◆ Logging in

◆ Upgrading Red Hat Linux

Starting with a Boot Disk

In most cases, you can install Red Hat Linux directly from your CD drive. All you should need to do is reconfigure the settings in your BIOS menu to boot directly from that drive, as described near the end of Chapter 2. However, there are situations where you need a boot disk:

◆ You're unable to set your BIOS to boot from your CD.

◆ Your CD is unable to read the boot files from the first Red Hat installation CD.

◆ You're installing Red Hat Linux from another source, such as a remote computer through the network (covered in Chapter 4). If you can boot from a CD, you may prefer to create the fairly small `boot.iso` CD for this purpose.

If you need to install Red Hat Linux from a boot floppy, you may need anywhere from one to four 1.44MB floppy disks, depending on your installation method and hardware.

You can create these floppies from `.img` files in the `/image` directory of the first Red Hat installation CD. The key files in this directory are summarized in Table 3.1.

TABLE 3.1: RED HAT LINUX INSTALLATION IMAGES

IMAGE FILE	DESCRIPTION
`bootdisk.img`	Standard boot disk for all local and network installations.
`drvblock.img`	Driver disk for block (storage) devices.
`drvnet.img`	Driver disk for network adapters.
`pcmciadd.img`	Driver disk for PCMCIA hardware.
`boot.iso`	All-in-one boot disk with drivers; while this does not fit on a single 1.44MB floppy, it can be installed on a CD.

This section is closely related to (and is somewhat repetitive of) the boot disk section in Chapter 4.

Creating a Boot or Driver Disk

Red Hat Linux provides four utilities that help you create boot and driver floppies. Two of them (**dd**, **cat**) work in Linux; the other two (**RAWRITE.EXE**, **RAWWRITEWIN.EXE**) work in Microsoft Windows. The Linux utilities are standard commands that you can run from other Linux or Unix computers; the image files and Microsoft utilities are available on the first Red Hat Linux installation CD.

If you're currently running a Linux computer, use these steps to create a boot disk. Remember, you'll probably also need one or more driver disks, as described in the following sections.

1. At a command-line interface, find the image files. For example, if you use the command

    ```
    # mount /mnt/cdrom
    ```

    to mount the first Red Hat Linux installation CD, the image files will be located in the `/mnt/cdrom/images` directory.

2. Insert a 1.44MB disk into a floppy drive. You do not need to use the `mount` command on that drive.

3. Use one of the following commands to convert the boot disk image, `bootdisk.img`, to a series of files on your floppy disk (`/dev/fd0` is the device associated with the first floppy drive on your computer):

    ```
    # dd if=/mnt/cdrom/images/bootdisk.img of=/dev/fd0
    # cat /mnt/cdrom/images/bootdisk.img > /dev/fd0
    ```

4. Repeat these steps with any driver disks that you might require from the `images` directory.

If you're in Microsoft Windows and want to create a boot disk from the command-line interface, use these steps to create that disk. Remember, you'll probably also need to repeat the process for one or both driver disks, as described in the following sections.

1. Insert the first Red Hat installation CD into a drive. Let's assume it's drive F:, but if your drive letter is different, substitute accordingly.

2. Access a MS-DOS prompt. Click Start ➤ Run. In the Run dialog box that appears, type **CMD** in the text box and press Enter. This should open a command prompt window.

3. In the command prompt window, type **F:** and press Enter.

4. Start the `RAWRITE.EXE` utility and run the following commands; insert a 1.44MB disk into your floppy drive when prompted:

    ```
    F:\>/DOSUTILS/RAWRITE.EXE
    Enter disk image source file name: /IMAGES/BOOTDISK.IMG
    Enter target diskette drive: A:
    Please insert a formatted diskette into drive A: and press -ENTER-:
    ```

5. Repeat the process with other required disk images in the `IMAGES` directory.

You can also use Microsoft Windows to create a boot disk by using the graphical `RAWWRITEWIN.EXE` utility. Remember, you'll probably also need one or both driver disks, as described in the sections that follow.

1. Insert the first Red Hat installation CD into a drive. Let's assume the CD is using drive H:, but if your drive letter is different, substitute accordingly.

2. Access the utility. Open Microsoft Windows Explorer. Click Start ➢ Run. In the Run dialog box that appears, type **EXPLORER** in the text box and press Enter. This should open Microsoft Windows Explorer.

3. Navigate to the H: drive, and then access the RAWRITEWIN folder, which is inside the DOSUTILS folder. You can then double-click on the RAWRITEWIN.EXE utility. (Yes, the spelling of the RAWRITEWIN folder differs from the RAWRITEWIN.EXE utility.)

4. This opens the RawWrite dialog box, shown in Figure 3.1. Click the Write tab if necessary. Click on the button to the right of the Image File text box; you should be able to access the image file of your choice from the H:\IMAGES directory in the Open dialog box.

FIGURE 3.1

Creating a boot floppy with RawWrite

5. Insert a 1.44MB disk into the floppy drive and click Write. Repeat this process with other required disk images.

Analyzing the Red Hat Boot Floppy

Whatever method you use to create it, the purpose and contents of the Red Hat Linux 9 boot floppy remain the same. It's created from the bootdisk.img file in the images directory on the first Red Hat installation CD and is used to boot your computer. On this floppy, the syslinux.cfg file provides a roadmap to what comes next, as shown in Figure 3.2.

Take a careful look at this file. Table 3.2 describes the key commands and should help you interpret the syslinux.cfg file.

FIGURE 3.2

The Linux Boot roadmap

```
default linux
prompt 1
timeout 600
display boot.msg
F1 boot.msg
F2 options.msg
F3 general.msg
F4 param.msg
F5 rescue.msg
F7 snake.msg
label linux
  kernel vmlinuz
  append initrd=initrd.img
label text
  kernel vmlinuz
  append initrd=initrd.img text
label expert
  kernel vmlinuz
  append expert initrd=initrd.img
label ks
  kernel vmlinuz
  append ks initrd=initrd.img
label lowres
  kernel vmlinuz
  append initrd=initrd.img lowres
_
```

TABLE 3.2: COMMANDS IN *SYSLINUX.CFG*

COMMAND	DESCRIPTION
default	Specifies the default boot option, in this case, default linux.
prompt	Sets out the boot: prompt.
timeout	Configures the delay time, in tenths of a second, before the boot disk automatically starts the default option; normally set to 600, or one minute.
display	Points to the initial message file to display on the screen.
Fx *option*.msg	Sets the function key associated with a particular message file.
label *command*	Specifies the actions associated with a particular command.
kernel	Sets the name of the compressed kernel image on the boot disk.
append	Adds the parameters with which the boot disk loads the kernel.
initrd	Specifies the Initial RAM disk.
text	Starts installation in text mode; see Chapter 4.
expert	Starts installation in expert mode, where you specify the hardware drivers.
ks	Starts the installation with a Kickstart file; see Chapter 5.
lowres	Starts the installation in a low-resolution 640×400 graphics mode with a basic VESA (SVGA) driver.

As you can see, the default is to load the compressed Linux kernel, `vmlinuz`, with the Initial RAM disk. As you can see in Figure 3.2, other options add different parameters.

TIP   You can use a Red Hat Linux boot floppy as a rescue disk. Using the techniques described in Chapter 11, it can help you recover from a number of failures, such as corrupted boot configuration files.

Analyzing the Storage Device Driver Disk

You can't install Red Hat Linux unless Anaconda detects a hard drive attached to your computer. The standard boot disk (from `bootdisk.img`) often recognizes standard IDE, SCSI, and even some USB hard drives that are connected to a PC; the required drivers are integrated into the compressed kernel.

That is why you may want to create a 1.44MB floppy from the `drvblock.img` file in the `images` directory of the first Red Hat Linux installation CD. Use any of the techniques described earlier in this chapter to create this disk. It loads five files onto a floppy, which we briefly describe in Table 3.3.

TABLE 3.3: FILES IN THE STORAGE DEVICE DRIVER DISK (*DRVBLOCK.IMG*)

FILE	DESCRIPTION
`modinfo`	Contains a list of device drivers and descriptions
`modules.cgz`	Has a compressed version of all drivers listed in `modinfo`
`modules.dep`	Includes a list of dependencies; in other words, other drivers required by each device
`pcitable`	Configures PCI settings for each device
`rhdd-6.1`	Labels this driver disk: "Supplemental Block Device Drivers"

Analyzing the Network Device Driver Disk

You can't install Red Hat Linux over a network unless Anaconda detects a network card on your computer. The standard boot disk (from `bootdisk.img`) does not include any network drivers, so you need a supplemental driver disk for network installations.

You can create a 1.44MB floppy from the `drvnet.img` file in the `images` directory of the first Red Hat Linux installation CD. Use any of the techniques described earlier in this chapter to create this disk. It loads five files onto a floppy, which are functionally similar to those on the storage device driver disk described in Table 3.3. While the contents have changed, the filenames are the same as before.

Analyzing the PCMCIA Driver Disk

Installing Red Hat Linux on a laptop computer often creates special issues. Laptops often rely on PCMCIA cards, as specified by the Personal Computer Memory Card International Association to connect to networks, SCSI devices and more. These credit card–sized adapters are sometimes known as PC Cards. Naturally, Red Hat provides many of the major PCMCIA socket, network, and SCSI drivers in the `pcmciadd.img` file.

You can create a 1.44MB floppy from the `pcmciadd.img` file in the `images` directory of the first Red Hat Linux installation CD. Use any of the techniques described earlier in this chapter to create this disk. It loads five files onto a floppy, which are functionally similar to those on the storage device driver disk described in Table 3.3. Although the contents have changed, the filenames are the same as before.

The Boot ISO

There is one more file of note in the `/images` directory of the first Red Hat Linux installation CD: `boot.iso`. You can create a boot CD from this 3.5MB file, using the techniques described for the `cdrecord` command in Chapter 14. It's suitable for simultaneous network installations where you don't want to run around loading and unloading boot and driver disks.

When you burn the `boot.iso` image onto a CD, the contents appear quite similar to the standard Red Hat boot floppy. There are two major differences: the files are all in an `isolinux` subdirectory, and the drivers associated with the aforementioned driver disks are combined in the Initial RAM disk image file, `initrd.img`.

Checking the Installation CDs

Before you start installing Red Hat Linux from the installation CDs, you should check the integrity of those CDs to ensure that all of the packages on the CDs are whole. One bad package out of the nearly 1500 available on the Red Hat CDs can stop your installation cold.

There are two basic options for checking your CDs. One involves starting the boot process with the `linux mediacheck` command; the other uses a statistical check based on the binary code on the CD.

NOTE   I've gone through the Red Hat installation process without the check—and after doing all the work required to configure Red Hat Linux, I've seen an installation stop cold at the third CD because of a single bad package. I had no choice but to start from scratch.

Inspecting CDs with *mediacheck*

To check your Red Hat Linux installation CDs, boot your computer from a boot floppy or the first installation CD. At the boot prompt shown in Figure 3.3, run the `linux mediacheck` command.

NOTE   In the `linux mediacheck` installation screens, you can switch between options with the Tab key and proceed to the next step by pressing the Enter key on your keyboard.

Anaconda then proceeds to install a basic kernel. The first prompt that you see, shown in Figure 3.4, allows you to test the integrity of your CDs. If you select Skip, Anaconda proceeds to the installation process. Select OK; it's important to check your CDs.

NOTE   If you're using a CD created from a downloaded `.iso` file, you don't need to run the `linux mediacheck` command. You'll get the prompt shown in Figure 3.4 automatically. See the introduction for more information on downloading and creating Red Hat Linux installation CDs.

FIGURE 3.3

Starting with a `mediacheck`

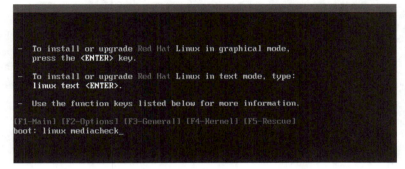

FIGURE 3.4

Anaconda offers to check your CD.

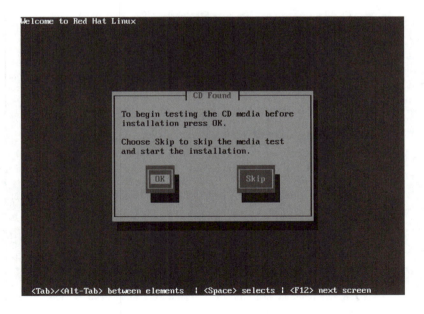

This mode isn't limited to the CDs for Red Hat Linux 9. I used Red Hat Linux 9's `mediacheck` feature to inspect a Red Hat Linux 8 installation CD. In the next screen (Figure 3.5), you can select whether to test the CD currently in the drive or eject it in favor of testing a different installation CD.

FIGURE 3.5

Ready to test

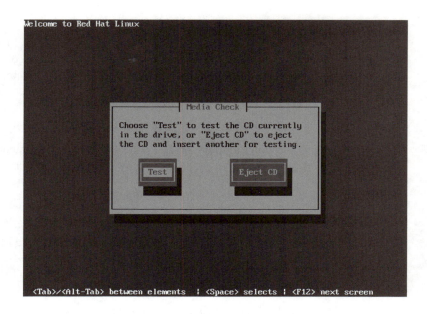

Insert the desired Red Hat installation CD, highlight Test, and press Enter. The test normally takes several minutes, at which point Anaconda identifies the CD and assigns it a grade of Pass or Fail. If necessary, reflect on the results and press Enter. Anaconda takes you to a slightly different screen, shown in Figure 3.6, where you can set up a different Red Hat installation CD for testing or insert the first Red Hat installation CD and then proceed with installation.

FIGURE 3.6

Continue testing or start the installation

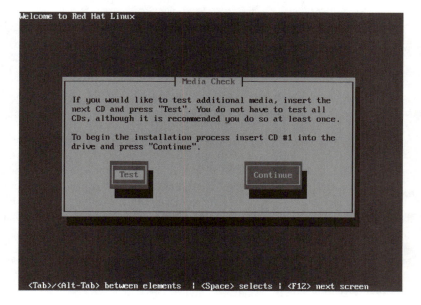

Checking CDs with *md5sum*

You can directly check the MD5 signature associated with each Red Hat installation CD. MD5 is an algorithm for checking digital signatures. You can apply the `md5sum` command from within Linux to a downloaded Red Hat Linux installation CD, in `.iso` format. For example, if you've downloaded the first installation CD as a file named *disc1*.iso, run the following command:

```
# md5sum disc1.iso
abb3dd2cd1cd1b92b5e85b0d556b8e12 disc1.iso
```

The 32-digit alphanumeric number that you get should match the number of the specified CD in the `MD5SUMS-ftp.i386` file. It is available from the same FTP directory as the large `.iso` files of the Red Hat Linux installation CDs. See the introduction for additional information.

Installing Red Hat Linux, Step by Step

Now that you've checked your CDs, you're ready to start installing Red Hat Linux 9 on your computer. The actual installation process does not have to be nearly as complex as I'll portray in this chapter—I'm just trying to give you a feel for everything that Anaconda can do for you. I've divided this process into several sections:

◆ "Selecting Installation Prompt Options" describes what you can do at the first installation `boot:` prompt.

◆ "Configuring Basic Parameters" allows you to examine your choices with your keyboard and mouse, as well as the language used by Anaconda during the installation process.

◆ "Setting Up Hard Drives" takes a detailed look at how you can configure different types of partitions in different formats using Disk Druid.

◆ "Configuring Installation Details" permits you to examine the nitty-gritty configuration details of the Red Hat Linux installation.

◆ "Selecting Package Groups" takes a look at the various package groups that you can install with Red Hat Linux as well as the individual package options.

◆ "Managing Post-Installation Steps" helps you configure the X Window and create a custom boot disk for your new system.

These steps assume that you're installing Red Hat Linux from the installation CDs. If you would rather install Red Hat Linux over a network connection, read Chapter 4.

This section assumes you've already changed the BIOS per Chapter 2 to boot from the first Red Hat installation CD. If you haven't, make sure your BIOS at least boots first from your floppy drive, or create a boot disk. Also keep in mind that this installation is based on a desktop computer with Microsoft Windows 98 currently installed. I've applied `fips` to the hard drive per Chapter 2 to create an empty partition with approximately 6GB of free space.

NOTE *It's possible to start the graphical installation process over an NFS (Network File System) connection. For more information on setting up an NFS-based network installation, see Chapter 4, and then return here for the graphical installation steps.*

Selecting Installation Prompt Options

You can start the installation process by booting your computer from one of two sources: the first Red Hat installation CD, or a boot disk. Either media will get you to the same start screen, shown in Figure 3.7. When you see this screen, press F2 within 60 seconds. Otherwise, Red Hat Linux starts graphical-mode installation automatically.

FIGURE 3.7

The installation prompt

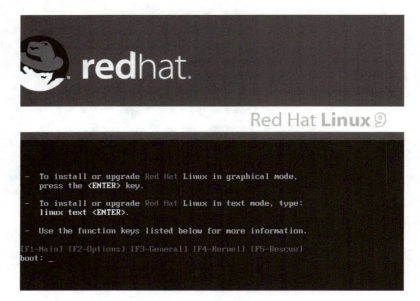

As you can see, several menus are available. We'll examine the different *installation* screens. The selections on the first screen are basic: you can choose to install Red Hat Linux in graphical or text mode. We examine graphical mode in this chapter and text mode in Chapter 4. When you press F5, Anaconda takes you to the Rescue Mode Help screen, which is unrelated to installation and is covered in Chapter 11.

When you're ready, you can press Enter to start graphical-mode installation, or type **text** and press Enter to start text-mode installation. In most cases, those are the best options.

However, if you have problems during installation, you may want to start again and try something else. Therefore, proceed to the "Installer Boot Options" section to examine the variety of commands that you can run at the `boot:` prompt.

INSTALLER BOOT OPTIONS

From the installation prompt screen in Figure 3.7, press F2. This takes you to the Installer Boot Options menu shown in Figure 3.8. Different options from this menu are briefly described in Table 3.4.

FIGURE 3.8

Installer Boot
Options

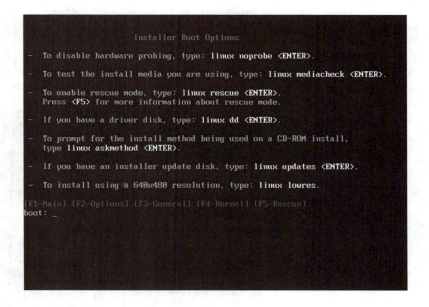

```
                        Installer Boot Options

-  To disable hardware probing, type: linux noprobe <ENTER>.

-  To test the install media you are using, type: linux mediacheck <ENTER>.

-  To enable rescue mode, type: linux rescue <ENTER>.
   Press <F5> for more information about rescue mode.

-  If you have a driver disk, type: linux dd <ENTER>.

-  To prompt for the install method being used on a CD-ROM install,
   type linux askmethod <ENTER>.

-  If you have an installer update disk, type: linux updates <ENTER>.

-  To install using a 640x480 resolution, type: linux lowres.

[F1-Main] [F2-Options] [F3-General] [F4-Kernel] [F5-Rescue]
boot: _
```

TABLE 3.4: INSTALLER BOOT OPTIONS

OPTION	DESCRIPTION
linux noprobe	Starts the installation process without automatic hardware detection; you'll need to select the drivers for any SCSI hard disks and network cards from a list.
linux mediacheck	Begins the installation process with the text-mode prompts that allow you to check the integrity of the Red Hat installation CDs; by default, continues in graphical mode.
linux rescue	Boots a basic Linux system in rescue mode that tries to detect a current Linux installation. See Chapter 11 for more information.
linux dd	Starts the installation process with a prompt for a driver disk; useful for third-party drivers.
linux askmethod	Begins the installation process; allows you to select the language and keyboard, and then allows you to select from local or network installation options.
linux updates	Supports an upgrade using a custom installer update disk.
linux lowres	Starts the installation in low-resolution graphics mode, 640×400; also known as VGA (Video Graphics Adapter).

You can run any of these installation options in text mode; just substitute **text** for **linux**.

GENERAL BOOT/KERNEL PARAMETER HELP

Press F3 in the Red Hat Linux installation start screen. This takes you to the General Boot Help menu, shown in Figure 3.9. This does not include any formal specific options; however, there is a lot more that you can do at the `boot:` prompt.

FIGURE 3.9

General Boot Help

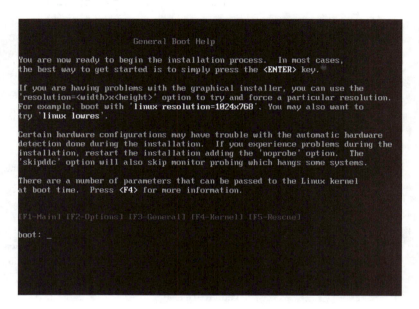

```
                              General Boot Help

You are now ready to begin the installation process.  In most cases,
the best way to get started is to simply press the <ENTER> key.

If you are having problems with the graphical installer, you can use the
'resolution=<width>x<height>' option to try and force a particular resolution.
For example, boot with 'linux resolution=1024x768'. You may also want to
try 'linux lowres'.

Certain hardware configurations may have trouble with the automatic hardware
detection done during the installation.  If you experience problems during the
installation, restart the installation adding the 'noprobe' option.  The
'skipddc' option will also skip monitor probing which hangs some systems.

There are a number of parameters that can be passed to the Linux kernel
at boot time.  Press <F4> for more information.


[F1-Main] [F2-Options] [F3-General] [F4-Kernel] [F5-Rescue]

boot: _
```

There are additional arguments that you can add after `linux` or `text` at the boot prompt. For example, the `linux upgradeany` command searches for and offers to upgrade any computer where Linux is detected, independent of what might be found in the `/etc/redhat-release` file. Several other arguments not covered in Table 3.4 are described in Table 3.5.

TABLE 3.5: BOOT PROMPT INSTALLATION ARGUMENTS

ARGUMENT	DESCRIPTION
`apm=off`	Disables Advanced Power Management (APM) during the installation process.
`display=`*ip_addr*`:0`	Forwards the installation display to a computer with an IP address of *ip_addr*. To make this work, be sure the receiving computer allows remote X Window access; see Chapter 15 on the `xhost` command for more information.
`expert`	Prompts for a driver disk; supports partitioning of removable drives. If you're installing on a SCSI hard drive, you'll need to supply at least the associated driver disk.
`ide=nodma`	Disables DMA (Direct Memory Access) addressing on IDE (Integrated Drive Electronics) devices such as hard drives.

Continued on next page

TABLE 3.5: BOOT PROMPT INSTALLATION ARGUMENTS *(continued)*

ARGUMENT	DESCRIPTION
isa	Prompts you to confirm that Anaconda has detected the correct ISA (Industry Standard Architecture) drives or similar devices.
mem=*xyz*M	Assigns a specific amount of memory; on some older computers, you may need to limit the RAM available to Anaconda to 128MB. On computers where RAM is shared with the video card, you may have to specify the available memory.
nmi_watchdog=1	Adds kernel debugging messages in one of the message screens described later.
nopcmcia	Avoids installing PCMCIA controllers; if you're installing Red Hat Linux from a CD that's not controlled through a PCMCIA connection, you don't need Anaconda to look for the PCMCIA controller.
nousb	Keeps Anaconda from installing USB support.
reboot=b	Modifies the kernel reboot method; some installations may otherwise hang just before the final step.
resolution=*a*x*b*	Specifies an installation video mode such as 640 × 480 or 1024 × 768.
serial	Starts serial console support during installation.
skipddc	Avoids the ddcprobe command, which is otherwise used to detect the monitor and graphics card. See Chapter 15 for more information on ddcprobe.
upgradeany	Looks for Linux installations to upgrade, independent of the contents of /etc/redhat-release.

NOTE *The* apic *argument that supported installation on computers with the Intel 440GX chipset BIOS is no longer available or required; support is now set up automatically.*

When you press F4, Anaconda takes you to the Kernel Parameter Help menu, shown in Figure 3.10. It includes information similar to the General Boot Help menu; Tables 3.4 and 3.5 include several arguments that you can pass to the kernel. Some are direct, such as mem=128M; others, such as noprobe, work indirectly by allowing you to specify the hardware address of key components of your PC.

Configuring Basic Parameters

Now we're actually ready to start the installation. Unless you have specific issues addressed by the previous section, just press Enter at the installation boot: prompt to start the Red Hat Linux installation process in graphical mode.

NOTE *If you've started the installation by entering* **linux mediacheck** *at the boot prompt, or you are starting from a CD created from a downloaded* .iso *file, Anaconda prompts you to check the integrity of your CDs, as described earlier.*

FIGURE 3.10

Kernel
Parameter Help

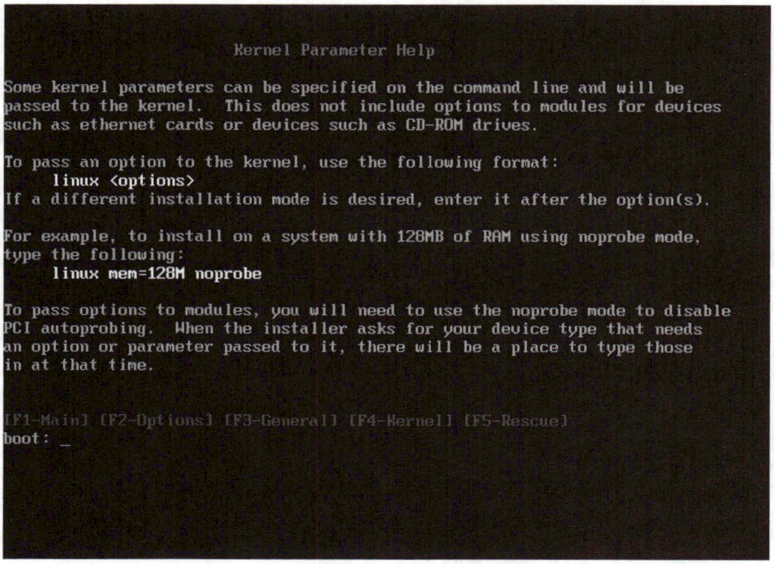

```
                        Kernel Parameter Help

Some kernel parameters can be specified on the command line and will be
passed to the kernel.  This does not include options to modules for devices
such as ethernet cards or devices such as CD-ROM drives.

To pass an option to the kernel, use the following format:
        linux <options>
If a different installation mode is desired, enter it after the option(s).

For example, to install on a system with 128MB of RAM using noprobe mode,
type the following:
        linux mem=128M noprobe

To pass options to modules, you will need to use the noprobe mode to disable
PCI autoprobing.  When the installer asks for your device type that needs
an option or parameter passed to it, there will be a place to type those
in at that time.



[F1-Main] [F2-Options] [F3-General] [F4-Kernel] [F5-Rescue]
boot: _
```

Anaconda probes your system to see if it meets the requirements for a graphical installation. As described in the REALEASE-NOTES file on the first installation CD, this requires at least 128MB of RAM. I tried a graphical installation with 64MB of RAM. It is allowed, but painfully slow, and I gave up early in the process. Anaconda automatically defaults to a text-mode installation if you have less than 64MB of RAM.

Next, it checks your system for the other requirements associated with a graphical installation: a video card, monitor, and mouse. You should see messages similar to the following:

```
Running anaconda, the Red Hat Linux system installer - please wait...
Probing for video card: Intel 810
Probing for monitor type: S/M 955DF
Probing for mouse type: Generic - Wheel Mouse (PS/2)
Attempting to start native X Server
Waiting for X server to start...log located in /tmp/X.log
1...2...3...4...5.... X server started successfully.
```

The messages you see list the hardware detected by Anaconda. If you have problems, note the location of the log file: /tmp/X.log. This message is a little unusual; the file actually disappears once Red Hat Linux is installed. We'll take a look at this file shortly.

If the hardware on your system passes the test, you'll see the first Anaconda installation screen, shown in Figure 3.11.

The basic graphical installation screen includes some help notes in the left-hand pane. If you click Release Notes, this opens the Release Notes window, shown in Figure 3.12. This includes the test from the RELEASE-NOTES file on the first Red Hat Linux installation CD.

FIGURE 3.11

The graphical
installation begins.

FIGURE 3.11

The graphical
installation begins.

FIGURE 3.12

Release Notes

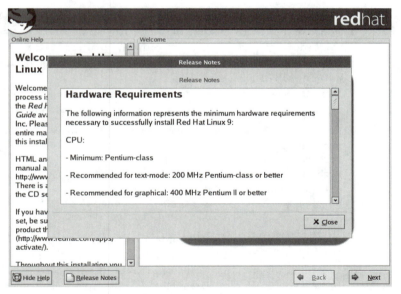

Read the Release Notes. They can help you learn more about Red Hat 9. When you've finished, click close to exit the release notes, and then click Next to continue. Anaconda takes you to the Language Selection screen, shown in Figure 3.13, which lets you select from 20 languages or dialects for the remainder of the installation process. This does not determine the languages that are loaded or used once Red Hat Linux is installed; we'll look at that step later. The rest of this chapter assumes that you're proceeding in English. Click Next to continue.

FIGURE 3.13

Selecting an
installation language

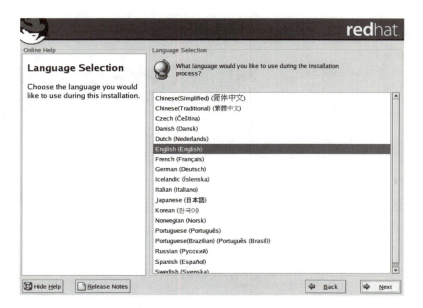

Now we'll look at the Keyboard Configuration screen shown in Figure 3.14, which lets you select
from 55 types of keyboards for your system. If Anaconda detected your keyboard, it should be highlighted. Your selection determines the default keyboard once Red Hat Linux is installed. You can
change the default keyboard after installation by using the `redhat-config-keyboard` utility described
in Chapter 19. Select the keyboard that most closely matches your system and click Next to continue.

FIGURE 3.14

Choosing a keyboard

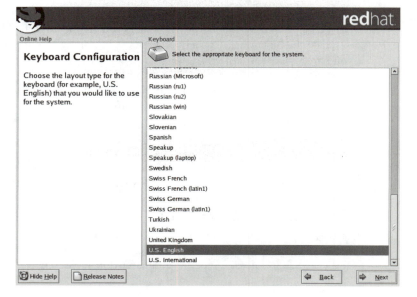

Next, we examine the Mouse Configuration screen, shown in Figure 3.15. This screen title is misleading; you can configure several different types of *pointing devices* with Anaconda.

FIGURE 3.15

Selecting a
pointing device

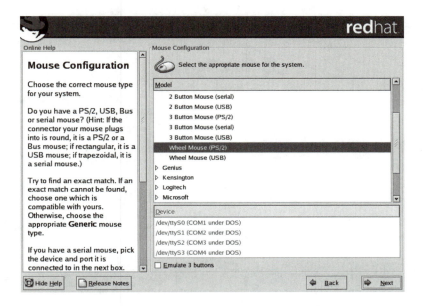

A pointing device can be a mouse, a touchpad, a trackball, or even a tablet. Red Hat Linux can even work with pointing devices connected through a USB (Universal Serial Bus) port. If you're configuring a pointing device that is connected to a serial port, the Device text box is active, and you can select the appropriate serial port device.

If you have a two-button mouse, you should activate the Emulate 3 Buttons option. This allows you to simulate the functionality of a middle mouse button by pressing both buttons together. However, if you have a mouse wheel, try pressing on it. If it clicks, Red Hat may already recognize it as a third button.

If Anaconda detected your pointing device, it should be highlighted on your screen. You can change the default pointing device after Red Hat Linux is installed with the `redhat-config-mouse` utility described in Chapter 19. Select the pointing device that most closely matches your system and click Next to continue.

If you're installing on a computer that includes a previous version of Red Hat Linux, you may see an Upgrade Examine screen. Upgrades are covered near the end of this chapter. If you see the screen shown in Figure 3.16, select Perform A New Red Hat Linux Installation and click Next to continue.

Selecting an Installation Type

Four basic types of installations are available, as shown in Figure 3.17. Each option supports a different kind of computer, and they are associated with different software package groups. The basic features of each installation type are summarized in Table 3.6.

FIGURE 3.16

Installing, not upgrading

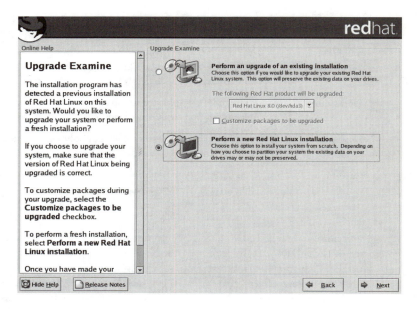

FIGURE 3.17

Selecting an installation type

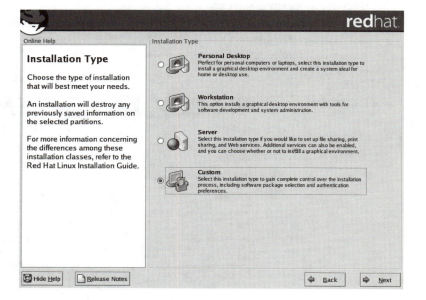

NOTE   *The size requirements are bigger than the requirements that you might see during the installation process. Additional files are installed based on dependencies, which are explained in detail in Web Chapter 5.*

TABLE 3.6: INSTALLATION TYPE

OPTION	DESCRIPTION
Personal Desktop	Configures a graphical desktop environment for PC desktop or laptop use. The default configuration installs nearly 1700MB of files.
Workstation	Configures a graphical desktop environment with software development and system administration tools. The default configuration requires about 2100MB of space for files.
Server	Configures a text-based desktop environment for a PC used as a server. The default configuration requires about 850MB of space for files.
Custom	Sets up an installation process that is completely customizable. The default configuration installs nearly 1500MB of files.

The sizes listed are defaults. They do not include space for a swap partition or any additional personal or third-party files or applications. However, you can further customize the packages to be installed, which can change the required disk space. Select the installation type suited for your needs. For the purpose of this chapter, we'll explore the Custom installation type. The other installation types use most of the same steps. After you select Custom, click Next to continue.

Setting Up Hard Drives

In the next several steps, we'll set up partitions on selected hard drives connected to your computer and recognized by Linux. Once you've selected an installation type, you get to choose whether to let Anaconda set up partitions for you or to proceed directly to Disk Druid. This screen is shown in Figure 3.18.

FIGURE 3.18

Choosing automatic or manual partitions

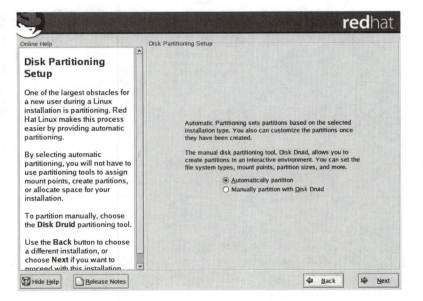

We'll select automatic partitioning and then continue on to Disk Druid to illustrate what Anaconda can do for you. If you select Manually Partition With Disk Druid, Anaconda skips the next step. Make your selection and click Next to continue.

Anaconda asks for your input as to where it should apply automatic partitions. As you can see in Figure 3.19, you have several options, which are explained in Table 3.7.

FIGURE 3.19

Configuring automatic partitioning

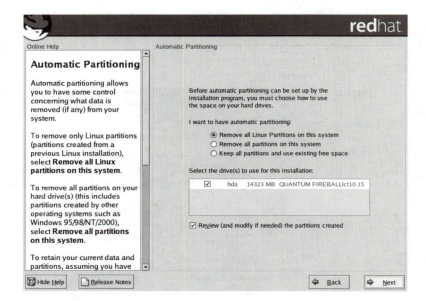

TABLE 3.7: AUTOMATIC PARTITIONING OPTIONS

OPTION	DESCRIPTION
Remove All Linux Partitions On This System	Deletes all currently configured partitions that are formatted to Linux filesystems. Applied to all selected hard drives.
Remove All Partitions On This System	Deletes *all* partitions on the selected hard drives. If you have another operating system such as Microsoft Windows, this action deletes that operating system.
Keep All Partitions And Use Existing Free Space	Does not delete any partitions. Attempts to configure partitions for Red Hat Linux in any hard drive space that is not allocated to a partition.
Select the Drive(s) To Use For This Installation	Lists the recognized hard drives on your computer. Automatic partitioning applies only to the drives that you select. Device names such as hda are explained in Chapter 2.
Review (And Modify If Needed) The Partitions Created	If checked, the next installation step illustrates Anaconda's proposed partition configuration in Disk Druid.

WARNING   *If you're installing Red Hat Linux as a server and want to dual-boot with another operating system such as Microsoft Windows, pay attention! Anaconda defaults to the Remove All Partitions On This System option, which would delete all Microsoft Windows partitions on your computer.*

For the purpose of this installation, we proceed by selecting Remove All Linux Partitions On This System. We also select the option Review (And Modify If Needed) The Partitions Created. (If you don't select this option, Anaconda skips the upcoming Disk Druid menu.) Make your selections and click Next to continue.

Before Anaconda removes any partitions, it sends you a warning message. If you've directed Anaconda to delete Linux partitions, the message is shown in Figure 3.20.

FIGURE 3.20

You'll see this warning before Anaconda removes partitions.

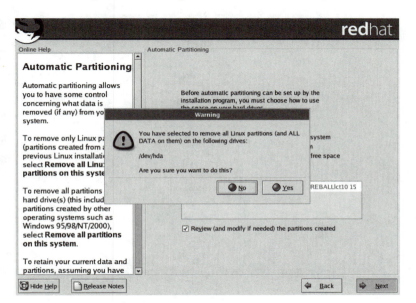

If you've directed Anaconda to delete all partitions, you should get a similar warning. Make sure you're actually ready to delete the noted partitions. If you are, click Yes to continue.

NOTE   *You may also get a warning about a /boot partition. If you already have another operating system, such as Microsoft Windows, on your computer, Anaconda probably can't install the /boot partition in the most desirable area of your hard drive, below the 1024th cylinder. The BIOS on some older computers won't be able to find your Linux boot files if the /boot partition is located above this cylinder on your hard drive. Even if your computer is affected, there are at least two ways to work around this issue. You can boot Linux from a boot floppy, or you can install a third-party bootloader such as Partition Magic or System Commander.*

Setting Up Partitions with Disk Druid

Disk Druid is Anaconda's semi-automated disk-partitioning utility. The results of Disk Druid's automatic partitioning on this desktop computer are shown in Figure 3.21.

FIGURE 3.21

Disk Druid at work

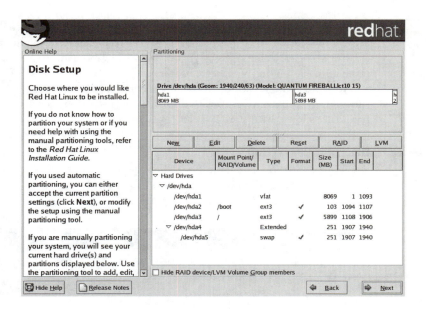

As you might guess, this is a dual-boot installation; /dev/hda1 happens to be a partition formatted to Microsoft's FAT32 filesystem. The swap partition, configured on /dev/hda5, is twice the size of the RAM on this desktop computer.

NOTE *If you have Microsoft Windows on the computer where you're installing Red Hat Linux, Anaconda shows both FAT16 and FAT32 partitions as type vfat.*

The Disk Druid screen is organized into sections. The top includes a map of current partitions as configured on recognized hard drives on your computer. It's followed by a series of command buttons that we'll explore momentarily. The bottom of the screen includes data on each drive and partition, as explained in Table 3.8.

TABLE 3.8: DISK DRUID DRIVE DEFINITIONS

COLUMN	DESCRIPTION
Device	Lists the device file for each hard drive and partition
Mount Point/RAID/Volume	Specifies the directory mounted on the partition
Type	Notes the filesystem of the partition
Format	Specifies drives to be formatted (if checked).
Size	Lists the size of the partition, in megabytes
Start	Notes the starting cylinder of the partition
End	Notes the ending cylinder of the partition

At the bottom of the screen, you can choose to Hide RAID Device/LVM Group Members. If you activate this option, the partitions in a RAID (Redundant Array of Inexpensive or Independent Disks) array or a Logical Volume Group are not shown. For more information on RAID, see Chapter 14; for more information on LVM, see Chapter 7.

Now let's examine each of the command options shown in Figure 3.21. We'll use the configuration shown in the following sections to illustrate our discussion. Since there is currently no room on the hard drive shown, we'll start by deleting a partition.

DELETING A PARTITION

To delete a partition, highlight it and click Delete. In the example shown in Figure 3.21, we've highlighted /dev/hda3 and clicked Delete. Before Disk Druid deletes the partition, it asks for confirmation, as shown in Figure 3.22.

FIGURE 3.22

Confirming a deleted partition

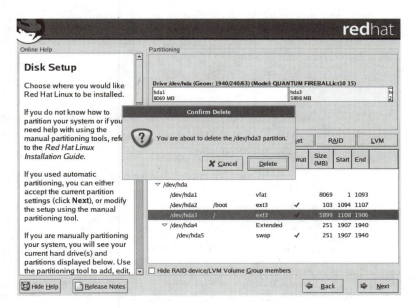

Now we have free space available from the deleted partition.

ADDING A PARTITION

You need free space on the available hard drives before you can add a partition. If you have free space on your hard drive, click New. This opens the Add Partition dialog box, shown in Figure 3.23. Each item in the figure is explained in Table 3.9.

FIGURE 3.23

Adding a partition

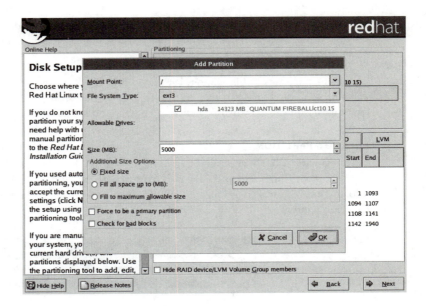

TABLE 3.9: OPTIONS IN THE ADD PARTITION DIALOG BOX

OPTION	DESCRIPTION
Mount Point	Specifies the directory to be mounted on the partition; for mountable directories, consult the discussion on the Filesystem Hierarchy Standard in Chapter 7. This is not applicable if the filesystem type is LVM, RAID, or swap.
File System Type	Sets the format for the partition; you're allowed to select form the Linux ext2 or ext3 standard, the Linux swap format, a Logical Volume Manager (LVM) physical volume, a software RAID volume, or a Microsoft Windows–style vfat format.
Allowable Drives	Notes the hard drive device associated with the partition.
Size (MB)	Specifies the size of the partition, in megabytes.
Fixed Size	Sets the partition size as specified.
Fill All Space Up To (MB)	If there is free space on your hard drive, the size of this partition grows up to the specified limit.
Fill To Maximum Allowable Size	Fills any remaining free space on the hard drive.
Force To Be A Primary Partition	Generally, you'll want the partition with the /boot directory to be on a primary partition below cylinder 1024.
Check For Bad Blocks	Sets up a physical check of the partition for unreadable sectors.

TIP   When you set up partitions on a hard drive, remember the limit of 16 partitions on an IDE hard drive and 15 partitions on a SCSI hard drive. If you exceed this limit, you won't find the problem until after it looks as if installation is complete.

For the purpose of this chapter, I've added four LVM partitions, four software RAID partitions, and a root (/) directory partition in the remaining space. You'll see how this works when we demonstrate what you can do when you click the RAID and LVM buttons.

EDITING A PARTITION

Editing a partition is very similar to adding a partition. For example, Figure 3.24 illustrates what happens when I highlight and edit the partition with my root (/) directory. The screen contains information identical to that in Figure 3.23. Please refer back to Table 3.9 for details on the Edit Partition window.

FIGURE 3.24

Editing an existing partition

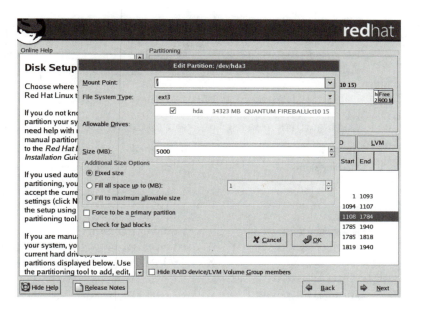

WARNING   Anaconda will not install Red Hat Linux 9 on hard drives with bad blocks.

RESETTING THE PARTITION TABLE

Any changes that you make aren't written until the partitions are formatted. If you want to return to the original partition table on your hard disk, click Reset. You'll get a chance to confirm your intent. Once you do, the partition table reverts to the configuration when you started Disk Druid.

MAKING RAID

Once you've configured software RAID partitions, you can create a RAID array. Ideally, the software partitions in a RAID array should be on different physical hard drives. Then the failure of one hard drive does not destroy your data in a RAID 1 or RAID 5 array. For more information, see Chapter 14.

Click RAID. Disk Druid takes you to the RAID options screen shown in Figure 3.25. As you can see, this window contains three options, which are described in Table 3.10.

FIGURE 3.25

Disk Druid software RAID options

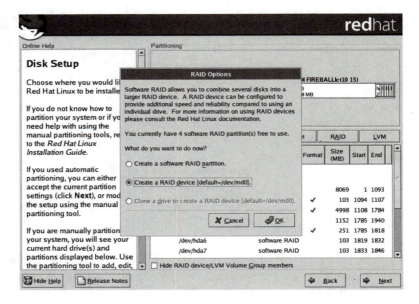

TABLE 3.10: SOFTWARE RAID CONFIGURATION MENU OPTIONS

OPTION	DESCRIPTION
Create A Software RAID Partition	Opens the Add Partition window with a software RAID filesystem type.
Create A RAID Device	Opens the Make RAID Device window, where you can assign software RAID formatted partitions to a RAID device.
Clone A Drive To Create A RAID Device	If you have two different physical hard drives, you can clone a RAID device from one drive to the other.

You already learned how to create a software RAID partition in the "Adding a Partition" section. If you have more than one hard drive on your computer and want to get serious about RAID, I recommend that you read one of the hardware RAID HOWTOs at www.tldp.org.

For the purpose of this installation, I've selected the Create A RAID Device option. After I click OK, Disk Druid takes me to the Make RAID Device window, shown in Figure 3.26.

FIGURE 3.26

Making a RAID device

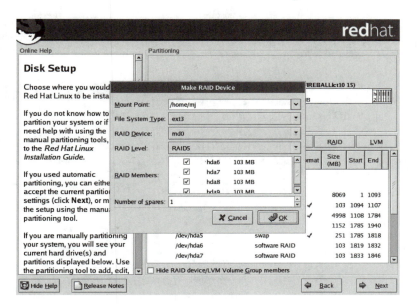

As shown in the figure, I've created a RAID device for the /home/mj directory. This is a RAID 5 device, formatted to the Linux ext3 filesystem. Since RAID 5 requires a minimum of three member partitions, it's possible to set this up with one spare partition. If one partition goes bad, RAID 5 will rebuild the required data on the spare partition automatically.

MAKING LVM

Once you've configured LVM physical volumes, you can create a LVM volume group. LVM is more practical on a single hard drive. As you can add and delete LVM physical volumes from a group, you can grow or compress the size of a partition assigned to a directory such as /usr. For more information, see Chapter 7.

Click LVM. Disk Druid takes you to the Make LVM Volume Group screen, shown in Figure 3.27. Each configurable option in the figure is explained in Table 3.11.

TABLE 3.11: MAKE LVM VOLUME GROUP OPTIONS

OPTION	DESCRIPTION
Volume Group Name	Sets the name of the LVM volume group
Physical Extent	Specifies the chunk of disk space associated with this volume group
Physical Volumes To Use	Lists LVM-formatted physical volumes (PV)

FIGURE 3.27

Making a LVM
volume group

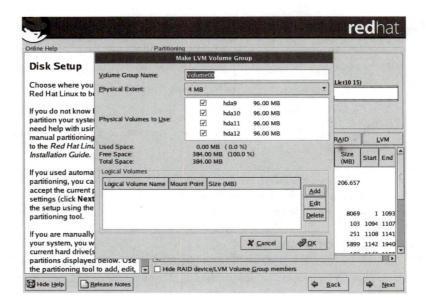

Make sure the physical volumes that you want to use for this volume group (VG) are checked. Name the volume group, and then click Add. This opens the Make Logical Volume window, shown in Figure 3.28; the options are described in Table 3.12.

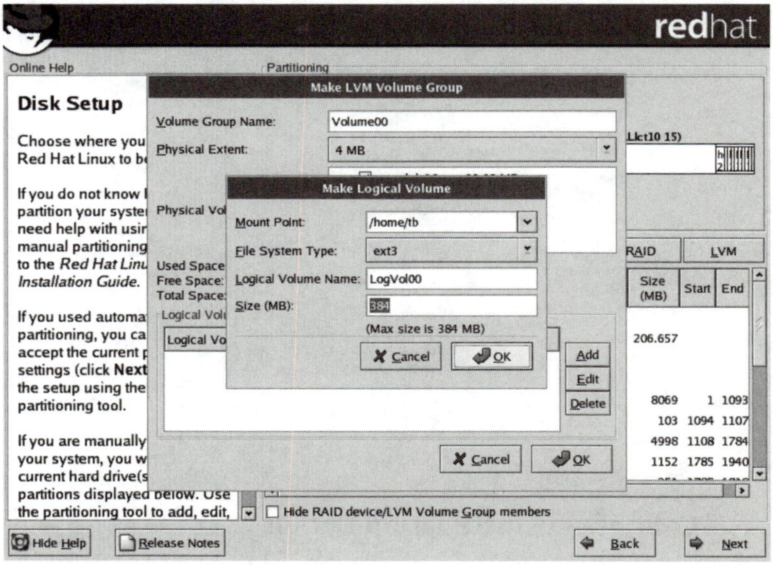

FIGURE 3.28

Making a logical
volume

TABLE 3.12: MAKING A LOGICAL VOLUME

OPTION	DESCRIPTION
Mount Point	The directory to be mounted on the logical volume (LV)
File System Type	The format associated with the LV
Logical Volume Name	An arbitrary name for the LV
Size (MB)	The size to be allocated to the LV, which includes the PVs that you've added to the LV

Once you've created the LV, click OK. This returns you to the Make LVM Volume Group window. You'll note that the amount of free space is reduced by the PVs that you've allocated to the new LV. When you've finished creating LVs, click OK to return to the main Disk Druid window.

LEAVING DISK DRUID

The final result is shown in Disk Druid, which includes your new partitions, RAID device arrays, and LVM volume groups, as shown in Figure 3.29. When you're ready, click Next to move beyond Disk Druid.

FIGURE 3.29

Disk Druid displays the revised partition table.

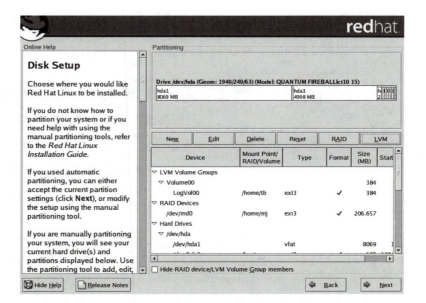

Configuring Installation Details

Now we'll explore the details of the Red Hat Linux installation process between Disk Druid and package group selection. The topics are wide and varied, starting with bootloader configuration and ending with authentication configuration.

BOOTLOADER CONFIGURATION

After you finish going through Disk Druid, it's time to configure the bootloader, which is what you see when you first boot your computer. Anaconda takes you to the Boot Loader Configuration screen, shown in Figure 3.30.

FIGURE 3.30

The Boot Loader Configuration screen

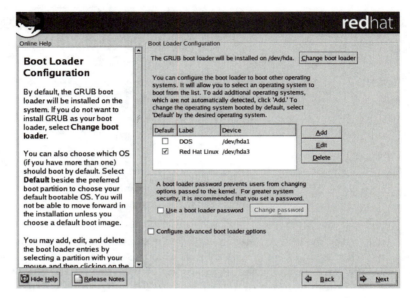

The default is GRUB, the Grand Unified Bootloader. The message at the top of the screen tells us that GRUB will be installed on the Master Boot Record (MBR) of the first IDE hard drive (`/dev/hda`). If you have a reason to use a different bootloader, click Change Boot Loader to open the Change Boot Loader window, shown in Figure 3.31.

NOTE   *The terms bootloader and boot loader are used interchangeably in Red Hat Linux.*

With Red Hat Linux, you can install the GRUB or LILO (Linux Loader) as your bootloader. If you already have a bootloader installed that you don't want to overwrite, select the Do Not Install A Boot Loader option. Make your choice and click OK, or click Cancel to retain the default bootloader. This returns you to the main Boot Loader Configuration screen.

NOTE   *You can use GRUB or LILO in concert with another boot loader, such as Partition Magic, System Commander, or Microsoft Windows NTLDR. Choose to install a boot loader, select Configure Advanced Boot Loader Options, and install GRUB or LILO on the partition with the /boot directory, as described in the next section.*

In the middle of the screen, you can see that Anaconda is installing Red Hat Linux in a dual-boot configuration. There is a Microsoft Windows operating system installed on partition device `/dev/hda1` labeled DOS, and the main Red Hat Linux files are installed on the partition labeled `/dev/hda3`. Red Hat Linux is the default, which in the default GRUB configuration means that GRUB starts Linux automatically if you don't make a selection in the GRUB menu within 10 seconds.

FIGURE 3.31

Selecting a boot-loader

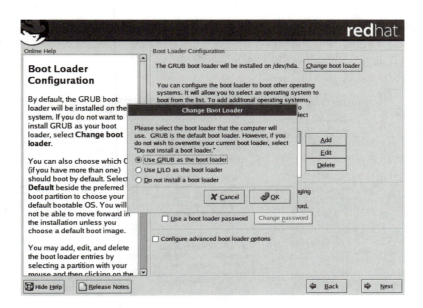

You can change a setting associated with DOS or Red Hat Linux by highlighting the setting and selecting Edit. This opens the Image window, shown in Figure 3.32, where you can edit the label, change the partition device, and set the associated operating system as the default. Make any desired changes and click OK to return to the Boot Loader Configuration screen.

FIGURE 3.32

Bootloader image properties

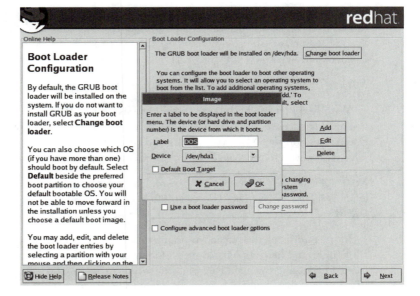

You can protect your bootloader with a password. If you want to set a password, click the Use A Boot Loader Password option. This opens the Enter Boot Loader Password window shown in Figure 3.33, which prompts you to enter a desired password twice. This password keeps others from changing your bootloader configuration file when your computer restarts.

FIGURE 3.33

Enter a Boot Loader Password

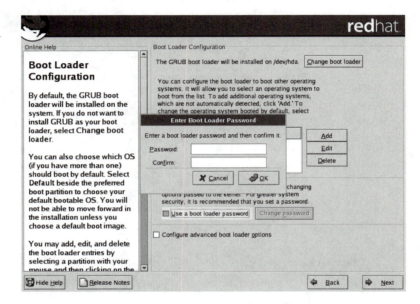

Finally, activate the Configure Advanced Boot Loader Options at the bottom of the screen, and click Next to continue.

ADVANCED BOOT LOADER CONFIGURATION

If you activated Advanced Boot Loader Options, you'll now see the Advanced Boot Loader Configuration screen, shown in Figure 3.34. It allows you to configure several more things associated with your bootloader, as described in Table 3.13. Make any desired changes and click Next to continue.

NETWORK CONFIGURATION

Now you can configure any network cards detected by Anaconda. By default, network cards are set to automatically get their network parameters from a Dynamic Host Configuration Protocol (DHCP) server. If you have a DHCP server on your network, it can assign a hostname and give your computer the IP addresses of your network gateway and DNS servers.

Even if you have a home network, you may already have a DHCP server. Many high-speed Internet routers/cable modems/DSL adapters are equipped with a DHCP server. Consult your hardware documentation for information.

We show the Network Configuration screen in Figure 3.35 and explain the basic options in Table 3.14. The two network devices shown in this figure are Ethernet network adapters, eth0 and eth1.

FIGURE 3.34

The Advanced
Boot Loader
Configuration
window

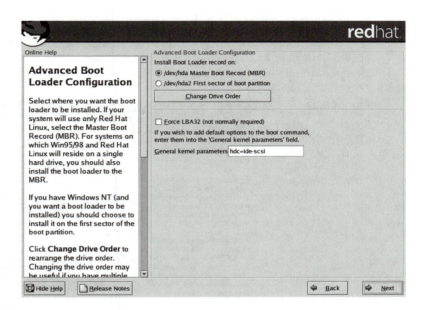

FIGURE 3.34

The Advanced
Boot Loader
Configuration
window

TABLE 3.13: ADVANCED BOOT LOADER CONFIGURATION OPTIONS

OPTION	DESCRIPTION
Install Boot Loader Record On	You can configure the bootloader on the MBR of a hard drive, which will run when the BIOS points to that drive. If you have another bootloader on the MBR, you can load the bootloader on the first sector of the boot partition.
Change Drive Order	If you have more than two physical hard drives, you may need to rearrange the drive order to make sure that your BIOS looks in the right drive for your bootloader. You can read more about this BIOS hard drive limitation in Chapter 2.
Force LBA32 (Not Normally Required)	If you had to mount the /boot directory on a partition above the 1024th cylinder on your hard drive, this may help your BIOS find your Linux boot files. This generally isn't required on newer hard drives.
General Kernel Parameters	If you need to pass parameters to the Linux kernel during the boot process, this is a good place to specify them. In the example shown in Figure 3.34, Anaconda added the SCSI emulation module for my CD writer automatically.

FIGURE 3.35

The Network Configuration window

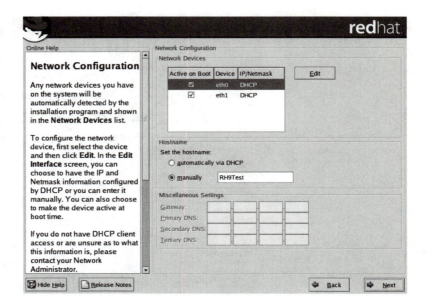

TABLE 3.14: NETWORK CONFIGURATION OPTIONS

OPTION	DESCRIPTION
Active On Boot	Activates the associated network device during the boot process, if there's a checkmark.
Edit	Starts the Edit Interface *Device* window for the highlighted device, where you can configure your network cards manually with a static IP address.
Hostname	Allows you to assign a hostname to this computer; otherwise, the DHCP server on your network performs this task.
Gateway	Notes the gateway IP address for messages outside your network. You can set it if you've configured your network cards manually.
Primary DNS	Lists the IP address of a DNS server for your network. You can set it if you've configured your network cards manually.
Secondary DNS	Lists the IP address of another DNS server for your network.
Tertiary DNS	Lists the IP address of another DNS server for your network.

If you prefer to assign static IP addresses to your network card, highlight the desired device and click Edit. This opens the Edit Interface *Device* window, shown in Figure 3.36.

FIGURE 3.36

Changing IP address information for a network device

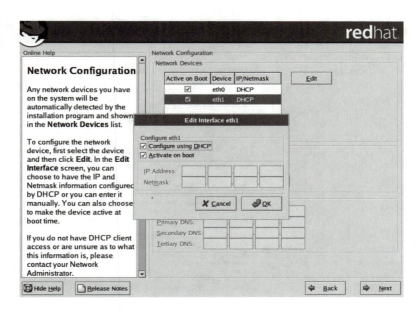

To set a static IP address, deselect the Configure Using DHCP option. You can then enter the IP address and netmask of your choice. For guidance on IP addresses on private networks, read Chapter 20. Make any desired changes and click OK to return to the Network Configuration screen.

If you change your mind after Red Hat Linux is installed, you can edit your configuration with the `redhat-config-network` utility described in Chapter 19.

When you've finished, click Next to continue.

FIREWALL CONFIGURATION

Now you're ready to configure a firewall for Red Hat Linux. This is especially important on a gateway computer, which may provide the link between your LAN and the Internet. In that situation, the gateway computer is the best place for a firewall to protect your LAN from the potential ravages of the Internet. For Red Hat Linux 9, this creates an `iptables`-based firewall in `/etc/sysconfig/iptables`. One possible configuration for a gateway computer is shown in Figure 3.37; configuration options are explained below.

High Configures a high security firewall that blocks almost all incoming traffic. The exception is messages from an external DNS server, which supports connections to the Internet.

Medium Sets up a medium security firewall that blocks traffic on TCP/IP ports 0 through 1023. It also blocks traffic on the ports that allow access to an NFS server, the local X Window Server, and the X Font Server.

No Firewall Disables all `iptables` firewall commands on this computer.

Use Default Firewall Rules Applies the default High or Medium security firewalls without modification to all network cards on this computer.

FIGURE 3.37

Configuring a firewall

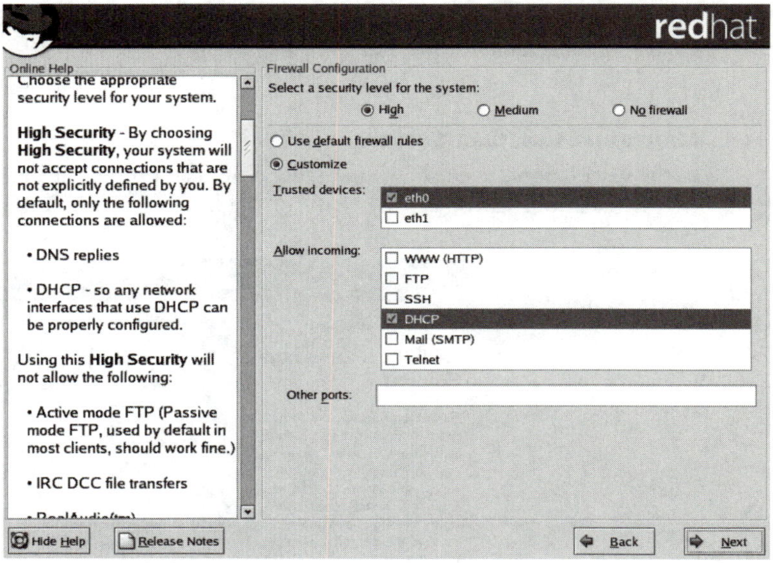

Customize   Allows you to specify different rules for one or more network cards on this computer.

Trusted Devices   Lists the network devices on this computer, in this case, `eth0` and `eth1`. It's common to turn off a firewall on the Ethernet card that's connected to the LAN as opposed to one connected to the Internet; in this case, `eth0` is a trusted device.

Allow Incoming   If you have a server on your computer, you may want to allow incoming traffic from other networks. For example, if you have a web server on your computer, you may want to allow incoming data through the TCP/IP port associated with WWW (HTTP) traffic (see Chapter 30). The other options relate to the File Transfer Protocol (FTP) (see Chapter 27), Secure Shell (SSH) (see Chapter 22), a Mail server such as sendmail (see Chapter 26), or Telnet (see Chapter 23).

By default, even the high security firewall allows incoming traffic associated with DNS (Domain Name Service) servers to help you navigate the Internet and DHCP (Dynamic Host Configuration Protocol) servers, which allows you to get IP addressing information from outside your LAN. For more information on both these services, see Chapter 24.

Other Ports   If you want to allow access through your firewall to a different server, you should enter the associated ports and protocols in the associated text box. For example, if you want to allow connections to a secure web server using the HTTPS protocol, you could enter the following in the Other Ports text box:

```
https:tcp,https:udp
```

You can change your firewall settings after Red Hat Linux is installed by using the GNOME Lokkit wizard described in Chapter 16, `redhat-config-securitylevel` in Chapter 19, or the `iptables` commands described in Chapter 22. Make any desired changes and click Next to continue.

NOTE   *This does not affect any firewalls associated with the* `xinetd` *service explained in Chapter 23 or individual network services discussed throughout the book.*

ADDITIONAL LANGUAGE SUPPORT

In the installation screen shown in Figure 3.38, you can set the default language for Red Hat Linux after installation. As you can see, some of the languages include a wide variety of national dialects.

FIGURE 3.38

Selecting languages

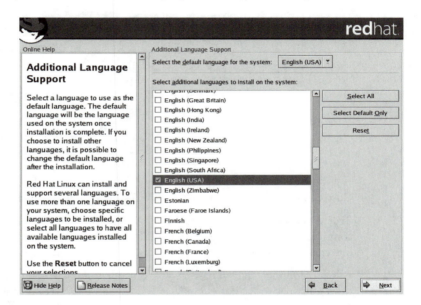

If you need different or additional languages for your installation, select them accordingly. If you've configured Anaconda to install more than one language, you can choose the default from these languages by clicking the drop-down arrow adjacent to the Select The Default Language For The System box. You can change the default language after Red Hat Linux is installed by using `redhat-config-language`, which is described in Chapter 19. Make any desired changes and click Next to continue.

SELECTING A TIME ZONE

In this installation screen, you can configure the basic time settings for your computer. After installation, you can go further. If you go through the `firstboot` utility described later in this chapter or `redhat-config-time` in Chapter 19, you can set this computer to synchronize its clock with a central time server.

The Time Zone Selection screen includes two tabs. The Location tab is shown in Figure 3.39.

FIGURE 3.39

Setting a time zone location

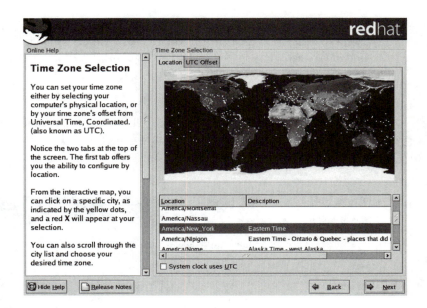

You can select the time zone associated with your location by clicking on the map, or by selecting the location from the scroll window. Unless your computer is in a dual-boot configuration with another operating system such as Microsoft Windows, you should activate the System Clock Uses UTC option. Make your selections and click the UTC Offset tab, shown in Figure 3.40. UTC is a French acronym that corresponds to Greenwich Mean Time.

FIGURE 3.40

The UTC Offset tab

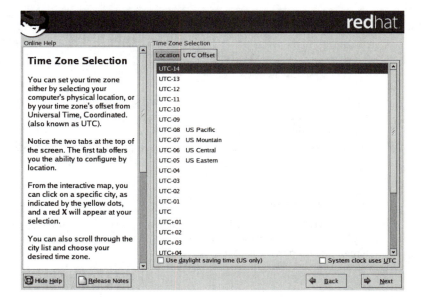

On the UTC Offset tab, select the offset that matches your time zone; for example, the U.S. West Coast is 8 hours behind Greenwich Mean Time, which corresponds to UTC-8. For the United States, you can then activate the Use Daylight Saving Time (US Only) option. Make your choices and click Next to continue.

SETTING A ROOT PASSWORD

The root user is also known as the *superuser*; the root user can do anything on your Linux computer. In the Root Password installation screen shown in Figure 3.41, type your desired root password twice. Red Hat requires the root password that you enter during this process to be at least 6 alphanumeric characters.

FIGURE 3.41

Setting a root password

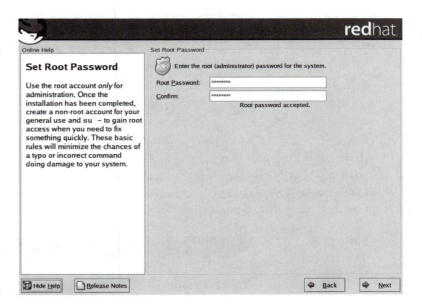

The best passwords include a combination of numbers and upper- and lowercase letters; it can take days or even weeks for a PC-based cracking program to find that kind of password. Such passwords need not be difficult to remember; I like to create passwords as acronyms for a favorite sentence. For example, Ieic3teM could stand for "I eat ice cream 3 times every Monday."

Enter your desired root password and click Next to continue.

NON-CUSTOM INSTALLATIONS

If you selected a Personal Desktop, Workstation, or Server installation type, Anaconda now moves to a couple of different installation screens. First, all of these installation types skip the Configure Authentication screen discussed in the next section.

Continued on next page

NON-CUSTOM INSTALLATIONS *(continued)*

If you selected a Personal Desktop or Workstation installation, Anaconda now gives you a Personal Desktop or Workstation Defaults screen. It lists some of the software that Anaconda will install by default with Red Hat Linux. The Workstation Defaults screen is shown below. The look and feel of the Personal Desktop Defaults screen is nearly identical. If you've selected either of these installations, you can accept the current package list; in this case, you'll proceed directly to the Ready To Install screen (see the section "Ready to Install"). Otherwise, select the Customize The Set Of Packages To Be Installed option; in that case, you'll proceed to the first Package Group Selection screen (see the section "Selecting Package Groups").

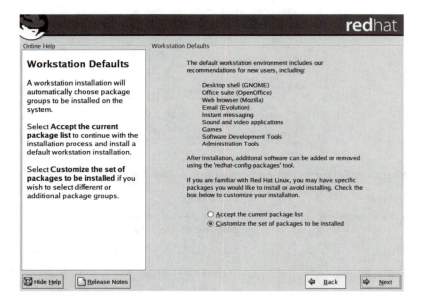

CONFIGURING AUTHENTICATION

Now that you're in password mode, Anaconda takes you to the next step of authentication. The Authentication Configuration screen is where you configure how Red Hat Linux checks the credentials of a user. The installation screen, shown in Figure 3.42, includes four tabs: NIS, LDAP, Kerberos 5, and SMB. The options associated with each tab are described in Table 3.15.

FIGURE 3.42

The Authentication Configuration window

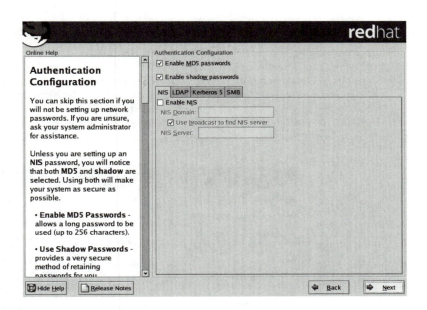

OPTION	DESCRIPTION	TAB
Shadow Passwords	Enables the Shadow Password Suite, with passwords protected in /etc/shadow.	N/A
MD5	Allows the MD5 form of password encryption.	N/A
Enable NIS	Triggers use of the Network Information Service (NIS), which provides a common database of usernames and passwords for a LAN; for more information, see Chapter 28.	NIS
NIS Domain	Enter the name of the NIS domain in this text box.	NIS
Use Broadcast To Find NIS Server	Select this option to send a broadcast message to other computers on your network to identify the NIS server.	NIS
NIS Server	Sets the name of the NIS server for your network, if you disable the broadcast option.	NIS
Enable LDAP	Enables use of a Lightweight Directory Assistance Protocol (LDAP) server for authentication and related LAN databases.	LDAP
LDAP Server	Sets the name of the server with the LDAP database.	LDAP
LDAP Base DN	Allows you to look up account information with the LDAP Distinguished Name (DN).	LDAP
Use TLS Lookups	Lets your computer use Transport Layer Security (TLS) to send encrypted usernames and passwords to an LDAP server.	LDAP

Continued on next page

TABLE 3.15: AUTHENTICATION CONFIGURATION OPTIONS *(continued)*

OPTION	DESCRIPTION	TAB
Enable Kerberos	Allows the use of the Kerberos 5 system, developed at MIT; supports strong encryption of usernames and passwords.	Kerberos 5
Realm	Permits you to access a Kerberos-enabled network.	Kerberos 5
KDC	Lets you access a Key Distribution Center (KDC) server, which issues Kerberos authentication tickets.	Kerberos 5
Admin Server	Allows you to access a Kerberos server using the kadmind utility.	Kerberos 5
Enable SMB Authentication	Allows you to use an SMB (Samba) server, such as a Microsoft Windows server operating system, for authentication.	SMB
SMB Server	Lets you specify the name of the SMB server with username and password information.	SMB
SMB Workgroup	Permits you to specify the workgroup or domain associated with the SMB authentication server.	SMB

Unless you have a network with special needs for one of these other services, the default configuration should be sufficient. For example, Figure 3.43 illustrates how you could connect your system to the username and password database on a Samba Server named Master1 on a domain or workgroup named Group1.

FIGURE 3.43

Configuring Samba Authentication

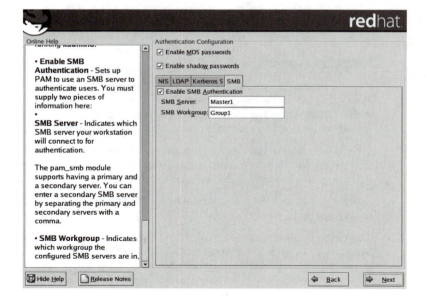

Make any desired changes and click Next to continue.

Selecting Package Groups

Finally, it's time to select what you're going to install with Red Hat Linux. You've configured everything else except your graphics system. You should now be looking at the Package Group Selection installation screen, shown in Figure 3.44.

FIGURE 3.44

Selecting package groups

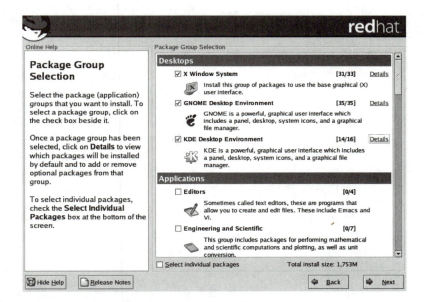

If you're unfamiliar with Linux, let's step back a moment. Red Hat organizes software into a package known as an RPM (Red Hat Package Manager). There are nearly 1500 RPMs on the Red Hat installation CDs. Many of these RPMs depend on each other; for example, you can't use most of the packages associated with the GNOME desktop unless you've also installed the Linux X Window Server.

When you install Red Hat Linux, even experienced users do not normally want to pick and choose between 1500 packages during the installation process. That's one reason why Red Hat has organized the RPMs into package groups displayed in the Package Group Selection installation window.

In other words, an RPM is also known as a package, and Red Hat bundles common RPMs together into package groups.

The Red Hat package groups correspond to the comps.xml configuration file on the first Red Hat Linux installation CD, in the /RedHat/base directory. Web Chapter 5, which can be found on the Sybex website at www.sybex.com, examines this file in detail.

Select the package groups of your choice. If you don't want to install a package group such as Games and Entertainment, you can deselect it to save space for other purposes. If you need more details about the packages in each package group, see Web Chapter 5.

The Anaconda graphical installation organizes package groups into five different categories. There are three desktop groups, as shown in Figure 3.44; Table 3.16 summarizes these groups.

TABLE 3.16: DESKTOP PACKAGE GROUPS

PACKAGE GROUP	DESCRIPTION
X Window System	Installs the basic XFree86 Server, fonts, and several GUI configuration files
GNOME Desktop Environment	Adds the packages required to use the GNOME Desktop
KDE Desktop Environment	Includes the packages required to use the KDE Desktop

Take a look at the numbers to the right of each package group. For example, in Figure 3.44, look at the numbers associated with the KDE Desktop Environment package group. That tells you that 14 of 16 packages in this package group will be installed. To the right of this number, click Details. This opens the Details For 'KDE Desktop Environment' window, shown in Figure 3.45.

FIGURE 3.45

KDE Desktop Environment package group details

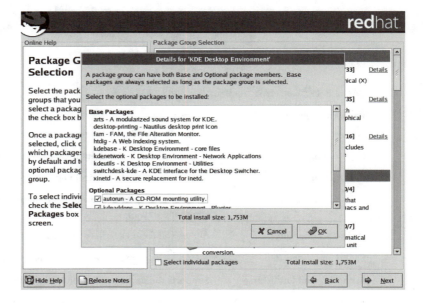

In the Details For 'KDE Desktop Environment' window, packages are organized in two categories: Base and Optional. Base packages are required for the KDE desktop to work. Optional packages add features.

The next category of package groups is Applications; part of the list is shown in Figure 3.46. Applications range from basic text editors to Internet connection utilities to games. The package groups in this category are summarized in Table 3.17.

FIGURE 3.46

Applications package groups

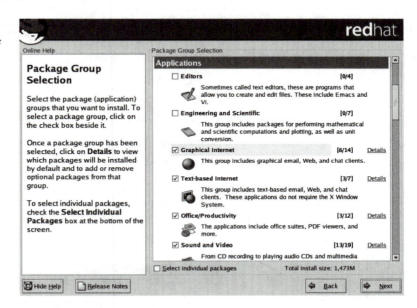

TABLE 3.17: APPLICATIONS PACKAGE GROUPS

PACKAGE GROUP	DESCRIPTION
Editors	Includes the packages for enhanced vi and Emacs
Engineering and Scientific	Adds programs for mathematical calculations and graphs
Graphical Internet	Installs a variety of graphical network communication tools
Text-based Internet	Incorporates network communication tools that you can use at the command line
Office/Productivity	Allows you to add a variety of office applications and suites
Sound and Video	Adds a series of multimedia packages, viewers, and configuration tools
Authoring and Publishing	Supports the packages that allow you to create DocBook packages
Graphics	Installs a number of graphical programs and support libraries
Games and Entertainment	Adds various video and board games

One important category for Linux administrators is Servers. Different servers can help you provide services for websites, e-mail, file services, databases, newsgroups, and more. Part of the list is shown in Figure 3.47. Each package group in this category is summarized in Table 3.18.

FIGURE 3.47

Servers package groups

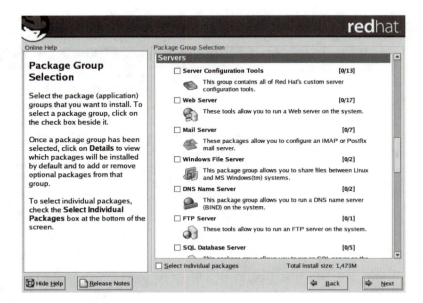

TABLE 3.18: SERVERS PACKAGE GROUPS

PACKAGE GROUP	DESCRIPTION
Server Configuration Tools	Installs several Red Hat graphical configuration tools
Web Server	Adds Apache and related packages for serving web pages to browsers on other computers
Mail Server	Incorporates various e-mail servers and utilities
Windows File Server	Allows you to connect your computer to a Microsoft Windows network as a client and as a server
DNS Name Server	Includes the software required to set up a Domain Name Service (DNS) server or a related caching nameserver
FTP Server	Adds the vsFTP file server, which also supports anonymous access
SQL Database Server	Installs packages that allow you to configure the PostgreSQL and MySQL server databases
News Server	Adds the InterNet News package, which supports a Usenet-style newsgroup system
Network Servers	Installs a variety of network servers, including DHCP, NIS, and Telnet

There are several Linux development package groups. Even if you're not a developer, you may eventually use many of the packages in these groups. For example, to compile the Linux kernel, you need packages from the Kernel Development and Development Tools package groups. The list of Development package groups is shown in Figure 3.48; Table 3.19 describes each package group in this category.

FIGURE 3.48

Development package groups

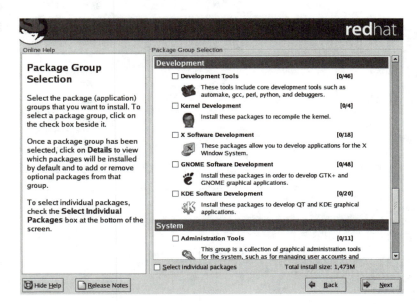

TABLE 3.19: DEVELOPMENT PACKAGE GROUPS

PACKAGE GROUP	DESCRIPTION
Development Tools	Includes package tools, language libraries, and more
Kernel Development	Installs headers and kernel source code
X Software Development	Adds development libraries, headers, and documentation associated with the Linux XFree86 graphics system
GNOME Software Development	Incorporates development libraries, headers, include files, and more associated with the GNOME Desktop Environment
KDE Software Development	Incorporates development libraries, headers, include files, and more associated with the KDE Desktop Environment

---

System is the final category of package groups. This category includes administrative, system, and printing tools. The list is shown in Figure 3.49; Table 3.20 summarizes each of the package groups.

FIGURE 3.49

System package groups

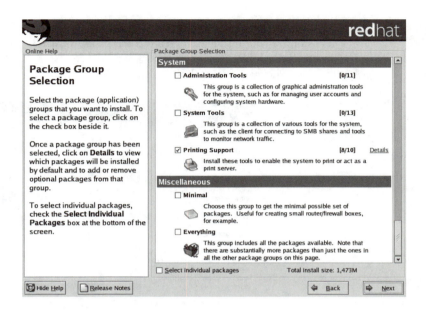

TABLE 3.20: SYSTEM PACKAGE GROUPS

PACKAGE GROUP	DESCRIPTION
Administration Tools	Installs graphical utilities that allow you to administer passwords, packages, kernel parameters, and more
System Tools	Allows you to administer a variety of applications, such as amanda-client for backups and gnome-lokkit for firewalls
Printing Support	Includes the packages required to install the Common Unix Print System (CUPS)

Finally, at the bottom of the Package Group Selection list, also shown in Figure 3.49, are two final Miscellaneous options:

Minimal   Deselects all package groups. After Red Hat Linux is installed, you can then install just the packages that you need. This is one option that can promote security; in general, if it isn't installed on your computer, it can't serve as a security hole.

Everything   Selects all package groups and requires about 5GB of space just for files.

For the purpose of this chapter, we've activated the Select Individual Packages option. Click Next to continue.

Selecting Individual Packages

You can customize your installation even further: by individual RPM. This is not as daunting a task as it may seem; once you've selected package groups, the corresponding RPM in the Individual Package Selection screen shown in Figure 3.50 is also installed.

FIGURE 3.50

Selecting individual RPM packages

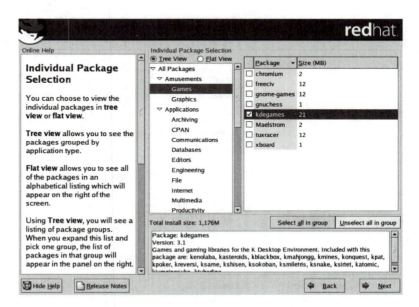

As you can see in the figure, the kdegames RPM package is slated for installation. As of this writing, this happens by default when we choose to install the KDE Desktop Environment package group. The other games packages shown would be checked if we also selected the Games and Entertainment package group. You can find out more about a package; when you highlight it, a description appears in the bottom right pane.

Assume you're working for a company that does not allow games on its PCs. Therefore, you want to remove the kdegames RPM. Deselect it. Feel free to browse some of the other package categories shown. When you're ready, click Next to continue.

You may see the following message flash across your screen:

```
checking dependencies in packages selected for installation...
```

A *dependency* is where one package won't work without another. For example, Linux applications such as the Mozilla web browser, the XFree86 X Window Server, and the OpenOffice suite won't work unless you install the Perl programming language.

If there are dependencies in your selected RPM packages, you'll see an Unresolved Dependencies screen similar to the one shown in Figure 3.51.

FIGURE 3.51

Unresolved
Dependencies

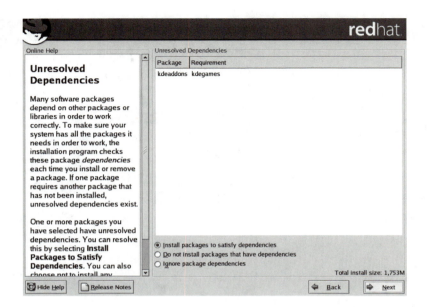

We deselected the kdegames RPM package. Now we see the reason it was selected in the first place: the kdeaddons RPM won't work without it. (The kdegames RPM includes some language libraries required for kdeaddons.) In addition, the kdeaddons RPM package adds to the functionality of Konqueror (the KDE web browser), noatun (a KDE media player), and Kate (a KDE text editor).

Now you have to make a choice. Do you violate company policy and install the kdegames RPM on this computer? Or do you accept the partial loss in functionality of the noted KDE applications? This choice is reflected in the three options shown in Figure 3.51:

Install Packages To Satisfy Dependencies   Installs all packages listed in the Unresolved Dependencies window.

Do Not Install Packages That Have Dependencies   Does not install any of the packages listed in the Unresolved Dependencies window.

Ignore Package Dependencies   Retains your original choices. However, you now know that the software installed with the kdeaddons RPM may not work.

The choice you make depends in this case on the software needs and policies of your company or organization. Do you sacrifice functionality, or would you rather convince your management to make an exception to the no games policy? Make your selection and click Next to continue.

Ready to Install

Finally, we're ready to let Anaconda install Linux on a computer! Anaconda includes the partitions we've defined, the package groups that we've selected, and the other settings that we've chosen. As you can see in Figure 3.52, when you click Next, Anaconda begins installing Red Hat Linux 9 to your specifications.

FIGURE 3.52

Ready to install

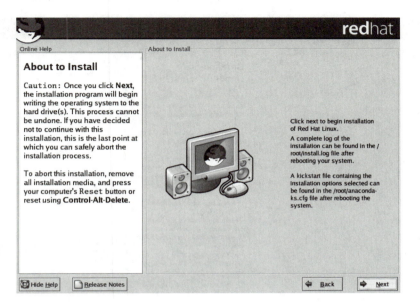

Make a note of the listed files. Once installation is complete, you'll be able to review the installed RPMs in /root/install.log. The /root/anaconda-ks.cfg file can help you duplicate this installation on other computers, using the Kickstart system described in Chapter 5.

When you're ready, click Next to continue.

Anaconda Installs Red Hat Linux

Finally, Anaconda begins the installation process. First, you'll see a series of messages such as:

```
Formatting / file system . . .
Formatting /boot file system . . .
Transferring install image to hard drive
Setting up RPM transaction
Starting install process, this may take several minutes
Preparing to install . . .
```

This is where Anaconda formats the partitions with the selected file system directories. Next, it transfers the basic installation template as an image, to your hard drive. It sets up the list of RPMs to be installed, and then starts to transfer data from the installation source—in this case, the Red Hat installation CDs to your hard drive. Then you'll see a screen like the one in Figure 3.53, which constantly updates the progress of the installation.

There are three Red Hat Linux installation CDs. (Please read the disclaimer about the Publisher's Edition two-CD set at the beginning of this chapter and in the introduction to the book.) As the installation progresses, Anaconda may require access to the second and third CDs. Installation stops with a message similar to the one shown in Figure 3.54. Follow the instructions and click OK to continue.

FIGURE 3.53

The installation in progress

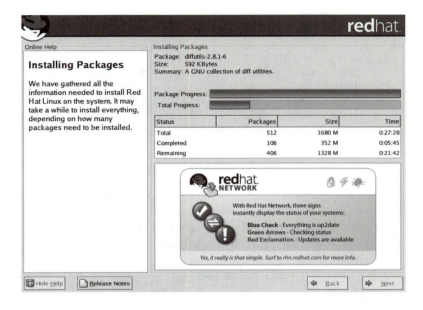

FIGURE 3.54

Time for another CD

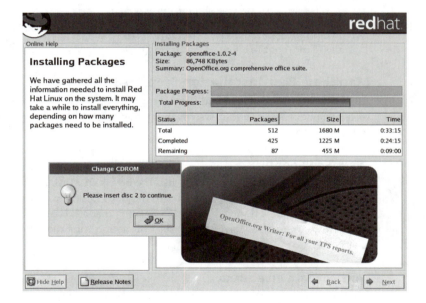

This is a good chance to examine what the installation process is doing to your system. Go to the second virtual console. Press Ctrl+Alt+F2. At the command prompt, check for disk usage:

```
-/bin/sh-2.05b# df
Filesystem 1K-blocks    Used Available Use% Mounted on
rootfs           6120    3594      2176  63% /
/dev/root.old    6120    3594      2176  63% /
/tmp/cdrom     653312  653312         0 100% /mnt/source
/tmp/hda3     5037736 1648884   3132948  35% /mnt/sysimage
/tmp/hda2      102486    8608     88586   9% /mnt/sysimage/boot
```

This output tells us that Anaconda has mounted the root (/) directory partition on the /mnt/sysimage directory. It has also mounted the partition with the /boot directory on /mnt/sysimage/boot.

You can use bash shell commands (described in Chapters 6, 7, and 8) to navigate these directories to see what Anaconda has installed so far. In fact, if there is a problem, examine the contents of /mnt/sysimage/root/install.log. This log identifies the current RPM that Anaconda is attempting to install on your system. If your installation freezes, there may be a problem with that particular RPM on your CD.

Once all desired RPM packages are installed, you'll see the following messages, which get Anaconda ready for the next steps in the process and installs the bootloader on your MBR. *At this time*, you can also find the bootloader configuration file in the second virtual console in the /mnt/sysimage/etc directory. Once you've completed your installation, you can find the file in the expected location, in the /etc directory. If you're using GRUB, it's in the grub.conf file.

```
Performing post install configuration
Installing bootloader
```

Managing Post-Installation Steps

Anaconda has installed Red Hat Linux on your computer. But your work is not done. You still need to create a boot disk for your system and configure graphics. The next screen you should see is shown in Figure 3.55.

CREATING A BOOT DISK

It's a good idea to create a boot disk. It is the best rescue disk available, customized for your system.

If you have a floppy drive, select Yes in the Boot Disk Creation screen and click Next. You'll be prompted to insert a floppy disk, with a warning that all data on that disk will be erased. Follow the instructions and click Make Boot Disk. This action runs the mkbootdisk command described in Chapter 11.

CONFIGURING A VIDEO CARD

If you've installed X Window software, Anaconda now prompts you to configure your graphics system, as shown in Figure 3.56. You can skip this process and configure it later with the redhat-config-xfree86 utility described in Chapter 15.

FIGURE 3.55

Creating a Boot Disk

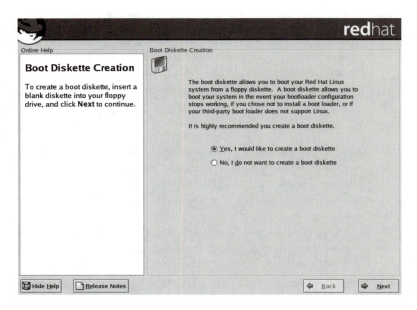

FIGURE 3.56

Configuring the
Linux Graphical
Interface

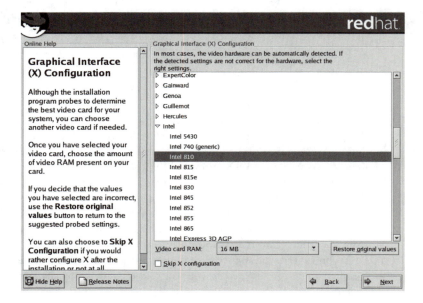

If Anaconda detected your hardware at the start of this process, it highlights the graphics card that it detected, along with the amount of RAM on that card. The options in the Graphical Interface (X) Configuration screen are detailed here:

Video Card   Select the video card that most closely matches your hardware. Anaconda may have selected one for you. Cards are organized by manufacturer. If you don't see your card, it may be under the manufacturer labeled Other at the top of the list. Alternatively, almost all newer video cards can be configured as a generic video card.

This section includes three generic cards: Generic VGA Compatible; Unsupported VGA Compatible; and VESA Driver (Generic), which is equivalent to SVGA.

NOTE   The Video Graphics Adapter (VGA) standard is a standard associated with older graphics cards and a monitor resolution of 640 × 480. SVGA stands for Super VGA, and is associated with a resolution of 800 × 600. These standards are maintained by the Video Electronics Standards Association (VESA); the standard VESA driver is associated with SVGA video cards. Many unrecognized high-performance cards such as those that conform to XGA and SXGA standards can use VESA mode.

Video Card RAM   Set the RAM to the capacity of your video card. If your video card shares regular RAM, make sure this matches the associated setting in your BIOS. Anaconda allows you to set your video RAM in increments between 256KB and 128MB.

Restore Original Values   If you've made a number of changes and want to return to the original detected configuration, click this button.

Skip X Configuration   If you do not want to configure your graphics system at this time, enable this option and click Next. You can still configure your graphics system later with `redhat-config-xfree86`.

In most cases, you won't need to make any changes. Make any desired changes and click Next to continue.

CONFIGURING A MONITOR

If you still want to configure the X Window system on your computer, the next thing you'll see should be similar to the Monitor Configuration screen shown in Figure 3.57.

When Anaconda probed your system, it may have detected a monitor. If it did, you'll see it highlighted here under the DDC Probed Monitor section. If this is the wrong monitor, select your monitor from the list, which is classified by manufacturer and model. If you don't see your monitor on the list, you can select from a wide variety of generic monitors.

Every monitor has a horizontal sync and vertical sync rate. Check the documentation for your monitor *carefully*! If the numbers you set here exceed the capabilities of your monitor, the signals from your video card could blow out your monitor's circuitry.

If you experiment and would rather return to the values detected by Anaconda, click Restore Original Values. In most cases, you won't need to make any changes. Make any desired changes and click Next to continue.

CUSTOMIZING GRAPHICS

We've arrived at the last step! Now you get to put together the configuration settings for your video card and monitor. Figure 3.58 shows the Customizing Graphics Configuration screen.

FIGURE 3.57

Monitor
Configuration

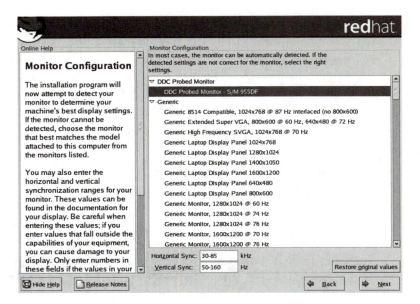

FIGURE 3.58

Customizing
your graphics
configuration

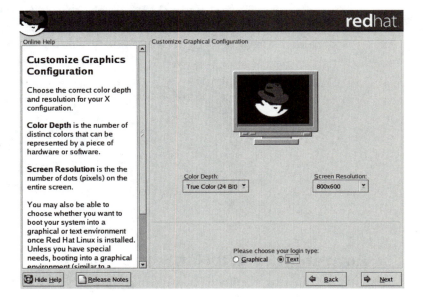

The options in this screen are:

Color Depth Specifies the number of bits of color associated with each pixel. For example, 24 bits is "true color" because it supports rendering of up to $2^{24} = 16,777,216$ different colors. Depending on the capabilities of your video card and monitor, you may be able to set 8 bit (256 colors) or 16 bit (65,536 colors) for each pixel.

Screen Resolution   Sets the number of pixels to be displayed on your monitor. The screen resolution is set in a *horizontal* × *vertical* format. For example, 800 × 600 resolution represents 800 pixels in the horizontal dimension and 600 pixels in the vertical dimension on your monitor. Available resolutions depend on the size of the monitor and the RAM associated with your video card.

Please Choose Your Login Type   Configures the Linux boot sequence; this affects the `id` variable in `/etc/inittab`, which you can change as described in Chapter 11. If you select Graphical, Linux boots into a graphical login screen; if you select Text, Linux allows you to log in at a text-based virtual console. These options are not available if you've selected a Personal Desktop or Workstation installation; both default to a graphical login interface.

Make your selections and click Next to continue. Finally, the installation is complete, as shown in Figure 3.59. Click Exit to reboot your computer.

FIGURE 3.59

Installation is complete!

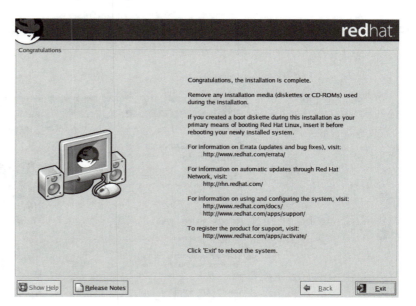

Running the Red Hat Setup Agent

The installation process may seem long enough already. Red Hat has moved several configuration activities from installation to a new program known as the Red Hat Setup Agent, also known as `firstboot`.

The first time you reboot your computer, you should see your chosen bootloader. By default, the bootloader is GRUB, which is shown in Figure 3.60. Remember, we installed Red Hat Linux in a dual-boot configuration.

FIGURE 3.60

The GRUB
bootloader

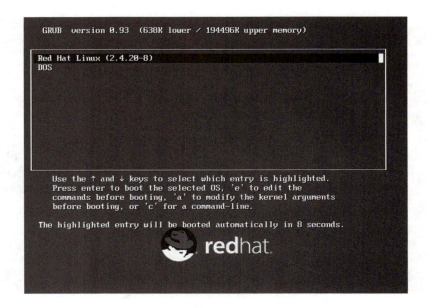

As described near the end of the installation process, there are two possible login modes: text and graphical. A typical text login looks like the following:

```
Red Hat Linux release 9 (Shrike)
Kernel 2.4.20-8 on an i686

RH9Test login:
```

However, if you selected a graphical login type at the end of the installation process, you'll be taken to the Red Hat Setup Agent shown in Figure 3.61. The Red Hat Linux boot process won't allow any detours before you're allowed to log in at a graphical screen.

The Red Hat Setup Agent allows you to configure user accounts, set up connections to a time server, probe for a sound card, register with the Red Hat Network, and add extra software.

If you selected a text login, you can start the Red Hat Setup Agent with the firstboot command.

NOTE *If you selected a text-mode login, you're in runlevel 3. Run the* telinit 5 *command and log into the Linux GUI. You can then run* firstboot *in a GUI command-line interface.*

Click Forward to continue.

Creating a Regular User

You're encouraged to create a personal user account, as shown in Figure 3.62. Enter a login name in the Username text box. Then add identifying information in the Full Name text box. Type in the same password twice in the last two text boxes and click Forward to continue (Vaclav Havel is the recently departed president of the Czech Republic).

FIGURE 3.61
The Red Hat
Setup Agent

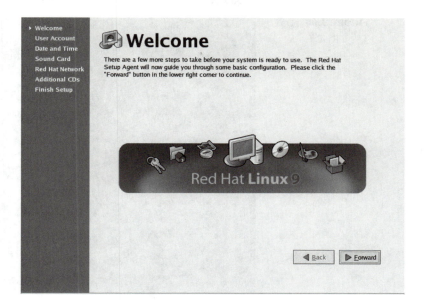

FIGURE 3.62
Creating a
regular user

Add the user of your choice and then click Forward to continue.

Specifying a Date and Time

Yes, you already specified a date and time during the Red Hat Linux installation process. The difference here is that this `firstboot` screen allows you to synchronize your computer with a central time server. Place a checkmark in the Enable Network Time Protocol option, as shown in Figure 3.63.

FIGURE 3.63

Specifying a
time server

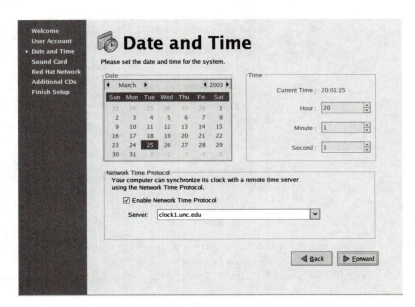

If your computer is connected to the Internet, you may want to select an NTP server from what may be the authoritative website on NTP, `www.eecis.udel.edu/~ntp`, located at the University of Delaware; it includes a link to a list of active NTP servers around the world. You can change your settings later with the `redhat-config-time` utility described in Chapter 19. Note that I've pointed my computer to a timeserver located at the University of North Carolina (UNC).

To make sure that that the NTP daemon continues working the next time you start Linux, the Red Hat Setup Agent activates the NTP daemon, `ntpd`, at runlevels 3 and 5. It also supplies a path through any firewall that you may have created. For more information on runlevels, read Chapter 11. For more information on firewalls, read Chapter 22.

Specify the time server of your choice and click Forward to continue. If you're connected to the Internet, `firstboot` now tries to contact your selected time server.

Sound Card

The Red Hat Setup Agent automatically tries to detect any sound cards that might be located on your computer. If it succeeds, you'll see a sound card vendor, model, and module, as shown in Figure 3.64. If you have speakers connected to your sound card, you can click the Play Test Sound button.

FIGURE 3.64

firstboot detects a sound card.

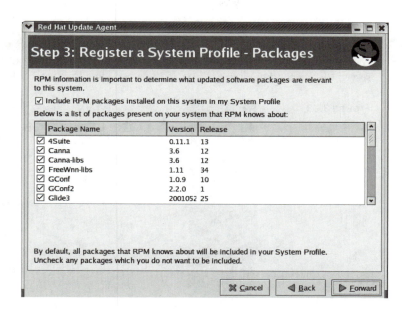

Once firstboot finishes playing the sound, you'll see the prompt asking "Did you hear the sample sound?" If you didn't, click No, and you'll get a message telling you that the sound card was not activated. Otherwise, click Yes to return to the Setup Agent, and then click Forward to continue.

Registering with the Red Hat Network

When you register your computer with the Red Hat Network, you can set up your computer to receive the latest software upgrades and patches. The Red Hat Setup Agent describes the options in Figure 3.65.

As of this writing, six levels of service are available: Demo, Basic, Enterprise, Enterprise Linux AS Developer, Enterprise Linux WS Basic, and Enterprise Linux ES Basic. The Demo level is free but requires regular registration and renewal. To register for the Basic service level, you'll need to purchase a Red Hat Linux 9 boxed set or a subscription on the Red Hat Network at rhn.redhat.com. Similar requirements apply to the Enterprise service levels. Red Hat also provides network-based support to educational institutions; see the Red Hat Network website for more information.

We'll proceed with registering for a Demo account. Select Yes, I Want To Register My System With Red Hat Network and click Forward to continue. This opens the Red Hat Network Configuration window, shown in Figure 3.66. As you can see, this window includes three tabs.

FIGURE 3.65

Registering your
computer with the
Red Hat Network

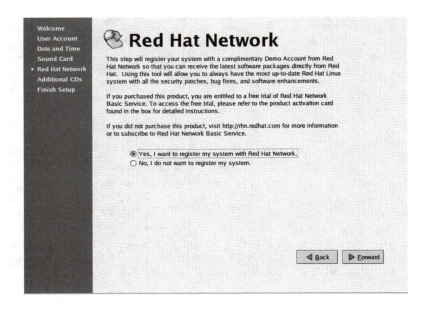

FIGURE 3.66

Red Hat Network
Configuration

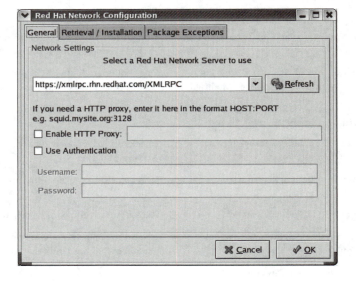

On the General tab, enter the Red Hat network server appropriate for your service level. One may already be provided for you in the text box. If you're setting up a Demo account, use the default server as shown. If your computer connects to the Internet through a proxy server, enter the connection information as required. Now click the Retrieval/Installation tab, shown in Figure 3.67; the options are described in Table 3.21.

FIGURE 3.67

Specifying packages
to update

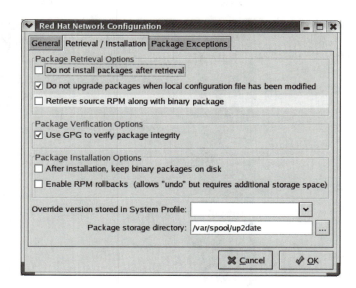

TABLE 3.21: RED HAT NETWORK RETRIEVAL/INSTALLATION OPTIONS

OPTION	DESCRIPTION
Do Not Install Packages After Retrieval	Downloads newer packages from the database to the specified Package Storage Directory; does not install those packages.
Do Not Upgrade Packages When Local Configuration File Has Been Modified	Does not upgrade the package of a service that you've configured. Allows you to test the upgraded package in a controlled manner.
Retrieve Source RPM Along With The Binary Package	Downloads the source code along with each package.
Use GPG To Verify Package Integrity	Checks each downloaded package using GNU Privacy Guard (see Chapter 22).
After Installation, Keep Binary Packages On Disk	Keeps the RPM package after installation.
Enable RPM Rollbacks	Allows you to return to the original pre-upgraded configuration.
Override Version Stored In System Profile	Ignores the Red Hat Network profile associated with a previous version of Red Hat Linux that may have files on this computer.
Package Storage Directory	Specifies the directory for RPMs.

Now click the Package Exceptions tab, shown in Figure 3.68. Here, you can specify the packages and filenames that won't be upgraded through the Red Hat Network, at least not without your approval. Note that upgraded `kernel*` RPMs are on this list.

FIGURE 3.68

The do not
upgrade list

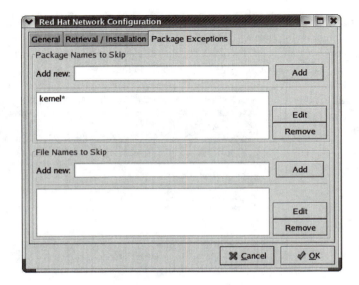

FIGURE 3.68

The do not
upgrade list

When you've finished making Red Hat Network Configuration changes, click OK. This opens
the Red Hat Update Agent described in Chapter 10. Click Forward to continue. The first time you
run the Update Agent, you'll see Step 1, a Red Hat privacy statement. Read it and click Forward to
continue. This brings you to Step 2, the Login screen shown in Figure 3.69.

FIGURE 3.69

Red Hat Update
Agent login

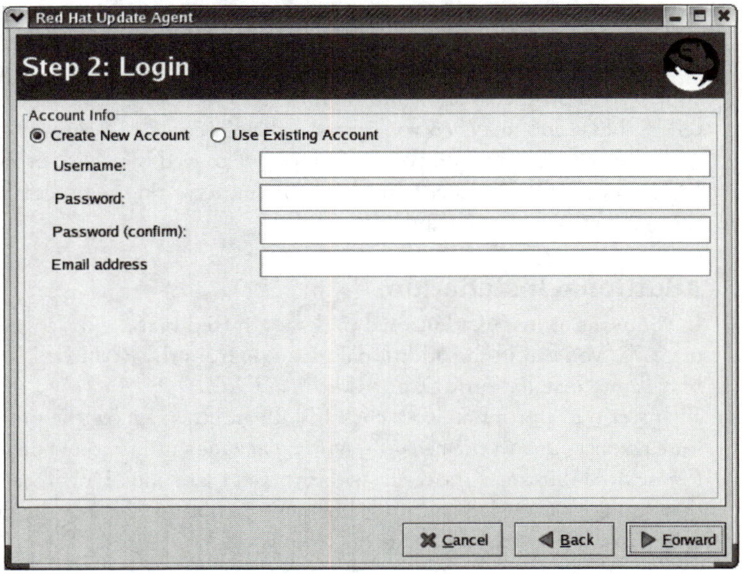

Enter your login information and click Forward to continue. You can set up a new login through this screen, or log into an existing Red Hat Network account. This brings you to Step 3, where you register your computer. Figure 3.70 illustrates my system profile that I've submitted to the Red Hat Network. Change the settings if desired and click Forward to continue.

FIGURE 3.70

Registering a
System Profile

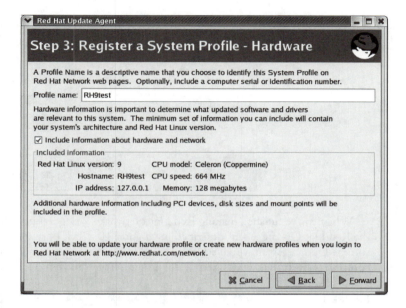

At this point, the Red Hat registration wizard collects a list of your RPMs and includes them in your system profile, as shown in Figure 3.71. You can deselect any packages that you don't want to tell Red Hat about. When you're ready, click Forward to continue.

If you're willing to send your system profile to Red Hat, click Forward to continue in the next screen. If you successfully register with the Red Hat network, the process should continue as described with the up2date utility in Chapter 10.

Additional Installation

If you want to install additional packages in Red Hat Linux, this is your chance. As shown in Figure 3.72, you can install additional packages from the Red Hat Linux Documentation CD, the Red Hat Linux Installation CD, or Additional CDs.

Insert the appropriate CD, click Install, and then follow the prompts. This section uses the software associated with the redhat-config-packages utility to organize the installation of new software. Figure 3.73 illustrates the result with the Red Hat Linux Documentation CD. Select any documents that you want to install and press Forward to continue. Follow the prompts and firstboot automatically installs the desired documents from CD.

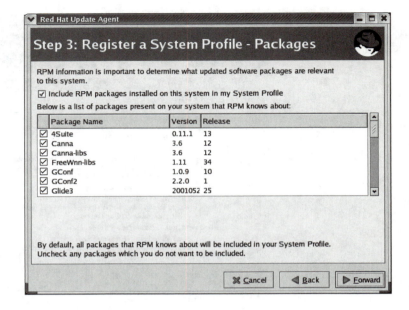

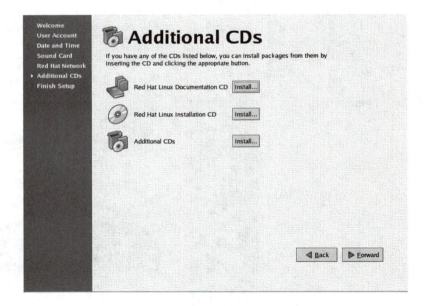

FIGURE 3.73

Installing Red Hat documents

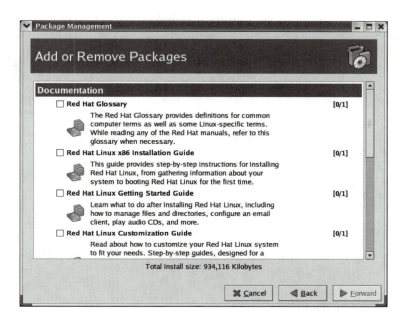

If you want to add more RPMs from the installation CDs, insert the first Red Hat installation CD and click Install. This starts the `redhat-config-packages` utility described in Chapter 19. Click Forward to continue.

At this point, you should see the Finish Setup screen shown in Figure 3.74. As noted, your system is now ready to set up and use.

FIGURE 3.74

Setup is finished.

Troubleshooting the Installation

A standard method for troubleshooting is to gather all available data. Red Hat Linux is a popular operating system. People exchange information about problems online all the time. Once you've collected data, you can identify the symptoms of the problem and work with the Linux community through your local user group or online.

You can obtain a lot of troubleshooting data by accessing the virtual consoles available during the installation process. The data you collect may indicate one of several major problems, as described in the following section.

Installation Virtual Consoles

One of the key tools for troubleshooting a problem installation is the *virtual consoles*. Once the graphical installation process begins, you can access five different installation virtual consoles.

When you're having a problem with installation of Red Hat Linux, the problem may not be obvious. There are several text installation screens that can provide valuable messages. You can get to these screens with the Ctrl+Alt+F*n* command, where *n* is the virtual console number: 1, 2, 3, 4, 5, or 7. Once you've reviewed the messages, you can return to the installation screen with the Ctrl+Alt+F7 command. Table 3.22 describes the installation screens.

TABLE 3.22: RED HAT INSTALLATION SCREENS

SCREEN	DESCRIPTION
Ctrl+Alt+F1	Looks at the detection messages for the local video card, monitor, and mouse.
Ctrl+Alt+F2	Opens a bash shell with limited command capabilities; for example, the df command can show mounted directories and partitions. Other bash commands are described in Chapters 6, 7, and 8 of this book.
Ctrl+Alt+F3	Views the installation log, with messages related to hardware detection; trouble reading CDs or loading drivers may be found here. During the installation process, this information is recorded in /tmp/anaconda.log.
Ctrl+Alt+F4	Goes to the system message log, with messages such as formatting and mounting directories on partitions. During the installation process, this information is recorded in /tmp/syslog.
Ctrl+Alt+F5	Notes other messages, such as filesystem labels, blocks, formats, and journals. Accessible only after Anaconda formats partitions.
Ctrl+Alt+F7	Returns to the graphical installation screen.

NOTE *When changing screens during the installation process, some keyboards require that you use the Ctrl and Alt keys on the left side of the keyboard.*

Installation virtual consoles and log files in the /tmp/syslog directory are stored in a RAM disk; thus, they are deleted once you reboot your computer or finish the installation process.

GRAPHICS-DETECTION MESSAGES

Early in this chapter, we reviewed messages in the first console associated with a successful installation. But problems are possible, especially if you have non-conforming graphics hardware. First, let's take a look at a message on my laptop that does not have enough memory:

```
You do not have enough RAM to use the graphical installer. Starting text mode.
```

This message is straightforward; if you see it, you need a computer with additional memory to perform a graphical installation. Fortunately, text-mode installation (covered in Chapter 4) is sufficient for most purposes. Sometimes graphics hardware does not conform, as indicated by the following messages:

```
Running anaconda, the Red Hat Linux system installer - please wait...
Probing for video card: Unsupported VGA Compatible
Probing for monitor type: Unknown monitor
Probing for mouse type: Generic - Wheel Mouse (PS/2)
Attempting to start native X Server
Waiting for X server to start...log located in /tmp/X.log
1...2...3...4...5...X SERVER FAILEDAttempting to start VESA driver X server X
➡ startup failed, falling back to text mode
```

These messages are also fairly straightforward, suggesting that this computer does not include graphics hardware that conforms even to the VESA (SVGA) standard.

LOG FILES

We have surprisingly easy access to log files during the installation process, through the second virtual console. Press Ctrl+Alt+F2 to open a bash prompt:

```
-/bin/sh-2.05b#
```

Here you can enter the bash commands of your choice. Any files installed so far are accessible through this interface. Earlier, we saw the message for the /tmp/X.log file. Open it with the vi /tmp/X.log command. The file should look similar to Figure 3.75.

Note the comments at the bottom of the file, pointing you to /tmp/ramfs/X.log, which provides additional information about the graphics problem on this computer. Other important log files are readily available in the /tmp directory, as explained in Table 3.23.

TABLE 3.23: LOG FILES DURING THE INSTALLATION PROCESS

FILE	DESCRIPTION
anaconda.log	Hardware-detection log associated with the third virtual console
isoinfo	MD5 checksum for the current CD
modules.conf	List of installed modules
syslog	Boot log; corresponds to dmesg (see Chapter 11)
X.log	Graphical configuration log file
XF86Config.text	Preliminary X Window configuration file

FIGURE 3.75

An X
Configuration log

```
XFree86 Version 4.3.0 (Red Hat Linux release: 4.3.0-2)
Release Date: 27 February 2003
X Protocol Version 11, Revision 0, Release 6.6
Build Operating System: Linux 2.4.20-3bigmem i686 [ELF]
Build Date: 27 February 2003
Build Host: porky.devel.redhat.com

        Before reporting problems, check http://www.XFree86.Org/
        to make sure that you have the latest version.
Module Loader present
OS Kernel: Linux version 2.4.20-8BOOT (bhcompile@porky.devel.redhat.com) (gcc ve
rsion 3.2.2 20030222 (Red Hat Linux 3.2.2-5)) #1 Thu Mar 13 17:31:38 EST 2003
Markers: (--) probed, (**) from config file, (==) default setting,
        (++) from command line, (!!) notice, (II) informational,
        (WW) warning, (EE) error, (NI) not implemented, (??) unknown.
(++) Log file: "/tmp/ramfs/X.log", Time: Wed Mar 26 11:54:54 2003
(++) Using config file: "/tmp/XF86Config.test"
(EE) Failed to load module "glx" (module does not exist, 0)
(EE) Failed to load module "record" (module does not exist, 0)
error opening security policy file /etc/X11/xserver/SecurityPolicy
Could not init font path element unix/:7100, removing from list!
cat: //.Xauthority: No such file or directory
```

HARDWARE-DETECTION MESSAGES

Several; hardware-detection messages are available in the third virtual console. During the installation process, you can get to this console with the Ctrl+Alt+F3 command, or you can see the entire list of messages in the second virtual console in /tmp/anaconda.log. Just remember, as installation proceeds, Anaconda constantly adds information to this file.

If you're having a hardware problem, it will normally be fairly obvious; for example, the following message indicates a problem that Anaconda has reading one of my CD-ROM drives:

```
<4>hdb: cdrom_decode_status: error=0x51{DriveReady SeekComplete Error}
```

While this message could indicate a problem with the CD media or hardware, it does tend to identify the problem.

Sometimes hardware messages are subtler:

```
/tmp/yenta_socket.o: init_module
Hint: insmod errors can be caused by incorrect module parameters, including
➥ invalid IO or IRQ parameters.
You may find more information in syslog or the output from dmesg.
```

I knew that the yenta_socket.o module is related to my PCMCIA hardware; it took additional research to find that my boot disk was missing the i82365 PCMCIA module. It's like the dog that didn't bark; I didn't figure out the problem until I realized that Anaconda never loaded the key PCMCIA module. I wouldn't have figured that out had I not been familiar with the hardware on my laptop.

THE SYSTEM MESSAGE LOG

The standard Linux installation message log is filled with fairly standard boot messages. It is less likely that you'll see a problem here. For example, any hardware that isn't detected simply does not show up in the system message log.

Thus, in order to find problems through this log, you need to be a bit of a detective. For example, you know there's a problem if you see a message detecting only 128MB of memory when you have 512MB installed.

This log is associated with the fourth installation virtual console, which you can access with the Ctrl+Alt+F4 command. You can also review the messages from the second virtual console in the /tmp/syslog file. Keep in mind that, as installation proceeds, Anaconda constantly adds information to this file.

OTHER MESSAGES

Anaconda formats your partitions just before it actually starts to install Red Hat Linux. If you haven't configured partitions with sufficient space, you'll get an error message and will have to start the process again. Standard file size requirements associated with each installation option are described earlier in Table 3.6.

You can take a look at this console after Red Hat Linux starts to install packages on your computer by using the Ctrl+Alt+F5 command. We've shown a view in Figure 3.76, which includes messages on how Anaconda has formatted the root (/) directory filesystem.

FIGURE 3.76

Anaconda format messages

```
This filesystem will be automatically checked every 28 mounts or
180 days, whichever comes first.  Use tune2fs -c or -i to override.
tune2fs 1.32 (09-Nov-2002)
Setting maximal mount count to -1
Setting interval between check 0 seconds
mke2fs 1.32 (09-Nov-2002)
Filesystem label=
OS type: Linux
Block size=1024 (log=0)
Fragment size=1024 (log=0)
26104 inodes, 104391 blocks
5219 blocks (5.00%) reserved for the super user
First data block=1
13 block groups
8192 blocks per group, 8192 fragments per group
2008 inodes per group
Superblock backups stored on blocks:
        8193, 24577, 40961, 57345, 73729

Writing inode tables: done
Creating journal (4096 blocks): done
Writing superblocks and filesystem accounting information: done

This filesystem will be automatically checked every 27 mounts or
180 days, whichever comes first.  Use tune2fs -c or -i to override.
tune2fs 1.32 (09-Nov-2002)
Setting maximal mount count to -1
Setting interval between check 0 seconds
```

Later in this process, Anaconda presents a GRUB prompt that lets you modify your bootloader configuration. However, the GRUB configuration file, grub.conf, is accessible through the second virtual console, as we described earlier in the "Anaconda Installs Red Hat Linux" section.

Package Status

One all too common problem with Linux installations is an RPM package that wasn't copied correctly. It could be the 1000th package in the installation process. If suddenly Anaconda finds a problem with a specific package, the installation stops. Unless you have alternate media (such as duplicate CDs) at hand, you may have no recourse but to restart the installation.

Once installation proceeds, you can track the status of the installation on the screen. Both graphics- and text-mode installations identify the package currently being installed. There is one more source; once installation starts, you can find the current list through the second virtual console, in the `install .log` file located in the `/mnt/sysimage/root` directory.

If you can identify the package with the problem, you may be able to replace it. You could replace it in the list of packages on the CD, or if you're more fortunate, you could download the package again to a central network installation source.

Especially if you've downloaded your Red Hat installation CDs over the Internet, there are many possible causes. There could be a momentary power surge somewhere on the Internet. You could be downloading to a hard drive with a bad sector. You might copy the CD files onto a disk with a flaw. The possible causes go on and on. While installing Red Hat Linux from downloaded CDs is usually trouble-free (I do it all the time), it does have its share of risks.

Logging In

Now you and your computer are ready for Linux. If you're a Linux expert (or want to be), you're probably logging in from the command-line interface, as shown here:

```
Red Hat Linux release 9 (Shrike)
Kernel 2.4.20-8 on an i686

RH9Test login: username
Password:
Last login: Wed Mar 19 15:33:00 on tty1
[username@RH9Test username]#
```

Now you're ready for a command-line interface, which is the main focus of most of this book.

Alternatively, if Linux is relatively new to you, you might be logging in at a graphical login prompt, such as the one shown in Figure 3.77.

Many Linux administrators take full advantage of the graphical user interface. The default Red Hat GUI is GNOME (GNU Network Object Model Environment). It's easy to start a command-line interface in GNOME. Right-click on any open area of the desktop, and select New Terminal in the menu that appears. This opens the default GNOME terminal command-line interface, shown in Figure 3.78.

FIGURE 3.77
Graphical Login
Screen

FIGURE 3.78
GNOME with a
command-line
terminal

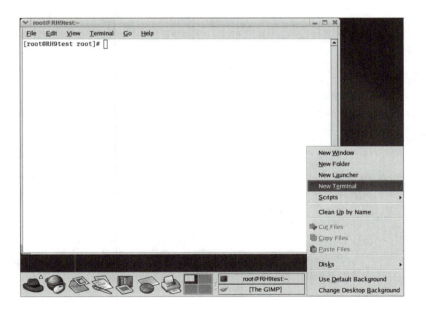

Now you're ready to learn all about Linux!

Upgrading Red Hat Linux

If you've installed Red Hat Linux before on the local hard drive, you may just want to upgrade. A good upgrade can save your configuration and data files in their current locations. While you should always back up your data prior to upgrading any operating system, life is a lot less troublesome when you don't have to spend time restoring from a backup.

Normally, Anaconda will detect a previous installation of Red Hat Linux on your computer from the /etc/redhat-release file. If it doesn't, you can enter the following at the Anaconda boot prompt:

```
boot: linux upgradeany
```

Allowable Upgrades

You can use the Red Hat Linux 9 installation CDs to upgrade from versions 6.2 and above. There's a special issue if you're trying to upgrade a version of Red Hat Linux with Ximian GNOME. If this is your situation, Red Hat recommends one of the following options:

◆ Remove Ximian GNOME before starting the upgrade.

◆ Upgrade to Red Hat Linux 9, and then reinstall Ximian GNOME.

◆ Upgrade to Red Hat Linux 9, and then upgrade all Ximian GNOME RPMs with their counterparts from the Red Hat Linux installation CDs.

If you currently use Ximian GNOME, upgrade to Red Hat Linux 9, and don't take one of these actions, Red Hat warns that GNOME will be unstable.

MAKING AN UPGRADE

Upgrades start in the same way as a regular installation. The issues with booting Anaconda from a CD or a floppy don't change. The first few steps of a graphical installation are the same. The first place we diverge from a regular installation is just after configuring a mouse. If Anaconda detects a previous version of Red Hat Linux, it will identify it in the Upgrade Examine screen shown in Figure 3.79. We've activated the Customize Packages To Be Upgraded option.

Click Next to continue. The following screen allows you to update your bootloader from a previous version of GRUB or from LILO. As you can see in Figure 3.80, you can skip the update process or create an entirely new bootloader configuration. Make your selection and click Next to continue.

Now Anaconda takes some time to examine the packages currently on your system. It goes through the list, looking for packages to upgrade. If you've enabled the Customize Packages To Be Upgraded Option earlier, the next step takes you to the Individual Package Selection menu, shown in Figure 3.81. You can browse through the menus; packages with a check mark are to be upgraded.

In this case, the only daemon that requires upgrading is the LPRng, which is the older Line Print Daemon. As you can read in Chapter 25, CUPS is the new default print service. Therefore, you can make a decision on upgrading that package. Make your choices and click Next to continue. If there are dependencies, you'll get a chance to look at them, in the same way as with the regular Anaconda installation process (this screen is shown back in Figure 3.51). Otherwise you'll see the About To Upgrade screen, shown in Figure 3.82. When you're ready, click Next to continue and start the upgrade.

FIGURE 3.79

Finding an earlier version of Red Hat

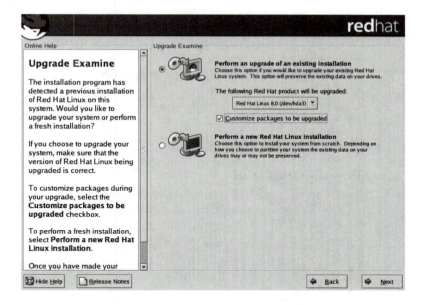

FIGURE 3.80

Updating the bootloader

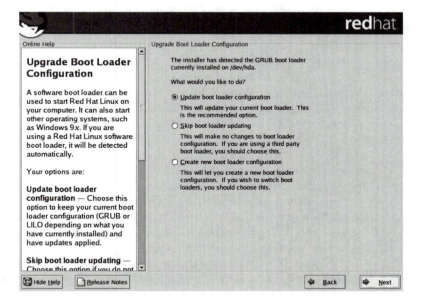

FIGURE 3.81

List of upgraded packages

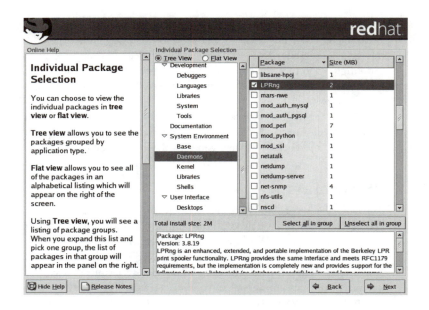

FIGURE 3.82

Ready to upgrade

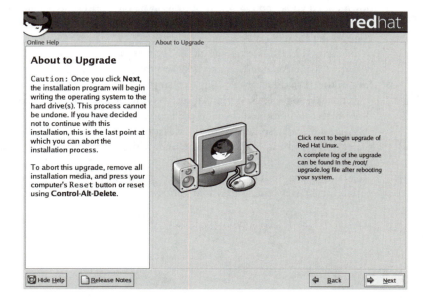

The upgrade proceeds as if it were an installation. The process is relatively short; if you've upgraded from a relatively up-to-date system, Anaconda may end up upgrading a small number of packages.

If the upgrade affects any services with configuration files, you should be able to find the original configuration files with an `.rpmsave` extension. For example, if your upgrade affects the Apache web server, you should see the original `httpd.conf` file in the `/etc/httpd/conf` directory saved as `httpd.conf.rpmsave`.

Once the upgraded packages are installed, you're prompted to create a boot disk. This is needed especially if Anaconda has installed a new kernel during the upgrade process. Follow the remaining prompts, and click Exit when you see the Congratulations, The Installation Is Complete message.

Summary

You have a lot of choices to make when you install Red Hat Linux on a computer. Normally, a Red Hat Linux installation need not be complex. In most cases, all you need to do is set your computer to boot from the CD drive, insert the first Red Hat Linux installation CD, follow some fairly straight-forward prompts, and you too can install Red Hat Linux in under an hour.

In this chapter, we examined a number of variations of Red Hat Linux installations. If you have aspirations of becoming a Linux administrator, we hope this chapter has helped you learn how to handle a variety of situations during the installation process.

This chapter showed you how to create boot and driver disks. We illustrated various ways to test downloaded CDs and examined options available during the installation process. We also showed you how to navigate the Red Hat Setup Agent to help users who select a graphical login screen finish configuring Linux as a desktop.

Many good resources are available for troubleshooting an installation, and you can use these resources while Anaconda is at work. You can take advantage of these resources by viewing the log files in the `/tmp` directory and by accessing installation virtual consoles.

Once you log into Red Hat Linux, you'll want to be ready with a command-line interface to learn more with this book and through the Linux community.

Anaconda can also help you upgrade from Red Hat Linux 6.2 and above. It allows you to customize the packages to be upgraded, lets you update the bootloader, and saves any configuration files that you had previously modified.

The next chapter takes a more advanced look at Red Hat Linux installations, using text mode, with a focus on installing Red Hat Linux over a network.

Chapter 4

Installing Linux Over a Network

THIS CHAPTER IS FOR Linux system administrators and others with several Linux computers connected in a network. While the installation process shown in Chapter 3 is attractive, it takes a lot of time to install from CDs, especially on multiple computers. You can save time by installing Red Hat Linux over a network. One added benefit is that you don't have to sit around waiting to insert other Red Hat installation CDs on your computers.

In this chapter, we assume that you've already prepared your computer per the requirements of Chapter 2. For example, if you're planning a dual-boot between Red Hat Linux and Microsoft Windows, you've used the techniques in that chapter to set aside free disk space with sufficient room for Linux.

We'll look at installing Linux from three types of network servers: NFS (Network File System), FTP (File Transfer Protocol), and web (via Apache). We'll learn how to set up the Red Hat Linux installation files on each of these servers. While you could set up these servers on different operating systems, we'll go through the basics of setting up each service. Detailed configuration of each service is covered in future chapters.

Also in this chapter, we'll look at the details of the network installation process, from boot disks to a step-by-step analysis of text-mode installation. Why text mode? It's faster—after all, your time is valuable. We'll also examine the subtle differences you'll run into when upgrading an existing Linux installation. Finally, we'll look at methods to help you troubleshoot a network installation.

Once you've read Chapters 4 and 5, you'll be ready to install Red Hat Linux on several computers simultaneously. This chapter covers the following topics:

- ◆ Preparing an NFS server
- ◆ Preparing an HTTP server
- ◆ Preparing an FTP server
- ◆ Installing Linux over a network
- ◆ Troubleshooting a network installation

Preparing an NFS Server

In this section, we'll look at configuring an NFS server with the Red Hat installation files from the CDs. When you've configured the server, you'll be able to use the shared NFS directory after Red Hat Linux is installed for the RPM packages that you may need in the future.

This assumes you already have a Linux or Unix computer, with the appropriate NFS services installed. We'll look at the basic commands that you need to set up an NFS installation server, but the details of how NFS works are not covered in this chapter. If you want to know more about NFS, see Chapter 28.

We also assume that you're making changes as the root user.

Copying Files

The first step is to set up a directory with the Red Hat Linux installation files. You'll need a `/RedHat` directory, with `base` and `RPMS` subdirectories. You need to copy the files in the `/RedHat/base` directory from the first Red Hat installation CD. You'll also need to copy the RPM packages from all three installation CDs to the `/RedHat/RPMS` directory.

This is actually a fairly easy process:

1. Find room for the Red Hat installation files. You'll need nearly 2GB of space.

2. Create a separate directory. Make sure it's in a partition with sufficient space. For more information on managing partitions, see Chapter 7. For the purpose of this exercise, I've named the directory `/mnt/inst`.

    ```
    # mkdir /mnt/inst
    ```

3. Mount the first Red Hat Linux 9 installation CD:

    ```
    # mount -r /dev/cdrom /mnt/cdrom
    ```

4. Copy the applicable files from the CD:

    ```
    # cp -ar /mnt/cdrom/RedHat /mnt/inst
    ```

5. Unmount the first installation CD. Mount the second Red Hat installation CD. Copy the applicable files from that CD:

    ```
    # umount /mnt/cdrom
    # mount -r /dev/cdrom /mnt/cdrom
    # cp -ar /mnt/cdrom/RedHat /mnt/inst
    ```

6. Repeat step 5 with the third Red Hat installation CD:

    ```
    # umount /mnt/cdrom
    # mount -r /dev/cdrom /mnt/cdrom
    # cp -ar /mnt/cdrom/RedHat /mnt/inst
    ```

Now you're ready with a Red Hat Linux installation source.

You could also install Red Hat Linux from `.iso` files on a shared NFS directory. I don't include that option in this book, since I believe that it is not as useful. While you can mount `.iso` files like regular Red Hat installation CDs, that approach does not provide a single source for RPM packages after Red Hat Linux is installed.

Sharing Directories

If you've installed NFS on your computer, you can now export the shared directory with the Red Hat Linux installation files. Exports are documented in the /etc/exports configuration file. Open it in the text editor of your choice.

NOTE *Several text editors are available in Linux. For more information on the* vi *text editor, see Chapter 6.*

Based on the previous section, we'll share the /mnt/inst directory with the Red Hat Linux installation files. It's not difficult; just follow these steps:

1. Add the following line to /etc/exports:

   ```
   /mnt/inst       *(ro,sync)
   ```

   Make sure that there are no spaces after the asterisk; NFS may misinterpret them. Save your changes to /etc/exports.

2. Next, export the shared directory with the following command:

   ```
   # exportfs -a
   ```

3. Now you can make sure that NFS is ready to share your directory. Stop the service. If NFS isn't yet running, the following messages may look like they're creating error messages. Don't worry about it.

   ```
   # service nfs stop
   ```

4. Copy the applicable files from the CD (this process will probably take several minutes):

   ```
   # service nfs start
   ```

5. Check your exports. Show the directories that can be mounted with the following command:

   ```
   # showmount -e
   ```

6. If you've installed a firewall during the installation process, it's easiest to disable it. While you could punch holes in the firewall, that requires more complex skills (see Chapter 23). For now, this "flushes" all firewall rules from your Linux computer:

   ```
   # iptables -F
   ```

   (If you have a slightly older version of Linux, you may need to use the ipchains -F command.)

Now you've set up a directory with Red Hat Linux installation files, and have shared it using NFS.

NOTE *If you want to continue sharing the installation directory the next time you boot Linux, the* chkconfig --level 2345 nfs on *command can help. For more information on* chkconfig, *see Chapter 13.*

Installation Parameters

To use the NFS directory that you've shared, you'll need two things: the address of the NFS server and the location of the /RedHat directory. The address of the NFS server could be a computer name, such as NFSserver, or a fully qualified domain name, such as www.example.com. But this requires a working DNS (Domain Name Service) server, which may not apply to all networks.

Alternatively, you can use the IP address of the NFS server. If you don't know that address, run the ifconfig command. It should give you output similar to Figure 4.1.

FIGURE 4.1

IP address
information

```
[root@RH9Test root]# ifconfig
eth0      Link encap:Ethernet  HWaddr 00:40:F4:3C:05:58
          inet addr:10.252.113.63  Bcast:10.252.113.255  Mask:255.255.255.0
          UP BROADCAST RUNNING MULTICAST  MTU:1500  Metric:1
          RX packets:191 errors:0 dropped:0 overruns:0 frame:0
          TX packets:117 errors:0 dropped:0 overruns:0 carrier:0
          collisions:0 txqueuelen:100
          RX bytes:37979 (37.0 Kb)  TX bytes:10859 (10.6 Kb)
          Interrupt:5 Base address:0x8000

lo        Link encap:Local Loopback
          inet addr:127.0.0.1  Mask:255.0.0.0
          UP LOOPBACK RUNNING  MTU:16436  Metric:1
          RX packets:4210 errors:0 dropped:0 overruns:0 frame:0
          TX packets:4210 errors:0 dropped:0 overruns:0 carrier:0
          collisions:0 txqueuelen:0
          RX bytes:286966 (280.2 Kb)  TX bytes:286966 (280.2 Kb)

[root@RH9Test root]# █
```

The important piece of information is the IP address; in Figure 4.1, it's 10.252.113.63 For more information on IP addressing and the other concepts in this section, see Chapter 20. To summarize, once you've set up shared directories on a running NFS server, you need the following bits of information during the installation process:

The IP address of the NFS server   If you have a working DNS server for your network, you could substitute the computer name or fully qualified domain name of the server.

The location of the /RedHat directory   Based on the actions taken earlier in this chapter, that is /mnt/init. If you've set up the Red Hat installation files in a different directory, the location changes accordingly.

You'll get a chance to see how this works in the section "Text Mode: Step by Step," later in this chapter.

Preparing an Apache Web Server

In this section, we'll look at configuring an Apache web server with the Red Hat installation files from the CDs. Once you've completed these steps, you'll be able to use a directory on your website after Red Hat Linux is installed for the RPM packages that you may need in the future.

In this section, we assume that you have a Linux or Unix computer, with the appropriate Apache (httpd) services already installed. We'll look at the basic commands that you need to set up an Apache (`httpd`) installation server; however, we don't address the details of how Apache is configured. To learn more about Apache, read Chapter 30.

Once again, we assume that you're making changes as the root user.

Copying Files

The first step is to set up a directory with the Red Hat Linux installation files. You'll need a `/RedHat` directory, with `base` and `RPMS` subdirectories. Copy the files in the `/RedHat/base` directory from the first Red Hat installation CD. Then, copy the RPM packages from all three installation CDs to the `/RedHat/RPMS` directory.

This is actually a fairly easy process:

1. Find room for the Red Hat installation files, preferably associated with the `/var` directory. You'll need nearly 2GB of space.

2. Create a separate directory. Make sure it's in a partition with sufficient space. For more information on managing partitions, see Chapter 7. For the purpose of this exercise, I've named the directory `/var/www/html/inst`.

   ```
   # mkdir /var/www/html/inst
   ```

3. Mount the first Red Hat Linux 9 installation CD: (this will probably take several minutes)

   ```
   # mount /dev/cdrom /mnt/cdrom
   ```

4. Copy the applicable files from the CD:

   ```
   # cp -ar /mnt/cdrom/RedHat /var/www/html/inst
   ```

5. Unmount the first installation CD. Mount the second Red Hat installation CD. Copy the applicable files from that CD:

   ```
   # umount /mnt/cdrom
   # mount /dev/cdrom /mnt/cdrom
   # cp -ar /mnt/cdrom/RedHat /var/www/html/inst
   ```

6. Repeat step 5 with the third Red Hat installation CD:

   ```
   # umount /mnt/cdrom
   # mount /dev/cdrom /mnt/cdrom
   # cp -ar /mnt/cdrom/RedHat /var/www/html/inst
   ```

Now you're ready with a Red Hat Linux installation source.

Unlike with NFS or a hard disk–based installation, you can't use an Apache server to install Red Hat Linux from `.iso` files.

Sharing Directories

If you've installed the Apache web server on your computer, you can now share the associated directory. By default, standard files are stored in `/var/www/html`. Assuming you used the directories cited in the previous section, all you need to cite during the Red Hat Linux installation process is the `/inst` directory.

The process is simpler than for NFS. All you need to do is make sure Apache is started with the command

```
# service httpd start
```

and then check to see if you get the "Test Page" when you navigate to `http://localhost` in the web browser of your choice.

Once you've created the share, you'll be able to download individual Red Hat RPM packages via your web server. Figure 4.2 shows how this is possible. Navigate to `http://yourwebserver/inst/RedHat`, and then click on the RPMs directory, and then you can click on the RPMs that you've loaded in the previous section. You should be able to download the RPMs to your local computer.

FIGURE 4.2

Accessing RPMs through a browser

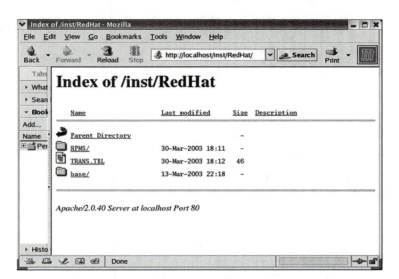

As with NFS, make sure that a firewall on the local computer isn't blocking access to your web server. The easiest way to do this is to "flush" the current rules in your firewall with the following command:

```
# iptables -F
```

If you have a slightly older Linux, you may need to use the `ipchains -F` command.

Now you've set up a directory with Red Hat Linux installation files, and have shared it using the Apache web server.

NOTE   *If you want to continue running Apache the next time you boot Linux, use the* `chkconfig --level 2345 httpd on` *command. See Chapter 13 for more information on* `chkconfig`.

Installation Parameters

To use the Apache directory that you've configured, you'll need two things: the address of Apache web server and the location of the /RedHat directory. The address of the Apache web server could be a computer name, such as Webserver, or a fully qualified domain name, such as www.example.com. However, this requires a working DNS (Domain Name Service) server, which may not apply to all networks.

Instead, you can use the IP address of the web server. If you don't know that address, run the ifconfig command. Find the IP address information for your computer as described earlier with Figure 4.1.

For more information on IP addressing and the other concepts in this section, see Chapter 20. To summarize, once you've set up shared directories on a running web server, you need the following bits of information during the installation process:

The IP address of the Apache web server   If you have a working DNS server on your network, you could substitute the computer name or fully qualified domain name of the server.

The location of the /RedHat directory   Based on the actions taken in the previous section, that is /inst.

You'll get a chance to see how this works in the section "Text Mode: Step by Step."

Preparing an FTP Server

In this section, you'll learn how to configure an FTP server with the Red Hat installation files from the CDs. You'll also learn how to connect to the same FTP server after Red Hat Linux is installed for the RPM packages that you may need in the future.

We assume that you already have a Linux or Unix computer, with the appropriate FTP services installed. On Red Hat Linux, that includes the vsftpd-* or (for older versions of Red Hat Linux) wu-ftpd-* and anonftp-* RPM packages. We don't delve into the details of how FTP servers are configured in this chapter; to learn more about that process, read Chapter 27.

In this section, we assume that you're making changes as the root user.

Copying Files

The first step is to set up a directory with the Red Hat Linux installation files. You'll need a /RedHat directory, with base and RPMS subdirectories. Copy the files in the /RedHat/base directory from the first Red Hat installation CD. Then, copy the RPM packages from all three installation CDs to the /RedHat/RPMS directory.

This is a fairly easy process:

1. Find room for the Red Hat installation files, preferably associated with the /var directory. You'll need a partition with nearly 2GB of space.

2. Create a separate directory. Make sure it's in a partition with sufficient space. For more information on managing partitions, see Chapter 7. For the purpose of this exercise, I've named the directory /var/ftp/pub/inst.

   ```
   # mkdir /var/ftp/pub/inst
   ```

3. Mount the first Red Hat Linux 9 installation CD:

```
# mount /dev/cdrom /mnt/cdrom
```

4. Copy the applicable files from the CD:

```
# cp -ar /mnt/cdrom/RedHat /var/ftp/pub/inst
```

5. Unmount the first installation CD. Mount the second Red Hat installation CD. Copy the applicable files from that CD:

```
# umount /mnt/cdrom
# mount /dev/cdrom /mnt/cdrom
# cp -ar /mnt/cdrom/RedHat /var/ftp/pub/inst
```

6. Repeat step 5 with the third Red Hat installation CD:

```
# umount /mnt/cdrom
# mount /dev/cdrom /mnt/cdrom
# cp -ar /mnt/cdrom/RedHat /var/ftp/pub/inst
```

Now you're ready with a Red Hat Linux installation source.

Unlike with NFS or a hard disk–based installation, you can't use an FTP server to install Red Hat Linux from .iso files.

Sharing Directories

If you've installed the FTP server packages on your computer, you can now share the associated directory. By default, standard files are stored in /var/ftp/pub. Assuming you used the directories cited in the previous section, all you need to cite during the Red Hat Linux installation process is the /inst directory.

The process is simpler than for NFS. Just make sure the FTP server is started with the command

```
# service vsftpd start
```

and then check to see if you get the appropriate directories after logging into that FTP server.

NOTE   *Prior to Red Hat 9,* vsftpd *was an* xinetd *service, which you can activate as described in Chapter 23.*

Once you've created the share, you'll be able to download individual Red Hat RPM packages from the FTP server. For more information, see Chapter 10.

As with the other servers, make sure that a firewall on the local computer isn't blocking access to your web server. The easiest way to do this is to "flush" the current rules in your firewall with the following command:

```
# iptables -F
```

If you have a version of Linux with a version 2.2.*x* kernel, you may need to use the ipchains -F command.

NOTE   *The* ipchains *command is most closely associated with Linux kernel version 2.2. However, there are computers with Linux kernel version 2.4 that run* ipchains. *This includes the default versions of Red Hat Linux 7.1 and 7.2.*

Now you've set up a directory with Red Hat Linux installation files, and have shared it using an FTP server.

NOTE *If you want to continue running Apache the next time you boot Linux, use the* `chkconfig --level 2345 vsftpd on` *command. For more information on* `chkconfig`*, see Chapter 13.*

Installation Parameters

To use the FTP directory that you've configured, you'll need two things: the address of the FTP server computer and the location of the `/RedHat` directory. The address of the FTP server could be a computer name, such as `Webserver`, or a fully qualified domain name, such as `www.example.com`. However, this requires a working DNS (Domain Name Service) server, which may not apply to all networks.

Instead, you can use the IP address of the FTP server. If you don't know that address, run the `ifconfig` command. Find the IP address information for your computer as described earlier with Figure 4.1.

For more information on IP addressing and the other concepts in this section, see Chapter 20. To summarize, once you've set up shared directories on a running FTP server, you need the following bits of information during the installation process:

The IP address of the FTP server   If you have a working DNS server on your network, you could substitute the computer name or fully qualified domain name of the server.

The location of the `/RedHat` directory   Based on the actions taken in the previous section, that is `/pub/inst`.

You'll get a chance to see how this works in the section "Text Mode: Step by Step."

Installing Linux over a Network

When you're installing Red Hat Linux over a network connection, you generally aren't going to use the Red Hat installation CDs. Therefore, you need a boot disk. Red Hat provides boot disk images that you can write to floppies and CDs.

Once you have the boot disk, you can start the Red Hat Linux network installation process. In this chapter, we proceed with text-mode installation, since we covered graphical mode in Chapter 3. In any case, graphical-mode installations aren't allowed if you're installing from an FTP or Apache server.

The Red Hat Linux installation program is known as Anaconda. You can customize the Anaconda installation process to omit installation options such as games. For more details, read Chapter 5.

Making Boot Disks

Red Hat provides boot disk images on the first installation CD, in the `/images` directory. You can even use the first installation CD itself as a network boot disk. There are two basic files that you can use to create an installation boot disk; several driver images are also available that you can use to create 1.44MB driver floppy disks.

The appropriate files in the `/images` directory are briefly described in Table 4.1.

TABLE 4.1: BOOT IMAGES

FILENAME	DESCRIPTION
bootdisk.img	Used to create a standard boot floppy for local and network installations.
drvblock.img	Contains additional block device drivers; may be needed for many SCSI hard drives.
drvnet.img	Includes additional network device drivers.
pcmciadd.img	Adds additional PCMCIA drivers for many laptop computers.
boot.iso	Includes data from all boot and driver disks; since it's too big for a 1.44MB floppy, it's set up to be recorded on a CD.

You can write an .img file to a 1.44MB floppy disk in one of three basic ways. If you have a Linux computer, you can use the **cat** or **dd** command. For example, you can use either of the following commands to write the contents of **bootdisk.img** to a 1.44MB floppy drive. These commands assume that you've mounted the first Red Hat Linux installation CD on the **/mnt/cdrom** directory:

```
# dd if=/mnt/cdrom/images/bootdisk.img of=/dev/fd0
# cat /mnt/cdrom/images/bootdisk.img > /dev/fd0
```

A second approach is to write the contents of these image files to a 1.44MB floppy drive in Microsoft Windows. The key utility is on the first Red Hat Linux installation CD, in the **/dosutils** directory. The command-line version of this interface is **RAWRITE.EXE**. In Microsoft Windows, open an MS-DOS command-line window. Insert your first Red Hat Linux installation CD. If your CD is on drive E, run the following commands:

```
E:\>DOSUTILS\RAWRITE
Enter disk image source file name: E:\IMAGES\BOOTDISK.IMG
Enter target diskette drive: A:
Please insert a formatted diskette in drive A: and press -ENTER- :
```

You can also create a boot CD from the **boot.iso** file. For more information, refer to the **cdrecord** command described in Chapter 14. You can even start a network installation using the first Red Hat Linux 9 installation CD; just remember to start the installation using the **linux askmethod** or **text askmethod** command.

Text Mode: Booting

Now we'll examine a text-mode network installation. As described in the last section, there are three basic options for boot disks:

◆ A floppy disk written from the **bootdisk.img** file

◆ A CD written from the **boot.iso** file

◆ The first Red Hat Linux installation CD

In all of these cases, you'll see the menu shown in Figure 4.3.

FIGURE 4.3

Red Hat Linux
installation menu

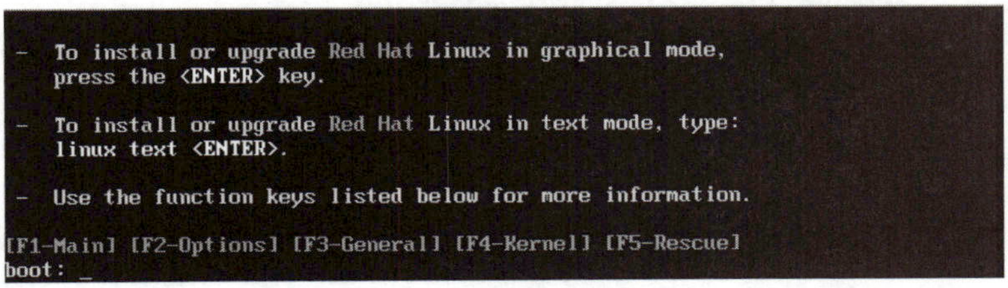

```
-   To install or upgrade Red Hat Linux in graphical mode,
    press the <ENTER> key.

-   To install or upgrade Red Hat Linux in text mode, type:
    linux text <ENTER>.

-   Use the function keys listed below for more information.

[F1-Main] [F2-Options] [F3-General] [F4-Kernel] [F5-Rescue]
boot: _
```

We installed Red Hat Linux in graphical mode in Chapter 3. That chapter was more focused on regular users. Now we'll look at the administrative side of things in more detail. As you can see from the initial menu, several other menus are available. You can get to the Installer Boot Options menu by pressing F2. The menu is shown in Figure 4.4.

FIGURE 4.4

Installer Boot
Options

```
                    Installer Boot Options
-   To disable hardware probing, type: linux noprobe <ENTER>.

-   To test the install media you are using, type: linux mediacheck <ENTER>.

-   To enable rescue mode, type: linux rescue <ENTER>.
    Press <F5> for more information about rescue mode.

-   If you have a driver disk, type: linux dd <ENTER>.

-   To prompt for the install method being used on a CD-ROM install,
    type linux askmethod <ENTER>.

-   If you have an installer update disk, type: linux updates <ENTER>.

-   To install using a 640x480 resolution, type: linux lowres.

[F1-Main] [F2-Options] [F3-General] [F4-Kernel] [F5-Rescue]
boot: _
```

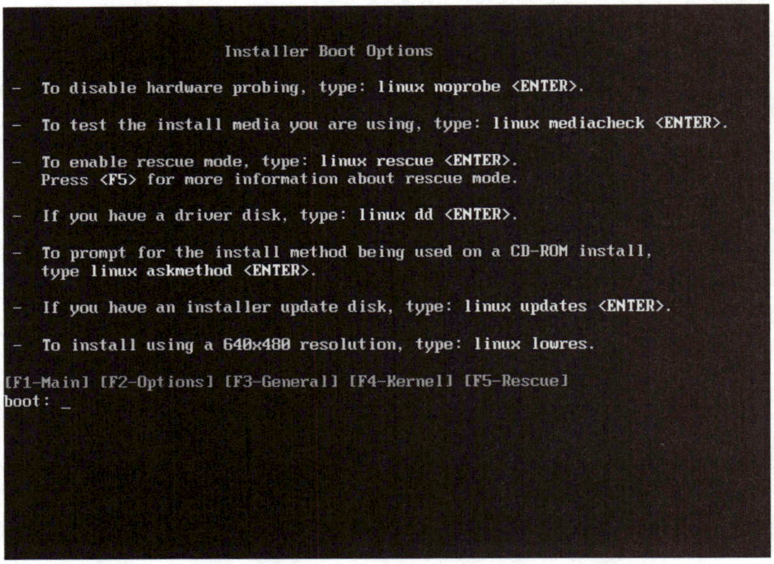

This menu lists some of the available options for what you can enter at the boot: prompt. Table 4.2 describes these options.

TABLE 4.2: INSTALLER BOOT OPTIONS

OPTION	DESCRIPTION
linux noprobe	Disables detection of key hardware components; if you select this option, be prepared to use driver disks.
linux mediacheck	Adds an additional step to the process, where the integrity of media such as installation CDs are tested against embedded MD5 checksums.
linux rescue	Starts a process that detects current Linux partitions on your system; can be used to recover from a number of different boot failures (for details, see Chapter 11).
linux dd	Adds an additional step to the process, prompting for a driver disk; when you use the standard Red Hat bootdisk.img floppy, Linux prompts for the driver disk automatically.
linux askmethod	If you're starting the installation process from the first Red Hat installation CD, allows you to select a network installation source.
linux updates	Allows you to use an update floppy disk; mostly for upgrades.
linux lowres	Starts a graphical-mode installation process in a screen with 640 × 480 resolution.

NOTE *If you want to start the installation in text mode, just substitute* text *for* linux *in one of the options in Table 4.2. Alternatively, you can start the installation in text mode by using the* linux text *or* text *commands.*

In other words, if you're starting the installation process from the bootdisk.img floppy or the boot.iso CD, you'll want to enter the following:

boot: **linux text**

Alternatively, if you're starting the installation process from the first installation CD, enter this:

boot: **text askmethod**

One of the things you can do at the boot prompt is to specify the parameters of some hardware. Figure 4.5, the Kernel Parameter Help screen, provides the basics of what you can do. For more information, run the man bootparam command on another Linux computer.

Text Mode: Step by Step

Now that you've started the installation process, let's examine how this works, step by step. We'll describe the text-mode process in detail, based on starting from a bootdisk.img installation floppy. The other startup methods are less complex.

TIP *This is a very long section. If you're planning to read it all at once, it might help to take a break before you begin.*

1. Boot your computer with the Red Hat Linux installation floppy, created from the bootdisk.img file, using the techniques described earlier in the "Making Boot Disks" section.

FIGURE 4.5

Kernel
Parameter Help

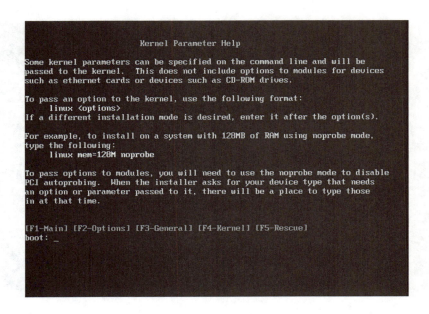

```
                         Kernel Parameter Help

Some kernel parameters can be specified on the command line and will be
passed to the kernel.  This does not include options to modules for devices
such as ethernet cards or devices such as CD-ROM drives.

To pass an option to the kernel, use the following format:
     linux <options>
If a different installation mode is desired, enter it after the option(s).

For example, to install on a system with 128MB of RAM using noprobe mode,
type the following:
     linux mem=128M noprobe

To pass options to modules, you will need to use the noprobe mode to disable
PCI autoprobing.  When the installer asks for your device type that needs
an option or parameter passed to it, there will be a place to type those
in at that time.



[F1-Main] [F2-Options] [F3-General] [F4-Kernel] [F5-Rescue]
boot: _
```

2. When you see the prompt, enter the following:

   boot: `linux text`

NOTE   *If you're using the first Red Hat Installation CD, enter* **text askmethod** *at the* boot: *prompt.*

You'll see a series of messages installing a basic kernel and the text-mode version of the
Anaconda installation program.

3. Select a language from the Choose A Language screen, shown in Figure 4.6. While English is
   the default, you can install Red Hat Linux with prompts in some 18 different languages and
   dialects. You can use the Up and Down arrow keys to make your selection. When you've
   selected your language, use the Tab button to highlight OK, and then press Enter or F12 to
   continue.

NOTE   *With the various text-mode menus, you can use the arrow and Tab keys to navigate between selections. Once you've
made your selection, you can press F12, or highlight OK and press Enter or the spacebar to continue. If there are settings
that you can toggle, highlight the desired setting and press your spacebar.*

4. Select a keyboard from the Keyboard Type screen, shown in Figure 4.7. While the us keyboard
   is the default, you can set up a Red Hat Linux installation on over 60 different keyboards, many
   of them customized for other languages. Once you've selected your keyboard, press F12 to
   continue.

FIGURE 4.6

Choosing a language

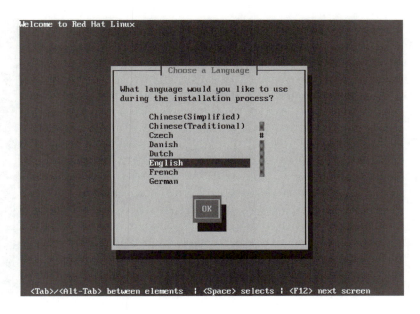

FIGURE 4.7

Choosing a
keyboard type

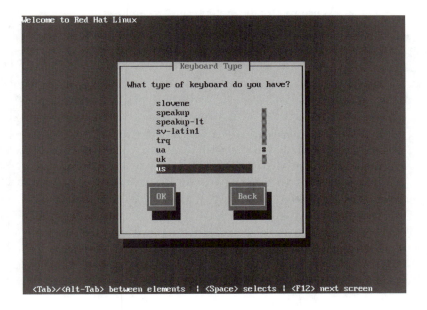

5. Select from the network installation methods shown in Figure 4.8. As we described earlier, you can install from an NFS, an FTP, or an HTTP (Apache) server. Make your selection and press F12 to continue.

FIGURE 4.8

Specifying an installation method

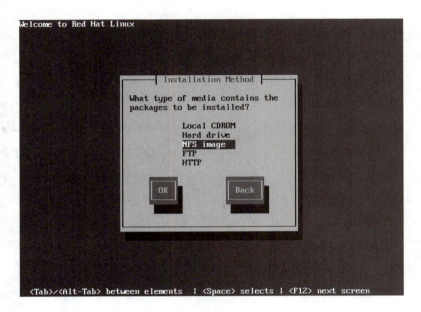

<NOTE> *If you have more than one network card, you'll see a menu where you're allowed to select between your cards, such as* eth0 *and* eth1. *There's no easy way to tell which card is connected to which network. If you select the wrong card, you'll see an error message in the next few steps. Some trial and error may be required; if you select the wrong network card, use the Back options in the menus, and then try the other card.*

6. Additional drivers may be required with the bootdisk.img-based installation floppy, as shown in Figure 4.9. Select Use A Driver Disk and press Enter to continue. If you don't see the No Driver Found screen, that means you probably started from the first Red Hat installation CD or the boot.iso-based CD; in that case, skip ahead to step 10.

7. Now that you need a new driver, you can select a driver disk, as shown in Figure 4.10. You can use one of the driver floppies that you may have created earlier in the section "Making Boot Disks." In that case, select fd0. If you can use the first Red Hat installation CD as a driver disk, select the device associated with your CD, usually hdb or hdc. After you make your selection, press F12 to continue.

FIGURE 4.9

The No Driver
Found screen

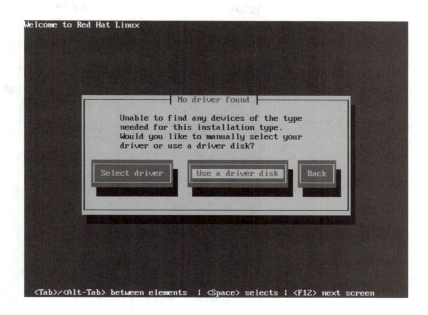

FIGURE 4.10

Selecting a driver
disk source

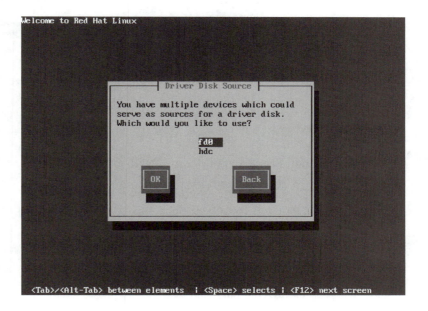

8. At the prompt shown in Figure 4.11, insert the driver disk (floppy or CD) appropriate for your network card or hard drive. If you need both, you'll be prompted to repeat the process with the other disk.

FIGURE 4.11

Insert a driver disk.

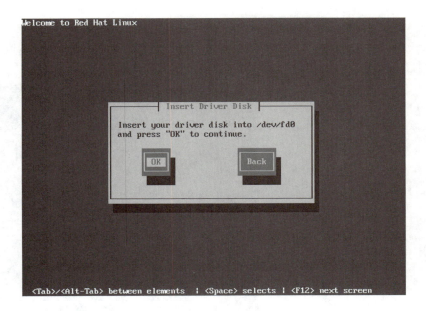

9. If you need a different driver disk, you'll see the Error screen shown in Figure 4.12. Select Load Another Disk and press Enter to continue. If you continue to see the same message, your driver disk may be corrupt or may not support your hardware. Return to step 7. If you don't see the Error screen, proceed to step 10.

FIGURE 4.12

Prompt for another driver disk

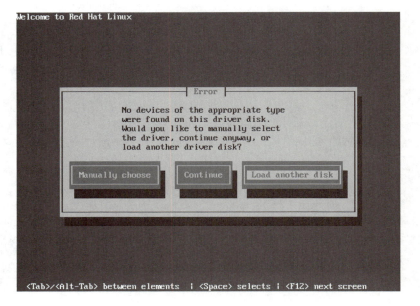

10. Now that you have installed drivers for your network card and hard drive, you're ready to set up the connection to the network server. In the Configure TCP/IP screen shown in Figure 4.13, you'll need to set up TCP/IP settings for your computer.

FIGURE 4.13

Configuring
TCP/IP

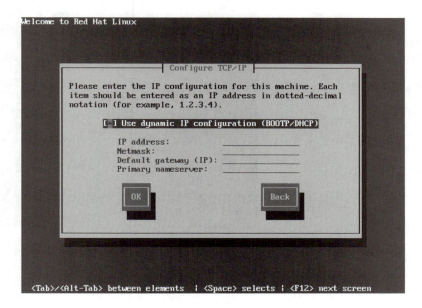

If there is a DHCP (Dynamic Host Configuration Protocol) server available for your network, you can keep the Use Dynamic IP Configuration (BOOTP/DHCP) setting active; otherwise, you'll need to set up key IP address information for your system. In that case, highlight the setting and press the spacebar to deselect it. For more information on IP addressing, see Chapter 20. Make your selections and press F12 to continue. If you have a second network card, you'll repeat this step with that card.

TIP   If you have a home network, you may already have a DHCP server. Many hardware routers, such as those associated with cable modems or DSL adapters, include their own DHCP server. If you have one of these components, check the documentation associated with that router. Make sure the assigned IP addresses matches the subnet you've configured for your network.

11. What you'll do next varies slightly depending on whether you're installing from an NFS, an Apache HTTP, or an FTP server. In any of these cases, you'll need to cite the name or IP address of the server, as well as the location of the installation files. Figures 4.14, 4.15, and 4.16 illustrate what you might enter for each of these types of servers, based on the server setup instructions earlier in this chapter. For example, Figure 4.14 works if you've installed the `RedHat` directory as part of the `/mnt/inst` directory on the NFS server. Figures 4.15 and 4.16 are based on the settings described earlier for copying installation files to an HTTP or a FTP server.

FIGURE 4.14
NFS Setup

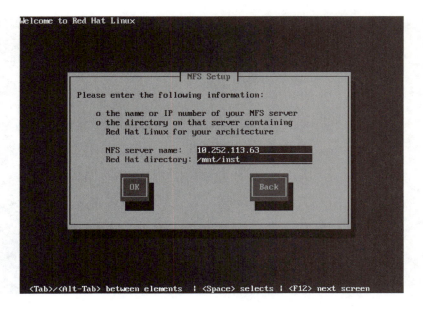

FIGURE 4.15
HTTP Setup

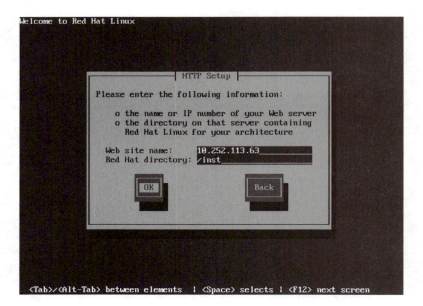

FIGURE 4.16

FTP Setup

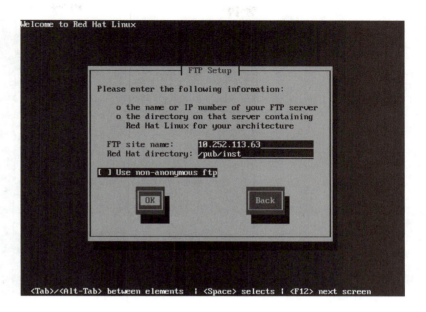

If you're installing from an FTP server, you'll see in Figure 4.16 that you can install from a non-anonymous FTP server, that is, where you have a user account with a password. If you select this option, you'll be prompted for your username and password.

12. If you're successful connecting to any network server, you'll eventually see the following message:

```
Running anaconda, the Red Hat Linux System installer - please wait
```

followed by the welcome screen shown in Figure 4.17. The steps that follow are independent of the installation server that you're using. Select OK to continue.

NOTE   If you ever install a Red Hat Linux beta, about this time you'll see a warning to that effect, along with an opportunity to stop the installation process.

13. Select a mouse from the Mouse Selection screen, shown in Figure 4.18. You can select from nearly 40 types of pointing devices, including several that connect to USB interfaces. In most cases, if you select a two-button mouse, the Emulate 3 Buttons option is automatically selected.

NOTE   The Emulate 3 Buttons option lets you simulate the functionality of a middle mouse button by pressing the left and right buttons simultaneously. You can select or deselect this option by highlighting it and pressing the spacebar.

14. If you're installing Red Hat Linux on a computer that already has a previous version of Red Hat, you'll see the System To Upgrade screen shown in Figure 4.19. If you're planning to upgrade an existing installation of Red Hat Linux, select it. Or, you can set up a fresh installation of Red Hat Linux in the same space by selecting Reinstall System.

FIGURE 4.17

The welcome screen

FIGURE 4.18

Selecting a mouse

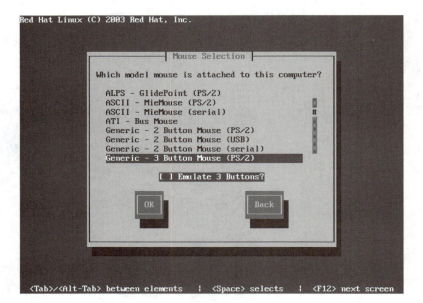

FIGURE 4.19

Option to upgrade

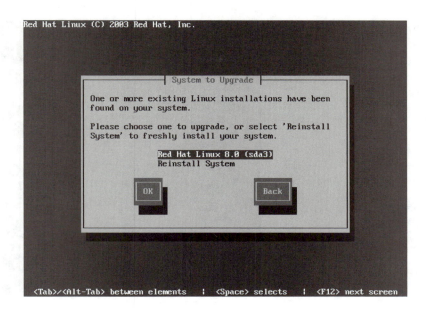

If you choose to upgrade an existing Red Hat Linux installation, read the next section. Otherwise, select Reinstall System and press F12 to continue.

15. Select an Installation Type. As shown in Figure 4.20, you have four options. Each option is associated with different default package groups, as described in the "Installation Options" sidebar. For the purpose of this chapter, we'll select a Server installation; the steps associated with the other options are nearly identical. Make your selection and press F12 to continue.

FIGURE 4.20

Installation Type options

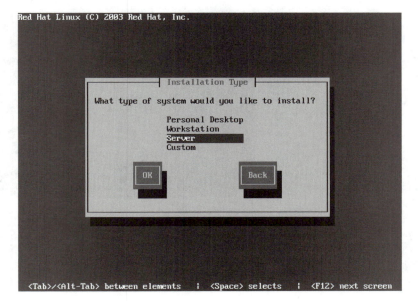

INSTALLATION OPTIONS

There are four standard Red Hat Linux installation options: Personal Desktop, Workstation, Server, and Custom. While customized installations are possible in each case, each option is associated with a set of default package groups. Each package group includes a set of RPM packages, documented in the `comps.xml` file, and described in Web Chapter 5, which can be found on the Sybex website at www.sybex.com.

Older versions of Red Hat Linux included a Laptop installation option, which incorporated packages associated with standard laptop hardware. These packages are now incorporated in the Personal Desktop and Workstation installation options.

For your reference, the package groups that are installed by default are listed here.

Group	Personal Desktop	Workstation	Server	Custom
Administration Tools	*	*	*	
Authoring and Publishing				
DNS Name Server				
Development Tools		*		
Editors	*	*		
Engineering and Scientific				
FTP Server				
GNOME Desktop Environment	*	*		*
GNOME Software Development		*		
Games and Entertainment	*	*		
Graphical Internet	*	*		*
Graphics	*	*		*
KDE Desktop Environment				
KDE Software Development				
Kernel Development				
Mail Server				
Network Servers				
News Server				
Office/Productivity	*	*		*
Printing Support	*	*	*	*
SQL Database Server				
Server Configuration Tools			*	
Sound and Video	*	*		*
System Tools				
Text-based Internet	*	*	*	*
Web Server			*	

Continued on next page

INSTALLATION OPTIONS *(continued)*				
Group	Personal Desktop	Workstation	Server	Custom
Windows File Server			*	
X Software Development		*		
X Window System	*	*		*
Approximate Size of installed files	1700MB	2100MB	850MB	1500MB

16. Next, you'll select the Disk Partitioning Setup, as shown in Figure 4.21. If you select Auto-partition, Red Hat Linux automatically configures partitions for you, based on the required packages, your RAM, and the size of available partitions on your hard drive(s). If you select Disk Druid, skip to step 18. Make your selection and press Enter to continue.

FIGURE 4.21

Disk Partitioning
Setup

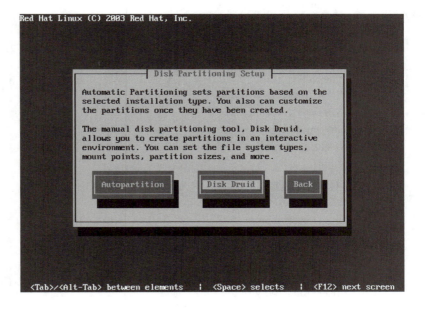

NOTE *If this is a new hard disk, you may see a warning that the partition table is unreadable. You'll be given an opportunity to initialize the drive. You'll have to answer yes to install Red Hat Linux on this hard drive.*

17. If you've chosen to let Red Hat autopartition your system, you'll see the Automatic Partitioning window, shown in Figure 4.22. If you're installing Red Hat Linux on a computer with Linux and Microsoft Windows partitions, be careful. The default option for a Server installation would delete your Microsoft Windows operating system. The options are described in Table 4.3. Make your selection and press F12 to continue.

FIGURE 4.22

Automatic
Partitioning

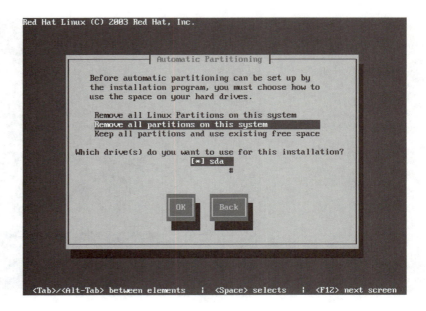

TABLE 4.3: AUTOMATIC PARTITIONING OPTIONS

OPTION	DESCRIPTION
Remove All Linux Partitions On This System	Deletes all partitions formatted to Linux filesystems; does not affect partitions formatted to other filesystems, such as those associated with Microsoft Windows.
Remove All Partitions On This System	Deletes all partitions on this computer.
Keep All Partitions And Use Existing Free Space	Assumes that you have unpartitioned free space on your hard drive(s); if you don't, this option leads to an error message.
Which Drive(s) Do You Want To Use For This Installation?	If you have more than one physical hard drive, you're allowed to select the drives where Red Hat Linux is to be installed.

18. You're asked to confirm your selection, as shown in Figure 4.23. If you're satisfied with your choice, select Yes and press Enter to continue.

19. You're taken to a Disk Druid screen, where you can review the choices made by Anaconda's Automatic Partitioning. The default Server configuration on a computer with 192MB of RAM and a 4GB hard drive is shown in Figure 4.24. When space permits, Red Hat normally assigns twice the amount of RAM as a swap partition.

FIGURE 4.23
You'll see this warning before you delete partitions.

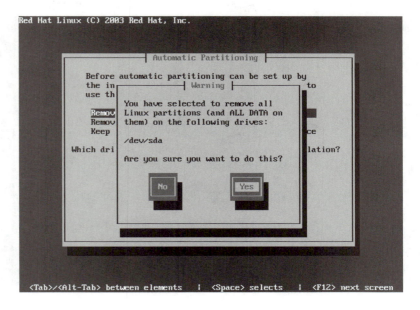

FIGURE 4.24
Disk Druid

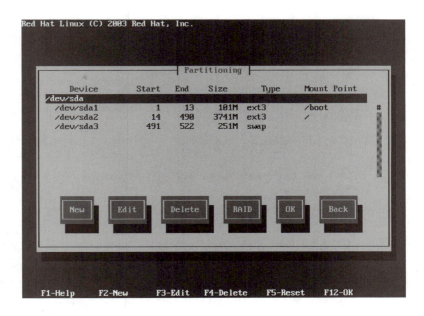

20. You can edit configured partitions. For example, if you had the configuration shown in Figure 4.24, you could highlight /dev/sda2, associated with the root (/) directory. You could then use the Tab key to highlight Edit and press Enter; this would take you to the Add Partition window, where you can change the settings associated with /dev/sda2. Figure 4.25 shows this menu, and Table 4.4 describes the options.

FIGURE 4.25

Editing a configured partition

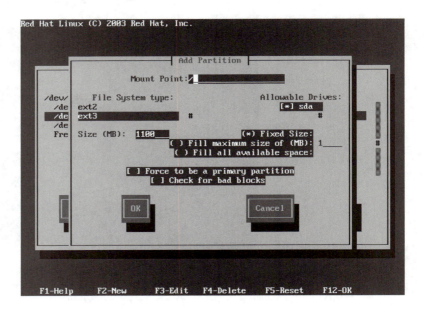

TABLE 4.4: Options in the Add Partition Window

OPTION	DESCRIPTION
Mount Point	Specifies the directory to be mounted on the partition; for mountable directories, consult the discussion on the Filesystem Hierarchy Standard in Chapter 7.
File System Type	Sets the format for the partition; you're allowed to select form the Linux ext2 or ext3 standards, the Linux swap format, a Logical Volume Manager (LVM) volume, a software RAID volume, or a Microsoft Windows–style vfat format.
Allowable Drives	Notes the hard drive device associated with the partition.
Size (MB)	Specifies the size of the partition, in MB; this can be fixed, growable to a specific size, or can be set to fill any remaining free space on the hard drive.
Force To Be A Primary Partition	Generally, you'll want the partition with the /boot directory to be on a primary partition below cylinder 1024.
Check For Bad Blocks	Sets up a physical check of the partition for unreadable sectors.

21. You can also add new partitions. For example, I've added a partition for the /var directory to help control the remaining free space, as shown in Figure 4.26.

FIGURE 4.26

Adding a partition

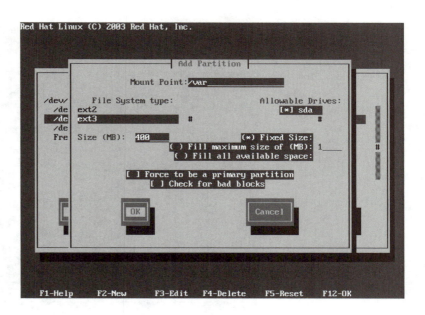

22. If you've configured two or more software RAID partitions, you can configure a RAID device. Back in the main Disk Druid screen shown in Figure 4.24, select RAID and press Enter. If you have sufficient available software RAID partitions, you'll see the Make RAID Device menu, shown in Figure 4.27.

FIGURE 4.27

The Make RAID Device menu

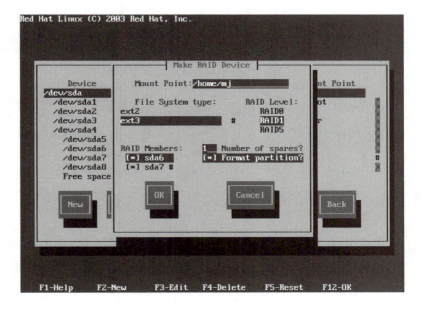

In this case, I've created a RAID1 level device, with three RAID member partitions: `sda6`, `sda7`, and `sda8`. Since RAID1 requires only two partitions, one is used as a spare. For more information on RAID, see Chapter 14.

NOTE *The Red Hat Linux text-mode menus don't allow you to manually configure Logical Volume Manager filesystems. However, it's possible in the graphical-mode installation shown in Chapter 3 as well as Kickstart installations shown in Chapter 5.*

PARTITION SIZES

One important decision during Red Hat Linux installation is on the size and number of your partitions. As described in Chapters 3 and 7, you can mount different directories on physically separate hard drive partitions. This can protect you, because an overload on many partitions may not crash your computer.

If you have less than 2GB or 3GB available on your hard drive, the choices are simple. You don't have much extra room on your hard drive and are therefore pretty much limited to separate partitions for a root (/) and /boot directory and a swap partition. This and several typical partition configurations are described in Chapter 7.

If you have more space, you have more flexibility. You may be able to configure separate partitions for several different directories. As described in Chapter 7, some directories should not be mounted on separate partitions.

Some examples of directories you might want to mount are shown below and include the *minimum* space required when you install everything in Red Hat Linux (this may be larger than the size of the files installed in the particular directory). Remember, you'll likely need additional room for users, applications, and log files. For example, large websites may produce gigabytes of log files every day!

Directory	Description
/boot	Contains the boot files, including the Linux kernel; the default 100MB size should be sufficient.
/	The top-level root (/) directory; includes all directories not mounted on separate partitions. When other directories shown are mounted on separate partitions, the remaining directories under root (/) contain about 110MB of files under the "Everything" installation.
/home	Includes home directories for all users except root; when selecting a size, you need to consider longer-term needs of current and future users.
/home/mj	Limits the amount of space available for a specific user; you can also do this with quotas described in Chapter 9.
/opt	Contains files for many third-party applications; about 17MB of files are installed via the "Everything" installation.
/tmp	Includes files that are automatically deleted on a regular basis; suitable for downloads. About 5MB of files are installed via the "Everything" installation.
/usr	Contains many programs and lots of data; an "Everything" installation requires over 5300MB of space. Some third-party programs may also require space in this directory.
/var	Includes directories for log files and print spools; should leave several hundred MB of empty space in this directory. About 210MB of files are installed via the "Everything" installation.

23. Create and delete additional partitions as desired. I've created the series of partitions shown in Figure 4.28. When you've finished, press F12 to continue.

FIGURE 4.28

A partition
configuration

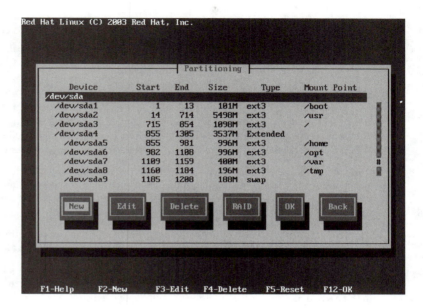

24. Now you can select your bootloader. You have three choices, as shown in Figure 4.29. The default is GRUB, the Grand Unified Boot Loader, which is the default described in Chapter 11. The main alternative is LILO, the Linux Loader, which was the default on older versions of Red Hat Linux. You can choose to use another bootloader, such as those associated with the proprietary Partition Magic or System Commander programs. Since Red Hat has deprecated LILO, we will stick with the default GRUB bootloader. Make your selection and press F12 to continue.

NOTE   The terms boot loader and bootloader are used interchangeably.

NOTE   It's possible use a floppy disk as a bootloader. Just be sure to create a boot disk in step 40 after Red Hat Linux actually installs packages on your system.

25. If there are special parameters associated with your kernel, you can enter them in the second Boot Loader Configuration screen, shown in Figure 4.30. You can enter kernel parameters described earlier in the section entitled "Text Mode: Booting." Red Hat Linux may do this automatically for you. For example, in the corresponding graphical screen in Chapter 3, Red Hat included the hdc=ide-scsi parameter, which is required for many IDE CD drives. Make any required selections and press F12 to continue.

FIGURE 4.29

Selecting a bootloader

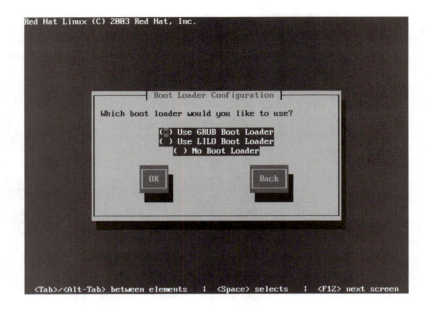

FIGURE 4.30

Here's your chance to add special kernel parameters.

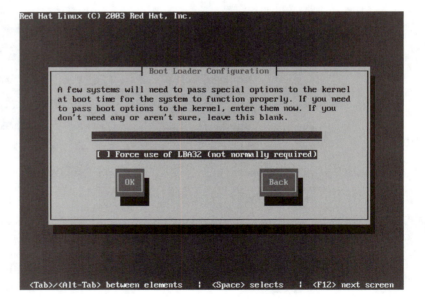

NOTE   *Generally, you won't need to activate the Force Use Of LBA32 option. Logical Block Addressing (LBA) allows Linux to see beyond the 1024th cylinder on your hard drive. It's active by default on most computers and is detected automatically by GRUB. Even if it isn't active, it does not matter as long as the partition with your /boot directory is located below that cylinder limit.*

26. If you're using GRUB, you can set a password. This prevents users with physical access to your computer from booting it in single-user mode to change your root password. This is an excellent idea. Activate the Use A GRUB Password option, and enter the password of your choice, as shown in Figure 4.31, then press F12 to continue.

FIGURE 4.31

Creating a GRUB password

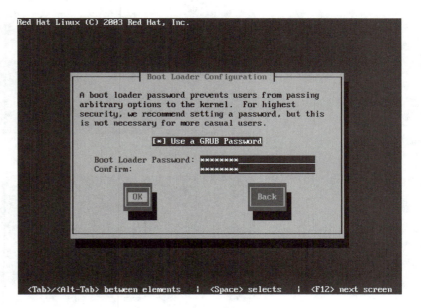

NOTE   *If your passwords don't match, you'll see a warning to that effect. After pressing Enter, you're then taken to the original screen where you can try to set your password again.*

27. Next, you can select the default operating system for your computer. If you're only using Red Hat Linux on your computer, this does not matter; you get only one choice. However, if Anaconda detects more than one operating system on your computer, you get to set a default. For example, the screen shown in Figure 4.32 allows you to select between the operating systems labeled DOS and Red Hat Linux.

In this case, the operating system on the partition labeled /dev/sda1 is Microsoft Windows NT 4. For more information on how this works in GRUB, see Chapter 11. Select the default operating system of your choice, use the Tab key to select OK, and then press Enter to continue.

FIGURE 4.32

Selecting a default operating system

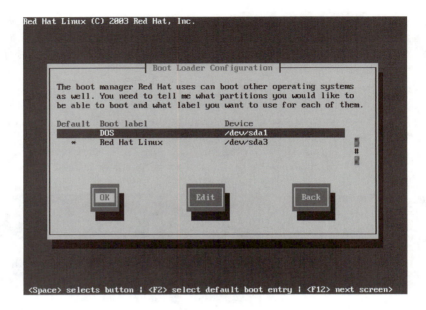

28. Now you can set the location of your bootloader. Typically, it should be placed on the Master Boot Record (MBR) of your hard drive. However, if you already have a different bootloader on your computer, you may want to choose First Sector Of Boot Partition, which corresponds to the partition with the /**boot** directory. Typical choices are shown in Figure 4.33. Make your selection and press F12 to continue.

FIGURE 4.33

Locating the bootloader

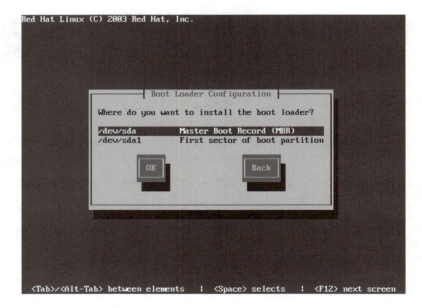

NOTE   *If you have more than two hard drives, be careful. The BIOS on a typical PC can only find the /boot directory if it's on one of the first two IDE (hda, hdb) or SCSI (sda, sdb) hard drives. The SCSI drive must have an ID Number of 0 or 1. If you have both IDE and SCSI hard drives, it must be on the first one of these drives; the SCSI drive must have a ID number of 0.*

29. Now you can complete your network configuration. Since you're installing from a network server, you've already entered basic IP address information for this computer. If you're satisfied with the settings shown in Figure 4.34, press F12 to continue. (Note that the configuration in this case is for the network card labeled eth0.) Otherwise, deselect Use BOOTP/DHCP, which allows you to change the settings shown in Table 4.5.

FIGURE 4.34

Configuring network settings

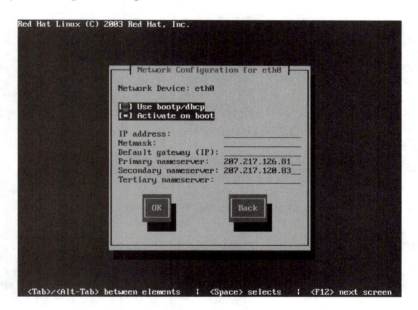

NOTE   *If you have more than one network card, you get to repeat step 29 with the next card.*

30. If you set a static IP address, you'll now see a Hostname Configuration window, where you can assign a hostname for your computer. Do so and press F12 to continue.

31. Next, you can configure a firewall for your computer. It's generally not necessary for computers inside a LAN that's already protected by a firewall. However, if you're installing Red Hat Linux on a computer that is also connected to another network such as the Internet, a firewall is critical. As shown in Figure 4.35, three firewall configurations are available. For the purpose of this installation, we'll configure a high-security firewall. Highlight this option, and press the spacebar to select it.

TABLE 4.5: NETWORK CONFIGURATION SETTINGS

SETTING	DESCRIPTION
Use BOOTP/DHCP	Makes the computer look for a DHCP server on a local or remote network; the BOOTP protocol makes it possible to get IP address information from a DHCP server on a remote network.
Activate On Boot	Sets the computer to activate this network configuration when you start Linux.
IP Address	Configures the IP address associated with this network card; for more information on IP addressing, see Chapter 20.
Netmask	Short for network mask or subnet mask; for more information, see Chapter 20.
Default Gateway (IP)	Notes the IP address of the computer or router that is also connected to an external network such as the Internet.
Primary Nameserver	Configures a DNS server for this network; the IP address can be outside your LAN.
Secondary Nameserver	Configures a DNS server for this network; the IP address can be outside your LAN.
Tertiary Nameserver	Configures a DNS server for this network; the IP address can be outside your LAN.

FIGURE 4.35

Configuring the firewall

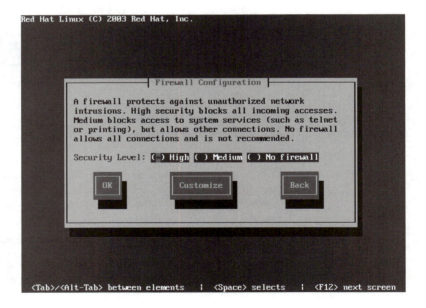

NOTE *Even the standard Red Hat high-security firewall allows the computer to get information from a DNS server, which is essential for browsing the Internet. This holds true as long as you've listed the IP address for at least one* nameserver *earlier in the installation process.*

32. Now we'll customize the firewall. Alternatively, you can customize the firewall after installation using the techniques described in Chapter 22. After selecting High, use the Tab key to highlight Customize, and then press Enter. That opens the Firewall Configuration - Customize screen, shown in Figure 4.36. The options shown in Figure 4.36 are described in Table 4.6. Make the desired changes and press F12 to return to the basic Firewall Configuration screen in Figure 4.35. Press F12 again to continue.

FIGURE 4.36

Customizing a firewall

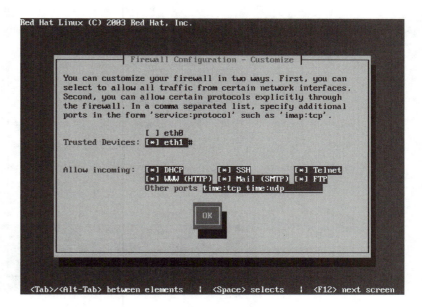

TABLE 4.6: FIREWALL CONFIGURATION CUSTOMIZATION OPTIONS

OPTION	DESCRIPTION
Trusted Devices	Lets you activate a network card as a trusted device; important if you have more than one network card. Any firewall you create won't stop any traffic that passes through that trusted device. It's common to activate this option for a network card connected to an internal network.
DHCP	Allows incoming DHCP information. You're allowing an external DHCP server to assign IP address information for computers on your network; essential for BOOTP access.
SSH	Permits Secure Shell access; you're allowing encrypted remote connections using this service, as described in Chapter 23.
Telnet	Permits Secure Shell access; you're allowing clear-text remote connections using this service, as described in Chapter 23.
WWW	Allows incoming requests to a web server on your network.

Continued on next page

TABLE 4.6: FIREWALL CONFIGURATION CUSTOMIZATION OPTIONS *(continued)*

OPTION	DESCRIPTION
Mail	Allows incoming requests to an outgoing e-mail server on your network.
FTP	Permits incoming requests to an FTP server on your network.
Other Ports	You can allow in data through one of the other TCP/IP ports described in /etc/services; the format is in the service:protocol format, such as time:tcp, time:udp.

33. In this step, you can customize the language packages installed with Red Hat Linux. As you can see in Figure 4.37, English (USA) is installed by default. Support for 120 different languages and or dialects is available. If you choose Select All, support for all languages will be installed. If you choose Reset, support for only English (USA) will be installed. Make your choices and press F12 to continue.

FIGURE 4.37

Selecting supported languages

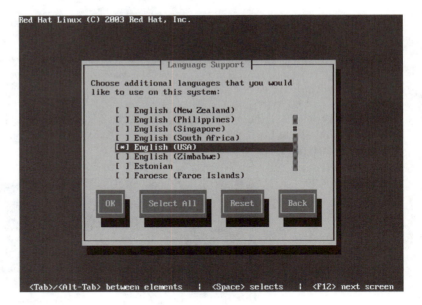

NOTE *If you select more than one language, you'll see a Default Language screen, where you select the default language for your system.*

34. Next, you can select the hardware clock settings and time zone for your computer. The options are shown in Figure 4.38. If you select Hardware Clock Set To GMT, you should set the clock in your PC's BIOS to Greenwich Mean Time. In addition, you need to select the time zone most closely associated with your location.

FIGURE 4.38

Selecting a time zone

NOTE *The advantage of activating the Hardware Clock Set To GMT option is that Linux can then adjust your clock for daylight saving time. However, if you have another operating system on your computer, such as Microsoft Windows, this setting would alter that clock.*

35. Now you need to select a root password for your system. This is the password that you'll use to log into the root or superuser account. Make your selections, as shown in Figure 4.39, and then press F12 to continue.

FIGURE 4.39

Creating a root password

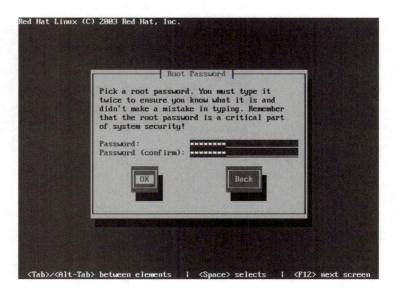

DIVERGING STEPS

After step 35, what you see varies, depending on the installation type. If you selected a Personal Desktop or Workstation installation back in step 15, you'll see a screen where you can customize your software selection. If you activate this option, you'll get to step 36 and a view similar to Figure 4.41. Otherwise, skip to step 39.

If you selected a Custom installation, you'll see the Authentication Configuration screen shown in Figure 4.40. The associated options are shown below.

If you selected a Server installation, proceed to step 36.

Option	Description
Use Shadow Passwords	Enables the shadow password suite, with passwords protected in /etc/shadow.
Enable MD5 Passwords	Allows the MD5 form of password encryption.
Enable NIS	Triggers use of the Network Information Service (NIS), which provides a common database of usernames and passwords for a LAN; for more information, see Chapter 28.
NIS Domain	Enter the name of the NIS domain in this text box.
Request Server via Broadcast	Select this option to send a broadcast message to other computers on your network to identify the NIS server.
Or Use:	Sets the name of the NIS server for your network if you disable the broadcast option.
Enable LDAP	Enables use of a Lightweight Directory Assistance Protocol (LDAP) server for authentication and related LAN databases.
LDAP Server	Sets the name of the server with the LDAP database.
LDAP Base DN	Allows you to look up account information with the LDAP Distinguished Name (DN).
Use TLS Connections	Lets your computer use Transport Layer Security (TLS) to send encrypted usernames and passwords to an LDAP server.
Enable Kerberos	Allows the use of the Kerberos 5 system, developed at MIT; supports strong encryption of usernames and passwords.
Realm	Permits you to access a Kerberos enabled network.
KDC	Lets you access a Key Distribution Center (KDC) server which issues Kerberos authentication tickets.
Admin Server	Allows you to access a Kerberos server using the kadmin utility.

36. It's time to select the package groups that will be installed, as shown in Figure 4.41. The default groups are customized for the type of installation, as described in the "Installations Options" sidebar earlier in this chapter. You can further customize your installation by selecting or deselecting the package groups of your choice. Each package group is described in more detail in Web Chapter 5.

FIGURE 4.40

Authentication Configuration

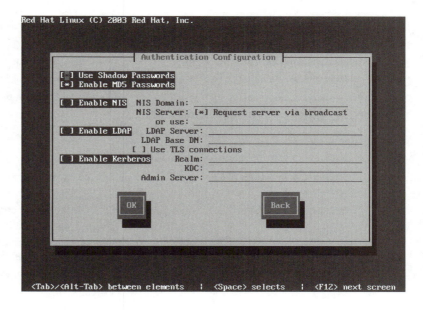

FIGURE 4.41

Selecting package groups

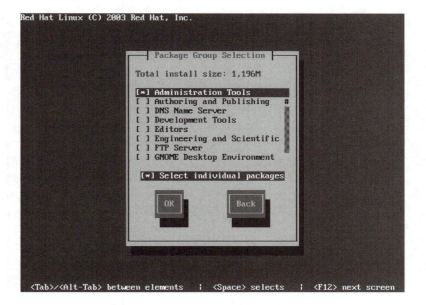

If you need to customize your installation further, you can activate the Select Individual Packages option. For the purpose of this chapter, I've done this to continue on to step 37.

NOTE   *The package groups that you install aren't final; you can always install individual packages using the* `rpm` *command described in Chapter 11 and the* `redhat-config-packages` *utility described in Chapter 19.*

37. You can select individual packages to install. For example, as Figure 4.42 shows, you can select individual packages within the Editors package group. The current size of each package (and group) is shown in the right side of the figure, which can help if you're concerned about available space on your hard drive. Make your selections and press F12 to continue.

FIGURE 4.42

Selecting individual packages

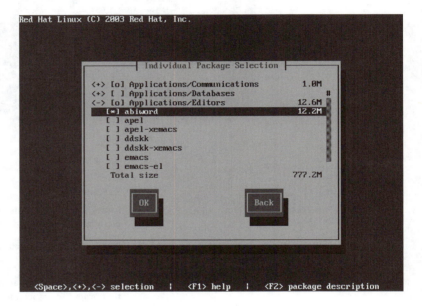

38. Anaconda checks your selected packages for dependencies. An example is shown in Figure 4.43, which lists unsatisfied dependencies. Based on the figure, the `control-center` and `firstboot` packages won't work unless you also install the `metacity` and `xscreensaver` packages. The options are described in Table 4.7. Normally, you'll select the Install Packages To Satisfy Dependencies option, and press F12 to continue.

FIGURE 4.43

Satisfying package
dependencies

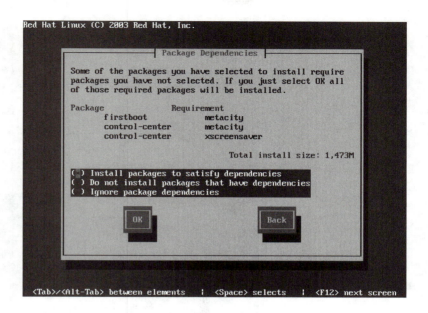

TABLE 4.7: PACKAGE DEPENDENCY OPTIONS

OPTION	DESCRIPTION
Install Packages To Satisfy Dependencies	Adds the packages in the Requirement column to the installation list.
Do Not Install Packages That Have Dependencies	Removes the packages from the Package column from the installation list.
Ignore Package Dependencies	Does not change the package installation list; there is a risk that programs associated with the cited packages may fail.

39. You get one last chance to stop before Anaconda starts installing Red Hat Linux on your system, as shown in Figure 4.44. The cited file, /root/install.log, will include a complete list of installed packages. If you're ready, highlight OK and press F12 to continue.

FIGURE 4.44

You're ready to install Red Hat Linux.

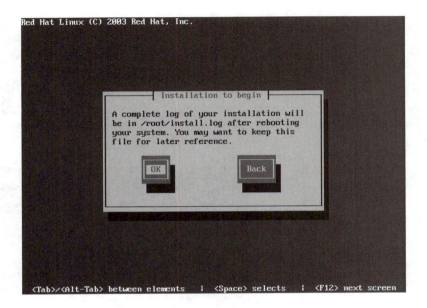

Now Anaconda formats your selected partitions. It may take several minutes to start the installation process. Figure 4.45 shows the installation process in action. You can track the current status of the installation.

FIGURE 4.45

The installation process at work

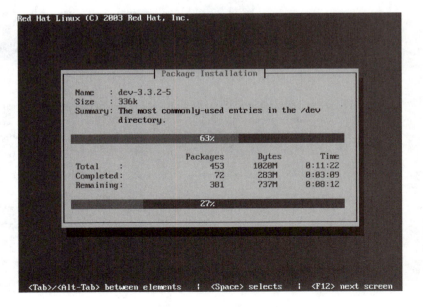

Once the installation process is complete, Anaconda performs a postinstall configuration automatically. Depending on the speed of your network and the number and size of packages that you've installed, the entire installation process could take a few minutes or several hours. Finally, we're ready for the next step.

40. At this point, we're ready to create a boot disk. It's a good idea; if you ever accidentally damage your bootloader or MBR, it can help you start Red Hat Linux. In the menu shown in Figure 4.46, choose Yes to create a boot disk. In the following menu, select Make Boot Disk when you've inserted a floppy disk in the drive.

FIGURE 4.46

Creating a boot disk

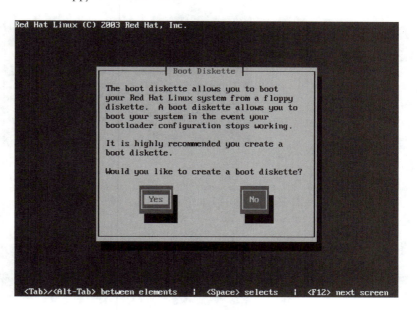

41. Now we're moving into the home stretch—configuring the graphics system. The Video Card Configuration menu, shown in Figure 4.47, illustrates what Red Hat Linux was able to detect for your video card. If you don't want to configure your graphics system at this time, you can select Skip X Configuration and press Enter. You'll be taken to step 45.

FIGURE 4.47

Configuring your
video card

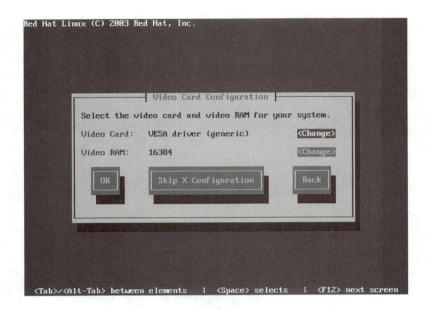

42. If you're not satisfied with the current configuration, you can change it. For example, you can highlight the Change option for the video card and press Enter. This opens the Video Card menu, shown in Figure 4.48.

FIGURE 4.48

Selecting a
video card

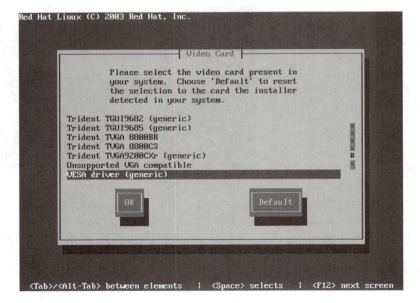

There are a whole series of video cards available; most are proprietary. If you can't find the make and model for your card, you can try a different card from the same manufacturer, or you can select Unsupported VGA Compatible or VESA Driver (Generic). These options correspond to default VGA and SVGA drivers. Select an appropriate driver and press F12 to continue.

NOTE   *VGA is short for Video Graphics Array, the basic color system for most monitors built today. One slightly higher but still common standard is SVGA, short for Super VGA. The Red Hat SVGA driver is VESA, which is short for the Video Electronics Standards Association; VESA also represents the group of standards associated with SVGA.*

43. Red Hat Linux may not detect all of the RAM associated with your video card. In that case, you can highlight the Change option associated with Video RAM and press Enter. This opens the Video RAM menu, shown in Figure 4.49. Select the amount of Video RAM associated with your video card and press F12 to return to the Video Card configuration menu. If you're satisfied with the overall configuration, press F12 again to continue.

FIGURE 4.49

Specifying your Video RAM

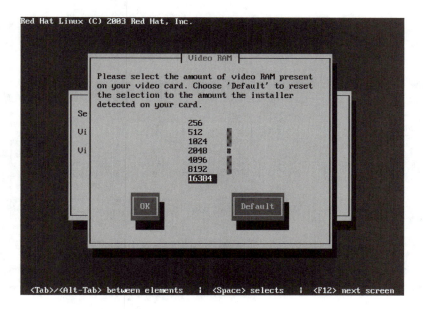

44. When you configure a video card, you also need to configure a monitor. In the Monitor Configuration screen, shown in Figure 4.50, you can specify a make and model for your monitor, as well as the allowable horizontal (HSync Rate) and vertical sync rates (VSync Rate).

FIGURE 4.50

Configuring your
monitor

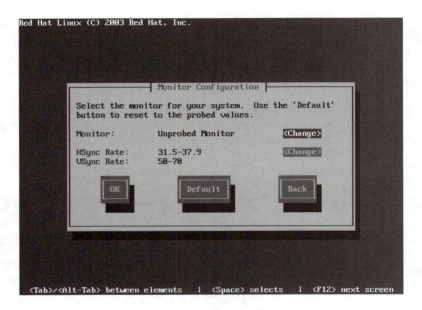

45. If you're not satisfied with the current configuration, you can change it. For example, you can highlight the Change option for the Monitor and press Enter. This opens the Monitor menu, shown in Figure 4.51.

FIGURE 4.51

Specifying a
Monitor

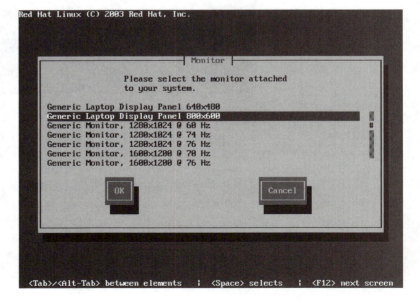

As you can see, there are a whole series of monitors; most are proprietary. If you can't find the make and model for your monitor, you can try a different card from the same manufacturer. In addition, a substantial number of generic monitors are available, including several for laptop computers. Select an appropriate monitor and press F12 to return to the Monitor Configuration window.

46. Next, you'll get to change allowable monitor sync rates, as shown in Figure 4.52. The horizontal sync rate is the amount of time it takes for your system to redraw one horizontal line on your screen; typically it's listed in KHz. The vertical sync rate is the amount of time it takes for your system to redraw the entire screen; typically that is listed in Hz. If you want to make a change, highlight the Change option associated with the HSync and VSync Rates and press Enter.

FIGURE 4.52

Setting monitor sync rates

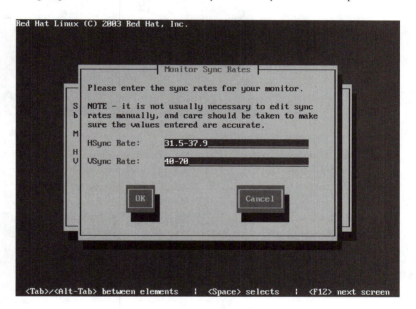

WARNING   *Be careful! Where possible, check the documentation for your monitor. If you specify horizontal or vertical rates that are too high, signals from the video card could permanently damage your monitor.*

Change the rates as desired and press F12 to return to the Monitor configuration menu. If you're satisfied with the overall configuration, press F12 again to continue.

47. Next, you'll get to specify several defaults. As shown in the X Customization menu in Figure 4.53, you can specify a color depth, resolution, and default login mode.

FIGURE 4.53

Selecting graphical
startup defaults

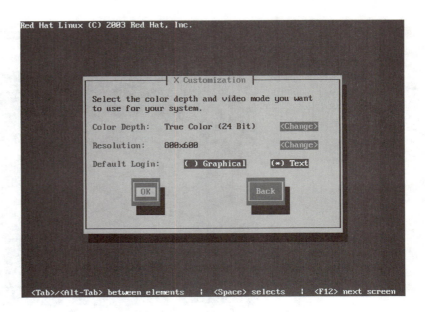

48. If you're not satisfied with the current configuration, you can change it. For example, you can highlight the Change option for Color Depth and press Enter. This opens the Color Depth menu, shown in Figure 4.54. Select the color depth of your choice and press F12 to return to the X Customization menu.

FIGURE 4.54

Selecting a color
depth

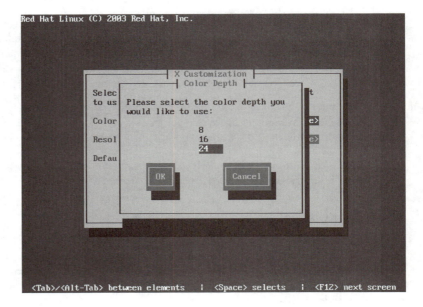

49. Now you can change the resolution, as shown in Figure 4.55. Highlight the preferred default resolution of your choice and press Enter.

FIGURE 4.55

Specifying a monitor resolution

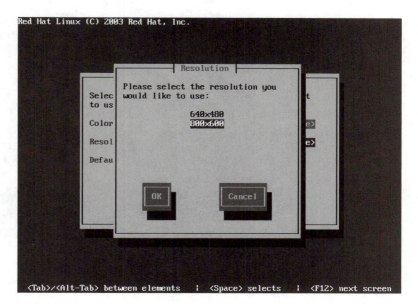

Available resolutions are based on the memory in your video card, your specified color depth, and the specifications of your monitor. Select the resolution of your choice and press F12 to return to the X Customization menu.

50. Also in the X Customization menu, you can change the Default Login mode for your Linux system. This changes the default runlevel in your /etc/inittab file, described in Chapter 11. You can set up a login at the text or graphical consoles. For a view of available graphical consoles, see Chapter 15. Make any desired changes and press F12 to continue.

51. Finally, installation and preliminary configuration are complete. You should see the screen shown in Figure 4.56. When you press Enter, Anaconda reboots your computer. The next thing you should see after reboot is the bootloader that you selected during the process.

NOTE   *If you configured a login at the graphical console in step 50, Red Hat Linux reboots and starts the* firstboot *utility. The steps and views are identical as described in the section on the Red Hat Setup Agent towards the end of Chapter 3.*

Text-Mode Upgrades

It's also possible to upgrade a previous version of Red Hat Linux. If Anaconda detects the previous version, you'll see the System To Upgrade menu. We looked at it briefly earlier, in step 14 of the full installation process. For your convenience, we'll review the menu here in Figure 4.57. We won't go through the full step-by-step process, since many of the steps are similar to the previously described text-mode installation.

FIGURE 4.56

Installation is complete.

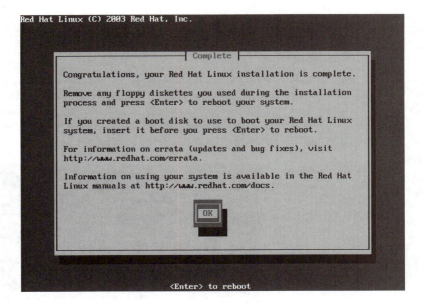

FIGURE 4.57

The System To Upgrade screen

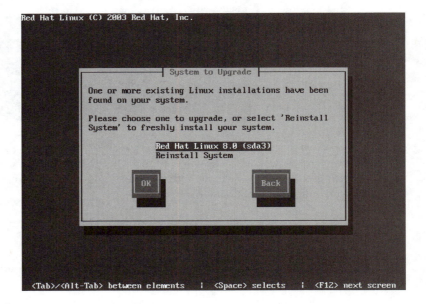

In this case, Anaconda has found the /boot directory associated with Red Hat Linux 8.0 installed on the /dev/sda3 partition. If you simply want to upgrade your packages to Red Hat Linux 9, select this option and press F12 to continue.

NOTE *If you're upgrading from a version of Linux with partitions formatted to the second extended filesystem (ext2), you're given the opportunity to convert to the Red Hat 9 default third extended filesystem (ext3). For more information on filesystems, see Chapter 7.*

Next, you'll be able to choose whether you want to customize the packages that you might want to upgrade. For example, if you're upgrading from Red Hat 7.2, you might not be ready to move your web server from Apache version 1.3.*x* to 2.0.*x*. In that case, you will want to customize the upgrade, as shown in Figure 4.58. Otherwise, Anaconda automatically installs new versions of packages, when available. Make your selection and press F12 to continue.

FIGURE 4.58

The Customize Packages To Upgrade screen

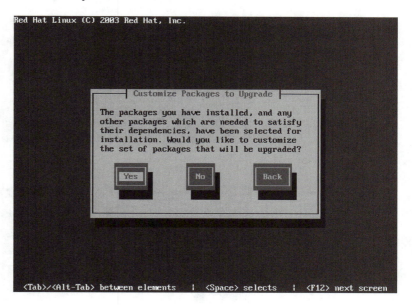

The screen that follows allows you to upgrade or install a new bootloader. As shown in Figure 4.59, you have three choices, which are described in Table 4.8. If you have a special bootloader configuration file, such as one with special kernel entries, you may not want to wipe it out with the Create New Boot Loader Configuration option.

TABLE 4.8: CHOICES IN UPGRADING A BOOTLOADER

OPTION	DESCRIPTION
Update Boot Loader Configuration	Upgrades the bootloader package without changing the configuration file.
Skip Boot Loader Updating	Does not upgrade the bootloader package, and does not change the configuration file.
Create New Boot Loader Configuration	Installs a new bootloader package; you'll have to change the configuration file.

FIGURE 4.59

Upgrading the boot-loader

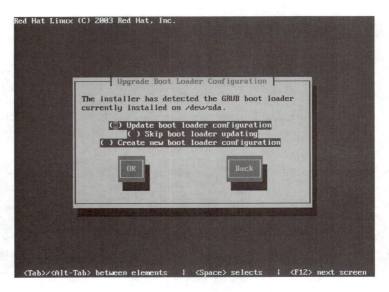

We'll select the first option. Select the option of your choice and press F12 to continue. Assuming that you're customizing packages to be upgraded, Anaconda proceeds to read the current packages on your system. That process took nearly 20 minutes for me when upgrading a Red Hat Linux 8.0 system without a GUI.

Once the upgrade assessment process is complete, you're taken to the Individual Package Selection screen, shown in Figure 4.60. The packages selected in this menu are limited to the planned upgrades. For example, as you can see in the figure, for this particular system, Anaconda will upgrade the ash shell.

FIGURE 4.60

Upgrades and selecting individual packages

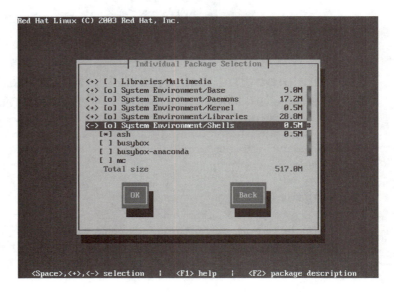

You can select or deselect the packages of your choice. If you're upgrading a server, pay particular attention to the System Environment/Daemons category. If you have a reliable service such as Apache or Samba, you may not want to upgrade it, at least at this time. Make any changes you need and then press F12 to continue.

Anaconda proceeds to check for dependencies. If it finds any, it goes through a process similar to that described back in Figure 4.43. This process may also take several minutes. When it completes, you'll see the Upgrade To Begin screen, shown in Figure 4.61. Once you press F12, Anaconda starts the upgrade process.

FIGURE 4.61

The upgrade is about to begin.

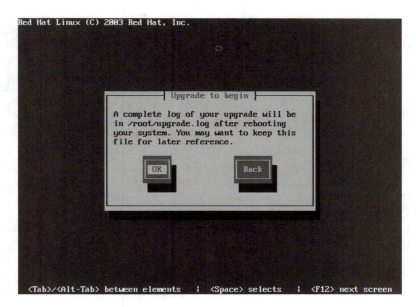

Troubleshooting a Network Installation

If you're unable to install Red Hat Linux over a network, there are a number of things that you can check. First, most network problems are physical. Red Hat Linux installs a firewall by default, and that firewall may also cause problems. If you don't have correct address settings, your computer won't be able to find the installation server. Finally, there are special issues related to network installations of Red Hat Linux on a laptop.

Checking the Messages

When you're having a problem with a network installation of Red Hat Linux, the problem may not even be with the network. Several text installation screens can provide valuable messages. You can get to these screens with the Ctrl+Alt+F*n* command, where *n* is a number between 2 and 5. I've described these screens in Table 4.9.

TABLE 4.9: RED HAT INSTALLATION SCREENS

SCREEN	DESCRIPTION
Ctrl+Alt+F1	Returns to the main installation screen.
Ctrl+Alt+F2	Opens a bash shell with limited command capabilities; for example, the df command can show mounted directories and partitions. Other bash commands are described in Part II of this book.
Ctrl+Alt+F3	Views the installation log, with messages related to hardware detection; if you're having trouble reading CDs or loading drivers, check here.
Ctrl+Alt+F4	Goes to the system message log, with messages such as formatting and mounting directories on partitions.
Ctrl+Alt+F5	Notes various messages such as filesystem labels, blocks, formats, and journals.

Checking the Network

Again, most network problems are physical. When you have a condition where your network is not working, that inevitably means you end up checking your cables, connections, and other hardware components.

There are a number of commands that you can use to test physical connections as well. For example, when you use the ping command on the IP address of another computer, you're testing the connectivity between your computers. Basic network troubleshooting techniques are described in Chapter 21.

The Firewall on the Server

Red Hat Linux installs a firewall by default. However, if you accept the default installation, you won't be able to access installation files from that computer, at least using the network protocols (NFS, HTTP, and FTP) discussed in this chapter. If you're still having network problems, it's worth logging into and checking the server computer with the Red Hat Linux installation files.

If that server is also running Red Hat Linux 7.3 and above, there are a couple of simple commands that you can use to check for a firewall:

```
# iptables -L
```

This iptables command lists any current rules that apply to that computer. If there are existing rules, you can "flush" them from the current configuration with the following command:

```
# iptables -F
```

When the installation is complete, you can reenable the firewall with the service iptables restart command. Firewalls are covered in more detail in Chapter 22.

Address Settings

Users who are less familiar with IP addressing may make mistakes. For example, if you've set a static IP address for your computer, you need to make sure that you have several things right:

◆ The IP address of the computer should be on the same network as your LAN.

◆ The network mask (or subnet mask) of the computer should match that of every other computer on the LAN.

While it's useful to have the correct default gateway and DNS server IP addresses, those aren't absolutely necessary for a successful network installation of Red Hat Linux. For more information on how IP addressing works, see Chapter 20.

A Laptop Installation over a Network

Installing Red Hat Linux on a laptop computer is usually trouble-free. However, there are some differences from the standard network installation. Laptop network cards are generally located in a PC Card slot (also known as PCMCIA, based on the standards of the Personal Computer Memory Card International Association).

PC Cards require their own drivers, loaded from a driver disk created from the `pcmciadd.img` file. As we discussed earlier in this chapter, driver image files are located on the first Red Hat Linux installation CD, in the `/images` directory.

Many PCMCIA network cards are available; the files in the Red Hat driver disk may not always cover what you need. For example, you need drivers for both the PCMCIA slot and the PCMCIA network card. If you're having problems, open the installation log screen with the Ctrl+Alt+F3 command. You may be able to identify your problem here.

Summary

In this chapter, we installed Red Hat Linux over a network. You need a second computer to hold the installation files. We looked at the process for configuring three network services: NFS, HTTP, and FTP. The step-by-step process is fairly straightforward. Details of each service are described in later chapters.

Then we looked at the various options for boot and driver disks. We then looked at the network installation process, in text mode, in a step-by-step fashion. We also took a brief look at the upgrade process.

If you have trouble with a network installation, you may be able to get clues to the problem using the installation message screens. If you have a network problem, most problems are physical; there are also a number of commands that you can use to inspect your network. One common mistake is to leave an active firewall on the installation server, which can block communication. Another common mistake is based on errors in IP address information. Finally, special problems can occur when you install Red Hat Linux on a laptop computer.

In the next chapter, we'll look at automating the installation process with Kickstart. Once you've set up a Kickstart file, you'll be able to install Red Hat Linux on a several computers simultaneously, using the same network installation server.

Chapter 5

Kickstarting Linux

IN PREVIOUS CHAPTERS, YOU learned to install Linux from local and remote sources. There are many ways to customize Red Hat Linux; all require extensive user input. Thus, if you're an administrator responsible for installing Red Hat Linux on a group of computers, you could spend a lot of time installing and customizing Linux on every last computer. For this reason, Red Hat has developed the Kickstart system to automate the installation process. With it, you can manage the installation of package groups, or even individual RPM packages, on each of your computers.

As you've seen in Chapters 3 and 4, packages are collected together in groups such as the GNOME Desktop Environment and Graphics. These package groups are organized in the comps .xml file on the first Red Hat installation CD, in the /RedHat/base directory. We'll examine this file in detail; you can edit the file to customize how your users install Red Hat Linux.

You've learned about dependencies. The software in some packages and package groups won't work unless other software is installed. These dependencies are also documented in comps.xml.

When you install Red Hat Linux 9 on your computer, Anaconda leaves a default Kickstart file, anaconda-ks.cfg, in your /root directory. You can use this file to create a standard Kickstart file for your other computers. In addition, Red Hat includes the detailed GUI Kickstart Configurator, which can help you customize the Kickstart file that you need.

Once you've created a Kickstart file, you can set it up on a boot floppy. All you need to do is reboot your computer with the floppy. Once the basic kernel is loaded, it can get Red Hat Linux installation files locally or through your network. This chapter covers the following topics:

◆ Grouping packages: comps.xml

◆ Analyzing the default Kickstart configuration

◆ Working with the GUI Kickstart Configurator

◆ Kickstarting from a floppy

Grouping Packages: *comps.xml*

Anaconda, the Red Hat Linux installation program, uses the comps.xml file to set up your installation. This file is located on the first installation CD, or the network source, in the /RedHat/base directory. It is written in XML, which is primarily used for web pages. It includes tags that are functionally similar to the standard language of web pages, HTML.

NOTE *Once Red Hat Linux is installed (on a standard Intel type PC), you can also find* `comps.xml` *in the* `/usr/share/comps/i386` *directory. If possible, open this file in a text editor to follow the descriptions in the first part of this chapter.*

The `comps.xml` file includes four basic sections. First are mandatory package groups that are normally installed with every Red Hat Linux installation. Then you have individual package groups, which you can select during the installation process. Third, these groups are organized in categories, which you can see during the graphical installation process or through the `redhat-config-packages` utility described in Chapter 19. Finally, there is a list of dependencies, which are packages required by others.

Once you understand `comps.xml`, you can edit this file. For example, you can add stanzas with your own special package groups. You can also delete or hide stanzas that you don't want users to install on their computers, such as Graphics or Games.

NOTE *Red Hat Linux is organized through the Red Hat Package Manager (RPM). Red Hat software is collected together in RPM files, which end with* `.rpm`. *When RPM packages are collected together in* `comps.xml`, *they are organized in package groups.*

Basic *comps.xml* Stanzas

There's a standard organization to each stanza in the `comps.xml` file. Like HTML, each stanza is enclosed with a starting *tag* such as `<group>` and an ending tag such as `</group>`. Each group has an identifier, as in the following:

```
<id>dialup</id>
```

Next, these lines determine whether a user is allowed to select the group, and whether it's installed by default:

```
<uservisible>false</uservisible>
<default>true</default>
```

This combination means that this particular group is installed by default. Since this package group isn't visible to the user during the installation process, Anaconda will automatically install it.

If you don't see either tag, `<uservisible>` is true and `<default>` is false. In other words, the associated package group is visible but not selected during the installation process.

Each group includes a name and a description; the `comps.xml` file includes versions of the following lines in different languages. These commands list the name of the KDE package group, the name in German, and an abbreviated description in the same language:

```
<name>KDE Desktop Environment</name>
<name xml:lang="de">KDE Desktopumgebung</name>
<description>KDE ist eine leistungsstarkes</description>
```

Some groups depend on others. For example, the Graphics group depends on the `base` and `base-x` groups, as documented by the following commands (we omitted several commands for clarity):

```
<group>
    <id>graphics</id>
    <name>Graphics</name>
    <grouplist>
        <groupreq>base</groupreq>
        <groupreq>base-x</groupreq>
    </grouplist>
</group>
```

Finally, there are the packages associated with each group, as delineated by the `<packagelist>` tag. Some packages are "mandatory," meaning that the package can't function without them. For example, the Windows File Server package group can't function without the `samba-client` and `samba` RPM packages:

```
<packagelist>
        <packagereq type="mandatory">samba-client</packagereq>
        <packagereq type="mandatory">samba</packagereq>
</packagelist>
```

Other packages are classified as default or optional. Users who select individual packages during the installation process can select or deselect these packages.

Finally, most of the `comps.xml` file includes a list of dependencies. For example, here is a list of dependencies for the `m4` macro processor described in Chapter 26:

```
<package>
    <name>m4</name>
    <dependencylist>
        <dependency>bash</dependency>
        <dependency>info</dependency>
        <dependency>glibc</dependency>
    </dependencylist>
</package>
```

Don't edit the dependency list unless you know what you're doing. Otherwise, you or your users could end up installing programs without required foundation software such as shells or language compilers.

Mandatory Groups

There are two mandatory package groups in comps.xml: Core and Base. The Core group includes RPM packages that Linux can't live without; some of these packages are listed in Table 5.1. For a full list, see Web Chapter 5, which can be found on the Sybex website at `www.sybex.com`.

TABLE 5.1: SOME CORE LINUX PACKAGES

PACKAGE	DESCRIPTION
basesystem	The first package installed in Red Hat Linux; it should never be deleted.
bash	The Bourne Again Shell; it's the default Red Hat Linux command interpreter.
cpio	An archiving utility; see Chapter 14.
e2fsprogs	The basic Linux filesystem management commands.
filesystem	The standard directory layout.
glibc	Standard C language libraries.
grub	The default Linux bootloader; see Chapter 11.
hotplug	For USB and IEEE1394 devices.
iputils	A package that includes basic networking commands such as ping.
kbd	For managing a console, fonts, and the keyboard.
kernel	The Linux kernel.
libgcc	A package that supports the GNU C language compiler.
passwd	A package that includes the passwd command.
procps	System Information utilities, such as ps.
raidtools	For configuring a software RAID device.
rpm	A package that includes the Red Hat Package Manager; see Chapter 10.
setup	Some basic /etc configuration files, such as passwd, group, profile.
vim-minimal	The vi editor.

The Base group includes RPM packages that make Red Hat Linux useful to administrators. A very few of these packages are listed in Table 5.2. For a full list of packages, see Web Chapter 5.

TABLE 5.2: SOME BASE LINUX PACKAGES

PACKAGE	DESCRIPTION
at	Supports the at and batch commands described in Chapter 13.
bind-utils	Contains commands for checking DNS (Domain Name Service) servers; see Chapter 24.
crontabs	For regularly scheduled jobs; see Chapter 13.
dhclient	Contains the DHCP (Dynamic Host Configuration Protocol) client.
ftp	Contains the FTP (File Transfer Protocol) command-line client.

Continued on next page

TABLE 5.2: SOME BASE LINUX PACKAGES *(continued)*

PACKAGE	DESCRIPTION
kudzu	Contains the Red Hat hardware probing tool.
nfs-utils	Contains Network File System (NFS) commands; see Chapter 28.
openssh-clients	For SSH (Secure Shell) client connections.
quota	Allows you to set quotas; see Chapter 9.
sudo	Lets you configure certain users with root privileges.
telnet	Contains the Telnet command-line client.
up2date	Contains the Red Hat Update Agent; see Chapter 10.
ypbind	Contains the NIS (Network Information Service) client; see Chapter 28.

These package groups together include nearly 450MB of files. There is incidentally one other group in `comps.xml` that is always installed: Dialup Networking Support. Now let's take a look at the other package groups that we see during the Red Hat Linux installation process.

Package Groups

In this section, we'll look at each package group in some detail. It should help you decide on a standard set of software packages to install on your computers. A complete list of packages in each of these groups is available in Web Chapter 5.

You may not see all of these groups during the Red Hat Linux installation process; as noted earlier, you can configure `comps.xml` to leave out one or more groups from the display.

The order of packages in this section corresponds to the `comps.xml` file available as of this writing. It may change when Red Hat Linux 9 is released. And the order is different from what you see during the Red Hat Linux installation process.

Some package groups depend on others. For example, the Office/Productivity package group won't work unless the X Window System package group is also installed. One component of this group, OpenOffice, requires installation of a number of other packages, as shown in the dependencies section of the `comps.xml` file.

PRINTING SUPPORT

It may seem strange to have the Printing Support package group this early in the `comps.xml` file. The fonts associated with this package are required for the GUI. Naturally, Printing Support also includes basic drivers and utilities associated with both the CUPS and LPD services described in Chapter 25. This group is installed by default.

X WINDOW SYSTEM

The X Window System package group includes the XFree86 Server and associated packages required to configure a basic GUI on your Linux computer. It includes some basic `redhat-config-*` utilities for managing the date, the network, the service runlevel configuration, sound, users, printers, and of course, the X Window.

You need this group if you want to install a desktop such as GNOME or KDE. It's installed by default, and requires the Printing Support package group, primarily for its fonts.

Other commands in `comps.xml` may refer to this group by its ID; for example, the following command refers to the `<id>` of the X Window System:

```
<id>base-x</id>
```

DIALUP NETWORKING SUPPORT

The Dialup Networking Support package group includes the basic text utilities required to make a connection via telephone modem. Other GUI Internet connection utilities depend on this package (see Chapters 16, 17, and 21). This package group is always installed as a part of Red Hat Linux 9.

GNOME DESKTOP ENVIRONMENT

The GNOME Desktop Environment package group contains the software you need to run the GNOME desktop. It includes basic applications such as text editors, calculators, and more.

You should install GNOME or KDE for users who want a GUI desktop environment. It won't work unless you install the X Window System package group. GNOME is the default Red Hat Linux desktop, and we cover it in Chapter 16.

KDE DESKTOP ENVIRONMENT

The KDE Desktop Environment package group contains the software you need to run the KDE desktop. It also includes basic applications such as text editors and calculators. And like the GNOME Desktop Environment package group, it won't work unless you install the X Window System package group. KDE, which is the most popular desktop for other Linux distributions, is covered in Chapter 17.

GRAPHICAL INTERNET

The Graphical Internet package group includes basic GUI utilities associated with Internet connections. They include the Mozilla web browser and the Evolution mail manager, as well as several chat and related utilities. While this isn't a book on GNOME or KDE, many of these utilities are described in Chapters 16–18.

TEXT-BASED INTERNET

There are a number of handy utilities that you can use to connect to the Internet from a text console. For example, `lynx` is a web browser with a surprising array of features, and `pine` is a competent e-mail client that has been deprecated; `mutt` is a good alternative.

SOUND AND VIDEO

This is an all-in-one package group for controlling, configuring, and commanding a sound card. It includes several tools for recording multimedia or data on CDs and DVDs.

GRAPHICS

The Graphics package group includes several utilities for managing pictures, screenshots, and other graphics. This includes The GIMP and associated data, which is briefly covered in Chapter 18. I've used The GIMP extensively to create screenshots for this book.

If you want graphics, naturally you'll need the X Window System package group.

OFFICE/PRODUCTIVITY

This package group includes two fully featured office suites: OpenOffice and KOffice. It also includes office-style applications associated with GNOME Office, plus a couple of other applications, such as a project manager, in the same category. These suites are briefly described in Chapter 18.

MAIL SERVER

This package group includes several mail servers. Optional packages can help you manage discussion lists, filter unwanted e-mail, and more. For more information on the sendmail and IMAP mail servers, see Chapter 26.

NETWORK SERVER

The Network Server package group includes a variety of servers that can be useful for managing a LAN. Available servers range from DHCP (for managing IP address information) to `telnet-server` (to allow incoming Telnet connections). More information on these servers can be found in Parts V–VII of this book.

NEWS SERVER

The News Server package group consists of only one package, InterNetNews (`inn`). This server allows you to set up a news server similar to Usenet discussion list servers that you can access through some mail managers. When you look at the dependency list in `comps.xml`, you'll see that `inn` also requires the `inews` package for newsfeeds.

WINDOWS FILE SERVER

The Windows File Server package group is also fairly simple; all you need is the `samba` and `samba-client` packages to connect to and share with other computers on a Microsoft Windows–based network. When you look at the dependencies, you can see that it requires the `samba-common` RPM package. Samba is covered in Chapter 29.

SERVER CONFIGURATION TOOLS

Red Hat has recently created several configuration tools, starting with `redhat-config-*`, where * represents the function. This package group allows you to use these tools to configure a number of servers. Although it isn't specified in `comps.xml`, most of these tools won't work unless you're running an X Window interface.

NOTE   One tool that does work without the X window is `redhat-config-xfree86`, which creates its own GUI even from the regular command-line interface.

FTP SERVER

The FTP Server package group is straightforward. It includes one package, the Very Secure FTP Daemon. It allows you to set up an FTP server with a decent level of security. We cover FTP configuration in Chapter 23.

SQL DATABASE SERVER

The SQL Database Server package group allows you to run a database server, which uses the Structured Query Language. The available servers, PostgreSQL and MySQL, are both foundations for a relational database server. These servers are not covered in this book. For more information, see *Mastering MySQL 4* by Ian Gilfillan (Sybex, 2002).

WEB SERVER

The Web Server package group includes two different web servers, Apache (`httpd`) and TUX, which are discussed in Chapter 30. This package group also includes a number of Apache modules.

DNS NAME SERVER

The DNS Name Server package group includes two packages: `bind` is the standard DNS server on Linux, and the `caching-nameserver` package supports a DNS server cache on a computer. DNS is covered in more detail in Chapter 24.

AUTHORING AND PUBLISHING

The Authoring and Publishing package group covers Linux's native publishing format, DocBook. It's a format for marking up text files that allows you to transform your document into one of several formats, including HTML, RTF, and TeX. The DocBook system is not covered in this book. For futher reading, try *DocBook: The Definitive Guide* from O'Reilly.

ENGINEERING AND SCIENTIFIC

The Engineering and Scientific package group includes a series of packages for calculations. Some relate to linear algebra, to help you solve complex equations. Since this is not an engineering book, we won't cover these packages.

EDITORS

Two of the most popular Linux text editors are part of the Editors package group: `vi` and Emacs. If you install `emacs` or its GUI cousin, `xemacs`, Red Hat Linux automatically installs the associated package groups which follow. Entire books have been written about both of these editors; I cover `vi` briefly in Chapter 6.

For more information on Emacs, see the *GNU Emacs Manual* by Richard M. Stallman (GNU Press; 2002).

EMACS

The Emacs group includes the Emacs text editor and a couple of packages for editing the LISP and SGML computer languages.

XEMACS

The Xemacs group includes three packages for making Emacs work within a GUI.

SYSTEM TOOLS

The System Tools package group includes a wide variety of client and diagnostic software. For example, as shown in Chapter 22, Ethereal allows you to read clear-text messages on your network. As we explain in Chapter 29, you can use a number of tools associated with `samba-client` to read shared directories on a Microsoft Windows–based network.

ADMINISTRATION TOOLS

The Administration Tools package group includes those `redhat-config-*` utilities that don't fit into other groups. Naturally, this includes a broad range of tools, from keyboard configuration to user management. For more information on these tools, see Chapter 19.

GAMES

Linux has games that you can install as part of the GUI. I don't personally install them, since I don't want to learn how to play another version of Freecell. However, some administrators feel that games can help the novice user become more comfortable with Linux. This package group includes games associated with both the GNOME and KDE desktops.

ISO8859 SUPPORT

There are two different ISO8859 font sets that you can install. ISO8859-2 is associated with Eastern European languages; ISO8859-9 is associated with the Turkish languages. These groups include fonts at 75 and 100 dpi (dots per inch).

NOTE *ISO is the International Organization for Standardization (*`www.iso.ch`*). As strange as it sounds, the acronym does not match the official title (nor does it match the French translation of the title).*

INDIVIDUAL LANGUAGE SUPPORT

There are a number of other package groups that may allow you to use Linux in your native tongue. Each individual language group includes fonts; many include spell checkers and translated man pages. As of this writing, support is available for the Cyrillic alphabet, as well as Brazilian Portuguese, British English, Canadian English, Catalan, Chinese, Czech, Danish, Dutch, Estonian, Finnish, French, German, Greek, Hebrew, Hungarian, Icelandic, Italian, Japanese, Korean, Norwegian, Polish, Portuguese, Romanian, Russian, Serbian, Slovak, Slovenian, Spanish, Swedish, Turkish, and Ukrainian.

NOTE   *Some of these languages require different font sets; for example, Ukrainian requires the Cyrillic alphabet package; Turkish requires the ISO8859-9 package.*

DEVELOPMENT TOOLS

If you do any sort of software development work, you'll need at least some of the packages from the Development Tools package group. While this is not a programming book, you'll need some of these packages to recompile the Linux kernel in Chapter 12.

Prominent packages include `automake`, which allows you to create `Makefile`-style configuration scripts; `binutils`, which includes binary management utilities; and `gcc`, the GNU C language compiler. This package group also depends on the installation of the Development Libraries package group.

DEVELOPMENT LIBRARIES

The Development Libraries package group includes many development programs for a wide variety of applications. These libraries range from `kudzu-devel`, which supports the Red Hat hardware management utility, to `openssl-devel`, which lets you configure the SSH server described in Chapter 23. If you're working on improvements to any of these applications, you may need to install this package group.

KERNEL DEVELOPMENT

If you're planning to modify or reconfigure the Linux kernel, you'll need to install the Kernel Development package group. This group includes the `kernel-source` package; it also depends on the installation of the Development Tools package group. For more information on these packages and managing the kernel, see Chapter 12.

LEGACY SOFTWARE DEVELOPMENT

Red Hat has relatively recently upgraded the GNU C language compiler packages. You may still be using software that requires older versions of this package. These legacy packages are organized in the Legacy Software Development package group.

X SOFTWARE DEVELOPMENT

If you're working on the XFree86 software, you may need to install the X Software Development package group. This group includes the packages you need to develop applications for the X Window system. Since there are other desktops, this group does not require the software associated with the GNOME or KDE Software Development packages.

GNOME SOFTWARE DEVELOPMENT

If you're developing applications for the GNOME desktop, you'll need to install the GNOME Software Development package group. A couple of key packages include `gtk+-devel`, The GIMP toolkit (GTK+), and `fontconfig-devel`, for managing fonts on your desktop. While GTK+ was created for The GIMP, it's also used to develop GNOME applications.

KDE Software Development

If you're developing applications for the KDE desktop, you'll need to install the KDE Software Development package group. A couple of key packages include `cups-devel`, for the CUPS print server, and `qt-devel`, for the Qt language toolkit. Qt is the KDE version of the GTK+ toolkit, used to develop KDE applications.

NOTE   Qt is a C++ language toolkit for creating GUI applications. Developed by TrollTech (`www.trolltech.com`), it is not related to QuickTime from Apple. In this case, Qt is not an acronym.

Package Group Categories

The `comps.xml` file organizes each package group into one of several categories. You've seen how it works in Chapter 3. The standard categories are described in Table 5.3.

TABLE 5.3: PACKAGE GROUP CATEGORIES

CATEGORY	DESCRIPTION
Applications	Allows the installation of a variety of package groups, including Graphical Internet, Editors, and Office Suites
Desktops	Configures the installation of the X Window and GNOME and/or KDE Desktop environments
Development	Permits you to add various development tool package groups
Servers	Lets you select from several different server package groups, including web, mail, and FTP services
System	Allows you to set up administrative or system tools and/or printing support

For example, the Desktops category, as shown below, includes the package groups that you may want or need to install the GUI on your computer:

```
<category>
      <name>Desktops</name>
      <subcategories>
        <subcategory>base-x</subcategory>
        <subcategory>gnome-desktop</subcategory>
        <subcategory>kde-desktop</subcategory>
      </subcategories>
</category>
```

The Desktops category includes `base-x`, `gnome-desktop`, and `kde-desktop`. Based on their `<id>` variables (near the top of the `comps.xml` file), this corresponds to the following package groups: X Window System, GNOME Desktop Environment, and KDE Desktop Environment.

Dependencies

When there's a dependency, a software package (such as kernel source code) won't work unless a second package (such as a C language compiler) is installed. Dependencies are a substantial part of the `comps.xml` file. For example, the following stanza lists three dependencies for the `XFree86-75dpi-fonts` package:

```
<package>
    <name>XFree86-75dpi-fonts</name>
    <dependencylist>
      <dependency>bash</dependency>
      <dependency>XFree86-font-utils</dependency>
      <dependency>chkfontpath</dependency>
    </dependencylist>
</package>
```

Normally, Red Hat Linux won't install the `XFree86-75dpi-fonts` package unless you're already installing the bash shell, the `XFree86-font-utils` package for installing fonts, and the `chkfontpath` package for configuring font directories.

Before Anaconda starts installing Red Hat Linux, it checks all dependencies. In this case, if you aren't already installing the dependent packages, Anaconda tries to select them for installation for you. You can then accept or reject Anaconda's selections.

Editing Examples

You can create your own package groups. For example, Netscape is no longer included in the Red Hat Linux CDs. But if you've downloaded or created a Netscape RPM, you could include it in the `/RedHat/RPMS` directory for a network installation.

You could then create a Netscape group by adding the following commands:

```
<group>
    <id>netscape</id>
    <name>Netscape Browser</name>
    <description>This group is for Netscape.</description>
    <uservisible>true</uservisible>
    <default>false</default>
    <packagelist>
      <packagereq type="optional">netscape</packagereq>
    </packagelist>
</group>
```

Those commands are enough to make Netscape an optional Package Group selection during the Red Hat Linux text-mode installation process. To make Netscape available during the graphical installation process, you need to include it in one of the group categories by inserting the following commands:

```
<subcategories>
    <subcategory>netscape</subcategory>
</subcategories>
```

Analyzing Your Default Kickstart Configuration

When you install Red Hat Linux, the configuration that you selected is saved in anaconda-ks.cfg, in the /root directory. In this section, we'll break down an example of this file from my desktop computer. The start of this file is shown in Figure 5.1.

FIGURE 5.1

A typical
anaconda-ks.cfg file

```
# Kickstart file automatically generated by anaconda.

install
lang en_US.UTF-8
langsupport --default en_US.UTF-8 en_US.UTF-8
keyboard us
mouse genericwheelps/2 --device psaux
xconfig --card "Intel 810" --videoram 16384 --hsync 30-85 --vsync 50-160 --resol
ution 800x600 --depth 24 --startxonboot --defaultdesktop gnome
network --device eth0 --bootproto static --ip 10.252.113.64 --netmask 255.255.25
5.0 --gateway 10.252.113.113 --nameserver 207.217.126.81 --hostname RH81Test
network --device eth1 --bootproto static --ip 10.252.113.63 --netmask 255.255.25
5.0 --gateway 10.252.113.113 --nameserver 207.217.126.81 --hostname RH81Test
rootpw --iscrypted $1$vjHyUL9r$SnE5M/ha2mT/ge/o.0Sm/1
firewall --medium --trust=eth0
authconfig --enableshadow --enablemd5
timezone America/New_York
bootloader --location=mbr --append hdc=ide-scsi
# The following is the partition information you requested
# Note that any partitions you deleted are not expressed
# here so unless you clear all partitions first, this is
# not guaranteed to work
#clearpart --linux --drives=hda
"anaconda-ks.cfg" 48L, 1669C
```

Each Kickstart file can be divided into several categories of commands. We'll look at my anaconda-ks.cfg file in the following sections. The order of commands in your Kickstart file may not match what you see here.

Once you've finished editing this file, save it as ks.cfg. You'll learn how to set it up on a floppy disk toward the end of this chapter.

Preinstallation Commands

You can set up parameters for your installation. For example, you might note the date and time the installation started. The /etc/motd file is shown each time you log into Linux:

```
#pre
echo "My Kickstart Installation started on `/bin/date`" >/etc/motd
```

Preinstallation commands should be placed near the end of your Kickstart file, just before any %post installation commands you might have.

More extensive scripts are of course possible, but they are limited by the commands available through the disk with the Kickstart file. As you'll see toward the end of this chapter, the Kickstart file is normally copied to the Red Hat installation boot disk, which includes a basic kernel with a limited number of bash shell commands.

Basic Configuration

Only a few basic commands are required to start the Red Hat Linux installation process. The following commands are taken from my `anaconda-ks.cfg` file:

```
install
lang en_US.UTF-8
langsupport --default en_US.UTF-8 en_US.UTF-8
keyboard us
mouse genericwheelps/2 --device psaux
timezone America/New_York
bootloader --location=mbr --append hdc=ide-scsi
```

If you're planning to install Linux on a series of other computers, it's best if you're using the same language, keyboard type, and mouse. If that's your situation, you probably won't make any changes. But just in case, let's examine these commands, one at a time.

INSTALL

The first command looks simple; in fact, it's too simple to support an automated installation. In other words, this command doesn't specify the source of the Red Hat installation files:

```
install
```

You could set up Kickstart to look for installation files on your CD or from a hard drive with one of the following commands:

```
cdrom
harddrive --partition=hdb1 --dir=/install
```

For the purpose of this section, let's assume that the `/RedHat` installation directory is part of the `/install` directory and that the server has an IP address of 192.168.0.1.

The `harddrive` command looks for the `/RedHat` directory on the second IDE hard disk on your computer, on the first primary partition (`hdb1`), in the `/install` directory. Or you could install from an NFS shared directory from the remote computer with the following command:

```
nfs --server=192.168.0.1 --dir=/install
```

Alternatively, you can install from Red Hat installation files on a remote FTP or web server, using one of the following commands:

```
url --url ftp://username:password@192.168.0.1/install
url --url http://192.168.0.1/install
```

If you're installing from an anonymous FTP server, the username and password are not required.

TIP *If you're installing Red Hat Linux with a static IP address configuration, some computers may have trouble finding installation files from the network. You can set up DHCP access, using the commands described in the "Network Settings" section later in this chapter.*

LANG **AND** *LANGSUPPORT*

The next commands specify the language to use during the installation process, as well as the language files to install with Red Hat Linux. For example, the following command installs Red Hat Linux using standard U.S. English:

```
lang en_US.UTF-8
```

A number of other language codes are available; you can find a list in the `locale.alias` file in the `/usr/X11R6/lib/X11/locale` directory. If you're running an automated installation, you probably won't see any of the installation screens, anyway. However, to install U.S. English as the language you see when you start Red Hat Linux, use the following command:

```
langsupport --default en_US.UTF-8 en_US.UTF-8
```

Other available languages include French (`fr_FR`), German (`de_DE`), and Korean (`ko_KR.eucKR`). The language you installed on your computer should be shown in your `anaconda-ks.cfg` file. You can choose from several other languages; check the Red Hat Linux customization guide, which is available on the Red Hat documents CD or online from `www.redhat.com`.

NOTE   *To get to the online Red Hat Linux 9 manuals, navigate to* `www.redhat.com/docs/manuals/linux/` `RHL-9-Manual/`.

KEYBOARD

The `keyboard` command in your Kickstart file is straightforward. The standard U.S. keyboard requires the following command:

```
keyboard us
```

The `keyboard` command in your `anaconda-ks.cfg` file should match your installation. But just in case, several dozen types are available, such as French (`fr`) and Spanish (`es`). A complete list is available in the Red Hat customization guide.

MOUSE

The `mouse` command in your Kickstart file represents your pointing device. It could be a touchpad or a tablet. For example, the following command represents a generic PS/2 mouse, connected to the standard PS/2 port (`psaux`):

```
mouse genericwheelps/2 --device psaux
```

If you want to configure a two-button mouse to emulate a third middle button, add the `--emulthree` switch to the end of this command. As described in Chapter 3, pressing the two mouse buttons together functions as a third button.

There are other mouse types, such as a standard USB mouse (`genericusb`), a Microsoft mouse (`microsoft`), or a Logitech mouse (`logitech`). A complete list is available in the Red Hat customization guide.

TIMEZONE

The `timezone` command is straightforward; it specifies the time zone associated with your computer. If Linux is the only operating system that you're installing, you should set the hardware clock to Greenwich Mean Time (`--utc`), which allows Linux to handle changes for daylight saving time. A typical `timezone` command looks like this:

```
timezone --utc America/New_York
```

NOTE   *UTC stands for Universal Coordinated Time, which satisfies those who don't want to refer to the city of Greenwich in the United Kingdom.*

BOOTLOADER

You need a bootloader such as GRUB or LILO to start Red Hat Linux. The `bootloader` command specifies the location, along with other kernel parameters that may be required:

```
bootloader --location=mbr --append hdc=ide-scsi
```

This command tells Kickstart to install your bootloader on the Master Boot Record (`mbr`). It also sends a configuration message to the kernel, for a CD-Writer. It allows Linux to make the secondary master IDE drive (`hdc`) look like a SCSI drive (`ide-scsi`).

NOTE   *For more commands that you can* `--append` *to the kernel, run the* `man bootparam` *command.*

Graphics

The graphics command in a Kickstart file, `xconfig`, can appear complex. It's easier than it looks. Since you don't have to configure an X Window system in Red Hat Linux, the `xconfig` command isn't required.

Let's analyze the `xconfig` command from my Kickstart file:

```
xconfig --card "Intel 810" --videoram 16384
➡  --hsync 30-85 --vsync 50-160 --resolution 800x600
➡  --depth 24 --startxonboot --defaultdesktop gnome
```

This specifies a specific video card, the Intel 810. If your other computers also have the same card and monitor, you should be able to keep these settings for your Kickstart file. However, in case you need to make changes, we've listed some `xconfig` settings in Table 5.4.

TABLE 5.4: KICKSTART *XCONFIG* SETTINGS

SETTING	DESCRIPTION
`--card` *"name"*	Specifies the make and model of the video card
`--videoram` *amount*	Notes the amount of video RAM
`--hsync` *range*	Lists the range for horizontal frequency, in KHz

Continued on next page

TABLE 5.4: KICKSTART *XCONFIG* SETTINGS *(continued)*

SETTING	DESCRIPTION
`--vsync range`	Lists the range for vertical synchronization, in MHz
`--resolution horxvert`	Specifies the resolution on the monitor
`--depth num`	Notes the number of colors per pixel
`--defaultdesktop gnome`	Sets up GNOME as the default GUI desktop
`--startxonboot`	Starts the X Window when installation is complete
`--noprobe`	Specifies that the installation process should not probe the monitor

TIP   If you don't want to configure the X Window with this Kickstart file, add the `skipx` *command. Otherwise, Anaconda stops the installation process to let you configure the X Window.*

Network Settings

In this section, we assume that you have a network card in your computers. But in most cases, the Kickstart process uses Red Hat installation files from a remote computer on a network. Therefore, you'll need a command similar to the following to configure a network card on your computer:

```
network --device eth0 --bootproto dhcp
```

This command assumes that you have an Ethernet network card, and a DHCP server on your network. If the DHCP server is on a remote network, you'll need to use the BOOTP protocol; just replace **dhcp** with **bootp** in the previous command. For more information on Ethernet, see Chapter 20; for more information on DHCP servers and BOOTP, see Chapter 24.

Alternatively, you could specify static IP address information. As you'll recall from Chapter 3, that includes an IP address (`--ip`), network mask (`--netmask`), gateway address (`--gateway`), and the IP address of a DNS server (`--nameserver`). You can also specify the hostname (`--hostname`) for this computer with the following command:

```
network --device eth0 --bootproto static --ip 192.168.12.20 --netmask
➥ 255.255.255.0 --gateway 192.168.12.11 --nameserver 207.217.126.81
➥ --hostname RH9test
```

NOTE   The `network` *command in a Kickstart file must be on one line.*

The Root Password

Every Red Hat Linux installation requires you to set a root password. This is a simple command, which can be configured in one of two ways:

```
rootpw Big747Ap
rootpw --iscrypted $1$ZIvDlQpJ$ptS2UJkTRngOTacYN22vR1
```

The first method includes the password in clear text, which is acceptable if you're using a local Kickstart file. However, it's possible to use a remote Kickstart file; in that case, it's best to encrypt the password, as we've done in the second example.

Firewalls

You can configure a firewall in the Kickstart file. As you've seen during the installation process, there are three basic firewalls:

```
firewall --high
firewall --medium
firewall --disabled
```

Assuming you want a standard high-security firewall, you can customize it. For example, if you have two network cards, eth0 and eth1, you may want to disable the firewall on one of the cards with the following command:

```
firewall --high --trust=eth1
```

There are several standard services that you can let through your firewall, including DHCP configuration messages (`--dhcp`), Secure Shell connections (`--ssh`), Telnet connections (`--telnet`), incoming e-mail (`--smtp`), incoming requests for web pages (`--http`), and incoming connections to an FTP server (`--ftp`).

You can let other services through the firewall, as long as you know the port number and associated protocol. For example, the following command sets up a high-security firewall that allows outside requests for regular and secure web pages:

```
firewall --high --http --port 443:tcp
```

The numbers are TCP/IP ports that are defined in `/etc/services`, as described in Chapter 20.

Authentication Options

Authentication involves checking the credentials of a user. Normally, this means just the username and password. However, you can configure this process in a number of ways. The default Kickstart command sets up shadow passwords with MD5 encryption:

```
authconfig --enableshadow --enablemd5
```

Several authentication options are available. For example, you can set up NIS support (`--enablenis`), specify the NIS domain name (`--nisdomain=name`), allow Kerberos passwords (`--enablekrb5`), and check passwords on a Samba or Microsoft Windows server (`--enablesmbauth`). More options are shown in the Red Hat Linux customization guide.

Hard Drive Partition Setup

When Anaconda writes your configuration to `anaconda-ks.cfg`, the hard drive settings are disabled by default. If you're satisfied with the following commands, delete the hash marks (#) to activate them:

```
#clearpart --linux --drives=sda
#part /boot --fstype ext3 --size=100 --ondisk=sda
```

```
#part / --fstype ext3 --size=700 --grow --ondisk=sda
#part swap --size=192 --grow --maxsize=384 --ondisk=sda
```

The first command (`clearpart`) deletes all data from any existing Linux-formatted partitions (`--linux`) on the first SCSI hard drive (`sda`). A standard server installation deletes all data from all formatted partitions (`--all`).

The next command sets up a partition (`part`) for the /boot directory. It's to be formatted (`--fstype`) to the ext3 filesystem, with a size of 100MB, on the first SCSI hard drive (`--ondisk=sda`).

The next command configures the root (`/`) directory with a size of at least 700MB on the first SCSI hard drive. However, the growable flag (`--grow`) is set, which allows the partition to fill available space on the first SCSI hard drive.

The final command in this set configures the swap partition, with a size of at least 192MB and a maximum size (`--maxsize`) of 384MB on the first SCSI hard drive.

More extensive hard drive configurations are possible. For example, the following commands configure separate partitions for the /boot, /usr, /home, root (/), and /var directories, as well as a swap partition:

```
#clearpart --linux
#part /boot --fstype ext3 --noformat --onpart hda2
#part /usr --fstype ext3 --size=2500
#part /home --fstype ext3 --size=1000
#part / --fstype ext3 --size=1000
#part /var --fstype ext3 --size=500
#part swap --size=256
```

Furthermore, the following commands configure a RAID array of four different partitions and two physical volumes suitable for Logical Volume Management (LVM):

```
#part raid.44 --size=100
#part raid.42 --size=100
#part raid.40 --size=100
#part raid.38 --size=100
#part pv.36 --size=100
#part pv.34 --size=100
```

Finally, the following `raid` command sets up the /home/mj directory on a RAID5 array of three partitions (with one spare). The `volgroup` and `logvol` commands configure an LVM group for the /home/ez directory:

```
#raid /home/mj --fstype ext3 --level=RAID5 --spares=1 raid.44 raid.42 raid.40 raid.38
#volgroup Volume00 pv.36 pv.34
#logvol /home/ez --fstype ext3 --name=LogVol00 --vgname=Volume00 --size=192
```

Packages and Groups

When you see the `%packages` command, the items that follow specify the packages and groups that will be installed. The first lines in this section should look similar to the following, which specifies five package groups.

```
%packages --resolvdeps
@ Administration Tools
@ Authoring and Publishing
@ DNS Name Server
@ Graphical Internet
@ Text-based Internet
```

The first line, with the `--resolvdeps` switch, ensures that Red Hat Linux installs all dependent packages with your selections. Otherwise, Anaconda stops the installation process to ask if you want to resolve dependencies.

These commands search through the `comps.xml` file described in the first part of this chapter for groups with the given names, per the `<name>` variable in the `comps.xml` file. Some of the packages in each group—as indicated by `<packagereq type="mandatory">`—must be installed. Other packages may be `"default"` or `"optional"`. You may have selected or deselected some of these packages during the Red Hat Linux installation process. Your choices lead to a list of RPM package names in the following format:

```
printman
libtool-libs
-gnomemeeting
gdbm
gnome-audio
tk
bzip2-libs
-ncftp
```

From this list, the `printman`, `libtool-libs`, `gdbm`, `gnome-audio`, `tk`, and `bzip2-libs` RPMs are installed. The `gnomemeeting` and `ncftp` RPMs are normally part of one of the installed package groups (Graphical Internet and Text-Based Internet); the minus sign (-) in front of each name means they are not installed through this Kickstart file.

Postinstallation Commands

Once Linux is installed, Kickstart proceeds to the postinstallation script at the end of the file. You can run the full range of available scripts; the default language is based on the bash shell. To specify a different scripting language, use a command like the following:

```
%post --interpreter /usr/bin/python
```

You can copy more configuration files from a remote computer; for example, the following script copies the `XF86Config` file from the computer with the noted IP address:

```
mkdir /mnt/source
mount 192.168.0.1:/etc /mnt/source
cp /mnt/source/etc/X11/XF86Config /root
```

This assumes that you've shared the `/etc` directory via NFS on the computer with the noted IP address.

One other simple command ensures that the system reboots after the Kickstart installation process is complete:

```
reboot
```

Other Commands

A substantial number of commands are available for Kickstart files. Table 5.5 lists the basic Kickstart commands.

TABLE 5.5: OTHER KICKSTART COMMANDS

COMMAND	DESCRIPTION
auth	Lets you specify authentication options; same as `authconfig`.
bootloader	Specifies the bootloader location; `--useLilo` installs LILO instead of GRUB.
clearpart	Removes current partitions; you can specify `--linux` or `--all`.
device	Allows you to set hardware parameters for a specific device.
driverdisk	If you need a separate driver disk, you can load it onto an existing partition; e.g.,: `driverdisk hda2 --type=vfat`.
firewall	Lets you set up a basic firewall configuration.
install	Allows you to specify basic installation parameters, including the source of Red Hat installation files.
interactive	Runs through the Kickstart file interactively; same as `autostep`.
keyboard	Specifies the keyboard type.
lang	Notes the language of the installation.
langsupport	Specifies the language(s) you want to install.
logvol	Adds a logical volume partition.
mouse	Adds a pointing device.
network	Configures the local network card.
part	Creates a specified partition; same as `partition`.
raid	Configures a software RAID device.
reboot	Reboots the system after the installation is complete.
rootpw	Specifies the root password for this system.
skipx	Skips the X Window configuration process.
text	Runs the installation in text mode.
timezone	Specifies the time zone for this computer.

Continued on next page

TABLE 5.5: OTHER KICKSTART COMMANDS *(continued)*

COMMAND	DESCRIPTION
upgrade	Upgrades an existing Linux system.
volgroup	Sets up an LVM group.
xconfig	Notes X Window and graphics card configuration details.
zerombr	Overwrites any existing partition tables, including all bootloaders.

NOTE *Many of these commands have a wide variety of switches. We've covered the ones we consider to be important in this chapter. If you need more information, refer to the Red Hat Linux 9 configuration guide.*

Working with the GUI Kickstart Configurator

There's another way to create a custom Kickstart configuration file: using the GUI Kickstart Configurator. You can start it in a GUI such as GNOME or KDE. Open a command-line interface and run the `redhat-config-kickstart` command to open the Kickstart Configurator, shown in Figure 5.2.

NOTE *If you need more information on starting a command-line interface in GNOME or KDE, refer to Chapter 16 or 17.*

FIGURE 5.2

The Kickstart Configurator

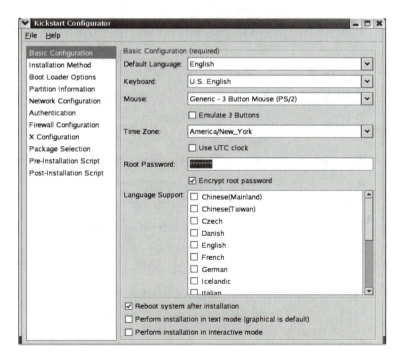

As you can see, the left-hand column contains 11 menus, which we'll look at in the following sections. If you've installed Red Hat Linux or read the first parts of this chapter, you should already be familiar with many of the options.

If you want to start from an existing configuration, click File ➤ Open File. You can then select a file, such as /root/anaconda-ks.cfg, from the menu that appears.

The Basic Configuration Menu

The Basic Configuration menu is shown in Figure 5.2. It includes a number of basic settings, which are briefly described in Table 5.6.

TABLE 5.6: KICKSTART CONFIGURATOR, BASIC CONFIGURATION OPTIONS

OPTION	DESCRIPTION
Default Language	Specifies the language you want to use during the installation process; some 20 languages are available.
Keyboard	Specifies a keyboard type; you can select from over 50 keyboards.
Mouse	Selects the mouse or other pointing device for your computer.
Emulate 3 Buttons	If you have a two-button mouse, this option allows you to simulate a middle mouse button by pressing both mouse buttons at the same time.
Time Zone	Specifies your current time zone.
Use UTC Clock	Select this option if you've set your hardware clock to Greenwich Mean Time and are not dual-booting with an operating system such as Microsoft Windows.
Root Password	Enter your desired root password here.
Encrypt Root Password	Encrypts the root password that you enter in the Kickstart file.
Language Support	Installs fonts and language files for your running Linux computer.
Reboot System After Installation	Adds the reboot command to the Kickstart file.
Perform Installation In Text Mode	Runs the installation process in text mode.
Perform Installation In Interactive Mode	Allows you to debug a Kickstart installation process.

The Installation Method Menu

In the Kickstart Configurator, select Installation Method. You should see the options shown in Figure 5.3.

FIGURE 5.3

The Kickstart
Configurator's
Installation
Method menu

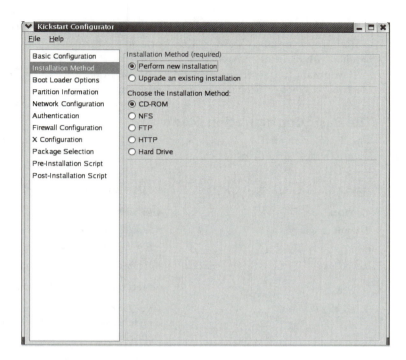

These options are fairly self-explanatory; you can configure Kickstart to install a fresh copy or upgrade Red Hat Linux. You can also specify a local (CD-ROM or Hard Drive) or network (FTP, HTTP, NFS) source for the installation files.

The Boot Loader Options Menu

The Boot Loader Options menu allows you to configure the type and location of the bootloader on your system. As we discussed in Chapter 11, there are two basic Linux bootloaders: GRUB and LILO. As you can see in Figure 5.4, this menu contains four sections.

If you already have a third-party bootloader (from Partition Magic or System Commander, for example), you can install GRUB or LILO on the first sector of the boot partition. If you prefer LILO and are upgrading Linux on this computer, you can keep LILO by selecting Upgrade Existing Boot Loader.

You can select GRUB or LILO as your bootleader. If you select LILO, you can have it read your hard disks in `linear` mode, which can help with larger hard drives. You can also force the use of `lba32` mode, which can help Linux look beyond the 1024th cylinder on older hard drives for the startup files in your `/boot` directory.

FIGURE 5.4

The Boot Loader
Options menu

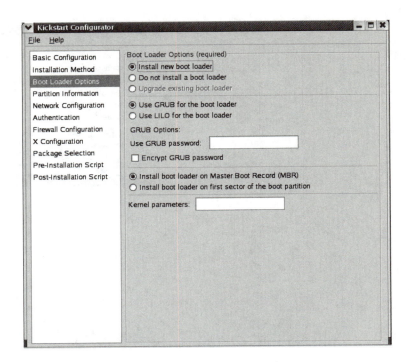

Normally, you'll install the bootloader on the Master Boot Record. If you prefer to use another bootloader, you can install GRUB or LILO on the first sector of the partition with your /boot directory.

You can also pass hardware parameters to the kernel. This is most commonly used when Linux has trouble detecting hardware automatically. You can specify a wide variety of parameters here, as defined in the bootparam man page.

NOTE *In Linux, a "man page" is a manual, typically for commands or configuration files. For example, to read the man page for* /etc/fstab, *open a Linux command-line interface and run the* man fstab *command.*

There is one more option related to bootloaders, which we discuss in the next section.

The Partition Information Menu

You can configure most of the partitions that you need in the Partition Information menu, shown in Figure 5.5.

FIGURE 5.5

The Partition
Information menu

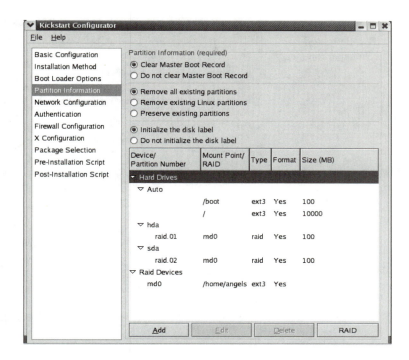

The first parts of this menu allow you set basic parameters for your hard disk. The Clear Master Boot Record option erases any existing bootloader from your hard disk. It is equivalent to Kickstart's `zerombr=yes` command.

If the hard disks have existing partitions, you can choose to delete just the Linux partitions, or all partitions on all detected hard drives. If you're installing Linux on computers with new hard drives, you'll also want to select Initialize The Disk Label.

NOTE *If you're upgrading Red Hat Linux, you're normally using existing partitions; all of the options in this menu are then deactivated.*

Click Add to open the Partition Options dialog box, shown in Figure 5.6. If you're familiar with Disk Druid from Chapter 3, the options here should look familiar. If you need more information on most of these options, read Chapter 3.

In addition to what is shown in Disk Druid, this dialog box contains the following two options:

Use Recommended Swap Size Red Hat can configure a recommended swap partition. It's normally twice the size of your RAM.

Use Existing Partition If you know the partition layout of the target computer, you can specify a partition such as `hda1`. See Chapter 2 for partition-naming conventions.

FIGURE 5.6

The Partition
Options dialog box

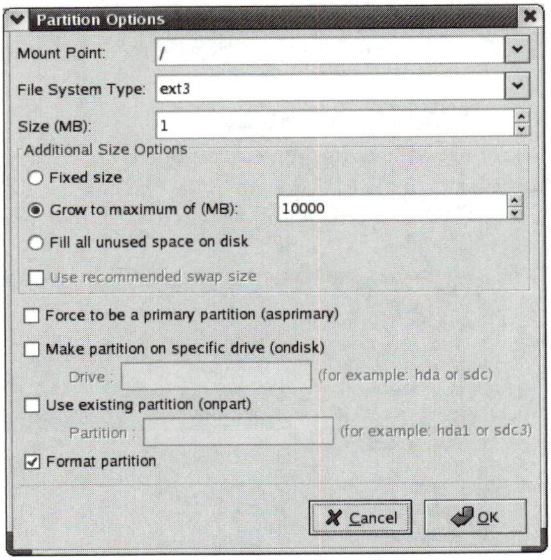

As of this writing, the Kickstart Configurator does not support the creation of volume groups for LVM partitions. You can still add LVM criteria to the actual Kickstart file, as we explained earlier.

You can also set up RAID devices. If you've configured RAID partitions, click RAID. In the RAID Options window, select Create A RAID Device and click OK to continue. This opens the Make RAID Device dialog box, shown in Figure 5.7.

FIGURE 5.7

The Make RAID
Device dialog box

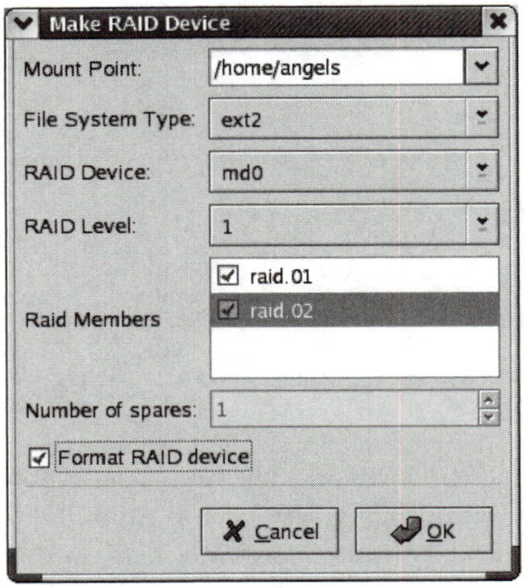

If you have a sufficient number of RAID partitions, this dialog box supports creating RAID devices at levels 0, 1, and 5. For more information on RAID requirements at these levels, see Chapter 14.

The Network Configuration Menu

To configure Ethernet network cards on your computer, use the Network Configuration menu. If you have a different type of network card, you'll have to edit the Kickstart configuration file directly. As you can see in Figure 5.8, the buttons allow you to add, edit, or delete various network devices.

FIGURE 5.8

The Network
Configuration menu

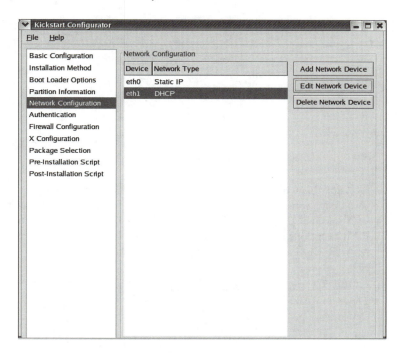

When you add or edit a network device, it opens the Network Device Information dialog box, as shown in Figure 5.9.

You can configure a number of different settings for each network device:

Network Device   Click the drop-down arrow to set this to one of 17 Ethernet network devices, between eth0 and eth16.

Network Type   You can select a network type for Static IP configuration; or you can get data for this network device from a local DHCP server, or a remote DHCP server using BOOTP. If you choose to set a Static IP network type, you can configure network address information for that device.

IP Address The IP version 4 address for the network card

Netmask The network mask for your LAN

Gateway The IP address of the computer or router that connects your network to an external network such as the Internet

Name Server The IP address of a DNS server connected to your network

FIGURE 5.9

Editing a Network Device

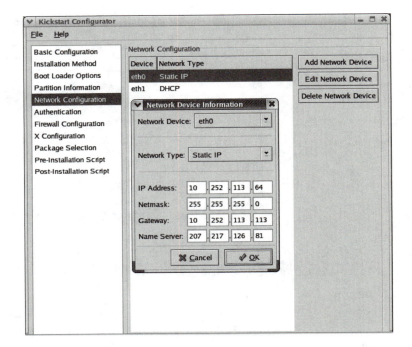

More information on each of these settings is available in Chapter 20.

The Authentication Configuration Menu

As we described earlier, authentication normally describes how a computer checks usernames and passwords. The basic menu is shown in Figure 5.10.

By default, Kickstart configures two types of password security. Shadow passwords are part of the Shadow Password Suite described in Chapter 9. MD5 is a form of encryption applied to user passwords.

As you can see in Figure 5.10, this window includes a series of tabs that represent various forms of authentication. They are briefly described in Table 5.7.

FIGURE 5.10

The Authentication
Configuration menu

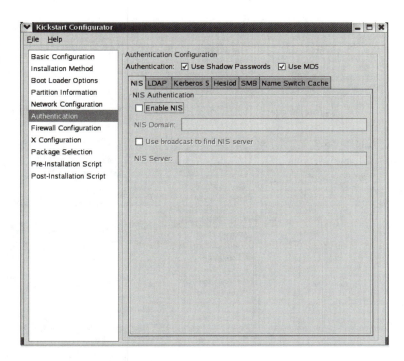

TABLE 5.7: THE KICKSTART CONFIGURATOR AUTHENTICATION OPTIONS

OPTION	DESCRIPTION
NIS	Network Information Service provides a common database of usernames and passwords for a LAN; for more information, see Chapter 28.
LDAP	The Lightweight Directory Assistance Protocol is also used for authentication and related LAN databases.
Kerberos 5	Developed at MIT, Kerberos 5 provides strong encryption for checking user credentials.
Hesiod	Functionally similar to NIS, `hesiod` uses DNS to distribute information kept in basic configuration files.
SMB	The SMB (Samba) option allows you to use other servers for authentication on a Microsoft Windows–based network.
Name Switch Cache	The associated daemon, `ncsd`, supports authentication via NIS.

The Firewall Configuration Menu

The Firewall Configuration menu should look familiar if you've installed Red Hat Linux in either Chapters 3 or 4. As you can see in Figure 5.11, you can choose from three basic firewall configurations: High, Medium, or Disabled.

FIGURE 5.11

The Firewall Configuration menu

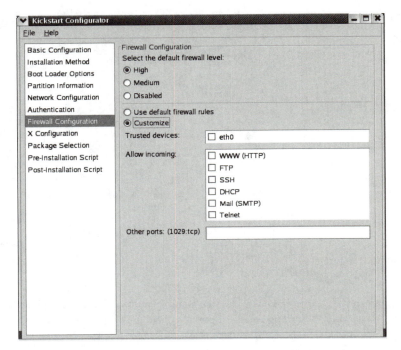

If you choose to configure a firewall, you can customize it. You can exclude a network card such as `eth0` from the firewall by checking the device name in the Trusted Devices text box. In addition, you can allow incoming network traffic to several different types of servers: web (WWW), FTP, a Secure Shell (SSH), DHCP, incoming mail (SMTP), and Telnet.

The Other Ports text box lets you add other ports based on `/etc/services`.

The X Configuration Menu

The X Configuration menu should look familiar if you know about the `redhat-config-xfree86` tool. If you choose to configure the X Window through Kickstart, select Configure The X Window System. This activates the three tabs shown in Figure 5.12.

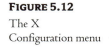

FIGURE 5.12

The X
Configuration menu

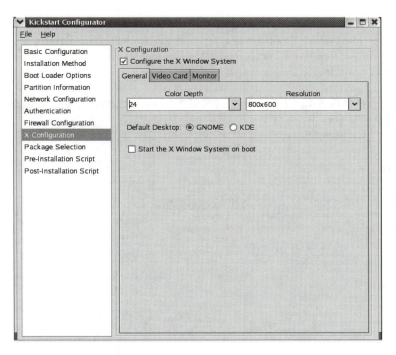

On the General tab, you can select an overall Color Depth and Resolution for your system. Be careful; some systems can handle a color depth of 24 bits per pixel; others are designed for 32 bits per pixel. Assuming your computer reflects the target hardware, it's best to take a working configuration from the `xconfig` command in your `anaconda-ks.cfg` file.

The other options are self-explanatory. If you've installed GNOME or KDE, you can make set of these as your default desktop. If you enable the Start The X Window System On Boot option, Linux opens one of the display managers described in Chapter 15.

The Video Card and Monitor tabs include the same database that is available through `redhat-config-xfree86`. You can find more information on this system in Chapter 15. By default, Kickstart probes for your video card and monitor, or you can activate the settings, including the monitor horizontal and vertical sync, using this tool.

The Package Selection Menu

The Package Selection menu allows you to select from the standard package groups in the `comps.xml` configuration file. As shown in Figure 5.13, the window is organized in the same way as Red Hat's graphical installation tool.

Select the package groups of your choice. Details of each group are available in the `comps.xml` file.

Unless you know what you're doing, select Automatically Resolve Dependencies. That option ensures that foundation software gets installed. Otherwise, a lot of the software installed with Red Hat Linux may not work.

FIGURE 5.13

The Package
Selection menu

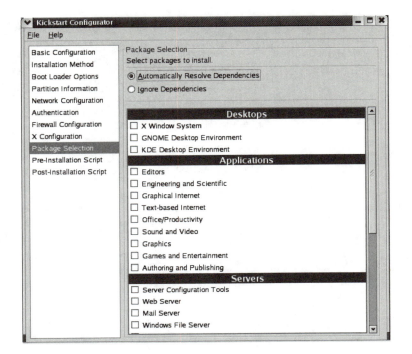

The Pre-Installation Script Menu

As we explained earlier, a preinstallation script helps you set parameters for the installation. Since the script is run before Red Hat Linux is installed, the range of available commands is limited. You can use the Kickstart Configurator to create a preinstallation script, as shown in Figure 5.14.

The default script language is bash. If you want to use commands in a different language, activate the Use An Interpreter text box and then enter the location of another language module, such as /usr/bin/python. Test your scripts; if there's an error, your Kickstart installation may fail.

The Post-Installation Script Menu

A postinstallation script helps you add parameters for each configuration. You can also use the Kickstart Configurator to create a postinstallation script, as shown in Figure 5.15.

FIGURE 5.14

The Pre-installation
Script menu

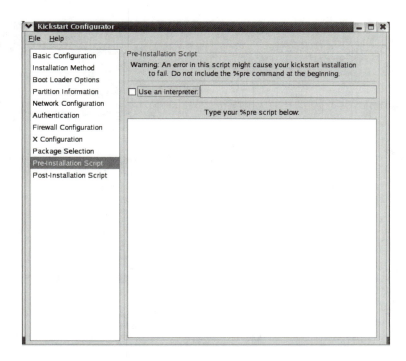

FIGURE 5.15

The Post-
Installation
Script menu

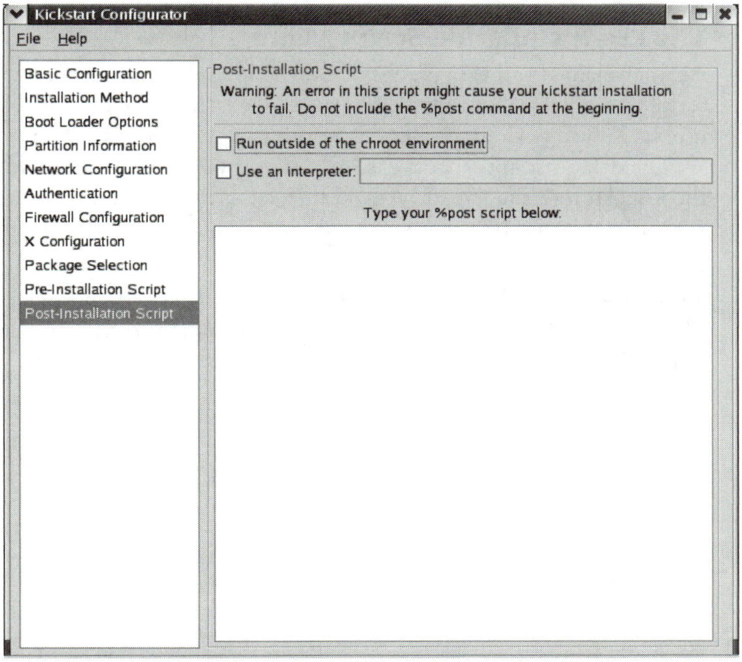

Postinstallation scripts are run in a `chroot` environment. In other words, during the installation process, the standard Linux root directory is mounted on the `/mnt/sysimage` directory. The `chroot` environment makes `/mnt/sysimage` look like your root directory.

For more information on the `chroot` environment, see Chapter 27. Once again, it's important to test your scripts. If there's an error, your Kickstart installation may fail.

The Next Steps

Once you've made your changes, you'll want to save your configuration to a Kickstart file. To do so, click File ➤ Save File and save the file in the directory of your choice. As you'll see in the next section, it helps to name the file `ks.cfg`.

If there are things that you could not add to your configuration file, such as LVM partitions, open `ks.cfg` in a text editor and do so now. We examined the basic configuration and commands of a Kickstart file earlier in this chapter.

Kickstarting from a Floppy

Now that you have a Kickstart file, you should be able to start the Red Hat Linux installation process from the installation boot floppy. Once Red Hat finds and loads your Kickstart file, it may need a driver disk. After it activates needed drivers, Anaconda proceeds to install Red Hat Linux automatically, using the instructions from your Kickstart file. You can then remove the installation and driver disks, and use them to start the process on another computer.

In other words, you can install Red Hat Linux on several computers simultaneously.

Files on a Boot Floppy

Kickstart files are typically small enough to include with the standard Red Hat Linux installation floppy disk. The standard files from the `bootdisk.img` boot floppy are shown in Figure 5.16. Note that I've included my `ks.cfg` file on this floppy.

FIGURE 5.16

Files on the installation boot floppy

```
[root@RH9Test root]# \ls -l /mnt/floppy/
total 1414
-rwxr-xr-x    1 root     root          342 Mar 13 21:58 boot.msg
-rwxr-xr-x    1 root     root          957 Mar 13 21:58 general.msg
-rwxr-xr-x    1 root     root       570110 Mar 13 21:58 initrd.img
-rwxr-xr-x    1 root     root         1305 Mar 27 14:38 ks.cfg
-r-xr-xr-x    1 root     root         7836 Mar 13 21:58 ldlinux.sys
-rwxr-xr-x    1 root     root          730 Mar 13 21:58 options.msg
-rwxr-xr-x    1 root     root          869 Mar 13 21:58 param.msg
-rwxr-xr-x    1 root     root          531 Mar 13 21:58 rescue.msg
-rwxr-xr-x    1 root     root          549 Mar 13 21:58 snake.msg
-rwxr-xr-x    1 root     root         5420 Mar 13 21:58 splash.lss
-r-xr-xr-x    1 root     root          435 Mar 13 21:58 syslinux.cfg
-rwxr-xr-x    1 root     root       855693 Mar 13 21:58 vmlinuz
[root@RH9Test root]#
```

Create a Red Hat Linux installation floppy, using the techniques described in Chapter 3. Rename any Kickstart file that you've created as `ks.cfg`. Copy this file to the installation floppy.

Unfortunately, there isn't enough room to include drivers on the installation boot floppy. If you need additional drivers, you can use the installation boot floppy and the Red Hat Linux installation CD.

NOTE *Some companies buy PCs without CD drives to prevent users from loading their own software.*

If your computer does not have a CD drive, you'll need more floppy disks for any drivers that Linux needs to load. As described in Chapter 2, other floppies can be created from the first Red Hat installation CD, from files in the `/images` directory. Depending on your configuration, you may need floppies created from one or more of the following: `drvnet.img`, `drvblock.img`, and `pcmciadd.img`.

The Installation Procedure

You're ready with your installation floppies. Insert the Red Hat Linux installation floppy with your Kickstart file into the appropriate drive. If possible, insert the first Red Hat Linux installation CD. Restart your computer, and boot from the installation floppy or the CD. When you see the first installation screen, you'll see the boot prompt, where you can enter the following command:

```
[F1-Main] [F2-Options] [F3-General] [F4-Kernel] [F5-Rescue]
boot: linux ks=floppy
```

If you've configured your `ks.cfg` file properly and booted from the CD, you should be able to remove the floppy and the CD after your computer reads in the startup kernel and appropriate drivers. The installation should proceed automatically.

If you don't boot from a CD, you'll have to insert the appropriate driver floppy disks when prompted. The prompts will be similar to the driver screens shown in Chapter 4.

Testing Kickstart

Kickstart is useful for installing Red Hat Linux on a group of computers with similar or identical hardware configurations. If you're going to install Kickstart on a large number of computers, it's important to test your installation first.

If you're planning to install Red Hat Linux on a large group of computers, you could stay in the office all night to make sure everything goes right, or you could test your Kickstart installation process on one or two computers. Then you can use Kickstart to install Red Hat Linux on the other computers on your network with additional confidence.

Summary

In previous chapters, we found that the installation of Red Hat Linux can be an involved process. Anaconda, the Red Hat installation program, can require considerable user input. In this chapter, you learned how to install Red Hat Linux automatically, using Kickstart. With an appropriate Kickstart file, you can insert a floppy and a CD into a PC and then type a simple command, and the installation proceeds automatically.

To demonstrate how to configure a Kickstart file, we examined the `comps.xml` file, which organizes Red Hat Linux packages into several groups.

Then we examined the default Kickstart configuration for a computer, which is saved in the `/root` directory in `anaconda-ks.cfg`. This file, with some modifications, allows Kickstart to create the same configuration on another computer.

The Kickstart Configurator provides a GUI interface for creating a custom Kickstart file. While creating a basic configuration saves you time, you may need to add a few more commands to the resulting file in a text editor.

Once you're satisfied with your Kickstart file, you can save it to `ks.cfg` on a Red Hat Linux installation boot floppy. You can use the first Red Hat Linux installation CD or a driver floppy for required drivers. If `ks.cfg` is properly configured, a simple command starts the installation. Unless you need to insert a separate driver floppy, you should be able to leave the computer. Red Hat Linux is installed automatically.

In the next chapter, we'll begin our journey through the nitty-gritty of Linux, the command-line interface. We'll examine the basic commands required to navigate around and administer Linux in the chapters that follow.

Part 2

Linux Fundamentals

In this Part, you will learn how to:
- ◆ Use Linux at the command-line interface
- ◆ Work with Linux files and filesystems
- ◆ Manage a Linux shell

Chapter 6

Starting at the Command Line

WHILE RED HAT LINUX includes a number of integrated GUI tools, the best way to control
Linux is from the command-line interface. Command-line tools have more options than GUI tools.
Since they don't include the overhead of a desktop such as GNOME or KDE, they are faster. And
there is still a strong bias in the Linux community toward the command line. Therefore, if you really
want to learn Linux, you should learn how to use the command-line interface.

This chapter shows you the workings of a number of different commands based on the
Bourne Again Shell (bash), discussed in Chapter 8. Some commands help you navigate different
Linux directories; others help you create and delete Linux files. Commands are available to help
you read or search through files in different ways. Some commands allow you to use the characteristics of a file to your advantage.

One of the keys to the command-line interface is the vi editor, which may be the only editor
you have available if you're troubleshooting problems such as boot failures. This chapter covers the
following topics:

◆ Exploring navigational commands

◆ Setting up files and directories

◆ Managing files

◆ Manipulating files

◆ Using the vi editor

◆ Understanding other text editors

Exploring Navigational Commands

There are two basic navigational commands for getting around the shell. The cd command lets you
navigate between directories. The ls command tells you the contents of a directory (including other
directories). But before you run around different Linux directories, the pwd command can tell you
where you are. Output from a navigational command depends on the absolute path, which specifies
your directory location relative to the top-level root (/) directory.

pwd

The pwd command (short for *present working directory*) is simple. Type it at the command-line interface, and you'll see the absolute path to your current directory. For example:

```
# pwd
/etc/httpd/conf
```

The output tells you that you're currently in the /etc/httpd/conf directory, which happens to be the default location for Apache configuration files.

cd

The change directory command is known as cd. Those of you familiar with MS-DOS may find a number of similarities between MS-DOS and Linux cd commands. Typical cd commands are shown in Table 6.1.

NOTE *Linux is case sensitive. Please note that the small capitals in the tables of this chapter represent lowercase letters.*

TABLE 6.1: *CD* COMMANDS

COMMAND	RESULT
cd ..	Moves up one directory level. For example, if you're currently in the /home/mj directory, this moves you to the /home directory.
cd ../..	Moves up two directory levels. For example, if you're currently in the /etc/rc.d/rc0.d directory, this moves you to the /etc directory. You can move up additional directory levels, up to the root (/) directory.
cd /home/mj	Navigates to the home directory of user mj.
cd ~	Navigates to your home directory. Works for any user.

NOTE *If you're relatively new to Linux, remember to use the forward slash /, and not the backslash \, when you cite directory, computer, or even domain names.*

ls

The ls command is versatile. Not only does it allow you to list the files and directories in your current directory, but with the proper options, you can also find the permissions and size of a file. The command allows you to check ownership, differentiate between file types, and sort the result in several ways. You can review some examples of this command in Table 6.2.

Perhaps the most important command in this series is ls -l, which lists all files in the current directory, including size, owner, and permissions. Figure 6.1 shows an example of the result of this command.

TABLE 6.2: *LS* COMMANDS

COMMAND	RESULT
ls	Lists in alphabetical order all nonhidden files in the current directory.
ls -a	Lists all files in the current directory, including hidden files.
ls -r	Lists in reverse alphabetical order all nonhidden files in the current directory.
ls -F	Lists all files by type. The character at the end of each file indicates the file type. For example, a forward slash (/) represents a directory, an asterisk (*) is associated with an executable file, and an "at" (@) represents a linked file.
ls -i	Lists files with inode numbers. An inode number represents the location of a file on a volume. Two or more files with the same inode number are two different names for the identical file.
ls -l	Lists all the files in the current directory, including the current directory (.) and the parent directory (..). Also lists the size, owner, and permissions associated with each file in what is known as *long listing format*.
ls -t	Lists files by the last time they were changed; most recent files are listed first.
ls -u	Lists files by the last time they were accessed; most recent files are listed first.

FIGURE 6.1

A long listing
(ls -l) in the
current directory

```
-rw-r--r--    1 root     root          35 Feb 25 18:18 updfstab.conf
-rw-r--r--    1 root     root         870 Feb 25 18:18 updfstab.conf.default
lrwxrwxrwx    1 root     root          34 Mar 26 10:19 vfontcap -> ../usr/share
/VFlib/2.25.6/vfontcap
lrwxrwxrwx    1 root     root          37 Mar 26 13:41 vfontcap.ja -> ../usr/sh
are/VFlib/2.25.6/vfontcap.ja
drwxr-xr-x    3 root     root        4096 Mar 26 10:24 vfs
drwxr-xr-x    2 root     root        4096 Mar 26 13:41 vsftpd
-rw-------    1 root     root         125 Feb 28 14:21 vsftpd.ftpusers
-rw-------    1 root     root         361 Feb 28 14:21 vsftpd.user_list
-rw-r--r--    1 root     root         864 Feb 25 10:53 warnquota.conf
-rw-r--r--    1 root     root       23964 Jan 25 22:09 webalizer.conf
-rw-r--r--    1 root     root       23930 Jan 25 22:09 webalizer.conf.sample
-rw-r--r--    1 root     root        4022 Jan 25 03:18 wgetrc
drwxr-xr-x    2 root     root        4096 Mar 26 14:43 wordtrans
drwxr-xr-x   17 root     root        4096 Mar 26 11:05 X11
-rw-r--r--    1 root     root         289 Feb 24 19:10 xinetd.conf
drwxr-xr-x    2 root     root        4096 Mar 26 13:38 xinetd.d
drwxr-xr-x    2 root     root        4096 Mar 26 10:31 xml
-rw-r--r--    1 root     root        4912 Feb 20 10:08 xpdfrc
-rw-r--r--    1 root     root         361 Mar 26 10:47 yp.conf
-rw-r--r--    1 root     root        1626 Jan 25 03:38 ypserv.conf
drwxr-x---    2 root     root        4096 Mar 26 13:43 zebra
[root@RH9Test etc]# []
```

As you can see, the long listing includes the permissions, user owner, group owner, size, modification time, and name of each file in the current directory.

Path Management

When you describe the location of a file, you specify either the *absolute* path or the *relative* path. An absolute path describes the location of a file relative to the root (/) directory. For example, you can type the following command to get to the scripts that start a number of Linux daemons:

```
# cd /etc/rc.d/init.d
```

The forward slash in front of the first directory makes this the absolute path. You can type this command from anywhere in Linux to get to this directory. Sometimes, you may accidentally type the command without the forward slash:

```
# cd etc/rc.d/init.d
```

In this case, Linux looks for these directories under your home directory. For example, if your home directory is /home/mj, this command makes Linux look for the /home/mj/etc/rc.d/init.d directory. Unless you keep a copy of these files deep in your home directory, Linux won't find anything.

Absolute and relative paths apply to other commands as well. For example, you can list the daemons in the /etc/rc.d/init.d directory with the following command:

```
# ls /etc/rc.d/init.d
```

However, if you use the relative path, your current directory matters. For example, if the output from the pwd command is /home/mj, the following command won't work unless you have an /home/mj/etc/rc.d/init.d directory:

```
# ls etc/rc.d/init.d
```

Setting Up Files and Directories

Creating a file in Linux is easy. You can copy from an existing file or save to the filename of your choice from an editor or another application. There's even a special command that allows you to set up an empty file. It's also easy to delete a file—so easy that some commands for deleting files can be dangerous.

Although a Linux directory is just a special file, Linux includes specific commands for creating and deleting directories. First, we'll look at the file management commands, and then we'll examine the commands for creating and deleting directories.

touch

There are times when you simply need to set up an empty file in Linux. For example, before you can activate a quota for a user or a group, you need to create an empty **aquota.user** or **aquota.group** file in the target directory. Creating empty files is easy with the **touch** command. The following commands create these files in the /home directory:

```
# touch /home/aquota.user /home/aquota.group
```

The **touch** command can also be used to change the timestamp associated with an existing file. When you use the command without a switch, the last access time of the file is changed to the current time. For example, suppose it's 11:21 on April 15 and you run the following command:

```
# touch /root/f0601.tif
```

When you run the `ls -l` command on the `f0601.tif` file, you see the following output:

```
-rw-r--r--   1 root root    883823 Apr 15 11:21 f0601.tif
```

Other switches, such as `-t`, can change the access time associated with a file as desired.

cp

The simplest version of the copy command is `cp file1 file2`. Issuing this command copies the contents of `file1` and places them in destination `file2`. The destination file will have a new creation date and inode number. Other copy commands can overwrite destination files. You can even use a switch for the `cp` command to copy the contents of one or more subdirectories. See Table 6.3 for examples of how the `cp` command works.

TABLE 6.3: *CP* COMMANDS

COMMAND	RESULT
`cp file1 file2`	Copies the contents of source `file1` to destination `file2`. The destination file has a new creation date and inode number.
`cp file* Dir1`	Copies multiple files to a directory.
`cp -f file1 file2`	If you already have a file named `file2`, this command overwrites its contents without prompting.
`cp -i file1 file2`	If you already have a file named `file2`, this command prompts you for confirmation before overwriting this file.
`cp -p file1 file2`	Copies the contents of source `file1` to destination `file2`. The destination file has the same inode number and creation date as the source file.
`cp -r Dir1 Dir2`	Copies the contents of the directory named `Dir1`, including subdirectories, to `Dir2`. The effect is recursive; in other words, if there are subdirectories under `Dir1`'s subdirectories, their files and directories are also copied.
`cp -u file1 file2`	If you already have a file named `file2` and `file1` is newer, this command overwrites its contents without prompting.

NOTE *An* inode *is the identifier used on each Linux partition for a file. Every file gets its own inode. The inode includes metadata about the file, which includes the permissions, size, last access time, and the disk block where the file is located. If the inode is misaligned or corrupted, Linux won't be able to find the associated file. In addition, identical files have the same inode number. But because you can't have the same inode number on different partitions, the* `cp -p file1 file2` *command doesn't work if you're copying a file from one partition to another.*

mv

If you want to rename a file in Linux, you move it. The `mv` command changes the name of a file. Unless you're moving a file to a different volume, everything about the file, including the inode number, stays the same. There are four key move commands, as shown in Table 6.4.

TABLE 6.4: *MV* COMMANDS

COMMAND	RESULT
mv *file1 file2*	Changes the name of a file from file1 to file2. If the source and destination files are located on the same volume, the files retain the same inode number.
mv *file* Dir1*	Moves multiple files to a directory.
mv -f *file1 file2*	If you already have a file named file2, this command overwrites its contents without prompting.
mv -i *file1 file2*	If you already have a file named file2, this command prompts you for confirmation before overwriting this file.

TIP   Some Linux users create files that start in lowercase, such as file1, and directories that start with a capital letter, such as Dir1. This is far from an absolute rule; standard Linux directories start in lowercase letters, such as /bin.

rm

You can use rm to remove files and directories. This is one of the reasons that many Linux administrators are advised to run Linux in root or superuser mode only when necessary; small mistakes in this command can easily delete all of your Linux files. For example, suppose you want to remove a group of temporary directories in your root (/) directory: a.tmp, b.tmp, and c.tmp. You want to use the rm -r *.tmp command, but instead you type the following:

```
# rm -r * .tmp
```

Because there is a space between the asterisk and the .tmp, the shell assumes that you want to recursively delete all directories and then delete the file named .tmp. The result is not good.

For this reason, Red Hat configures the following as an alias for the root user:

```
alias rm='rm -i'
```

The alias ensures that whenever you use the rm command (even rm -r), the shell prompts you for confirmation before you delete any files. Some Linux distributions set up this alias as a shell variable for root users. The key rm commands are shown in Table 6.5.

TIP   You can find default aliases with the alias command.

TABLE 6.5: *RM* COMMANDS

COMMAND	RESULT
rm *file1*	Deletes file1 without prompting for confirmation. However, this command does not supersede an alias rm='rm -i', which requires confirmation.

Continued on next page

TABLE 6.5: *RM* COMMANDS *(continued)*

COMMAND	RESULT
rm -d *Dir1*	Deletes *Dir1* without prompting for confirmation. However, this command does not supersede an alias rm='rm -i', which requires confirmation.
rm -i *file1*	Deletes *file1* after prompting for confirmation from the user.
rm -f *file2*	If you already have a file named *file2*, this command overwrites its contents without prompting. It even supersedes an alias rm='rm -i'.
rm -r *	Removes files recursively; if there are any subdirectories in the current directory, this command deletes them (and all of their files) as well. However, this command does not supersede an alias rm='rm -i', which requires confirmation.

ADMINISTERING AS ROOT

One of the raging debates in the Linux community is whether it's sensible for a Linux administrator to log in as the root user. Errors as root can damage or destroy the files on your system. In addition, logging in as root may expose the root password to someone who has put a "Trojan horse" program on your system.

On the other hand, Red Hat has made it safer to use the root account. Good aliases make it more difficult to accidentally delete key files. Defaults such as root_squash in NFS prevent root users on other computers from sabotaging your system. You can further protect your system with passwords for the GRUB bootloader and your BIOS. Because the people I know at Red Hat use the root account regularly, I do the same in this book.

If you do log in as the root user, remember to be careful. Don't leave your system without logging out; otherwise, someone could change your password and access your system at his or her leisure. And don't expose your system to services that can read or even control what you do as root, such as AT&T's Virtual Network Computing (VNC) environment.

ln

Instead of just copying or moving a file, you can link it. Links are common, especially for those programs that start at various runlevels. When you link a file, you're creating another path to a currently existing file. For example, if both you and a colleague are working on a file named **project**, you can create a linked file in your home directory. Assume the **project** file is in the /home/jm directory. To create a link to a file in mj's home directory, you use the following command:

```
# ln /home/jm/project /home/mj/project
```

When you work on either file, the change and results are visible and accessible to those who access both directories. This is sometimes known as a *hard link*. With a hard link, because both files retain the same inode number, both files are identical. If the original file is deleted, the hard-linked file remains in place. It retains all the information from the original file.

NOTE   *The* `ln file1 file2` *command produces the same result as the* `cp -p file1 file2` *command. Unless the files are located on different partitions,* `file1` *and* `file2` *retain the same inode number.*

One useful option for links is *symbolic mode*, which allows you to see the linked file. For example, if you run the following command:

```
# ln -s /home/jm/project /home/mj/project
```

you will see the linked file when you run a long listing (`ls -l`) of that file. This is known as a *soft link*. If the original file is deleted, the soft-linked file points to an empty file. The information in the original file is lost.

mkdir and *rmdir*

As you'd expect, the `mkdir` command lets you create directories. The directory that you create does not have to be based in your current directory. You can make several levels of directories if you choose. You can also assign the permissions of your choice to the directory that you create. The key `mkdir` commands are shown in Table 6.6.

TABLE 6.6: *MKDIR* COMMANDS

COMMAND	RESULT
`mkdir -p Dir1/Dir2`	Creates a directory named *Dir2*. If *Dir1* does not exist, the `-p` switch tells Linux to create that directory as well. Both are created as subdirectories of the current directory.
`mkdir -m 755 /usr/Dir3`	Creates a directory named *Dir3* as a subdirectory in the /usr directory. The permissions (755) are rwx for the owner and r-x for other members of the group and everyone else.

The `rmdir` command allows you to delete empty directories. The directory that you remove does not have to be based in your current directory. You can delete several levels of directories if the directory that you delete empties others. For example, with the following command, you can delete the directories named *Dir1* and *Dir3*:

```
# rmdir -p Dir1/Dir3
```

This command deletes directory *Dir3* if it is empty. If the only "file" in directory *Dir1* is *Dir3*, this command also deletes directory *Dir1*.

Managing Files

Linux includes a number of commands to help you read files in different ways. You can verify different types of files, and you can read files from the top or from the bottom. This read can be limited to a few lines, or it can set you up to page through the entire file. You can also count the lines, words, and alphanumeric characters within a file. In addition, Linux lets you search through a file using the search term of your choice.

Because it is difficult to define words or lines in binary files, most of these commands work best with text files.

file

Although some distributions differentiate between file types by color, there are no standard extensions in Linux. Executable files don't end in `.exe`, and document files may not end in `.doc`. The `file` command allows you to view the type of each file. You can see how this works in Figure 6.2.

FIGURE 6.2

Reviewing different file types

```
boot.log:        ASCII English text
cron:            ASCII text
cups:            directory
dmesg:           ASCII text
gdm:             directory
httpd:           directory
ksyms.0:         ASCII text
lastlog:         Non-ISO extended-ASCII text, with no line terminators
maillog:         ASCII text
mailman:         setgid directory
messages:        ASCII English text
news:            directory
pgsql:           empty
rpmpkgs:         ASCII text
samba:           directory
scrollkeeper.log: ASCII text
secure:          ASCII text
spooler:         empty
squid:           directory
vbox:            directory
wtmp:            GLS_BINARY_LSB_FIRST
XFree86.0.log:   ASCII English text
zebra:           directory
[root@RH9Test log]# []
```

As you can see in Figure 6.2, you are not able to see the file type if you don't have the proper permissions.

cat

The concatenate (`cat`) command sends the text of a file to standard output. You can use the `cat` command on any file. The following command sends the text of the file to your screen:

```
# cat file
```

This command is flexible; you can even use it to read multiple files, in sequence, with the `cat file1 file2` command.

head and tail

The `head` and `tail` commands are like two sides of a coin. The `head` command provides you with a view of the first few lines of a file; the `tail` command provides you with a view of the last few lines of that same file. You can regulate the amount of the file that you see with switches. For example, use the following command to see the first 15 lines of the `bully.txt` file:

```
# head -n15 bully.txt
```

If you substitute `tail` for `head`, you see the last 15 lines of this file. Table 6.7 lists more switches you can use with these commands.

TABLE 6.7: *HEAD* AND *TAIL* COMMANDS

COMMAND	RESULT
head 400b bully.txt	You see the first 400 bytes of the file known as `bully.txt`.
tail 4k bully.txt	You see the final 4KB of the file known as `bully.txt`.
head 3m bully.txt	You see the first 3MB of the file known as `bully.txt`.
tail -n22	You see the final 22 lines of the file known as `bully.txt`.

more and *less*

The `more` and the `less` commands aren't opposites, like `head` and `tail`. They both start at the beginning of a text file. When you run these commands on a text file, you review the contents of the file one page at a time. The `less` command is more versatile; unlike `more`, it allows you to scroll up and down any large text file by using the Page Up and Page Down keys on your keyboard.

Because they can read text a little bit at a time, these commands can open a file more quickly than a text editor like `vi`. The `less` command also has some of the advantages of the `vi` editor, since you can use some `vi` commands to search through a file.

Each command includes two sets of options. A command like the following sets up the file named `bigfile` with line numbers:

```
# less -N bigfile
```

Once the text file is open, you can run other commands, as described in Table 6.8.

TABLE 6.8: COMMANDS USED AFTER *LESS* IS APPLIED TO A TEXT FILE

COMMAND	RESULT
space	Pressing the spacebar on your keyboard scrolls forward one page in your screen.
page up	Scrolls back one page on your screen.
page down	Scrolls forward one page on your screen.
#z	"#" represents a number. For example, 8z scrolls forward eight lines in the file. If you do not use a number, this command is equivalent to the `space` command.
/abc	Searches through the file for the text string abc. This is a command from the Linux `vi` text editor.

The `more` and `less` commands are also known as pagers because they allow you to review text files one page at a time using the Page Up and Page Down keys on your keyboard. When you've finished, just press the q key to exit from this "browse" mode.

Permissions

As shown in the output from `ls -1`, each file is associated with owners, groups, and a series of permissions. (For an example of this setup, see Figure 6.1.) The permissions associated with a file are assigned to owners, groups, and everyone else on your Linux computer. Take a look at the following entry, which is the output from an `ls -1` command applied to a hypothetical file named abc:

```
-rwxrw-r-- 1 root root  1213 Feb 2 09:39 abc
```

Permissions are based on the characters on the far-left end of the output. The 10 characters determine what different users can do with this file.

If the first character is not a dash (-), it's not a regular file. It could be a directory (d) or a file that is linked (1) to another.

The remaining characters can be grouped in threes. The subsequent three characters shown are rwx. In other words, the owner of the file named abc can read (r), write (w), and execute (x) this file.

The next three characters shown are rw-. Users in the same group as the file owner can read this file (r) or edit and write to this file (w). These users cannot execute the file.

The final three characters are r-. Users that don't belong to the same group as the file owner can read this file. They can't write to it, nor can they execute it if it's a script.

You can set up these permissions on any file using the following command:

```
# chmod 764 abc
```

Permissions are set with a three-number code. In the preceding command, the first number (7) sets permissions for the owner, the second (6) for the other users in the owners group, and the third (4) for everyone else. Each number represents all permissions given to the owner, group, or everyone else, as described in Table 6.9.

TABLE 6.9: NUMERIC PERMISSIONS

PERMISSION	NUMBER	BASIS
r	4	= r(4)
w	2	= w(2)
x	1	= x(1)
rx	5	= r(4) + x(1)
rw	6	= r(4) + w(2)
wx	3	= w(2) + x(1)
rwx	7	= r(4) + w(2) + x(1)

Look at the permissions associated with the file named abc again. Because the first number is 7, the owner of this file has read (r), write (w), and execute (x) permission to this file. Since the second number is 6, other users in the owner's group have read (r) and write (w) permissions on this file. Since the third number is 4, everyone else has just read (r) permissions on this file.

TIP *Two closely related commands are* chown *and* chgrp, *which the root user can use to change the owner and group owner of a file. For example, the* chown mj abc *command makes user* mj *the owner of the file* abc.

umask

When you create a new file or directory, the permissions you get depend on the value of what is known as the umask. Type umask at the command-line interface, and you'll see the current numeric *masked* value of your permissions:

```
# umask
0022
```

To understand this number, you need a clear idea of the numeric value of permissions. The first number in the umask is currently unused. So the actual umask is 022.

Now let's look at an example. If you gave everyone permissions to your files and directories, you would have read, write, and execute permissions for all users. As discussed in the previous section, these permissions correspond to the number 7 (r+w+x = 4+2+1). When applied to all users, they correspond to 777. You could set up the same permissions for all users on the abc file with the following command:

```
# chmod 777 abc
```

By convention, this corresponds to a umask of 000. However, umask does not allow you to configure execute (x=1) permissions on any file. Therefore, a umask of 022 corresponds to permissions of 644, or rw-r--r--; in other words, for new files, the owner has read and write permissions, the members of the group that own the file have read permissions, and all other users have read permissions.

Manipulating Files

Several commands are available that allow you to learn about and search for and through different files. The wc command allows you to get a count of the number of lines, words, and characters in a file. The find and locate commands let you search for specific files. The grep command enables you to search through a file for a text string without opening it. The slocate and egrep commands are variations on these commands.

wc

The wc command is fairly straightforward. With any text file, you have a certain number of lines, words, and characters. Using the wc command, you can find all three characteristics. For example, you can check the showoff text file as follows:

```
# wc showoff
1914    9298    76066
```

These numbers correspond to the number of lines, words, and characters in this file, respectively. You can get any individual figure based on the commands shown in Table 6.10.

TABLE 6.10: EXAMPLES OF THE *WC* COMMAND

COMMAND	RESULT
wc -l showoff	Number of lines in the file showoff
wc -w showoff	Number of words in the file showoff
wc -c showoff	Number of characters in the file showoff

find

The find command looks through directories and subdirectories for the file(s) of your choice. For example, if you want to find a file named fig0606.tif, you use the following command:

```
# find / -name fig0606.tif
```

This command searches in the root directory and all subdirectories for the fig0606.tif file. The search can take quite some time. If you have more information, you may want to substitute a lower-level directory for the root (/).

With the find command, you can also use wildcards, such as the asterisk (*) and question mark (?), in your search term.

locate and slocate

An alternative to find is the locate command. This command searches through a database of your files. By default, if you keep Linux running on your computer, the database associated with the locate command is refreshed every day at 4:02 A.M. If you're searching for a file that wasn't created since the last database update, the locate command finds files much more quickly.

In Red Hat Linux, the locate command is actually soft-linked to the more secure slocate command. The database is updated per the /etc/cron.daily/slocate.cron script. Take a look at the default command in that script:

```
/usr/bin/updatedb -f "nfs,smbfs,ncpfs,proc,devpts" \
➥-e "/tmp,/var/tmp,/usr/tmp,/aft,/net"
```

As you can see from the updatedb man page, the -f switch excludes a number of filesystem types, and the -e switch excludes a number of directories that should be accessible only to the root user. You can customize this script to exclude other directories, such as /root, or filesystem types, such as vfat.

Once you have a locate database, it is more flexible; for example, if you use the following command, it returns all files that include the text string fig0:

```
# locate fig0
```

The locate command works as if asterisks are assumed before and after the search term.

grep

The grep command is a handy way to search through a file. As a system administrator, you may have long lists of users. If you want to search through your /etc/passwd file for a user named michael jang, try the following command:

```
# grep "michael jang" /etc/passwd
mj:x:500:500:michael jang:/home/mj:/bin/bash
```

This response tells you that there is a user named michael jang. It also includes the home directory and default shell for that user. If the search string exists in more than one line, you'll see those lines as well. You can even use grep to search through a series of files with commands like the following:

```
# grep mj *
# grep -c bash /etc/passwd
```

The first command looks for the string mj in all files in the current directory. The second command, with the -c switch, counts the number of lines that include the word *bash*.

Command Combinations

It's a common practice to use more than one Linux command in a line. For example, if you're using the find command and you know that the result will have a large number of files, you can use a command like grep to search through the result. Specifically, let's say you want to find some of the .html files on your system. You might start with the following command:

```
# find / -name *.html
```

However, you might get discouraged when you see hundreds of files flashing past you on your terminal screen. An alternative is to combine commands like this:

```
# find / -name *.html | grep bookmark
```

This command searches through the results of the find command for the text string "bookmark". Only those files with both strings are output to the screen. Other possible command combinations include the following:

```
# who | grep mj
# ps aux | grep mozilla
```

The first command, who, lists all users currently logged onto your Linux system. When you pipe (|) the result to the grep mj command, you'll find the number of times that user mj is currently logged onto your system.

The second command, ps, lists the processes currently running on your Linux system. The three switches, aux (a dash is not required for ps command switches), leads to a very long list of processes, because it includes all processes run by all users (a), each associated with the username (u), independent of the virtual terminal (x). You need a tool like grep to search through these processes. This combined command returns all processes with the word *mozilla*.

Using the *vi* Editor

Linux relies on a large number of text files for configuration. Therefore, you need a text editor to configure Linux. The vi editor may seem old. It certainly isn't the most popular editor even in the

Linux community. The one- or two-letter commands are cryptic, but if you ever need to rescue your system with a boot disk, vi may be the only editor at your disposal.

It is easy to open a file with vi. For example, if you want to open the /etc/inittab file, use this command:

```
# vi /etc/inittab
```

There are three basic ways to work in vi. Command mode is the default; you use insert mode when you want to insert text; and with a few special characters, execute mode can be used to run regular shell commands.

Command Mode

When you open a file in vi, the first mode is command mode. This is what you use to scroll through text, search for different text strings, or delete specific characters, words, or lines.

One aid in vi is line numbers, which you can activate by typing the following in the editor, which should lead to a result that looks similar to Figure 6.3:

```
:set nu
```

FIGURE 6.3

vi with line numbers

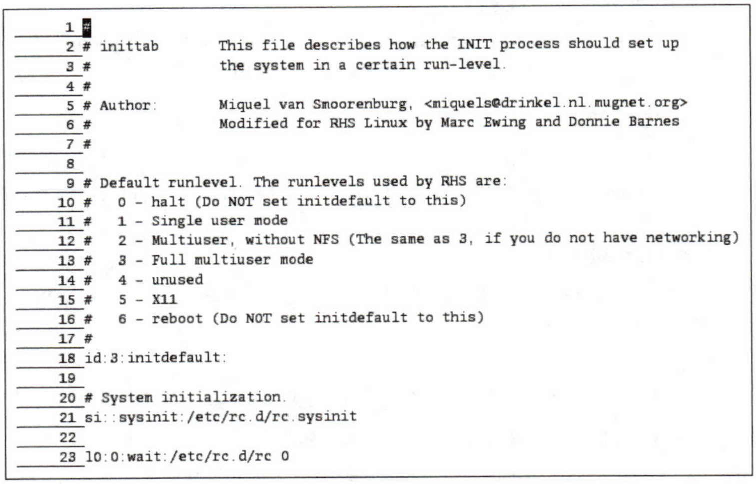

```
    1 #
    2 # inittab        This file describes how the INIT process should set up
    3 #                the system in a certain run-level.
    4 #
    5 # Author:        Miquel van Smoorenburg, <miquels@drinkel.nl.mugnet.org>
    6 #                Modified for RHS Linux by Marc Ewing and Donnie Barnes
    7 #
    8
    9 # Default runlevel. The runlevels used by RHS are:
   10 #   0 - halt (Do NOT set initdefault to this)
   11 #   1 - Single user mode
   12 #   2 - Multiuser, without NFS (The same as 3, if you do not have networking)
   13 #   3 - Full multiuser mode
   14 #   4 - unused
   15 #   5 - X11
   16 #   6 - reboot (Do NOT set initdefault to this)
   17 #
   18 id:3:initdefault:
   19
   20 # System initialization.
   21 si::sysinit:/etc/rc.d/rc.sysinit
   22
   23 l0:0:wait:/etc/rc.d/rc 0
```

GETTING AROUND

Although current versions of vi allow you to use the directional keys on your keyboard (arrows, Page Up, Page Down), this editor was designed for older U.S. keyboards that did not have these keys. Four lowercase letters take the place of the navigational arrows on the standard U.S. keyboard:

h	Left arrow
j	Down arrow
k	Up arrow
l	Right arrow

The alternatives to the Page Up and Page Down keys are Ctrl+B (back) and Ctrl+F (forward), respectively.

If you already know the line number you want, the G command can help. When used alone, it takes you to the last line in the file. When used with a line number, such as 20G, it takes you to the desired line. As with Linux shells, case makes a difference, so make sure that you're using the uppercase G for this command.

DELETING TEXT

It is easy to delete text in vi. Three deletion commands are associated with the current location of the cursor:

x	Deletes the current character, even if that character is a blank space or a tab
dw	Deletes the current word
dd	Deletes the current line

If you accidentally delete something, the u command reverses the last command entered.

SEARCHING FOR TEXT

It is easy to search for text in vi. Just start with a forward slash. For example, if you want to search for the word *dollar* in a file, type the following:

```
/dollar
```

The cursor highlights the first place this word is found in the file. To proceed to the next instance of this word, type **n**. Just remember, case matters in a search in the vi editor.

Insert Mode

When you want to insert text into a file, use insert mode. There are several ways to do this, relative to the current location of the cursor (see Table 6.11).

TABLE 6.11: INSERT MODE OPTIONS

COMMAND	ACTION	COMMENT
i	Insert	Everything you type is inserted, starting at the current position of the cursor.
a	Append	Everything you type is inserted, starting one character after the current position of the cursor. This is closely related to A, where everything you type is inserted, starting at the end of the line with the cursor.
o	Open	Everything you type is inserted, starting one line below the current position of the cursor. Closely related is O (uppercase), where everything you type is inserted, starting one line above the current position of the cursor.
cw	Change word	Deletes the word (or space) that corresponds to the current position of the cursor. You get to insert text starting with that word.

In any case, getting out of insert mode is easy; just press the Esc key on your keyboard.

Execute Mode

You can run regular shell commands from inside the vi editor. Just type :!, followed by the command. For example, if you were creating a script, you might need to know the directory location of a certain file. You could list the files in the /etc/cron.daily directory with the following command:

```
:!ls /etc/cron.daily
```

Regular execute mode starts with the colon (:). Several file management commands are associated with execute mode, including :q (to exit a file) and :w (to write the current text to the file). A number of basic commands for vi in all modes are shown in Table 6.12.

TIP   If you want to exit from vi without saving any changes, use the !q command.

TABLE 6.12: BASIC *VI* COMMANDS

COMMAND	DESCRIPTION
a	Starts insert mode after the current cursor position.
A	Starts insert mode by appending at the end of the current line.
cw	Deletes the current word and then enters insert mode to allow you to replace that word.
dw	Deletes the current word without entering insert mode.
dd	Deletes the current line.
G	Moves the cursor to the end of the line.
15G	Moves the cursor to the fifteenth line.
h	Moves the cursor left one space.
I	Enters insert mode.
o	Enters insert mode by opening a line directly below the current cursor.
O	(Uppercase O) Enters insert mode by opening a line directly above the current cursor.
:q	Exits from vi. If you have made changes and want to quit without saving, use :q!.
r	Replace; the next character that you type replaces the current character.
:set nu	Activates line numbers for the current file.
u	Undoes the last change.
:w	Writes the current file.
Esc	Exits from insert mode.
/system	Searches for the word system in the current file.

Understanding Other Text Editors

Obviously, vi is not the only text editor available in Linux. Three other major text editors are emacs, pico, and joe. None of these editors are currently installed in Red Hat Linux by default. Because this is not a book on text editors, we cover those three only briefly.

emacs

The emacs editor may be the most popular text editor used in the Linux/Unix world today. Once you've installed the emacs RPM, you can use it to open text files, just as you can with vi. For example, to open up /etc/inittab in emacs, just run the following command:

```
# emacs /etc/inittab
```

NOTE   *RPM is the Red Hat Package Manager, the standard way Red Hat organizes software; this system is covered in Chapter 10.*

As you can see in Figure 6.4, opening emacs in a GUI brings up a menu-driven interface. If you want to know more about emacs, start the tutorial with the Ctrl+h t command.

FIGURE 6.4

The emacs editor

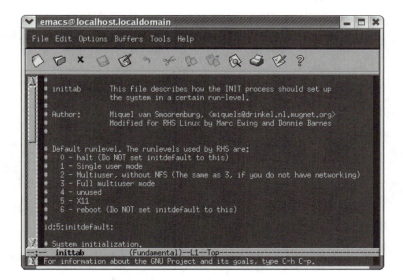

pico

Another popular Linux/Unix editor is pico, which is installed as part of the pine e-mail RPM package. Once you've installed the pine RPM, you can use pico to open text files. For example, to open /etc/inittab in pico, just run the following command:

```
# pico /etc/inittab
```

As you can see in Figure 6.5, opening `pico` in a GUI brings up a Control character-driven interface. The control character, as shown in Figure 6.5, is a ^. For example, the exit command shown is ^X, which you can run with the Ctrl+x command.

Some of the available commands are shown at the bottom of the screen. As you can see, help and additional commands are available through the Get Help screen, which you can access with the Ctrl+g command.

FIGURE 6.5

The `pico` editor

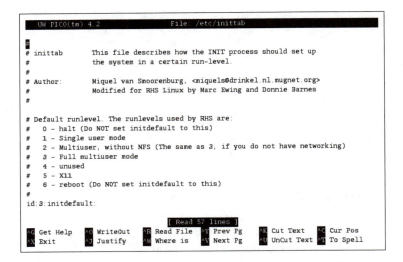

joe

Another popular Linux/Unix editor is `joe`, also known as "Joe's own editor." Once you've installed the `joe` RPM, you can use it to open text files. For example, to open up /etc/inittab in `joe`, just run the following command:

```
# joe /etc/inittab
```

Opening `joe` in a GUI brings up a Control character-driven interface. Unfortunately, the F1 key does not bring up help; the Ctrl+k h command is required. Some of the available commands are shown at the top of the screen, as you can see in Figure 6.6.

FIGURE 6.6

The joe editor

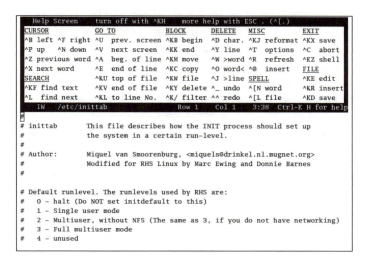

Summary

In this chapter, we looked at some of the basic commands that you can use at the command-line interface. Navigational commands can help you get around the Linux directory structure. Other commands can help you create, copy, move, delete, and link files and directories.

You can manage files by classifying their file types. You can also read the text in each file in a number of different ways. Linux lets you manipulate text files by counting lines, words, and characters; searching for specific files on your system; and searching for text within specific files. Command combinations help you focus on the information that you need.

Perhaps the most important Linux text editor is vi. While it is not the most popular text editor, it may be all you have available if you ever have to rescue your Linux system. The vi editor includes three modes: command, insert, and execute. Other major Linux editors include emacs, pico, and joe.

Now that you know some basic shell and vi editing commands, you're ready for Chapter 7, where you'll learn about the structure of Linux directories and the setup of some key configuration files. The next chapter also will help you learn how to manage, format, label, and troubleshoot different hard disk partitions. With Logical Volume Management, you can even expand and contract virtual partitions to meet your needs.

Chapter 7

A Filesystem Primer

EVERYTHING IN LINUX IS configured as a file. In Chapter 6, you worked with regular files and links to other files. As you learned, directories are just special types of files. In addition, hardware device drivers and partitions are represented by files. The organizational system for Linux files is known as the Filesystem Hierarchy Standard (FHS).

Filesystems are typically mounted on specific partitions. Linux servers often include several filesystems on different partitions. You can create partitions with fdisk or Disk Druid, and format them to one of several standards. When you document the result in /etc/fstab, during the boot process Linux mounts the partitions as specified.

When you divide a hard drive into different partitions, you lose some flexibility; it isn't easy to expand the space available to a dedicated filesystem such as /home. The Logical Volume Management (LVM) system makes it possible to expand the size of a filesystem. This chapter covers the following topics:

- ◆ Understanding the Filesystem Hierarchy Standard

- ◆ Managing partitions

- ◆ Using formats and journals

- ◆ Mastering /etc/fstab

- ◆ Exploring Logical Volume Management

Understanding the Filesystem Hierarchy Standard

When you install Linux, you can mount all of the Linux directories on a single partition. Alternatively, you can set up just about any Linux directory as a distinct filesystem by mounting it in a separate partition.

Establishing separate partitions limits risks to your system. For example, web servers such as Apache can accumulate log files that can consume gigabytes of space, easily crowding out all free space on your hard drive. Your users would no longer be able to save files, there would be no room for Linux to prepare print jobs, and chaos would undoubtedly result.

However, if you mount the right directory in a separate partition, your users can still work and save files even if the partition with the log files becomes full.

The Basic Linux Directory Structure

Before you select partitions for your Linux system, you first need to be familiar with the options in Linux directories. Red Hat Linux organizes files into directories according to the Filesystem Hierarchy Standard (FHS):

/   The top-level root directory. All other directories are below the root directory in the filesystem hierarchy. In other words, they are *subdirectories*. Any directory not mounted in a separate partition is automatically part of the root directory volume.

/bin   Contains basic command-line utilities. You should not configure this directory in a separate partition. If you do, you won't be able to access these utilities in `linux rescue` mode.

/boot   Includes the commands and files required for Linux to boot on your computer, such as the Grand Unified Bootloader (GRUB), the Initial RAM disk, and the Linux kernel. If you have a larger drive (over 8GB), it is generally a good idea to mount **/boot** in a separate partition. This helps to ensure that your Linux boot files remain accessible when you start your computer.

/dev   Lists available device drivers. For example, if you mount a floppy drive, you might mount `/dev/fd0` onto a directory such as `/mnt/floppy`. You should not mount this directory in a separate partition.

/etc   Contains basic Linux configuration files, including those related to passwords, daemons such as Apache and Samba, and the X Window.

/home   Includes home directories for all but the root user. If you mount this directory in a separate partition, leave enough room for each of your users to add files.

/initrd   Configures an empty directory used by the Initial RAM disk during the boot process. Do not mount this directory in a separate partition. If you delete this directory, Red Hat Linux will not boot; you'll get a `kernel panic` message. This directory is not a formal part of the FHS.

/lib   Lists program libraries needed by a number of different applications as well as the Linux kernel. You should not mount this directory in a separate partition.

/lost+found   Contains orphan files. Utilities such as `fsck` place empty unidentifiable files (or parts of files) in this directory. This directory is not a formal part of the FHS.

/misc   Notes a common mount point for shared NFS directories. This directory is not a formal part of the FHS.

/mnt   Contains the mount point of removable media, such as floppy (`/mnt/floppy`), CD-ROM (`/mnt/cdrom`), and Zip (`/mnt/zip`) drives.

/opt   Includes the standard locations for third-party applications such as Sun StarOffice or Corel WordPerfect.

/proc Includes all kernel-related processes that are currently running. Some of the files in this directory list current resource allocations; for example, /proc/interrupts lists currently allocated interrupt request (IRQ) ports.

/root The home directory for the root user. The /root directory is a subdirectory of the root (/) directory. Do not mount this directory separately.

/sbin Contains many system administration commands. Do not mount this directory separately.

/tftpboot Supports diskless workstations, also known as remote terminals. The diskless workstation mounts this directory from the Linux terminal server. This directory is not a formal part of the FHS.

/tmp Serves as a dedicated storage location for temporary files; also a good place to download files. By default, the /etc/cron.daily/tmpwatch script empties files older than 10 days from this directory.

/usr Includes programs and data available to all users; contains many subdirectories. For example, the programs associated with the OpenOffice suite are installed in /usr/bin.

/var Contains variable data, including log files and print spools. On Linux servers, this directory is frequently mounted on a separate partition.

NOTE The top-level root directory, /, is different from the home directory of the root user, /root. In fact, /root is a subdirectory of /.

You'll want to mount some of these directories on separate hard drive partitions. For example, by mounting /home on a separate partition, you ensure that this directory will always have access to the space on that partition. In addition, by mounting /var on a separate partition, you can keep runaway log files from crowding out space needed by files in other directories. In the sections that follow, we discuss this approach in greater depth.

Partition Schemes

You now know that Linux provides a variety of ways to set up partitions. To help guide your efforts, there are a few standard partition schemes. By default, when you install Red Hat Linux, you will set up at least two directories on separate partitions: the root (/) directory and /boot. The /boot directory is commonly mounted on its own partition because many Linux installations cannot start if the files in the /boot directory are stored above hard drive cylinder 1024.

NOTE For most newer computers, configuring the /boot directory above cylinder 1024 can work with LBA enabled; see Chapter 3, for more information. (LBA stands for Logical Block addressing, which is the way a BIOS looks at the cylinders, heads, and sectors of a hard drive.)

When you install Red Hat Linux in the Server configuration, the default includes several more mounted directories: /home, /usr, and /var. Other configurations may be appropriate if you're installing different Linux directories on different physical hard drives. Table 7.1 contains a short list of possible Linux partition configurations.

TABLE 7.1: POSSIBLE LINUX PARTITION CONFIGURATIONS

MOUNTED DIRECTORIES	COMMENT
/, swap	Typical configuration for a computer with one small hard drive.
/, /boot, swap	Typical configuration for a computer with a large hard drive. This is the default configuration for the Red Hat Linux 9 Personal Desktop and Workstation installation.
/, /boot, /var, swap	Possible configuration where log file size, such as from a web server, is an issue. This can prevent runaway log files from crowding out all free space on your Linux computer.
/, /boot, /home, swap	Possible configuration for a Linux server with home directories for a number of other users. With other measures such as quotas, this can help regulate the amount of space taken by individual users.

Managing Partitions

When you partition a hard drive, you organize it into sections, which can then be formatted. Every hard drive requires at least one partition. In fact, you can divide a standard hard drive into 15 or 16 different partitions, depending on whether it is an IDE (Integrated Drive Electronics) or SCSI (Small Computer Systems Interface) drive.

You can configure three different types of partitions on a hard drive:

Primary partition   You can create up to four different primary partitions on an IDE or a SCSI hard drive. One primary partition must be active; it should include a bootloader such as GRUB, the Linux Loader (LILO), or the Windows NT/2000/XP bootloader.

Extended partition   If you need more partitions, you can convert one primary partition into an extended partition. The extended partition then can be further subdivided into logical partitions.

Logical partition   An extended partition can be subdivided into the logical partitions that you need. You can have up to 11 logical partitions on a SCSI hard drive or up to 12 logical partitions on an IDE hard drive.

In Chapter 3, you used Disk Druid to create different partitions during the Red Hat Linux installation process. However, Disk Druid is not available once Linux is installed; your only option is to use the fdisk utility.

Adding Partitions with *fdisk*

The fdisk utility is the traditional tool for managing partitions. While functionally similar to the MS-DOS tool of the same name, the Linux fdisk utility looks different and is much more versatile. It can help you manage the empty space on an existing drive. It lets you configure up to four primary partitions on a hard drive. You can use fdisk to change the type of partition to one of over 100 different types, including FAT32, Novell NetWare, Linux Logical Volume Manager, Linux Swap, and, of course, a standard Linux partition.

ADDING A NEW HARD DRIVE

As a Linux administrator, you need to know how to add new hard drives to your servers. Once you've physically connected your hardware, make sure your PC recognizes it through your BIOS or other means. If your PC doesn't recognize it, there may be a problem with the new hard disk or the connections.

Once you've added a new hard drive, you need to set it up and configure it. The basic hard drive configuration utility is fdisk. Take a look at Figure 7.1, which illustrates a configuration with two different physical hard drives.

FIGURE 7.1

fdisk shows
two hard drives

```
[root@RH9Desk root]# fdisk -l

Disk /dev/sda: 4293 MB, 4293596160 bytes
255 heads, 63 sectors/track, 522 cylinders
Units = cylinders of 16065 * 512 = 8225280 bytes

   Device Boot    Start      End    Blocks   Id  System
/dev/sda1   *         1       13    104391   83  Linux
/dev/sda2            14      474  3702982+   83  Linux
/dev/sda3           475      522   385560    82  Linux swap

Disk /dev/sdb: 1073 MB, 1073741824 bytes
128 heads, 32 sectors/track, 512 cylinders
Units = cylinders of 4096 * 512 = 2097152 bytes

Disk /dev/sdb doesn't contain a valid partition table
[root@RH9Desk root]#
```

As you can see, the fdisk -l command lists partition tables on the local computer. In this case, there are two different physical SCSI hard disks, designated /dev/sda and /dev/sdb. The /dev/sda hard drive includes a number of different partitions.

Note the number of cylinders in /dev/sda. Because that is the same number as the last cylinder of the last /dev/sda partition, you know that no room is available for additional partitions on the first SCSI hard drive.

As shown in Figure 7.1, no partitions are associated with /dev/sdb. As noted by the output from fdisk -l, the second SCSI hard drive does not contain a valid partition table. It's time to do something about that. Use fdisk to open up the second SCSI hard drive with the following command:

```
# fdisk /dev/sdb
```

NOTE *Depending on the value of your PATH variable, you may need to specify the full path to a command such as* fdisk. *If the* fdisk *command does not work by itself, try* /sbin/fdisk. *For more information on PATH, see Chapter 8.*

If this is a completely new hard drive, you'll see a message telling you the hard drive does not contain a valid partition table. If you don't see this message, it probably means that someone has used the hard drive before. In either case, the next thing you'll see is the fdisk utility prompt:

```
Command (m for help):
```

Now press the m command to see the options available within the fdisk utility. The more important commands are described in Table 7.2.

TABLE 7.2: *FDISK* COMMANDS

COMMAND	RESULT
a	Sets or unsets the bootable flag. You need to make at least one primary partition on one of your first two hard drives bootable.
d	Deletes a partition. Before a partition is actually deleted, you need to select the partition number.
l	Lists known partition types. Over 100 different partition types are available.
m	Shows available fdisk commands.
n	Configures a new partition.
p	Lists the current partition table.
q	Exits fdisk without saving changes.
t	Allows you to change the partition system ID. You'll also need the partition number and the ID of the partition type you want, based on the known partition types (which you can find with the l command).
v	Verifies the current partition table.
w	Writes your changes and exits from fdisk. No changes are written to the partition table until you execute this command.

Now let's return to the task at hand: configuring a new hard drive. You're in the fdisk utility, and the first thing to do is to create a new partition. Issue the n command. The fdisk utility lets you choose whether you're creating a primary or an extended partition. If you already have an extended partition, fdisk allows you to create a logical partition.

```
Command (m for help): n
Command action
      e   extended
      p   primary partition (1-4)
```

Start by creating a primary partition with the p command. Make it the first primary partition, and start it with the first available cylinder. You can specify the size of the partition in cylinders, KBs, or MBs. The sequence is shown in Figure 7.2. The first partition is configured as 100MB, starting with cylinder number one. As you can see, 100MB in this case corresponds to 49 cylinders.

You can continue this process until you've configured the space you need or you've allocated all of the space on the new hard drive. Once you've finished configuring partitions, save your changes with the w command. If you want to start again, exit without saving by using the q command.

Before you can use your new partition, you need to format it to a system such as ext2, ext3, or VFAT. Details on this process are available later in this chapter.

FIGURE 7.2

Creating a new partition

```
[root@RH9Desk root]# fdisk /dev/sdb
Device contains neither a valid DOS partition table, nor Sun, SGI or OSF disklabel
Building a new DOS disklabel. Changes will remain in memory only,
until you decide to write them. After that, of course, the previous
content won't be recoverable.

Warning: invalid flag 0x0000 of partition table 4 will be corrected by w(rite)

Command (m for help): n
Command action
   e   extended
   p   primary partition (1-4)
p
Partition number (1-4): 1
First cylinder (1-512, default 1): 1
Last cylinder or +size or +sizeM or +sizeK (1-512, default 512): +100M

Command (m for help): p

Disk /dev/sdb: 1073 MB, 1073741824 bytes
128 heads, 32 sectors/track, 512 cylinders
Units = cylinders of 4096 * 512 = 2097152 bytes

   Device Boot    Start      End    Blocks   Id  System
/dev/sdb1              1       49    100336   83  Linux

Command (m for help): █
```

MANAGING AN EXISTING HARD DRIVE

If you installed Red Hat Linux on a very large hard drive, you may have some extra space available. Remember, you can configure up to 15 or 16 different partitions on your hard drive, depending on whether it is an IDE or a SCSI drive. In this section, we'll toggle a bootable partition, add a new extended partition, and then add and delete a logical partition.

It's easy to make a partition bootable. Once in the fdisk utility, run the a command. Select the appropriate primary partition, and fdisk adds the bootable label. Figure 7.3 illustrates this process.

FIGURE 7.3

Making a partition bootable

```
[root@RH9Desk root]# fdisk /dev/sdb

Command (m for help): p

Disk /dev/sdb: 1073 MB, 1073741824 bytes
128 heads, 32 sectors/track, 512 cylinders
Units = cylinders of 4096 * 512 = 2097152 bytes

   Device Boot    Start      End    Blocks   Id  System
/dev/sdb1              1       49    100336   83  Linux

Command (m for help): a
Partition number (1-4): 1

Command (m for help): p

Disk /dev/sdb: 1073 MB, 1073741824 bytes
128 heads, 32 sectors/track, 512 cylinders
Units = cylinders of 4096 * 512 = 2097152 bytes

   Device Boot    Start      End    Blocks   Id  System
/dev/sdb1      *       1       49    100336   83  Linux

Command (m for help): ▯
```

You can install a bootloader such as GRUB or LILO on a bootable partition on one of the first two hard drives on your computer.

Based on the configuration shown back in Figure 7.2, there are 463 free cylinders still available on the new hard drive. The space under the Boot column is empty. And this is specifically labeled as a Linux partition.

Now that you're more familiar with `fdisk`, creating extended and logical partitions is fairly easy. However, you can also select different cylinders. Figure 7.4 shows one set of commands that you could use to create an extended and a logical partition.

FIGURE 7.4

Adding extended and logical partitions

```
Command (m for help): n
Command action
   e   extended
   p   primary partition (1-4)
e
Partition number (1-4): 4
First cylinder (50-512, default 50): 200
Last cylinder or +size or +sizeM or +sizeK (200-512, default 512): 512

Command (m for help): n
Command action
   l   logical (5 or over)
   p   primary partition (1-4)
l
First cylinder (200-512, default 200): 200
Last cylinder or +size or +sizeM or +sizeK (200-512, default 512): +300M

Command (m for help): p

Disk /dev/sdb: 1073 MB, 1073741824 bytes
128 heads, 32 sectors/track, 512 cylinders
Units = cylinders of 4096 * 512 = 2097152 bytes

   Device Boot      Start         End      Blocks   Id  System
/dev/sdb1               1          49      100336   83  Linux
/dev/sdb4             200         512      641024    5  Extended
/dev/sdb5             200         343      294896   83  Linux

Command (m for help):
```

Note how the cylinders of the first logical partition, `/dev/sdb5`, are contained within the cylinders of the extended partition. All logical partitions must fit within the space available to an extended partition.

Revising Partition Labels

You can use `fdisk` to configure partitions for swap space for LVM, or even for other operating systems.

When you use the Linux `fdisk` utility to create a new partition, it sets up the new partition with a Linux label by default. You can configure such partitions to the basic Linux formats: ext2, ext3, xfs, reiserfs, and so forth. However, there are a number of other ways to label a partition.

Use `fdisk` to open the hard drive with the partition you want to change. The following is based on Figure 7.4.

Now use the `t` command within `fdisk` to change the partition label. You'll need to select the partition number and then enter the hex code associated with the desired system. For example, the following commands changes the `/dev/sdb5` logical partition to the Linux swap system:

```
Command (m for help): t
Partition number (1-5): 5
```

```
Hex code (type L to list codes): 82
Changed system type of partition 5 to 82 (Linux swap)
```

As you can see in Figure 7.5, you can set a partition to be usable by a wide variety of operating systems.

FIGURE 7.5

Available `fdisk` partition systems

```
Command (m for help): t
Partition number (1-5): 5
Hex code (type L to list codes): l

 0  Empty            1c  Hidden Win95 FA 70  DiskSecure Mult bb  Boot Wizard hid
 1  FAT12            1e  Hidden Win95 FA 75  PC/IX           be  Solaris boot
 2  XENIX root       24  NEC DOS         80  Old Minix       c1  DRDOS/sec (FAT-
 3  XENIX usr        39  Plan 9          81  Minix / old Lin c4  DRDOS/sec (FAT-
 4  FAT16 <32M       3c  PartitionMagic  82  Linux swap      c6  DRDOS/sec (FAT-
 5  Extended         40  Venix 80286     83  Linux           c7  Syrinx
 6  FAT16            41  PPC PReP Boot    84  OS/2 hidden C:  da  Non-FS data
 7  HPFS/NTFS        42  SFS             85  Linux extended  db  CP/M / CTOS / .
 8  AIX              4d  QNX4.x          86  NTFS volume set de  Dell Utility
 9  AIX bootable     4e  QNX4.x 2nd part 87  NTFS volume set df  BootIt
 a  OS/2 Boot Manag  4f  QNX4.x 3rd part 8e  Linux LVM       e1  DOS access
 b  Win95 FAT32      50  OnTrack DM      93  Amoeba          e3  DOS R/O
 c  Win95 FAT32 (LB  51  OnTrack DM6 Aux 94  Amoeba BBT      e4  SpeedStor
 e  Win95 FAT16 (LB  52  CP/M            9f  BSD/OS          eb  BeOS fs
 f  Win95 Ext'd (LB  53  OnTrack DM6 Aux a0  IBM Thinkpad hi ee  EFI GPT
10  OPUS             54  OnTrackDM6      a5  FreeBSD         ef  EFI (FAT-12/16/
11  Hidden FAT12     55  EZ-Drive        a6  OpenBSD         f0  Linux/PA-RISC b
12  Compaq diagnost  56  Golden Bow      a7  NeXTSTEP        f1  SpeedStor
14  Hidden FAT16 <3  5c  Priam Edisk     a8  Darwin UFS      f4  SpeedStor
16  Hidden FAT16     61  SpeedStor       a9  NetBSD          f2  DOS secondary
17  Hidden HPFS/NTF  63  GNU HURD or Sys ab  Darwin boot     fd  Linux raid auto
18  AST SmartSleep   64  Novell Netware  b7  BSDI fs         fe  LANstep
1b  Hidden Win95 FA  65  Novell Netware  b8  BSDI swap       ff  BBT
Hex code (type L to list codes): []
```

Later in this chapter, you'll take the final steps to get new partitions ready for data. But first, partitions have labels that help Linux use `/etc/fstab` to mount the partitions that you need. Let's take a look.

Using Formats and Journals

As you've seen in Figure 7.5, there are many ways to format a filesystem for different operating systems. In addition, there are several ways to format a partition for Linux. The latest versions of Linux include journaling features, which promote quick recovery from drive crashes. Each of these procedures set up different types of labels for your partitions.

Basic Linux Formats

As you've learned, you can format a filesystem in several different ways. While the current default for Red Hat Linux is the third extended filesystem, ext3, a number of other Linux filesystems are available that you may want to use. Table 7.3 lists the major Linux filesystem formats.

Linux is moving toward journaling filesystems. A journal records all pending changes, such as data to be written to disk. If a drive crashes, Linux can check the journal for pending changes. No disk check is required, which can save considerable time.

TABLE 7.3: MAJOR LINUX FILESYSTEM FORMATS

FORMAT	DESCRIPTION
ext2	The second extended filesystem, which was the standard for Red Hat Linux through 2001. If you have older systems with ext2 partitions, they are easy to convert to ext3.
ext3	The third extended filesystem, which is the current default for Red Hat Linux. Includes a journal, which records all pending changes, such as data to be written to disk.
reiserfs	The Reiser filesystem, which is based on different designs from the Linux extended filesystems.
xfs	The Silicon Graphics filesystem, which supports extremely large hard drives.

Several other Linux type filesystems are available, including ext, bfs, minix, xia, and jfs. None of these filesystems are commonly used on the Linux operating system today.

Formatting a Partition

Linux configures the mkfs command as a front end to format Linux partitions. If a partition has been previously formatted, all you need is that command, and Linux will reformat the partition to the same filesystem. Otherwise, you'll need to specify the type of filesystem to be built by including the -t switch. You can also check for bad blocks before formatting with the -c switch.

The commands are fairly straightforward. For example, the following commands format the /dev/sdb1 partition to the noted filesystems:

```
# mkfs -t ext2 /dev/sdb1
# mkfs -t ext3 /dev/sdb1
# mkfs -t vfat /dev/sdb1
# mkfs -t reiserfs /dev/sdb1
```

Another way to create an ext3 filesystem is with the following command (the -j creates a journal);

```
# mkfs -j /dev/sdb1
```

Alternatively, if you're formatting a partition for Linux swap space, use the mkswap command. For example, if you want to set up /dev/sdb5 as a swap partition, the command is straightforward:

```
# mkswap /dev/sdb5
```

Tuning

It's easy to convert an older partition formatted to the ext2 filesystem to ext3. In fact, the ext3 filesystem is virtually identical to ext2. The only difference is that ext3 partitions include a journal.

Therefore, if you create a journal for an ext2 filesystem, it automatically becomes an ext3 filesystem. All you need is the tune2fs -j command. For example, the following command converts the /dev/hda1 partition from ext2 to ext3:

```
# tune2fs -j /dev/hda1
```

Disk Management

Two very similar disk management commands are available in Linux: du and df. The directory usage (du) command lists the amount of space used by each file in and below your current directory. The disk free (df) space command lists the amount of space available on each hard drive volume. Figure 7.6 shows the output you get if you run the du command in a Linux user's home directory.

FIGURE 7.6

Output from du

```
16        ./.gnome-desktop
12        ./.metacity/sessions
16        ./.metacity
4         ./.gimp-1.2/brushes
4         ./.gimp-1.2/generated_brushes
4         ./.gimp-1.2/gradients
192       ./.gimp-1.2/palettes
4         ./.gimp-1.2/patterns
4         ./.gimp-1.2/plug-ins
4         ./.gimp-1.2/modules
4         ./.gimp-1.2/scripts
4         ./.gimp-1.2/tmp
4         ./.gimp-1.2/curves
4         ./.gimp-1.2/levels
4         ./.gimp-1.2/fractalexplorer
4         ./.gimp-1.2/gfig
4         ./.gimp-1.2/gflare
4         ./.gimp-1.2/gimpressionist/Brushes
4         ./.gimp-1.2/gimpressionist/Paper
4         ./.gimp-1.2/gimpressionist/Presets
16        ./.gimp-1.2/gimpressionist
564       ./.gimp-1.2
4         ./book
1120      .
[root@RH9Desk root]#
```

The number you see on the left is the size of the file, in kilobytes, which is the default from both the df and du commands. The applicable file is shown on the right. For example, you may see the following:

```
1941    ./.gimp/tmp
```

The first dot (.) means that you start in your current directory. The slash (/) navigates to a subdirectory, in this case .gimp. In other words, this line means there are 1941 kilobytes of disk space dedicated to the .gimp/tmp subdirectory.

The df command shows how full each filesystem is on your computer. As you can see in Figure 7.7, the df -m command assesses each filesystem and displays the results in megabytes. It includes any other filesystems, such as your floppy or CD-ROM drives that are currently mounted.

The -m switch gives you results in megabytes, and the -k switch gives you results in kilobytes.

FIGURE 7.7

Output from df -m

```
[root@RH9Test root]# df -m
Filesystem          1M-blocks     Used Available Use% Mounted on
/dev/sda5                 494       85       383  19% /
/dev/sda1                  99       10        84  10% /boot
/dev/sda3                 726       17       672   3% /home
none                       62        0        61   0% /dev/shm
/dev/sda2                1984     1244       640  67% /usr
/dev/sda6                 548       51       470  10% /var
/dev/cdrom                640      641         0 100% /mnt/cdrom
//laptop2/downloads    22889     8792     14097  39% /root/downloads
/dev/fd0                    1        2         0  95% /mnt/floppy
[root@RH9Test root]#
```

Extended Partition Data

Linux includes a substantial amount of data with each partition, which you can access with commands such as `e2label` and `dumpe2fs`. When you install Red Hat Linux, Linux partitions that you create during the installation process are automatically given appropriate label data. For example, I can get the following from this command:

```
# e2label /dev/sda1
/boot
```

As you will see later in this chapter, labels can be important. The default /etc/fstab uses disk labels. You can also find disk labels in the GRUB configuration file. But when you configure a new partition with `fdisk` and format it with `mkfs`, neither command adds a label. So if you want to mount the /home/mj directory on the /dev/sdb1 partition, you should also label it with the following command:

```
# e2label /dev/sdb1 /home/mj
```

Alternatively, you can get more information about a partition with the `dumpe2fs` command. Look at Figure 7.8, which illustrates a partition with the /home/mj label.

FIGURE 7.8

Find filesystem data with `dumpe2fs`

```
dumpe2fs 1.32 (09-Nov-2002)
Filesystem volume name:   <none>
Last mounted on:          <not available>
Filesystem UUID:          3922f241-1d2a-42d8-b891-d0a104b2306f
Filesystem magic number:  0xEF53
Filesystem revision #:    1 (dynamic)
Filesystem features:      has_journal filetype sparse_super
Default mount options:    (none)
Filesystem state:         clean
Errors behavior:          Continue
Filesystem OS type:       Linux
Inode count:              26208
Block count:              104448
Reserved block count:     5222
Free blocks:              97006
Free inodes:              26197
First block:              1
Block size:               1024
Fragment size:            1024
Blocks per group:         8192
Fragments per group:      8192
Inodes per group:         2016
Inode blocks per group:   252
Filesystem created:       Fri Mar  7 07:01:03 2003
Last mount time:          n/a
--More--
```

You can even check the last time this partition was mounted with the Last Mount Time variable from the `dumpe2fs` output; in this case n/a means that no directory has been mounted on this platform.

Mounting Directories

Before you can read or write to a Linux partition, you need to mount it. Without any help, you need to specify the partition, the directory being mounted, and the format associated with the partition. A typical syntax of the `mount` command is as follows:

```
# mount -t format partition directory
```

The *format* is the way the partition is configured, such as ext2, ext3, or vfat. The *partition* is the hard drive device being mounted, such as /dev/sda1 or /dev/hda1. And the *directory*, also known as the mount point, is the part of the Linux directory structure allocated to that partition, such as /boot, /home, or /var.

In other words, you could mount the /home/mj directory on the /dev/sdb1 partition that has been formatted to the ext3 filesystem with the following command:

```
# mount -t ext3 /dev/sdb1 /home/mj
```

This is more complicated than is normally required. With the list of formats in the /etc/filesystems configuration file, the mount command can look through this file and find a format that matches the /dev/sdb1 partition. So all you need is the following command:

```
# mount /dev/sdb1 /home/mj
```

You can make this even simpler. If you add the following line to your /etc/fstab configuration file, you need to specify only the partition or the directory:

```
/dev/sdb1    /home/mj      ext3  defaults  1 2
```

In this case, either of the following commands would work:

```
# mount /dev/sdb1
# mount /home/mj
```

Sometimes it's important to unmount a directory. For example, Linux locks the CD drive on many computers until you unmount the relevant directory with a command such as:

```
# umount /mnt/cdrom
```

Note that this command is spelled umount, not *unmount*.

Troubleshooting

The failure of a filesystem can be more troubling than problems booting Linux. As you'll see in Chapter 11, there are established methods for getting around boot problems. However, filesystem problems are more difficult to diagnose. They can be a sign of corrupted files, misaligned blocks, troubled configuration files, or even bad hardware.

Filesystem problems normally require troubleshooting during the boot process. Linux may have trouble mounting a specific partition, or a check of the filesystem integrity fails in some way. In either case, you may see a message that the fsck operation failed and that you need to type in the root password to gain access to Linux. An example of this situation is shown in Figure 7.9.

The fsck command is an important tool. It is used by Linux periodically to automatically check most of the partitions on your system. If you don't have a filesystem integrity problem, you may just need to adjust a parameter and remount a filesystem, such as the root (/) directory.

FSCK

The fsck command is used to check and repair Linux filesystems. As with mkfs, it is a front end to commands that are dedicated to relevant filesystems, such as fsck.ext2, fsck.ext3, and fsck.reiserfs. If the filesystem format is known, the fsck command is all you need. If the partition is formatted to ext3, the `fsck.ext3` command is called automatically. Several key switches for this command are shown in Table 7.4.

FIGURE 7.9

Linux's response to a filesystem problem

```
Initializing USB keyboard:                                    [  OK  ]
Initializing USB mouse:                                       [  OK  ]
Checking root filesystem
/: clean, 73416/463072 files, 308960/925745 blocks
                                                              [  OK  ]
Remounting root filesystem in read-write mode:                [  OK  ]
Activating swap partitions:                                   [  OK  ]
Finding module dependencies:                                  [  OK  ]
Checking filesystems
fsck.ext3/dev/sdb1:
The superblock could not be read or does not describe a correct ext2
filesystem.  If the device is valid and it really contains an ext2
filesystem (and not swap or ufs or something else), then the superblock
is corrupt, and you might try running e2fsck with an alternate superblock:
    e2fsck -b 8193 <device>

/boot: clean, 41/26104 files, 12727/104391 blocks
: Bad magic number in super-block while trying to open /dev/sdb1
                                                              [FAILED]

*** An error occurred during the file system check.
*** Dropping you to a shell; the system will reboot
*** when you leave the shell.
Give root password for maintenance
(or type Control-D to continue): _
```

TABLE 7.4: *FSCK* COMMAND SWITCHES

SWITCH	EXPLANATION
-a	Automatically repairs target filesystems without prompts. Should be used only within /etc/rc.sysinit.
-b *superblock*	Use a different superblock. Optional superblocks can be found via the dumpe2fs command.
-A	Check all filesystems listed in /etc/fstab.
-R	When -A is used, skip the root (/) directory filesystem.
-y	When fsck suggests a solution, it sets a default answer of "yes."

WARNING   *Do not run* fsck *on a mounted partition. It can lead to severe filesystem damage.*

If you suspect a problem, you can run fsck on any unmounted partition. Generally, you should accept the default suggestions for repairing any filesystem problems. While some data may be lost, this process should make your partition bootable again. At that point, you should be able to reboot Linux cleanly.

NOTE   *Incidentally, the pronunciation of* fsck *varies; some may say* ef es *check, while others may talk about running the* fisk *command on a partition.*

AUTOMATED PARTITION CHECKS

The `fsck` command is no longer run periodically by default. However, you can change this by using the `tune2fs -c count /dev/partition` command. To find the mount count information for a specific partition, use the `dumpe2fs` command. The relevant output is shown in Figure 7.10.

FIGURE 7.10

Periodic partition check information

```
Inode blocks per group:   255
Filesystem created:       Wed Mar 26 05:06:00 2003
Last mount time:          Wed Mar 26 15:16:24 2003
Last write time:          Wed Mar 26 15:16:24 2003
Mount count:              8
Maximum mount count:      -1
Last checked:             Wed Mar 26 05:06:00 2003
Check interval:           0 (<none>)
Reserved blocks uid:      0 (user root)
Reserved blocks gid:      0 (group root)
First inode:              11
Inode size:               128
Journal UUID:             <none>
Journal inode:            8
Journal device:           0x0000
First orphan inode:       0


Group 0: (Blocks 1-8192)
  Primary superblock at 1, Group descriptors at 2-2
  Block bitmap at 3 (+2), Inode bitmap at 4 (+3)
  Inode table at 5-259 (+4)
  0 free blocks, 2014 free inodes, 2 directories
--More--
```

MOUNTING AND REMOUNTING

One of the options in the rescue modes discussed in Chapter 11 is to mount filesystems such as root (/) in read-only mode. Once you've made the necessary changes, you can mount that filesystem in read-write mode. Alternatively, you may want to mount a filesystem with programs such as /usr in read-only mode.

Eventually, you may want to change the /etc/fstab configuration file and reboot Linux. However, you can test your changes first by remounting the directory with the desired options. For example, if you want to remount the root (/) directory in read-write mode, use the following command:

```
# mount -o remount,rw /
```

Or if you want to remount /usr in read-only mode, you could use the following command:

```
# mount -o remount,ro /usr
```

Remember, changes with this command apply only until you reboot Linux, unless you also revise the /etc/fstab file accordingly.

Mastering */etc/fstab*

Linux uses /etc/fstab during the boot process to mount partitions and directories in different ways. As shown in Figure 7.11, a number of parameters are associated with each filesystem. These parameters determine how filesystems are mounted, the way data is read, which user permissions are associated with the filesystem, and more.

FIGURE 7.11

/etc/fstab defines how directories are mounted

```
LABEL=/              /                  ext3     defaults             1 1
LABEL=/boot          /boot              ext3     defaults             1 2
none                 /dev/pts           devpts   gid=5,mode=620       0 0
LABEL=/home          /home              ext3     defaults             1 2
none                 /proc              proc     defaults             0 0
none   █             /dev/shm           tmpfs    defaults             0 0
LABEL=/usr           /usr               ext3     defaults             1 2
LABEL=/var           /var               ext3     defaults             1 2
/dev/sdb1            /home/mj            ext3     defaults             1 2
/dev/sda7            swap               swap     defaults             0 0
/dev/cdrom           /mnt/cdrom         iso9660  noauto,owner,kudzu,ro 0 0
/dev/fd0             /mnt/floppy        auto     noauto,owner,kudzu   0 0
~
~
~
~
~
~
~
~
~
~
```

As you can see, there are six different fields in each /etc/fstab line. Table 7.5 describes these fields, which are listed from left to right.

TABLE 7.5: */ETC/FSTAB* FIELDS

COLUMN	FIELD	DESCRIPTION
1	Label	The filesystem, such as /usr, or partition, such as /dev/sdb1, to be mounted.
2	Mount Point	The directory where the partition or filesystem is to be mounted.
3	Format	The Filesystem format type, such as ext2, ext3, or reiserfs.
4	Mount Options	The defaults option includes rw (read-write), suid (SUID permissions), dev (terminals and block devices such as drives), exec (binary files), auto (automatically mounted), nouser (only root can mount), and async (data is read and written asynchronously).
5	Dump Value	If 1, the filesystem is automatically written to disk.
6	Filesystem Check Order	Filesystems that need fsck. The root (/) filesystem should be 1; others on the local computer should be 2; swap, virtual, CD, floppy, and remote directories should be 0.

In most cases, a listing such as LABEL=/ is checked against the partition data on your computer to find the actual partition device, such as /dev/hda3, to be mounted.

Other mount options are available, such as usrquota and grpquota (for setting quotas), noauto (to make sure Linux doesn't look for a CD or floppy when it boots), and user (to let any user mount a filesystem, such as a CD-ROM).

Exploring Logical Volume Management

Without Logical Volume Management (LVM), the decision on how to partition your hard drives during the Red Hat Linux installation is critical. Once drives are partitioned, there is no easy way to expand the available space.

For example, assume you've set up the /home directory in a separate partition. You've planned ahead and assumed that you'll have enough space for 10 users. But your company expands, and suddenly, you need space on /home for 20 users. Without LVM, there is no easy way to expand the size of the /home partition. You would need to back up the files from /home, find a partition with the space that you need, and then restore the files to that new partition.

LVM allows you to reallocate chunks of disk space between different filesystems. So with LVM, if you have extra room in a filesystem such as /var, you can reallocate that space to /home.

You can create a LVM volume group during the installation of Red Hat Linux, as described in Chapter 3. You can also create and manage a LVM volume group using the techniques described in the following sections. Even if you've already created a LVM volume group when you installed Red Hat Linux, read on. LVM does not help unless you can use the commands described in this section to increase and decrease the size of your *logical volumes*.

Fundamentals

LVM is essentially a mapping of different physical sections of a hard drive. Once collected together into a logical volume, filesystems such as /home and /usr can be mounted on that volume. Logical volumes can be reorganized to include additional hard drive space.

That is the short version of what you can do with LVM. To really understand what happens in LVM, start with some fundamental definitions:

Physical volume (PV)   A *physical volume* (PV) usually corresponds to a standard primary or logical partition on a hard drive.

Physical extent (PE)   A *physical extent* (PE) is a chunk of disk space. Physical volumes are divided up into a number of equal sized PEs.

Logical extent (LE)   A *logical extent* (LE) is a chunk of disk space. The size of an LE in an LVM system is the same as the size of PEs on that system. Every LE corresponds to a specific PE.

Logical volume (LV)   A *logical volume* (LV) is a collection of LEs. You can mount filesystems such as /usr and /boot on an LV.

Volume group (VG)   The LVs on your system, collected together, form a *volume group* (VG). When you configure an LVM system, most commands are applied to a VG.

Creating a Physical Volume

If you're implementing LVM for the first time, it may be more convenient to configure it on a new hard drive. After installing the drive, do not install any partitions on it yet. You can create a PV on an entire hard drive. For example, if the hard drive is the slave on the secondary IDE connector, the Linux device is /dev/hdd. To create a PV on that disk, run the following command:

```
# pvcreate /dev/hdd
```

Alternatively, if you've already set up partitions with a utility such as fdisk, you can set up PVs on specific partitions. First, run fdisk to change the system ID of the desired partition. Once you're in the fdisk menu, the following commands would change hypothetical partition number 10 on a hard drive:

```
Command (m for help): t
Partition number (1-15): 1
Hex code (type L to list codes): 8e
```

Don't use this command on any partition where you want to keep the data. Once the type is changed to Linux LVM, you can then create a physical volume with a command such as:

```
# pvcreate /dev/hdd1
```

Once you've configured two or more PVs, the next step is to create a volume group.

Creating a Volume Group

A VG is a collection of PVs that are configured on one or more hard drives. You can create a VG from existing PVs. When you add more PVs, you can add them to existing VGs.

It's easy to create a VG. You can even give that VG the name of your choice, such as programs, with a command such as:

```
# vgcreate programs /dev/sdc1 /dev/sdd1
```

Once you have a VG, it's easy to add PVs with a slightly different command:

```
# vgextend programs /dev/sde1
```

Now you can organize a VG into chunks that you can set up in a PV.

Creating a Logical Volume

Finally, you can create a logical volume where you can mount a filesystem such as /home or /var. But first, you need to know the size of a PE in your volume. You can do this and more with the vgdisplay command. Using the VG created in the previous section, this requires a command like:

```
# vgdisplay programs
```

A sample output is shown in Figure 7.12. As you can see, this includes information on the maximum number of logical and physical volumes for this group, the size of this volume group, and the size of PEs in this group (in the figure, it's 4MB).

FIGURE 7.12

Volume group details

```
[root@RHL9 root]# vgdisplay programs
--- Volume group ---
VG Name                programs
VG Access              read/write
VG Status              available/resizable
VG #                   0
MAX LV                 256
Cur LV                 0
Open LV                0
MAX LV Size            255.99 GB
Max PV                 256
Cur PV                 2
Act PV                 2
VG Size                392 MB
PE Size                4 MB
Total PE               98
Alloc PE / Size        0 / 0
Free  PE / Size        98 / 392 MB
VG UUID                QqCvYP-KzSI-6ynj-0ny6-zjmr-l3Lu-Z5kHeF


[root@RHL9 root]#
```

Now you can create an LV of the size that you need, with a command such as the following:

```
# lvcreate -l num_of_PEs programs -n logicvol
```

From the above example, the name of the new LV is `logicvol`. You know that each PE is 4MB in size. If you wanted to set up a 200MB `logicvol` LVM partition, substitute 50 for *num_of_PEs*.

This creates a new device, `/dev/programs/logicvol`. You can now format and mount that device just like any other hard drive partition. For example, the following commands format it to the ext3 filesystem and mount it on the `/tmp` directory:

```
# mkfs -j /dev/programs/logicvol
# mount -t ext3 /dev/programs/logicvol /tmp
```

Now it's easy to increase the size of `/dev/programs/logicvol`. Assuming you have spare PEs, just use the `lvextend` command. The following example increases the size of `/dev/programs/logicvol` to 300MB:

```
# lvextend -L300M /dev/programs/logicvol
```

Summary

In this chapter, we examined how files and filesystems work in Linux. Files are organized in a distinct structure known as the Filesystem Hierarchy Standard (FHS). Different directories in the FHS have different functions; you can mount many of these directories on their own partitions.

The basic Linux partition management utility is `fdisk`. With this utility, you can manage the empty space on existing or newly installed hard drives. You can create and size new partitions, and set or change them for different Linux formats.

Once you have a new partition, you can format it with the `mkfs` command. It's easy to format a partition to the Red Hat Linux standard format, the ext3 filesystem. Just use the `mkfs -j` command.

You can even convert an existing ext2 partition to an ext3 partition by using the `tunefs -j` command. Red Hat Linux uses `fsck` to troubleshoot partitions on a regular basis.

The key filesystem configuration file is `/etc/fstab`, which defines how different partitions are mounted and checked.

Now with Logical Volume Management, you can vary the size of a partition based on the way you configure partitions into volume groups.

Now that you understand the basics of filesystems, the next chapter continues our exploration of the shell. You'll learn all the details you need to make the shell work effectively for you.

Chapter 8

Making the Shell Work for You

In the previous two chapters, we examined many of the fundamental commands that you need to navigate and administer Red Hat Linux. In this chapter, you'll learn the tricks of the trade that can help make the shell work for you.

The default Red Hat Linux shell is bash (short for the Bourne Again Shell). While several other shells are available, bash is the default shell created by the Free Software Foundation (`www.fsf.org`), and is therefore the shell most commonly associated with Linux.

If you are already familiar with a different shell such as Korn, C, or Z, it's okay to install the applicable RPM packages and use it. They're easy to start; the ksh, csh, and zsh commands start these shells automatically, usually at a different prompt. Like other Unix-style operating systems, Linux works well with other shells. However, if Linux is your first foray into Unix-style operating systems, I highly recommend that you learn to use bash. It is the default Linux shell, and most online Linux documentation assumes that you use bash commands.

In this chapter, you'll learn to manage the basics of bash. Then you'll examine the secrets of the shell, which can help you make different bash commands work together in a complex harmony. Finally, you'll take advantage of *environment* and *shell* variables, which can ease your transition to the bash shell. This chapter covers the following topics:

◆ Managing the shell

◆ Configuring the shell

◆ Discovering the secrets of the shell

Managing the Shell

The Bourne Again Shell (bash) is a user interface to the Linux operating system. You use bash commands to run programs, manage your files, and interact with your hardware through the Linux kernel. You can configure bash with a number of local and system-wide files and variables.

Shells such as bash are also known as command-line interpreters, which is a user interface that responds to specific commands, such as ls, cd, or cp. Shells also respond to programs or scripts that you create.

As you move around the command line, keep in mind that Linux is case sensitive. In other words, the ls command lists the files in your current directory, whereas the LS, Ls, or lS commands are meaningless in any current Linux shell.

Two ways the bash shell can help you are based on its history of previous commands and the ease with which you can complete a longer command. These characteristics are known as *interactivity* and *command completion*.

Interactivity

Interactivity allows you to run through previous commands. It also allows you to interact with current commands. You can use basic keys, such as the Home and arrow keys, to correct typos; alternatively, you can even use commands that you've used in a text editor.

INTERACTIVITY AND HISTORY

You can interact with a history of Linux commands. Open a command-line interface and type the history command. If you've previously used the command-line interface, you'll see a result similar to that shown in Figure 8.1.

FIGURE 8.1

A history of previous commands

```
 80   mount
 81   fdisk -l
 82   quota
 83   df
 84   alias
 85   mount
 86   mkdir /mnt/source
 87   mount '//laptop3/redhat' /mnt/source
 88   ls
 89   df
 90   ps
 91   vi /etc/passwd
 92   cat /etc/inittab
 93   fdisk -l
 94   switchdesk kde
 95   man dumpe2fs
 96   rpm -q kernel-source
 97   redhat-config-xfree86
 98   mount
 99   df
100   mozilla &
101   alias
102   history
[root@RH9Desk root]#
```

By default, you can repeat previous commands in several ways. The easiest way is to use the Up and Down arrow keys on your keyboard. Go to your command-line interface. When you press the Up arrow key, you'll see the previous commands that you used, in reverse order. The list may even include commands that you used during previous sessions. You can reverse the process with the Down arrow key.

Alternatively, if you remember the first letter of a recent command, use an exclamation point (!) to recall that earlier command. For example, based on the output of the history command shown in Figure 8.1, if you type !r the shell recalls the last time you used a command that started with the letter *r*—in this case, redhat-config-xfree86—and runs that command.

This feature is flexible; you can add a bit more information, such as !rp. Based on the history shown in Figure 8.1, the shell would respond by running the `rpm -q kernel-source` command. The feature lets you go back quite a bit. If you type the `env | more` command, you should find a `HISTSIZE=1000` line, which means that you can go back and rerun any of the past 1000 commands.

INTERACTIVITY AND EDITORS

You can also interact with the details of a current or a previous command. For example, take the following command, which includes a typographical error:

```
# rpm -Vvh /mnt/cdrom/RedHat/RPMS/sendmail-*
```

You realize that you should have typed the `rpm -Uvh` command, but you don't want to retype the entire command. Fortunately, you don't have to erase the entire command. You can use basic keys such as the Left and Right arrows and the Home key to move the cursor toward the beginning of the command.

Alternatively, you can use the commands that you know in a text editor. For example, if you want to set `vi` as the default command-line editor, run the following command:

```
# set -o vi
```

NOTE *The* `set` *command is counterintuitive; while* `set -o editor` *enables that* `editor`, `set +o editor` *disables it. For this command,* `editor` *can be* `emacs` *or* `vi`.

Now you can use `vi` editor commands. By default, you're in *insert mode* at the command-line interface. As we discussed in Chapter 6, you can switch to *command mode* by pressing the Esc key. Then you can apply the `vi` commands of your choice to that line. Some useful `vi` commands not described in Chapter 6 are shown in Table 8.1.

TABLE 8.1: MORE *VI* COMMANDS

COMMAND	DESCRIPTION
Home	Moves to the beginning of a line
b	Moves left one word
w	Moves right one word

Remember, other `vi` commands are available as well, such as `cw`, which deletes the current word and starts insert mode.

Command Completion

The bash shell allows you to use the Tab key to complete commands. You need to type only part of a command. For example, to use the `ypdomainname` command to find the NIS domain name for your system, type the following letters:

```
# ypd
```

When you press the Tab key, bash completes the command for you. If there is more than one available command that starts with **ypd**, press the Tab key again, and you'll see a list of these commands.

Configuring the Shell

There are two sets of configuration files for any shell. Some are system-wide; in other words, they affect all users on your Linux computer. Others are user specific and are stored in a user's home directory.

Depending on your distribution, there are two basic system-wide configuration files for bash: **/etc/bashrc** and **/etc/profile**. Each of these files contains two different kinds of variables: *shell variables*, which remain constant only within a specific shell such as bash, and *environment variables*, which stay with you even if you change shells.

In other words, shell variables are local, and environment variables are global.

Shell Variables

The default Red Hat Linux **/etc/bashrc** configuration file, shown in Figure 8.2, sets two basic shell variables: a default value for **umask**, and the prompt that you see with the cursor at the command-line interface.

FIGURE 8.2

/etc/bashrc

```
/etc/bashrc

# System wide functions and aliases
# Environment stuff goes in /etc/profile

# by default, we want this to get set.
# Even for non-interactive, non-login shells.
if [ "`id -gn`" = "`id -un`" -a `id -u` -gt 99 ]; then
    umask 002
else
    umask 022
fi

# are we an interactive shell?
if [ "$PS1" ]; then
    if [ -x /usr/bin/tput ]; then
      if [ "x`tput kbs`" != "x" ]; then # We can't do this with "dumb" terminal
        stty erase `tput kbs`
      elif [ -x /usr/bin/wc ]; then
        if [ "`tput kbs|wc -c `" -gt 0 ]; then # We can't do this with "dumb" te
rminal
          stty erase `tput kbs`
        fi
      fi
    fi
    case $TERM in
    xterm*)
        if [ -e /etc/sysconfig/bash-prompt-xterm ]; then
            PROMPT_COMMAND=/etc/sysconfig/bash-prompt-xterm
"/etc/bashrc" 56L, 1497C
```

These configuration files work with customizable files in each user's home directory. By default, they include **.bash_history**, **.bash_logout**, **.bash_profile**, and **.bashrc**. While you can customize each of these files, they contain several defaults. The periods in front of each of these files hides them from normal searches. You can view hidden files with the **ls -a** command.

.bash_history Includes a history of your previous bash commands. Some administrators do not like this file, because crackers may be able to get clues to your system from the commands that you used. You can discontinue this process by adding HISTFILESIZE=0 to your .bash_profile file as shown in Figure 8.3.

FIGURE 8.3

You can find a lot of previous commands in your .bash_history.

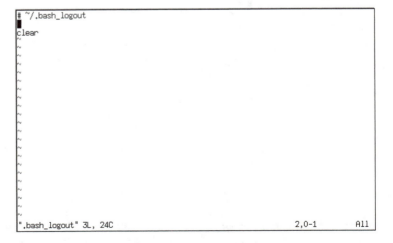

```
mount '//laptop3/redhat' /mnt/source
mkdir /mnt/source
mount '//laptop3/redhat' /mnt/source
ls
df
ps
vi /etc/passwd
cat /etc/inittab
fdisk -l
switchdesk kde
man dumpe2fs
rpm -q kernel-source
redhat-config-xfree86
mount
df
mozilla &
alias
history
mount -o username=michael '//laptop3/ml3' book
quota
vi /etc/bashrc
vi .bash_profile
vi .bash_history
```

.bash_logout Sets commands for when you exit a shell. By default, this includes the clear command, which wipes out your previous commands from the current terminal window. A sample of the simple default .bash_logout file is shown in Figure 8.4.

FIGURE 8.4

A home directory .bash_logout

```
# ~/.bash_logout
█
clear
~
~
~
~
~
~
~
~
~
~
~
~
~
~
~
~
~
~
~
~
~
".bash_logout" 3L, 24C                                    2,0-1        All
```

.bash_profile   Calls the .bashrc file for more configuration data. Adds the ~/bin directory to yourPATH as shown in Figure 8.5. If you add the HISTFILESIZE=0 variable, remember to add it to the export list in this file.

FIGURE 8.5

A home directory .bash_profile

```
# .bash_profile

# Get the aliases and functions
if [ -f ~/.bashrc ]; then
        . ~/.bashrc
fi

# User specific environment and startup programs

PATH=$PATH:$HOME/bin
BASH_ENV=$HOME/.bashrc
USERNAME="root"

export USERNAME BASH_ENV PATH

~
~
~
~
~
~
~
".bash_profile" 15L, 234C
```

.bashrc   Calls the /etc/bashrc file for basic configuration data. For the root user, this file adds aliases for the rm, mv, and cp commands to help prevent accidental deletion of a file, as shown in Figure 8.6.

FIGURE 8.6

A home directory .bashrc

```
# .bashrc

# User specific aliases and functions

alias rm='rm -i'
alias cp='cp -i'
alias mv='mv -i'

# Source global definitions
if [ -f /etc/bashrc ]; then
        . /etc/bashrc
fi
~
~
~
~
~
~
~
~
~
~
".bashrc" 12L, 176C                                    2,0-1        All
```

When you run the **export** command on a shell variable, you're essentially making it into a global, or an environment, variable. Global variables are also available to your programs.

NOTE *Remember, if you don't document your variables in the* .bash *files in your home directory, your setup will revert to the original configuration the next time you log into Linux.*

Environment Variables

There are a large number of default environment variables, which you can review with the env command. Some are set through /etc/profile. These variables include colors for filenames, settings for the secure shell, and default terminal and display variables. We've listed some of the standard environment variables in Table 8.2.

TABLE 8.2: OTHER MAJOR DEFAULT ENVIRONMENT VARIABLES

VARIABLE	COMMENT
SHELL	The default shell.
LANG	The default language.
BASH_ENV	Environment variables for the bash shell, normally in ~/.bashrc.
DISPLAY	The console used for the X-Window. DISPLAY=:0 corresponds to console F7; DISPLAY=:1 corresponds to F8; DISPLAY=server:0 sends GUI applications to a remote computer.
COLORTERM	The default terminal in a GUI, normally gnome-terminal.
PATH	Linux automatically searches through all directories in your path for a desired command, in the order shown from the output to the echo $PATH command. /etc/profile automatically adds several directories to the root user's PATH.
USER	Automatically set to the username of the currently logged-in user.
LOGNAME	Normally set to $USER.
MAIL	Set to the standard mail directory for a specific $USER.
HOSTNAME	Set to the output of the /bin/hostname command.
HISTSIZE	Sets the number of commands remembered by the history command.
INPUTRC	Sets defaults for keyboard mapping. See /etc/inputrc for details.

It's easy to reset environment variables. One of the most important of these is the PATH. Say you've added a number of scripts to the /opt/data/db/programs directory and do not want to cite the full directory path every time you want to run one of these programs. The following command adds this directory to your PATH:

```
# PATH=$PATH:/opt/data/db/programs
```

Now if you want to run a program such as /opt/data/db/programs/script1, all you need to do is type script1 and press Enter. But remember, to make the change permanent you'll need to revise the .bash_profile configuration file in your home directory to reflect the change to your PATH. To find the current directories in your PATH, run the echo $PATH command.

The Secrets of the Shell

You can use a number of techniques with the bash shell. For example, you can direct the output of one command to a file or even to another command. The shell enables you to set up aliases to define the commands of your choice. You can also move a running program to the background, which saves you the trouble of opening up another virtual terminal or console.

The bash shell is flexible; there are different ways to manage input to bash commands. For example, two different kinds of *wildcard* characters help you represent more than one file. And Linux allows you to use three different kinds of quote characters to manage the input to a command.

Other secrets allow you to easily move to any home directory, set aliases that can ease administration, and move up and down the Linux directory tree quickly.

Data Streams

Linux includes three data streams: data goes in, data comes out, and errors go out a different direction. These concepts are also known as standard input (*stdin*), standard output (*stdout*), and standard error (*stderr*). Standard input normally comes from a keyboard entry to a command. For example, if you run the `ls c*` command, `c*` is standard input to the `ls` command.

Standard output is the result of a command. For example, the files that you see after typing `ls` are standard output (stdout), which is normally directed to your monitor.

If there is no standard output, there may be an error message. This is the standard error data stream, which is also normally directed to your monitor.

There are two basic ways to redirect stdin, stdout, and stderr. You can pipe one of these data streams to another command, or you can redirect one of these streams to or from a file.

REDIRECTING INPUT AND OUTPUT

Normally, standard input comes from a keyboard. But if you already have a file full of data, you don't need to type everything again—you can simply redirect that file of data with the left-facing arrow (<)to your program. For example, the following command directs the **database_data** file to the **database_program**:

```
# database_program < database_data
```

In many cases, you'll want to save standard output in a file. For example, the following command using the right-facing arrow (>) saves standard output from the `ls` command to the file named **filelist**:

```
# ls > filelist
```

This overwrites any data in the file named **filelist**. Alternatively, a double right-facing arrow (>>) appends data to the end of the file named **filelist**:

```
# ls >> filelist
```

You can combine these redirection arrows in the same command. For example, if the **database_program** generates a lot of output, you can save it for later analysis:

```
# database_program < database_data > database_output
```

Standard error output can help you diagnose trouble with a program. For example, if you have a program that runs in the middle of the night, you may want to redirect the standard error stream from this program to a file so that you'll have some clues if something goes wrong. For example, the following command redirects errors to a file named `errorlog`:

```
# database_program < database_data 2> errorlog
```

Similarly, you can ensure that the previous contents of the `errorlog` file are not overwritten with the following command:

```
# database_program < database_data 2>> errorlog
```

TIP   When you look at standard errors, be careful with the 2> or the 2>>. No space is allowed between these characters.

FILE DESCRIPTORS AND DATA STREAMS

This sidebar is for the programmers. When a process in the shell works with a file, it sets up a file descriptor. These are program system calls which help manage that process.

There are three standard file descriptors: 0, 1, and 2. File descriptor 0 corresponds to standard input, or the right-facing arrow (>). File descriptor 1 corresponds to standard output, or the left-facing arrow (<). File descriptor 2 corresponds to standard error, which is represented by 2> in the bash shell.

INPUT AND OUTPUT PIPES

Just as you can redirect stdin, stdout, and stderr to and from specific files, you can also *pipe* these data streams to other commands. If you want to review permissions on a large number of files, you might use two different commands:

```
# ls -l > tempfiles
# more tempfiles
```

The first command takes your current file listing and stores the result in a file named `tempfiles`. The second command allows you to read the `tempfiles` file, one screen at a time. Because your file list probably changes frequently, you should delete the `tempfiles` file as it becomes out of date.

But this is also inefficient. You can combine these commands with a pipe (|), which is the character above the backslash on a U.S. keyboard. For example, the following command does the work of the previous two:

```
# ls -l | more
```

The pipe (|) takes the standard output from the `ls -l` command and sends the results as standard input to the `more` command. You don't need to create or delete any temporary files.

Running in the Background

Linux is a multitasking system. When you don't have additional terminals or virtual consoles available, you can still run multiple programs from a single command line. For example, some of the steps in compiling a kernel can take nearly an hour. When you run that program in the background, you don't have to wait to run other programs.

There are two ways to make programs run in the background. For example, let's assume you have a script in your current directory named `test`. This script starts an alarm in an hour. You want to run `test`, but you want to keep working while you wait. To do this, you can run the following command:

```
# ./test &
```

The ampersand (**&**) sends program execution to the "background." The program continues to run, and you are returned to the command-line interface.

NOTE   *The* `./programname` *command is used to run programs in the current directory. It's the easiest way to run local programs if the current directory is not in your PATH.*

Alternatively, if you're running a program to calculate the value of pi to an infinite number of digits, such a program might take a while to complete. If you forget to use the ampersand (**&**), you will need another way to send the program to the background. The Ctrl+Z command suspends a running program; the **bg** command then sends the program to the background.

Special Shell Characters

Special shell characters regulate standard output. You may already have some special characters assigned to you in your shell. To check, run the **stty -a** command, which leads to output similar to Figure 8.7.

FIGURE 8.7

Special shell characters

```
[root@RH9Desk root]# stty -a
speed 38400 baud; rows 24; columns 80; line = 0;
intr = ^C; quit = ^\; erase = ^?; kill = ^U; eof = ^D; eol = M-^?; eol2 = M-^?;
start = ^Q; stop = ^S; susp = ^Z; rprnt = ^R; werase = ^W; lnext = ^V;
flush = ^O; min = 1; time = 0;
-parenb -parodd cs8 hupcl -cstopb cread -clocal -crtscts
-ignbrk brkint -ignpar -parmrk -inpck -istrip -inlcr -igncr icrnl ixon -ixoff
-iuclc ixany imaxbel
opost -olcuc -ocrnl onlcr -onocr -onlret -ofill -ofdel nl0 cr0 tab0 bs0 vt0 ff0
isig icanon iexten echo echoe echok -echonl -noflsh -xcase -tostop -echoprt
echoctl echoke
[root@RH9Desk root]#
```

The output shows a number of special characters and settings. In the output, the carat (^) corresponds to the Ctrl key on your keyboard. For example, the `intr = ^C` setting means that the Ctrl+c command interrupts a running program. Some of the default special characters are described in Table 8.3. These are only defaults; you can customize the special characters that you use for different commands.

TIP   *The way you type a shell character varies from what you see in the output from the* `stty -a` *command. For example, the* `eof` *character appears as* ^D *(uppercase D); you actually run the Ctrl+d command (lowercase d) to exit from the terminal.*

TABLE 8.3: SPECIAL SHELL CHARACTERS

CHARACTER	DESCRIPTION
^C	Interrupts and stops a running program.
^\	Sends the quit command.
^D	Stops standard input; exits from a console.
^Z	Suspends a currently running program.

There are also a number of settings with and without a hyphen in front. For example, while an igncr setting would ignore a carriage return, the -igncr setting corresponds to "Don't ignore a carriage return." In other words, when you press Enter on your keyboard, the shell gives you a new prompt. The echo setting means that what you type on your keyboard is seen in the terminal.

You can assign different sets of special characters with the stty command. For example, to suspend a program with Ctrl+x (instead of Ctrl+z), run the following command:

```
# stty susp ^X
```

WARNING *The* stty *command can be dangerous. For example, if you were to enter the* stty -echo *command, anything you typed later would not be shown on the screen. You'd have to enter the* stty echo *command to restore your original configuration. Imagine the frustration if a cracker were to enter* stty -echo *in a login profile!*

Tildes and Home Directories

One key character in the bash shell is the tilde (~). It represents the home directory of the currently logged-on user. On most standard U.S. keyboards, you can find this character on the same key as the back quote (`), just above the Tab key.

You can use the tilde with most bash shell commands. For example, users can navigate to their own home directories with the cd ~ command. Alternatively, a user can list the files in his or her home directory with the ls ~ command. Other examples are shown in Table 8.4.

TABLE 8.4: COMMAND EXAMPLES WITH THE TILDE (~)

COMMAND	RESULT
cd ~	Navigates to your home directory.
cd ~/.kde	Moves to the .kde subdirectory of your home directory. For example, if your username is mj, this moves you to the /home/mj/.kde directory.
ls ~	Lists the files in your home directory.
tar czvf homebk.tar.gz ~	Backs up the files in your home directory.
~/yourprogram	Runs the program named yourprogram in your home directory.

This also can be useful in your Linux scripts, as the tilde (~) can help you configure a script to be useful for all users on your Linux server.

Connecting the Dots

The dot is nearly as important of a tool as the slash in the bash shell. While a single dot (.) represents the current directory, a double dot (..) can help you navigate to the parent directory.

You can use these dots with many bash commands. For example, the `ls .` command lists the files in the current directory, and the `ls ..` command lists the files in the parent directory.

You can even use the dot to run programs in the current directory. For example, if you're in the `/etc/rc.d/init.d` directory with the service scripts, you may not want to enter the full directory path for every command. For example, you could run the `./iptables` status command to check the current situation with your firewall.

Wildcards

There are two other special characters in Linux commands, which are variations on the Microsoft concept of wildcards. The characters are the asterisk (*) and the question mark (?). The asterisk represents any number of numbers or letters. Each question mark represents one alphanumeric character. For example, if you were to run the following command, you'd get a list of all files that start with the letter a:

```
# ls a*
```

If you have a file named a, it would be part of this list. In contrast, if you were to run the following command, you'd get a list of all files with two alphanumeric characters starting with a:

```
# ls a?
```

If you have a file named a, it would not be a part of this list. However, the files named ab, ac, and ad would. You can also perform more complex file searches with commands like the following:

```
# ls ?at?
```

This command returns files with names like cate, kata, and mate. It would not return files with names like Catherine, matador, or cat.

You can even define special characters in more detail with brackets ([]). For example, if you want to see all files in your directory between f0801.tif and f0806.tif, you can run either of the following commands:

```
# ls f080[1-6].tif
# ls f080[123456].tif
```

TIP   *In the world of Linux, the techniques associated with using wildcards are also known as globbing.*

Slashes in the Shell

There are forward slashes (/) and backslashes (\). A single forward slash represents the root directory. Additional forward slashes, such as those in `/etc/rc.d/init.d`, help you navigate to subdirectories.

The backslash is a special character. For example, if you wanted to look for an asterisk (`*`) in your `/etc/shadow` file, you might try the following command:

```
# grep * /etc/shadow
```

Unfortunately, this command looks for the name of every file in the current directory in the `/etc/shadow` file.

The problem is that the asterisk is a wildcard, which looks for almost everything, depending on the context. That's where the backslash can help. When you put the backslash in front of a special character, it "escapes" the meaning of that character.

In other words, the following command actually looks for asterisks in the `/etc/shadow` file:

```
# grep \* /etc/shadow
```

The backslash is handy for other situations, such as listing two-word directories such as Microsoft's `My Documents`. For example, if you've mounted a Microsoft Windows drive from a remote computer on the `/mnt/win1` directory, you might try to list the files in the directory with the following command:

```
# ls /mnt/win1/My Documents
```

This command looks for two separate directories: `/mnt/win1/My` and `Documents`. The problem is the space between the two words *My* and *Documents*. But when you add a backslash, the shell ignores the space and returns the list of files in the mounted `My Documents` directory:

```
# ls /mnt/win1/My\ Documents
```

Quotes

There are three types of quote characters on your keyboard: the single quote (`'`), the double quote (`"`), and the back quote (`` ` ``). When applied to standard input, they perform different functions.

The difference between these characters is in how they affect variables, such as `$NAME`, and shell commands, such as `date`. With any pair of quotes, the shell sends everything inside the quotes to the command. In the following example, the `echo` command is used. In detail, the difference is as follows:

Single quotes   The shell does not process any variables or commands.

Double quotes   The shell processes variables, such as `$NAME`, but does not process any commands.

Back quotes   The shell tries to process every word in quotes as a command. If there are variables, they are evaluated first, and then processed as a command. Thus, if `$NAME` were in back quotes, it is processed, and then the result is evaluated as a command.

You can see how this works in the following examples. Assume `NAME=Michael`. Remember, `date` is a command that returns the current date and time. The first command has no quotes. The shell interprets the `$NAME` variable, but does not run the `date` command:

```
# echo Welcome $NAME, the date is date
Welcome Michael, the date is date
```

The next command encloses the input in single quotes. This prevents the shell from interpreting any variables or commands:

```
# echo 'Welcome $NAME, the date is date'
Welcome $NAME, the date is date
```

The following command encloses the input in double quotes. The result is similar to the output without quotes:

```
# echo "Welcome $NAME, the date is date"
Welcome Michael, the date is date
```

The final command here includes back quotes for the command. The shell interprets the command:

```
# echo "Welcome $NAME, the date is `date`"
Welcome Michael, the date is Fri Jan 17 15:52:02 EST 2003
```

Aliases

One of the most useful shell variables is the alias. When you type the `alias` command, you get a list of commands that you can substitute for others. Example aliases for the root user are shown in Figure 8.8.

FIGURE 8.8

A list of aliases

```
[root@RH9Desk root]# alias
alias cp='cp -i'
alias l.='ls -d .* --color=tty'
alias ll='ls -l --color=tty'
alias ls='ls --color=tty'
alias mv='mv -i'
alias rm='rm -i'
alias which='alias | /usr/bin/which --tty-only --read-alias --show-dot --show-ti
lde'
[root@RH9Desk root]#
```

As discussed earlier, this list shows aliases for the `cp`, `mv`, and `rm` commands, which can help prevent the accidental deletion of a file. It's easy to create other aliases. For example, the following command makes `rx` an alias for the `redhat-config-xfree86` command:

```
# alias rx=redhat-config-xfree86
```

Now you can type the `rx` command, and the bash shell calls up the `redhat-config-xfree86` utility. You can reverse the process with the `unalias` command. For example, the following command deletes the alias for `redhat-config-xfree86`:

```
# unalias rx
```

TIP   You can create aliases for complex commands that you run frequently. For example, the alias le='ls -ltr /etc | more' *command could be a timesaver when you need to look through the* /etc *configuration files. If you want to make the alias change permanent, add the change to the* .bashrc *file in your home directory.*

Summary

While the bash shell includes a large number of commands, the details of the bash shell are fairly straightforward. Interactivity makes it easy to recall previous commands. Command completion allows you to find the command that you need with just a couple of strokes of the Tab key.

Shell and environment variables are maintained in some basic configuration files in the /etc and individual users' home directories. These variables determine the basic setup of the command-line interface. Other variables determine the size of your history, the default terminal, standard e-mail directories, and more.

There are a number of secrets associated with the shell. They include the three basic data streams: standard input, standard output, and standard error. Also, you can run commands in the background. Special shell characters set terminal parameters and allow you to use the Ctrl key to do different things on your keyboard. The tilde (~) represents any user's home directory.

Dots and double dots can help you navigate through the Linux filesystem hierarchy. Wildcards help you identify files and commands even when you don't know the complete name . While forward slashes help you navigate directories, backslashes escape the meaning of characters such as asterisks and spaces. Single, double, and back quotes let you process variables and commands in different ways. Aliases make it possible to rename commands that you might otherwise forget.

That completes Part II, where we have examined the fundamentals of Linux. In Part III, we'll look at a number of basic administrative functions. Chapter 9 begins this process by looking at how you administer users and groups. Red Hat Linux promotes security by helping you administer users and groups with the Shadow Password Suite, quotas, and the User Private Group scheme.

Part 3

Basic Linux Administration

In this Part, you will learn how to:
- ◆ Administer users and groups securely
- ◆ Install and manage packages with RPM
- ◆ Configure the startup and shutdown process
- ◆ Recompile kernels
- ◆ Work with the administrative nitty-gritty details
- ◆ Back up your system

Chapter 9

Administering Users and Groups Securely

ONE OF THE KEY TASKS for a Linux administrator is to maintain users and groups. Even if the computer is a workstation with one dedicated user, chances are that you'll want to maintain at least a root and a regular account on that computer.

You configure users and groups in several basic files in the /etc directory. Red Hat Linux allows you to create users by editing these files directly, or you can use some basic commands. In either case, there are other commands and configuration files that you can use to manage the life of a user account and the associated password.

The Shadow Password Suite allows Linux to provide an additional layer of protection, by user and by group. Quotas can help you regulate the amount of space and/or the number of files that users are allowed on your system.

Red Hat Linux includes a different way of organizing groups, known as the User Private Group scheme. It enhances user security, because users get their own exclusive group. If needed, it still allows you to set up individual groups with a shared directory. This chapter covers the following topics:

◆ Basic user and group management

◆ Creating users

◆ Using the Shadow Password Suite

◆ Setting quotas

◆ Creating user private groups

Basic User and Group Management

Everyone on a Linux system needs a user account. Every account has rights and privileges that vary depending on the command and the directory. Linux user accounts are organized into groups. While default users are the only member of their default groups, you can organize users into new groups, and you can configure rights and privileges that vary differently by group.

In Red Hat Linux, user accounts are organized in /etc/passwd. Their passwords are made more secure in /etc/shadow. For Red Hat Linux groups, the analogous files are /etc/group and /etc/gshadow.

When creating a new account, the default parameters are configured in /etc/login.defs; configuration files are normally copied to the new user's home directory from the /etc/skel directory.

NOTE *Regular users will want their own accounts, and generally, you want to minimize risks by keeping them away from root user privileges. However, if you're the administrator for your Linux computer, you may want to sign in as the root user, for the reasons discussed in Chapter 6.*

/etc/passwd

Linux users can be classified into three groups: administrative, service, and regular users. Every user has rights and privileges. Regular and administrative users have usernames, passwords, and home directories. All users are configured through a line in the /etc/passwd file, as shown in Figure 9.1.

FIGURE 9.1

/etc/passwd

```
ftp:x:14:50:FTP User:/var/ftp:/sbin/nologin
nobody:x:99:99:Nobody:/:/sbin/nologin
ntp:x:38:38::/etc/ntp:/sbin/nologin
apache:x:48:48:Apache:/var/www:/sbin/nologin
rpc:x:32:32:Portmapper RPC user:/:/sbin/nologin
vcsa:x:69:69:virtual console memory owner:/dev:/sbin/nologin
nscd:x:28:28:NSCD Daemon:/:/sbin/nologin
sshd:x:74:74:Privilege-separated SSH:/var/empty/sshd:/sbin/nologin
rpm:x:37:37::/var/lib/rpm:/bin/bash
mailnull:x:47:47::/var/spool/mqueue:/sbin/nologin
smmsp:x:51:51::/var/spool/mqueue:/sbin/nologin
rpcuser:x:29:29:RPC Service User:/var/lib/nfs:/sbin/nologin
nfsnobody:x:65534:65534:Anonymous NFS User:/var/lib/nfs:/sbin/nologin
pcap:x:77:77::/var/arpwatch:/sbin/nologin
xfs:x:43:43:X Font Server:/etc/X11/fs:/sbin/nologin
named:x:25:25:Named:/var/named:/sbin/nologin
gdm:x:42:42::/var/gdm:/sbin/nologin
desktop:x:80:80:desktop:/var/lib/menu/kde:/sbin/nologin
postfix:x:89:89::/var/spool/postfix:/sbin/nologin
squid:x:23:23::/var/spool/squid:/dev/null
webalizer:x:67:67:Webalizer:/var/www/html/usage:/sbin/nologin
mj:x:500:500:Michael Jang:/home/mj:/bin/bash
jm:x:501:501:The Other User:/home/jm:/bin/bash
```

The last two lines in this figure contain entries for regular users. As you can see, usernames are associated with services such as ftp, apache, and squid. Each entry includes seven columns delineated by colons (:). Table 9.1 describes each of these columns.

/etc/shadow

Red Hat Linux includes the /etc/shadow file for additional password security. By default, this file is readable only to the root user. If you use standard commands to create new users, basic information is also added to this file, based on the defaults in /etc/login.defs (which we discuss later in this chapter). Take a look at /etc/shadow in Figure 9.2.

TABLE 9.1: /ETC/PASSWD **ENTRIES**

COLUMN	FUNCTION	COMMENT
1	Username	Login name.
2	Password	If this field contains an x, the encrypted password is stored in /etc/shadow.
3	User ID	Red Hat User IDs start at 500.
4	Group ID	Red Hat Group IDs normally match User IDs.
5	Extra information	Commonly used for a user's real name.
6	Home directory	Normally /home/*username*.
7	Default shell	The shell a user sees after logging in.

FIGURE 9.2

/etc/shadow

```
ftp:*:11919:0:99999:7:::
nobody:*:11919:0:99999:7:::
ntp:!!:11919:0:99999:7:::
apache:!!:11919:0:99999:7:::
rpc:!!:11919:0:99999:7:::
vcsa:!!:11919:0:99999:7:::
nscd:!!:11919:0:99999:7:::
sshd:!!:11919:0:99999:7:::
rpm:!!:11919:0:99999:7:::
mailnull:!!:11919:0:99999:7:::
smmsp:!!:11919:0:99999:7:::
rpcuser:!!:11919:0:99999:7:::
nfsnobody:!!:11919:0:99999:7:::
pcap:!!:11919:0:99999:7:::
xfs:!!:11919:0:99999:7:::
named:!!:11919:0:99999:7:::
gdm:!!:11919:0:99999:7:::
desktop:!!:11919:0:99999:7:::
postfix:!!:11919:0:99999:7:::
squid:!!:11919:0:99999:7:::
webalizer:!!:11919:0:99999:7:::
mj:$1$Yp6h.q5K$Lb7moiDvzbDCDWn0RIJZo/:11920:0:99999:7:::
jm:$1$vfwW4pCG$PrEpYyZhZkq879zHfKnDF1:11920:0:99999:7:::
```

As you can see, the last two lines contain entries for the same regular and service users that were shown in /etc/passwd. In this case, each user entry includes eight columns delineated by colons (:). Table 9.2 describes each of these columns.

/etc/group

The Red Hat Linux group configuration file is simpler than those for users; they include only four columns. In Figure 9.3, you can see the same two regular usernames in /etc/group that you saw in /etc/passwd and /etc/shadow. In /etc/group, they are group names. You may note that the group ID for groups mj and jm matches the user IDs for the users with the same names in the previous two configuration files.

TABLE 9.2: */ETC/SHADOW* ENTRIES

COLUMN	FUNCTION	COMMENT
1	Username	Login name.
2	Password	Encrypted password.
3	Number of days	Last time the password was changed, in days, after January 1, 1970.
4	Minimum password life	You can't change a password for at least this amount of time, in days.
5	Maximum password life	You have to change a password after this period of time, in days.
6	Warning period	You get a warning this many days before your password expires.
7	Disable account	If you don't use your account this many days after your password expires, you can't log in.
8	Account expiration	If you don't use your account by this date, you won't be able to log in. May be in YYYY-MM-DD format, or in the number of days after January 1, 1970.

FIGURE 9.3

/etc/group

```
rpc:x:32:
floppy:x:19:
vcsa:x:69:
nscd:x:28:
sshd:x:74:
rpm:x:37:
mailnull:x:47:
smmsp:x:51:
slocate:x:21:
rpcuser:x:29:
nfsnobody:x:65534:
pcap:x:77:
xfs:x:43:
named:x:25:
gdm:x:42:
desktop:x:80:
postdrop:x:90:
postfix:x:89:
squid:x:23:
webalizer:x:67:
mj:x:500:
jm:x:501:
Sharing:x:600:jm,mj
```

Note the final entry, the Sharing group. As you can see, users mj and jm are members of that group. Table 9.3 describes the columns in /etc/group.

TABLE 9.3: *ETC/GROUP* ENTRIES

COLUMN	FUNCTION	COMMENT
1	Group name	By default, Red Hat users are members of groups with the same name.
2	Password	If you see an "x" in this column, see /etc/gshadow for the actual encrypted password.
3	Group ID	By default, Red Hat users have the same ID as their groups.
4	Members	Includes the usernames of others that are members of the same group.

/etc/gshadow

The Red Hat Linux /etc/gshadow configuration file for groups is analogous to the /etc/shadow file for users. It specifies an encrypted password for applicable groups, as well as administrators with privileges for a specific group. A sample /etc/gshadow file is shown in Figure 9.4.

FIGURE 9.4

/etc/gshadow

```
rpc:x::
floppy:x::
vcsa:x::
nscd:x::
sshd:x::
rpm:x::
mailnull:x::
smmsp:x::
slocate:x::
rpcuser:x::
nfsnobody:x::
pcap:x::
xfs:x::
named:x::
gdm:x::
desktop:x::
postdrop:x::
postfix:x::
squid:x::
webalizer:x::
mj:!::
jm:!::
Sharing:Ihcj.tdyhi6fIdyh:mj,jm
```

Note the differences from /etc/group with respect to the Sharing group. Table 9.4 describes the columns in /etc/shadow.

TABLE 9.4: */ETC/SHADOW* ENTRIES

COLUMN	FUNCTION	COMMENT
1	Group name	You can create additional groups.
2	Password	The encrypted group password, added with the gpasswd command.
3	Group administrator	The user allowed to manage users in that group.
4	Group members	Includes the usernames that are members of the same group.

/etc/skel

Users have a default set of configuration files and directories. You examined some of these files as they related to the bash shell in Chapter 8. The default list of these files is located in the /etc/skel directory, which you can easily inspect with the ls -la /etc/skel command, as shown in Figure 9.5. The list changes depending on what you have installed.

FIGURE 9.5

Default home files in /etc/skel.

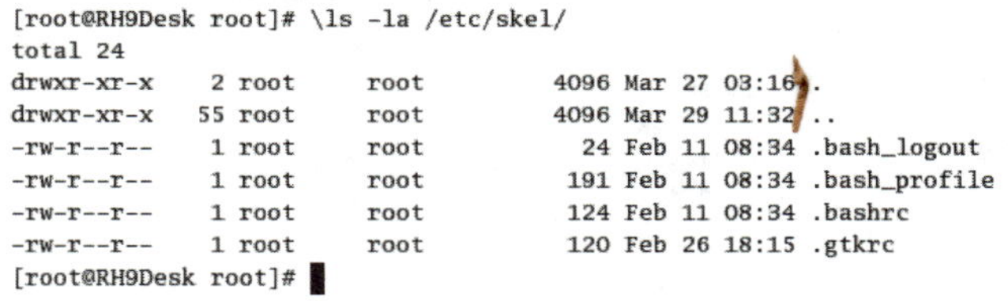

```
[root@RH9Desk root]# \ls -la /etc/skel/
total 24
drwxr-xr-x    2 root     root       4096 Mar 27 03:16 .
drwxr-xr-x   55 root     root       4096 Mar 29 11:32 ..
-rw-r--r--    1 root     root         24 Feb 11 08:34 .bash_logout
-rw-r--r--    1 root     root        191 Feb 11 08:34 .bash_profile
-rw-r--r--    1 root     root        124 Feb 11 08:34 .bashrc
-rw-r--r--    1 root     root        120 Feb 26 18:15 .gtkrc
[root@RH9Desk root]#
```

TIP   *If you have a list of standard files, such as corporate policies for new users, you may want to copy them to* /etc/skel. *All new users will get a copy of these files in their home directories.*

/etc/login.defs

When you create a new user, the basic parameters come from the /etc/login.defs configuration file. The version included with Red Hat Linux includes settings for e-mail directories, password aging, user ID and group ID numbers, and creating a home directory. The default variables in this file are almost self-explanatory:

```
MAIL_DIR    /var/spool/mail    # Default mail directory
PASS_MAX_DAYS 99999            # Password max life
PASS_MIN_DAYS 0                # Password min life
PASS_MIN_LEN 5                 # Min password length
PASS_WARN_AGE 7                # Warning before expiration
UID_MIN       500              # Lowest User ID number
UID_MAX       60000            # Highest User ID number
GID_MIN       500              # Lowest Group ID number
GID_MAX       60000            # Highest Group ID number
CREATE_HOME                yes
```

Needless to say, these settings can be further refined through other configuration files. For example, you can manage the allowed lifetime settings for passwords by editing /etc/shadow. You can review a copy of this file in Figure 9.6.

FIGURE 9.6

/etc/login.defs

```
# *REQUIRED*
#   Directory where mailboxes reside, _or_ name of file, relative to the
#   home directory.  If you _do_ define both, MAIL_DIR takes precedence.
#   QMAIL_DIR is for Qmail
#QMAIL_DIR      Maildir
MAIL_DIR        /var/spool/mail
#MAIL_FILE      .mail

# Password aging controls:
#       PASS_MAX_DAYS   Maximum number of days a password may be used.
#       PASS_MIN_DAYS   Minimum number of days allowed between password changes.
#       PASS_MIN_LEN    Minimum acceptable password length.
#       PASS_WARN_AGE   Number of days warning given before a password expires.
PASS_MAX_DAYS   99999
PASS_MIN_DAYS   0
PASS_MIN_LEN    5
PASS_WARN_AGE   7

# Min/max values for automatic uid selection in useradd
UID_MIN                  500
UID_MAX                60000
# Min/max values for automatic gid selection in groupadd
GID_MIN                  500
GID_MAX                60000

# If defined, this command is run when removing a user.
#USERDEL_CMD    /usr/sbin/userdel_local
# If useradd should create home directories for users by default
CREATE_HOME     yes
```

Administering User Accounts

Linux administrators do three basic things with user accounts. They add new users. They delete users. They manage the access parameters of existing users. While a Red Hat Linux graphical tool is available for this purpose (see redhat-config-users in Chapter 19), most administrators perform these functions from the command-line interface.

THE COMMAND LINE VS. GUI ADMINISTRATIVE DEBATE

Linux administrators generally prefer tools at the command-line interface. While this may appear archaic to a Microsoft Windows administrator, there are good reasons to use command-line tools:

◆ Command-line tools are more versatile. Generally, more options are available when you use a command-line tool than when you use a GUI.

◆ Command-line tools are faster. You don't have to wait for Linux to process the GUI or to place another GUI tool on your screen.

◆ GUI tools are just front ends. In other words, Linux GUI tools take the entries you make and run the corresponding command in the shell.

◆ GUI tools are another layer of software—which is another way things can go wrong.

◆ GUI tools don't show all errors. While command-line interface tools give you error messages that you can see at the console, GUI tools may not show these errors on a graphical desktop.

Adding Users

There are three basic ways to add users in Red Hat Linux:

◆ Edit the `/etc/passwd` file directly, adding desired files to new users' home directories.

◆ Work with some of the commands designed for this purpose, such as `useradd`.

◆ Open the graphical front end, `redhat-config-users`, which is covered in Chapter 19.

Alternatively, the `newusers` command lets you add a whole group of users based on a batch file configured to the same format as `/etc/passwd`.

THE DIRECT METHOD

It's instructive to go through the steps required to create a new user . It can help you appreciate all of the parameters associated with existing users. For this example, assume you're creating an account for James K. Polk (U.S. president 1845–1849), and plan to assign him user ID and group IDs 600. (If 600 is already taken, substitute a different unused number between 500 and 60000.) Follow these steps to set up the user account:

1. Open `/etc/passwd` in a text editor.

2. Start a new line. The easiest way to do this is by copying the applicable information from a current user.

3. Change the username, user ID, group ID, and home directory. Insert **jkp** as the username in the first column, **600** in the third column for the user ID, **600** in the fourth column for the group ID, **James K Polk** in the fifth column, and **/home/jkp** as the user's home directory in the sixth column. Make sure that the information you enter (except for the shell) is unique relative to other entries in your `/etc/passwd` file. Save your changes to this file.

4. Open `/etc/shadow` in a text editor. Create a new line by copying the applicable information from a current user. Insert **jkp** for the new user in the first column. Save your changes to this file. This is a read-only file; in `vi`, the `wq!` command overrides read-only settings.

5. Open `/etc/group` in a text editor. Create a new line by copying the applicable information from a current group. For this user, insert **jkp** as the group name in the first column and **600** as the group ID in the third column.

6. Set up your new user's home directory. For user jkp, the appropriate command is

   `mkdir -p /home/jkp`

7. Give your new user access to his home directory. In this case, assign ownership with these commands:

   `chown jkp /home/jkp`
   `chgrp jkp /home/jkp`

8. Assign a new password with the `passwd jkp` command. Give the new password to your new user. Tell him to assign a new password to himself with the `passwd` command.

9. Copy the basic initialization files, which are normally stored in the `/etc/skel` directory. (We covered these files, such as `.bashrc` and `.bash_profile`, in Chapter 8.) Change your identity to the new user with the

   ```
   su - jkp
   ```

   command. Copy these files with the

   ```
   cp /etc/skel/.* /home/jkp
   ```

   command.

10. Copy any subdirectories in `/etc/skel` to `/home/jkp`. For example, you can copy the `/etc/skel/.kde` directory with the command

    ```
    cp -r /etc/skel/.kde /home/jkp
    ```

11. Change the user and group ownership of the files that you copied from `/etc/skel`.

12. Log out from the jkp user account and tell your new user about his new username and password.

13. Assuming you're using the default Shadow Password Suite, run the `pwconv` and `grpconv` commands. These commands are discussed later in this chapter.

USING *USERADD*

It's a lot easier to use the `useradd` command to create a new user. For example, to set up a new account for jkp, all you need to do is type in the following command:

```
# useradd jkp
```

This command sets up user jkp with the defaults as described earlier in the `/etc/login.defs` configuration file. It also copies the files from `/etc/skel` and modifies the ownership of these files. You still need to assign a new password for jkp, as described in step 8 of the previous section.

Inspect your `/etc/passwd`, `/etc/shadow`, and `/etc/group` configuration files to verify that the `useradd` command added entries for jkp to these files.

Using *newusers*

The `newusers` command is designed to handle a large number of users from a batch file of usernames and passwords, in the same format as the `/etc/passwd` file. The only difference is that the password column requires an encrypted password, which you can copy from the `/etc/passwd` or `/etc/shadow` entry for a known user. If you create a list of new users in a file named `new-batch`, you can then set up these users with the following command:

```
# newusers new-batch
```

The `new-batch` file must be in the same format as `/etc/passwd`; the passwords must be entered in clear text. Therefore, if you save this batch file, make sure it's secure. You might want to hide it, encrypt it, or delete it. A list of usernames and clear text passwords is a very tempting tool for anyone who wants to crack your system.

TIP *It's easy to copy text like an encrypted password. Try it yourself. Open* `/etc/shadow` *in the text editor of your choice. Highlight the password. Exit from the editor. Right-click your mouse. You should see an exact copy of what you just highlighted. Open up the file of your choice. In insert mode, when you right-click your mouse again, you should see another copy of the encrypted password.*

Deleting Users

You can delete users directly, or you can use the `userdel` command. You can even deactivate a user temporarily, while retaining the files in that user's home directory.

TIP *It's easy to deactivate a user. Just substitute an asterisk (*) for the target user's password in* `/etc/passwd`*. That user won't be able to log into her account with any password. This works even if you're using the default Red Hat Linux Shadow Password Suite.*

THE DIRECT METHOD

Deleting users is easier than adding them. You just need to ensure that the user's entries are deleted from the respective configuration files, and then delete that user's home directory. The basic steps are as follows:

◆ Delete the user's entry from `/etc/passwd`.

◆ Delete the user's entry from `/etc/group`.

◆ Delete the user's entry from `/etc/shadow`.

◆ Delete the user's entry from `/etc/gshadow`.

◆ Delete the user's home directory after saving the files you need.

DELETING WITH COMMANDS

When working with commands, two steps are required to delete a user. The `userdel` command is straightforward. If you have a user named James K. Polk who just left your company, you'll want to deactivate his account. Retrieve and save any files you need from his home directory, and then run the following command:

```
# userdel -r jkp
```

This command deletes jkp's information from the `/etc/passwd` file. The `-r` switch deletes the `/home/jkp` directory, including any files and directories that it may contain.

But you also need to delete that user's group with the `groupdel` command, as shown here. Otherwise, the next user that you add will have a user ID and a group ID that differ from each other, which can cause problems when you manage new users in the future.

```
# groupdel jkp
```

Managing User Access with *chage*

You can manage user passwords with the `chage` command. It can help you specify the information described in the earlier discussion on `/etc/shadow`, based on regulating the lifetime of a password.

In fact, chage changes the settings in this file. You can review the switches associated with chage in Table 9.5.

TABLE 9.5: *CHAGE* COMMANDS

COMMAND	RESULT
chage -m *days user*	Sets the minimum life of a password to *days* days.
chage -M *days user*	Sets the maximum life of a password to *days* days.
chage -I *days user*	Sets the number of *days* that an account can be inactive before it's locked.
chage -E *date user*	Sets the *date* after which an account is inaccessible.
chage -W *days user*	Sets an advance warning, in *days*, of an upcoming required password change.
chage -l *user*	Lists the current user's password and account information. Can be run by regular users on their own accounts.

The date can be in YYYY-MM-DD format, or in the number of days after January 1, 1970.

The Shadow Password Suite

The Shadow Password Suite features all of the commands related to managing Linux users and groups, including those already addressed in this chapter. By default, Red Hat Linux uses this suite to provide additional security through encrypted passwords in the /etc/shadow and /etc/gshadow files. These files require commands to convert passwords to and from the companion /etc/passwd and /etc/group configuration files.

These encrypted password files have more restrictive permissions than /etc/passwd or /etc/group; only the root user is allowed to even view these files, and they are not writeable by default.

However, these additional security provisions may not do you much good unless your passwords are strong, as we explain the next section.

NOTE   One of the major password–testing programs is known as crack. A version of it is available as part of the cracklib* *RPM packages. You should use it only to test the security of your users' passwords.*

Strong Passwords

By default, Red Hat Linux discourages the use of simple passwords, such as dictionary words, or simple patterns, such as *abcd*. Readily available password-cracking programs can decipher such passwords in minutes. In contrast, the best passwords are based on a combination of upper- and lowercase letters and numbers; such passwords can take weeks for the same programs to decipher. One easy way to set up such passwords is based on a favorite sentence; for example, Ira3mmoW could stand for "I ran a 3 minute mile on Wednesday."

NOTE   When you use the passwd *command, you get to type in the new desired password twice. If your passwords don't match, you'll see a warning to that effect. After pressing Enter, you're then taken to the original prompt where you can try again.*

Converting User Passwords

Two commands are associated with converting user passwords in the Shadow Password Suite: `pwconv` and `pwunconv`.

pwconv   Converts an existing `/etc/passwd` file. Passwords that currently exist in `/etc/passwd` are replaced by an "`x`"; the encrypted password, username, and other relevant information are transferred to the `/etc/shadow` file. If you've recently added new users by editing the `/etc/passwd` file in a text editor, you can run this command again to convert the passwords associated with any new users. This works even if other passwords are already encrypted in `/etc/shadow`.

pwunconv   Passwords are transferred back to `/etc/passwd`, and the `/etc/shadow` file is deleted. Be careful, because this also deletes any password-aging information (see the `chage` command described earlier) otherwise saved in `/etc/shadow`.

Converting Group Passwords

As we discussed earlier, you can configure group administrators in `/etc/group` and assign associated passwords with `gpasswd`. Once you have group passwords, you may have the same security concerns as with regular user passwords. Two commands are associated with converting user passwords in the Shadow Password Suite: `grpconv` and `grpunconv`.

grpconv   Converts an existing `/etc/group` file. The relevant information is transferred to `/etc/gshadow`.

grpunconv   Reverses the process of the `grpconv` command; like `pwunconv`, this command also deletes any existing `/etc/gshadow` file.

Quotas

Quotas keep individual users or groups from consuming all of the space available on a partition. Disk quotas are commonly used by Linux administrators to regulate the amount of space occupied by any single user for e-mail, website files, FTP files, and more. This prevents any particular user from uploading so much data that it crowds out a critical directory such as **/boot** or root (/). Without sufficient free space for these directories, Linux might even crash.

You can configure quotas with limits on the number of inodes. Each inode is associated with a specific file. Alternatively, you can set absolute limits in kilobytes. In other words, you can limit the number of files that a user or group can put on your system, or you can place an absolute limit on the amount of data that user or group can place on your system.

Quotas allow you to monitor the pattern of use of your system.

Configuration

By default, the quota RPM package is installed and is active in Red Hat Linux. If you're not sure, run the command

```
rpm -q quota
```

If the packages are installed, you'll see the package name and version number in the standard output on your screen. If necessary, see Chapter 10 for instructions on how to install RPM packages such as **quota-***.

Quotas are normally active in the kernel. Once they're active, you can configure quotas on a specific partition for users and/or for groups. In either case, you'll need to remount the target directory with active quota settings shown in `/etc/fstab`. Once you've configured those settings, you can activate quotas yourself; they are activated in subsequent reboots in `/etc/rc.d/rc.sysinit`.

KERNEL NOTES

While the default Red Hat Linux kernel enables quotas, that setting may not apply for kernels that you download from other sources. Fortunately, checking the appropriate kernel setting is easy.

When you download the source code for a kernel, the files are saved to the `/usr/src/linux` or `/usr/src/linux-2.4` directories. Red Hat Linux kernels are downloaded to a different directory, which is linked to `/usr/src/linux-2.4`. For more information on kernel sources, see Chapter 12.

NOTE *The next big Linux Kernel release is scheduled for sometime in 2003. (As of this writing, it may be called 2.6 or 3.0.) Once released, the source code will probably be associated with the* `/usr/src/linux-2.6` *or the* `/usr/src/linux-3.0` *directory. Many of the features of that future kernel have already been incorporated into the kernel included with Red Hat Linux 9.0.*

Once you've identified the directory with your source code, there should be a `.config` file in that directory. If it isn't there, it means that this kernel has not been compiled for your computer. In that case, search this file for the `CONFIG_QUOTA` setting with the following command:

```
# grep CONFIG_QUOTA /usr/src/linux-2.4/.config
```

If the directory with your kernel source code is different, change this command accordingly. You should see one of the following results in the standard output:

```
CONFIG_QUOTA=y
CONFIG_QUOTA=n
```

In other words, quota support is active (y) or not active (n). If quota support is not active, you'll need to compile it into your kernel. See Chapter 12 for more information.

NOTE *The version number of the kernel should be associated with the settings that you find in your bootloader configuration file, normally* `/boot/grub/grub.conf`*. For more information on the relationship between a bootloader and the kernel, see Chapter 12.*

USER QUOTAS

To create a quota for specific users, follow these six basic steps:

1. Modify `/etc/fstab` to activate quota options for the filesystem of your choice.

2. Enable the change by remounting the filesystem.

3. Create the `aquota.user` file at the top of the subject filesystem. For example, if you're creating quotas on `/home`, create `/home/aquota.user`.

4. Scan the appropriate filesystem and create basic quota files with the `quotacheck` command.

5. Use `edquota` to apply quota limits for a specific user.

6. Finally, activate quotas with the `quotaon` command.

We explain these steps in more detail in the following sections.

Modifying /etc/fstab and Remounting

It's easy to modify `/etc/fstab` for quotas. Take a typical line from this configuration file, which in this case sets up `/home` as a filesystem on a separate partition:

```
LABEL=/home   /home  ext3  defaults  1 2
```

Fortunately, there's room in `/etc/fstab` to add the User Quota setting, `usrquota`. Space is scarce in `/etc/fstab`, since the boot process may not work if you let this code wrap to the next line. So with the User Quota setting, this `/etc/fstab` line would read as follows:

```
LABEL=/home   /home  ext3  defaults,usrquota  1 2
```

Now you can activate the change by remounting the `/home` directory. Fortunately, you do not need to change runlevels or reboot with the rescue disk to make this work; all you need to activate `/etc/fstab` changes on `/home` is the following command:

```
# mount -o remount /home
```

Creating the Quota File

It's easy to create the quota file that you need with the `touch` command. As we're creating quotas on the `/home` filesystem in this section, create an empty `aquota.user` file in the `/home` directory. The easiest way to do this is with the `touch` command:

```
# touch /home/aquota.user
```

It's important to set the security on this file so it's accessible only to the root user. Since this file need not be executable, you can do this with the following command:

```
# chmod 600 /aquota.user
```

Making the quotacheck

Now you're ready to create appropriate quota files with the `quotacheck -avum` command. This scans (`-a`) `/etc/mtab` for filesystems with enabled quotas, creates verbose (`-v`) output, looks for user quotas (`-u`), and remounts the scanned filesystem (`-m`).

Using edquota for a User

Next, you can set up quotas for a specific user. Run the `edquota` command for the user of your choice. For example, if you want to set quotas on user ez, run the following command:

```
# edquota ez
```

By default, this opens up the quota information file for user ez in the `vi` editor, as shown here:

```
Disk quotas for user ez (uid 512)
  Filesystem blocks   soft   hard inodes soft hard
  /dev/sda3       4      0      0      1    0    0
```

As you can see, there are four blocks of data (in KB) and one inode used in ez's home directory. You can set hard and soft limits in each category. But what are hard and soft limits?

Soft limit A soft limit is the maximum amount of space or inodes allocated to a user. If there is no grace period, this acts as a hard limit. You can set a grace period with the `edquota -t` command.

Hard limit If there is a grace period, the hard limit is the absolute limit on the amount of space or inodes allocated to a user.

Now if you want to set a 100MB soft limit and a 110MB hard limit, edit the quota for ez to look like the following:

```
Disk quotas for user ez (uid 512)
  Filesystem blocks    soft   hard inodes soft hard
  /dev/sda3       4 100000 110000      1    0    0
```

Enabling Quotas

The last step, enabling quotas, is the simplest. You've already done the necessary configuration work. Just run the following command to enable quotas for all configured users on the `/home` filesystem:

```
# quotaon /home
```

Alternatively, you can deactivate quotas on the same filesystem with the `quotaoff /home` command.

GROUP QUOTAS

Creating group quotas is as easy as creating user quotas. The differences can be summarized in the same six steps:

1. Modify `/etc/fstab` to activate quota options for the filesystem of your choice. For group quotas, add the `grpquota` setting to the options for the target filesystem.

2. Enable the change by remounting the filesystem with the `mount -o remount filesystem` command.

3. Create the `aquota.group` file at the top of the subject filesystem. For example, if you're creating quotas on `/home`, create `/home/aquota.group`.

4. Scan the appropriate filesystem and create basic quota files with the `quotacheck` command. Use the `-avgm` switches; `-g` configures group quotas.

5. Use `edquota` to apply quota limits for a specific group.

6. Finally, activate quotas with the `quotaon` command.

ACTIVATION IN *RC.SYSINIT*

Once you've configured quotas in Red Hat Linux, the operating system can take over the next time you reboot. Quota checking and activation commands are included in the default `/etc/rc.d/rc.sysinit` startup script. The relevant section is shown in Figure 9.7, which also attempts to convert the quota files associated with Linux kernel version 2.2 (`quota.user` and `quota.group`).

FIGURE 9.7

rc.sysinit
activates quotas

```
# check remaining quotas other than root
if [ X"$_RUN_QUOTACHECK" = X1 -a -x /sbin/quotacheck ]; then
        if [ -x /sbin/convertquota ]; then
                # try to convert old quotas
                for mountpt in `awk '$4 ~ /quota/{print $2}' /etc/mtab` ; do
                        if [ -f "$mountpt/quota.user" ]; then
                                action $"Converting old user quota files: " \
                                        /sbin/convertquota -u $mountpt && \
                                                rm -f $mountpt/quota.user
                        fi
                        if [ -f "$mountpt/quota.group" ]; then
                                action $"Converting old group quota files: " \
                                        /sbin/convertquota -g $mountpt && \
                                                rm -f $mountpt/quota.group
                        fi
                done
        fi
        action $"Checking local filesystem quotas: " /sbin/quotacheck -aRnug
fi

if [ -x /sbin/quotaon ]; then
    action $"Enabling local filesystem quotas: " /sbin/quotaon -aug
fi
"/etc/rc.d/rc.sysinit" 794L, 22605C                          550,2-16        69%
```

Applying Quotas to Other Users

You can set up common quotas for a number of different users. The edquota command allows you to set up the same quotas for a list of users. Assuming you've already set up quotas for user ez, the following command copies the identical limits for the other users that follow, in this case, mj, jm, and tp:

```
# edquota -up ez mj jm tp
```

Quota Monitoring

Now that you've set up quotas, you can get reports on who is using disk space and inodes, and how much space they occupy. The repquota command gives you quota reports by users (-u) or groups (-g). You can also get a report on all filesystems with the repquota -a command.

If you want to check up on an individual user (-u) or group (-g), use the quota command. Individual users can check their own status with this command.

User Private Groups

Red Hat Linux has a unique way of organizing users and groups, which promotes security. This section describes the Red Hat User Private Group scheme, and then details a scenario where you can create a secure group with a common directory.

The Red Hat Scheme

As noted in the beginning of the chapter, everyone's user ID number usually matches their group ID number in /etc/passwd. But this is generally true only for Red Hat Linux and allied distributions. The other scheme is where every user has the same group ID number, which is usually 100. In other words, in other distributions every user belongs to the same group by default.

The Red Hat scheme is more suitable for a number of configurations. For example, it allows the users of an ISP to keep their files hidden from other users of that ISP. Yet, you can still configure a shared directory for selected users.

Creating a Shared Directory

Sometimes you want users to be able to share files. Some users may be in a common department, or they may be working on a common project. You can set up a group and a directory where all imported files are readable by all members of that group.

The easiest way to illustrate this process is with an example. Say you need to set up a group and a shared directory for project members Tom, Adnan, Carlos, and Libby. In the following steps, you'll create the users, a common group, and a shared directory. Then you'll set the group ID (SGID) bit, which allows any user in the group to copy files to the shared directory, and makes it readable by the other members of the group.

1. Give Tom, Adnan, Carlos, and Libby accounts on your system with the `useradd` *username* command. Remember to assign passwords to each user.

2. Use the `groupadd project` command to create the project group. Edit `/etc/group` to add your new users to that group.

3. Set up a new shared directory, called `/home/project`. Give it full permissions (`rwx`) for the user and group that own this directory with the `chmod 770 /home/project` command.

4. Configure the SGID bit on the directory with the `chmod g+s /home/project` command. This allows all users in the group that owns the directory to have ownership-level permissions.

5. Feel free to log in as one of the users. Copy files from the home directory of a user to `/home/project`. Log in as a different user in the same group. Can you do anything with the file copied by the first user?

TIP   It's possible to combine the two `chmod` *commands; the* `chmod 2770 /home/project` *command configures the noted permissions and adds the SGID bit to that directory.*

Summary

In this chapter, we examined the basics of how users and groups are managed in Red Hat Linux. We began with the configuration files. While `/etc/passwd` and `/etc/group` contain basic information about users and groups, `/etc/shadow` and `/etc/gshadow` include encrypted passwords and password age parameters in more secure files. New users are assigned a home directory with a copy of the files in `/etc/skel`, based on the parameters shown in `/etc/login.defs`.

You can create users and groups directly, by editing the appropriate configuration files. You can create them more efficiently with commands such as **useradd** and **groupadd**. Users and groups can be deleted with the nearly parallel **userdel** and **groupdel** commands. And you can manage how user passwords are regulated with the **chage** command.

This system of users, groups, and associated commands is known as the Shadow Password Suite. With the appropriate strong passwords, this suite can improve the security of your user and group accounts. The `pwconv` and `grpconv` commands convert `/etc/passwd` and `/etc/group` to conform to this suite. The `pwunconv` and `grpunconv` commands reverse this process.

You can manage the demands of your users with quotas. Linux quotas can limit users by inodes or by the space their files occupy on a specific partition. Quotas are easily configurable once you've modified `/etc/fstab` to incorporate quotas on desired filesystems. And once they're configured, Red Hat Linux automatically activates your quotas when it boots.

Finally, the Red Hat User Private Group scheme provides additional security by isolating every user in his or her own unique individual group. However, you can still organize users in a common group with a shared directory.

In the next chapter, you'll learn all about the Red Hat way of managing packages with the Red Hat Package Manager. This system has been so successful that it has been adapted by a number of other competitive Linux distributions.

Chapter 10

Managing Packages with RPM

THE RED HAT PACKAGE Manager (RPM) provides a standardized way to group the software that you need for various utilities and applications. RPMs make it possible for Red Hat to organize Linux into fewer than 2,000 packages instead of tens of thousands of files.

You'll find that using RPMs to add new programs and applications is an easy process. The RPM is so successful that it has been adapted as the primary package manager by other competitive Linux distributions, including SuSE and SCO (formerly Caldera).

As an administrator, you'll want to install, upgrade, remove, and maintain many different RPM packages. RPMs also include dependency information, which helps you install any prerequisite packages you might need. When Red Hat adds new features or provides more secure software, you may want to upgrade what you have as well.

While the RPMs that you install are in binary format, Red Hat provides the source code for each package. You can use the `rpmbuild` command to organize and build these packages into the binary files that anyone can install. Alternatively, you can build binary RPMs from the other standard package system, known colloquially as the *tarball*.

One of the advantages of RPMs is that you can verify the integrity of packages and files. If a file has been modified without your knowledge, the correct `rpm` command identifies the altered file.

The RPM system is rich with features. This chapter just scratches the surface, providing what I believe are the most important RPM skills to the Linux administrator.

Red Hat also stores the latest RPMs through a system known as Rawhide. Alternatively, you can use `up2date` to update the RPMs of your choice based on a current database of upgradeable RPMs. This chapter covers the following topics:

- ◆ Installing and upgrading, simplified
- ◆ Using source RPMs
- ◆ Understanding the verify and list process
- ◆ Introducing a special agent: `up2date`

Installing and Upgrading, Simplified

Installations and upgrades form the essence of managing RPM packages. When you install an RPM, you're adding new software to your system. When you're upgrading an RPM, you're updating the associated software with the latest features.

Before you install or upgrade an RPM, you should know whether the desired package is already on your system. The RPM query can also give you descriptive information about the package, and verify and list the files associated with the package.

You can install or upgrade RPMs from local or remote sources. There are provisions to include username/password combinations when you access a binary RPM from a remote location.

RPM packages include dependency information. For example, the kernel source code RPM needs the GNU C language compiler. Since the kernel source is dependent, you should install the compiler before installing the source code.

If you're looking for a specific file, install the standard Red Hat Linux database of RPMs. This can help you identify packages that you might need to install.

Queries

The query mode of the `rpm` command has many dimensions. In its simplest form, you can run this command to find the version of an installed package. With additional switches, you can use it to view summary information, list the files, verify the contents, and more.

A SIMPLE QUERY

The simplest query takes the form of `rpm -q` *packagename*. For example, you can locate the installed version of the setup RPM, which contains a number of basic configuration files. Just run the following command:

```
# rpm -q setup
setup-2.5.25-1
```

INFORMATION QUERIES

Queries can provide more information about a package. For example, the `rpm -qi` *packagename* command helps you get the summary information associated with the **setup** RPM. The output, as shown in Figure 10.1, can reveal a lot of good information about a specific package.

IDENTIFYING THE OWNER

Suppose you've heard that upgrades are available for a certain file but you don't know what RPM package to use. In this case, just use the `rpm -qf` *filename* command to identify the name of the package. For example, if you need to identify the RPM package that owns the */etc/passwd* configuration file, run the following command:

```
# rpm -qf /etc/passwd
setup-2.5.25-1
```

Note that you need the full path to the file in question.

FIGURE 10.1

An RPM package summary information

```
[root@RH9Desk root]# rpm -qi setup
Name        : setup                  Relocations: (not relocateable)
Version     : 2.5.25                      Vendor: Red Hat, Inc.
Release     : 1                       Build Date: Mon 17 Feb 2003 11:49:35
 AM EST
Install Date: Mon 31 Mar 2003 03:10:13 PM EST      Build Host: daffy.perf.redhat
.com
Group       : System Environment/Base    Source RPM: setup-2.5.25-1.src.rpm
Size        : 34827                       License: public domain
Signature   : DSA/SHA1, Mon 24 Feb 2003 12:56:03 AM EST, Key ID 219180cddb42a60e
Packager    : Red Hat, Inc. <http://bugzilla.redhat.com/bugzilla>
Summary     : A set of system configuration and setup files.
Description :
The setup package contains a set of important system configuration and
setup files, such as passwd, group, and profile.
[root@RH9Desk root]# []
```

LISTING THE FILES IN AN RPM

If you're not sure about a package, you can list the files within by using the `rpm -ql` *packagename* command. That list confirms whether certain configuration files or commands are part of that package. If you're upgrading, that information can help you understand what is at risk when you upgrade. Listing the files in the **setup** RPM provides a good example, as shown in Figure 10.2.

FIGURE 10.2

A list of files in an RPM package

```
[root@RH9Desk root]# rpm -ql setup
/etc/bashrc
/etc/csh.cshrc
/etc/csh.login
/etc/exports
/etc/filesystems
/etc/group
/etc/host.conf
/etc/hosts.allow
/etc/hosts.deny
/etc/inputrc
/etc/motd
/etc/passwd
/etc/printcap
/etc/profile
/etc/profile.d
/etc/protocols
/etc/securetty
/etc/services
/etc/shells
/usr/share/doc/setup-2.5.25
/usr/share/doc/setup-2.5.25/uidgid
/var/log/lastlog
[root@RH9Desk root]# []
```

TIP   Package upgrades are always a risk. If you've configured a daemon and then overwrite it with an upgrade, you may lose your custom configuration. While RPM is supposed to save configuration files with the .rpm* *extension, it is still a good practice to back up key configuration files. In some cases, installing two versions of the same package is safer than upgrading. You'll see an example of where this is true when you upgrade the Linux kernel in Chapter 12.*

RPMs AND CPUs

Many RPMs are built for specific CPUs. For example, many RPMs have an extension such as `.i386.rpm` or `.noarch.rpm`. While Red Hat Linux 9 can't be installed on computers with Intel 386–level CPUs, RPMs with the `.i386.rpm` extension can be installed on all Red Hat Linux computers with Intel-compatible Pentium-level CPUs.

RPMs with other extensions are optimized for their CPUs. When possible, you should install the RPM associated with your CPU. To find your CPU identifier, type the `uname -p` command. Table 10.1 shows several optional extensions.

TABLE 10.1: RPM EXTENSIONS

EXTENSION	CPU
noarch.rpm	Does not depend on the CPU; can be installed on all computers.
i386.rpm	Based on the Intel 386 CPU, these RPM packages can be installed on all Intel-compatible computers.
i486.rpm	For computers with the Intel 486 CPU (now obsolete).
i586.rpm	For computers with the Intel 586 CPU.
i686.rpm	For computers with the Intel 686 CPU.
ia64.rpm	For computers with the Intel Itanium 64-bit CPU.
alpha.rpm	For computers with the HP Alpha CPU, originally developed by the former Digital Equipment Corporation.
athlon.rpm	Based on the AMD Athlon CPU.
ppc.rpm	For computers with the Apple PowerPC CPU.
s390.rpm	For IBM servers based on the S/390 CPU.
sparc.rpm	For computers with the Sun Microsystems SPARC CPU.

The Basic Installation

Installing a new RPM package is simple. Just use the `rpm -i` *packagename-versionnumber* command, and if that package is not already on your system, it is automatically installed. Normally, you'll be installing new RPMs from a source such as the Red Hat Linux installation CDs, mounted on /mnt/cdrom. Once the source is mounted, you might run the following command to install the **setup** RPM package:

```
# rpm -i /mnt/cdrom/RedHat/RPMS/setup-*
```

The asterisk is an appropriate wildcard, because RPM packages are updated frequently but the actual name of the package usually remains constant. If multiple packages start with **setup-***, this command installs all of them.

If you have a favorite online source for RPM packages, you can install them directly from the source. For example, if you want to install the `lynx` RPM package from the `RedHat/RPMS` directory on a server named abcd, run the following command:

```
# rpm -ivh ftp://abcd/RedHat/RPMS/lynx-*
```

As the `-i` extension installs, the `-v` and `-h` extensions set up verbose output with hashing, so you can monitor the progress of the installation. Some FTP servers require usernames and passwords. If you were installing the `lynx` RPM package, with a username of anonymous and a password of efgh, you could use the following command:

```
# rpm -ivh ftp://anonymous@ftp.redhat.com/pub/redhat/linux/rawhide/i386/RPMS/
➥lynx-*
Password for anonymous@ftp.redhat.com:
```

The password that you enter at the prompt is not shown on the screen. While you could add the password to the `rpm` command, it isn't advisable, since the password would appear on your screen and be transmitted in clear text over the Internet.

You can even use this command to install the latest version of multiple packages. But this command often does not work over the Internet; if you want to install a package reliably, download it first. The Rawhide packages discussed near the end of this chapter are the latest packages available from Red Hat.

NOTE   *When Red Hat develops a later version of an RPM package, it stores it in Rawhide. You can find these packages on the Red Hat FTP server (and mirror sites). As of this writing, they're stored in the* `/pub/redhat/linux/rawhide/` *`cputype`/RedHat/RPMS* *directory, where* `cputype` *represents the CPU for your system, such as* `i386` *or* `sparc`.

Upgrades

There are always risks associated with upgrades. You may accidentally overwrite configuration files that you've customized for your computer and/or your network. Or perhaps the upgraded software has interaction problems with other applications installed on your system.

However, there are often good reasons to upgrade an RPM package. Sometimes, you or your users need updated features. You may be upgrading software to address a security alert. Or you may need upgraded software (such as compilers) to handle upgraded versions of other new packages, such as kernels.

Two switches are associated with upgrades: `-U` and `-F`. Both switches can upgrade an RPM package. The difference is what happens if there is no installed RPM package to upgrade. In that case, the `rpm -U packagename` command installs the new package, and the `rpm -F packagename` command does not.

Generally, it is a good practice to include the `-v` (verbose) and the `-h` (hash mark) switches whenever you upgrade or freshen an RPM package. For example, if you're upgrading an installed version of the `lynx` RPM from a mounted CD, the following command can help you monitor the progress of the installation (with hash marks), as well as any error messages that might appear:

```
# rpm -Uvh /mnt/cdrom/RedHat/RPMS/lynx-*
```

Dependencies

When you try to install or upgrade an RPM, you may get an error message. Perhaps the most common rpm error message is based on dependencies.

An RPM dependency occurs when one package will not work unless a different package is already installed. The source code for the package lists other RPM packages that it needs—in other words, packages that it depends upon. You can see an example of a dependency from when I tried to install the kernel-source RPM:

```
# rpm -Uvh /mnt/cdrom/RedHat/RPMS/kernel-source-*
warning: /mnt/cdrom/RedHat/RPMS/ kernel-source-2.4.20-11.i386.rpm: Header V3 DSA
➥ signature: NOKEY, key ID 89da07a
error: Failed dependencies:
   gcc >= 2.96-98 is needed by kernel-source-2.4.20-11
Suggested resolutions:
   gcc-3.2.2-5.i386.rpm
```

The output suggests that I need to install the gcc (GNU C Compiler) package first. You could install both packages simultaneously, or install gcc first. If this seems like a lot of trouble, you could also use the rpm --nodeps switch to ignore the dependency. As long as you install gcc before you actually use the kernel-source package, this should not be a problem. One way to do that is with the following commands:

```
# rpm -Uvh --nodeps /mnt/cdrom/RedHat/RPMS/kernel-source-*
# rpm -Uvh /mnt/cdrom/RedHat/RPMS/gcc-3*
```

Deletions

It's easy to delete an RPM package by using the -e switch. You don't even have to know the version number of the package. For example, the following command deletes the kernel-source RPM:

```
# rpm -e kernel-source
```

Since you do not need to cite the path to delete an RPM, it is easy to delete multiple packages with the same command:

```
# rpm -e kernel-source gcc
```

A Database of RPMs

Say you're looking for a file or a command, and discover that it isn't yet installed on your computer. You know that Red Hat Linux files are organized by RPM packages. In some cases, it isn't too difficult to figure out the right RPM to install; for example, commands such as smbclient are part of the samba-client-* RPM package. However, if you're looking for the RPM associated with some obscure program library, finding the right package can be more difficult.

This is where the Red Hat Linux database can help. Once installed, the rpmdb-redhat-* RPM can help you find the RPM package associated with every file that you can install in the current version of Red Hat Linux.

As an example, if you're looking for the package associated with /etc/exports, the following command will work, once the **rpmdb-redhat-*** RPM package is installed:

```
# rpm --redhatprovides /etc/exports
setup-versionnumber
```

Making Source RPMs Work

A key feature of Linux is the easy accessibility to the source code. Since Red Hat Linux is built on RPM packages, that means access to the *source RPMs* (SRPMs). An SRPM includes the code and instructions needed to build a *binary RPM*, which you can then install on your Red Hat Linux computer.

Processing source code now requires the `rpm-build` RPM package. While the `rpm` command still provides legacy support for managing SRPMs, you'll need to use the `rpmbuild` command for this purpose in the future.

To understand how to use a source RPM, you need to know the default directory structure and understand that `.spec` files are used to build a binary RPM.

Directories

By convention, SRPMs are easy to identify; they have the `.src.rpm` extension. SRPMs include specification and other files, which you can set up in various `/usr/src/redhat` subdirectories. Any SRPM that you build into a binary file is also set up in the same directory structure. The five key SRPM directories are shown in Table 10.2.

TABLE 10.2: SOURCE RPM DIRECTORIES

DIRECTORY	FUNCTION
/usr/src/redhat/BUILD	Any source code that you process is unpacked and built here.
/usr/src/redhat/RPMS	Binary RPMs that you create from an SPRM are found here.
/usr/src/redhat/SOURCES	Contains the actual source code.
/usr/src/redhat/SPECS	Includes the files that control the RPM build process.
/usr/src/redhat/SRPMS	Includes SRPMs created during the build process.

To break an SPRM down into these directories, you need to install it. For example, if you want to work with the `anonftp` package, you'll need to install the associated `.src.rpm` file. For example, if you've mounted an SRPM Red Hat CD, you might use the following command:

```
# rpm -i /mnt/cdrom/RedHat/SRPMS/anaconda-*.src.rpm
```

The Spec File

The key to managing an SRPM is in its spec file. Once you've installed an SRPM, you should be able to find its spec file in the `/usr/src/redhat/SPECS` directory. This file controls how packages are built, and configures commands when an RPM is installed or deleted.

The key sections in a spec file are `%prep`, `%build`, and `%install`. They allow you to build source and binary RPMs. One important variable is *Requires* or *BuildRequires*, which lists other packages that you should install first. Other typical sections in a `.spec` file include:

`%define` Includes basic parameters such as the location of the top-level directory for that package. For example, you might see a `ROOT /var/ftp` line in this section. The section includes basic summary information for the RPM. When this RPM is installed, this is what a user will see in response to the `rpm -qi` *packagename* command.

`%package` Lists packages that depend on this particular RPM.

`%description` Provides more information for the `rpm -qi packagename` command.

`%prep` Includes preparation commands for archives and patches.

`%setup` Contains processing commands for unpacking archives.

`%build` Builds the code to be compiled.

`%install` Adds the commands that actually build the files and install the package in well-defined directories.

`%clean` Includes basic commands for deleting any intermediate files from your system.

`%post` Contains post-installation scripts, such as a script that modifies a user account.

`%postun` Contains scripts after you remove a package.

`%pre` Contains pre-installation scripts, such as a script that prepares a directory.

`%preun` Contains scripts before you remove a package.

`%triggerin` Contains parts of other packages you've copied.

`%config` Lists configuration files for `/etc`.

Spec files are not as difficult as they may look. For the most part, they include regular Linux commands and descriptions, which you can modify in a text editor.

Building Binaries from a Tarball

You can create an RPM from a tarball. But first, you need a spec file. As you've seen in the previous section, this can be a little difficult.

NOTE A tarball is a single file that is a package, or an archive, of a group of files. When you "unpack" a tarball, the files in the package are copied to the computer. In that way, a tarball is similar to a Microsoft Windows compressed "zip" file archive. Tarballs are typically available in a compressed format, with extensions such as `.tar.gz`, `.tgz`, and `.tar.bz2`.

One way to learn more about this process is to read different spec files. For example, take the following excerpts from a `dosemu.spec` file:

```
%define vimver 5.8
%define vim vim58
Summary: A DOS emulator.
```

```
Name: dosemu
Version: 1.1.1
Release: 3
Exclusivearch: %{ix86}
License: distributable
Group: Applications/Emulators
Source0: ftp://ftp.dosemu.org/dosemu/dosemu-%{version}.tar.bz2
...
Patch0: dosemu-0.66.7-config.patch
...
%package -n xdosemu
Requires: dosemu = %{PACKAGE_VERSION}
Summary: A DOS emulator for the X Window System.
Group: Applications/Emulators
```

This file was taken from a `dosemu-*.src.rpm` package. The system is fairly straightforward; from the code, you can find the release version, the URL for the source and related patch(es), and the summary description. You can also see that the `xdosemu` package requires `dosemu`, which sets up an RPM dependency.

Building a Binary RPM

All you need to create a binary RPM is the source code (which you can get from a source RPM or a tarball) and a spec file. You can create a spec file from scratch, or modify an existing spec file from a source RPM.

There are two basic ways to build a binary RPM:

```
# rpmbuild -ba packagename.spec
# rpmbuild -bb packagename.spec
```

The first command (`rpmbuild -ba`) creates binary and source RPM packages. The second command (`rpmbuild -bb`) creates only the binary RPM package.

NOTE   *The* `rpm -ba` *and* `rpm -bb` *commands no longer work starting with Red Hat Linux 9. Their functionality has been moved to the* `rpmbuild` *command, from the* `rpm-build-*` *RPM.*

RPM Security

Once you've learned to use RPMs, it's easy to become too dependent. A cracker might post a virus or a Trojan horse on an RPM posted online. The `rpm` command includes ways to check the integrity of an RPM, using the Pretty Good Privacy (PGP) system (see the next section). You can also verify the contents of a package, or even a specific file.

RPM and Pretty Good Privacy

The RPM system uses one of the security standards associated with e-mail security, known as Pretty Good Privacy (PGP). Developed by Phil Zimmerman, PGP provides a private- and public-key system. With Red Hat Linux, the GNU way of using PGP is known as the GNU Privacy Guard (GPG).

The key to all of this is the Red Hat GPG key. It should be installed by default as `/usr/share/doc/rpm-`*version*`/RPM-GPG-KEY`. If it isn't there, you can get it from at least one of the following sources:

◆ From the Red Hat Linux installation CDs, in the main directory. If you install CDs in the default location, the key will be in `/mnt/cdrom/RPM-GPG-KEY`.

◆ From `www.redhat.com`. As of this writing, it is available at `www.redhat.com/solutions/security/news/publickey.html`.

Next, import the GPG public key. For example, if you're importing from the installation CD, you should import to the `/var/lib/rpm/Pubkeys` file with the following command:

```
# rpm --import /mnt/cdrom/RPM-GPG-KEY
```

NOTE   *The* `rpm --import` *command is fairly new. If you're using an older version of Red Hat Linux (before 7.3), you may need to use the* `gpg --import` *publickey command.*

Verifying a Package

Now you can verify any RPM package for a genuine Red Hat Linux signature. For example, it may be a good idea to verify the integrity of the kernel sources before recompiling. To perform this task on a `kernel-sources` RPM in the `/tmp` directory, run the following command:

```
# rpm -K /tmp/kernel-source-*.rpm
/tmp/kernel-sources-versionnumber.rpm: (sha1) dsa sha1 md5 gpg OK
```

This verifies the integrity of the `kernel-source` RPM to the noted encryption schemes, including GPG.

Verifying a File

It's useful to check files against the original configuration. For example, if a cracker changes a file on your computer, you want to know about it. There are a number of standard things about every file you can check against the original. The data associated with every file installed through an RPM package is stored in the RPM database in the `/var/lib/rpm` directory.

If you suspect that a certain command isn't working quite as it should, you can check it against the RPM database. Let's take the `mount` command as an example. You can check the integrity of `mount` with the following command:

```
# rpm -Vf /bin/mount
```

If you don't see any output, the command matches what was originally installed.

Alternatively, if someone tampered with the `mount` command, you might see output similar to the following:

```
# rpm -Vf /bin/mount
SM5....T    /bin/mount
```

This command checks nine different attributes of /bin/mount. If you see one of the letters shown in Table 10.3, the file differs from the original in some way. In this particular case, there are changes to the file size, permissions, the MD5 checksum, and the file modification time.

TABLE 10.3: *RPM* FILE VERIFICATION ISSUES

OUTPUT	FAILED TEST
S	File size mismatch
M	Mode (different permissions and file type)
5	MD5 checksum wrong
L	Symbolic link incorrect
D	Device number wrong
U	User ownership changed
G	Group ownership changed
T	File modification time mismatch
?	Unreadable file
c	Configuration file flag

In some cases, a "failure" is not a problem. For example, if you've revised your /etc/inittab file, you'll see what looks like a verification failure:

```
# rpm -Vf /etc/inittab
..5....T c /etc/inittab
```

However, this particular "failure" may not mean that a problem exists. For example, I got this result after modifying the initdefault variable in this configuration file. In other words, the checksum (5) changed because I changed the content of the file; and the file modification time (T) is different from when Red Hat Linux was installed on my computer.

Updating RPMs

Red Hat keeps the most up-to-date RPMs available in a storehouse known as Rawhide. It's easy to access with any FTP client. As of this writing, you can find Rawhide RPMs on the Red Hat FTP server in the /pub/redhat/linux/rawhide directory.

If you want to upgrade a specific RPM, download it from Rawhide to a directory such as /tmp. Back up your current configuration as it relates to that package. If possible, use the rpm command to install (-i) and not upgrade (-U) the new package. If you have a problem, it's easier to restore the original configuration. You'll see an example of this process when you learn to upgrade the Linux kernel in Chapter 12.

A Special Agent: *up2date*

One alternative to Rawhide is the Red Hat Update Agent, also known by its text command, `up2date`. This section assumes you've registered for the Red Hat Network as discussed in Chapter 3. When you registered, you sent a list of installed RPM packages on your system. With the Red Hat Update Agent, you can check the Red Hat database for newer RPM packages, and have them installed as desired.

You can start the Red Hat Update Agent by running the `up2date` command at the command-line interface. Figure 10.3 assumes that you've already registered your computer on the Red Hat Network and started `up2date` in a GUI.

Otherwise, you may see the Red Hat Network Configuration window, and windows to log into the Red Hat Network and transmit basic information and a list of packages installed on your computer. For details, see Chapter 3.

FIGURE 10.3

Starting the Red Hat Update Agent

Assuming you've already registered, you should now see the Channels dialog box, as shown in Figure 10.4. As you can see, this dialog box lists the channel for Red Hat Linux 9. Click Forward to continue.

NOTE   *If you have an active Red Hat "Demo" account, you're limited to one computer on that account. You'll need to delete the current computer on that account before you can register the new computer.*

Next, `up2date` reviews the available RPM packages on the Red Hat network and compares them to what you have installed. Assuming you've designated RPM packages to be skipped during the registration process, and there are updates of those packages available, you should see something similar to Figure 10.5 (kernel version 2.4.21 was not available as of this writing). This gives you a chance to install these packages. Make any desired choices, and then click Forward to continue.

FIGURE 10.4

Red Hat update channels

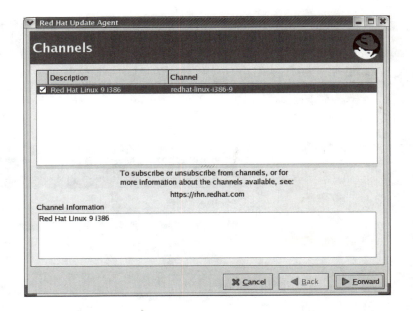

FIGURE 10.5

Packages Flagged to Be Skipped

The next step allows you to review available updates—in other words, newer RPM packages that you might install. Figure 10.6 configures the update of the Mozilla web browser (your choices will probably not be identical). Make your selections, and then click Forward to continue.

As described earlier, there can be RPM dependencies. If other packages need to be installed, `up2date` lists them for you.

Assuming you wish to proceed, click Forward to continue. The Red Hat Update Agent will begin downloading the desired and dependent RPM packages, similar to what is shown in Figure 10.7.

FIGURE 10.6

Available Package Updates

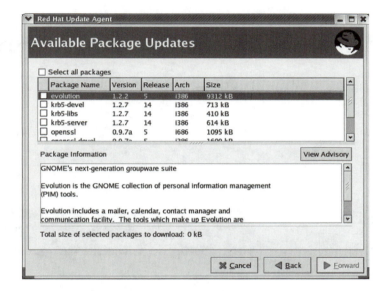

FIGURE 10.7

RPM package retrieval

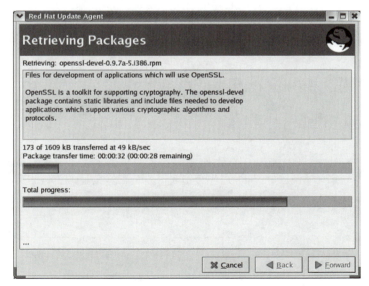

Now that the packages are on your Linux computer, `up2date` will begin installing them. Your system should look similar to Figure 10.8. Once installation is complete, you'll see a dialog box that lists the RPM packages that `up2date` installed on your computer.

FIGURE 10.8

RPM package installation

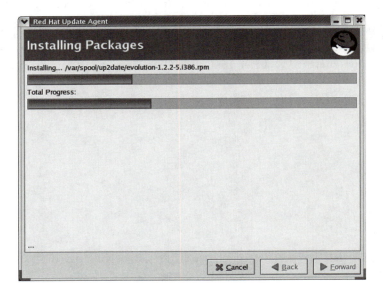

Summary

If you want to install new software in Red Hat Linux, you need to know how to manage RPM packages. You can use the `rpm` command to upgrade or install new packages locally from a source such as a CD, or remotely from a FTP or HTTP server.

The `rpm` command is flexible. With the right switches, you can query the status, the list of files, or even ownership of a package. A properly configured RPM package lists dependencies. For example, if you need the GNU C Compiler for something like the Linux kernel source, the `rpm` command won't let you install the `kernel-source` package first, at least not by default. If you need to find the right RPM, the `rpmdb-redhat-*` RPM package provides a database of all RPMs associated with your current Red Hat Linux distribution.

Linux is associated with easy accessibility to the source code. Red Hat Linux supports this with source RPMs. Once you've installed the `rpm-build` package, you can use the `rpmbuild` command to create binary RPMs from the source. All you need is a properly configured `.spec` file.

Spec files are included with Red Hat Linux SRPMs, and you can modify them to meet your needs. Alternatively, you can create your own `.spec` file to create a binary RPM from a tarball package.

It may be a bit too easy to become dependent on RPMs and ignore security issues. Therefore, Red Hat Linux supports the Pretty Good Privacy system. All you need is a genuine `RPM-GPG-KEY` file, available from several sources. Then you can verify the integrity of any RPM package with the `rpm -K` *packagename* command. If you suspect a problem with a specific file or command, you can even verify the integrity of that specific file with the `rpm -Vf` *filename* command.

If you're looking for the latest RPMs, check the Rawhide directory on your favorite FTP server. Red Hat posts the latest updates here first. Alternatively, you can use the Red Hat Update Agent to automate this process.

In the next chapter, you'll learn to analyze the boot process in detail. As you learn about the Linux boot process, you'll gain skills that can help you troubleshoot various kinds of boot problems. Finally, you can use the Red Hat installation CD's `linux rescue` mode to get around most boot problems so you can repair any damaged files.

Chapter 11

Configuring and Troubleshooting the Boot Process

SOMEDAY, RED HAT LINUX may have problems booting on your computer. If you see a message such as `kernel panic`, don't panic! You may not even have to restore your system from a backup. If you know the basic boot configuration files, you can quickly and easily diagnose and solve most boot problems.

To understand how Linux boot configuration files work, you need to understand the basic boot process, from hardware detection through runlevel management.

Then you can get into the nitty-gritty of the key boot configuration files for managing hardware, for finding your kernel, for starting your terminals, and for initializing services at the appropriate runlevel.

If you have a problem, the boot disk that you created during installation (you did create one, didn't you?) will normally get you around most problems. Otherwise, the Red Hat Linux installation boot disk, even the one on CD, can offer you a rich variety of rescue modes. This chapter covers the following topics:

◆ Exploring the basic boot process

◆ Understanding the default configuration files

◆ Troubleshooting and using rescue disks

Exploring the Basic Boot Process

Before getting into the nitty-gritty of Red Hat Linux configuration files, it's important to have a "big picture" overview of the process. While small changes can keep Red Hat Linux from booting, an understanding of the big picture can help you identify the problem quickly.

When you start your Linux computer, three basic steps are involved in the process. Hardware is initialized through your Basic Input/Output System (BIOS) and is then detected by Linux. The BIOS points to the Linux bootloader. Once the bootloader starts, it opens the kernel. Next, it starts `init`, the so-called "first program," which then loads your kernel, and moves to initialize other startup programs. Finally, Linux finds the default runlevel and starts all associated processes.

We provide detailed information on each of these processes later in this chapter.

Initializing Hardware

While this is not a book on computer hardware, it's helpful to know some basics. Then it's easy to determine if you have a hardware problem or a Linux problem.

Everything on a standard PC starts with the BIOS. The first step, associated with a series of beeps, is known as the power-on self-test (POST), which checks connections to basic hardware. It looks for other BIOSes related to IDE and SCSI hard drives. It may also detect other basic hardware on your system.

TIP   *If you're interested in the Linux+ certification exam from CompTIA, you need to know a lot more about PC hardware. For more information, see the* Complete PC Upgrade and Maintenance Guide, *2003 Edition (Sybex).*

After Linux initiates the loading process through the bootloader, it begins to detect hardware using the `kudzu` utility. Then it adds modules related to your hardware, using settings stored in `/etc/modules.conf`. You can analyze the results with the `dmesg` command. If you're having a hardware problem, a little detective work with `dmesg` output can help you identify the trouble.

Bootloaders

There are two basic Linux bootloaders, the Grand Unified Bootloader (GRUB) and the Linux Loader (LILO). GRUB is the default for Red Hat Linux. LILO is now obsolete, and will probably be removed in some future release of Red Hat Linux.

In either case, the bootloader is used for four purposes:

1. To select an operating system (if more than one is installed on your computer)

2. To identify the partition with the appropriate boot files

3. To locate the kernel

4. To run the Initial RAM disk to set up the kernel and associated modules

Runlevels

A *runlevel* is a specific way to organize initialized software in Linux. Different services are started and stopped at different runlevels. When you start Red Hat Linux, it looks to `/etc/inittab` to determine the default runlevel, which then points to an associated subdirectory of `/etc/rc.d` to identify the services to kill and start.

Understanding the Default Configuration Files

To recap, there are key startup configuration files for hardware, for the bootloader, and for runlevels. The hardware configuration files help you determine what was detected. The bootloader enables you to trace the location of the kernel, the Initial RAM disk, and any other operating systems on your computer. The directories for each runlevel help you customize the processes that start and stop on your Linux computer.

Hardware Detection

Once GRUB or LILO finds your boot files, the next step is to make a connection between the Linux kernel and your computer's hardware. The Linux hardware detection process consists of several parts. First, Linux takes data related to basic hardware from your BIOS. Next, it uses the kudzu utility to look for new hardware on your system. Assuming you have a default modular kernel, it then inserts any modules related to specialized hardware from the /etc/modules.conf file. You can inspect the messages related to this process with the dmesg command.

KERNEL CONNECTIONS

The dmesg command should show you how your kernel interacts with your hardware as Linux starts on your computer. It starts with your BIOS; uses related information to find your CPU, hard drives, PCI (Peripheral Component Interconnect) devices, and communications ports; starts the appropriate filesystems on the right partitions; and finally configures other basic devices related to keyboards and mice. Figure 11.1 shows an excerpt from my dmesg output.

FIGURE 11.1

Excerpt from dmesg

```
Linux version 2.4.20-8 (bhcompile@porky.devel.redhat.com) (gcc version 3.2.2 200
30222 (Red Hat Linux 3.2.2-5)) #1 Thu Mar 13 17:54:28 EST 2003
BIOS-provided physical RAM map:
 BIOS-e820: 0000000000000000 - 000000000009f800 (usable)
 BIOS-e820: 000000000009f800 - 00000000000a0000 (reserved)
 BIOS-e820: 00000000000ca000 - 00000000000cc000 (reserved)
 BIOS-e820: 00000000000dc000 - 00000000000e0000 (reserved)
 BIOS-e820: 00000000000e4000 - 0000000000100000 (reserved)
 BIOS-e820: 0000000000100000 - 000000000bef0000 (usable)
 BIOS-e820: 000000000bef0000 - 000000000befc000 (ACPI data)
 BIOS-e820: 000000000befc000 - 000000000bf00000 (ACPI NVS)
 BIOS-e820: 000000000bf00000 - 000000000c000000 (usable)
 BIOS-e820: 00000000fec00000 - 00000000fec10000 (reserved)
 BIOS-e820: 00000000fee00000 - 00000000fee01000 (reserved)
 BIOS-e820: 00000000fffe0000 - 0000000100000000 (reserved)
0MB HIGHMEM available.
192MB LOWMEM available.
On node 0 totalpages: 49152
zone(0): 4096 pages.
zone(1): 45056 pages.
zone(2): 0 pages.
Kernel command line: ro root=LABEL=/
Initializing CPU#0
--More--
```

From the sample output, you can identify one CPU and 128MB of memory. If you actually have more than one CPU and additional RAM installed, this output tells you that Linux did not detect this additional hardware.

KUDZU

The current version of Kudzu is the culmination of Linux efforts to support plug-and-play hardware. In the past, using plug-and-play hardware on Linux was at best an uncertain venture. Now it manages any new hardware that you throw at it without a hitch.

Kudzu works by looking at the various ports on your computer. If it detects and recognizes new hardware, it adds the relevant information, such as device and driver names, to /etc/sysconfig/hwconf.

If special hardware drivers are required, specifications are added to /etc/modules.conf. Linux reads this file during the boot process to load the required drivers the next time you start your computer.

If you've just added new hardware and want to make sure Red Hat Linux detects it properly, just run the kudzu command. If additional configuration is required, you could be taken to a text version of redhat-config-mouse (See Chapter 19); the steps look similar to the deprecated mouseconfig utility. In rare cases, you may be prompted to add information such as IRQ ports, I/O addresses, or DMA channels.

KERNELS AND HARDWARE

Linux makes it easy to see how the Linux kernel views your hardware. Just look in the /proc directory. As shown in Table 11.1, various files in /proc can give you additional information on the hardware that is connected to Red Hat Linux.

TABLE 11.1: SELECTED HARDWARE FILES IN /PROC

FILE	DESCRIPTION
apm	Advanced power management battery status
cpuinfo	Detected CPUs
dma	Assigned DMAs
ide	Directory specifying attached IDE devices
interrupts	Assigned IRQs
ioports	Assigned I/O addresses
modules	Installed driver modules; same as lsmod output
partitions	Basic partition information
pci	Detected PCI devices
scsi	Directory specifying attached SCSI devices

The information is quite detailed. For example, take a look at the /proc/cpuinfo file in Figure 11.2. Not only does it show the rated and the effective speed of the CPU, but it also shows the cpu family, which helps you find the optimized Linux kernel to use for your system. In this case, I'd use the kernel-*versionnumber*.i686.rpm package. You'll see how this helps in the next chapter.

FIGURE 11.2

Kernel information on the CPU

```
processor       []: 0
vendor_id       : GenuineIntel
cpu family      : 6
model           : 11
model name      : Intel(R) Pentium(R) III Mobile CPU        1200MHz
stepping        : 1
cpu MHz         : 1386.351
cache size      : 32 KB
fdiv_bug        : no
hlt_bug         : no
f00f_bug        : no
coma_bug        : no
fpu             : yes
fpu_exception   : yes
cpuid level     : 2
wp              : yes
flags           : fpu vme de pse tsc msr pae mce cx8 sep mtrr pge mca cmov pat p
se36 mmx fxsr sse
bogomips        : 2366.82

~
~
~
"/proc/cpuinfo" [readonly] 19L, 401C
```

The */etc/modules.conf* Settings

Sometimes Red Hat Linux needs a little help with kernel configuration settings. There are cases where default plug-and-play settings for different components might interfere with each other. That's where the /etc/modules.conf configuration file steps in. It's where Linux stores driver, device, and address settings for various hardware components. Take the following excerpt from my /etc/modules.conf file:

```
alias eth0 pcnet32
alias usb-controller usb-uhci
options sb io=0x220 irq=5 dma=1 dma16=5 mpu_io=0x330
```

Note how this defines drivers for the first Ethernet card, the USB controller, and a SoundBlaster (sb) card. As Linux detects more and more hardware, the importance of this file will decline over time.

When you change the /etc/modules.conf file, you can test the results immediately. For example, if you're trying to find the right settings for the SoundBlaster card, you could use the following command:

```
# modprobe sb
```

If you don't see an error message, check the lsmod command again. Your sound card is probably now installed. Otherwise, check the error messages carefully for clues on your next step, which is probably to try different hardware settings.

Listing Modules

You can verify whether Red Hat was able to detect your hardware. Besides reviewing the earlier discussion on the /proc directory, you can review installed modules with the lsmod command. For example, this command on my computer lists a series of modules in Figure 11.3.

FIGURE 11.3

1smod lists installed modules.

```
[root@RH9Desk root]# lsmod
Module                  Size  Used by    Not tainted
smbfs                   44368  1  (autoclean)
ide-cd                  35708  0  (autoclean)
cdrom                   33728  0  (autoclean) [ide-cd]
parport_pc              19076  1  (autoclean)
lp                       8996  0  (autoclean)
parport                 37056  1  (autoclean) [parport_pc lp]
autofs                  13268  0  (autoclean) (unused)
pcnet32                 18240  1
mii                      3976  0  [pcnet32]
keybdev                  2944  0  (unused)
mousedev                 5492  1
hid                     22148  0  (unused)
input                    5856  0  [keybdev mousedev hid]
usb-uhci                26348  0  (unused)
usbcore                 78784  1  [hid usb-uhci]
ext3                    70784  2
jbd                     51892  2  [ext3]
BusLogic               100796  3
sd_mod                  13452  6
scsi_mod               107128  2  [BusLogic sd_mod]
[root@RH9Desk root]#
```

As you can see, each module has a file size in bytes. Some modules depend on others; for example, note how the mii module is required for the **pcnet32** network driver module. In other words, if you tried to remove the mii module with the following command, you'd get an error message:

```
# rmmod mii
mii: Device or resource busy
```

If you remove the **pcnet32** network card from your computer, Linux won't install either module the next time you start your computer. Alternatively, you could shut down networking and then remove the modules in order:

```
# rmmod pcnet32
# rmmod mii
```

You could install modules just as easily; for example, if you need to install a new 3Com Ether-Link network card and Linux isn't detecting it, you might try installing the associated module with the following command:

```
# insmod 3c589_cs
```

If successful, you won't see any error messages; check the result with the 1smod command. You should see the network card module in the output.

The Bootloader

As we mentioned earlier, the default Red Hat Linux bootloader is known as GRUB. It is a significant improvement over LILO in a number of ways, including:

◆ It can be password-protected.

◆ It is easy to edit during the boot process. You can try different boot parameters without permanent changes to the GRUB configuration file.

◆ It can boot Windows NT operating systems from the Master Boot Record area of your hard drive.

♦ It supports Logical Block Addressing (LBA) mode, which can help your computer find the /**boot** files, especially if they are beyond the 1024th cylinder on your hard drive.

LILO is now deprecated; Red Hat plans to remove LILO from Red Hat Linux, probably in the near future. Therefore, this older bootloader is not covered in this book.

Take a look at a typical GRUB configuration file in Figure 11.4, from /**boot/grub/grub.conf**.

FIGURE 11.4

Dual-boot GRUB

```
# grub.conf generated by anaconda
#
# Note that you do not have to rerun grub after making changes to this file
# NOTICE:  You have a /boot partition.  This means that
#          all kernel and initrd paths are relative to /boot/, eg.
#          root (hd0,0)
#          kernel /vmlinuz-version ro root=/dev/sda2
#          initrd /initrd-version.img
#boot=/dev/sda
password --md5 $1$6Thul/$aaGq2O8r.MXTj2KLuR8QV1
default=0
timeout=10
splashimage=(hd0,0)/grub/splash.xpm.gz
title Red Hat Linux (2.4.20-8)
        root (hd0,0)
        kernel /vmlinuz-2.4.20-8 ro root=LABEL=/
        initrd /initrd-2.4.20-8.img
title DOS
        rootnoverify (hd0,0)
        chainloader +1
_
_
```

The variables shown in Figure 11.4 are explained in Table 11.2.

TABLE 11.2: SELECTED GRUB VARIABLES

VARIABLE	COMMENT
password	Password-protects GRUB. With the --md5 switch, the password can be entered in encrypted format.
default	Specifies the default operating system. If default=0, the operating system shown in the first stanza boots automatically if there is no user input.
timeout	Sets the time limit before GRUB starts the default, in seconds.
splashimage	Notes the default GRUB image.
title	Sets the option as shown in the GRUB menu.
root	Specifies the partition with the /boot files.
kernel	Notes the location of the Linux kernel.
initrd	Points to the location of the Initial RAM disk.
rootnoverify	Specifies the partition with boot files for a sensitive operating system such as Windows XP.
chainloader	With +1, looks for boot files in the first sector of the noted partition.

The root variable in GRUB may be confusing, because it actually refers to the partition with the /boot directory. Note the data associated with root, such as (hd0,0) or (hd0,1). This data points to the partition with the boot files for that operating system.

If you're having trouble with hardware, use the hardware modules described earlier as much as possible. However, you may need to give Linux some help finding hardware critical to the boot process, such as a hard drive or a SCSI controller for a hard drive. In that case, you should specify a module in the kernel line. For example, if you want to specify an IRQ of 9, an IO address of 0x330, and a SCSI ID of 7 for an older Adaptec controller, add the following command to the kernel line in your grub.conf configuration file:

```
kernel /vmlinux-2.4.20-2.2 ro root=LABEL=/ aha152x=0x330,9,7
```

The boot hard disk is shown as a comment as /dev/sda. Therefore, root (hd0,1) points to Linux boot files on the first SCSI hard drive, on the second partition, also known as /dev/sda2. Similarly, the root (hd0,0) setting points to DOS boot files on the first SCSI hard drive, on the first partition (/dev/sda1).

NOTE   *For convenience,* /etc/grub.conf *is linked to the actual bootloader configuration file,* /boot/grub/grub.conf.

TIP   *The word root has several meanings in Linux. There is the root user, with a home directory of* /root. *There is the top-level root directory, associated with the forward slash,* /. *And in GRUB, the root variable actually points to the partition with the* /boot *directory. So when you see* / *in the GRUB configuration file, it's really the* /boot *directory.*

ADDING A PASSWORD TO GRUB

If you forgot to add a GRUB password during Red Hat Linux installation, it's easy to add a secure MD5 password to GRUB. Just use the grub-md5-crypt command. When prompted, enter the password of your choice. You'll get a strange-looking series of characters that you can copy to the GRUB configuration file, in the format shown in Figure 11.2.

It's easy to copy this password from the command line. Just use your mouse to highlight the password. Open /etc/grub.conf in a text editor. Right-click your mouse in the desired location, and then Linux automatically inserts the highlighted MD5 password. Alternatively, if you're in the GNOME terminal, a right-click opens a pop-up menu that allows you to copy and paste the highlighted text.

/etc/inittab

Linux now initializes the key files, processes, and applications on your system. The governing configuration file is /etc/inittab. Open it in your favorite text editor. The key variable in this file is initdefault; the other variables just set up important parts of the Linux environment. My /etc/inittab file is shown in Figure 11.5.

The initdefault variable sets the default runlevel, which starts when you boot Linux. For example, the following line configures your computer to start in runlevel 3.

```
id:3:initdefault
```

```
#
# inittab        This file describes how the INIT process should set up
#                the system in a certain run-level.
#
# Author:        Miquel van Smoorenburg, <miquels@drinkel.nl.mugnet.org>
#                Modified for RHS Linux by Marc Ewing and Donnie Barnes
#

# Default runlevel. The runlevels used by RHS are:
#   0 - halt (Do NOT set initdefault to this)
#   1 - Single user mode
#   2 - Multiuser, without NFS (The same as 3, if you do not have networking)
#   3 - Full multiuser mode
#   4 - unused
#   5 - X11
#   6 - reboot (Do NOT set initdefault to this)
#
id:3:initdefault:

# System initialization.
si::sysinit:/etc/rc.d/rc.sysinit

l0:0:wait:/etc/rc.d/rc 0
l1:1:wait:/etc/rc.d/rc 1
l2:2:wait:/etc/rc.d/rc 2
l3:3:wait:/etc/rc.d/rc 3
l4:4:wait:/etc/rc.d/rc 4
l5:5:wait:/etc/rc.d/rc 5
l6:6:wait:/etc/rc.d/rc 6

# Trap CTRL-ALT-DELETE
ca::ctrlaltdel:/sbin/shutdown -t3 -r now

# When our UPS tells us power has failed, assume we have a few minutes
# of power left.  Schedule a shutdown for 2 minutes from now.
# This does, of course, assume you have powerd installed and your
# UPS connected and working correctly.
pf::powerfail:/sbin/shutdown -f -h +2 "Power Failure; System Shutting Down"
```

There are six standard Red Hat Linux runlevels, as shown in Table 11.3 (runlevel 4 is not used by Red Hat). In the next section, we'll explore what happens when Linux boots in runlevel 3.

TABLE 11.3: STANDARD RED HAT LINUX RUNLEVELS

RUNLEVEL	FUNCTION
0	Halt; shuts down Linux; init stops all services currently running on your computer.
1	Single-user mode; no networking; init starts just the programs needed to allow one user to log into your Linux system; as you'll see later in this chapter, you can go into single-user mode to fix critical files and more.
2	Multiuser mode; no NFS access; init starts the programs that allow multiple users to log into your Linux system simultaneously.
3	Multiuser mode with networking; init starts the network daemons on your computer after the multiuser runlevel.
5	Graphical login; init starts your network programs, and then starts X Window programs that can be split between client and server,
6	Reboot; shuts down Linux and restarts your computer at the runlevel defined by the id command in /etc/inittab.

Other Linux distributions may use different standard runlevels.

WARNING *Do not set your default runlevel to 0 or 6. If you do, your computer will either shut down or go into a continuous reboot cycle when you start Linux.*

The standard Red Hat Linux `/etc/inittab` file includes several other important commands. The following command

```
si::sysinit:/etc/rc.d/rc.sysinit
```

runs the `rc.sysinit` script, which activates configured networks, quotas, fonts; mounts filesystems; activates Logical Volume Management (LVM) and RAID partitions; loads hardware modules; and more. In short, `rc.sysinit` sets the stage for Linux to activate services.

To help Microsoft Windows users, `/etc/inittab` associates the Ctrl+Alt+Del key combination with the `shutdown` command.

TIP *If you're setting up a Linux server, you may want to comment out the `ca::ctrlaltdel:/sbin/shutdown -t3 r now` command. You don't want the frustration of one user to halt the system for everyone.*

By default, Red Hat Linux uses `/etc/inittab` to set up six virtual terminal consoles, `tty1` through `tty6`. You can access different virtual consoles by pressing Ctrl+Alt+F*n*, where *n* is the number of the console. Red Hat Linux allows you to configure up to 12 virtual consoles, with commands such as the following in `/etc/inittab`:

```
1:2345:respawn:/sbin/mingetty tty1
```

This command configures the first virtual console (`tty1`) whenever Linux starts runlevels 2, 3, 4, or 5.

TIP *If you've just edited `/etc/inittab`, you may not need to reboot. For example, if you've added a virtual console, the `telinit q` command forces Linux to reread `/etc/inittab`.*

THE FIRST PROCESS: *INIT*

Closely related to `/etc/inittab` is the first process, `init`. It works at several different runlevels, primarily scripts in the `/etc/rc.d` directory. For example, if you run the `init 5` command, Linux runs the scripts in the `/etc/rc.d/rc5.d` directory.

Starting a Runlevel

Now we'll look at how Red Hat Linux starts a runlevel with the `initdefault` variable. As we described earlier, it's common for Red Hat Linux to start in runlevel 3, full multiuser mode. When Linux reads the desired runlevel, it starts the associated script. In this case, the following command starts all of the scripts associated with runlevel 3:

```
l3:3:wait:/etc/rc.d/rc 3
```

This command points to a set of scripts at the associated runlevel, and then executes kill and start scripts, in that order. It's easy to compare two different runlevels. Just examine the list of scripts in the appropriate directories. Figure 11.6 compares the scripts from runlevel 3 with runlevel 1.

NOTE   The kill and start scripts that you see on your computer vary with the services that you've installed, and those that you've activated in that runlevel.

FIGURE 11.6

Resource control scripts

```
[root@RH9Desk root]# \ls /etc/rc.d/rc3.d/
K05saslauthd   K95firstboot    S13portmap     S28autofs      S90cups
K15httpd       S05kudzu        S14nfslock     S55sshd        S90xfs
K20nfs         S06vmware-tools S17keytable    S56rawdevices  S95anacron
K24irda        S08iptables     S20random      S56xinetd      S95atd
K35smb         S09isdn         S24pcmcia      S80sendmail    S97rhnsd
K35winbind     S10network      S25netfs       S85gpm         S99local
K74ntpd        S12syslog       S26apmd        S90crond
[root@RH9Desk root]# \ls /etc/rc.d/rc1.d/
K03rhnsd       K15gpm          K35smb         K74apmd        K88syslog      K96pcmcia
K05anacron     K15httpd        K35winbind     K74ntpd        K90network     S00single
K05atd         K20nfs          K44rawdevices  K75netfs       K91isdn        S17keytable
K05saslauthd   K24irda         K50xinetd      K80random      K92iptables
K10cups        K25sshd         K60crond       K86nfslock     K95firstboot
K10xfs         K30sendmail     K72autofs      K87portmap     K95kudzu
[root@RH9Desk root]# []
```

The directories are fairly straightforward; kill scripts start with a K, while start scripts begin with an S. These scripts are executed in the order shown. But there are differences. Runlevel 3 starts over 25 services, many related to networking. Runlevel 1 kills just about every available service, except those needed for single-user mode. No networking or multiuser configurations are required in single-user mode.

NOTE   Remember, a script such as S05kudzu *starts a service and a script such as* K15httpd *kills a different service. For more information on service management, see Chapter 13.*

Troubleshooting and Using Rescue Disks

As a system administrator, you'll need to examine and edit a number of configuration files. When changes are made, mistakes are possible. For example, if you make a mistake in editing the GRUB configuration file, you might see the following message the next time you boot Linux:

```
root (hd0,1)
 Filesystem type is ext2fs, partition type 0x83
kernel /vmlinuz-2.4.20-8 ro root=LABEL=/

Error 15: File not found

Press any key to continue
```

This is just one of many possible boot problems. Sometimes the boot disk floppy that you created during the installation process can help. If you've misplaced this disk, the `mkbootdisk` command can help.

However, the boot disk may not help you in every case. And if you don't have a boot disk, Red Hat Linux has other automated recovery options. You can use any standard installation boot disk, even the first installation CD, to rescue your Linux system. Depending on the problem, you could select the automated recovery process, or start Linux in single-user mode.

TIP   There's an optimized rescue CD that Red Hat sometimes makes available for download from `ftp.redhat.com`*. It includes text editors such as* `emacs` *and* `pico`*, as well as network utilities such as Telnet and FTP. Look for a file named* `rescue-cd.iso` *on the Red Hat FTP site. Use the techniques described in Chapter 14 to set up your CD.*

The Specialized Boot Disk

The easiest way to get around the specified problem is with a boot disk. The boot disk that you should have created during Red Hat Linux installation is customized for this purpose. As long as you haven't changed the way partitions are organized, the custom boot disk should start your Linux system.

It's easy to create a new boot disk with the `mkbootdisk` *versionnumber* command, where you use the version number associated with your Linux kernel. For example, if the kernel shown in the `/boot` directory is `vmlinuz-2.4.21-13`, the following command creates a customized boot disk on a 1.44MB floppy:

```
# mkbootdisk 2.4.21-13
Insert a disk in /dev/fd0. Any information on the disk will
➥ be lost. Press <Enter> to continue or ^C to abort:_
```

Just remember to test your customized boot disk as soon as possible. You don't want problems with this disk when you're trying to rescue your Linux system.

Rescue Mode

Customized boot disks don't solve all possible Linux boot problems. Fortunately, you're not out of luck. Even if you've lost your customized boot disk, Red Hat's `linux rescue` mode will normally get you into your Linux system. Once you've started Linux, you can restore or repair any damaged files that you have.

TIP   To use `linux rescue` *mode, you need access to the Red Hat Linux installation files. If you're starting from a network boot disk, you need the address and location of the* `/RedHat` *directory. See Chapter 4 for examples.*

You can start `linux rescue` mode from any Red Hat Linux installation boot disk. If you don't have one available, you can download it from `ftp.redhat.com` or associated mirror sites. You can even create installation boot disks on a Microsoft Windows computer using the `RAWRITE.EXE` utility discussed in Chapter 3. Just type `linux rescue` at the `boot:` prompt for installing Red Hat Linux:

```
boot: linux rescue
```

At this point, you may wonder if you did the right thing, because Red Hat Linux takes you through the first two steps of a standard installation: language and keyboard type. If you used a Red

Hat Linux installation floppy, you're taken to Figure 11.7, where you'll also need to enter the location (local or network) of the Red Hat Linux installation files. Refer to Chapter 4 if you need more information.

FIGURE 11.7

Enter the location of the Red Hat Linux installation files here

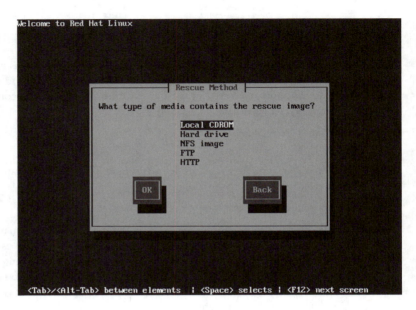

Now `linux rescue` mode presents a menu with three different options:

Continue   If you select Continue, Red Hat Linux searches your hard disk for your installation. All located filesystems are mounted as subdirectories of `/mnt/sysimage`. I think of this as automatic rescue mode.

Read-Only   The Read-Only option is almost identical, except that located filesystems are mounted in read-only mode. You can think of this as read-only rescue mode.

Skip   The Skip option proceeds directly to a root shell prompt in single-user mode. No attempt is made to look through available filesystems. I view this as a manual rescue mode.

Once you've made the necessary changes, type the `exit` command. Repeat as needed until you see messages regarding termination signals. Linux should unmount all filesystems and then automatically reboot your computer.

AUTOMATIC RESCUE MODE

If automatic rescue mode is successful, Red Hat Linux mounts all appropriate filesystems from `/etc/fstab` on `/mnt/sysimage`. In this case, the `df` command reflects the mounted directories, as shown in Figure 11.8.

FIGURE 11.8

Rescue mode
mounts

```
# df
Filesystem          1k-blocks     Used Available Use% Mounted on
rootfs                   2401      592      1672  26% /
/dev/root.old            2401      592      1672  26% /
/tmp/cdrom             659488   659488         0 100% /mnt/source
/dev/sda2             3771316  1434048   2145696  40% /mnt/sysimage
/dev/sda1              101089     9483     86387  10% /mnt/sysimage/boot
# _
```

In Figure 11.8, the CD is mounted on /mnt/source, /dev/sda2 is mounted on /mnt/sysimage, and /dev/sda1 is mounted on /mnt/sysimage/boot. While it's easy to see that /dev/sda1 is associated with /boot and /dev/sda2 is associated with root (/), you can confirm this with the e2label *partitiondevice* command:

```
# e2label /dev/sda1
/boot
```

But what if automatic rescue mode can't mount all of your filesystems? In this case, you might see an error message such as the following:

```
Error mounting filesystem on sdc1: Invalid argument
```

Simply continue with automatic rescue mode. Linux mounts as many filesystems as it can. In this case, you can work on any damage to an unmounted filesystem such as /dev/sdc1.

If you have one or more unmounted filesystems, the first two things to check are the fstab configuration file and the integrity of the format itself. At this point, you can use the vi editor to check fstab, but since the root (/) directory is actually mounted on /mnt/sysimage, you'll need the following command to open up fstab:

```
# vi /mnt/sysimage/etc/fstab
```

Alternatively, to clean up a damaged, unmounted filesystem, use the fsck *devicename* command. For example, to check /dev/sdc1, run the following command:

```
# fsck /dev/sdc1
```

TIP *If you want to access the Linux man pages in* linux rescue *mode, run the* chroot /mnt/sysimage *command. This restores your top-level root (/) directory to the top of the hierarchy, activating the standard paths to the Linux man pages.*

READ-ONLY RESCUE MODE

The only difference between read-only and automatic rescue mode is that all filesystems are mounted in read-only mode. This may be the best choice if you have a large number of filesystems, such as with a typical server installation of Red Hat Linux.

You can remount any desired filesystem in read-write mode. For example, the following command remounts partition device /dev/sda2 on the root (/) directory in read-write mode:

```
# mount -w -o remount /dev/sda2 /
```

NOTE *This command is equivalent to the* mount -o remount,rw / *command described in Chapter 7.*

MANUAL RESCUE MODE

Sometimes `linux rescue` mode can't find any of your filesystems. Don't panic; the problem could be as simple as an error in the name of /etc/fstab. Manual rescue mode is most appropriate here.

This mode loads a minimal root image and the kernel to a RAM disk, and then sends you to a root shell prompt (#). No filesystems are mounted; you have access only to a basic set of commands, such as `mount`, `mkdir`, `mv`, `cp`, `rm`, `fdisk`, and `fsck`. Once you've mounted a directory, you can also use the `vi` editor to change the files that you need.

But remember, this is a minimalist version of Linux. You don't have all the commands that you might be used to at this level.

In manual rescue mode, the first step is to mount the partition associated with your root (/) directory in a temporary location such as /mnt/sysimage. This should allow you access to additional commands from directories such as /bin, /sbin, and /usr/sbin.

Single-User Mode

There's one other method, known as *single-user mode*, that you can use to log into a damaged Linux system. If Linux can find your root (/) directory filesystem, it can start Linux in this mode. As described earlier, single-user mode, also known as runlevel 1, requires only two services.

Once you've made any required changes, you don't have to reboot. The `exit` command automatically moves you to the default runlevel as defined in /etc/inittab. Alternatively, the `init 3` or `init 5` commands can immediately start those respective runlevels. Single-user mode is also useful for changing the root password. If you forgot the password, run the `passwd` command in single-user mode. The password that you enter becomes the new root password.

Sometimes you'll encounter a problem such as a bad /etc/fstab file or an unmountable filesystem during the boot process. In this case, you'll see a prompt similar to that shown in Figure 11.9. When you enter the root password at the prompt, Linux starts in single-user mode.

FIGURE 11.9

Dropping to single-user mode

```
Setting clock  (utc): Sat Mar 29 13:39:37 EST 2003     [  OK  ]
Loading default keymap (us):                           [  OK  ]
Setting hostname RH9Desk:                              [  OK  ]
Initializing USB controller (usb-uhci):                [  OK  ]
Mounting USB filesystem:                               [  OK  ]
Initializing USB HID interface:                        [  OK  ]
Initializing USB keyboard:                             [  OK  ]
Initializing USB mouse:                                [  OK  ]
Checking root filesystem
WARNING: couldn't open /etc/fstab: No such file or directory
/:
The superblock could not be read or does not describe a correct ext2
filesystem.  If the device is valid and it really contains an ext2
filesystem (and not swap or ufs or something else), then the superblock
is corrupt, and you might try running e2fsck with an alternate superblock:
    e2fsck -b 8193 <device>

fsck.ext2: Is a directory while trying to open /
                                                       [FAILED]

*** An error occurred during the file system check.
*** Dropping you to a shell; the system will reboot
*** when you leave the shell.
Give root password for maintenance
(or type Control-D to continue): _
```

You can also start single-user mode from the GRUB menu. As described earlier, it's easy to protect GRUB with a password. If you don't see GRUB editing options as shown in Figure 11.10, enter the **p** command, and then enter the GRUB password.

FIGURE 11.10

GRUB editing commands

FIGURE 11.11

Modifying GRUB for single-user mode

Highlight the Linux operating system of your choice, and then press the a command to modify the kernel arguments. GRUB should take you to a line such as the following:

```
grub append> ro root=LABEL=/
```

At this point, you can add a command to the end of this line, such as `single`, `1`, or `init=/bin/sh`, as shown in Figure 11.11.

When you press Enter, Red Hat Linux proceeds to boot in single-user mode, runlevel 1. At this point, you can `fsck` unmounted drives, edit configuration files, check the status of LVM partitions, and more.

Summary

In this chapter, you learned about the Linux boot process. The basic process starts with the computer BIOS. Once it detects basic hardware on your system, it points to the Linux bootloader (GRUB), where you can select an operating system. When you select Red Hat Linux, the bootloader starts the kernel. The `/etc/inittab` file then starts the processes associated with the default runlevel.

It helps to have the customized boot disk that you created during Linux installation or with the `mkbootdisk` command. It can help you start Linux even when you have a number of different problems in the boot process. However, `linux rescue` mode, using one of the Red Hat Linux installation boot disks, is also a viable option. In various `linux rescue` modes, you can `fsck` partitions, edit configuration files, and more. Alternatively, you can start Linux in single-user mode, which can help you address other problems, such as a lost root password.

NOTE *In Red Hat parlance, it's common to refer to a partition check by its command, i.e., you can* `fsck` *(pronounced "fisk") a partition.*

In the next chapter, you will learn about the Linux kernel in detail. Once you understand the basics, it is not difficult to modify, recompile, and implement a new Linux kernel.

Chapter 12

Upgrading and Recompiling Kernels

THE THOUGHT OF RECOMPILING a kernel strikes fear into many Linux users. It is true; errors can lead to an unbootable system. If you don't have an appropriate backup, recovery can be difficult. But with a few simple precautions, you can avoid risks when you recompile a kernel. Once you understand the basic steps, it is not a difficult process.

There is an easy way to upgrade a kernel: just install the next version of the Red Hat kernel RPM that's customized for your CPU. The Red Hat RPM automatically updates your bootloader so you can start Linux with either the old or the new kernel.

The Red Hat kernel RPM may not include the very latest upgrades. The latest Linux kernels are available in tarball format; alternatively, minor upgrades only require a patch. Both options are described in this chapter.

You can customize and recompile the kernel already on your computer, or you can download, customize, and recompile a new kernel. The wide variety of options makes this process seem more difficult than it really is. In this chapter, you'll learn about three different "make" kernel configuration tools.

This chapter includes a detailed analysis of what you can change, based on the GUI kernel configuration tool. This tool is organized into configuration menus, storage devices, networking, other hardware support, and other software support categories.

I've included a number of different kernel version numbers. The Linux kernel version released with Red Hat 9 is 2.4.20. Some version numbers in this chapter may be higher, which can reflect the changes that you or a colleague may already have made.

Once you've made the desired changes, you need to compile your new kernel. It's a straightforward, step-by-step process. After compiling the kernel, you'll want to copy it to the appropriate directories. At least for now, you'll also want to configure it into your bootloader as though the old and new kernels were two different operating systems. This chapter covers the following topics:

◆ Why bother?

◆ Choosing the easy way

◆ Exploring tarball and patch alternatives

- ◆ Setting up configuration menus
- ◆ Understanding kernels, section by section
- ◆ Compiling your new configuration
- ◆ Updating the bootloader

Why Bother?

The kernel that comes with Red Hat Linux works for most hardware and software applications. But there are several good reasons why you might want to change your kernel:

Drivers   You want to take advantage of a new driver. It may be for hardware that you just installed, or for a filesystem that you want to try.

Bugs   You've learned that your current Linux kernel does not work in some way that affects how you run this operating system.

Features   You've heard about a new kernel. Perhaps it provides improved hardware support, such as for an IEEE 1394 FireWire video recorder. Maybe it allows you to connect to an 802.11a wireless network.

Security   You may want to protect yourself against a newly discovered security breach.

Size   It's possible to speed up your system by removing unneeded drivers, thereby reducing the size of your kernel.

When you want to change your kernel, you should consider the following options, in order:

1.   Recompile your existing kernel. New kernels and associated source code can consume a lot of space. A newer kernel may not work as well with the software you have in place. You may be able to do what you need with the existing kernel.

2.   Patch your existing kernel. You can perform small upgrades of Linux kernels with a patch. When applied, the patch is incorporated into your current kernel source code. For example, a single patch can upgrade your kernel from version 2.4.20 to 2.4.21.

3.   Install a new kernel. Once the new kernel package is installed, you should also configure and compile the new kernel.

KERNEL VERSION NUMBERS

Linux kernels are stored in the /boot directory with a name such as `vmlinuz-2.4.23`. All kernels include a version number in a *major.minor.patch* numbering format. In this case, the first number (2) refers to the second major release of the Linux kernel. The second number (4) has two meanings: it's the fourth minor release of the specified major kernel, and since it's an even number, it's a production-ready version of the kernel. The third number (23) refers to the twenty-third patch to the specified minor release.

Continued on next page

KERNEL VERSION NUMBERS *(continued)*

Red Hat Linux kernels have version numbers that look slightly different, such as 2.4.23-10. You can see that there's an extra number; this is the build number. Each "build" can incorporate a small number of new drivers or bug fixes. Some Red Hat kernels include a number with a "pp," a "pre-patch," which is a test release of a kernel.

If you're installing a new kernel on a production computer, avoid odd minor numbers; for example, kernel version 2.5.22 is a beta release not suitable for the real world. In addition, pre-patch (pp) kernel releases may also be fraught with risk.

"Upgrading" the Easy Way

Red Hat makes it easy to "upgrade" a kernel. If you're willing to use the "stock" Red Hat packaged kernel RPM, you can install the next version of your kernel with little trouble.

Furthermore, if you install a Red Hat kernel RPM, the new kernel is added to your bootloader as if it were a different operating system. If you have problems with the new kernel, all you need to do is reboot and select the older kernel in your bootloader.

Installing the Newest Red Hat Kernel

While you might be used to upgrading RPMs, it's best to install the latest kernel RPM. Yes, that means you'll have two Linux kernels installed, side by side. One example is shown in Figure 12.1. RPMs on this network are mounted on the /mnt/source directory.

FIGURE 12.1

Installing a new kernel RPM

```
[root@RHL9 root]# rpm -ivh /mnt/source/RPMS/kernel-2.4.20-8.i686.rpm
error: Failed dependencies:
        SysVinit < 2.84-13 conflicts with kernel-2.4.20-8
        pam < 0.75-48 conflicts with kernel-2.4.20-8
        vixie-cron < 3.0.1-73 conflicts with kernel-2.4.20-8
        cups < 1.1.17-13 conflicts with kernel-2.4.20-8
[root@RHL9 root]# rpm -Uvh /mnt/source/RPMS/SysVinit-2.84-13.i386.rpm
Preparing...                ########################################### [100%]
   1:SysVinit              ########################################### [100%]
[root@RHL9 root]# rpm -Uvh /mnt/source/RPMS/pam-0.75-48.i386.rpm
Preparing...                ########################################### [100%]
   1:pam                   warning: /etc/pam.d/system-auth created as /etc/pam.
d/system-auth.rpmnew
########################################### [100%]
[root@RHL9 root]# rpm -Uvh /mnt/source/RPMS/vixie-cron-3.0.1-74.i386.rpm
Preparing...                ########################################### [100%]
   1:vixie-cron            ########################################### [100%]
[root@RHL9 root]# rpm -e cups cups-drivers
warning: /etc/xinetd.d/cups-lpd saved as /etc/xinetd.d/cups-lpd.rpmsave
warning: /etc/cups/printers.conf saved as /etc/cups/printers.conf.rpmsave
warning: /etc/cups/classes.conf saved as /etc/cups/classes.conf.rpmsave
[root@RHL9 root]# rpm -ivh /mnt/source/RPMS/kernel-2.4.20-8.i686.rpm
Preparing...                ########################################### [100%]
   1:kernel                ########################################### [100%]
[root@RHL9 root]#
```

As you can see, higher kernel versions sometimes require you to upgrade and even temporarily remove other packages. Upgrades are riskier, because it's more difficult to go back. However, none of these packages are as essential to Linux as the kernel. So in the worst case, you can remove the upgraded packages and then reinstall the original RPMs.

Several Red Hat `kernel-*` RPMs are available, and they can be customized by CPU. Red Hat Linux kernel RPM files are organized in the following format:

```
kernel-versionnumber.cputype.rpm
```

Red Hat customizes kernels for the CPU types shown in Table 12.1. Red Hat may not provide the latest Linux kernel in RPM format customized for your CPU. To find your *cputype*, use the following command:

```
# uname -p
```

NOTE   *For the rest of this chapter, I'll substitute* x *for* versionnumber *in files and directories.*

TABLE 12.1: CUSTOM RED HAT KERNELS

CPU TYPE	DESCRIPTION
alpha	From the HP alpha CPU, developed by the former Digital Equipment Corporation
athlon	For the AMD Athlon CPU
i386	Generic Intel kernel, good for i386, i586, and i686 CPUs
i586	Intel 586 CPU
i686	Intel 686 CPU
ia64	Intel Itanium 64-bit CPU
ppc	Power PC CPU
ppc64	Power PC, 64-bit CPU
s390	Specialty CPU for an IBM server
s390x	A 64-bit version of the s390
sparc	Developed by Sun Microsystems, primarily for the Solaris operating system

NOTE   *Keep good records of the RPMs you've installed. Start with* `/root/install.log`, *which is a list of RPMs installed when you installed Red Hat Linux on your computer.*

It's easy to install a new kernel RPM. Typical steps are illustrated in Figure 12.1. The commands that you use will likely be different. For example, if the kernel RPM filename is `kernel-2.4.22.i686.rpm`, located in the `/mnt/source` directory, just run the following command:

```
# rpm -ivh /mnt/source/kernel-2.4.22.i686.rpm
```

If you see the `Failed dependencies` error shown in Figure 12.1, install packages listed in your error message first. The actual packages that you may need to install or upgrade will depend on the requirements of the new kernel and what you already have installed.

When you install another kernel, you're installing several files in the /**boot** directory. These files are stored side by side with files associated with your old kernel. These files are summarized in Table 12.2.

TABLE 12.2: KERNEL-RELATED /*BOOT* FILES

FILE	DESCRIPTION
config-*	Kernel configuration file
initrd-*	Initial RAM disk; allows the kernel access to drivers at the start of the boot process
module-info-*	A list of available hardware modules for this kernel
System-map-*	A memory map with different functions
vmlinux-*	The kernel
vmlinuz-*	A compressed version of the kernel

And that's it! Your new kernel is automatically installed. Wasn't that easy? In the next section, you'll see what the newly installed kernel does to your bootloader.

Bootloader Updates

The Red Hat Linux kernel RPMs automatically update your active bootloader, whether it be GRUB or LILO. Detailed information on each bootloader is available in Chapter 11. A revised `grub.conf` file with two different kernels is shown in Figure 12.2.

FIGURE 12.2

An updated GRUB bootloader

```
# grub.conf generated by anaconda
#
# Note that you do not have to rerun grub after making changes to this file
# NOTICE:  You have a /boot partition.  This means that
#          all kernel and initrd paths are relative to /boot/, eg.
#          root (hd0,0)
#          kernel /vmlinuz-version ro root=/dev/sda2
#          initrd /initrd-version.img
#boot=/dev/sda
default=1
timeout=10
splashimage=(hd0,0)/grub/splash.xpm.gz
title Red Hat Linux (2.4.20-9)
        root (hd0,0)
        kernel /vmlinuz-2.4.20-9 ro root=LABEL=/
        initrd /initrd-2.4.20-9.img
title Red Hat Linux (2.4.20-8)
        root (hd0,0)
        kernel /vmlinuz-2.4.20-8 ro root=LABEL=/
        initrd /initrd-2.4.20-8.img
title DOS
        rootnoverify (hd0,1)
        chainloader +1
"/etc/grub.conf" 23L, 705C
```

This particular `grub.conf` file makes it look as if you have a choice between three different operating systems:

◆ Red Hat Linux (new kernel number)

◆ Red Hat Linux (old kernel number)

◆ DOS (typically, a version of Microsoft Windows)

Remember, the kernel is the core of the operating system. Thus, when you install a new kernel, you've actually installed another version of Linux. Yet both kernels still use most of the same utilities, programs, and commands.

You may also note the `default=1` command, which actually points to the second stanza as the default operating system. In other words, if you don't select a different operating system in 10 seconds (`timeout`), GRUB automatically boots your old Red Hat Linux kernel.

You can see the result in Figure 12.3, which shows the associated GRUB menu. Note that the second listing for Red Hat Linux, with the original kernel number, is highlighted.

FIGURE 12.3

The revised
GRUB menu

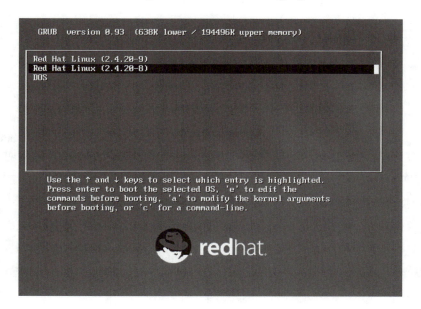

NOTE   *The default Red Hat Linux bootloader is GRUB. The Red Hat installation program saves a version of LILO in* `/etc/lilo.conf.anaconda`. *If you make a copy of this file in* `/etc/lilo.conf`, *the Red Hat kernel RPM will automatically upgrade LILO as well.*

Tarballs and Patches

One drawback to using Red Hat kernel RPMs is that they may not incorporate the very latest features into the latest kernel. If you need the absolute latest kernel, you're probably going to have to download and process a tarball package. More information on the `tar` command is available in Chapter 14; we'll go through the process step by step here.

Download Sources

The Linux kernel is under constant development. As new features emerge, a loose team of volunteers headed informally by Linus Torvalds decides when new kernels are ready for test and production release. You can download their work from the `kernel.org` Internet sites. If you can't get to `www.kernel.org` or `ftp.kernel.org`, you can select from mirror websites all over the world, as listed in `www.kernel.org/mirrors`.

I've demonstrated a download of Linux kernel 2.4.20 from `zeus-pub.kernel.org` in Figure 12.4. This particular package is large; at around 33MB, it might take a few hours to download on a regular telephone modem.

FIGURE 12.4

Downloading a kernel tarball

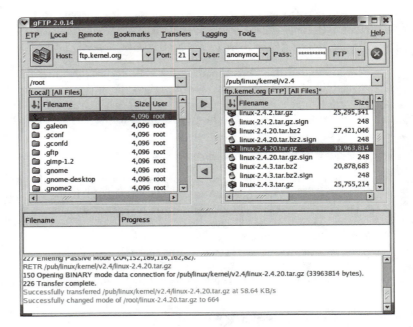

Setup

Now that you've downloaded the kernel tarball package, the setup process is easy. The package that you've downloaded should have a name similar to `linux-x.tar.gz`. With that in mind, follow these steps:

1. Copy the kernel tarball package to the `/usr/src` directory. For example, if the package is in the current directory, run the following command:

   ```
   # cp linux-x.tar.gz /usr/src
   ```

2. Navigate to `/usr/src` and unpack the tarball. The following commands should open up a large number of files in the `/usr/src/linux-x` directory:

```
# cd /usr/src
# tar xzvf linux-x.tar.gz
```

3. Navigate to the `/usr/src/linux-x` directory. Later in this chapter, you'll learn how to open and use a Linux kernel configuration menu. You'll then compile and install your new kernel.

The Patch Alternative

Installing and compiling a new kernel may seem like a lot of trouble, just to upgrade for the latest changes. Let's assume your computer has Linux kernel 2.4.20 installed. If you just want to incorporate the new security features available in Linux kernel 2.4.21, there is an alternative: you can install a kernel patch.

NOTE   *We assume that you've already installed the source code for the current kernel via the* `kernel-source-*` *RPM. The other required RPM packages are described later in this chapter, in Table 12.3.*

You can download kernel patches from the `kernel.org` Internet or mirror sites described earlier. As of this writing, they're available from the same directories as regular kernels, with a simple name: `patch-x.gz`.

Once you've downloaded the patch, copy it to the `/usr/src` directory. Then you can upgrade your kernel with the following command:

```
# zcat patch-x.gz | patch -p0
```

This command reads from the compressed patch file, identifies the differences with the current Linux kernel's source code, and updates files as needed. If there are problems, they're documented in `*.rej` files in your kernel source directory, `/usr/src/linux-x`.

NOTE   *Patches don't always work well with Linux kernels built by Red Hat; Red Hat may have already incorporated some of the contents of the patch, leading to errors during the upgrade process.*

You can then customize, compile, and install your patched kernel as described later in this chapter.

Customizing a Kernel

Customizing the kernel is a long process. In this section, you'll look at the basic steps. Later in the chapter, you'll go through the graphical configuration menu in detail. First, you'll edit the `Makefile` to label your new kernel. Then, once you've cleaned up your source files, you'll save your current configuration.

Next, you'll customize your kernel, using what you've learned earlier in this chapter. When you've saved your new configuration, you'll organize dependencies and create a new kernel image.

At this point in the process, you will have made the changes you want to the kernel; activated the settings you need; included appropriate hardware as modules; minimized the size of the kernel by deactivating items that you don't need; and saved your changes. The next step will be to compile and create your new kernel.

Kernels vary. The steps you need to take may vary. The first thing you should do is read the README file in the /usr/src/linux-x directory for any major changes in procedure.

Preparing the Source

You may have downloaded a new kernel. Perhaps you just want to change some settings on the kernel that you're currently using. In either case, you need to prepare the source code.

Remember, the source code is located in the /usr/src/linux-x directory, where x stands for the linux-*versionnumber* of your kernel. Navigate to this directory. Read the following sections in sequence.

TIP   It's important to follow these instructions in the right order when revising and recompiling your Linux kernel. If you have problems, refer to the Linux Kernel HOWTO *at* www.tldp.org.

THE *MAKEFILE*

Open the file named Makefile from the /usr/src/linux-x directory in your favorite text editor. The first four lines in this file should look similar to:

```
VERSION = 2
PATCHLEVEL = 4
SUBLEVEL = 20
EXTRAVERSION = something
```

If you're new to Linux kernels, this may be confusing. The labels in the Makefile are not consistent with the standard kernel numbering format: PATCHLEVEL is the minor version revision level of the kernel, and SUBLEVEL is the patch revision level of the kernel.

EXTRAVERSION is what Linux adds to the end of the kernel files that you can transfer to the /boot directory at the end of this process. It also helps you identify your new kernel in a bootloader such as GRUB.

Change the EXTRAVERSION variable to something you'll recognize. For the purpose of this chapter, I'm editing my Makefile with the following:

```
EXTRAVERSION = sugaree
```

TIP   Be very careful with the EXTRAVERSION *variable; an extra space after* sugaree *would create an error during the kernel module configuration process.*

SAVING THE CURRENT KERNEL CONFIGURATION

If you've never revised your kernel before, Red Hat already has your current kernel configuration on file. As described earlier, it's located in the /boot/config-x file. This is also true if you've installed a different Red Hat Linux kernel from a "stock" kernel RPM.

If you've recompiled your kernel before, your current configuration should be in the hidden file, .config, in the /usr/src/linux-x directory. Save it now. The step described in the next section deletes that file.

In either case, back up your current configuration. These files are small enough to fit on a regular floppy disk.

CLEANING THE SOURCE

Now that your `Makefile` is ready, it's time to clean the source code. If you aren't already there, navigate to the `/usr/src/linux-x` directory. The following command uses the `Makefile` script to clean files and directories that would interfere with compiling the kernel source code:

```
# make mrproper
```

TIP   *Each of the* `make` *commands in this chapter may run through thousands of lines of code. While some may take minutes, others may take hours, especially on slower computers. Be patient.*

A STANDARD STARTING POINT

When you download a kernel from a non–Red Hat source such as `ftp.kernel.org`, you may have to adjust several hundred settings to match the current Red Hat configuration. That process can be painful.

Alternatively, you can set a Red Hat starting point for your kernel; some might call this a *baseline configuration*. There are four basic options for your baseline Linux kernel; each is mutually exclusive:

The saved `.config` file   If you saved the `.config` file earlier, you can restore it to the `/usr/src/linux-x` directory.

The `/boot/config-x` file   This file contains the configuration of your kernel when you installed it from an RPM, or when you installed Red Hat Linux. You can copy this to the `/usr/src/linux-x/.config` file.

Your current configuration   Use the `make oldconfig` command to set up your current configuration in the `/usr/src/linux-x/.config` file.

The appropriate file in `/usr/src/linux-x/configs`   The `configs` subdirectory includes a series of configuration files, customized for different CPUs. You can copy the file closest to your kernel to the `/usr/src/linux-x/.config` file.

Customizing the Configuration

You've seen three menus that you can use to customize your kernel configuration: `make config`, `make menuconfig`, and `make xconfig`. Select one and make the desired changes to your kernel, using the techniques and criteria described earlier. Generally, you'll want to:

- Use modules. Make sure they're enabled in the Loadable Module Support menu. The alternative is to use a monolithic kernel, which may be too big for your system.

- Be sure to cite the correct CPU in the Processor Type And Features menu.

- Remove unneeded devices and modules. This can minimize the size of your kernel and associated driver files. For example, if you're not planning to connect a Ham Radio to your Linux computer, you won't need the modules associated with Amateur Radio Support.

◆ If in doubt, don't remove it. Assuming you're starting from a baseline or standard kernel configuration, many of the settings are interdependent. If you remove the wrong device, you might make this kernel unusable.

NOTE *Previous kernels required symmetric multiprocessing (SMP) support, even for computers with one CPU. That is no longer required for the kernel included with Red Hat Linux 9.*

When you've made your changes, save your configuration. By default, the `make` tools save your settings to the `.config` file in the `/usr/src/linux-x` directory.

Creating Dependencies

Now you can force your source code to read your Linux kernel configuration. The following command resolves all dependencies. It takes the settings from your new `.config` file and uses them to customize your source code:

```
# make dep
```

NOTE *The* `make dep` *process took 5 minutes on my 660MHz computer. Your experience depends in part on the speed of your CPU and the size of your kernel.*

Making a Kernel Image

Now that the dependencies are satisfied, you're ready to "make" the kernel image. This process can take minutes or even all night, depending on the speed of your CPU. You want the image to be compressed so that you can fit it on a boot or rescue floppy disk. To create a compressed kernel image, run the following command:

```
# make bzImage
```

You'll see a very long series of messages. When this command is complete, watch for the following message:

```
warning: kernel is too big for standalone boot from floppy
```

If this is what you see, you probably can't use the `mkbootdisk` command from Chapter 11 to create a boot floppy. If you're motivated to make your kernel smaller, you may want to start the `make xconfig` process again and remove more settings.

NOTE *The* `make bzImage` *process took 15 minutes on my 660MHz computer. Your experience depends in part on the speed of your CPU and the size of your kernel.*

You may not need a customized boot disk. In many cases, you can use the Red Hat Linux installation boot disk in rescue mode to boot your system. For more information on the `linux rescue` process, see Chapter 11.

TIP *The Red Hat Linux installation boot disk in* `linux rescue` *mode may not rescue all systems. You might need a customized boot disk for your new kernel.*

Make a note of the directory cited in the last message. You'll need it again in a moment. For now, assume you're recompiling kernel version 2.4.20-8:

```
/usr/src/linux-2.4.20-8/arch/i386/boot
```

NOTE   *If you're using a PC that does not use an Intel 32-bit CPU, the* i386 *in the directory may be different.*

After Compiling

Now you can move your kernel to the /boot directory and update your bootloader. As we noted earlier, the new kernel is in the /usr/src/linux-2.4.20-8/arch/i386/boot directory. Copy it to the /boot directory, and name it vmlinuz-2.4.20sugaree.

You also need to create an Initial RAM disk. Based on the noted kernel version and value of EXTRAVERSION, you can do so with the following command:

```
# mkinitrd /boot/initrd-2.4.20sugaree.img 2.4.20sugaree
```

Building Modules

At this point, we've assumed that you've configured module support into your kernel. The next step is to "make" your modules. The first command organizes the modules that you've configured in various /usr/src/linux-x subdirectories:

```
# make modules
```

NOTE   *The* make modules *process took 45 minutes on my 660MHz computer. As always, your experience depends in part on the speed of your CPU and the size of your kernel.*

The next command organizes your modules in the /lib/modules/2.4.20-4 directory:

```
# make modules_install
```

NOTE   *The* make modules_install *process took 30 minutes on my 660MHz computer.*

TIP   *If you see the* when making multiple links, last argument must be a directory *error message, check the* EXTRAVERSION *variable in the* /usr/src/linux-x/Makefile. *There may be an extra space at the end of that line.*

Now you're ready to get to the nitty-gritty of customizing the kernel, based on one of three different configuration menus.

Setting Up Configuration Menus

If you're going to customize your kernel in any way, you need a configuration menu. Different menus are available in text, terminal graphics, and GUI formats. Each of these menus requires a series of packages: the source code and language libraries for the kernel, and language libraries for graphical configuration screens.

Kernel RPM Packages

Several RPMs associated with building a kernel are available, as shown in Table 12.3. Some provide the source code; others are related to languages and libraries needed to configure and process the kernel. Install them using the `rpm` command described in Chapter 10.

TABLE 12.3: KERNEL RPM PACKAGES

PACKAGE	DESCRIPTION
`binutils-*`	Required binary utilities
`cpp-*`	A GNU C language preprocessor
`gcc-*`	The C language compiler
`glibc-devel-*`	For developing programs (such as the kernel) that require C language libraries
`glibc-kernheaders-*`	Kernel C language header files
`kernel-source-*`	Kernel source files
`ncurses-*`	A language library for presenting graphics on a terminal; required for `make menuconfig`
`ncurses-devel-*`	Header files for `ncurses` screens
`tcl-*`	TCL scripting language; designed for use with TK; required for `make xconfig`
`tk-*`	Widgets for GUIs designed to work with TCL; required for `make xconfig`

TIP *If you get a* `Failed dependencies` *message related to* `kernel-headers`, *install the* `glibc-kernheaders-*` *RPM package. Many dependencies explicitly cite the RPM package that you need. Dependencies related to* `kernel-headers` *do not.*

If you're reconfiguring an existing kernel, you don't need to install the `kernel-x.cputype.rpm` package. You'll actually be creating a new kernel from some of the other packages when you compile it later in this chapter.

If you're willing to customize your kernel in text mode, you don't need the `ncurses*` or `tcl-*` or `tk-*` RPM packages. But a kernel contains a huge number of settings that you can customize, which makes the graphical kernel configuration screens a terrific convenience. You'll see this for yourself in the following section.

Make Menus

Now that you have the right RPM packages installed, it's time to examine the three different menus available for customizing your kernel. Start by navigating to the directory with your Linux kernel's source files, `/usr/src/linux-versionnumber`. For convenience, we'll call it the `/usr/src/linux-x` directory for the rest of this chapter.

TIP   *By default, Red Hat Linux links the* `/usr/src/linux-2.4` *directory to the default source code directory for your original kernel.*

You'll find a `Makefile` in `/usr/src/linux-x` that lets you configure your kernel. That file includes three different kernel configuration tools:

◆   `make config`

◆   `make menuconfig`

◆   `make xconfig`

We introduce these tools briefly in the following sections. Then we'll use `make xconfig` to analyze what you can configure in your kernel in detail.

Before moving on, navigate to the `/usr/src/linux-x` directory on your computer. The `make` commands shown won't work unless you're in that directory.

WHY A MENU?

You can edit your configuration file directly. As described earlier, your first kernel configuration is documented in the `config-x` file, in your `/boot` directory. This file includes all kinds of settings, such as:

```
CONFIG_MODULES=y
CONFIG_3C359=m
# CONFIG_IRDA_DEBUG is not set
```

In other words, the `CONFIG_MODULES` setting, which lets your kernel use modular drivers, are integrated into the kernel. The `CONFIG_3C359=m` command makes this particular network card driver into a module; when Red Hat detects this card, it will be able to use the `insmod` command (see Chapter 11) to use this driver. Unused elements such as `CONFIG_IRDA_DEBUG` are left out of the kernel and modules; the hash mark (#) turns it into a comment, and your kernel ignores the line.

When you're done, you should save the file to `.config` in the `/usr/src/linux-x` directory. Then you'll be ready to compile and install your kernel, as described later in this chapter.

TIP   *If you've recompiled your kernel before, the settings are normally saved in the* `/usr/src/linux-x/.config` *file. One previous revision is saved in* `/usr/src/linux-x/.config.old`. *Nevertheless, this is a good time to back up your* `.config` *file to another directory.*

But because this file contains about 2000 lines, analyzing each line can be a time-consuming process. For that reason, three kernel tools are available to help.

MAKE CONFIG

When you're in the `/usr/src/linux-x` directory, the `make config` command starts a kernel configuration tool. It prompts you with a series of questions, as shown in Figure 12.5.

FIGURE 12.5

The `make config` process

```
[root@RH9Desk linux-2.4]# make config
rm -f include/asm
( cd include ; ln -sf asm-i386 asm)
/bin/sh scripts/Configure arch/i386/config.in
#
# Using defaults found in configs/kernel-2.4.20-i686.config
#
*
* Code maturity level options
*
Prompt for development and/or incomplete code/drivers (CONFIG_EXPERIMENTAL) [Y/n
/?]
*
* Loadable module support
*
Enable loadable module support (CONFIG_MODULES) [Y/n/?]
  Set version information on all module symbols (CONFIG_MODVERSIONS) [Y/n/?]
  Kernel module loader (CONFIG_KMOD) [Y/n/?]
*
* Processor type and features
*
Low latency scheduling (CONFIG_LOLAT) [Y/n/?]
Processor family (386, 486, 586/K5/5x86/6x86/6x86MX, Pentium-Classic, Pentium-MM
X, Pentium-Pro/Celeron/Pentium-II, Pentium-III/Celeron(Coppermine), Pentium-4, K
6/K6-II/K6-III, Athlon/Duron/K7, Elan, Crusoe, Winchip-C6, Winchip-2, Winchip-2A
/Winchip-3, CyrixIII/VIA-C3/VIA-C5) [Pentium-Pro/Celeron/Pentium-II] []
```

It starts by looking for a `.config` file in your `/usr/src/linux-x` directory. If that file does not exist, it uses `uname -p` to identify your CPU and find the corresponding file in the `/usr/src/linux-x/configs` directory. The settings in the selected file become your default values.

Alternatively, if you're modifying your kernel for the first time, you can use the installed configuration in `/boot/config-x`, where `x` represents the kernel version number. Copy it to `/usr/src/linux-x/.config` with the following command:

```
# cp /boot/config-x /usr/src/linux-x/.config
```

Next, you get a bunch of questions. For each question, you have up to four options. `Y` and `N` are straightforward. In many cases, you can select `M`, which makes the relevant driver module available in a file. And if you enter `?`, you open a help file related to the question.

But you need to answer hundreds of questions. If you just have to change the setting for the 366th question, you might miss it. If you pass a question, there is no way to go back. You just have to press Ctrl+C and start the process again. For this reason, the other two "make" menu options are more popular.

MAKE MENUCONFIG

When you're in the `/usr/src/linux-x` directory, the `make menuconfig` command should give you a low-resolution graphical menu. As long as you have the `ncurses*` RPM packages installed, as described earlier, you should see a menu similar to Figure 12.6.

FIGURE 12.6

The make
menuconfig
main menu

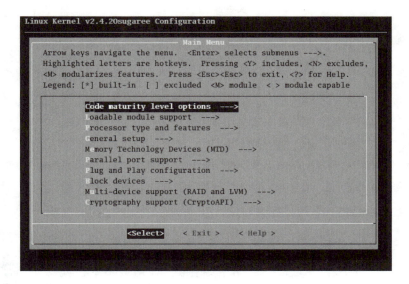

Like make config, this option looks for a .config file in the /usr/src/linux-x directory. If it does not exist, it uses the *.config file customized for your CPU in the /usr/src/linux-x/configs directory.

As you can see, kernel settings are organized into menus. You can highlight a setting and select Help at any time. Unfortunately, help is not available for every variable.

Highlight a menu option and press Enter to review detailed configuration options; for example, Figure 12.7 illustrates some available Wireless LAN devices. As you can see, some are available modules, while others are built into the kernel.

FIGURE 12.7

The Wireless LAN
kernel menu

```
Linux Kernel v2.4.20sugaree Configuration
┌─────────────────── Wireless LAN (non-hamradio) ───────────────────┐
│ Arrow keys navigate the menu.  <Enter> selects submenus --->.      │
│ Highlighted letters are hotkeys.  Pressing <Y> includes, <N> excludes, │
│ <M> modularizes features.  Press <Esc><Esc> to exit, <?> for Help. │
│ Legend: [*] built-in  [ ] excluded  <M> module  < > module capable │
│ ┌───────────────────────────────────────────────────────────────┐ │
│ │ [*] Wireless LAN (non-hamradio)                               │ │
│ │ <M>     STRIP (Metricom starmode radio IP)                    │ │
│ │ <M>     AT&T WaveLAN & DEC RoamAbout DS support               │ │
│ │ <M>     Aironet Arlan 655 & IC2200 DS support                 │ │
│ │ <M>     Aironet 4500/4800 series adapters                     │ │
│ │ <M>     Aironet 4500/4800 ISA/PCI/PNP/365 support             │ │
│ │ [*]       Aironet 4500/4800 PNP support                       │ │
│ │ [*]       Aironet 4500/4800 PCI support                       │ │
│ │ [*]       Aironet 4500/4800 ISA broken support (EXPERIMENTAL) │ │
│ │ [*]       Aironet 4500/4800 I365 broken support (EXPERIMENTAL)│ │
│ └───────────────────────────────────────────────────────────────┘ │
│              <Select>      < Exit >      < Help >                  │
└───────────────────────────────────────────────────────────────────┘
```

NOTE   *You can run* make menuconfig *on a Telnet or SSH connection from a remote computer. Depending on your point of view, this may be a convenience or a security risk. More information on Telnet and SSH is available in Chapter 23.*

As you can see, many other menus are available through make menuconfig. We illustrate these options in detail in the next section, since the make xconfig menus are easier to read in a book.

When you exit out of make menuconfig, you get a chance to save your new configuration. If you answer yes, this tool writes your new kernel configuration to /usr/src/linux-x/.config.

MAKE XCONFIG

When you're in the /usr/src/linux-x directory and a GUI, the make xconfig command should give you a high-resolution graphical menu. As long as you have the tcl-* and tk-* RPM packages installed, you should see a menu similar to Figure 12.8.

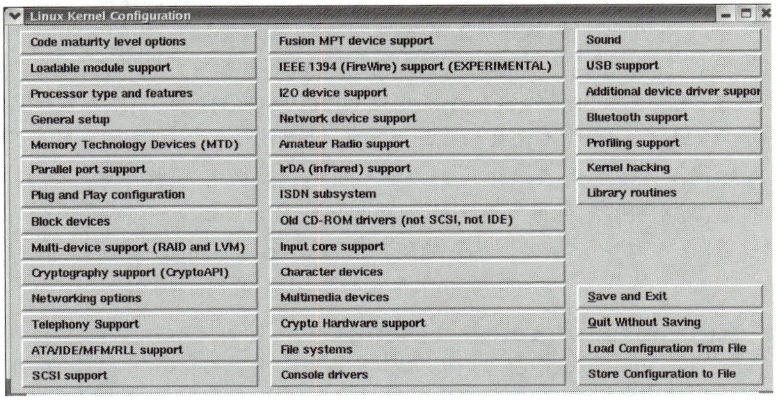

FIGURE 12.8

The Linux Kernel Configuration menu

Like make config, this option looks for a .config file in the /usr/src/linux-x directory. If it does not exist, it uses the *.config file customized for your CPU in the /usr/src/linux-x/configs directory. If you want to start with a different configuration file, the two buttons in the lower-right corner can help.

As you can see, different kernel settings are organized into different sections. We'll look at these sections in much more detail later in this chapter. When you're happy with your changes, click Save And Exit; otherwise, click Quit Without Saving.

Kernels, Section by Section

What follows is a section-by-section analysis of the Linux kernel, based on the make xconfig Linux Kernel Configuration menu. This is a fairly long section, so if you're reading this full chapter, you may want to take a break.

A total of 35 kernel menus are shown; I've organized them into six sections:

◆   Basic configuration menus help you configure the fundamental parts of the kernel, such as the CPU and ISA or PCI support. Be especially careful with these menus; errors can keep Linux from recognizing peripherals or even your CPU.

◆ Storage device menus help you work with connections related to all types of storage: hard drives, CDs, parallel port drives, and more. Be careful; you want to make sure Linux can recognize your hard disks.

◆ Networking menus allow you to configure basic network software and network hardware in detail.

◆ External hardware covers menus associated with hardware that is physically outside the computer box.

◆ Other hardware support is associated with hardware that does not easily fit into any of the other categories.

◆ Other software support includes critical components such as filesystems and libraries.

If you want to follow along on your Linux computer, navigate to the `/usr/src/linux-x` directory and run the `make xconfig` command. As you go through each section, click on the applicable button in the Linux Kernel Configuration menu.

Examine the hardware kernel settings with a critical eye. If you know that you'll never use the associated hardware, consider deactivating the setting. If you might add the noted hardware in the future, consider creating a module. These actions minimize the size of your kernel and can greatly improve the startup speed and performance of your system.

WARNING   If in doubt about an active or modular kernel setting, don't deactivate it. There are a number of innocuous-looking kernel parameters that are critical to the basic operation of Linux.

Basic Configuration Menus

I've arbitrarily organized several menus in this section. They include the basic parameters associated with starting Linux, recognizing hardware, setting up a CPU, and using experimental components in the kernel.

NOTE   Previous versions of the kernel included a Binary Emulation Of Other Systems menu, which allowed users to configure support to emulate other Unix-style systems, including UnixWare 7.x, SCO Open Server, and Solaris 2.x. This option is no longer available in the kernel included with Red Hat Linux 9.

CODE MATURITY LEVEL OPTIONS

If you're using Red Hat Linux in a production environment, make sure that the setting shown in Figure 12.9 is set to n. Otherwise, you might accidentally include experimental kernel drivers and settings.

FIGURE 12.9

Code Maturity Level Options

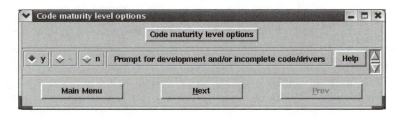

If you're a developer, be careful. It's a good idea to work on only one experimental driver at a time; if you have problems, you'll know the source. You can find more information on each variable by clicking the associated Help button. The help dialog box for this menu is shown in Figure 12.10.

FIGURE 12.10

Configuration help

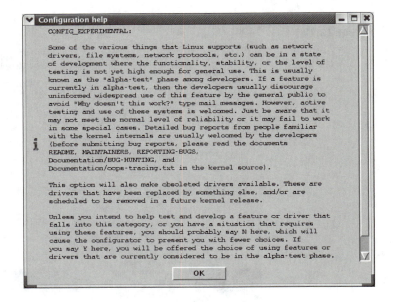

LOADABLE MODULE SUPPORT

Normally, when Red Hat Linux detects new hardware on your computer, it automatically installs the driver module, if available. This is possible in part to the Loadable Module Support options shown in Figure 12.11.

FIGURE 12.11

Loadable Module
Support

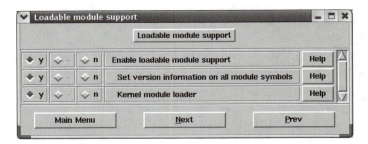

You should almost always answer yes to all of these options; they allow you to separate hardware driver modules from the kernel, use drivers from different sources, and load modules as needed.

Otherwise, you would have to include all possible drivers into the main kernel. This would make the kernel large and unwieldy. Some kernels without modules, also known as monolithic kernels, are so big that older PCs aren't able to load them when you try to boot Linux.

PROCESSOR TYPE AND FEATURES

You can customize the Linux kernel for your CPU. This loosely corresponds to the different kinds of `kernel-x.cputype.rpm` packages that you can install directly on your computer. As you can see in Figure 12.12, you can configure the kernel for a wide variety of CPUs.

FIGURE 12.12

Processor Type And Features options

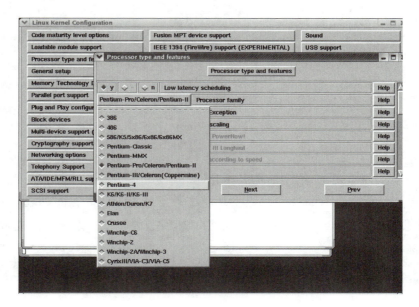

If you don't see your CPU in the list, find the closest available match. If you have an Intel 32-bit CPU, you can also try 386 for a basic kernel good for all current Intel 32-bit CPUs.

Once you've selected the processor, you should configure a number of other variables, including special modules that can support multiple CPUs and special features of Toshiba or Dell laptops.

GENERAL SETUP

The General Setup kernel menu shown in Figure 12.13 provides several basic hardware, binary, and networking options for the kernel. Look through the list of variables. They fall into a number of categories and some are fundamental to the kind of hardware on your computer. These categories include:

Networking support   Some programs require kernel networking support even if your computer never connects to another network or the Internet.

Basic hardware support   Normally, Linux kernels are configured with support for PCI, ISA, and PCMCIA cards.

Hot-pluggable support   Linux can be configured to support hardware that can be installed or removed while your computer is running.

Power management support   Linux supports the older Advanced Power Management (APM) system; support for the Advanced Configuration Power Interface (ACPI) standard is still experimental, that is, not ready for production computers.

FIGURE 12.13

General Setup

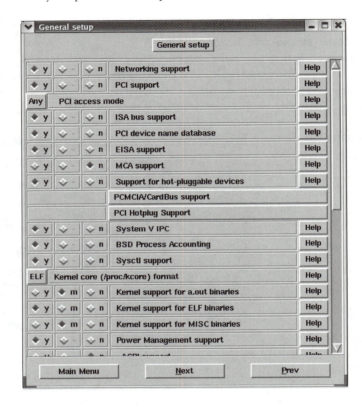

FIGURE 12.13

General Setup

NOTE   *In the General Setup menu, click on the PCMCIA/CardBus Support button. You'll see the submenu shown in Figure 12.14. If you're using Linux on a laptop computer, be sure that the appropriate bridges are active.*

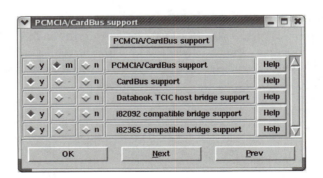

FIGURE 12.14

PCMCIA/CardBus Support

Storage Devices

Several Linux kernel menus organize the settings related to where you can store files and other information. If you have an external storage device, see the menus described in the "External Hardware" section.

MEMORY TECHNOLOGY DEVICES

In the Linux kernel, Memory Technology Devices (MTD) includes everything that can store information in a "solid state." Examples include the BIOS, camera flash cards, and ROM chips. Remember, some of these might be installed through a PCMCIA adapter. The basic menu is shown in Figure 12.15.

FIGURE 12.15

Memory Technology Devices

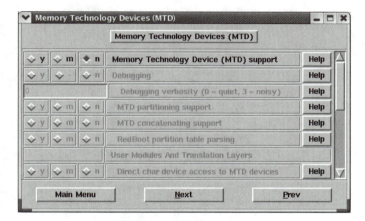

BLOCK DEVICES

Block devices allow you to mount a storage unit, such as a floppy or a hard drive, on a directory. Open the Block Devices menu, and you'll see something similar to Figure 12.16. Scroll down the menu. You'll see support for floppy drives, regular IDE hard disks, shared network drives, and RAM disks.

These settings are closely related to ones found on the ATA/IDE/MFM/RLL Support menu.

MULTI-DEVICE SUPPORT

As described in Chapter 3, Red Hat Linux supports RAID and LVM. Both systems require multiple partitions. Since Linux assigns a device to each partition, RAID and LVM are considered multi-device systems. If you ever intend to use RAID or LVM, you should activate these settings, as shown in Figure 12.17.

FIGURE 12.16

The Block Devices
menu

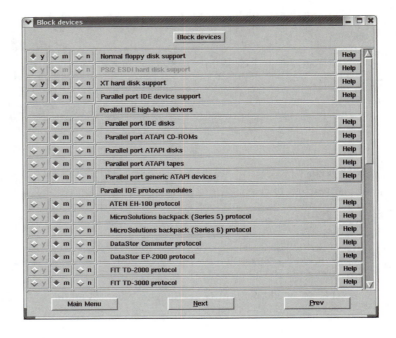

FIGURE 12.17

Multi-Device
Support options

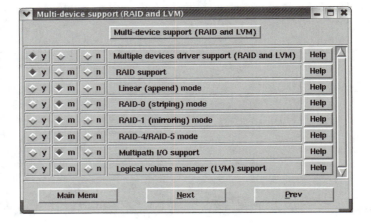

ATA/IDE/MFM/RLL SUPPORT

ATA, IDE, MFM, and RLL are a bunch of acronyms all related to standard PC hard disk and CD-ROM interfaces. As shown in Figure 12.18, there's an IDE, ATA And ATAPI Block Devices button that you can click to call up a submenu with variables for different drives and chipsets.

FIGURE 12.18
ATA/IDE/MFM/
RLL Support

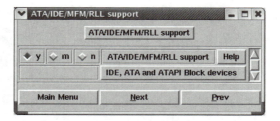

SCSI SUPPORT

The other major interface for storage devices is SCSI, the Small Computer Systems Interface. The SCSI Support kernel menu allows you to activate drivers or modules for basic SCSI hard drives, tape drives, and CD systems. At the bottom of the SCSI Support menu shown in Figure 12.19, there are two submenus:

◆ The SCSI Low-Level Drivers menu includes support for a number of specific SCSI hard drives and RAID devices.

◆ The PCMCIA SCSI Adapter Support menu accommodates PCMCIA cards that connect your computer to SCSI devices.

FIGURE 12.19
SCSI Support
options

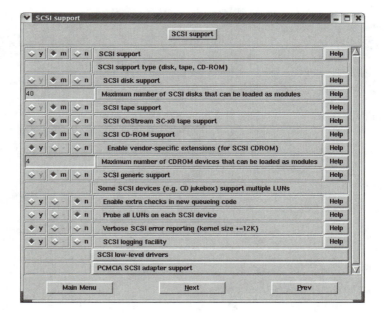

OLDER CD-ROM DRIVERS

Older CD-ROM drives were connected to sound cards. The Old CD-ROM Drivers (Not SCSI, Not IDE) menu includes access to the Linux drivers that were once used for these drives. A number of drivers are available, as shown in Figure 12.20.

FIGURE 12.20

The Old CD-ROM Drivers (Not SCSI, Not IDE) menu

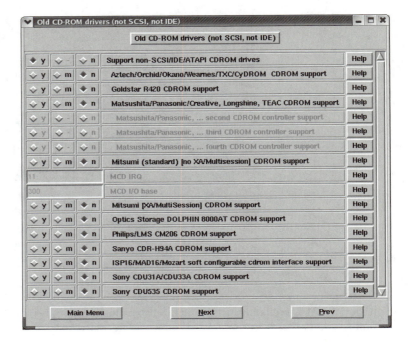

As you can see, older CD-ROM drivers are organized by make and model. If you have an older CD-ROM drive that's not on this list, check your documentation. Try the driver associated with a similar make or model. Just remember, these drivers are no longer supported and may not work well with the latest Linux production kernels.

Networking

Linux is built for networking. Naturally, it offers several networking-related kernel configuration menus. You can configure basic network software as well as specific devices in the various Networking menus. Not all of these menus are strictly related to networking.

More information on basic network protocols is available in Chapter 20. Other important reference chapters for Linux kernel network settings are Chapters 21 and 22.

NETWORKING OPTIONS

The Networking Options menu is primarily used to configure network software. While you can activate other protocol stacks such as IPX/SPX, many of the options are related to the primary network protocol for Linux and the Internet, TCP/IP. This is a large menu; part of it is shown in Figure 12.21.

FIGURE 12.21

Networking Options

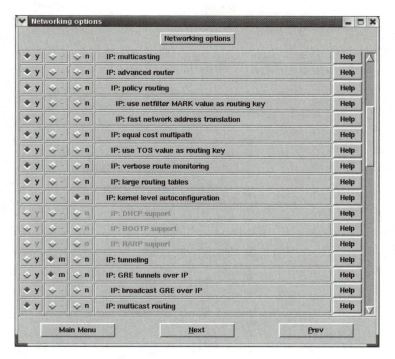

Many of these settings are not obvious; for example, the IP: DHCP Support option shown in Figure 12.21 is used only for remote Linux terminals. Remember, the help menus provide more information on each setting. Several submenus are available:

- The IP: Netfilter Configuration submenu allows your kernel to support firewalls using `iptables`, `ipchains`, or even `ipfwadm`. The `ipchains` commands are associated with Linux kernel 2.2; the `ipfwadm` commands are obsolete and are associated with Linux kernel 2.0. You can learn more about the current `iptables` firewalls in Chapter 22.

- The IPv6: Netfilter Configuration submenu allows you to configure firewalls if you're using this more advanced system of IP addressing, described in Chapter 20. Remember, IPv4 is still in common use today.

- The Appletalk Devices menu allows you to communicate with Apple computers over a TCP/IP network.

- The QoS And/Or Fair Queuing menu supports networks that allow you to prioritize messages, using "Quality of Service" parameters.

- The Network Testing menu lets you send preconfigured data packets to check the capacity of your system.

NETWORKING DEVICES

The Network Device Support kernel menu allows you to activate any number of drivers for different kinds of network adapters. This is also a substantial menu, as shown in Figure 12.22.

FIGURE 12.22

Network Device Support

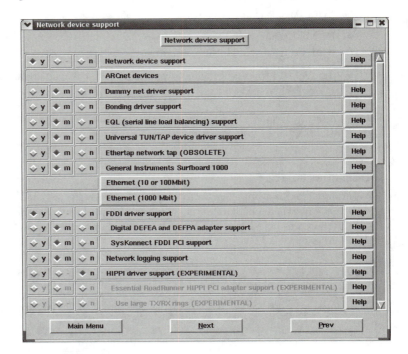

It includes a list of basic network drivers. There are several submenus with hardware-specific drivers. As you can see, network cards were developed for a number of different network systems, such as Ethernet. These submenus include:

◆ ARCnet Devices allows you to use network cards built for a specific type of LAN. ARCnet is a variation on Token Ring; because it's a slow network (2.5Mbps), it is generally not used today.

◆ Ethernet (10 Or 100 Mbit) lets you configure regular and Fast Ethernet adapters. If you don't see your adapter in this list, check your documentation for "clones." For example, many older network cards can use the Novell NE2000 driver.

◆ Ethernet (1000 Mbit) permits you to configure Gigabit Ethernet network adapters on your Linux computer.

◆ Wireless LAN (Non-Hamradio) allows you to configure basic wireless networking on your PC, mostly for devices that conform to the IEEE 802.11b standard. Bluetooth support is available under a separate menu. As of this writing, support for IEEE 802.11a devices is not available.

◆ The Token Ring Devices submenu lets you configure specific network adapters designed for this older network system. While Token Ring networks are not in common use, some believe that they are more reliable than Ethernet; thus, you might still find some of these networks in places like factories.

◆ Wan Interfaces permits you to configure network devices that connect two distant LANs in a Wide Area Network (WAN).

◆ PCMCIA Network Device Support allows you to accommodate network cards to this standard, primarily for laptop computers.

◆ The ATM Drivers submenu let you adapt network cards built for Asynchronous Transfer Mode (ATM) networks. ATM is a popular alternative to Fast and Gigabit Ethernet.

TIP   *If you're configuring your kernel for a network card that conforms to the PCMCIA or PC Card standard, check the PCMCIA Network Device Support menu.*

TELEPHONY SUPPORT

Modern telephone companies translate regular phone calls to data that's often sent over networks such as the Internet. This process is known as *telephony*. Linux supports a couple of telephony cards, primarily used to help larger businesses translate phone calls to data. The Telephony Support menu is shown in Figure 12.23.

FIGURE 12.23

Telephony Support

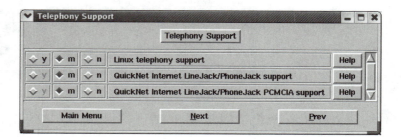

AMATEUR RADIO

You can configure the Linux kernel to support connections to amateur radios, as shown in the Amateur Radio Support menu in Figure 12.24.

Computers can be networked through amateur radios, using the AX.25 protocol. There is even an AX.25 Network Device Drivers submenu that allows you to configure this type of network connection.

FIGURE 12.24

Amateur Radio
Support

FIGURE 12.24

Amateur Radio
Support

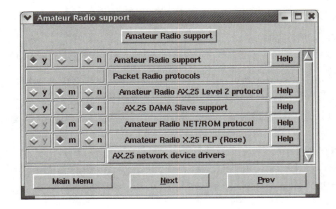

ISDN

Early digital computer connections over telephone networks were made using Integrated Services
Digital Network (ISDN) adapters. These connections are still popular in Europe, and are often the
only "high-speed" wired (128Kbps) option in rural areas of the United States of America. The basic
ISDN Subsystem menu shown in Figure 12.25 allows you to configure ISDN with several types of
networks and commands.

FIGURE 12.25

ISDN Subsystem

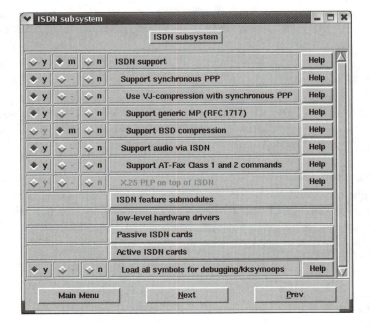

The Linux kernel ISDN Subsystem menu includes a number of submenus:

- The ISDN Feature Submodules submenu allows you to configure a virtual ISDN card and some commands that may be needed for European connections.

- The Passive ISDN Cards submenu lets you configure adapters that are generally used by consumers; they're associated with 128Kbps speeds.

- The Active ISDN Cards submenu allows you to configure higher-speed ISDN adapters.

FUSION MPT

Fusion MPT Device Support is a specialty menu for high-speed SCSI devices from LSI Logic. There is also an associated LAN driver, as shown in Figure 12.26.

FIGURE 12.26

Fusion MPT Device Support

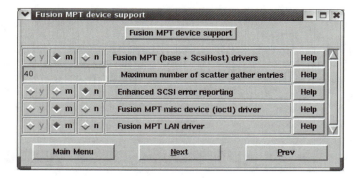

INFRARED

You can configure the Linux kernel to work with infrared devices that conform to the Infrared Data Association (IrDA) standard. As you can see from the menu in Figure 12.27, there are several infrared protocols for transmitting data. The Infrared-Port Device Drivers submenu allows you to include the appropriate hardware in the Linux kernel or modules.

BLUETOOTH

The Bluetooth specification is based on a radio technology for networks. The range is short—typically around 33 feet (10 meters). It's commonly used on portable devices such as handheld computers and cellular telephones. Several portable devices are built on Linux. Bluetooth technology can also be used to connect regular computers in networks. The kernel Bluetooth Support menu is shown in Figure 12.28.

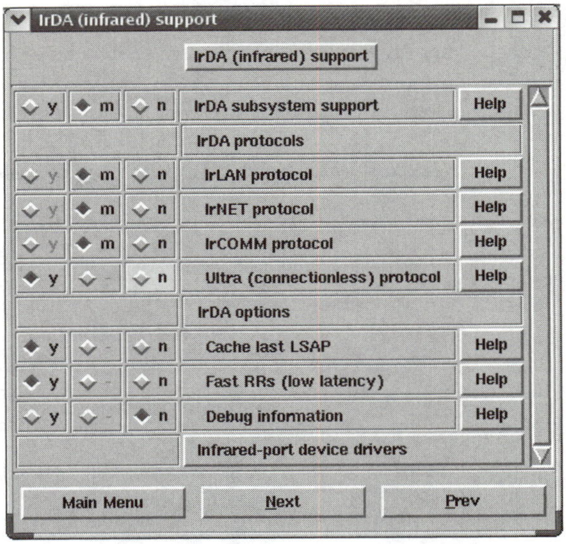

FIGURE 12.27
IrDA (Infrared) Support

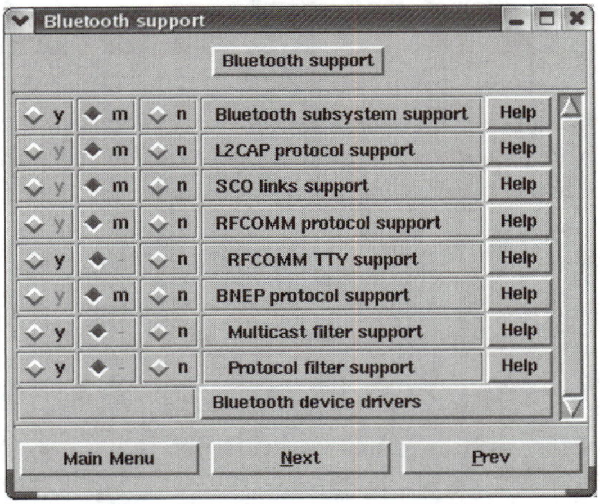

FIGURE 12.28
Bluetooth Support

The Bluetooth Device Drivers submenu allows you to use the basic Host Controller Interface (HCI). Different drivers are available for USB, serial ports, and the PCMCIA cards associated with various vendors.

External Hardware

There are three Linux kernel menus for external hardware. Two are related to relatively new standards: USB and IEEE 1394. The other menu addresses older external hardware: parallel port support.

PARALLEL PORT SUPPORT

The parallel port is commonly known as the printer port. As you can see in Figure 12.29, you can configure parallel port support in several ways. For example, IEEE 1284 transfer modes support standard bidirectional communication with a printer.

FIGURE 12.29

Parallel Port
Support

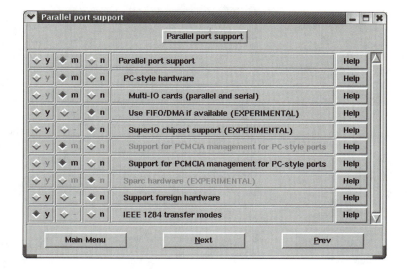

Remember, parallel ports aren't just for printers. For example, there are a number of hard disks and other storage devices that you can connect to the parallel port. It is also a way to sync computers and transfer data. More information is available under the Block Devices menu.

USB SUPPORT

It seems possible that all future external devices will conform to some USB or IEEE 1394 standard. New hardware in both areas is being released at a fast and furious pace. Linux developers are working steadily to keep up.

Linux support for USB is far from complete; kernel support for USB 2.0 standard devices is still experimental as of this writing. More information on Linux and USB is available in Chapter 2 and from www.linux-usb.org. As you can see from the main USB Support menu shown in Figure 12.30, kernel code is available for the major types of USB hardware.

The USB Serial Converter Support submenu allows you to configure serial port adapters. This lets you connect a serial device, such as an older mouse, to an USB port.

IEEE 1394 — FIREWIRE/iLINK

As discussed in Chapter 2, IEEE 1394 hardware is more popularly known by its trade names, FireWire and iLink. Linux support for these devices is still experimental. Associated devices use its high-speed (400Mbps+) capabilities, as shown in Figure 12.31.

NOTE *This menu is not active if you've deactivated the development drivers setting in the Code Maturity Level Options menu.*

FIGURE 12.30

USB Support

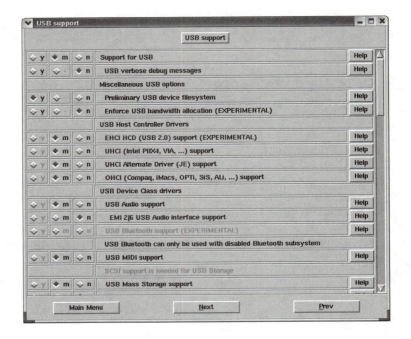

FIGURE 12.31

IEEE 1394
(FireWire) Support
(EXPERIMENTAL)

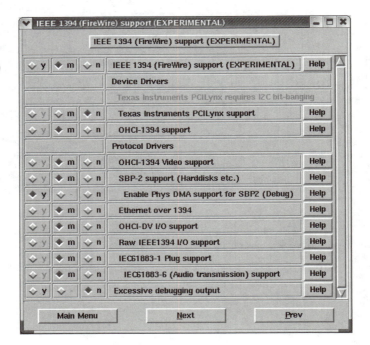

WARNING *Experimental code is not production-ready. In other words, testing is not complete, and the associated kernel components may not work and could even affect other parts of your system. Use it at your own risk.*

Other Hardware Support

Some hardware menus are difficult to put in any of the other categories. Several are related to the ways terminals and consoles work locally and remotely; there's also plug and play, and multimedia.

CHARACTER DEVICES

A character device transfers data to and from a user process, and is often associated with a serial port. The most common character device is a terminal. You can configure drivers for local virtual terminals as well as remote terminals. Some remote terminals can use serial and other physical ports. You can review these options in Figure 12.32.

FIGURE 12.32

Character Devices

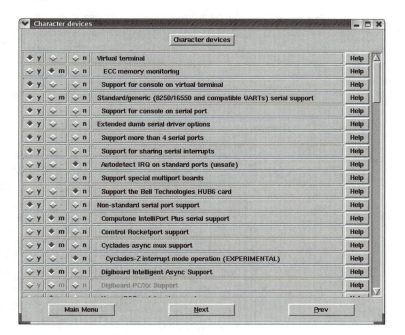

Character devices also include some surprising kernel settings, such as tape drives, graphics cards, mice, and joysticks. Several submenus are included:

◆ I2C Support is a serial bus protocol required to support a wide variety of hardware, including Video For Linux kernel settings.

◆ Hardware Sensors Support includes a number of devices designed to monitor hardware; it's based on the work of the Linux System Hardware Monitoring project at `www2.lm-sensors.nu/~lm78`.

◆ The Mice submenu allows you to configure support for basic pointing devices such as a mouse or touchpad.

◆ Joysticks relate to devices associated with the game port on a PC.

◆ Watchdog Cards are common with embedded devices; they're designed to force reboots if there is no input for some specified period of time.

◆ Ftape relates to older tape drives connected to the 34-pin floppy disk controller. It includes drivers for several makes and models.

◆ The PCMCIA Character Devices submenu lets you emulate serial ports.

CONSOLE DRIVERS

Console drivers are straightforward: they allow for consoles, or text-mode terminals, in a graphical screen. The Console Drivers menu is shown in Figure 12.33.

FIGURE 12.33

Console Drivers

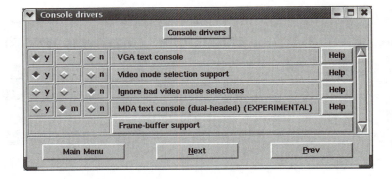

There is one submenu, Frame-Buffer Support. It allows applications to get to the graphical hardware through a buffer. It's experimental for Intel-based systems and generally is not required.

INPUT CORE SUPPORT

Input core support is required for Human Interface Device (HID) interaction with Linux. An HID is a physical interface that sends signals to your computer, including keyboards, mice, and joysticks. The Input Core Support menu is shown in Figure 12.34.

FIGURE 12.34

Input Core Support

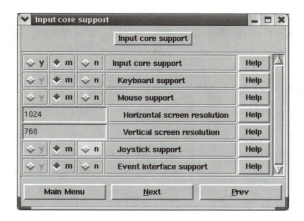

PLUG AND PLAY CONFIGURATION

Linux plug-and-play support in the kernel is straightforward. As shown in Figure 12.35, you can activate basic plug-and-play support, as well as the special commands required for ISA plug-and-play devices.

FIGURE 12.35

Plug And Play
Configuration

I2O DEVICES

I2O is the acronym for the Intelligent Input/Output architecture, which allows drivers to be split into modules for the hardware and operating system. I2O is commonly used with embedded devices; most users won't use or need to enable I2O devices in the Linux kernel. The I2O Device Support menu is shown in Figure 12.36.

FIGURE 12.36

I2O Device Support

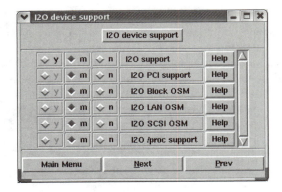

SOUND

Linux supports an impressive array of sound cards. While Linux does not support every sound card, you may be able to make some sound cards work by configuring an appropriate alternative, such as a SoundBlaster card. If you don't see a driver for your sound card in this menu, shown in Figure 12.37, check the documentation or consult the manufacturer of your sound card for advice.

FIGURE 12.37

Sound

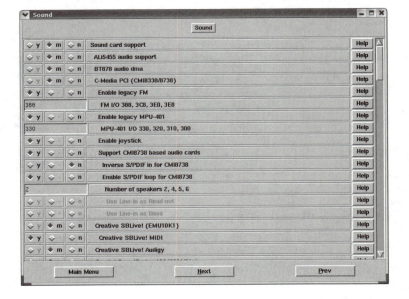

MULTIMEDIA

Closely related to sound is multimedia. The Multimedia Devices menu may not be quite what you'd expect. It includes a submenu for Video For Linux, which requires I2C serial support in the Character Devices menu. It also includes a submenu for Radio Adapters, which includes a list of regular radios that you can install on your computer. The Multimedia Devices menu is shown in Figure 12.38.

FIGURE 12.38

Multimedia Devices

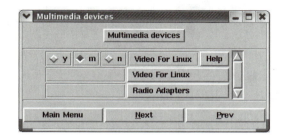

CRYPTOGRAPHY

There are hardware and software cryptography menus for the Linux kernel. The Crypto Hardware Support menu, shown in Figure 12.39, lets you include support for the Broadcom 5820 chipset, which supports secure web servers. Don't confuse this with the Cryptography Support menu shown in Figure 12.40.

FIGURE 12.39

Crypto Hardware Support

Other Software Support

The remaining kernel menus are software menus that can't be classified into any of the other categories. They include basic interfaces for encryption, filesystems, load profiling, kernel debugging, and libraries.

CRYPTOGRAPHY

The cryptography support options allow you to use strong encryption on Linux. It goes well beyond the Crypto Hardware Support described earlier, since that was limited to one chipset. The Cryptography Support (CryptoAPI) menu is shown in Figure 12.40.

FIGURE 12.40

Cryptography
Support
(CryptoAPI)

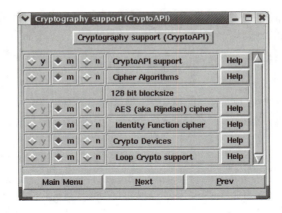

FILESYSTEMS

The Linux kernel File Systems menu allows you to configure the types of formats Linux can read, as well as quotas on each partition. Linux supports a number of filesystem formats, including many that you're familiar with from Chapter 7. The File Systems menu is shown in Figure 12.41.

FIGURE 12.41

File Systems

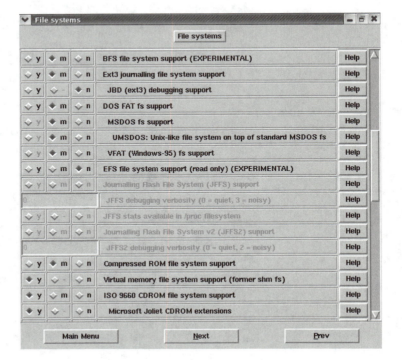

Be careful. Linux support for several filesystems is experimental. This includes the module that lets you write a file to a Microsoft NTFS style filesystem, which is labeled as "DANGEROUS."

NOTE *The terms* file systems *and* filesystems *are used interchangeably.*

WARNING *I would not activate the NTFS Write Support module. The associated help file suggests that you ". . .back up your NTFS volume first, since it will probably get damaged."*

PROFILING

The latest Linux kernels are incorporating support for profiling the performance of your system. It's based on the OProfile system described at `http://oprofile.sourceforge.net/about.php3`; it is currently "Alpha" level experimental software. This menu is not active if you've deactivated the development drivers setting in the Code Maturity Level Options menu. The Profiling Support menu is shown in Figure 12.42.

FIGURE 12.42

Profiling Support

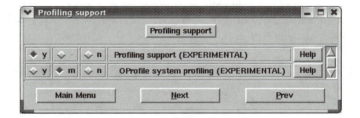

KERNEL HACKING

The Kernel Hacking menu, shown in Figure 12.43, supports drivers that can help you debug driver or other kernel problems. This menu is generally used by developers.

FIGURE 12.43

Kernel Hacking

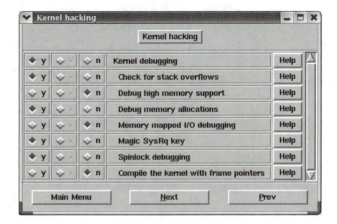

LIBRARY ROUTINES

The Library Routines menu shown in Figure 12.44 includes `zlib` compression and decompression support for data streams.

FIGURE 12.44

Library Routines

Bootloader Updates

While GRUB is the default bootloader for Red Hat Linux, LILO is still in fairly common use. When you recompile a kernel, you should set up your bootloader to boot from either kernel, as though they were two distinct operating systems. Although bootloader updates aren't a part of the "make" process, the steps you need to update either bootloader are fairly straightforward.

Updating GRUB

Assuming GRUB is your bootloader, open `/etc/grub.conf` in the text editor of your choice. If Red Hat Linux is the only operating system on your computer, the key commands are as follows:

```
default=0
title Red Hat Linux (2.4.20-8)
    root (hd0,1)
    kernel /vmlinuz-2.4.20-8 ro root=LABEL=/
    initrd /initrd-2.4.20-8.img
```

Now take the kernel that you just recompiled. The main compressed kernel file is `vmlinuz-2.4.20-sugaree`; the corresponding Initial RAM file is `initrd-2.4.20sugaree.img`. Since you've installed these files in the same `/boot` directory, none of the other parameters will change. You can add a second stanza with the newly compiled kernel:

```
default=0
title Red Hat Linux (2.4.20-8)
    root (hd0,1)
    kernel /vmlinuz-2.4.20-8 ro root=LABEL=/
    initrd /initrd-2.4.20-8.img
title Red Hat Linux (2.4.20sugaree)
    root (hd0,1)
    kernel /vmlinuz-2.4.20sugaree ro root=LABEL=/
    initrd /initrd-2.4.20sugaree.img
```

Remember, nothing more is required. When you reboot your computer, you'll see both titles in the GRUB menu, as shown in Figure 12.45. Since `default=0`, the old kernel in the first stanza is still the default. We described a similar version of `grub.conf` in Figure 12.2. For a detailed analysis of GRUB, see Chapter 11.

FIGURE 12.45

Revised GRUB

Updating LILO

If you use LILO as your bootloader, open /etc/lilo.conf in the text editor of your choice. If Red Hat Linux is the only operating system on your computer, the key commands are as follows:

```
default=linux
image=/boot/vmlinuz-2.4.20-8
    label=linux
    initrd=/boot/initrd-2.4.20-8.img
    read-only
    append="root=LABEL=/"
```

Now take the kernel that you just recompiled. The main compressed kernel file is `vmlinuz-2.4.20sugaree`; the corresponding Initial RAM file is `initrd-2.4.20sugaree.img`. Since you've installed these files in the same /**boot** directory, none of the other parameters will change. You can add a second stanza with the newly compiled kernel:

```
default=linux
image=/boot/vmlinuz-2.4.20-8
    label=linux
    initrd=/boot/initrd-2.4.20-8.img
```

```
        read-only
        append="root=LABEL=/"
image=/boot/vmlinuz-2.4.20sugaree
    label=linux-sugaree
    initrd=/boot/initrd-2.4.20sugaree.img
    read-only
    append="root=LABEL=/"
```

Save your changes. With LILO, you need to run the `lilo` command to write the changes to the MBR of your hard disk. Since the `default` setting is `linux`, LILO will still automatically boot your old kernel unless you specifically select the new one in the LILO boot menu.

Summary

The idea of upgrading and recompiling the Linux kernel strikes fear into many. While the steps are labor-intensive, there is nothing difficult about this process.

The easiest way to upgrade a kernel is to install a newer Red Hat Linux kernel RPM package. When installed and not upgraded, a new kernel automatically upgrades the bootloader as well. Alternatively, if the upgrade is small, you can download and install a patch.

If you want to change the configuration of a kernel, the process is long. Here's a summary of the basic steps:

1. Download the source code for the new kernel: tarballs from Internet sites such as `ftp.kernel.org` or Red Hat RPMs.

2. Install the RPMs associated with kernel tools such as `menuconfig` or `xconfig`.

3. Navigate to the directory with your kernel source code. Select a value for EXTRAVERSION in the `Makefile`. Back up any current hidden `.config` file. Clean the current source code with the `make mrproper` command.

4. Use a baseline configuration; some are available in `/boot`, others in the `configs` subdirectory. Alternatively, you could use the local `.config` file or create one with the `make oldconfig` command.

5. Open a kernel configuration editor using `make menuconfig` or `make xconfig`. Make your changes and save.

6. Set up the dependencies with the `make dep` command.

7. Create a compressed kernel image with the `make bzImage` command. Note the directory with the image.

8. Copy the kernel that you created to the `/boot` directory. Name it `vmlinuz-xEXTRAVERSION`, where *x* represents the version number of the kernel, and EXTRAVERSION is a variable in the `Makefile`.

9. Organize your kernel modules with `make modules` and `make modules_install`.

10. Create an Initial RAM disk for your new kernel with the `mkinitrd/boot/initrd-xExtraVersion` command.

11. Modify your bootloader: add a stanza with the new kernel and Initial RAM disk files.

In the next chapter, we'll pick up with other administrative functions. Job managers such as `cron` and `at` allow administrators to run programs on an automated basis. Other key administrative skills include log file analysis and service management.

Chapter 13

The Administrative Nitty-Gritty

ADMINISTERING COMPUTERS CAN BE a complicated job. Even in small organizations, there are users and groups to configure, backups to create, databases to maintain, and similar chores. Many administrative jobs are time-consuming exercises. If you run them during the day, they can overwhelm a system that's already trying to keep up with your users.

You could change your hours and run these jobs at night. But what if you're responsible for several facilities? Even Linux administrators deserve a personal life.

To support these tasks, Linux includes the at and cron daemons, which help you automate the tasks that you need to run, any time, on any schedule. While at is a onetime management tool, cron allows you to set up jobs to run on regular schedules.

If you don't have an immediate solution, the first place to start troubleshooting is with the log files. Linux logs—most of which are located in the /var/log directory—are a rich source of information on the activity of your system. Different log files can help you monitor security, login activity, daemon status, and more.

As a Linux administrator, you should be familiar with a number of basic commands. The ps, top, and kill commands help you manage processes. You can check current logins with who. The nice and renice commands help you prioritize what's running. The nohup command can also help you run commands even after logging out of your account. This chapter covers the following topics:

◆ Using the cron daemon

◆ Using the at daemon

◆ Managing services

◆ Troubleshooting with logs

◆ Managing processes and users

Using the *cron* Daemon

If you were a computer operating system and did not need sleep, you could back up users' files at night. You could also rotate logs and delete temporary files while others sleep.

The `cron` daemon (also known by its command script, `crond`) performs these tasks on an automated basis. When Linux starts, it runs `crond` as a background process. Every minute, it checks the appropriate configuration files to see if something needs to be run.

There are two groups of `cron` configuration files. One group is governed by a global configuration file, `/etc/crontab`. Another is based on those created by individual users with the `crontab` command.

Formatting *cron*

To understand how `cron` works, it's best to start with the basic `cron` configuration file, `/etc/crontab`. This file specifies several environment variables, including SHELL, PATH, and HOME. The following is a line-by-line analysis of this file:

```
SHELL=/bin/bash
```

The commands in this file are based on the bash shell.

```
PATH=/sbin:/bin:/usr/sbin:/usr/bin
```

When the commands in this file are located in the noted directories, the full directory path is not required. The PATH in `/etc/crontab` also determines the order in which the directories are searched. For example, if the `flight` command exists in both the `/sbin` and `/usr/bin` directories, `cron` runs the `/sbin/flight` command.

```
MAILTO=root
```

Every time `crond` actually does something, notification is mailed to the root user.

```
HOME=/
```

The home directory associated with this `/etc/crontab` configuration file is the root (`/`) directory.

```
# run-parts
```

The `run-parts` command runs every script file in the specified directory. This allows you to organize the scripts that you need to run on a periodic basis.

```
01 * * * * root run-parts /etc/cron.hourly
```

This command runs every script in the `/etc/cron.hourly` directory at one minute past every hour, every day.

```
02 4 * * * root run-parts /etc/cron.daily
```

This command runs every script in the `/etc/cron.daily` directory at 4:02 A.M., every day.

```
22 4 * * 0 root run-parts /etc/cron.weekly
```

This command runs every script in the `/etc/cron.weekly` directory at 4:22 A.M every Sunday.

```
42 4 1 * * root run-parts /etc/cron.monthly
```

This command runs every script in the `/etc/cron.monthly` directory at 4:42 A.M on the first day of every month

The numbers and asterisks in the commands may seem cryptic. Let's take a closer look.

The Syntax of *cron*

To use cron effectively, you need to understand the time and date fields on the left side of each command in a cron file. Table 13.1 shows the five fields, from left to right.

TABLE 13.1: *CRON* FIELDS

FIELD	ALLOWABLE RANGE
Minute	0–59
Hour	0–23, where 0 is midnight and 20 is 8 P.M..
Day	1–31
Month	1–12
Day of week	0–7, where 0 and 7 both represent Sunday.

An asterisk in any field is a wildcard. For example, if the first field contains an asterisk, that particular job is run every allowable minute.

If you want to specify a range such as every hour between 8:00 A.M and 4:00 P.M., set the second field to 8-16. Alternatively, you can run a job every other day by setting the third field to */2. As you can see, once you know each of the five fields (minute, hour, day, month, day of week), there is nothing cryptic about any of the cron command fields.

Standard *cron* Jobs

When you install Red Hat Linux, the standard configuration includes a set of cron jobs. This configuration allows you to organize cron jobs on an hourly, daily, monthly, and weekly basis. Each of these categories includes its own directory: /etc/cron.hourly, /etc/cron.daily, /etc/cron.weekly, and /etc/cron.monthly.

Take a look at several standard cron jobs that are run on a daily basis:

logrotate   Rotates logs periodically. For example, Red Hat Linux rotates five weeks of logs, and the /var/log/messages entries from the previous week are kept in the /var/log/messages.1 file.

slocate.cron   Refreshes the database associated with the locate command. By default, the database updates exclude directories that are networked from other computers, as well as several temporary directories.

tmpwatch   Deletes files in the /tmp and /var/tmp directories. By default, files in these directories are deleted if they haven't been accessed in 240 and 720 hours, respectively.

User *cron* Jobs

Linux users may want to schedule their own cron jobs. For example, someone may want to manage a database in the middle of the night. As long as that user is not on the /etc/cron.deny list (described later in this chapter), that user can start his or her own cron file by using the crontab -e command.

NOTE *While* `crontab` *uses the* `vi` *editor by default, you can set it to use another editor. For example, if you want to use* `emacs` *to edit your* `cron` *file, run the* `export EDITOR=emacs` *command.*

For example, assume you've configured a script named `goodback` to back up all the files in your home directory. You want to run `goodback` every Sunday morning at 1:36 A.M. Assume your username is ez, and your script is in your a default home directory (`/home/ez`). Log in as ez, and then run `crontab -e`. Assuming you're using the default `vi` editor, type i to enter insert mode, and type the following line:

```
36 1 * * 0     /home/ez/goodback
```

Once you've saved the file, you can check the contents with the `crontab -1` command. All user `cron` files are stored in the `/var/spool/cron` directory and are accessible by default to the owner and the root user.

NOTE *If you're creating a* `cron` *file, you should also assign the SHELL, PATH, and HOME variables. It's also a good idea to set the MAILTO variable, as it can notify you whenever* `cron` *actually runs one of your jobs. For guidance, see the earlier section, "Formatting* `cron`*," which detailed the default* `/etc/crontab` *file.*

SCRIPT MANAGEMENT

When you run a `cron` job, you're running a script. This is an executable file with commands that you could otherwise run at the command-line interface. You can also put any command that you use frequently into a file by using a text editor. Save the file and then use the `chmod +x` *script1* command to make it executable. Assuming, for example, the file is in the /path/to directory, you run it at any time by typing the /path/to/*script1* command. If you have several commands that you normally run at the same time, you could expand that one-line file to include several commands. This is a great timesaver.

Saving your scripts to a directory in your PATH is even more efficient. For example, say your username is tb. Run the `echo $PATH` command. You should see the /home/tb/bin directory in your PATH. If you save scripts such as *script1* to /home/tb/bin, all you'd need to do to run that script is run the *script1* command.

Just remember, if you're going to run *script1* as a `cron` job, you need to add the appropriate directory to the PATH as described earlier.

---

cron Security

By default, `cron` tools are available to all users. You can limit access to `cron` by creating `/etc/cron.allow` and/or `/etc/cron.deny` files. There are three possible scenarios for these files:

◆ Neither of these files exists, which means every user is allowed access to `cron`.

◆ Users listed in `/etc/cron.allow` are the only ones allowed access to `cron` tools. If you also have an `/etc/cron.deny` file, it is ignored.

◆ Users listed in `/etc/cron.deny` are not allowed to use `cron` tools. This assumes `/etc/cron.allow` does not exist.

Using the *at* Daemon

One of the drawbacks of a `cron` job is that it is scheduled to be run on a regular basis. Sometimes, you just want to run a specific task once and then forget it. That's where the `at` daemon comes in.

It's easy to set up an `at` job. You can specify the time when you want to run the program, or you can use the associated `batch` command to start the job when your computer is relatively free.

This daemon works more like the print process; jobs are spooled in the `/var/spool/at` directory and executed at the desired time.

Setting Up an *at* Job

The `at` daemon works almost as if it were a separate shell. When you run the `at` *time* command, it sends you to a command prompt where you can enter the commands and programs of your choice. The `at` *now + time* command works as well; the job is run after a specified time period has passed.

For example, assume you're working on a large database and want to process the data when nobody else will be using the system, say at 2:05 A.M. You've set up the `/home/mj/airplane` script to manage your database, and plan to process the results in the `/home/mj/air-safe` file. The normal way to do this is with the following commands:

```
# at 2:05 tomorrow
at> /home/mj/airplane > /home/mj/air-safe
at> Ctrl-D
```

There are a number of different ways to set up the time in the `at` *+ time* command, as shown in Table 13.2.

TABLE 13.2: *AT* DAEMON TIME PARAMETERS

PERIOD	EXAMPLE	COMMENT
Minute	`at now + 5 minutes`	The jobs will start in 5 minutes.
Hour	`at now + 1 hour`	The jobs will start in 1 hour.
Days	`at now + 3 days`	The jobs will start in 3 days.
Weeks	`at now + 2 weeks`	The jobs will start in 2 weeks.
Fixed	`at midnight`	The jobs will start at midnight.
Fixed	`at 10:30pm`	The jobs will start at 10:30 .P.M.
Fixed	`at 1:00 5/12/03`	The jobs will start on May 12, 2003, at 1 A.M.

Job Queue

Once you've entered a job, you can make sure that it's in the queue by using the `atq` command. As you can see, the output gives you the job number, the responsible user, and the time when the job is to be executed. The letter before the username (`a` or `b`) indicates whether it's an `at` or a `batch` job.

```
# atq
8    2003-03-08 02:05 a mj
```

It's easy to remove a job. Just use the `atrm` *jobnumber* command. For example, the following command deletes job 8 from the queue:

```
# atrm 8
```

Batch Jobs

The `batch` command is a specialized version of `at` that runs `at` jobs. By default, jobs created with this command run only when the demand on your CPU is below 80 percent of its capacity.

The `batch` command is equivalent to the `at -q b` command.

Security

Similar to the `cron` daemon, `at` uses the `/etc/at.allow` and `/etc/at.deny` files to regulate access to this system. By default, Red Hat Linux installs a blank `/etc/at.deny` file. This allows all users access to the `at` system.

As long as the `/etc/at.allow` file does not exist, only the users listed in `/etc/at.deny` are denied use to `at`. If you add users to `/etc/at.allow`, only those users are allowed to use the `at` command. In this case, the `/etc/at.deny` file is ignored.

Service Management

One key skill for Linux system administrators is service management. You can start and stop current services with the scripts in the `/etc/rc.d/init.d` directory. In addition, you can ensure that the services of your choice are active only at specific runlevels.

/etc/rc.d/init.d Scripts

The services that you install in Red Hat Linux have their own scripts in the `/etc/rc.d/init.d` directory. It's likely that you have a substantial number of scripts on your system; a sample from my desktop computer is shown in Figure 13.1.

FIGURE 13.1

Service scripts in
/etc/rc.d/init.d

```
[root@RH9Test root]# \ls /etc/rc.d/init.d/
aep1000   dhcrelay   kdcrotate   netfs      postgresql   smb           xfs
amd       firstboot  keytable    network    pxe          snmpd         xinetd
anacron   functions  killall     nfs        radvd        snmptrapd     ypbind
apmd      gpm        kprop       nfslock    random       spamassassin  yppasswdd
atd       halt       krb524      nscd       rawdevices   squid         ypserv
autofs    httpd      krb5kdc     ntpd       rhnsd        sshd          ypxfrd
bcm5820   innd       kudzu       ospf6d     ripd         syslog        zebra
bgpd      iptables   lisa        ospfd      ripngd       tux
crond     irda       lpd         pcmcia     saslauthd    vncserver
cups      isdn       mailman     portmap    sendmail     vsftpd
dhcpd     kadmin     named       postfix    single       winbind
[root@RH9Test root]#
```

Take a look at some of these scripts. Open them up in a text editor. Near the end of each script, you should see a series of commands similar to Figure 13.2. This particular script, `smb`, manages Samba. Some of the commands in different scripts do vary.

FIGURE 13.2

The innards of a service script

```
case "$1" in
  start)
        start
        ;;
  stop)
        stop
        ;;
  restart)
        restart
        ;;
  reload)
        reload
        ;;
  status)
        rhstatus
        ;;
  condrestart)
        [ -f /var/lock/subsys/smb ] && restart || :
        ;;
  *)
        echo $"Usage: $0 {start|stop|restart|reload|status|condrestart}"
        exit 1
esac
                                              96,1-8       97%
```

As you can see Figure 13.2, you can run several actions for that particular service, as shown in Table 13.3. The table simply reflects the actions shown in Figure 13.2; the actions associated with a different script will vary.

TABLE 13.3: SERVICE SCRIPT ACTIONS

ACTION	DESCRIPTION
start	Starts the service; equivalent to the service *script* start command.
stop	Starts the service; equivalent to the service *script* stop command.
restart	Shuts down the service, then starts it again; equivalent to the service *script* restart command.
reload	Makes the service reread any applicable configuration files without restarting; equivalent to the service *script* reload command.
status	Provides the current status of the service; equivalent to the service *script* status command.
condrestart	If the service is "locked," this switch shuts down the service, then starts it again; equivalent to the service *script* condrestart command.

For example, if you wanted to restart Samba, you could run one of the following two commands as the root user:

```
# /etc/rc.d/init.d/smb restart
# service smb restart
```

Activation at Different Runlevels

You can make a service start and stop at different runlevels. For example, take a look at Figure 13.3.

FIGURE 13.3

Services at runlevel 3

```
[root@RH9Test root]# \ls /etc/rc.d/rc3.d/
K05innd          K35vncserver    K65krb5kdc      S08iptables    S56rawdevices
K05saslauthd     K35winbind      K70aep1000      S09isdn        S56xinetd
K12mailman       K36lisa         K70bcm5820      S10network     S58ntpd
K15httpd         K45named        K74ypserv       S12syslog      S80sendmail
K15postgresql    K46radvd        K74ypxfrd       S13portmap     S80spamassassin
K20nfs           K50snmpd        K84bgpd         S14nfslock     S85gpm
K24irda          K50snmptrapd    K84ospf6d       S17keytable    S90crond
K25squid         K50tux          K84ospfd        S20random      S90cups
K28amd           K50vsftpd       K84ripd         S24pcmcia      S90xfs
K34dhcrelay      K54pxe          K84ripngd       S25netfs       S95anacron
K34yppasswdd     K65kadmin       K85zebra        S26apmd        S95atd
K35dhcpd         K65kprop        K95firstboot    S28autofs      S97rhnsd
K35smb           K65krb524       S05kudzu        S55sshd        S99local
[root@RH9Test root]#
```

You can see from the `/etc/rc.d/rc3.d` directory that Apache is killed when Linux starts runlevel 3 (`K15httpd`). If you want to start that service at runlevel 3, you need to change it into a start script. The standard method is the `chkconfig` command. To list the current runlevels associated with Apache (`httpd`), run the following command:

```
# chkconfig --list httpd
httpd    0:off  1:off  2:off  3:off  4:off  5:off  6:off
```

The output shows that Apache isn't started at any runlevel. To start it, you need to activate it at the desired runlevels. For example, the following command starts Apache at runlevels 3 and 5, in standard multiuser and GUI modes:

```
# chkconfig --level 35 httpd on
```

You can confirm the effect by listing the files at runlevels 3 and 5; in this case, you'll see the `S85httpd` start script in each directory (`/etc/rc.d/rc3.d` and `/etc/rc.d/rc5.d`). Alternatively, just run the following command:

```
# chkconfig --list httpd
httpd    0:off  1:off  2:off  3:on  4:off  5:on  6:off
```

Several graphical tools are available. For example, you can use `ntsysv --level` *runlevel* to view the services at different runlevels. For example, the `ntsysv --level 5` command could illustrate active services at runlevel 5, as shown in Figure 13.4.

Troubleshooting with Logs

To paraphrase an old song associated with a restaurant in Berkeley, California: "You can have almost any log you want…in a Linux restaurant." The menu of available log files is impressive. You can configure logs by service or the severity of the problem.

You've already seen the workings of installation log files in Chapter 3. In this section, you'll review log files to see what happened with many Linux services.

Log files are governed by the syslog and kernel log daemons, `syslogd` and `klogd`, as configured in `/etc/syslog.conf`. Both daemons are active by default.

FIGURE 13.4

Managing services with `ntsysv`

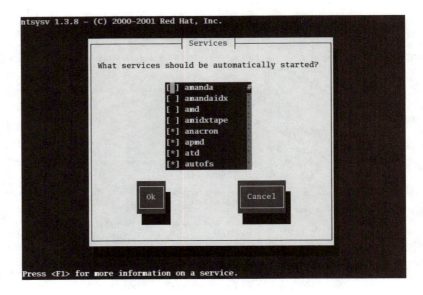

Log File Categories

You can use a system log file to diagnose a problem with installation, booting, specific services, and more. Logs can be further subdivided into eight categories, listed here in descending order of importance:

- `emerg` (emergency)
- `alert`
- `crit` (critical)
- `err` (error)
- `warning`
- `notice`
- `info`
- `debug`

Log files are organized as described in the Linux `/etc/syslog.conf` configuration file. Take a look at the default Red Hat Linux version of this file in Figure 13.5.

As you can see, most logs are located in the `/var/log` directory. If you activate kernel messages, they are normally sent to the console (your screen). Some daemons, such as Internet Network News (`innd`), include additional specifications in this file.

FIGURE 13.5

/etc/syslog.conf

```
# Log all kernel messages to the console.
# Logging much else clutters up the screen.
#kern.*                                                  /dev/console

# Log anything (except mail) of level info or higher.
# Don't log private authentication messages!
*.info;mail.none;news.none;authpriv.none;cron.none       /var/log/messages

# The authpriv file has restricted access.
authpriv.*                                               /var/log/secure

# Log all the mail messages in one place.
mail.*                                                   /var/log/maillog


# Log cron stuff
cron.*                                                   /var/log/cron

# Everybody gets emergency messages
*.emerg                                                  *

# Save news errors of level crit and higher in a special file.
uucp,news.crit                                           /var/log/spooler

# Save boot messages also to boot.log
local7.*                                                 /var/log/boot.log
```

Logs are maintained through a standard `cron` job, `logrotate`. As discussed earlier, it rotates log files on a weekly basis. Thus, the `/var/log/boot.log.1` file is from the previous week.

Take the first active line in this file, which specifies messages associated with several daemons. For example, the first statement, `*.info`, sends all messages of `info` level and higher (`notice`, `warning`, `err`, `crit`, `alert`, and `emerg`) to the appropriate log file.

System Logs

Now let's look at some of the system logs in the `/var/log` directory. The `dmesg` file consists of basic boot messages associated with starting Linux. The `message` file includes additional process messages after Linux boots on your computer. The `boot.log` file lists messages related to the starting and stopping of daemons. And `wtmp` helps you monitor logons.

GETTING THE REST OF THE *DMESG*

In Chapter 11, you learned about how `/var/log/dmesg` helps you determine whether Linux detected your hardware. There's one other critical item at the end of this file: whether Linux has properly mounted your filesystems and swap space. If the mount was successful, you should see messages similar to the following:

```
EXT3 FS 2.4-0.9.19, 19 August 2002 on ide0(3,6), internal journal
Adding Swap: 257032K swap-space (priority -1)
kjournald starting. Commit interval 5 seconds
```

This tells you that Linux has successfully mounted an ext3 filesystem with an internal journal on a partition. The kjournal daemon (`kjournald`) does the actual work of keeping the filesystem journal up to date. You'll see additional lines like this for each Linux partition.

OTHER /VAR/LOG/MESSAGES

Other messages associated with hardware and services are documented in /var/log/messages. A couple of examples are shown in the following excerpt:

```
Sep 23 11:03:00 RH9 kernel: sb: No ISAPnP cards found, trying standard ones...
Sep 23 11:03:00 RH9 kernel: SB 4.13 detected OK (220)
Sep 23 11:46:46 RH9 sshd(pam_unix)[1129]: session opened for user root by LOGIN(uid=0)
Sep 23 11:46:51 RH9 sshd(pam_unix)[1129]: session closed for user root
```

Each line in this file includes some basic characteristics—such as the date, time, hostname, and service associated with each message. If available, the username and process identifier are also listed.

You can see two important developments in the code. First, Red Hat Linux has detected a Sound Blaster sound card during the boot process. Next, someone has successfully accessed the RH9 computer through **sshd**, the Secure Shell daemon. As you'll see in Chapter 22, **sshd** is a critical tool that can help you administer a computer remotely.

But you may have a security breach. If the noted login is not authorized, a cracker may have broken into your system. See Chapter 22 for techniques that you can use to secure your Linux system.

NOTE   *In the Linux world, hackers are good people who just want to create better software. Crackers, on the other hand, are people who try to break into your system.*

ANALYZING THE /VAR/LOG/BOOT.LOG

When services or daemons start and stop, they are listed in /var/log/boot.log. Take the example shown in Figure 13.6. The first line shown is, in fact, the last message of a shutdown on January 15. The second message is the first daemon started when you boot Linux.

FIGURE 13.6

boot.log

```
Mar 26 10:54:04 RH9Test syslog: syslogd startup succeeded
Mar 26 10:54:04 RH9Test syslog: klogd startup succeeded
Mar 26 10:54:04 RH9Test portmap: portmap startup succeeded
Mar 26 10:54:05 RH9Test nfslock: rpc.statd startup succeeded
Mar 26 10:54:05 RH9Test keytable: Loading keymap:
Mar 26 10:54:05 RH9Test keytable:
Mar 26 10:54:05 RH9Test keytable:
Mar 26 10:54:05 RH9Test rc: Starting keytable:  succeeded
Mar 26 10:54:05 RH9Test random: Initializing random number generator:  succeeded
Mar 26 10:54:05 RH9Test rc: Starting pcmcia:  succeeded
Mar 26 10:54:06 RH9Test netfs: Mounting other filesystems:  succeeded
Mar 26 10:54:06 RH9Test apmd: apmd startup succeeded
Mar 26 10:54:06 RH9Test autofs: automount startup succeeded
Mar 26 10:54:10 RH9Test sshd: RSA1 key generation succeeded
Mar 26 10:54:10 RH9Test sshd: RSA key generation succeeded
Mar 26 10:54:15 RH9Test sshd: DSA key generation succeeded
Mar 26 10:54:15 RH9Test sshd:  succeeded
Mar 26 10:54:19 RH9Test xinetd: xinetd startup succeeded
Mar 26 10:54:20 RH9Test sendmail: sendmail startup succeeded
Mar 26 10:54:21 RH9Test sendmail: sm-client startup succeeded
Mar 26 10:54:21 RH9Test gpm: gpm startup succeeded
Mar 26 10:54:21 RH9Test crond: crond startup succeeded
Mar 26 10:54:24 RH9Test cups: cupsd startup succeeded
"/var/log/boot.log" 312L, 17876C
```

Some services are associated with other parameters. For example, the `keytable` parameter shown in Figure 13.6 loads the `keymap` associated with your keyboard. In addition, the `network` service initializes the loopback interface.

DETECTING REMOTE LOGINS

Login records are kept in a database file, `/var/log/wtmp`. You can use the `utmpdump` command to make this file readable. Take a look at Figure 13.7; this is part of the output when I ran `utmpdump /var/log/wtmp`. Note the login from IP address 128.99.1.64.

WARNING   *You should know the IP addresses for your LAN. If your network does not include some of the addresses shown in Figure 13.7, and you don't have any remote users, be afraid. Someone may have tried to break into your system. Chapter 22 includes techniques designed to block logins from suspicious networks.*

FIGURE 13.7

Checking login activity

```
               ] [Wed Mar 26 11:03:49 2003 EST]
[5] [02151] [x   ] [           ] [           ] [2.4.20-8        ] [0.0.0.0
               ] [Wed Mar 26 11:03:49 2003 EST]
[6] [02145] [1   ] [LOGIN   ] [tty1        ] [           ] [0.0.0.0
               ] [Wed Mar 26 11:03:49 2003 EST]
[6] [02149] [5   ] [LOGIN   ] [tty5        ] [           ] [0.0.0.0
               ] [Wed Mar 26 11:03:49 2003 EST]
[6] [02150] [6   ] [LOGIN   ] [tty6        ] [           ] [0.0.0.0
               ] [Wed Mar 26 11:03:49 2003 EST]
[6] [02146] [2   ] [LOGIN   ] [tty2        ] [           ] [0.0.0.0
               ] [Wed Mar 26 11:03:49 2003 EST]
[6] [02147] [3   ] [LOGIN   ] [tty3        ] [           ] [0.0.0.0
               ] [Wed Mar 26 11:03:49 2003 EST]
[6] [02148] [4   ] [LOGIN   ] [tty4        ] [           ] [0.0.0.0
               ] [Wed Mar 26 11:03:49 2003 EST]
[7] [02204] [:0  ] [root     ] [:0          ] [           ] [128.99.1.64
               ] [Wed Mar 26 11:04:33 2003 EST]
[8] [00000] [:0  ] [         ] [:0          ] [           ] [128.99.1.64
               ] [Wed Mar 26 11:05:34 2003 EST]
[7] [02333] [:0  ] [root     ] [:0          ] [           ] [128.99.1.64
               ] [Wed Mar 26 11:05:46 2003 EST]
[7] [02437] [/0  ] [root     ] [pts/0       ] [:0.0        ] [0.0.0.0
               ] [Wed Mar 26 11:06:01 2003 EST]
--More--
```

Daemon Logs

Most Linux daemons, such as `crond`, `httpd`, and `smbd`, are configured with log files in the `/var/log` directory. Each log file can provide clues as to the success or failure of any particular service. A clean example is shown in Figure 13.8, a view of the `/var/log/cron` file.

Figure 13.8 illustrates the date and time `cron` jobs were executed. You may recognize these as the standard `cron` jobs listed earlier in this chapter. While the times are different from those specified in `/etc/crontab`, it simply means that this particular Linux computer was not running at the specified time.

FIGURE 13.8

`/var/log/cron`

```
Mar 26 10:54:21 RH9Test crond[1944]: (CRON) STARTUP (fork ok)
Mar 26 10:54:26 RH9Test anacron[2037]: Anacron 2.3 started on 2003-03-26
Mar 26 10:54:26 RH9Test anacron[2037]: Will run job `cron.daily' in 65 min.
Mar 26 10:54:26 RH9Test anacron[2037]: Will run job `cron.weekly' in 70 min.
Mar 26 10:54:26 RH9Test anacron[2037]: Will run job `cron.monthly' in 75 min.
Mar 26 10:54:26 RH9Test anacron[2037]: Jobs will be executed sequentially
Mar 26 11:01:00 RH9Test CROND[2082]: (root) CMD (run-parts /etc/cron.hourly)
Mar 26 11:23:15 RH9Test crond[1958]: (CRON) STARTUP (fork ok)
Mar 26 11:23:19 RH9Test anacron[2035]: Anacron 2.3 started on 2003-03-26
Mar 26 11:23:19 RH9Test anacron[2035]: Will run job `cron.daily' in 65 min.
Mar 26 11:23:19 RH9Test anacron[2035]: Will run job `cron.weekly' in 70 min.
Mar 26 11:23:19 RH9Test anacron[2035]: Will run job `cron.monthly' in 75 min.
Mar 26 11:23:19 RH9Test anacron[2035]: Jobs will be executed sequentially
Mar 26 11:58:25 RH9Test crond[1961]: (CRON) STARTUP (fork ok)
Mar 26 11:58:30 RH9Test anacron[2039]: Anacron 2.3 started on 2003-03-26
Mar 26 11:58:30 RH9Test anacron[2039]: Will run job `cron.daily' in 65 min.
Mar 26 11:58:30 RH9Test anacron[2039]: Will run job `cron.weekly' in 70 min.
Mar 26 11:58:30 RH9Test anacron[2039]: Will run job `cron.monthly' in 75 min.
Mar 26 11:58:30 RH9Test anacron[2039]: Jobs will be executed sequentially
Mar 26 12:01:00 RH9Test CROND[2376]: (root) CMD (run-parts /etc/cron.hourly)
Mar 26 12:24:05 RH9Test crond[1959]: (CRON) STARTUP (fork ok)
Mar 26 12:24:09 RH9Test anacron[2037]: Anacron 2.3 started on 2003-03-26
Mar 26 12:24:10 RH9Test anacron[2037]: Will run job `cron.daily' in 65 min.
```

The following excerpt from `/var/log/httpd/access_log` tells you about one of the clients for your web server; for example, that particular client used the Lynx web browser from the U.S. eastern time zone during daylight saving time (-0400).

```
localhost.localdomain - -[23/Sep/2003:14:05:26 -0400] "GET / HTTP/1.0" 403 2898
➥ "-" "Lynx/2.8.5dev.7 libwww-FM/2.14 SSL-MM/1.4.1 OpenSSL/0.9.6b"
```

The following excerpt (from `/var/log/samba/smbmount.log`) shows a connection to a Microsoft Windows share through Samba:

```
[2003/09/23 13:53:32, 0] client/smbmount.c:send_fs_socket(383) mount.smbfs: entering
➥ daemon mode for service \\laptop2\downloads, pid 5711
```

As you add more daemons to your Red Hat Linux system, more log files will appear in the `/var/log` directory. However, log files don't have to be stored in `/var/log`; it's determined by the configuration files associated with each daemon.

Other Logs

The /var/log directory contains a number of other log files. As you add more services, more log files will appear. Therefore, Table 13.4 is not a comprehensive list.

TABLE 13.4: */VAR/LOG* LOG FILES

FILE	FUNCTION
ksyms	Exported kernel symbols, such as drivers and modules.
lastlog	Specifies last login time and location, based on the lastlog -u *username* command.
maillog	Anything related to mail servers, such as startup, shutdown, aliases, and errors related to sendmail.
news	A directory of log files related to the InterNetNews (INN) server.
rpmpkgs	Currently installed RPMs.
scrollkeeper	For documents, especially in GUIs.
secure	Anything related to secure connections, including ssh and xinetd.

Process Management

Anyone who manages a Linux computer needs to know how to manage processes.

A couple of key tools are available to help you manage Linux processes: who and ps. These commands help you keep track of who is connected and what processes are being run, respectively. In addition, the top command helps you monitor the demands that a service is placing on your computer. Finally, the nohup command can help you run another command and keep it going even after you log off your computer.

If any of your users are having a problem with any application, you can use the kill command to stop that application. If an important program or procedure is about to run, commands such as nice and renice can help you raise or lower the priority associated with the program of your choice.

Processes and *ps*

The ps command shows currently running processes or programs. When you type the ps command by itself, you see the processes associated with your setup. If you type the ps aux command, you can see everything running on your Linux system including daemons. Another useful variation is ps l, which returns a "long list" associated with each currently running process. Important categories from this command are shown in Table 13.5.

NOTE   ps *is one of the few commands that does not require a dash in front of command switches.*

If you have a program that's out of control, you need the PID number to kill that problem program. Alternatively, if you need to run a program that's stuck waiting for CPU resources, you can use its PID to raise its priority.

TABLE 13.5: *PS-AL* OUTPUT CATEGORIES

ITEM	EXPLANATION
PID	The process identifier. Every process is associated with a number known as a process identifier.
PPID	The parent process identifier. Every process has a parent except init. If you can't kill a process, you might be able to kill the parent process.
PRI	The priority value. Higher priority programs get attention from your CPU more quickly. The highest priority program has a PRI of -20. The lowest priority program has a PRI of 19.
STAT	The current status of the process. There are three options: Running (R), Sleeping (S), or Swapped (SW) to the swap partition.

Processes and *top*

The **top** command helps you identify the programs that are "hogging" resources, specifically your CPU and RAM memory. For example, Figure 13.9 shows what the **top** command can see on a system with a less than ideal amount of RAM.

FIGURE 13.9

top command output

```
 1:38pm  up  5:18,  1 user,  load average: 3.22, 1.78, 0.74
65 processes: 60 sleeping, 5 running, 0 zombie, 0 stopped
CPU states: 12.7% user,  7.6% system,  0.0% nice, 79.5% idle
Mem:    37552K av,    37028K used,    524K free,      0K shrd,     312K buff
Swap:  193528K av,    54264K used,  139264K free                14892K cached

  PID USER     PRI  NI  SIZE  RSS SHARE STAT %CPU %MEM   TIME COMMAND
 1221 root      14  -1 13724 3476  2520 D <   5.7  9.2  0:58 X
 1286 root      15   0  4688 3524  2652 R     3.9  9.3  0:23 gnome-terminal
 1270 root      15   0  5268 3992  3164 R     2.1 10.6  0:12 gnome-panel
 1450 root      15   0   788  748   592 R     1.7  1.9  0:05 top
 1452 root      15   0 14884  12M  9080 R     1.1 34.8  0:14 mozilla-bin
 1278 root      15   0  6940 3652  3044 S     0.9  9.7  1:04 rhn-applet-gui
    5 root      15   0     0    0     0 SW    0.5  0.0  0:05 kswapd
 1274 root      15   0  2684 1952  1836 S     0.1  5.1  0:01 magicdev
    1 root      15   0   400  368   348 S     0.0  0.9  0:04 init
    2 root      15   0     0    0     0 SW    0.0  0.0  0:00 keventd
    3 root      15   0     0    0     0 SW    0.0  0.0  0:00 kapmd
    4 root      34  19     0    0     0 SWN   0.0  0.0  0:00 ksoftirqd_CPU0
    6 root      15   0     0    0     0 SW    0.0  0.0  0:00 bdflush
    7 root      15   0     0    0     0 SW    0.0  0.0  0:00 kupdated
    8 root      24   0     0    0     0 SW    0.0  0.0  0:00 mdrecoveryd
   12 root      15   0     0    0     0 SW    0.0  0.0  0:01 kjournald
```

In our example, performance is slow, and you can hear the hard drive working constantly. The output shown in Figure 13.8 suggests that to reduce the load on your hard disk, you should either refrain from running the Mozilla web browser or add more RAM to your system.

If you're running a multiuser system, pay attention to users associated with troublesome processes.

Logins and *who*

As an administrator, you should check logons regularly; for example, the following output from `who` shows the same person logged on from two different locations:

```
mj      tty1    Mar 12 10:33
ywow    pts1    Mar 11 22:30 (192.168.0.12)
mj      pts0    Mar 11 22:45 (136.46.1.64)
```

Because user mj is logged on from the local computer and remotely from the computer at 136.46.1.64, you should be concerned that someone else is using mj's username and password to break into your system.

Process *kill*

By reputation, Linux doesn't crash. There are reports of users and websites powered by Linux running without reboots for months at a time. One reason behind this is that system administrators can manage troublesome programs with the `kill` command.

For example, if a program like Mozilla "locks up" on you while you're browsing the Internet, follow these steps to kill the program:

1. Open a command-line shell. If you can't open a command-line shell inside an X Window, start a new virtual console with the Ctrl+Alt+F*n* command, where *n* is a number between 1 and 6.

2. Run the `ps aux | grep mozilla` command. The number after your username is the PID of the process that is currently running Mozilla on your computer. Record that number. For purposes of this exercise, assume the number is 1789.

3. Run the `kill` *PIDnumber* command. Based on step 2, the actual command would be `kill 1789`. If the `kill` command doesn't work, run the `ps auxl | grep mozilla` command to find the PPID. You may need to kill those processes first.

4. As a last resort, use the `-9` switch, which kills the process even if it leaves other programs in your memory. In this case, you would use the `kill -9 1789` command.

nice and *renice*

The `nice` and `renice` commands let you run programs at different relative priorities. The priority of any program can range from -20 (highest) to 19 (lowest). The `nice` program starts another process with an adjusted priority. For example, you could set Mozilla to start after all others have finished by using the `nice -n 19 mozilla` command. If you have to focus Linux on one specific program, you need its PID. Once you find the program's PID (assume it's 1789 for this exercise), you can raise its priority with the `renice -10 1789` command.

NOTE   *To understand priorities, keep in mind that everything seems reversed in Linux. If you want to make a program more important, use a negative number.*

Leaving a *nohup*

If you can't run a program with the priority that you want, the nohup command can help. With nohup, you run a long command just before leaving your computer. For example, say you want to record an .iso file to a CD. You know that CDs take some time to record, but you need to pick up your child from school right now.

If your computer includes a CD recorder, the nohup command can help. If you want to take the redhatcd1.iso file and record it on a blank writeable CD, run the following command and log out of your user account, and the CD recording process will proceed automatically. Messages are written to the nohup.out file in the local directory.

```
# nohup cdrecord -v speed=4 dev=0,0,0 redhatcd1.iso
```

This assumes, of course, you don't shut down Linux on your computer. More information on the cdrecord command is available in the next chapter.

Summary

The cron daemon can help you run programs on an automated regular basis. Red Hat Linux configures standard cron jobs through /etc/crontab, configured by time period in directories such as /etc/cron.hourly and /etc/cron.weekly. Users can configure their own cron jobs with the crontab command; each user's configuration is stored in the /var/spool/cron directory. cron security is governed by the /etc/cron.allow and /etc/cron.deny files.

The at command is like cron, except it can help you run jobs on a onetime basis. The batch command is a variation of at that runs a specified job when the demands on your system are below 80 percent of capacity. Similar to cron, at command security is governed by the /etc/at.allow and /etc/at.deny files.

Another key to administering Linux is based on log files. Standard Linux log files are configured in /etc/syslog.conf and located in the /var/log directory. System logs help you trace detected hardware and analyze login activity. Daemon logs can help you monitor when daemons such as crond, httpd, and smbd are used. Other log files are available for tasks such as monitoring currently installed RPMs, secure connections, news servers, and more.

Everyone who administers a Linux computer needs to know several basic process and user management commands. The ps, top, and kill commands help you find and kill processes that are out of control. The who command can identify currently logged-in users. The nice and renice commands enable you to prioritize critical jobs.

In the following chapter, you'll extend your knowledge of Linux administration by learning the commands you need to back up all or part of your system.

Chapter 14

Backing Up Your System

DATA ON TODAY'S PERSONAL computers is fragile. Administrators are constantly worried about viruses that might affect data on a network. Events such as cracker attacks, power surges, mechanical failures, magnetic fields, and natural disasters can destroy some or all of the data on your hard drives.

The measures you take to back up your system depend on your situation. Backing up data for multiple users on multiple computers requires more care. To help recover from a disaster at your facility, you may choose to store data at a different site.

Several different types of backup media are available. You can back up critical data on CDs, or you can back up entire computers on one or more tape drives. Recordable DVDs are quickly becoming a viable alternative to tape drives. Alternatively, removable and external hard drives have the capacity and can easily be stored in remote locations.

On larger networks, backups to a central server may be an option. As an administrator, you may want one location to back up files from all servers on your network. As a workstation or desktop user, you may find it convenient to have a central backup server maintained by a responsible Linux administrator.

Depending on your backup mode and media, several backup commands are available to you, such as `tar`, `cpio`, `dump`, and `restore`. Alternatively, a properly configured Redundant Array of Independent or Inexpensive Disks (RAID) can also back up your data on other hard drives. In some cases, a RAID drive can be removed and stored in a secure remote location. This chapter covers the following topics:

- ◆ Exploring backup concepts
- ◆ Selecting your media
- ◆ Using backup and restore commands
- ◆ Understanding RAID

What You Need to Know about Backing Up

Selecting a backup strategy depends on the risks that you are willing to take. The risk equation for any computer backup consists of two parts. First, you need to understand what can happen to your data and computers. Disasters range from a corrupted file to the destruction of your main corporate facility. Second, you need to select a backup strategy to address each of these disasters. The strategy (and cost) varies depending on the importance of the data, your users' reactions to different disasters, and how fast you need to restore from backup. Finally, you must make sure that you can restore from any backup you create, before you really need it.

To understand these parts of the risk equation, you should examine various disaster scenarios and the available levels of data and computer backup.

Data Disaster Scenarios

The loss of even a single file can be a disaster for a user. The loss of a commercial airplane engineering drawing, a master's thesis, or even chapters for a book in production can be a life-changing event.

Information technology managers have to plan for every level of disaster, from the loss of a file to the effects of a nuclear war. (Yes, there are corporate IT managers who create backup plans for a nuclear war.) See Table 14.1 for several basic scenarios.

TABLE 14.1: DATA DISASTER SCENARIOS

SCENARIO	RECOVERY STRATEGY
Lost user file	Restore from backup of the /home filesystem.
Lost configuration file	Restore from backup of /etc.
Lost application file	Reload from backup, or reinstall the application.
Damaged partition	Restore partition from backup, or use an appropriate level of RAID.
Damaged hard drive	Restore hard drive from backup or an appropriate level of hardware RAID.
Damaged computer	Restore data from other computers or tapes/CDs/DVDs on site.
Damaged data facility	Restore from backups stored in a remote location.
Electromagnetic data loss	Restore from nonmagnetic backups.

This is far from a comprehensive list of possible disaster scenarios. For example, problems with a network can be just as difficult, especially if they prevent users from accessing their files or applications on a server. Of course, disaster planning for networks is beyond the scope of this book, but the principles are essentially the same.

Levels of Backup

You need to decide what data is critical to you. If you're a personal desktop user, you may have just a few critical files, such as documents. You may be able to back up these files every time you change them.

If you're a Linux administrator for a network of computers, you may be willing to spend a lot more money to protect and back up your data. However, with the amount of data stored in a network of computers, it may not be cost-effective to back up everything every night.

The following sections examine what you might do if you use a Linux computer as a personal desktop, administer a regular network, or administer a network where you have very time-sensitive data. What you actually do in practice may vary with the importance of the data and your available resources.

Your needs will also determine how often you do backups of time-sensitive data and the hard drives on a large group of computers.

PERSONAL DESKTOP USERS

Not all users back up their computers. Personal desktop users who just use their computers to browse the Internet may not have any irreplaceable data on their systems. For some home users, a disaster is just an inconvenience; all they need to do is reinstall their operating system and connect to the Internet once again. However, if you're a home user who keeps critical data such as financial records on your computer, consider yourself a Linux administrator and read the sections that follow.

In many cases, all these users need are backups of files on their home directories. Backups of configuration files in /etc can also help users restore many customized settings.

Some users prefer to back up all files and data on their Linux computers. That way, they can recover from any disaster without spending additional time reconfiguring their systems.

LINUX ADMINISTRATORS

If you're the Linux administrator responsible for a group of computers, timely backups are critical. For example, the data associated with the design of a new airplane evolves constantly.

Though it may not be too difficult to recover data from a lost day of work, the consequences of a lost week or month of design work for an airplane company can be rather expensive. In this case, you might configure a series of nightly backups on larger capacity media, such as DVDs or tape drives.

In this way, a Linux administrator can help tired engineers recover the data they accidentally deleted. If there's a larger disaster, the administrator can reinstall Linux, along with the appropriate engineering software, and then restore the design files to the appropriate directories.

TIME-SENSITIVE SITUATIONS

Computers are used in time-sensitive situations. For example, if you're the Linux administrator responsible for a financial services firm, timely backups are critical. For example, if you are unable to restore the data associated with sales in the stock market, the consequences can be expensive. Time-sensitive information suggests the need for real-time backups, such as those associated with RAID.

In this way, the failure of any hard disk does not affect the operation of the firm. With the use of removable hard disks, RAID data can also be copied and stored in external locations.

Backup Type and Frequency

The most straightforward backup is of everything on your computer. However, as the amount of data on individual hard disks moves into the hundreds of gigabytes, the amount of time required can stretch into dozens of hours.

Although Linux computers are multitasking, the load associated with a backup can affect performance for your users. That leaves you with two basic choices: back up your entire computer only on occasion (e.g., weekends), or back up only part of your data, such new files or the /home and /etc directories.

Many Linux administrators use a mix of the two philosophies—a complete backup available for a Linux computer, with daily backups for new files. There are two ways to make this happen:

Incremental backup   An incremental backup includes all files that were created or changed since the last full backup. As time increases since the last full backup, the size of an incremental backup gets progressively larger. Restoring a system requires only the data you saved in the full and the latest incremental backup.

Differential backup   A differential backup includes all files that were changed since the last backup of any type. Differential backups are almost always smaller than incremental backups. However, restoring a system from a differential backup can be more difficult. It requires the data you saved in the full backup, the incremental backup (if applicable), and all of the subsequent differential backups.

Because of the time associated with restoring data, many Linux administrators use some form of RAID. As you'll see later in the chapter, RAID can provide approximate real-time redundancy for your data.

Selecting Your Media

You can back up data anywhere you can record information. In some cases, you may even want to print out hard copies of key configuration files. Some personal desktop users may find 1.44MB floppy drives adequate. Workstation users may find that slightly larger capacity media such as 100MB Zip or 230MB Bernoulli drives meet their needs. In either case, users can back up just the critical files that they need, usually from their /home directory. Commands such as `tar` and `cpio` let you back up specific groups of files and or directories, as described later in this chapter.

For those with a need to back up gigabytes (GB) or even terabytes (TB) of data (1TB = 1000GB), there are three basic options: tape drives, writeable CDs/DVDs, and removable/external hard disks. If one tape or CD is not enough to back up your hard disk, hardware is available that organizes these systems into tape libraries and CD/DVD "jukeboxes." One way to use hard disks for backups is discussed later in this chapter, in the section "Understanding RAID."

All three types of media can be copied and transported to secure and remote locations. If your facility is destroyed by fire or some other disaster, the right media, properly stored, can help you restart your business or organization. Backups were tested on a large scale during the tragedies of September 11. Some businesses saved data in remote locations in real-time; others were able to get to their data in hours or days.

NOTE   A number of other third-party software solutions are available; you might need their support if you have the amount of data that justifies a "jukebox" or a high-capacity tape drive. You'll find a list of third-party backup software and hardware manufacturers at `www.storagesearch.com`*.*

Tape Drives

If you have the money, you can get a tape drive that can store your data nearly as fast as current IEEE 1394 hard drives. As of this writing, systems are available that can store nearly 30TB of data in over a 100 tape cartridges in a single box. With data transfer speeds of nearly 1000GB per hour, it is possible to fill this unit with a full backup in a single weekend.

Also available are lower capacity, less expensive tape drives with conventional interfaces, such as to parallel ports, IDE, and SCSI. Tape drives with these interfaces carry device names similar to hard drives with these connections.

There are also tape drives with USB and IEEE 1394 interfaces. As discussed in Chapter 2, support for IEEE 1394 and many USB interfaces is still experimental, and they may not work with Red Hat Linux 9.

CD/DVD Backups

Compared to tape drives, writeable CDs and even DVDs seem to pale by comparison. A CD can hold only around 650MB of data; a DVD can hold just over 6GB of data. But a number of "jukeboxes" are available that can write data to literally hundreds of disks.

In addition, CDs and DVDs hold a number of advantages over tape drives. In proper environmental conditions (i.e., don't store your CDs in a hot and humid environment!), CDs and DVDs can last for a decade or more. Unlike with tape drives or hard disks, you can't accidentally erase them with a magnet. They are not susceptible to the electromagnetic pulses associated with nuclear explosions.

Using Backup and Restore Commands

The commands you use depend in part on how you're backing up your data. Generic backups commonly use the `tar` or `cpio` commands. Alternatively, you might `dump` and `restore` data to and from a tape drive. Backups to local CDs are associated with the `mkisofs`, `cdrecord`, and `dvdrecord` commands. Some variations are required to back up and restore data through the network to remote locations.

Generic Backup Commands

Let's look at the two generic Linux commands for backing up a group of files. The `tar` command was originally developed to archive files and directories to tape drives; the `cpio` command also copies files and directories to and from an archive. With the right options, these commands can be used to back up files to most media.

NOTE   *You can also use the* `dd` *command to dump the contents of a directory directly to a device—for example, a floppy drive device such as* `/dev/fd0` *or a tape drive device such as* `/dev/st0`. *For more information on* `dd`, *see Chapter 3.*

ARCHIVING BY *TAR*

You examined the `tar` command for the first time in Chapter 10. It's simple to use. The format is easily compressed and downloadable. This command is the main alternative to the RPM system for packaging programs and applications. With the right options, it's functionally similar to the `.zip` file system associated with Microsoft Windows.

The `tar` command is designed to copy a series of files into a single large file. If you want to back up the files in mj's home directory, you might run the following command:

```
# tar cvzf mjbackup.tar.gz /home/mj
```

This command creates (c) a backup, listing every filename in the archive (v = verbose) in compressed format (z = zip) in the file (f) named `mjbackup.tar.gz`. Files in subdirectories of `/home/mj` are also saved to this archive. You can then save this archived file to a backup area such as a network share or a tape drive.

NOTE *Compressed tar archives often include the* `.tar.gz`, `.tgz`, *or* `.tar.bz2` *extensions. The first two extensions are both tar archives compressed with the* `gzip` *command. The last extension, based on the bzip2 "Burrows-Wheeler block sorting compression algorithm," is slightly more efficient at data compression.*

You can just as easily unarchive files with the following command:

```
# tar tkvzf mjbackup.tar.gz
```

This command lists (t) the files in your archive. When it restores, it does not overwrite your current files (k = keep old files). In verbose (v) mode, you see everything that happens. If you stored files in a zipped format, you need to restore from the zipped (z) format. Also, it is restoring from the backup file named `mjbackup.tar.gz`.

You can review some of the available `tar` switches in Table 14.2. Note that the first switch in the `tar` command should start with a c, t, or an x.

NOTE *The* `tar` *command is path dependent. If you save the files in a directory using the absolute path (with a leading forward slash, such as* `/home/mj`*), you can restore the files to that directory from any location on that computer. Alternatively, if you use the relative path (without a leading forward slash, such as* `home/mj`*), files may not be restored to their original locations; it depends on the present working directory.*

You can use a number of `tar` commands to create and extract archives. Some typical commands include the following. Read them over using the descriptions in Table 14.2.

```
# tar xzvf download.tar.gz
# tar czvf backup.tar.gz /somedirectory
```

TABLE 14.2: COMMAND OPTIONS FOR *TAR*

OPTION	FUNCTION
c	Creates an archive.
d	Compares files between an archive and a current directory.
f	Uses the following filename for the archive.
j	Compresses in bzip2 format to or from an archive.
k	Does not overwrite existing files.
r	Adds files to the end of an archive.
t	Lists files in a current archive.
v	Verbose; lists all files going in or coming out of an archive.
z	Zip. Compresses files to or from an archive in regular gzip format.

NOTE   *The* `tar` *command is similar to* `ps` *in that single-letter command options do not require a leading dash.*

ARCHIVING BY *CPIO*

The `cpio` command can help you archive a class of files, because unlike `tar`, it works with standard input and output. This use is suggested by its name (`cpio` = copy + input/output).

As with `tar`, it's fairly easy to archive known directories (along with the files in their subdirectories). For example, if you want to back up the files in mj's home directory, you run the following command:

```
# find /home/mj | cpio -o > mjarch.cpio
```

But there is a disadvantage; `cpio` takes from standard input and archives to standard output. Note how the standard input, all files in the /home/mj directory, are piped to the `cpio` command. Since this works with classes of files, you can use wildcards to set up a group of files as standard input as well. For example, the following command creates an archive from the .tif files in the current directory:

```
# find *.tif | cpio -o > mjtifs.cpio
```

Remember, the `find` command is flexible; the following command creates an archive from all the .tif files on your system:

```
# find / -name '*.tif' | cpio -o > mjtifs.cpio
```

It's easy to restore the files from a .cpio archive. The following command restores the files in the mjarch.cpio:

```
# cpio -i < mjarch.cpio
```

As with `tar`, the way `cpio` restores files saved from a directory depends on whether you used the absolute or relative path.

One of the advantages of `cpio` is the ability to send files directly to external sources. For example, the following commands send and restore the files from mj's home directory to a SCSI tape drive:

```
# find /home/mj | cpio -o > /dev/st0
# cpio -i < /dev/st0
```

A number of options are available for the `cpio` command. Some of the important options are shown in Table 14.3.

TABLE 14.3: *CPIO* COMMAND OPTIONS

OPTION	FUNCTION
-A	Appends to an existing archive. Closely associated with -F.
-F	Specifies archive filename. Can substitute for redirection arrow (>).
-i	Extracts from an archive file or device.
-o	Copies to an archive file or device.
-u	Replaces all files, even if they are newer.
-v	Verbose mode.

Tape *dump* and *restore*

The dump and restore commands make it easy to implement incremental and or differential backups. dump allows you to take the contents of a directory, and restore allows you to interactively return backed-up files to their original locations.

Although these commands are most commonly associated with tape drives, they work with other media as well. The examples shown in this section are based on using these commands to back up a home directory to a floppy disk.

ARCHIVING BY *DUMP*

The dump command has three basic levels of options. More are shown in the Appendix. You can set up a series of commands that starts with a full backup of a home directory, followed by differential backups. For example, if you want to back up the home directory of mao with dump to the /dev/nst0 tape drive, you run the following commands:

```
# dump 0f /dev/nst0 /home/mao
# dump 1f /dev/nst0 /home/mao
# dump 2f /dev/nst0 /home/mao
# dump 3f /dev/nst0 /home/mao
# dump 4f /dev/nst0 /home/mao
# dump 5f /dev/nst0 /home/mao
```

The first command, with the 0f option, sets up a full backup of the /home/mao directory. The commands that follow, when run in sequence, set up differential backups that save only those files that were changed since the previous backup.

TIP   *To speed the backup, you may be able to use the biggest block size allowed by your backup system (for instance, a tape drive). For example, the command* dump 0f /dev/nst0 /home/mao -b 2048 *uses a block size of 2048 bytes. You may want to experiment with larger block sizes to reduce backup time. But remember, you should also verify the results of your experiment with the appropriate* restore *command.*

Alternatively, you could start with a full backup, followed by incremental backups with a sequence of commands such as:

```
# dump 0f /dev/nst0 /home/mao
# dump 8f /dev/nst0 /home/mao
# dump 7f /dev/nst0 /home/mao
# dump 6f /dev/nst0 /home/mao
# dump 5f /dev/nst0 /home/mao
# dump 4f /dev/nst0 /home/mao
```

NOTE   *You don't need to run all six of these commands. With an incremental backup, you just need to make sure that the next number, such as* 4f, *is lower than the previous incremental backup command. Otherwise, the backup may not get recorded.*

If you're backing up an entire filesystem, you'll want to use the u option, which stores the history in /etc/dumpdates. For example, the following command backs up the entire root (/) directory filesystem:

```
# dump 0uf /dev/nst0 /
```

Take a look at the workings of a dump command on the files in the /home/mao directory in Figure 14.1.

FIGURE 14.1

dump output

```
[root@RH9Test root]# dump 0f /dev/fd0 /home/mao/
  DUMP: Date of this level 0 dump: Fri Mar 28 10:54:02 2003
  DUMP: Dumping /dev/hda3 (/ (dir home/mao)) to /dev/fd0
  DUMP: Added inode 8 to exclude list (journal inode)
  DUMP: Added inode 7 to exclude list (resize inode)
  DUMP: Label: /
  DUMP: mapping (Pass I) [regular files]
  DUMP: mapping (Pass II) [directories]
  DUMP: estimated 239 tape blocks.
  DUMP: Volume 1 started with block 1 at: Fri Mar 28 10:54:03 2003
  DUMP: dumping (Pass III) [directories]
  DUMP: dumping (Pass IV) [regular files]
  DUMP: Closing /dev/fd0
  DUMP: Volume 1 completed at: Fri Mar 28 10:54:10 2003
  DUMP: Volume 1 240 tape blocks (0.23MB)
  DUMP: Volume 1 took 0:00:07
  DUMP: Volume 1 transfer rate: 34 kB/s
  DUMP: 240 tape blocks (0.23MB) on 1 volume(s)
  DUMP: finished in 1 seconds, throughput 240 kBytes/sec
  DUMP: Date of this level 0 dump: Fri Mar 28 10:54:02 2003
  DUMP: Date this dump completed:  Fri Mar 28 10:54:10 2003
  DUMP: Average transfer rate: 34 kB/s
  DUMP: DUMP IS DONE
[root@RH9Test root]# []
```

There are a number of options available for the dump command. Table 14.4 shows some of the important options.

TABLE 14.4: *DUMP* COMMAND OPTIONS

OPTION	FUNCTION
0-9	Dump level. 0 = full backup. Differential backups use dump with increasing numbers (e.g., 1, 2, 3…). Incremental backups use dump with decreasing numbers (e.g., 8, 7, 6…).
A	Archives a table of contents for the backup.
f	Writes the backup to a file or device.
j *level*	Writes with compression; you need to specify a compression level such as 2 or 4.
T *date*	Uses the specified date instead of what is shown in /etc/dumpdates.
u	Updates /etc/dumpdates after a successful backup.

RECOVERING WITH *RESTORE*

There are two ways to restore from a backup created with the **dump** command: interactively or directly. In either case, you can restore an entire backup, or just the files that you need.

You can view a listing of files that were backed up with the **dump** command. As shown in Figure 14.2, the following command lists the files from the backup of mao's home directory:

```
# restore -tf /dev/fd0
```

FIGURE 14.2

Files on a backup

```
[root@RH9Test root]# restore -tf /dev/fd0
Dump    date: Fri Mar 28 10:54:02 2003
Dumped from: the epoch
Level 0 dump of / (dir home/mao) on RH9Test:/dev/hda3
Label: /
          2        .
     611688        ./home
     550464        ./home/mao
     550465        ./home/mao/.kde
     550466        ./home/mao/.kde/Autostart
     550467        ./home/mao/.kde/Autostart/Autorun.desktop
     550468        ./home/mao/.kde/Autostart/.directory
     550469        ./home/mao/.emacs
     550470        ./home/mao/.bash_logout
     550471        ./home/mao/.bash_profile
     550472        ./home/mao/.bashrc
     550473        ./home/mao/.gtkrc
[root@RH9Test root]# []
```

Alternatively, you can use restore mode to search through a current backup. As shown in Figure 14.3, the **-i** option brings you into interactive mode, where you can use some very basic Linux navigational commands. As of this writing, **restore** interactive mode doesn't allow you to use options such as -l for the **ls** command.

FIGURE 14.3

An interactive restore

```
[root@RH9Test root]# restore -if /dev/fd0
restore > ls
.:
home/

restore > cd /home/mao
restore > ls
./home/mao:
.bash_logout   .bashrc        .gtkrc
.bash_profile  .emacs         .kde/

restore > help
Available commands are:
        ls [arg] - list directory
        cd arg - change directory
        pwd - print current directory
        add [arg] - add `arg' to list of files to be extracted
        delete [arg] - delete `arg' from list of files to be extracted
        extract - extract requested files
        setmodes - set modes of requested directories
        quit - immediately exit program
        what - list dump header information
        verbose - toggle verbose flag (useful with ``ls'')
        prompt - toggle the prompt display
        help or `?' - print this list
If no `arg' is supplied, the current directory is used
restore > []
```

A number of options are available for the `restore` command. Table 14.5 lists some of the important ones.

TABLE 14.5: *RESTORE* COMMAND OPTIONS

OPTION	FUNCTION
-C	Compares a backup with current files.
-f	Specifies a file.
-i	Allows interactive recovery from a backup; several commands are available in restore mode.
-r	Rebuilds the data to a freshly formatted partition.
-t	Lists the filenames in the backup.

Backup Commands for CDs/DVDs

Before you can start recording data, you need to check whether Red Hat Linux recognizes your hardware. This is normally a simple exercise. Then you can create files suitable for CDs or DVDs, and then record them with the appropriate commands.

CHECKING HARDWARE

Before you can start backing up data to your writeable CD or DVD drive, you need to make sure it's actually working. Assuming Red Hat Linux has automatically detected the right drive, you should see the appropriate setting for it when you issue one of these commands:

```
# cdrecord --scanbus
# dvdrecord --scanbus
```

Linux uses SCSI drives for recording. But that's probably not a big deal if all you have is an IDE drive; in most cases, Red Hat Linux automatically configures SCSI emulation by default. In other words, it makes your IDE CD or DVD writer look like a SCSI drive.

From either of these commands, you should see output associated with an `scsibus`, similar to the following. Though this component is listed as a CD-ROM, it works as it should as a CD-RW drive:

```
0,0,0  0) 'LG  ' 'CD-RW CED-8083B ' '1.09' Removable CD-ROM
```

However, if you get a "No such file or directory" message, there's a problem. Red Hat may be having a bit of trouble adapting your system to SCSI emulation. It's not hard to do yourself. First, add the following line to `/etc/modules.conf`, which ignores IDE settings:

```
options ide-cd ignore=hdb
```

If your writeable CD or DVD drive is on a different IDE device such as `/dev/hdc`, substitute accordingly. You can check for your device with the `dmesg | grep hd` command. Add the SCSI emulation module with the following command, and you should be on your way:

```
# modprobe -a ide-scsi
```

To make it work, you'll need to link the appropriate SCSI device file, normally /dev/scd0, to /dev/cdrom, in /etc/fstab.

For example, you might change the following line in /etc/fstab from the first version to the second:

```
/dev/cdrom   /mnt/cdrom   iso9660   noauto,owner,kudzu,rw 0 0
/dev/scd0   /mnt/cdrom   iso9660   noauto,owner,kudzu,rw 0 0
```

Alternatively, you can link the device file directly with the following command:
```
# ln -s /dev/scd0 /dev/cdrom
```
If you get a "File exists" error, try the ls -l /dev/cdrom command. Linux may have already created the proper link for you.

MAKING AN IMAGE

The next step is to make an image file. Whether you're recording to a CD or a DVD, you can create the image file with the mkisofs command. As an example, assume you want to back up all the files and directories under /home. You might use the following command, where -r includes Rock Ridge extensions (which supports Unix-based filesystems), -J includes the Joliet filesystem (which makes files readable under Microsoft operating systems), -T preserves long filenames, and -o stands for output:

```
# mkisofs -J -r -T -o newcd.iso /home
```

This may create a very big file; if you're creating an image for a DVD, the file could easily be several gigabytes in size. It's a good idea to check the integrity of this file. One way to do this is to mount the image file as if it were a CD or DVD. For example, for CDs, the following command mounts your newly created newcd.iso image on /mnt/cdrom:

```
# mount -t iso9660 -o loop newcd.iso /mnt/cdrom
```

Alternatively, for DVDs, the following command lists the files in the appropriate image file:

```
# isoinfo -i newdvd.iso -l
```

NOTE *Commands for recording data on DVDs are still under development; thus the commands shown in this chapter are subject to change. For the latest information, see the official website of the* dvdrtools *project at* www.nongnu.org/dvdrtools.

BURNING THE IMAGE

Now we're ready to copy the image to a blank writeable CD. The cdrecord command can help. For the items cited in the previous section, you'd use this command:

```
# cdrecord -v speed=2 dev=0,0,0 newcd.iso
```

The -v option allows you to see what happens as Linux copies the image onto your CD. If there is a problem, these messages can also help you diagnose the cause. Figure 14.4 shows how to create a Red Hat installation boot CD from the boot.iso file described in Chapter 4. As you can see in the figure, a substantial number of useful messages are available when you run this command.

Alternatively, the command to copy the image to a blank writeable DVD is similar:

```
# dvdrecord -v speed=1 -dao dev=0,1,0 newdvd.iso
```

This records the newdvd.iso image, verbosely (-v), at first speed (speed = 1), in Disk at Once (-dao) mode, where data is written in a single operation.

FIGURE 14.4

The cdrecord

process

```
[root@RH9Test root]# cdrecord -v speed=2 dev=0,0,0 boot.iso
Cdrecord 2.0 (i686-pc-linux-gnu) Copyright (C) 1995-2002 J?rg Schilling
TOC Type: 1 = CD-ROM
scsidev: '0,0,0'
scsibus: 0 target: 0 lun: 0
Linux sg driver version: 3.1.24
Using libscg version 'schily-0.7'
cdrecord: Warning: using inofficial libscg transport code version (schily - Red
Hat-scsi-linux-sg.c-1.75-RH '@(#)scsi-linux-sg.c        1.75 02/10/21 Copyright
1997 J. Schilling').
atapi: 1
Device type    : Removable CD-ROM
Version        : 0
Response Format: 1
Vendor_info    : 'LG      '
Identifikation : 'CD-RW CED-8083B '
Revision       : '1.09'
Device seems to be: Generic mmc CD-RW.
Using generic SCSI-3/mmc CD-R driver (mmc_cdr).
Driver flags   : MMC SWABAUDIO
Supported modes: TAO PACKET SAO SAO/R96P SAO/R96R RAW/R16 RAW/R96P RAW/R96R
Drive buf size : 1024000 = 1000 KB
FIFO size      : 4194304 = 4096 KB
Track 01: data     3 MB
Total size:        4 MB (00:24.13) = 1810 sectors
Lout start:        4 MB (00:26/10) = 1810 sectors
Current Secsize: 2048
ATIP info from disk:
  Indicated writing power: 5
  Is not unrestricted
```

NOTE   *If you're in GNOME and insert a blank writable CD, Nautilus automatically opens a* burn:/// *window, where you can copy the files and folders that you want written to that CD. It includes a Write To CD button and easy to understand prompts.*

Understanding RAID

Two different labels are associated with RAID: Redundant Array of Independent Disks and Redundant Array of Inexpensive Disks. Neither works in this case, because they don't accurately describe how the software version of RAID works in Red Hat Linux.

A Redundant Array of Independent Disks implies that every disk in a RAID array is physically independent. If one disk fails, the others in the array can take over its functionality. Several versions of RAID exist where Linux can use the other working disk drives to reconstruct the data on any single failed disk drive. One version of RAID includes two separate hard disks with identical information.

You can also include "spare" hard disks in a RAID array. If there is a failure in any RAID 1 or RAID 5 hard disk, Linux can immediately begin rebuilding the data on the spare disk.

Using a RAID array provides three main advantages.

High availability   A RAID array always lets you get to your data. With appropriate hardware, you can even change a hard disk while the computer is on. This is not possible with a Red Hat Linux software RAID array.

Fault tolerance   With most hardware RAID arrays, the data is always accessible even if one hard disk fails. You can set up fault tolerance in a Red Hat Linux software RAID array, as long as you configure each RAID partition in the array on separate physical hard drives.

Failover   When a hard disk fails, a RAID system can automatically switch to a reserve hard disk. Data is automatically transferred to the backup hard disk or partition.

RAID Options

Three versions of RAID are associated with Red Hat Linux: RAID 0, RAID 1, and RAID 5. Briefly, RAID 0 can speed access to hard disks, without fault tolerance. RAID 1, since it has two separate disks with identical information, complete fault tolerance. RAID 5 is based on an array of three or more disks and also provides fault tolerance.

You learned to configure a basic RAID array during the Red Hat Linux installation, as discussed in Chapter 3.

NOTE   Although the latest Linux kernel also supports RAID 4, the Red Hat Linux installation program does not support configuring this version of RAID. There is one difference between RAID 4 and RAID 5. In RAID 4, all parity information is stored on one partition or hard disk. In RAID 5, parity information is distributed on all hard disks in the array.

RAID 0

This level of RAID includes two or more drives or partitions, grouped together. When these are separate physical drives, your computer can use the buffers on each drive. This is one way RAID 0 can speed reading and writing to your hard disks.

However, RAID 0 provides no data redundancy. In other words, if any disk or partition in a RAID 0 array fails, you lose all of the data in that array.

NOTE   RAID 0 is sometimes known as "striping without parity."

RAID 1

At this level, RAID is like a mirror. It includes two separate disks or partitions with identical data. When RAID 1 is used for two separate hard disks, either hard disk can be used. If one hard disk fails, the other hard disk is ready to step in. No data is lost.

The drawback to RAID 1 is that it takes longer to write data to disk. With RAID 1, writes are not complete until the data is written to both disks. The hardware version of RAID 1 is secure but expensive; if you were to implement RAID 1 on all of your computers, you would need to purchase and install twice as many hard disks.

NOTE   RAID 1 is sometimes known as "disk mirroring."

RAID 5

At this level, RAID requires three or more disks. RAID 5 stripes parity information evenly across all disks in the array. If one disk fails, Linux can reconstruct the "lost" information from the parity data on the remaining disks. Although data retrieval is slower when a RAID 5 disk fails, your system can still run.

If there is a spare hard disk available in a RAID 5 array, Linux immediately begins to write this lost information onto the spare disk.

This level of RAID is generally preferred in most cases. Data integrity is ensured. The space of only one disk is sacrificed to hold the parity information. And performance is good.

NOTE   RAID 5 is sometimes known as "disk striping with parity."

Software and Hardware RAID

The software RAID that you can configure in Red Hat Linux is a bit different from the hardware RAID, because it uses partitions, not separate physical disk drives. If you use RAID on Red Hat Linux, I highly recommend that you avoid using partitions from the same hard disk for any single RAID array. Otherwise, any failure of that hard disk could destroy all data in that RAID array.

Several hardware RAID systems are available, with their own software support for Linux. However, the principles discussed in this chapter work for any version of RAID associated with Red Hat Linux.

Dedicated RAID hardware can help ensure that your data survives any catastrophic physical failure on any single hard disk.

Creating RAID Partitions

You can create RAID partitions after installing Red Hat Linux. As an example, assume you have several SCSI hard disks available. You've installed Red Hat Linux on the first SCSI hard disk, /dev/sda. You have three other hard disks available for a RAID array, /dev/sdb, /dev/sdc, and /dev/sdd.

NOTE   You can also create RAID partitions during the Red Hat Linux installation process. See Chapters 3 or 4 for details.

After installation, the standard utility for creating new partitions is fdisk. For more information on the basics of this utility, please refer to Chapter 7.

To create a RAID array in Red Hat Linux, you need two or more partitions of approximately equal size. If you want your array to survive the failure of any physical hard drive, each of the partitions in a RAID array must be on a separate physical drive.

Once you have the partitions for a RAID array, you can use the fdisk utility to change the partition type to one suitable for a RAID array. For example, the commands shown in Figure 14.5 change the partition /dev/sdb1 to one that you can make part of a RAID array.

WARNING   Never change the file type of a partition with data you need, unless you've already backed it up in a secure location. When you use fdisk to change the file type, that action can destroy any data currently stored on that partition.

Once you've created the disks or partitions for your RAID array, you'll need to format them. As discussed in Chapter 7, you need the mkfs -j *partitiondevice* command to format your new partition to the ext3 filesystem. For example, the following command properly formats the partition just created:

```
# mkfs -j /dev/sdb1
```

FIGURE 14.5

Creating a RAID partition

```
[root@RHL9 root]# fdisk /dev/sdb

Command (m for help): p

Disk /dev/sdb: 128 heads, 32 sectors, 512 cylinders
Units = cylinders of 4096 * 512 bytes

   Device Boot    Start     End   Blocks   Id  System
/dev/sdb1           205     300   196608   83  Linux
/dev/sdb2            52     102   104448   83  Linux
/dev/sdb3             1      51   104432   83  Linux

Partition table entries are not in disk order

Command (m for help): t
Partition number (1-4): 1
Hex code (type L to list codes): fd
Changed system type of partition 1 to fd (Linux raid autodetect)

Command (m for help): █
```

Repeat the process to create the RAID partitions that you need. Remember to format all the partitions that you're using in your RAID array.

Configuring /etc/raidtab

When you have the RAID partitions that you need, the next step is to edit the RAID configuration file, /etc/raidtab. This file is fairly easy to configure. The following sections illustrate example configurations for RAID 0, RAID 1, and RAID 5 arrays.

There are several commands in /etc/raidtab that you may use for any of these arrays, as shown in Table 14.6.

TABLE 14.6: COMMANDS IN /ETC/RAIDTAB

COMMAND	FUNCTION
raiddev	RAID device filename.
raid-level	RAID array type, usually 0, 1, or 5.
nr-raid-disks	Number of disks assigned to this RAID array.
nr-spare-disks	Number of backup disks assigned to this RAID array.
persistent-superblock	If this =1, Linux can detect this RAID array.
chunk-size	Amount of data to be read/write, in KB.
parity-algorithm	How RAID 5 calculates parity.
device	Device name of a RAID partition.
raid-disk	Number assigned to a partition in a RAID array, in sequence, starting with 0.
spare-disk	Number assigned to a reserve partition in a RAID array, in sequence, starting with 0.

RAID 0 */ETC/RAIDTAB*

RAID 0 is disk striping without parity. Because there is no data redundancy, no spare disk partition is configured in this RAID array. The following excerpt from a RAID 0 /etc/raidtab file configures a RAID array of two partitions, /dev/sda1 and /dev/sdb1, with a fairly large chunk-size (16KB), to maximize data transfer speed:

```
raiddev        /dev/md0
raid-level   0
persistent-superblock        1
chunk-size   16

nr-raid-disks    2
nr-spare-disks   0

device       /dev/sda1
raid-disk    0
device       /dev/sdb1
raid-disk    1
```

RAID 1 */ETC/RAIDTAB*

RAID 1 is known as disk mirroring. Because this is the ultimate in redundancy, one spare disk partition is included in the following excerpt from /etc/raidtab. The two partitions in the array are /dev/sda2 and /dev/sdb2. The spare partition is /dev/sdc2.

```
raiddev        /dev/md1
raid-level   1
persistent-superblock        1
chunk-size   4

nr-raid-disks    2
nr-spare-disks   1

device       /dev/sda2
raid-disk    0
device       /dev/sdb2
raid-disk    1
device       /dev/sdc2
spare-disk   0
```

RAID 5 */ETC/RAIDTAB*

RAID 5 is known as striping with parity. This can be run with a large number of disks or partitions. Since it provides redundancy, two spare disk partitions are included in the following excerpt from /etc/raidtab. The four RAID partitions in the array are /dev/sda3, /dev/sdb3, /dev/sdc3, and /dev/sdd3. The spare partitions are /dev/sde3 and /dev/sdf3.

```
raiddev        /dev/md2
raid-level   5
persistent-superblock        1
```

```
chunk-size   4

nr-raid-disks    4
nr-spare-disks   2

device      /dev/sda3
raid-disk   0
device      /dev/sdb3
raid-disk   1
device      /dev/sdc3
raid-disk   2
device      /dev/sdd3
raid-disk   3
device      /dev/sde3
spare-disk  0
device      /dev/sdf3
spare-disk  1
```

Creating the RAID Device

OK, we're almost there! You've created the partitions you want in your RAID array. You've set them to the Linux RAID file type. You've formatted each partition. You've set up the configuration for the RAID array in /etc/raidtab. Now you're ready to create and format the RAID device.

For example, take the RAID 5 configuration created in the previous section. The RAID device file is /dev/md2. You'll want to create the file and then format it. You can then mount the filesystem of your choice on that partition. If you want to have it mounted automatically the next time you boot Linux, you'll also need to incorporate it into /etc/fstab.

The following commands create and then format the RAID device:

```
# mkraid -R /dev/md2
# mkfs -j /dev/md2
```

WARNING *The* mkraid -R raiddevice *command deletes all data from all partitions associated with the* raid-device *in* /etc/raidtab.

Mounting RAID

At this point, you're ready to mount your new RAID array on the filesystem of your choice. For example, if you want to set up RAID for your home directories, copy all files (including hidden files) from the /home directory to another location, mount your new RAID device on /home, and then restore the files. Assuming /tmphome exists, the following commands work for the /dev/md2 RAID device just created:

```
# cp -r /home /tmphome
# mount /dev/md2 /home
# cp -r /tmphome/home /
```

Finally, to make the change permanent, label your new device and then add an appropriate entry in/etc/fstab. For the directory and device shown, you first run the `e2label /dev/md2 /home` command, and then create a new entry such as the following in `/etc/fstab`:

```
LABEL=/home  /home   ext3 defaults 1 2
```

When you reboot, Linux should automatically mount the `/home` filesystem on your new RAID device, `/dev/md2`.

Summary

Data is fragile. Backups are important. Before you select a strategy for protecting your data, you need to consider various disaster scenarios. Standard scenarios range from the loss of a user's key file to complete data erasure and computer damage from an electromagnetic pulse.

Your response depends on the computers that you need to protect. If you're a personal desktop user, most disasters are just an inconvenience. Chances are all you need to back up are files in your home directory. Backups of configuration files in `/etc` can save time as you reinstall and then reconfigure Linux. Administrators who are responsible for groups of computers need more complete backups. In some situations, you'll need media that you can access quickly, because information such as financial data can be time-sensitive.

Three different types of backups are available: full, incremental, and differential. Full backups are complete backups of all files on entire computer systems. Incremental backups include all data since the last full backup. Differential backups include all data since the last backup of any type.

There are wide varieties of media suitable for backups. The main candidates are tape drives and writeable CDs/DVDs. If an individual tape or CD does not provide enough room, devices such as "jukeboxes" are available that collect large numbers of tape drives or CDs/DVDs together in one backup computer.

For tapes and other media, you can use generic backup and restore commands such as `tar`, `cpio`, `dump`, and `restore`. If you're backing up to CDs or DVDs, you'll need to create an image of the files you want to save with the `mkisofs` command. Then you can write to the appropriate drive with the `cdrecord` or `dvdrecord` command.

One alternative to backups is RAID. A Redundant Array of Independent Disks provides data redundancy. In other words, if any single hard drive fails, the right type of RAID ensures that no data is lost. Red Hat Linux supports three types of RAID: RAID 0, which does not provide redundancy; RAID 1, which mirrors one hard disk onto another; and RAID 5, also known as striping with parity. Hardware RAID is available for this purpose.

In Red Hat Linux, you can create a software RAID array from a series of partitions, formatted to the `Linux raid autodetect` file type. Once you've configured the device in `/etc/raidtab`, you can format and then mount your new RAID device. Just remember to label the partition with the `e2label` command. You also need to document that device in `/etc/fstab`, if you want Linux to mount it automatically the next time you boot.

Next, we'll look at Part IV, where we learn how to manage the X Window in Red Hat Linux. This starts in Chapter 15 with a detailed review of how to configure basic X Servers and X Clients. We'll examine configuration tools and the files they affect in detail. Then we'll look at how this can work for remote graphical applications.

Part 4

X Window Management

In this Part, you will learn how to:

- ◆ Manage X servers and X clients
- ◆ Work with GNOME
- ◆ Work with KDE
- ◆ Use GUI applications
- ◆ Understand Red Hat graphical front ends

Chapter 15

Managing X Servers and X Clients

NEWER LINUX USERS OFTEN prefer a graphical user interface (GUI). If they're not administrators, they don't need the flexibility of the command line. They do need optimized graphics to design airplanes, create movies, chart statistical data, and other tasks. Some are regular consumers who want an easy transition from another operating system. The two most common GUIs are GNOME (see Chapter 16) and KDE (see Chapter 17).

While most veteran Linux administrators prefer the command-line interface, they should recognize that many users have a legitimate need for the GUI. To this end, Red Hat Linux includes the X Client and X Server system developed by the XFree86 project (www.xfree86.org). Linux GUIs use this client-server structure.

You may have already configured the X Window and installed GNOME and/or KDE when you installed Red Hat Linux. As long as you've installed the basic X packages, you can use the basic xf86config or redhat-config-xfree86 tools to configure the X Window on your computer.

The critical X Window configuration file is XF86Config, in the /etc/X11 directory. It includes a number of sections that we'll analyze in detail. There are several other significant X Window configuration files that can help you customize your system. This chapter covers the following topics:

◆ Using the basic configuration tools

◆ Understanding the configuration files

◆ Troubleshooting the X Window

Using the Basic Configuration Tools

When you configure the X Window on your computer, you must configure several parts of your computer. Not only do you need to configure graphics, but also any input device that might interact with a graphical screen. These components include the following:

◆ Monitors with specifications for horizontal and vertical frequency, resolution, and refresh rates

◆ Video cards with a specified amount of memory

◆ A mouse or other pointing device for a GUI

◆ Keyboards to support a GUI

This data is documented in /etc/X11/XF86Config. You could edit this file directly. In fact, we'll review this file in detail later in this chapter. Unfortunately, the language within the file is a little obscure. Thus, most people use an X Window configuration tool to help with the process.

The X Window configuration tool is redhat-config-xfree86. Red Hat no longer includes three other formerly popular configuration tools, xf86config, Xconfigurator and XF86Setup. However, since xf86config is part of the X Window package that you can install from www.xfree86.org, we include a description of this tool in this chapter.

If Linux can detect your hardware, there is one simple alternative for creating an X Window configuration file: the X -configure command.

X WINDOW RPMS

Normally, if you want to install more packages, you just start the redhat-config-packages utility described in Chapter 19. This opens the Package Group Selection screen (see Chapter 3), where you can select different package groups. But that utility doesn't work unless you've already installed a GUI.

If you need to install X Window RPMs use the rpm command (refer to Chapter 10) to install the packages in the base-x group. You can find this group in the comps.xml file on the first Red Hat Linux installation CD, in the /RedHat/base directory. For your convenience, you can review a detailed list of these packages in Web Chapter 5, which can be found on the Sybex website at www.sybex.com.

X Window RPMs may not be enough. You'll need more for a GUI desktop. As explained in Chapters 3 and 4, the GNOME and KDE desktops require a different set of RPM packages. These can also be found in comps.xml in the gnome-desktop and kde-desktop groups.

xf86config

The traditional Linux X configuration tool, xf86config, works at the command-line interface. You don't need a GUI to start it. It allows you to configure the fundamental components: a mouse, keyboard, monitor, and video card.

NOTE *xf86config is not included with Red Hat Linux 9. However, it is still a standard tool included with the XFree86 packages that you can download from their home page at* www.xfree86.org.

If installed, you can run xf86config. It's not difficult to use, and includes a complete database of available video cards. Use these steps as a guideline, because they vary depending on your selections and hardware:

1. Back up your current /etc/X11/XF86Config file. That way, if you make a mistake during the process, you can restore your existing configuration.

2. Open a command-line interface and run the xf86config command to open the introductory screen shown in Figure 15.1. At the end of the introduction, there's a reference to SuperProbe; for Red Hat Linux, its functionality has been replaced by the ddcprobe command. Press Enter to continue.

```
This program will create a basic XF86Config file, based on menu selections you
make.

The XF86Config file usually resides in /usr/X11R6/etc/X11 or /etc/X11. A sample
XF86Config file is supplied with XFree86; it is configured for a standard
VGA card and monitor with 640x480 resolution. This program will ask for a
pathname when it is ready to write the file.

You can either take the sample XF86Config as a base and edit it for your
configuration, or let this program produce a base XF86Config file for your
configuration and fine-tune it.

Before continuing with this program, make sure you know what video card
you have, and preferably also the chipset it uses and the amount of video
memory on your video card. SuperProbe may be able to help with this.

Press enter to continue, or ctrl-c to abort.▯
```

3. As shown in Figure 15.2, the questions that follow allow you to select a basic mouse protocol, to emulate three buttons on a two-button mouse, and specify a device name. Run the `ls -l /dev/mouse` command in a separate virtual console (described in Chapter 11). If `/dev/mouse` is linked to the actual mouse port, that device should be sufficient. Press Enter to continue.

```
1.  Microsoft compatible (2-button protocol)
2.  Mouse Systems (3-button protocol)
3.  Bus Mouse
4.  PS/2 Mouse
5.  Logitech Mouse (serial, old type, Logitech protocol)
6.  Logitech MouseMan (Microsoft compatible)
7.  MM Series
8.  MM HitTablet
9.  Microsoft IntelliMouse

If you have a two-button mouse, it is most likely of type 1, and if you have
a three-button mouse, it can probably support both protocol 1 and 2. There are
two main varieties of the latter type: mice with a switch to select the
protocol, and mice that default to 1 and require a button to be held at
boot-time to select protocol 2. Some mice can be convinced to do 2 by sending
a special sequence to the serial port (see the ClearDTR/ClearRTS options).

Enter a protocol number: 4

If your mouse has only two buttons, it is recommended that you enable
Emulate3Buttons.

Please answer the following question with either 'y' or 'n'.
Do you want to enable Emulate3Buttons? y

Now give the full device name that the mouse is connected to, for example
/dev/tty00. Just pressing enter will use the default, /dev/mouse.

Mouse device: ▯
```

NOTE *Depending on the mouse protocol you select, you may get one or two additional questions, such as whether you want to enable* ChordMiddle *for a Logitech mouse, or if you want to make sure your Mouse Systems three-button mouse does not default to Microsoft compatible mode. For more information, see the documentation section of* www.xfree86.org.

4. Next, you can select from about 25 basic keyboards. Make a selection and press Enter to continue.

5. At this point, you can select a language type associated with your keyboard; languages from Albanian to Vietnamese are available. Make your selection and press Enter; you can then enter a special name for your configuration. Press Enter to continue. You should see the following message:

```
Please answer the following question with either 'y' or 'n'. Do you want to
select additional XKB options (group switcher, group indicator, etc)?
```

6. XKB options are interesting primarily for non-English users, especially for keyboards with multiple alphabets. Unfortunately, good documentation is lacking in this area, with the possible exception of Ivan Pascal's work at www.tsu.ru/~pascal/en/xkb. If you have a single-language keyboard, type **n** and press Enter to continue.

7. Next, you can set specifications for your monitor. Have the documentation for your monitor ready, with appropriate horizontal and vertical sync ranges. Make the appropriate entries when prompted. If in doubt, select the lowest available range. Enter an Identifier, and press Enter to continue.

8. Now you can configure your video card. Have the appropriate documentation ready, as described in Figure 15.3. Alternatively, you can type **y** to look at the list of available cards. If your card is on the list, xf86config then handles the needed configuration details for you.

FIGURE 15.3

xf86config and video cards

```
Now we must configure video card specific settings. At this point you can
choose to make a selection out of a database of video card definitions.
Because there can be variation in Ramdacs and clock generators even
between cards of the same model, it is not sensible to blindly copy
the settings (e.g. a Device section). For this reason, after you make a
selection, you will still be asked about the components of the card, with
the settings from the chosen database entry presented as a strong hint.

The database entries include information about the chipset, what driver to
run, the Ramdac and ClockChip, and comments that will be included in the
Device section. However, a lot of definitions only hint about what driver
to run (based on the chipset the card uses) and are untested.

If you can't find your card in the database, there's nothing to worry about.
You should only choose a database entry that is exactly the same model as
your card; choosing one that looks similar is just a bad idea (e.g. a
GemStone Snail 64 may be as different from a GemStone Snail 64+ in terms of
hardware as can be).

Do you want to look at the card database? █
```

9. Over 700 cards are available. Find the card and enter the corresponding number, or type **q** to continue. Confirm your card definition and press Enter to continue.

10. Enter the amount of memory on your video card as prompted; next enter the Identifier of your choice for the card.

11. Now you can select different resolutions for your monitor/video card system. For example, based on Figure 15.4, options 1, 2, or 3 allow you to change the default resolution associated with 8-, 16-, and 24-bit color. If you select option 4, skip to step 13.

FIGURE 15.4

xf86config
resolutions

```
For each depth, a list of modes (resolutions) is defined. The default
resolution that the server will start-up with will be the first listed
mode that can be supported by the monitor and card.
Currently it is set to:

"640x400" for 8-bit
"640x480" for 16-bit
"640x480" for 24-bit

Modes that cannot be supported due to monitor or clock constraints will
be automatically skipped by the server.

  1  Change the modes for 8-bit (256 colors)
  2  Change the modes for 16-bit (32K/64K colors)
  3  Change the modes for 24-bit (24-bit color)
  4  The modes are OK, continue.

Enter your choice: 3

Select modes from the following list:

  1  "640x400"
  2  "640x480"
  3  "800x600"
  4  "1024x768"
  5  "1280x1024"
  6  "320x200"
  7  "320x240"
  8  "400x300"
  9  "1152x864"
```

12. Select a new default resolution associated with the color setting. You can then select a "virtual screen" if desired. This allows you to configure a resolution (such as 1800×1400) bigger than what your monitor can handle. Return to step 11.

13. Select a default color depth. The standard options are 1, 4, 8, 16, 24, and possibly 32 bits.

14. If you're satisfied with your changes, let **xf86config** write the result to **/etc/X11/XF86Config**.

As you can see in Figure 15.5, other options are available.

NOTE   *Remember, Linux is case sensitive. The utility named* **xf86config** *is used to modify the X Window configuration file* **XF86Config**. *These are two different things.*

FIGURE 15.5

xf86config writes
a configuration file

```
I am going to write the XF86Config file now. Make sure you don't accidently
overwrite a previously configured one.

Shall I write it to /etc/X11/XF86Config? n

Please answer the following question with either 'y' or 'n'.
Shall I write it to the default location, /usr/X11R6/etc/X11/XF86Config? n

Do you want it written to the current directory as 'XF86Config'? y

File has been written. Take a look at it before running 'startx'. Note that
the XF86Config file must be in one of the directories searched by the server
(e.g. /etc/X11) in order to be used. Within the server press
ctrl, alt and '+' simultaneously to cycle video resolutions. Pressing ctrl,
alt and backspace simultaneously immediately exits the server (use if
the monitor doesn't sync for a particular mode).

For further configuration, refer to the XF86Config(5) manual page.

[root@RH9Test root]# []
```

redhat-config-xfree86

The tool for configuring the X Window on Red Hat Linux is redhat-config-xfree86. In most cases, you can even run it from the standard command-line interface; it probes your monitor and graphics card and opens the basic dialog boxes with a VESA interface.

NOTE   VESA is the basic graphical interface developed by the Video Electronics Standards Association. The associated generic settings are also known as Super VGA.

The redhat-config-xfree86 command detects your hardware. It includes sections for the overall display, the monitor, and the video card.

DETECTING HARDWARE

Before redhat-config-xfree86 opens the Display Settings window, it runs the ddcprobe command. You can run this command yourself. Figure 15.6 illustrates the effect on my desktop computer.

FIGURE 15.6

ddcprobe detects
a monitor and
video card

```
[root@RH9Test root]# ddcprobe

Videocard DDC probe results
Description:  Intel Corporation i810 Graphics Controller
Memory (MB):  1

Monitor DDC probe results
ID: SAM413b
Name: S/M 955DF
Horizontal Sync (kHZ): 30-85
Vertical Sync (HZ)  : 50-160
Width (mm): 360
Height(mm): 270
[root@RH9Test root]#
```

THE OVERALL DISPLAY

When `redhat-config-xfree86` opens, you'll see a Display Settings window similar to Figure 15.7. The Display tab allows you to select a resolution and color depth. The available settings are based on what the video card can do and reflect the limits of the monitor.

FIGURE 15.7

The Display tab

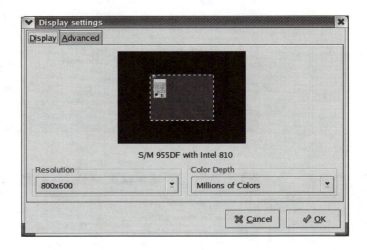

S/M 955DF with Intel 810

The top of the screen illustrates open GUI applications on your computer. This can help you get a feel for how the applications will look on your monitor. If you change the Resolution setting, the dotted lines around the applications change as well.

Resolution represents the number of dots that your video card sends to your monitor. The number is in horizontal × vertical format; 800 × 600 resolution means that there are 800 dots across in the horizontal plane and 600 dots in the vertical plane. For a list of other available resolutions, click on the Resolution drop-down arrow.

The Color Depth setting represents the number of colors available for each dot. For example, 16-bit color means that you can have any of $2^{16} = 65,536$ colors in each dot. For a list of other available color depths, click on the Color Depth drop-down arrow.

THE VIDEO CARD

Back in the `redhat-config-xfree86` Display Settings window, click the Advanced tab. As you can see in Figure 15.8, the lower half of this screen includes your Video Card settings (note how the detected video RAM is now correct).

You can further configure the video card. Click Configure in the Video Card section of the Advanced tab. You're taken to the Video Card Settings window, shown in Figure 15.9.

FIGURE 15.8

The Advanced tab

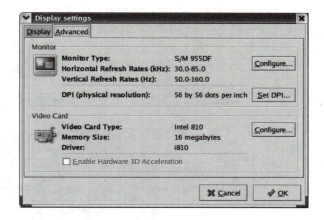

FIGURE 15.9

Video card settings

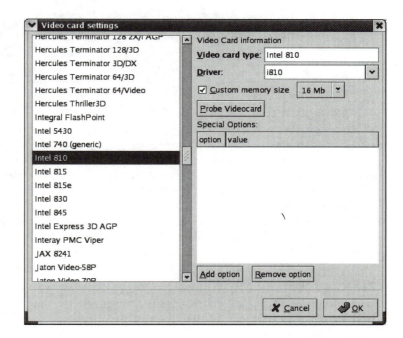

You can select from well over 600 makes and models of video cards. When you do, the Video Card Type and Driver appear automatically in the upper-right corner. In some cases, you'll see special option commands in the lower-right corner.

Alternatively, you can try clicking the Probe Videocard button. In many cases, `redhat-config-xfree86` can detect your video card and select the appropriate drivers automatically.

If you don't see a video card that matches your make and model, you have several options:

◆ Select the VESA Driver (Generic) card type. This assigns standard settings (SVGA) with the `vesa` driver that should work for most video cards built in the past several years.

◆ Select the Unsupported VGA Compatible card type. This assigns the `vga` driver to your system.

◆ Select Custom (at the top of the list). You may add a Linux driver from the video card manufacturer or a third party to the video modules directory, `/usr/X11R6/lib/modules/drivers`.

Whether you use a model-specific or a generic driver, be sure to check the Custom Memory Size setting. Revise it if it does not match the actual amount of graphics memory on your video card.

Several video cards allow you to configure various options, such as acceleration, depth, and orientation. You can use the Add Option button for this purpose. Make your selections and click OK to continue.

NOTE *If you want more information on the options available, get the make and model of your video card. Navigate to* `www.xfree86.org/4.3.0/RELNOTES.html`*, and look for the Video Drivers section. You'll see links for the make and model of your video card. Video card–specific* `XF86Config` *file options are also documented here.*

When you return to the Advanced tab of the Display Settings window, look at the Enable Hardware 3D Acceleration check box. If your video card has this capability, you should be able to activate the check box. Now let's look at your monitor.

THE MONITOR

The `redhat-config-xfree86` tool also allows you to configure X Server settings for your monitor. Once again, open the Advanced tab of the Display Settings window, then click the Configure button to open the Monitor Settings window, shown in Figure 15.10.

FIGURE 15.10

The Monitor
Settings window

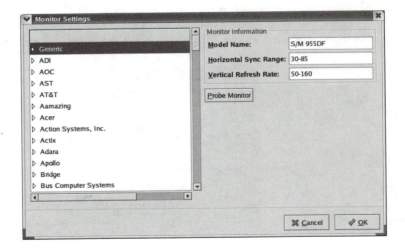

You can use `redhat-config-xfree86` to configure monitors from well over 100 manufacturers. If you see the manufacturer of your monitor, click the arrow adjacent to the name. This should open a selection of models made by that manufacturer.

Alternatively, you may find an exact match when you click the Probe Monitor button.

If you can't find an exact match, a large selection of Generic monitors is available; part of the current list is shown in Figure 15.11. As you can see, settings are available even for laptop computers.

FIGURE 15.11

Generic monitor settings

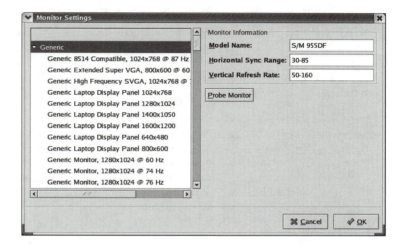

While you can customize the Horizontal Sync Range and Vertical Refresh Rate of your monitor, be careful. Check the documentation for your monitor. If the numbers you select are too large, you may exceed the capabilities and destroy your monitor. Although many monitors include protection against such overloads, why risk blowing out your new flat-panel or laptop screen?

When you complete your settings, click OK to return to the Advanced tab. Click the Set DPI button to open the Monitor DPI Settings window, shown in Figure 15.12.

FIGURE 15.12

The Monitor DPI Settings window

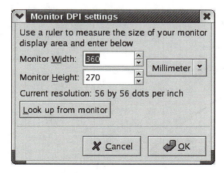

As you can see, you can customize the size of the picture on your monitor screen. Using the drop-down box, you can set the width and height of your monitor in millimeters or inches. If you click the Look Up From Monitor button, you get the current settings. Make any desired changes and click OK.

When you click OK in the Display Settings window, `redhat-config-xfree86` saves your changes to `/etc/X11/XF86Config`. Your settings take effect the next time you log into a GUI on this computer.

Auto X Configure

If neither `xf86config` nor `redhat-config-xfree86` is to your liking, you have one more option. If the XFree86 Server can detect your video card and monitor, there's a simple alternative. Try the following command:

```
# X -configure
```

If successful, it'll create the `XF86Config.new` file in the local directory. Back up your current `/etc/X11/XF86Config` file. You may be able to make additional changes to your `XF86Config` file, as described later in this chapter. When you're ready, overwrite your `/etc/X11/XF86Config` file with `XF86Config.new`. Run the `startx` command to test the result.

switchdesk

In Red Hat Linux, GNOME is the default desktop. If you use a variety of desktops, the `switchdesk` utility provides an easy way to start a different GUI. If you run `switchdesk` from inside a GUI, you'll see something similar to the Desktop Switcher window shown in Figure 15.13.

FIGURE 15.13

Desktop Switcher

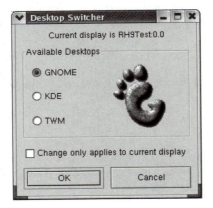

The Desktop Switcher window shows your installed GUIs; you can use it to switch between installed desktop environments such as GNOME and KDE.

You can also use `switchdesk` from the command-line interface. It's simple; for example, if you want to make KDE your default desktop, run this command:

```
# switchdesk KDE
```

LINUX GUI DESKTOPS

Several Linux GUI desktops are available. Some of the major options can be used by switchdesk:

◆ GNOME is the default Red Hat Linux GUI desktop; the acronym stands for the GNU Network Object Model Environment.

◆ KDE is the other major GUI desktop; the acronym stands for the K Desktop Environment.

◆ The fvwm (and fvwm95) window manager was the standard Red Hat GUI before GNOME and KDE. Because it requires only a small amount of memory, it suited the time when RAM was more expensive.

◆ Enlightenment is perhaps the most configurable of the major Linux GUI window managers.

◆ The twm window manager is very basic; on Red Hat Linux, it includes one console screen. It also serves as a failsafe desktop environment, with minimal tools and programs.

◆ The WindowMaker window manager is designed to be more intuitive; it looks vaguely like the GUI for the NeXTStep operating system.

Changing the Display Manager

A display manager is the login manager, which provides a graphical look and feel to users when they log into your Linux computer. Three major options are available for display managers. Two are associated with GNOME and KDE; the third is a generic X Window display manager.

You can select your preferred display manager in /etc/X11/prefdm. The key variable is about 10 lines into this file:

```
preferred=
```

Depending on your preferred display manager, you can set the preferred variable to *one* of the following lines:

```
preferred=gdm
preferred=kdm
preferred=xdm
```

These refer to the GNOME Display Manager, the KDE Display Manager, and the X Display Manager, respectively. Let's examine each in turn.

THE GNOME DISPLAY MANAGER

The GNOME Display Manager is shown in Figure 15.14.

Besides the straightforward login interface (which prompts you for a password), there are three menus:

Language   If you've installed the appropriate language packages, you can click Language and select that language for your session.

Session   This opens a menu that allows you to select from available desktops.

Reboot   This prompts for confirmation before rebooting the computer.

Shutdown   This prompts for confirmation before shutting down the computer.

You can configure the GNOME desktop manager. Open up a GUI and run the `gdmsetup` command to open a menu with five tabs, as shown in Figure 15.15.

These tabs can help you customize the GNOME Display Manager in several ways:

♦ The General tab allows you to configure basic local and remote login parameters.

♦ The Standard Greeter tab gives you control over the look and feel of this interface, normally used for remote graphical connections.

♦ The Graphical Greeter tab gives you a choice of several themes for the graphical gdm interface. You may be able to install new themes as they are developed by Red Hat, the GNOME project, or a third party such as Ximian.

♦ The Security tab lets you regulate root and remote logins, as well as available login menus.

♦ The XDMCP tab allows you to configure how this display manager communicates with remote users. XDMCP is the X Display Manager Control Protocol.

As described in Chapter 17, you can configure the KDE Display Manager through the KDE Control Center Login Manager setting. No equivalent configuration tool is available for the X Display Manager (xdm); however, it includes configuration files in the /etc/X11/xdm directory.

THE KDE DISPLAY MANAGER

You can also configure the KDE Display Manager, as shown in Figure 15.16. This manager also includes a straightforward login interface, and several options:

Session Type   Allows you to select from available desktops.

Go   Sends your typed-in username and password for verification.

Clear   Erases entries in the Username and Password text boxes.

Menu   Allows you to restart the X Server.

Shutdown   Brings up a window that allows you to send the Turn Off Computer (poweroff) or Restart Computer (reboot) commands.

FIGURE 15.16

The KDE Display Manager

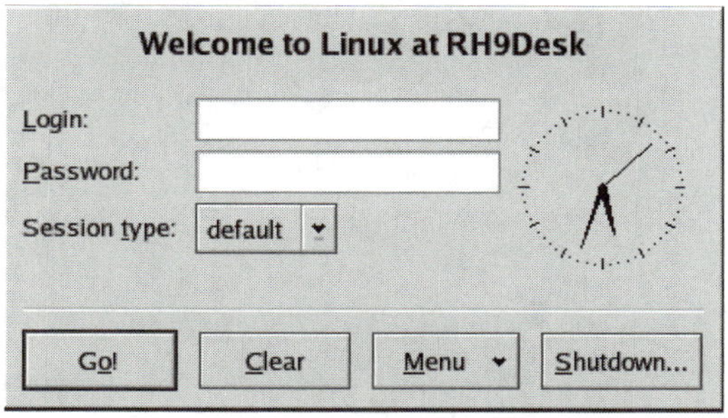

THE X DISPLAY MANAGER

Finally, you can configure the X Display Manager, as shown in Figure 15.17. This is the most straightforward of login interfaces; all you can do from this screen is log into this computer.

FIGURE 15.17

The X Display Manager

DEFINITIONS

You should keep in mind a number of definitions when talking about the X Window and the GUI. Several of these terms are closely related and are used interchangeably, which can be confusing.

Display manager   A graphical interface for logins. Common display managers include the X Display Manager (xdm), the GNOME Display Manager (gdm), and the KDE Display Manager (kdm).

Desktop   A window manager integrated with a series of tools and programs. The two most common desktops are GNOME and KDE. The GNOME desktop does not have to include the GNOME window manager. For example, older versions of Red Hat Linux configured an Enlightenment window manager on a GNOME desktop.

Graphical user interface (GUI)   A graphical interface through which a user can interact with a computer. A combination of an X Server and X Clients.

Window manager   A specialized X Client that controls the look and feel of and the interface to windows in a GUI.

X Client   An application that is run within a GUI; it can be run from the local or from a remote computer.

X Server   The drivers and programs that create the GUI on the local computer.

Understanding the Configuration Files

Several important configuration files and executable programs are related to the Linux X Window. Most of you know the command that starts the X Window from a command-line interface:

```
# startx
```

This program refers to other configuration files and programs, in the /etc/X11/xinit and /usr/X11R6/bin directories. The /etc files can be customized for individual users, as hidden files in their home directories.

By far, the most important X Window configuration file is /etc/X11/XF86Config; we'll discuss that file in some detail later in this section.

startx

There are three basic ways to get into the Linux GUI. You can edit the id variable in /etc/inittab to start in runlevel 5 when you boot Linux, or you can go into runlevel 5 from the text console with the init 5 command. (More information on /etc/inittab and init are available in Chapter 11.) Either of these methods brings you to one of the graphical login interfaces described earlier.

A third method is to run the startx command. This is actually an executable file in the /usr/X11R6/bin directory. You can open startx in any text editor. The start of this file is shown in Figure 15.18.

FIGURE 15.18

The startx file

```
# This is just a sample implementation of a slightly less primitive
# interface than xinit.  It looks for user .xinitrc and .xserverrc
# files, then system xinitrc and xserverrc files, else lets xinit choose
# its default.  The system xinitrc should probably do things like check
# for .Xresources files and merge them in, startup up a window manager,
# and pop a clock and serveral xterms.
#
# Site administrators are STRONGLY urged to write nicer versions.
#
# $XFree86: xc/programs/xinit/startx.cpp,v 3.14 2002/01/28 18:19:50 tsi Exp $

█

userclientrc=$HOME/.xinitrc
userserverrc=$HOME/.xserverrc
sysclientrc=/etc/X11/xinit/xinitrc
sysserverrc=/etc/X11/xinit/xserverrc
defaultclient=/usr/X11R6/bin/xterm
defaultserver=/usr/X11R6/bin/X
defaultclientargs=""
defaultserverargs=""
clientargs=""
serverargs=""
```

As you can see, this script includes several variables. It first looks for .xinitrc and .xserverrc files in the home directory of the requesting user. If these files aren't available, it uses defaults in the /etc/X11/xinit directory.

NOTE *The /etc/X11/xinit/xserverrc file does not exist by default on Red Hat Linux systems; instead, the* startx *command starts the X Server in the first available graphical console, with the* X :0 *command.*

The defaultclient and defaultserver are the default X Client and the default X Server; the default xterm client is used if you use switchdesk to make twm your default desktop. The other variables are intentionally left empty; if you're comfortable with programming code, you'll be able to see how these variables are assigned.

MORE X WINDOWS

It's possible to run different X Windows, locally and remotely. As described in Chapter 3, the X Window gets its own virtual console. If you're in a text screen and the GUI is running, you can access it with the Ctrl+Alt+F7 command.

If you have enough memory, you can run a second X Window in your local computer. The startx -- :1 command opens a second GUI, which you can access with the Ctrl+Alt+F8 command.

If you want to try a GUI application from another computer, set that computer to accept X commands from the remote computer. Disable your firewall, and let the remote computer in with the xhost +*computername* or xhost +*remoteipaddr* command. (*remoteipaddr* represents the IP address of the remote computer.) Then you can log into the remote computer and start a command such as gimp --display *youripaddr*:0.0 or xclock -display *youripaddr*:0.0.

The display switch is not consistent; with some commands such as xclock, it requires only one dash (-display); other commands such as gimp require a double-dash (--display). If in doubt, run the command with the -h switch such as xclock -h or gimp -h.

/etc/X11

The /etc/X11 directory contains a number of important configuration files and directories. Table 15.1 describes each of the files and subdirectories.

TABLE 15.1: */ETC/X11* FILES AND DIRECTORIES

FILE OR DIRECTORY	DESCRIPTION
applink	A directory with links to applications that appear in a GUI Start menu
desktop-menus	A directory with settings for various default GUI menus
fs	A directory with the Font Server configuration
gdm	A directory with GNOME Display Manager configuration files
lbxproxy	A directory for remote clients that want to use the low-bandwidth extension to the X Server (LBX)
prefdm	A file that selects the preferred display manager
proxymngr	A directory with configuration for use with proxy managers
rstart	A directory with a remote start client; based on rsh
serverconfig	A directory for X Server configuration settings
starthere	A directory with basic X desktop settings
sysconfig	A directory with a gnome-lokkit configuration file

Continued on next page

TABLE 15.1: */ETC/X11* FILES AND DIRECTORIES *(continued)*

FILE OR DIRECTORY	DESCRIPTION
twm	A directory with the twm configuration file, `system.twmrc`
X	A file linked to the X Server application
xdm	A directory with X Display Manager configuration files
XF86Config	The main X Server configuration file
xinit	A directory with default X configuration files called by `startx`; used if equivalent files are not available in the applicable home directory
xkb	A directory for keyboard configuration
Xmodmap	A default configuration file for keyboards
Xresources	A configuration file that calls fonts for the login screen
xserver	A directory with a `SecurityPolicy` configuration file
xsm	A directory that configures the X session manager

Local Configuration Files

You can set up X Window configuration files in users' home directories. As you've seen earlier, `startx` looks for two of them for settings to start the Linux X Window: `~/.xinitrc` and `~/.xserverrc`. The dot hides these filenames in your home directory.

NOTE   As described in Chapter 6, you can view the hidden files in any directory with the `ls -a` *command.*

As described earlier, Red Hat does not use the `xserverrc` file. Thus, the key configuration file is `~/.xinitrc`, which also calls several other files in the home directory.

NOTE   Remember, the tilde (~) represents the current user's home directory.

The other key files are `~/.Xclients` and `~/.Xclients-default`, which `switchdesk` modifies so `startx` knows the desktop you want. If you're interested in how these files work, read them for yourself. Use the `switchdesk` command as described earlier to set a different default desktop and see what that does to `~/.Xclients-default`.

XINITRC

When the `startx` command starts your X Server, it needs to call up fonts, keyboard settings, and default X Clients.

The `xinitrc` file is an executable shell script. You can use the default in the `/etc/X11/xinit` directory, or you can customize it, change its name to `.xinitrc`, and store it in your own home directory. The following is a detailed analysis of the default `xinitrc` file:

```
#!/bin/sh
# © 1999-2003 Red Hat, Inc.
```

```
userresources=$HOME/.Xresources
usermodmap=$HOME/.Xmodmap
userxkbmap=$HOME/.Xkbmap

sysresources=/etc/X11/Xresources
sysmodmap=/etc/X11/Xmodmap
sysxkbmap=/etc/X11/Xkbmap
```

These first lines represent the other configuration files needed through the rest of the script. You'll see in a moment that if the user* variable files aren't available, xinitrc uses just the sys* files.

```
# merge in defaults
if [ -f "$sysresources" ]; then
    xrdb -merge "$sysresources"
fi

if [ -f "$userresources" ]; then
    xrdb -merge "$userresources"
fi
```

These lines start by applying the $sysresources file, /etc/X11/Xresources. If there's a valid $userresources file (~/.Xresources), the settings from each file are combined.

```
# merge in keymaps
if [ -f "$sysxkbmap" ]; then
    setxkbmap `cat "$sysxkbmap"`
    XKB_IN_USE=yes
fi

if [ -f "$userxkbmap" ]; then
    setxkbmap `cat "$userxkbmap"`
    XKB_IN_USE=yes
fi
```

These lines serve the same purpose as the previous stanzas, except they apply to the noted Keyboard Map files, based in Xkbmap. However, that file doesn't normally exist in Red Hat Linux and are therefore ignored. In xinitrc, this is followed by a stanza related to a Sun Microsystems X Server, which Red Hat does not use and therefore also ignores. This is followed by:

```
# xkb and xmodmap don't play nice together
if [ -z "$XKB_IN_USE" ]; then
    if [ -f "$sysmodmap" ]; then
        xmodmap "$sysmodmap"
    fi

    if [ -f "$usermodmap" ]; then
        xmodmap "$usermodmap"
    fi
fi

unset XKB_IN_USE
```

This stanza checks for an Xmodmap file in /etc/X11/xinit, or a hidden version in your home directory. If it exists, it's used in place of the aforementioned Xkbdmap file. But remember, that file doesn't normally exist in Red Hat Linux.

```
# run all system xinitrc shell scripts.
for i in /etc/X11/xinit/xinitrc.d/* ; do
    if [ -x "$i" ]; then
        . "$i"
    fi
done
```

This stanza runs basic shell scripts in the noted directory, /etc/X11/xinit/xinitrc.d. These scripts can include files such as xinput and xmbind, which are described later.

```
if [ -f $HOME/.Xclients ]; then
    [ -x /usr/bin/ssh-agent -a -z "$SSH_AGENT_PID" ] && \
        exec ssh-agent $HOME/.Xclients || \
        exec $HOME/.Xclients
elif [ -f /etc/X11/xinit/Xclients ]; then
    [ -x /usr/bin/ssh-agent -a -z "$SSH_AGENT_PID" ] && \
        exec ssh-agent /etc/X11/xinit/Xclients || \
        exec /etc/X11/xinit/Xclients
else
```

These commands check for default clients in the Xclients file. They also set up an authentication agent for SSH, if previously configured. See Chapter 23 for more information.

```
        xclock -geometry 100x100-5+5 &
        xterm -geometry 80x50-50+150 &
        if [ -x /usr/bin/netscape -a -f /usr/share/doc/HTML/index.html ]; then
                netscape /usr/share/doc/HTML/index.html &
        fi
        if [ -x /usr/X11R6/bin/fvwm2 ]; then
                exec fvwm2
        else
                exec twm
        fi
fi
```

These commands set up default clients if no Xclients file is available. You might note that this stanza includes Netscape, which is no longer included with the Red Hat Linux CDs. This stanza also uses xclock, a generic Linux GUI clock, and xterm, a generic command-line interface window.

You can also create your own .xinitrc file in your home directory. Make sure to use the appropriate **chmod** command to make that file executable. For example, you could add the following information to .xinitrc:

```
#!/bin/bash
xclock &
xterm &
```

```
gimp &
exec twm
```

This file starts with #!/bin/bash, which assumes that the commands that follow are based on the bash shell. The remaining commands start the standard Linux graphical clock (xclock), a basic terminal command-line interface (xterm), and The GIMP (gimp), the GNU Image Manipulation Program. Finally, the code starts a simple window manager interface known as twm (twm). The result starts the programs with twm, as shown in Figure 15.19.

FIGURE 15.19

What you can do with .xinitrc

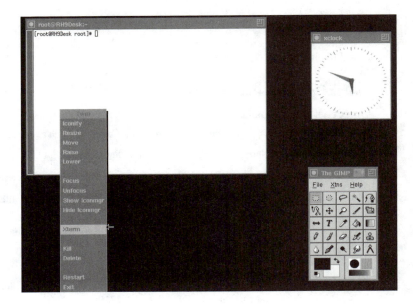

Xresources

There is normally an .Xresources file in users' home directories, as well as a default Xresources in /etc/X11. The default file goes through a series of steps to find your preferred desktop. Generally, if GNOME or KDE is not available, Xresources looks for a .wm_style file in your home directory that might call for an older window manager.

But these are details; the standard .Xresources file in your home directory sets a color scheme for basic X Clients in your GUI.

XF86Config

The /etc/X11/XF86Config file contains the main configuration settings for the X Server. Whenever you start a Linux GUI, the basic settings for resolution, pitch, graphics drivers, monitors, keyboards, and mice or other pointing devices are configured through this file. This file includes several major sections described here.

The first line in a file tells you if `XF86Config` was created through Anaconda:

```
# XFree86 4 configuration created by pyxf86config
```

or `redhat-config-xfree86`

```
# XFree86 4 configuration created by redhat-config-xfree86
```

NOTE *Prior to Red Hat Linux 8.0, the default X Server configuration file was* `/etc/X11/XF86Config-4`. *The -4 was added because Red Hat accommodated two different major versions of the XFree86 Server, 3.a.b and 4.x.y. Since Red Hat has now dropped version 3.a.b, it has also dropped the -4 suffix. The XFree86 version 4.x.y server now includes data for all but the oldest graphics cards.*

Many of the directives in `XF86Config` are listed in Table 15.2. The following subsections correspond to the typical sections that you might see in your `XF86Config` file.

TABLE 15.2: COMMON DIRECTIVES IN */ETC/X11/XF86CONFIG*

DIRECTIVE	DESCRIPTION
BoardName	Specifies the name assigned to the device, such as a video card
BusID	Notes the location of a PCI or AGP video card, if Linux doesn't detect it
DefaultDepth	Specifies the default number of color bits per pixel; normally 1, 4, 8, 16, 24, or 32
DisplaySize	Lists the horizontal and vertical size of the screen, in millimeters
Driver	Names a specific driver for the component
EndSection	Indicates the end of a group of commands
EndSubSection	Indicates the end of a SubSection group of commands
FontPath	Notes where X fonts can be found; may cite a specific file, or the TCP/IP port of the local font server, usually with unix/:7100
HorizSync	Shows the range of allowable horizontal synchronization rates for the monitor
Identifier	Allows interaction between command groups
InputDevice	May refer to keyboards or pointing devices such as a mouse or a touchpad
Load	Adds the specified module
Model Name	Represents the name of a specific model; goes with VendorName
Modes	Specifies the allowable monitor resolution(s)
Module	Lists servers and font modules to be loaded with your X Server
Monitor	Notes the monitor Identifier associated with a Screen
Option	Indicates one of the many options available for different hardware components
RgbPath	Notes a database file, in text format, which specifies the level of Red, Green, and Blue for different colors

Continued on next page

TABLE 15.2: COMMON DIRECTIVES IN */ETC/X11/XF86CONFIG (continued)*

DIRECTIVE	DESCRIPTION
Section	Indicates the beginning of a group of commands; should be labeled, and goes with EndSection
SubSection	Indicates the beginning of a group of commands inside a Section
VendorName	Specifies the name of a manufacturer
VertRefresh	Shows the range of allowable vertical refresh rates for the monitor
VideoRam	Indicates the amount of available Video RAM memory

SERVERLAYOUT

The ServerLayout section binds various InputDevice(s) and the Screen, which includes the combined configuration for the monitor and video card. The example shown here is in effect a summary of the configuration on my computer:

```
Section "ServerLayout"
      Identifier    "Default Layout"
      Screen    0    "Screen0" 0 0
      InputDevice    "Mouse0" "CorePointer"
      InputDevice    "Keyboard0" "CoreKeyboard"
      InputDevice    "DevInputMice" "AlwaysCore"
EndSection
```

In other words, this particular ServerLayout section combines the settings of Screen0, Mouse0, DevInputMice, and Keyboard0, as configured through Anaconda, the Red Hat Linux installation program.

FILES

The Files needed by your X Server relate to colors and fonts. The example here is taken from my computer:

```
Section "Files"
      RgbPath    "/usr/X11R6/lib/X11/rgb"
      FontPath    "unix/:7100"
EndSection
```

To translate, this Files section notes the location of RGB style colors for display. It also lists the standard TCP/IP port for the X Font Server, xfs. RGB (Red Green Blue) is the traditional standard for color graphics.

NOTE *RGB is not good enough for many artists and graphic designers. There is an alternative. Some Linux applications support the CMYK (Cyan, Magenta, Yellow, and Black) standard. This is good enough for several major movie studios, including DreamWorks and Disney. A couple of Linux CMYK programs are Houdini (www.sidefx.com) and Maya (www.aliaswavefront.com).*

MODULE

The `module` commands load font and server extension modules. The font modules shown below are straightforward; they load the Freetype (True Type clone) and Type1 fonts. A full list of available modules is shown in the `/usr/X11R6/lib/modules` directory.

```
Section "Module"
     Load "dbe"
     Load "extmod"
     Load "fbdevhw"
     Load "dri"
     Load "glx"
     Load "record"
     Load "freetype"
     Load "type1"
EndSection
```

INPUTDEVICE

An `InputDevice` is anything that a user directly touches to send information to a computer. Also known as a Human Interface Device (HID), these devices are primarily keyboards and mice, but can include trackballs, touchpads, and more. As you can see below, there's a separate `InputDevice` section for each component.

```
Section "InputDevice"
     Identifier "Keyboard0"
     Driver     "keyboard"
     Option     "XkbRules" "xfree86"
     Option     "XkbModel" "pc105"
     Option     "XkbLayout" "us"
EndSection
```

This first `InputDevice` specifies your keyboard, using the driver by the same name. The basic keyboard rules specify a layout, which conforms to those associated with the XFree86 Server. The model is associated with a standard 105-key keyboard, in a standard U.S. layout.

```
Section "InputDevice"
     Identifier "Mouse0"
     Driver     "mouse"
     Option     "Protocol" "IMPS/2"
     Option     "Device" "/dev/psaux"
     Option     "ZAxisMapping" "4 5"
     Option     "Emulate3Buttons" "no"
EndSection
```

The next `InputDevice` specifies a mouse, using a PS/2 connection. The device driver file is `/dev/psaux`, which is often linked to `/dev/mouse`. `ZAxisMapping` represents the up and down motion of a mouse wheel, which in this case corresponds to standard mouse buttons 4 and 5. These buttons aren't available on all mice. Button 4 corresponds to a scroll wheel on a three-button mouse. Button 5 corresponds to a button on the side of the mouse. If you have more than one mouse or pointing device, there may be another `InputDevice` section.

MONITOR

The `Monitor` section summarizes the basic settings associated with your monitor. The following settings from my computer are fairly straightforward; they identify the monitor model, the `DisplaySize` in millimeters, and the horizontal sync and vertical refresh rates. The `dpms` option represents the power-saving settings standard.

```
Section "Monitor"
      Identifier   "Monitor0"
      VendorName   "Monitor Vendor"
      ModelName    "S/M 955DF"
      DisplaySize  360     270
      HorizSync    30.0 - 85.0
      VertRefresh  50.0 - 160.0
      Option       "dpms"
EndSection
```

It's possible to configure two different monitors; each monitor gets its own section with customized settings. The monitor and video card together gets its own `Screen` section, as we describe later in this chapter.

DEVICE

The main device that supports any GUI is the video card. The following section identifies a specific card, with driver, and associated video RAM.

```
Section "Device"
      Identifier   "Videocard0"
      Driver       "i810"
      VendorName   "Videocard vendor"
      BoardName    "Intel 810"
      VideoRam     16384
EndSection
```

If you have more than one video card, each card gets its own separate section in your `XF86Config` file.

SCREEN

The `Screen` section combines the applicable video card (`Device`) and monitor settings from their respective sections. The name associated with the `Device` and `Monitor` lines is taken from their `Identifier` variables.

```
Section "Screen"
      Identifier "Screen0"
      Device     "Videocard0"
      Monitor    "Monitor0"
      DefaultDepth   24
      SubSection "Display"
            Depth     16
            Modes     "1024x768" "800x600" "640x480"
      EndSubSection
```

```
        SubSection "Display"
                Depth    24
                Modes    "800x600" "640x480"
        EndSubSection
EndSection
```

It's the combined video card and monitor that gets a dot pitch (`Depth`) and resolution (`Modes`). The following section configures two different `SubSection "Display"` stanzas. Note that each stanza has one `Depth` and possibly overlapping `Modes`.

DRI

The Direct Rendering Interface (DRI) takes advantage of the 3D acceleration available with higher-end video cards. It's associated with games as well as the higher-end graphics required for movies and computer-aided design models. The following `DRI` section is simple:

```
Section "DRI"
        Mode     0666
EndSection
```

The `0666` is associated with read and write file permissions, for all users. If you specify a group in `/etc/group`, you can limit 3D rendering access. For example, if there is a galley group in `/etc/group`, you could limit access with the following stanza:

```
Section "DRI"
        Group    "galley"
        Mode     0666
EndSection
```

Troubleshooting the X Window

If you have problems starting the Linux GUI, there are a number of things that you can check. Much of this chapter has focused on the basic X configuration tools; you can always start by rerunning these tools.

As with most other servers, many problems can show up in the log files, stored in the `/var/log` directory. Sometimes the display is actually someplace else—on another console, or even another computer. One common problem with starting the X Server is the fonts. If the X Font Server won't start, neither will the X Window.

Log Files

Two basic files are associated with events in the Linux X Window, and both are located in the `/var/log` directory. The `XFree86.0.log` file in this directory shows what happens when `startx` and associated commands interact with your configuration files, especially `XF86Config`. The `/var/log/messages` file can help you identify X Font Server problems.

Even if you're not having a problem, study these files. You might be surprised at the errors you find. What you learn can help you make your X Window start faster.

XFREE86.0.LOG

Take a look at an excerpt from this log file in Figure 15.20. If you've read the earlier section on the `XF86Config` file, you'll recognize many of the variables.

FIGURE 15.20

XFree86.0.log

```
Markers: (--) probed, (**) from config file, (==) default setting,
         (++) from command line, (!!) notice, (II) informational,
         (WW) warning, (EE) error, (NI) not implemented, (??) unknown.
(==) Log file: "/var/log/XFree86.0.log", Time: Sun Dec 22 09:47:01 2002
(==) Using config file: "/etc/X11/XF86Config"
(==) ServerLayout "Default Layout"
(**) |-->Screen "Screen0" (0)
(**) |    |-->Monitor "Monitor0"
(**) |    |-->Device "Videocard0"
(**) |-->Input Device "Mouse0"
(**) |-->Input Device "Keyboard0"
(**) Option "XkbRules" "xfree86"
(**) XKB: rules: "xfree86"
(**) Option "XkbModel" "pc105"
(**) XKB: model: "pc105"
(**) Option "XkbLayout" "us"
(**) XKB: layout: "us"
(==) Keyboard: CustomKeycode disabled
(**) |-->Input Device "DevInputMice"
(**) FontPath set to "unix/:7100"
(**) RgbPath set to "/usr/X11R6/lib/X11/rgb"
(==) ModulePath set to "/usr/X11R6/lib/modules"
(--) using VT number 7
"XFree86.0.log" 625L, 32662C                              31,10        2%
```

Make a note of those lines based on the configuration file, with the "(**)" in front. If there are problems, you can fix those in your XF86Config file. In my version of the file, I see lines such as:

```
(II) I810(0): Not using default mode "320x175" (bad mode
➥ clock/interlace/doublescan)
```

This is an informational (II) message, since it doesn't affect how things work. But look for warning (WW) and error (EE) messages.

LEARNING TO TROUBLESHOOT

Troubleshooting can be a difficult process. You can wait until trouble strikes; crises do have a tendency to focus the mind. Alternatively, you can experiment. Because the X Window depends on the XF86Config file, I learn about possible problems by experimenting on this file. If you know the linux rescue mode described in Chapter 11 and you are systematic, you too can learn this way.

Before experimenting with any configuration file, back it up. In this case, make sure your id variable in /etc/inittab is set to runlevel 3. If you run into problems with XF86Config, that will help you restart Linux at the command-line interface.

Try "commenting out" various commands in this file, by adding an "#" in front of the line, and then run startx. Sometimes your X Window will start fine, using other settings as defaults. Other times, your X Window might not start at all. Pay attention to the (EE) messages and their relationship to what you changed in the XF86Config file.

When you've finished, remember to restore the original configuration file.

/VAR/LOG/MESSAGES

The X Window can't start unless your X Font Server is running. It's a service controlled from the /etc/rc.d/init.d directory, like many other services.

NOTE *The main font configuration file is* /etc/font/font.conf.

The /var/log/messages file is fairly long. By default, it can hold the startup and shutdown messages for your Linux computer for up to a full week. If the problem is recent, start near the end of the file. The first message that you'll see during the startup process should look like this:

```
Dec 22 10:25:09 RH9Server kernel: Linux version 2.4.20-3
```

This will be followed up by an xfs startup message similar to the following:

```
Dec 22 10:25:09 RH9Server xfs: xfs startup succeeded
```

If you don't see this message, you may have a font problem. Look at the following possibilities:

◆ Check the status of the xfs service. If it's stopped, try starting it with the **service xfs start** command. Make sure xfs is set to start automatically with the appropriate **chkconfig** command, discussed in Chapter 13.

◆ Check the FontPath variable in /etc/X11/XF86Config. It should point to actual font files or TCP/IP port 7100.

◆ Make sure the files listed in the FontPath variable actually exist. If they don't, you may need to install some of the font RPM packages associated with XFree86. These packages have names in a format like XFree86-*-fonts-*.

◆ Check your firewall. If you're blocking local access to port 7100, the font server can't get information to your X Window.

NOTE *Don't confuse the X Font Server with the xfs file system developed by Silicon Graphics (SGI). Unfortunately, they do use the same acronym.*

Summary

In this chapter, you learned the basics of configuring the X Window. While many Linux experts have no desire or need for the graphical user interface, it is an important tool for many power users. It holds appeal for users who are converting from more graphical systems, such as Microsoft Windows.

You may have already configured the X Window during the Linux installation process. If you haven't or need to change your settings, two major tools can help: xf86config and redhat-config-xfree86. Red Hat uses redhat-config-xfree86; the alternative xf86config is available on other distributions or if you download new XFree86 servers from www.xfree86.org.

Several key configuration files are associated with the X Window, called through the startx script. You can create individual settings in your home directory, or allow startx to use generic settings in the /etc/X11 directory.

Perhaps the key configuration file is `/etc/X11/XF86Config`. It's helpful to know the basics of this file, so you can customize it as well as troubleshoot some of the problems you may encounter. While the X Window requires a working font server, `xfs`, you'll find most problems in the main X Window log file, `/var/log/XFree86.0.log`.

In the next chapter, we'll take a detailed look at the default desktop for Red Hat Linux, GNOME. It is a fully featured GUI, with virtually all of the features available on Microsoft Windows. Even if you don't use a GUI, you should know the benefits of GNOME in order to help your users.

Chapter 16

GNOME

WHILE LINUX ADMINISTRATORS MAY not need a graphical user interface (GUI), users who are converting from Microsoft Windows do. One of the goals within the GNU community is to make the Linux operating system competitive on the desktop. To this end, Linux needs a GUI that can help Microsoft Windows users feel comfortable.

To achieve this goal, Red Hat Linux has worked magic with GNOME, the GNU Network Object Model Environment. Not only does GNOME provide a high-performance GUI, but it also includes high-performance software such as office suites that can cost the Microsoft user hundreds of dollars. And of course, there are no licensing fees associated with Linux. As noted in Chapter 1, this has caused a number of companies and governments to consider replacing Microsoft Windows with Linux.

GNOME provides a GUI desktop, control applets, and several important applications. Many of these components can replace costly third-party applications that run only on Microsoft Windows. In this chapter, we'll take a brief look at the GNOME desktop, the Control Center, as well as the applications that come with GNOME on Red Hat Linux 9.

However, this chapter does not include a comprehensive introduction to GNOME. We won't look at common applications such as OpenOffice until Chapter 18. We'll also hold off on the `redhat-config-*` tools until Chapter 19.

In addition, the Red Hat implementation of GNOME allows you to use KDE applications and utilities, which are covered in Chapter 17. Many KDE tools are accessible directly through the GNOME Main Menu button. This chapter covers the following topics:

- ◆ Working with the basic GNOME interface
- ◆ Learning about GNOME extras

The Basic GNOME Interface

The standard GNOME desktop has all of the characteristics of today's GUI operating systems. It includes a panel, a Main Menu button, and icons. You can customize each of these components for your own needs, or even configure a standard interface for your GNOME installations. You can control and customize GNOME's look and feel through the GNOME Control Center. When you first start a GUI on Red Hat Linux, you'll probably see a desktop similar to Figure 16.1.

NOTE   *In Red Hat Linux, the panel is functionally equivalent to the Microsoft Windows taskbar; the Main Menu button (with the red hat icon) corresponds functionally to the Microsoft Start button.*

FIGURE 16.1

The GNOME desktop

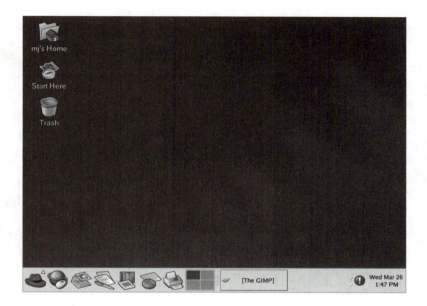

An Overview of GNOME

The basic GNOME desktop is deceptively simple. As you can see from Figure 16.1, it includes a way to navigate to your home directory (*username*'s home); a Start Here button that opens available applets, utilities, and applications; and a Trash folder. All three use Nautilus, which is an "Explorer"-style graphical shell that you use to manage your files, your GNOME configuration, and any GUI tools associated with your Linux system. We'll use Nautilus again later in this chapter. In the following sections, we'll examine the buttons on the panel and the GNOME Control Center.

THE GNOME PANEL

The GNOME panel is one place where you can call up a number of applications, switch between open programs, and even switch between open workspaces. I've included a view of my GNOME panel in Figure 16.2. In this case, the GNOME panel includes seven icons on the left, which are briefly described in Table 16.1.

NOTE   *A workspace is like a standard desktop, with its own icons and open programs. By default, GNOME includes four workspaces; the data for three are stored in spare video memory.*

FIGURE 16.2

The GNOME panel

TABLE 16.1: GNOME PANEL ICONS

ICON	DESCRIPTION
	Clicking this button opens the GNOME Main Menu, which provides access to available programs and utilities; it works like the Start button in Microsoft Windows.
	Opens the Mozilla web browser.
	Starts the Evolution personal information manager; functionally similar to Microsoft Outlook.
	Begins the OpenOffice Writer; functionally similar to Microsoft Word.
	Opens the OpenOffice Impress presentation manager; similar to Microsoft PowerPoint.
	Starts the OpenOffice Calc spreadsheet program; similar to Microsoft Excel.
	Begins the GNOME Print Manager.

GNOME WORKSPACES AND OPEN PROGRAMS

GNOME is flexible. You can place open windows in several workspaces. So instead of opening and closing windows, you can just switch workspaces to get to your applications. For example, I can have OpenOffice Writer in one workspace, OpenOffice Impress in a second, The GIMP image program in a third, and a terminal window in a fourth workspace. A view of the four workspaces appears in a thumbnail on the panel, as shown in Figure 16.3.

FIGURE 16.3

Four GNOME workspaces

To switch to another workspace, click on its corresponding thumbnail. To move an application to another workspace, click on the upper-left corner of the application. You'll see the drop-down menu shown in Figure 16.4.

FIGURE 16.4

Moving to
Workspace 2

You can also switch between open applications shown on the panel. For example, Figure 16.5 illustrates a screen where you can switch between three open applications.

FIGURE 16.5

Switching between
applications

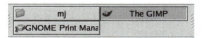

OTHER GNOME PANEL ITEMS

Finally, on the far right of the panel are two more icons. The red exclamation point is a Red Hat Network Alert Icon, which suggests that you need to use **up2date** to connect to the Red Hat network to upgrade some packages. (If it's a blue check mark, your system is up-to-date with the latest packages.). The **up2date** utility is covered in Chapter 10.

If you left-click on the date and time on the panel, you'll see the calendar for the current month; if you right-click on this area and select Adjust Date & Time from the pop-up menu, you'll open the **redhat-config-date** utility, which we discuss in Chapter 19.

It's easy to customize the GNOME panel. Right-click on an open area of the panel, and click Properties in the menu that appears. You'll see the Panel Properties window, shown in Figure 16.6.

There are a number of things that you can do with the properties of your GNOME panel. You can change the size and location of the panel. You can hide it by default until you hover the mouse near the panel. On the Background tab, you can set the background of the panel itself.

TIP   Many Linux administrators use a command line interface in GNOME. To start it, right-click the desktop. In the pop-up menu that appears, select New Terminal. This opens the **gnome-terminal** *command line window. Alternatively, you can open this command line interface by selecting Main Menu ➤ System Tools ➤ Terminal.*

FIGURE 16.6

The GNOME Panel
Properties window

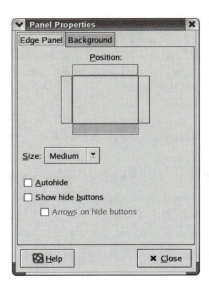

The GNOME Main Menu

Now we'll take a look at the GNOME Main Menu. Click on the red hat in the lower-left corner of the desktop. You should see a menu similar to that shown in Figure 16.7.

FIGURE 16.7

The GNOME
Main Menu

As you can see, the GNOME Main Menu opens a series of other commands and menus. They are briefly described in Table 16.2. We cover some of these menus in more detail in this and future chapters. Many programs under these menus are specifically associated with KDE, the K Desktop Environment, and will be covered in Chapter 17. Major applications from this menu, such as office suites and graphics, will be covered in Chapter 18. We discuss Red Hat–specific administration tools in Chapter 19.

TABLE 16.2: GNOME MAIN MENU COMMANDS AND SUBMENUS

MENU OR COMMAND	DESCRIPTION
Accessories	Opens a group of small programs, such as text editors and calculators.
Documentation	Enters any documents that you may have loaded from the Red Hat Linux documents CD.
Games	Starts any games that you may have installed.
Graphics	Accesses graphics applications for editing, screenshots, faxes, PDF readers, and more.
Internet	Includes a series of applications that you can use to communicate on a TCP/IP network such as the Internet.
Office	Opens a group of applications associated with the OpenOffice suite of programs; other office suites should be accessible through this menu.
Preferences	Allows you to customize your settings; mostly related to the desktop.
Programming	Opens access to a group of programming tools; strangely enough, Emacs is part of this group.
Sound & Video	Adds multimedia applications, including a CD writer.
System Settings	Includes access to many `redhat-config-*` administrative utilities; most require root-level access.
System Tools	Starts a menu with a variety of administrative tools.
Help	Opens a GNOME help session in a simplified browser.
Home Folder	Starts Nautilus with a view of the files in your home directory.
Network Servers	Provides access to shared folders from other computers, including Microsoft Windows computers via Samba.
Run Program	Opens a Run Program dialog box where you can type in the text name for an application.
Search For Files	Starts a front end to the Find command for file searches, starting from a specified directory.
Open Recent	Allows you to open recently accessed documents; normally uses OpenOffice.
Lock Screen	Starts a secure screensaver; to return to the desktop, you need your username and password.
Log Out	Exits GNOME.

If you don't see a specific menu, you may not have installed the associated package(s). For example, you won't see a Games menu unless you've installed associated packages such as kdegames-* or gnome-games-*.

The GNOME Control Center

Now we'll look at some more detailed configuration options for the GNOME desktop, available through the GNOME Control Center. You can open it from the Main Menu: click Main Menu ➤ Preferences ➤ Control Center. This opens a Nautilus window with a series of icons, shown in Figure 16.8. Every icon is associated with a graphical application that can help you work with GNOME. The Control Center icon opens a second Preferences window. We describe each of the other applets in the following sections.

FIGURE 16.8

The GNOME Control Center

NOTE   *The applets in the GNOME Control Center are also available in the Main Menu ➤ Preferences submenu.*

ABOUT MYSELF

The About Myself applet opens the User Information window, shown in Figure 16.9. It allows you to enter additional information related to your account, such as phone numbers and locations. This serves as a front end to the chfn command. The detailed information is accessible with the finger command.

FIGURE 16.9

User Information

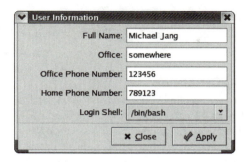

ACCESSIBILITY

The Accessibility applet opens the Keyboard Accessibility Preferences window, shown in Figure 16.10. If you want to change any features, activate the Enable Keyboard Accessibility Features option.

FIGURE 16.10

Keyboard
Accessibility
Preferences

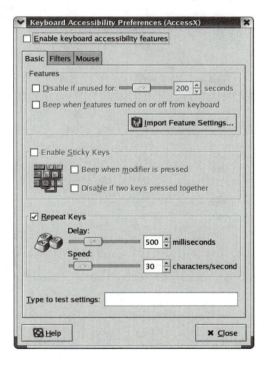

This window includes three tabs. The Basic tab allows you to customize standard settings for your keyboard. The Filters tab takes a look at input; for example, if your fingers shake when you type, the Enable Bounce Keys option can ignore duplicate pressed keys made within a few milliseconds. The Mouse tab allows you to manage the speed of the mouse pointer on the screen.

BACKGROUND

The Background applet starts the Background Preferences menu, shown in Figure 16.11. This allows you to customize the display or picture shown in the desktop background. To change the background picture, click on the picture shown under Select Picture.

FIGURE 16.11

Background
Preferences

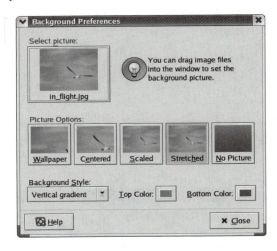

CD PROPERTIES

This applet opens the CD And DVD Preferences window, shown in Figure 16.12. As you can see, it allows you to set preferences when CDs or DVDs are inserted in their respective drives. By default, data CDs are automatically mounted, audio CDs are played with `gnome-cd`, and blank CDs get access to the Nautilus CD burner. You can set different CD or DVD commands in the respective Command text boxes.

FIGURE 16.12

CD And DVD
Preferences

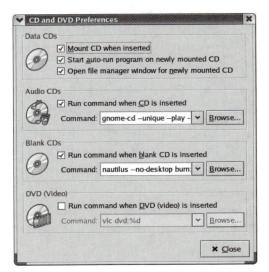

NOTE   *The Control Center icon opens a second Preferences window.*

FILE MANAGEMENT

The File Management applet allows you to manage the look and feel of file views in Nautilus. As shown in Figure 16.13, the File Management Preferences window contains four tabs:

◆ The Views tab allows you to customize the look and feel of files in Nautilus. By default, it is in Icon View, which can include thumbnail pictures of graphics files.

◆ The Behavior tab lets you determine what happens when you click on a file. For example, you can set your preferences to run executable files when clicked.

◆ The Icon Captions tab helps you adjust the information displayed with each icon.

◆ The Preview tab allows you to determine the behavior of a text, image, sound, and directory (folder) files when viewed through a Nautilus window.

FIGURE 16.13

File Management
Preferences

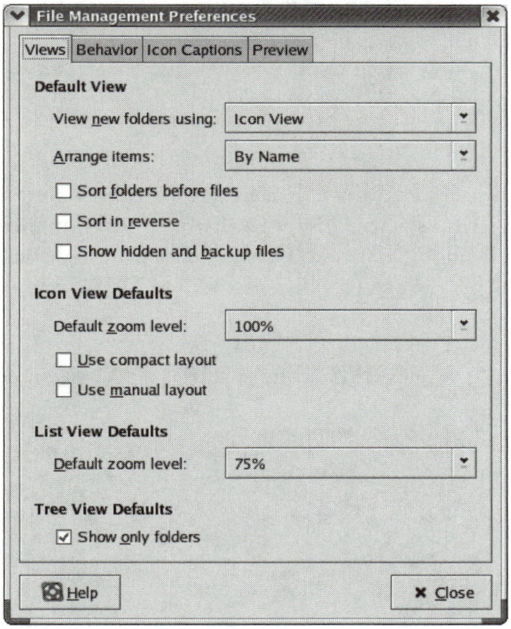

FILE TYPES AND PROGRAMS

The File Types And Programs window, shown in Figure 16.14, lets you associate different file types with specific applications. File identification depends on the extension, such as `.doc` or `.tif`. If you want to add or change the program associated with a particular file type, select it and click Edit.

FIGURE 16.14

File Types And
Programs

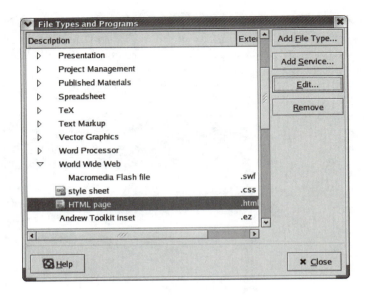

NOTE *The HTML page file type shown in Figure 16.14 can be found under Documents ➤ World Wide Web.*

FONT

The Font Preferences program window lets you configure the default font for various components on your desktop, as shown in Figure 16.15. You can still specify custom fonts in different applications and utilities, such as terminal windows.

FIGURE 16.15

Font Preferences

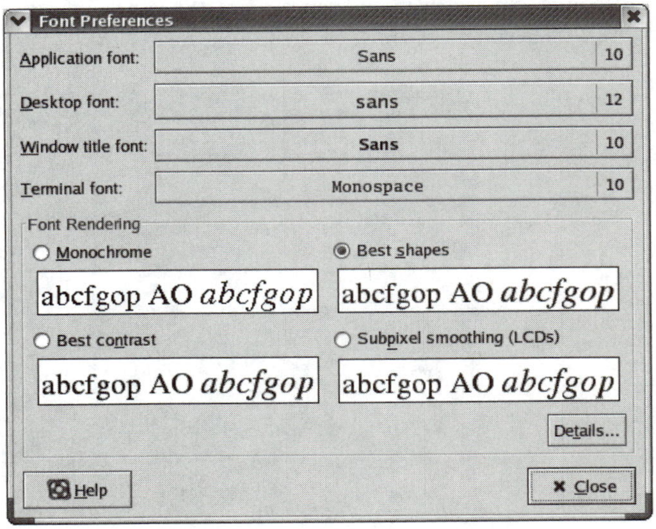

HANDHELD PDA

The Handheld PDA applet is a front end to `gnome-pilot`, which can be used for synchronizing data between GNOME and handheld devices that conform to the PalmPilot and PalmOS standards. When you open the applet for the first time, it starts a wizard, which helps you define the cradle, device, and allowed users. The GNOME Pilot Settings window is shown in Figure 16.16.

FIGURE 16.16

GNOME Pilot Settings

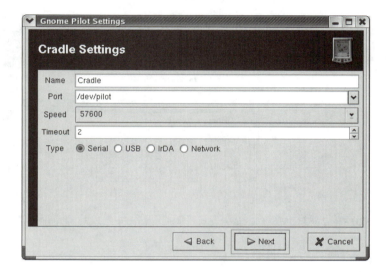

KEYBOARD

The Keyboard Preferences window, shown in Figure 16.17, permits you to customize how your keyboard responds to a key that you keep pressed, the way the cursor blinks, and whether a sound is associated with keyboard events.

FIGURE 16.17

Keyboard Preferences

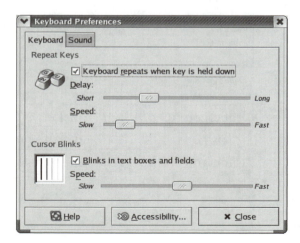

KEYBOARD SHORTCUTS

The Keyboard Shortcuts window that is shown in Figure 16.18 lists functions that you can perform with various control keys on your keyboard, including Shift, Ctrl, Alt, Tab, and Esc. There are two sets of defaults: one for the GNOME desktop, another for Emacs.

FIGURE 16.18

Keyboard Shortcuts

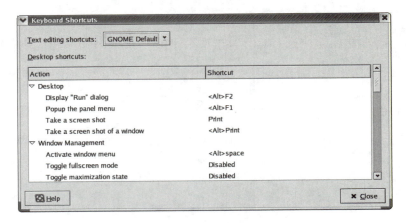

If you want to change a shortcut, highlight it, press the Backspace key, and then press the keys you want to use as a shortcut for that action.

LOGIN PHOTO

The Login Photo window is associated with the GNOME Display Manager (GDM) described in Chapter 15. It allows you to set a photo associated with the GDM standard greeter. It doesn't start unless you've logged in using GDM.

To make this work, you'll need to enable the Show Choosable User Images option in the GDM Setup menu on the Standard Greeter tab described in Chapter 15. Once set, the Select A Photo window shown in Figure 16.19 allows you to set a photo for that particular login situation.

FIGURE 16.19

Selecting a photo
for GDM

NOTE   *Login photo files are limited to 64KB.*

MENUS AND TOOLBARS

The Menu And Toolbars Preferences window, shown in Figure 16.20, allows you to modify the look and feel of icons and text in program menus.

FIGURE 16.20

Menu And Toolbar Preferences

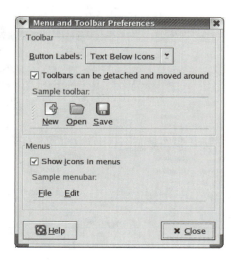

MOUSE PREFERENCES

The Mouse Preferences window, shown in Figure 16.21, allows you to manage the characteristics of your pointing device. It includes three tabs:

- ◆ The Buttons tab allows you change the orientation and double-click delay.

- ◆ The Cursors tab gives you a selection of different cursors.

- ◆ The Motion tab helps you manage the speed of the cursor as well as drag-and-drop behavior.

NETWORK PROXY

The Network Proxy Configuration window allows you to set the path for an external network connection, most likely to the Internet. If there is a proxy server for your network, you can set the addresses for the protocols shown in Figure 16.22. Alternatively, some administrators provide an Automatic Proxy Configuration link that you can enter in the Autoconfiguration URL text box.

PASSWORD

The Password applet is straightforward. It allows you to change the login password for the current user account. It serves as a front end to the `passwd` command, where you enter the current password, and then the new password twice.

PREFERRED APPLICATIONS

You can select a preferred web browser, text editor, and command-line interface terminal in the Preferred Applications window. The default web browser is Mozilla; there is no default text editor, and the default terminal is `gnome-terminal`. You can review the Preferred Applications window in Figure 16.23.

FIGURE 16.21

Mouse Preferences

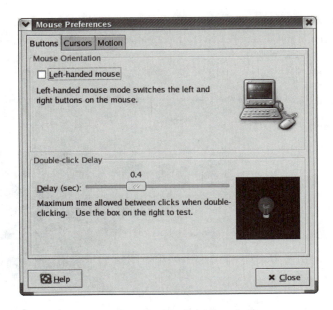

FIGURE 16.22

Network Proxy
Configuration

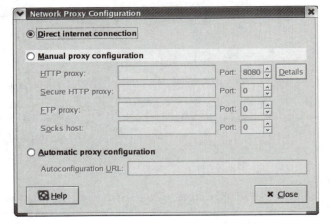

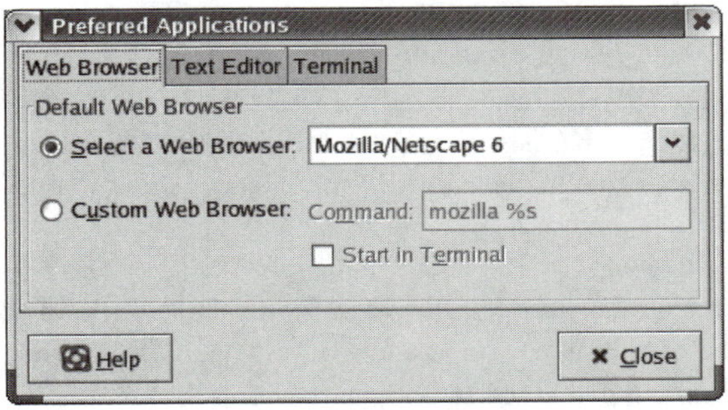

FIGURE 16.23

Preferred
Applications

SCREENSAVER

You can configure the screensaver of your choice through the Screensaver applet. The Screensaver Preferences window, shown in Figure 16.24, allows you to configure a random or specific screensaver pattern, along with delay times and screensaver performance settings.

FIGURE 16.24

Screensaver
Preferences

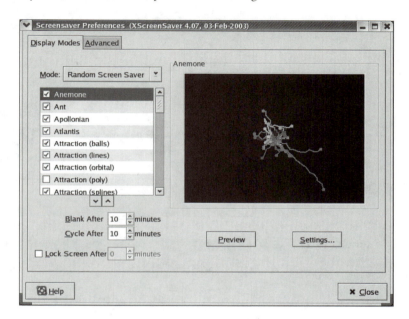

NOTE   GNOME does not allow screensaver access to the root user, unless you run the xhost +localhost *command. The* xhost *command, described in Chapter 15, allows network access to the named computers. In fact, GNOME discourages root access to their GUI. While I've used the root account for this book, I would not leave a root-enabled computer unattended, so I don't need a screensaver.*

SOUND

If you've configured a sound card on your computer, you can use the Sound applet to activate sounds on different events, such as e-mail receipt, logins, errors, and more. The Sound Preferences window, shown in Figure 16.25, allows you to specify different sounds for the specified events.

THEME

The Theme Preferences window, shown in Figure 16.26, is also straightforward. It shows the Red Hat "Bluecurve" theme that is now the default for Red Hat desktops. Click Details, and you can set different themes for controls, window borders, and icons.

WINDOWS

The Window Preferences window, shown in Figure 16.27, allows you to set the behavior of windows in your GUI. You can set what the window does when you double-click the title bar or the key associated with moving a particular window.

FIGURE 16.25

Sound Preferences

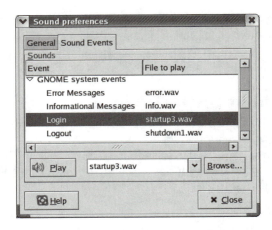

FIGURE 16.26

Theme Preferences

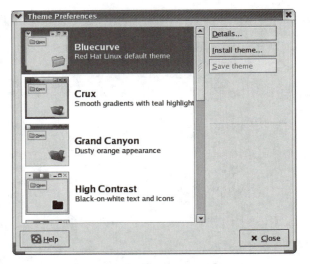

FIGURE 16.27

Window Preferences

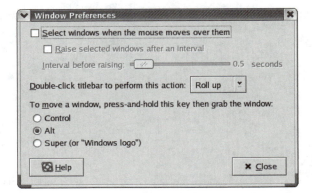

MORE PREFERENCES

The GNOME Control Panel includes a link to More Preferences, which opens a different window with the following three items: CD Database, Panel, and Sessions. We cover the associated preferences windows later in this chapter.

Learning about GNOME Extras

GNOME comes with a number of bonus applications, accessible through the Main Menu button. They fall into several categories: Accessories, Internet, Preferences, Multimedia, and System Tools. This is not a comprehensive list of programs available through the Main Menu button; many are covered in the following three chapters. While most are based on the work of the GNOME project, a few third-party utilities are included in this section as well.

Accessories

GNOME includes several accessories that help you with simple computing tasks. They're accessible through the Main Menu ➤ Accessories submenu. As you can see in Figure 16.28, there is a More Accessories submenu off the Accessories menu. Most of the utilities under this second menu are associated with KDE and are addressed in Chapter 17.

FIGURE 16.28

Accessories menus

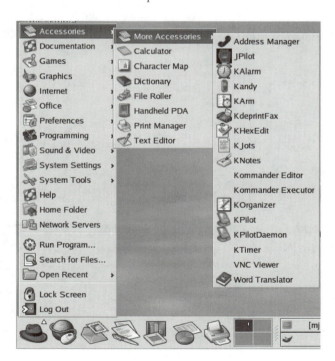

CALCULATOR

GNOME includes a simple scientific calculator, as shown in Figure 16.29. It responds to entries in a keyboard numeric keypad. You can copy the results to other GUI applications.

FIGURE 16.29

The GNOME
Calculator

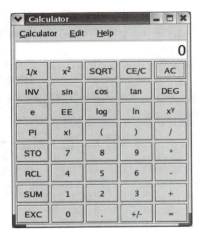

CHARACTER MAP

The Character Map application, shown in Figure 16.30, allows you to work with a number of non-English languages that still use Roman-style alphabets. It provides an interface where you can include special letters and accented characters in your documents.

FIGURE 16.30

The GNOME
Character Map

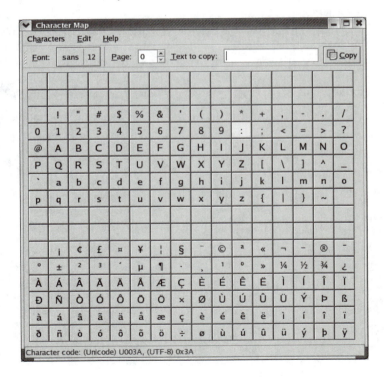

DICTIONARY

The GNOME dictionary provides access to the online dictionary server at `dict.org`. It uses TCP/IP port 2628, which is why there is no "www" or "http" in front of the URL. As long as you're connected to the Internet, it's easy to find the definitions that you need. An example is shown in Figure 16.31.

FIGURE 16.31

The GNOME
Dictionary

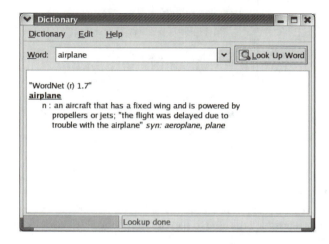

FILE ROLLER

The GNOME File Roller is functionally similar to various Zip utilities associated with Microsoft Windows. In other words, it can view and extract the files from within a compressed archive. An example view of the files within a `.tar.gz` archive is shown in Figure 16.32.

FIGURE 16.32

The GNOME
File Roller

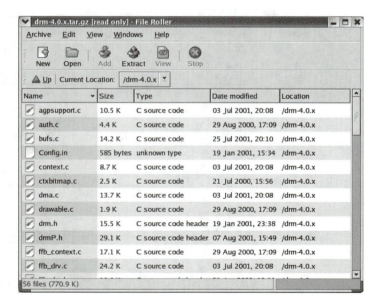

HANDHELD PDA

When you select Main Menu ➤ Accessories ➤ Handheld PDA, GNOME opens the Pilot Link utility described earlier in this chapter.

PRINT MANAGER

When you run Main Menu ➤ Accessories ➤ Print Manager, GNOME opens a print monitor that checks for documents in your print queue. If you want to know more about the applicable documents, click Edit ➤ Preferences. If you haven't configured a printer before, GNOME Print Manager starts the `redhat-config-printer` utility described in Chapter 25.

TEXT EDITOR

The `gedit` program is the standard GNOME GUI text editor. It's surprisingly versatile for a Linux text editor, especially when compared to `vi`. Figure 16.33 illustrates a `gedit` view of the `/etc/fstab` configuration file.

FIGURE 16.33

`gedit` at work

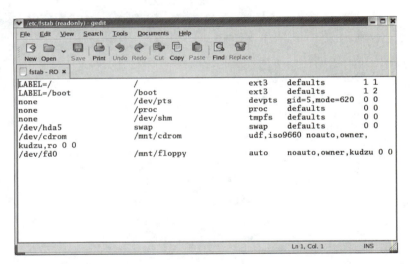

The `gedit` program is also quite customizable. Click Edit ➤ Preferences to open the Preferences menu. It allows you to customize the look and feel of text. For example, you can use it to modify fonts, colors, add line numbers, configure print settings, and add plugins.

VNC VIEWER

AT&T's Virtual Network Computing (VNC) provides a way to access remote graphical operating systems. You can start the VNC Client Viewer via Main Menu ➤ Accessories ➤ More Accessories ➤ VNC Viewer. VNC Viewer works in conjunction with a remote VNC Server.

The VNC Viewer program opens a small VNC Server window, where you can enter the IP address and password of the remote server. As you can see in Figure 16.34, I've used it to open up a fully functional view of a remote Windows 2000 computer.

FIGURE 16.34

VNC Viewer accesses remote operating systems.

Documentation

Red Hat Linux now includes a Documentation menu, which supports easy access to any Red Hat Linux 9 documents that you might have installed. You can access this menu via Main Menu ➢ Documentation as shown in Figure 16.35.

FIGURE 16.35

Documentation menu

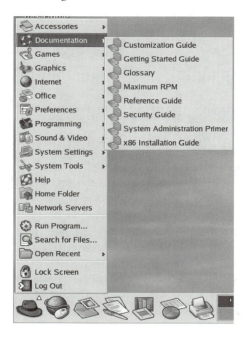

When you select one of the documents shown, Red Hat Linux opens it in the default web browser.

Games

If you've installed any standard GNOME or KDE games packages on your system, you'll be able to access them through Main Menu ➤ Games. We do not cover the startup or operation of any Linux games. There are some who believe that games can give Microsoft Windows users more comfort during any transition to Linux.

Internet Utilities

GNOME includes a number of utilities and applications for communicating on the Internet. The difference between a utility and an application in this case is somewhat arbitrary; we'll look at the Mozilla browser, the Ximian Evolution personal information manager, and the Gaim instant messaging (IM) utility in the Internet Applications section.

In this section, we'll examine more basic programs, including instant messengers, chat programs, and other miscellaneous connection utilities. Internet Utilities are accessible when you click Main Menu ➤ Internet; some are available through Main Menu ➤ Internet ➤ More Internet Applications, as shown in Figure 16.36. Many of these utilities were developed for KDE and will be covered in Chapter 17.

FIGURE 16.36

Internet menus

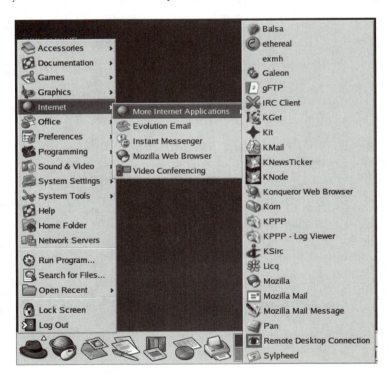

NOTE   *Many of the applications shown in Figure 16.36, such as Balsa and Ethereal, aren't part of GNOME or KDE and are covered in other chapters*

VIDEO CONFERENCING

You can start GnomeMeeting by selecting Main Menu ➤ Internet ➤ Video Conferencing. Gnome-Meeting is a fully featured H.323-compliant videoconferencing application. In other words, you can use it to connect to other videoconferencing clients, such as Microsoft's NetMeeting. It supports audio and video, which means you need a sound card and a "webcam" that is supported in Linux. The basic screen is shown in Figure 16.37.

FIGURE 16.37

GnomeMeeting

NOTE *For a list of supported webcams, see the Hardware HOWTO at* www.tldp.org/HOWTO/Hardware-HOWTO/other.html *and the QuickCam mini-HOWTO at* www.dkfz.de/Macromol/wedemann/mini-HOWTO-cqcam.html.

The first time you start GnomeMeeting, you should see a First Time Configuration Druid; otherwise, click Edit ➤ Configuration Druid to get the screen shown in Figure 16.38. You'll need your identifying information, your connection type (e.g., modem, ISDN, or DSL adapter), and sound and video device drivers. You can also use GnomeMeeting to connect your PC to the regular telephone network using a MicroTelco account from www.microtelco.com. You can modify your preferences later by clicking Edit ➤ Preferences.

EXMH

The exmh program is an X window user interface for for Unix-style e-mail mail handlers (MH). It's useful for searching through internal messages, as shown in Figure 16.39. If you have configured sendmail per Chapter 25, you'll be able to reply or forward any messages that you receive.

FIGURE 16.38

GnomeMeeting First
Time Configuration
Druid

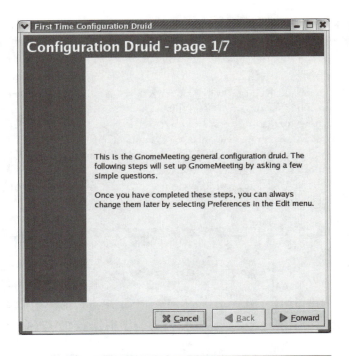

FIGURE 16.39

exmh handles mail.

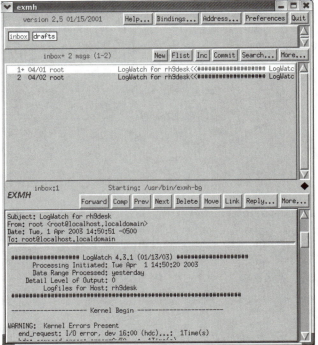

The first time you open exmh, it checks whether you have an MH account. If not, it goes through a wizard to set up your MH environment, and sets up a `.mh_profile` in your home directory.

GALEON

While the default Red Hat web browser is Mozilla, there's an alternative GNOME browser known as Galeon. The first time you open this browser, you're prompted to set it up using bookmarks from Netscape or Mozilla, toolbars, and proxy settings on your gateway (if any).

You can also integrate Galeon as the default client for normal (HTTP) web pages, secure (HTTPS) web pages, FTP sites, and GNOME help, and for browsing files in local directories.

As you can see in Figure 16.40, Galeon does not include Mozilla's functions in the left-hand pane; some might suggest that provides a cleaner interface. You can edit your preferences with the Settings ➤ Preferences command.

FIGURE 16.40

The GNOME Galeon browser

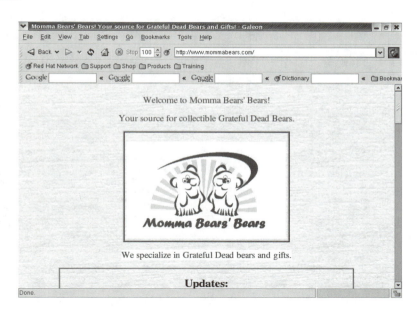

IRC

Linux includes an Internet Relay Chat (IRC) program, X-Chat, that allows access to many different chat servers, as you can see in Figure 16.41. Other groups may have their own IRC servers, which you can set up by clicking the New Server button.

Once you've configured X-Chat, select the chat server of your choice and click Connect. If the server is available, you're taken to a chat window similar to what is shown in Figure 16.42.

FIGURE 16.41

X-Chat and IRC

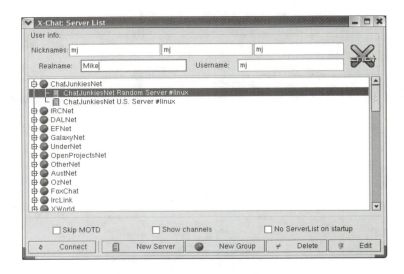

FIGURE 16.42

Chatting on IRC

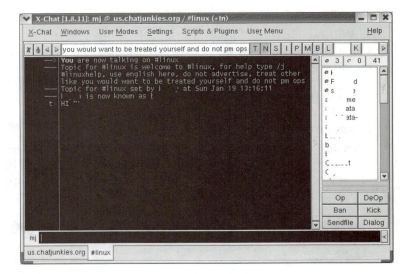

PAN

GNOME includes a graphical newsreader known as Pan. As shown in Figure 16.43, it allows you to read and post messages on different newsgroups.

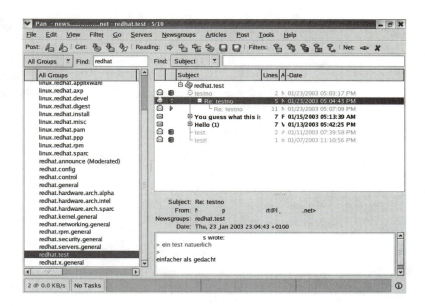

When you start Pan for the first time, you're prompted for basic login information, including your e-mail address, the SMTP server, and the name of the news server. If you're using sendmail on the local computer, you can use `localhost`; otherwise, use the outgoing e-mail server for your ISP.

If you want to change the look of your posts, click Tools ➢ Posting Profiles. If you want to change or add a news server, click Tools ➢ News Servers.

REMOTE DESKTOP CONNECTION

If you have a remote desktop server, you can connect to it with the Remote Desktop Connection utility, shown in Figure 16.44. It works with computers with VNC servers. The advantage of a remote desktop connection is that it takes you into a full-screen mode. Except for a small label at the top of the screen, your desktop environment appears identical to the remote computer.

FIGURE 16.44

Making a remote
desktop connection

SYLPHEED

Sylpheed is an e-mail client developed with the same basic tools as GNOME: GTK+ (GNOME Tool Kit). It's developed in Japan so it reportedly includes a strong Japanese language interface. It's a lightweight mail manager, unencumbered by any web browser. A configured version is shown in Figure 16.45.

FIGURE 16.45

The Sylpheed mail manager

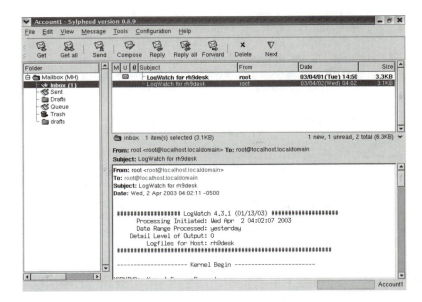

Sylpheed is fairly easy to configure. You start with the Configuration menu, which offers a series of menu command options, described in Table 16.3.

TABLE 16.3: SYLPHEED CONFIGURATION OPTIONS

OPTION	DESCRIPTION
Common Preferences	Includes folder locations, interfaces, reply defaults, auto-check times, and more
Filter Setting	Allows you to stop or forward messages with certain characteristics
Templates	Supports generic replies
Actions	Lets you specify commands, such as decoding for certain messages
Preferences For Current Account	Specifies the default account settings
Create New Account	Allows you to create a second e-mail account for Sylpheed
Edit Accounts	Lets you edit the settings for configured accounts
Change Current Account	Revises the default account

Internet Applications

In this section, we'll cover three basic applications commonly run by Linux users on the Internet. These are Red Hat default programs: the web browser, Mozilla; the Personal Information Manager, Evolution; and the Instant Messenger (IM) client, Gaim, which are accessible via Main Menu ➤ Internet.

MOZILLA

The default Red Hat web browser is Mozilla. It is a fully featured web browser, built on the code that Netscape re-released as open source in 1998. You can navigate between several features by clicking on the icons shown in the lower-left corner of the window (see Figure 16.46). From left to right, these icons are associated with a browser, mail and newsgroups reader, web page composer, address book, and IRC chat client.

FIGURE 16.46

Mozilla icons

Alternatively, there are control keys associated with each of these features, as described in Table 16.4.

TABLE 16.4: MOZILLA FEATURES

FUNCTION	FEATURE
Ctrl+1	Navigator (the browser)
Ctrl+2	Mail and Newsgroups
Ctrl+3	IRC Chat
Ctrl+4	Composer
Ctrl+5	Address Book

NOTE   When Marc Andreesen was working on the Netscape Web browser, the leading browser was Mosaic, and he wanted a "Mosaic Godzilla," which became the code name for the browser project: Mozilla.

The Mozilla Browser

The default Mozilla web browser has the same look and feel as Netscape, as shown in Figure 16.47. It includes commands associated with Netscape, such as the What's Related sidebar.

FIGURE 16.47

The Mozilla web
browser

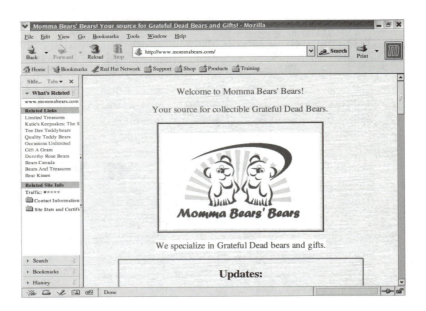

You can customize various Mozilla settings. Click Edit ➤ Preferences to open the Preferences
window shown in Figure 16.48. The options should be familiar to Netscape users.

FIGURE 16.48

Setting Mozilla
preferences

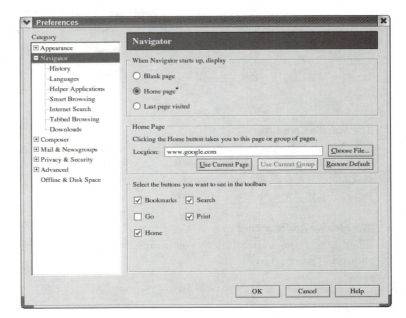

The Mozilla Mail and Newsgroup Reader

When you open the Mozilla Mail and Newsgroup reader for the first time, you're prompted to set up an e-mail or newsgroup account. If you want to add additional accounts, click Edit ➤ Mail And Newsgroups Account Settings. In the window that opens, click Add Account.

For an e-mail account, you need your name, e-mail address, incoming POP or IMAP e-mail servers, and your outgoing SMTP server. You should be able to get this information from the ISP associated with your e-mail address. More information on these mail protocols is available in Chapter 26.

Once configured, Mozilla includes hyperlinks for basic functions, as shown in Figure 16.49.

FIGURE 16.49

Mozilla and e-mail

The Mozilla Composer

The Mozilla Composer allows you to create and edit web pages. For example, the code shown in Figure 16.50 comes from the help files associated with the `redhat-config-httpd` utility. As you can see, you can review the web page in a normal view, with HTML tags, from the HTML source code, and preview how it will look in a browser.

The Mozilla Address Book

The Mozilla address book allows you to collect a variety of information for each of your contacts, as shown in Figure 16.51.

FIGURE 16.50

The Mozilla Composer

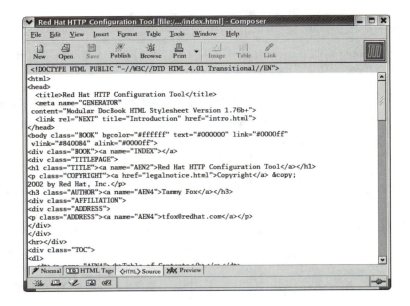

FIGURE 16.51

A Mozilla address book entry

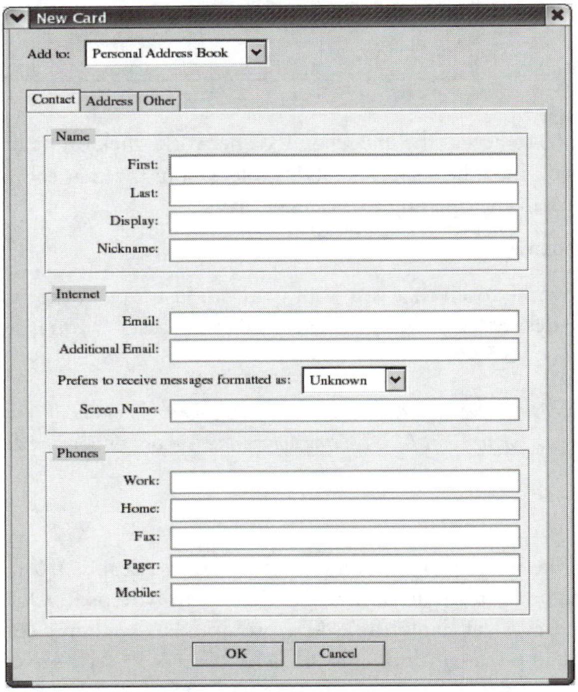

The Mozilla Chat Client

Mozilla chat, also known as ChatZilla!, is a link-based program. When you start Mozilla chat, you should see the screen shown in Figure 16.52. You can click on one of the Available Networks, which are actually in blue in a ChatZilla screen.

FIGURE 16.52

ChatZilla!

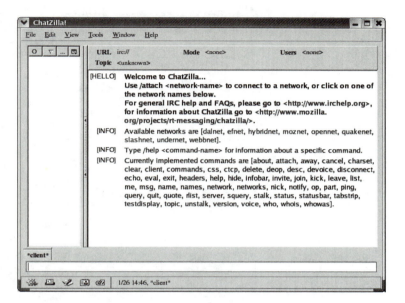

For example, to access the undernet IRC network, click on its link in the ChatZilla! window. Once it logs you into the server, you'll be able to join the chat room of your choice. In some cases, you'll see a link in the opening messages, such as

```
/join #phoenix
```

If you know the room that you want, you can just type in the associated command; in this case, substitute the desired chat room for phoenix. If successful, you'll see a room with users such as that shown in Figure 16.53.

TIP *If your chat client does not respond, you may have blocked communication with a firewall. You may be able to set up chat communications through port 6667, using appropriate* iptables *commands as described in Chapter 22.*

EVOLUTION

While the name of the program on the GNOME desktop is Evolution Email, it is so much more. It serves as a personal information manager, similar to Microsoft Outlook.

When you first start Evolution, you're prompted to configure your profile. Evolution can handle all types of standard e-mail, including POP, IMAP, and MH-style servers. It also requires that you identify your time zone, and it prompts you to import your address book and e-mail from other formats.

As you can see in Figure 16.54, the Evolution summary view lists the status of your local weather, e-mail, appointments, and upcoming tasks. One additional useful feature for Linux administrators is a list of the latest Red Hat errata.

FIGURE 16.53

Communicating with ChatZilla!

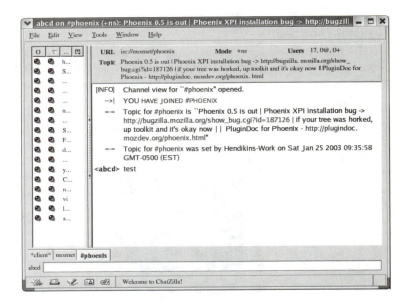

FIGURE 16.54

Ximian Evolution

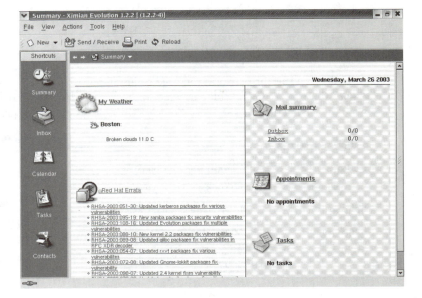

NOTE *Ximian (*`www.ximian.com`*) is an important player on the Linux desktop, developing GUI desktop tools for the Enterprise. They've also launched the Mono project, which is working toward an open source implementation of Microsoft's .NET platform.*

INSTANT MESSENGER

GNOME includes an instant messenger (IM) client, suitable for connections to a variety of servers, including those provided by America Online (AOL), Yahoo!, and the Microsoft Network (MSN). The official acronym is Gaim, which is short for a GNU version of some popular IM program (which I should not name). In reality, the acronym does not do Gaim justice, as unlike the proprietary IM programs, Gaim uses plug-ins, which are essentially program adapters, to connect to several different types of IM networks. The Gaim login screen is shown in Figure 16.55.

FIGURE 16.55

Gaim login screen

To access a specific network, you need to install one of the configured plug-ins. In Gaim, click Plugins to open the Gaim - Plugins window. In that window, click Load, which lists available plug-ins in the `/usr/lib/gaim` directory. Some of the more popular plug-ins are shown in Table 16.5.

TABLE 16.5: GAIM PLUG-INS

PLUGIN	INSTANT MESSAGE NETWORK
libicq.so	ICQ (a.k.a.: "I seek you")
libirc.so	Internet Relay Chat (IRC)
libmsn.so	Microsoft Network (MSN)
libyahoo.so	Yahoo! Messenger

For details on required login information, consult the IM provider of your choice. The Screen Name corresponds to your account; the Alias is what is typically seen in the IM chat area.

Preferences

Most of the utilities associated with the Main Menu ➤ Preferences submenu were covered earlier in this chapter, in the discussion on the GNOME Control Center. This section deals with the utilities associated with the Main Menu ➤ Preferences ➤ More Preferences submenu. These menus are shown in Figure 16.56.

FIGURE 16.56

Preferences menus

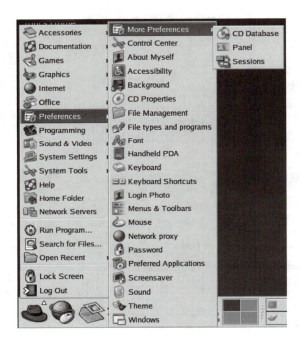

CD DATABASE

There are a series of CD Database (CDDB) servers that provide additional information about your favorite music CDs. When you open the CD Database Preferences window, you can configure access to these servers. Some are available through `www.freedb.org`; the home page for CDDB is `www.gracenote.com`.

PANEL

The Panel Preferences window allows you to configure the behavior of the GNOME panel, as well as any *drawers* that you configure within the panel. A drawer is similar to a Main Menu button, where you can configure links to the applications and menus of your choice.

SESSIONS

The Sessions window allows you to configure the programs that start when you enter the GNOME desktop. It also allows you to configure the behavior when GNOME starts, and monitors currently loaded programs. As shown in Figure 16.57, the window contains three tabs, described in Table 16.6.

FIGURE 16.57

GNOME Sessions management

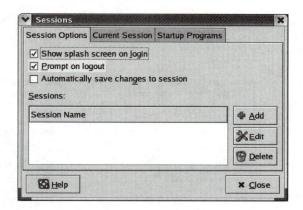

TABLE 16.6: GNOME SESSIONS

TAB	DESCRIPTION
Session Options	Manages behavior during the GNOME login and logout process
Current Session	Lists currently running programs in GNOME
Startup Programs	Notes the programs that start when GNOME starts

Multimedia

Several GNOME multimedia applications are available when you click Main Menu ➤ Sound & Video. As shown in Figure 16.58, these include various audio and CD players and sound control utilities. Some of the multimedia applications shown in this menu are associated with KDE and are therefore addressed in Chapter 17.

AUDIO PLAYER

The Audio Player is the X Multimedia System (XMMS). While the Media Player itself looks unimposing (see Figure 16.59), it allows you to set up a virtual recording studio where you can mix different sounds.

CD PLAYER

The GNOME CD Player is an easy-to-use player for audio CDs. As shown in Figure 16.60, it has the standard buttons that allow you to play and move between CD tracks.

FIGURE 16.58

Multimedia menus

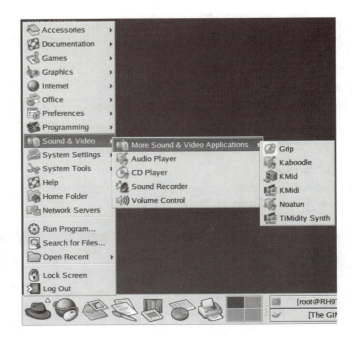

FIGURE 16.59

X Multimedia
System

FIGURE 16.60

GNOME CD Player

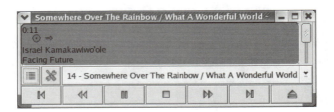

If you click on the name of the song, you'll be able to select the song of your choice from the CD tracklist. The two buttons to the left of the song name allow you to edit the track database and manage the preferences for the CD Player.

SOUND RECORDER

The Sound Recorder performs as advertised; it allows you to record sounds that come in through the sound card microphone port. You can also play any .wav file sounds that you've recorded. In addition, it includes a mixing function that lets you control the volume from multiple sources.

VOLUME CONTROL

The gnome-volume-control utility allows you to control the volume to and from a number of sources, as shown in Figure 16.61.

FIGURE 16.61

GNOME Volume Control

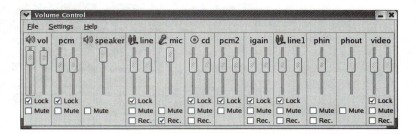

GRIP

Grip (GNOME rip) is a GNOME CD player and burner. It can take the tracks of your choice from CDs or downloads, and it allows you to configure the music of your choice for CD recording, in the desired order. As you can see in Figure 16.62, it includes several configuration tabs as well as standard CD functions at the bottom of the window. The tabs are briefly described in Table 16.7.

TABLE 16.7: GRIP CONFIGURATION TABS

TAB	DESCRIPTION
Track	Lists the audio tracks on the CD; double-click on a title to add it to the "Rip" list.
Rip	Allows you to record the audio tracks of your choice.
Config	Includes various configuration parameters for the CD, default recorders, encoders, and more.
Help	Displays help buttons related to various Grip functions.
About	Lists the version and home page for Grip.

FIGURE 16.62

The Grip CD player and burner

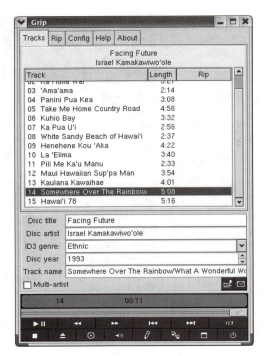

Files are normally saved in `.ogg` format in the `~/ogg` directory, and the `.m3u` format in a subdirectory associated with the name of the artist.

NOTE   *We do not in any way encourage or endorse the recording of music for illegal purposes. We only document the capabilities of various Linux programs in this book.*

System Tools

There are a wide variety of system tools available. Many are `redhat-config-*` tools which are primarily covered in Chapter 19. Others are covered in this section. The System Tools menus are shown in Figure 16.63.

X CD WRITER

The X-CD-Roast tool shown in Figure 16.64 allows you to copy and write music and data CDs. Before you use X-CD-Roast, you should first configure it from its Main Menu by clicking Setup. This allows you to verify detection of your CDs, modify the location of recorded image files, and more.

FIGURE 16.63

System Tools menus

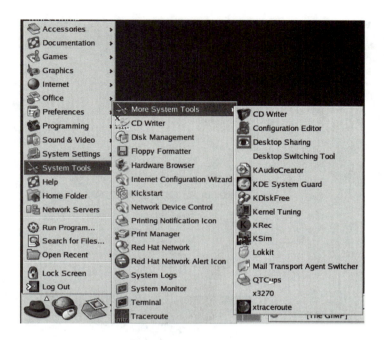

FIGURE 16.64

X-CD-Roast

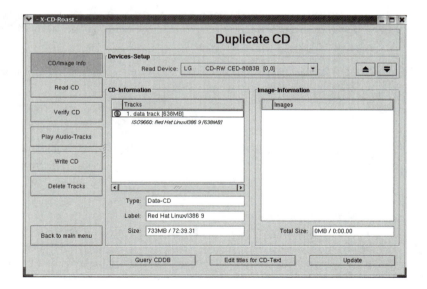

DISK MANAGEMENT

The User Mount Tool, shown in Figure 16.65, illustrates the current state of various Linux filesystems, based on `/etc/fstab`. You can use it to mount or format a filesystem such as `/mnt/floppy`.

FIGURE 16.65

The User Mount Tool

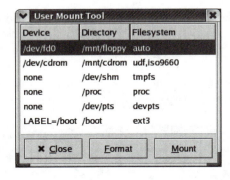

FLOPPY FORMATTER

The `gfloppy` tool allows you to format disks on an installed floppy drive. It allows you to select from installed floppy drives, specify data format and size, name the volume, and format in various modes.

HARDWARE BROWSER

The Hardware Browser illustrates detected devices on your computer, as shown in Figure 16.66. This browser is for information only; no configuration is possible in this window.

FIGURE 16.66

The Hardware Browser

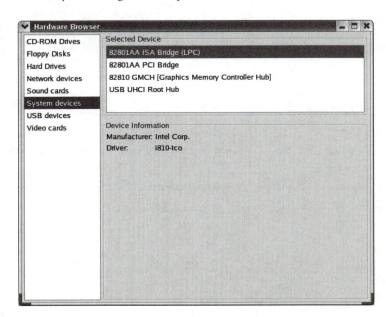

PRINTING NOTIFICATION ICON

When you select the Printing Notification Icon, you're activating drag-and-drop printing.

PRINT MANAGER

The GNOME Print Manager allows you to control and manage printers and print jobs. If you don't have any configured printers, it starts the `redhat-config-printers` utilty, which is covered in Chapter 25.

RED HAT NETWORK

The Red Hat Network configuration tool, shown in Figure 16.67, sets defaults for your `up2date` connection to the Red Hat network management servers. It includes three tabs, as described in Table 16.8.

FIGURE 16.67

Red Hat Network
Configuration

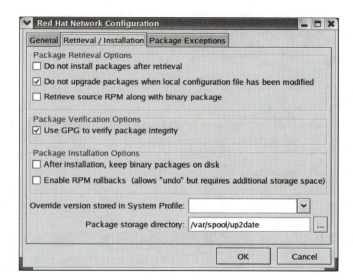

TABLE 16.8: RED HAT NETWORK CONFIGURATION TABS

TAB	DESCRIPTION
General	Cites the path to the secure Red Hat Network server, and any proxy services that might be required on your network
Removal / Installation	Configures settings for package retrieval, installation, and verification
Package Exceptions	Sets RPM packages and files to skip during the up2date process

NOTE *For more information on the Red Hat Network, see Chapters 3 and 10.*

RED HAT NETWORK ALERT ICON

The Red Hat Network Alert Icon utility adds a circular icon to your taskbar. One alert icon should already be there by default. The icon you see may include one of the following:

◆ A blue check mark indicates that the packages on your system are up to date.

◆ A green pair of arrows tells you that your system is communicating with the Red Hat Network.

◆ A red exclamation point lets you know that your system does not include the latest packages, according to the Red Hat Network.

SYSTEM MONITOR

The GNOME System Monitor allows you to monitor current processes, as well as CPU and swap partition usage. It's a customizable front end to the **top** command. The System Monitor tab illustrating system loads is shown in Figure 16.68.

FIGURE 16.68

GNOME System
Monitor

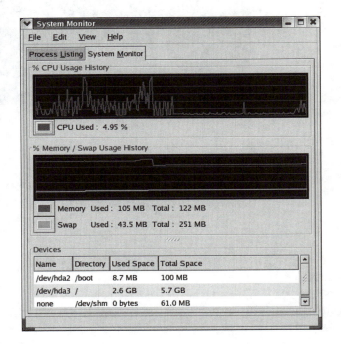

TERMINAL

GNOME Terminal is the standard command-line interface used on the GNOME desktop. With its black-on-white interface, it is easy to read; I've used it in most of the command-line based screenshots in this book.

TRACEROUTE

There are two system tools related to the `traceroute` command, which maps the path of your data from your computer to the destination. Figure 16.69 uses `xtraceroute` to illustrate the path of a connection between my computer in the United States to the website for Egypt Air.

FIGURE 16.69

Tracing a
network route

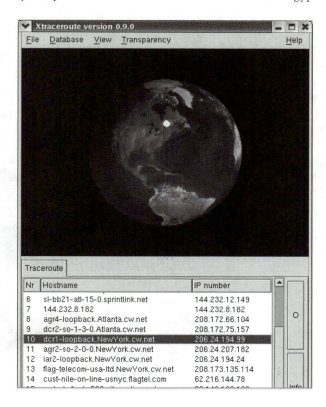

CD WRITER

The GNOME CD Writer is known as Gnome Toaster, as shown in Figure 16.70. It allows you to configure audio and data CDs. It includes an extensive array of preferences, and supports "drag and drop" copying.

CONFIGURATION EDITOR

GConf is in a sense a GNOME configurator for all the settings stored in users' home directories. Microsoft Windows users may recognize the Registry-style interfaces shown in Figure 16.71, and revisions can be nearly as dangerous to your ability to run GNOME. However, it is an all-in-one interface that allows you to edit GNOME settings without opening every last GNOME application.

More information on the workings of GConf is available from `developer.gnome.org/feature/archive/gconf/gconf.html`.

FIGURE 16.70

The GnomeToaster

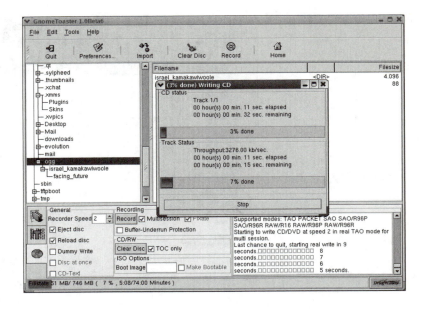

FIGURE 16.71

The GConf Editor

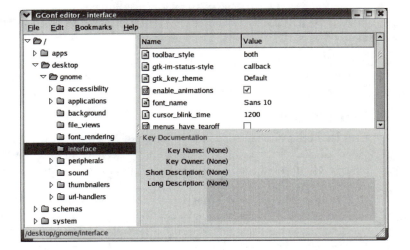

LOKKIT

The `lokkit` utility helps you configure firewalls. At the command-line interface, `lokkit` is functionally similar to the `redhat-config-firewall` tool described in Chapter 19. However, from the Main Menu button, it starts a firewall wizard that guides you through the configuration process. One example is shown in Figure 16.72, which allows you to let people on other computers access your local web server.

FIGURE 16.72
lokkit helps you configure a firewall.

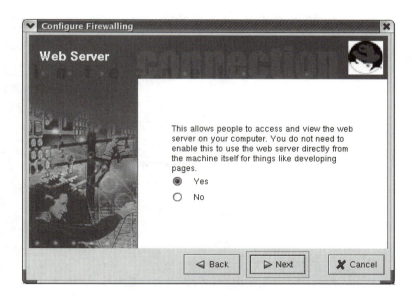

One weakness of the GUI version of lokkit is that it does not give you a chance to customize access through additional TCP/IP ports. For more information on firewalls, see Chapter 22.

x3270
The x3270 utility starts a terminal suitable for accessing IBM mainframe computers. It includes the function keys commonly associated with mainframe terminals.

Summary

This has been a basic introduction to the GNOME desktop, the default GUI for Red Hat Linux. GNOME includes many of the same tools that you might find in Microsoft Windows, and more. In fact, you can distribute open applications on four different desktops. It's easy to configure the GNOME desktop to your needs.

A substantial number of extras are available through GNOME. This includes a wide variety of software that could easily cost you hundreds of dollars. It includes the accessories that you need every day. The Internet applications consist of browsers, e-mail managers, and chat clients. The Sound and Video utilities allow you to manage, process, and record multimedia. And GNOME includes a number of system tools that help administrators manage their systems.

In the next chapter, we'll look at the most common Linux GUI desktop alternative, the K Desktop Environment (KDE). If you've used KDE before, you'll see how Red Hat has customized it with a similar look and feel to GNOME.

Chapter 17

KDE

As THERE ARE OTHER Linux distributions, there are other Linux GUI desktops. Perhaps the main alternative to GNOME is KDE, the K Desktop Environment. Both are quite popular among Linux users. In fact, many Linux users, myself included, prefer KDE. While the Red Hat default is GNOME, all of the major Linux distributions allow you to install either desktop environment.

Red Hat has integrated the "Bluecurve" theme into its implementations of both GNOME and KDE. It also has integrated a number of common tools into the main menus of both desktops. In Red Hat Linux, the two desktops are converging in functionality. Thus, your choice of desktop is a matter of personal preference.

While the rivalry between KDE and GNOME isn't as intense as, say, between Linux and Microsoft Windows, the desktops do come from different development environments. KDE uses the Qt toolkit , which was fairly recently released under open source licenses. Most KDE development is centered in Europe, which contributes to its popularity outside of North America. For example, KDE is being adapted by the government of the Federal Republic of Germany as its default desktop GUI.

In this chapter, we'll cover the basics of the KDE interface, along with the custom utilities associated with KDE. We'll take a detailed look at the capabilities of the KDE Control Center. As you'll see in this chapter, the people behind KDE have developed a number of excellent administrative tools that I believe rival the `redhat-config-*` tools in quality.

In addition, the Red Hat implementation of KDE allows you to use GNOME applications and utilities, which we covered in Chapter 16. If you've read Chapter 16, you'll see a lot of similarities in this chapter, which reflect Red Hat's work toward standardizing the Linux GUI. KDE (as well as GNOME and `redhat-config-*`) tools are easily accessible directly through the KDE K Menu button. This chapter covers the following topics:

- ◆ Working with the basic KDE interface
- ◆ Using the KDE Control Center
- ◆ Learning about KDE utilities

Working with the Basic KDE Interface

The standard KDE desktop has the same characteristics of other major GUI operating systems. It includes a panel, a K Menu button, and icons. You can customize each of these components to meet your own needs; alternatively, you can even configure a standard interface for your KDE installations. You can control and customize KDE's look and feel through the KDE Control Center. If you've installed and have set KDE as your default desktop, you'll probably start with a view similar to Figure 17.1.

NOTE *In Linux, the panel is functionally similar to the taskbar in Microsoft Windows. The K Menu button (represented by the red hat) corresponds functionally to the Microsoft Start button; in GNOME, it's called the Main Menu button. Red Hat uses the terms interchangeably; I do in this chapter as well.*

FIGURE 17.1

The KDE desktop

An Overview of KDE

The basic KDE interface is also quite simple. As you can see in Figure 17.1, it includes a Trash icon, a floppy disk manager, direct access to your home directory, and access to a Start Here directory. All of these icons use Konqueror, which is an "Explorer"-style graphical shell that you can use to manage your files as well as your KDE configuration. While the default Red Hat web browser is still Mozilla, Konqueror was developed by the KDE project.

When you start KDE for the first time, you'll see "Kandalf's Useful Tips." These tips are for the most part quite useful even for less experienced computer users.

NOTE *You'll find the middle mouse button useful in KDE. Try it on the desktop. What do you see? Try it again on an icon. What happens?*

In the following sections, we'll examine the buttons on the panel and the KDE Control Center.

THE KDE PANEL

The KDE panel is one place where you can call up a number of applications, switch between open programs, and even switch between open desktops. I've included a view of my KDE panel in Figure 17.2. In this case, the KDE panel includes six icons on the left, which are briefly described in Table 17.1.

NOTE *In KDE, there are four standard desktops, which are also known as* workspaces. *Each workspace gets its own icons and open programs. You don't see all four workspaces at once; the data for three are stored in spare video memory. You'll see later that KDE desktops are easily customizable.*

FIGURE 17.2

The KDE panel

TABLE 17.1: KDE PANEL ICONS

ICON	DESCRIPTION
	Clicking on this button opens the KDE Main Menu, which provides access to available programs and utilities; it works like the Start button in Microsoft Windows.
	Opens the Mozilla web browser.
	Starts the Evolution personal information manager; similar to Microsoft Outlook.
	Begins the OpenOffice Writer; similar to Microsoft Word.
	Opens the OpenOffice Impress presentation manager; similar to Microsoft PowerPoint.
	Starts the OpenOffice Calc spreadsheet program; similar to Microsoft Excel.
	Begins the GNOME Print Manager.

NOTE *The OpenOffice suite of applications is officially known as OpenOffice.org, or OOo, and is released under the GNU General Public License and the Sun Industry Standards Source Licence.*

KDE WORKSPACES AND OPEN PROGRAMS

KDE is flexible. You can place open windows in several different workspaces. So instead of opening and closing windows, you can just switch workspaces to get to your various applications. For example,

I can have The GIMP image program in one workspace, the OpenOffice Calc spreadsheet program in a second, a terminal window in a third, and OpenOffice Writer in a fourth workspace. A view of the four workspaces is shown in a thumbnail on the panel, as shown in Figure 17.3. Note that the active workspace is highlighted.

FIGURE 17.3

Four KDE
workspaces

To switch to another workspace, click on its corresponding thumbnail. To move an application to another workspace, click on the upper-left corner of the application. In the drop-down menu that appears, select To Desktop. You'll see the drop-down menu shown in Figure 17.4.

FIGURE 17.4

Moving to
Workspace 2

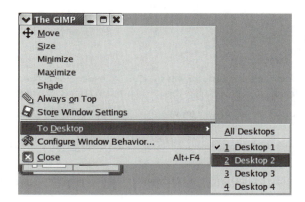

You can also switch between the open applications shown on the panel. For example, Figure 17.5 illustrates a screen where you can switch between three open applications.

FIGURE 17.5

Switching between
applications

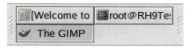

OTHER KDE PANEL ITEMS

Finally, on the far right of the panel are three more icons. The clipboard with a "K" is known as Klipper, the KDE clipboard tool, which allows you to copy and paste between applications. To configure Klipper, right-click on its panel icon and select Configure Klipper from the resulting menu.

The next space may include one of three icons: a red circle with an exclamation point, which means that you should connect to the Red Hat Network to check for updates; a green circle with arrows, which means your system is communicating with the Red Hat Network; or a blue check mark, which means your system is up-to-date. You can right-click the icon to check or configure your connection to the Red Hat Network. See the up2date section in Chapter 10 for more information on keeping your system up-to-date with the latest changes. Depending on running applications, you may find other icons in this area.

If you left-click on the time on the panel, you'll see the calendar for the current month; if you right-click on this area, you'll open a menu where you can configure the look and feel of the clock, the time zone, and the format.

It's easy to customize the KDE panel. Right-click on an open area of the panel and select Panel Menu ➢ Configure Panel. You'll see the KDE Control Module window, shown in Figure 17.6.

FIGURE 17.6

KDE's panel control module

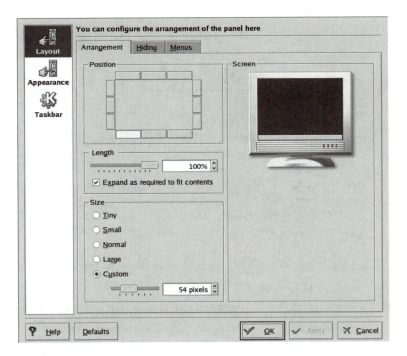

There are a number of things that you can do with the properties of your KDE panel. They are all related to the look, feel, and location of the panel, as well as the contents of the Main Menu commands.

The KDE Main Menu

Now we'll take a look at the KDE Main Menu. Click on the red hat in the lower-left corner of the desktop. You should see a menu similar to that shown in Figure 17.7.

FIGURE 17.7

The KDE
Main Menu

As you can see, the KDE Main Menu opens a series of other commands and menus. They are briefly described in Table 17.2. Some of these menus are covered in more detail in this and other chapters. Many programs under these menus are specifically associated with GNOME and are covered in Chapter 16. Major applications from this menu, such as office suites and graphics, will be covered in Chapter 18. Red Hat–specific administration tools will be covered in Chapter 19. Linux games are not covered in this book.

The three applets shown atop the KDE Main Menu in Figure 17.7 are recently used applications. By default, KDE stores up to the five most recently used applications.

TABLE 17.2: KDE MAIN MENU COMMANDS AND SUBMENUS

MENU OR COMMAND	DESCRIPTION
Accessories	Opens a group of small programs, such as text editors and calculators.
Documentation	Navigates to Red Hat documentation; described in Chapter 16.
Games	Moves to KDE or GNOME games that you may have installed.
Graphics	Accesses graphics applications for editing, screenshots, faxes, PDF readers, and more.
Internet	Includes a series of applications that you can use to communicate on a TCP/IP network such as the Internet.
Office	Opens a group of applications associated with the Open Office suite of programs; KOffice is also available through this menu, under the More Office Applications submenu.

Continued on next page

TABLE 17.2: KDE Main Menu Commands and Submenus *(continued)*

MENU OR COMMAND	DESCRIPTION
Other	Includes an interesting variety of KDE tools; many are useful in education.
Preferences	Allows you to customize your settings; mostly related to the desktop.
Programming	Opens access to a group of programming tools; strangely enough, Emacs is part of this group.
Sound & Video	Adds multimedia applications, including a CD writer.
System Settings	Includes access to many `redhat-config-*` administrative utilities; most require root-level access.
System Tools	Starts a menu with a variety of administrative tools, including many created for KDE.
Control Center	Opens the KDE Control Center, which is a nearly all-in-one configuration and information tool.
Find Files	Begins a find utility for files; lets you search within files and view their properties.
Help	Opens a KDE help session in a simplified browser.
Home	Starts Konqueror with a view of the files in your home directory.
Run Command	Opens a Run Command dialog box where you can type in the text name for an application.
Lock Screen	Starts a secure screensaver; to return to the desktop, you need your password.
Log Out	Exits KDE.

If you don't see a specific menu, you may not have installed the associated package(s). For example, you won't see a Games menu unless you've installed associated packages such as `kdegames-*` or `gnome-games-*`.

The KDE Control Center

Now we'll look at a fairly comprehensive configuration tool, the KDE Control Center. It allows you to configure the desktop—and a lot more. You can open it from the Main Menu: click Main Menu ➢ Control Center. This opens the Control Center window, shown in Figure 17.8. As you can see, the Control Center allows you to configure your computer in a number of areas, from Appearance & Themes to Web Browsing. Each tool in these areas will be covered in the following sections.

Whenever you make a configuration change, you should click the Apply button to write the changes to your `~/.kde` directory. (As described in Chapter 8, the ~ represents your home directory).

NOTE *Some applets in the KDE Control Center require administrative access. If you're working as a regular user (not root), you'll see an Administrator Mode button when required. If you want to make changes to these types of settings, click the Administrator Mode button and enter the root password in the Run As Root window that appears.*

FIGURE 17.8

The KDE Control
Center

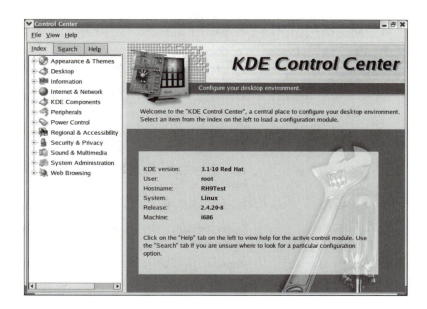

Appearance & Themes

The Appearance & Themes section of the KDE Control Center allows you to customize the look and feel of your KDE desktop. You can use the various functions shown in Figure 17.9 to customize everything from the desktop background to the look and feel of your windows (Window Decorations).

FIGURE 17.9

Appearance &
Themes

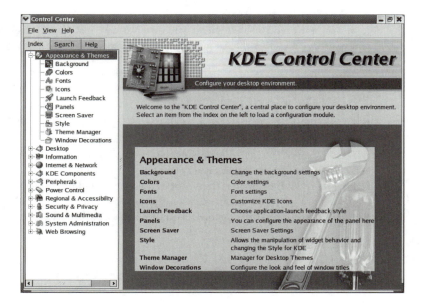

Background   The Background applet allows you to modify the look and feel of each desktop. In KDE, these are easily customizable. Unless you've activated the Common Background option in Figure 17.10, you can configure a different background and wallpaper for each desktop.

FIGURE 17.10

Configuring Desktop Backgrounds

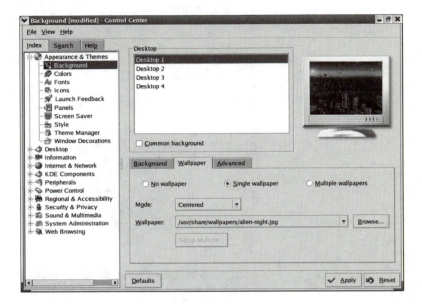

Colors   The Colors applet allows you to configure any number of color schemes for windows, title bars, menus, buttons, links, and more. There are over 25 color schemes available, and it's possible to import additional schemes, as shown in Figure 17.11.

Fonts   The Fonts applet allows you to configure different fonts for different types of locations on the KDE desktop, from menus, task bars, window titles, and more.

Icons   With the Icons applet, you can select from several icon themes for the KDE desktop.

Launch Feedback   The Launch Feedback applet is normally configured to show a busy cursor while a large program, such as OpenOffice, is loading on your desktop.

Panels   You can configure different colors for each button on your panel. Different colors are possible for the K Menu button, applications, window lists, and more on the panel. Tooltips provide a brief description of an icon after you've hovered a cursor above it.

Screen Saver   KDE is configured with a wide variety of screensavers, as shown in Figure 17.12. You can set the screensaver to start after a fixed period of inactivity, and require a password to return to your desktop.

FIGURE 17.11

Configuring
desktop colors

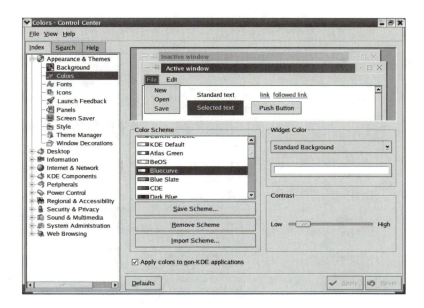

FIGURE 17.12

Configuring a
screensaver

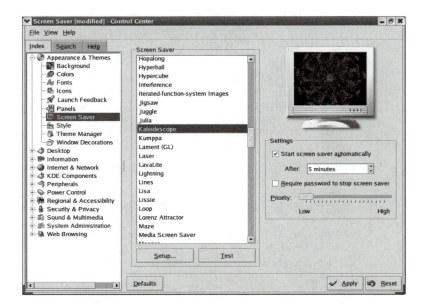

Style KDE allows you to configure the style associated with tabs, buttons, checkboxes, and more. You can select from about 20 different styles, and then configure different effects for the style of your choice.

Theme Manager You can configure an overall look and feel for your desktop with different themes, as shown in Figure 17.13. While the Bluecurve theme is the default on Red Hat KDE desktops, you can configure the theme of your choice, and customize where it applies on your desktop.

FIGURE 17.13

Configuring a theme for your KDE desktop

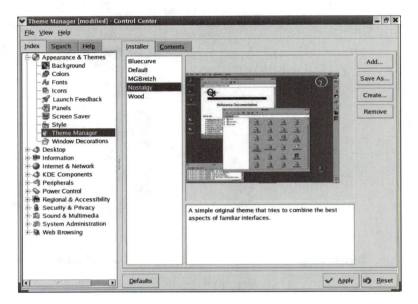

Window Decorations You can set up a different look and feel for window and title borders with the Window Decorations applet. Once again, the default theme is Red Hat's Bluecurve.

Desktop

The Desktop section of the KDE Control Center is essentially a continuation of the Appearance & Themes section, since it also allows you to customize the look and feel of your KDE desktop. You can use the functions shown in Figure 17.14 to customize everything from the font to the response of different windows to your mouse.

Appearance With the Appearance applet, you can set the standard font and text color for your KDE desktop.

Behavior Through the Behavior applet (see Figure 17.15) you can customize the look and feel of icons on the desktop and within file manager views in Konqueror. You can also customize the response to mouse clicks, as well as the device icons shown on the desktop.

Multiple Desktops By default, KDE includes four desktops. Through the Multiple Desktops applet, you can configure KDE with up to 16 different desktops.

FIGURE 17.14
The Desktop
control

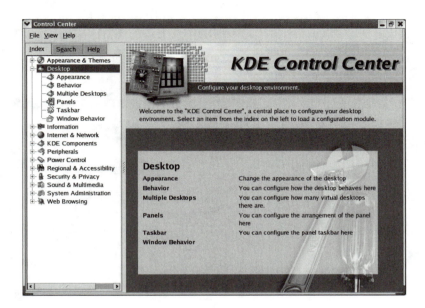

FIGURE 17.15
Desktop behavior

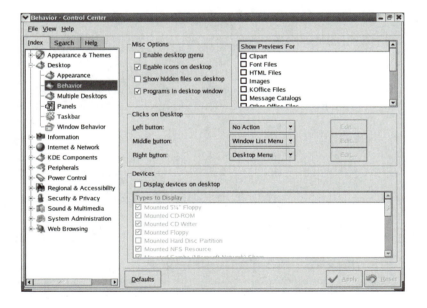

Panels   With the Panels applet, you can set the position and length of the panel, as well as the size of associated icons. You can set up the panel to be hidden. You're also allowed to set up different settings on the K Menu. The Panels applet is shown in Figure 17.16.

FIGURE 17.16

Customizing panels

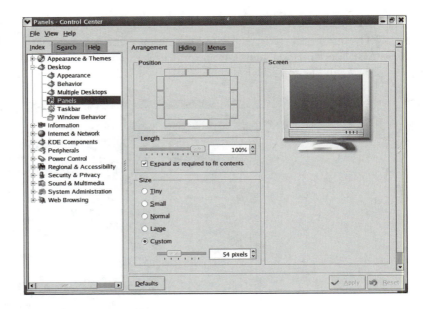

Taskbar   The Taskbar applet lets you determine the behavior of open applications, as well as the actions associated with left, middle, and right mouse button clicks.

Window Behavior   With the Window Behavior applet shown in Figure 17.17, you can customize how open windows respond to the mouse cursor and to being moved. Advanced settings allow you to set animation characteristics for open windows.

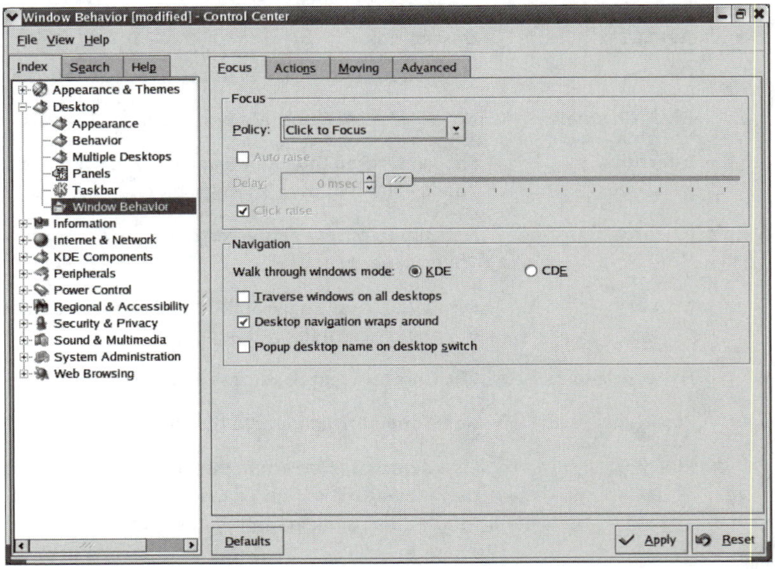

FIGURE 17.17

Setting window behavior

Information

The Information section of the KDE Control Center is essentially a graphical view of detected hardware system information, mostly from your **/proc** directory, described in Chapter 11. The list of hardware shown in Figure 17.18 is described in Table 17.3.

FIGURE 17.18

Hardware information

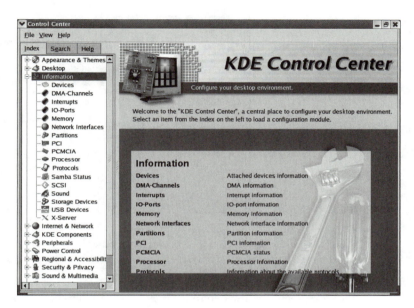

TABLE 17.3: KDE CONTROL CENTER HARDWARE INFORMATION

APPLET	DESCRIPTION
Devices	Lists detected device files from /proc/devices and /proc/misc.
DMA-Channels	Notes occupied Direct Memory Address channels; information is taken from /proc/dma.
Interrupts	Shows all taken Interrupt Request (IRQ) channels; information is taken from /proc/interrupts.
IO-Ports	Lists input/output addresses and associated hardware; information is taken from /proc/iports.
Memory	Displays current usage of RAM and swap space. Uses data from the top command; used in /proc/meminfo.
Network Interfaces	Illustrates current IP address and status information for detected network adapters.
Partitions	Notes directories mounted through /etc/fstab.
PCI	Lists detected PCI (Peripheral Component Interconnect) cards, controllers, and bridges; may include unconfigured hardware such as second network cards and Winmodems. Information is taken from /proc/pci.

Continued on next page

TABLE 17.3: KDE CONTROL CENTER HARDWARE INFORMATION *(continued)*

APPLET	DESCRIPTION
PCMCIA	Shows available controllers associated with laptop computers. PCMCIA devices are built to Personal Computer Memory Card International Association standards; they're also known as PC Cards. Information is taken from `/proc/pci`.
Processor	Displays the characteristics of detected CPUs; information is taken from `/proc/cpuinfo`.
Protocols	Provides definition for a number of protocols; an example is shown in Figure 17.19.
Samba Status	Illustrates Samba client and server connections, from other computers to shared Samba directories.
SCSI	Notes attached SCSI (Small Computer System Interface) devices.
Sound	Lists information associated with your sound card.
Storage Devices	Displays mounted storage devices, local and network; reflects the `mount` command.
USB Devices	Shows installed USB hardware.
X-Server	Illustrates your graphics configuration; information is taken from `/etc/X11/XF86Config`.

FIGURE 17.19

The KDE Control Center explains protocols.

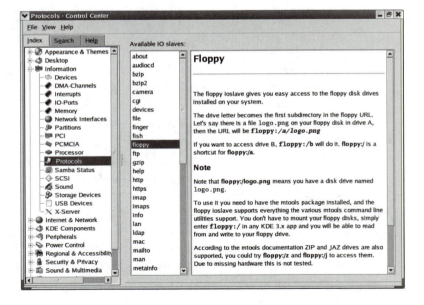

Internet & Network

The Internet & Network section of the KDE Control Center allows you to configure parameters for your network and shared directories. You can use the functions shown in Figure 17.20 to customize everything from your e-mail defaults to proxy servers. If you click on an item in this section and get an error message, you probably have not installed the associated package.

FIGURE 17.20

Internet & Network

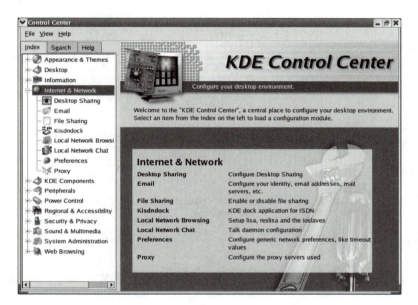

Desktop Sharing   The KDE Desktop Sharing applet is intended to support VNC (Virtual Network Computing) services (see Chapter 16). It is intended to allow others to make remote connections to your GUI.

Email   The Email applet allows you to create basic defaults for your outgoing e-mail, including name, e-mail address, organization, the reply-to address, and the outgoing (SMTP) mail server.

File Sharing   If you enable file sharing, users will be allowed to share files from their home directories over a network. Allowed methods include NFS (the Network File System described in Chapter 28) and Samba (described in Chapter 29).

Kisdndock   This applet allows you to configure any installed ISDN devices. ISDN (Integrated Services Digital Network) is an option for digital Internet connections that works nominally at about twice the speed of a regular telephone modem. Because ISDN is popular in Europe, it is not surprising that KDE, which is mostly developed in Europe, provides solid ISDN support.

Local Network Browsing   The Local Network Browsing applet lets you set up a default username and password for connecting to shared directories and printers over a Samba network. As discussed in Chapter 29, that is a common way to connect to shared printers and directories from Microsoft Windows computers.

Local Network Chat   The Local Network Chat applet allows you to configure the talk daemon for your local network.

Preferences   When you configure the Preferences applet, you're determining how KDE programs react when connecting to external networks such as the Internet. For example, you can set timeout values for slow websites and configure passive mode (which is required for connections to many FTP servers).

Proxy   Many networks are protected in part by a proxy server. If your computer is on such a network, you can use the Proxy applet to configure the settings associated with that server. You can then connect to an external network such as the Internet.

KDE Components

The KDE Components section lets you configure basic parameters associated with various KDE utilities. They range from the resources associated with your address book to the settings when you log out of the KDE desktop. The basic KDE components are shown in Figure 17.21.

FIGURE 17.21

KDE Components

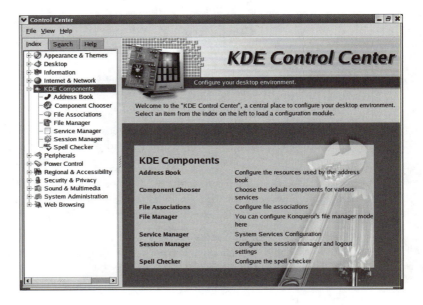

Address Book   The KDE Address Book can incorporate standard .vcf address book files; alternatively, it can convert address book entries from other files or LDAP (Lightweight Directory Assistance Protocol) databases.

Component Chooser   With the KDE Component Chooser, you can select the default e-mail client, embedded text editor, and terminal emulator.

File Associations   The KDE File Associations applet enables you to set applications associated with different file types. For example, Figure 17.22 shows the applications associated with .jpg image files.

FIGURE 17.22
KDE File
Associations

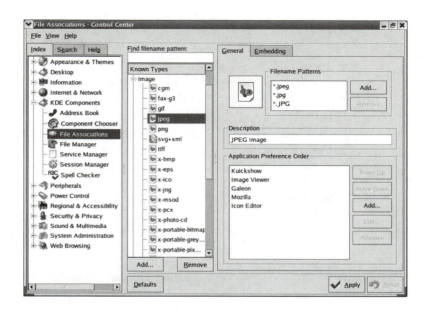

File Manager   You can use the KDE File Manager applet to configure the look and feel of files in Konqueror. This includes the font, the behavior when you open new directories, confirmations when you delete files, and previews/thumbnails of files below a configured size.

Service Manager   As Linux starts with various services and daemons, KDE also starts with services. Some KDE services are automatically loaded when you start this GUI; others are started as needed. You can configure these services through the Service Manager applet.

Session Manager   You can set the behavior of KDE when logging in and out. Specifically, you can configure whether KDE reopens the same utilities that were running whenever you logged out. You can also specify whether your computer exits within Linux, restarts, or shuts down.

Spell Checker   In the Spell Checker applet, you can configure the default spell checker for your system. Available spell checkers depend on the languages that you've installed, probably during the installation of Red Hat Linux.

Peripherals

The Peripherals section lets you configure four external devices: a digital camera, a keyboard, a mouse or other pointing device, and a printer. The KDE Control Center view of Peripherals is shown in Figure 17.23.

FIGURE 17.23

KDE Control Center Peripherals

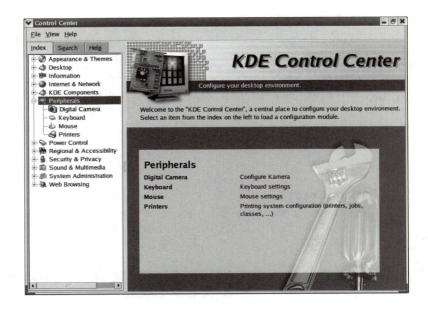

FIGURE 17.23

KDE Control Center Peripherals

Digital Camera   The Digital Camera applet allows you to configure and connect a digital camera to the KDE desktop. For example, Figure 17.24 illustrates how you can select and configure a camera connection.

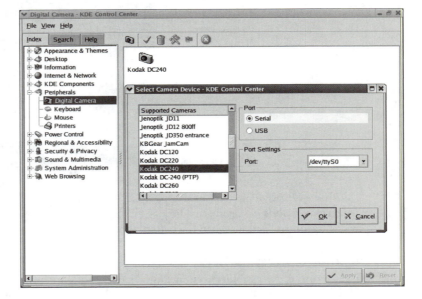

FIGURE 17.24

Configuring a camera with the KDE Control Center

Keyboard   With the Keyboard applet, you can set some basic parameters for keyboard response. This includes the repeat rate, the default condition of the Num Lock key, and the response of keys to other types of activity.

Mouse   You can use the Mouse applet to configure mouse keys, the effect of single and double clicks, and the behavior of the cursor. You can also make it possible to move the cursor with keys on the numeric keypad.

Printers   In KDE, you can send a print job to a variety of locations, including a fax or a file. With the Printers applet, you can configure the characteristics of each of these print locations, down to the color settings of the image.

Power Control

The Power Control section allows you to configure power management settings, including those associated with laptop batteries, if installed. The KDE Control Center view of this section is shown in Figure 17.25.

FIGURE 17.25

KDE Power Control

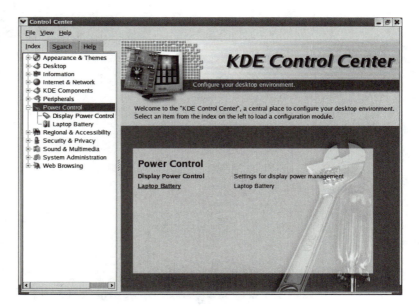

With the Display Power Control applet, you can configure standby, suspend, and power off modes, after certain periods of inactivity. Through the Laptop Battery applet, you can set up status checks, power control, and actions when the battery power falls to specified levels.

Regional & Accessibility

The Regional & Accessibility section allows you to configure formats associated with various nations and languages. It also lets you set up keyboards with bells and responses to different control keys. The

KDE Control Center Regional & Accessibility view is shown in Figure 17.26; the applets are described in Table 17.4.

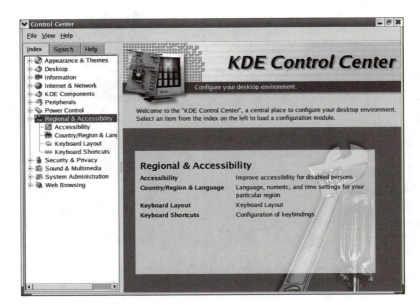

FIGURE 17.26

KDE Regional & Accessibility settings

TABLE 17.4: REGIONAL & ACCESSIBILITY APPLETS

APPLET	DESCRIPTION
Accessibility	Configures settings for keyboard bells, as well as sticky, slow, and bounce keys.
Country/Region & Language	Supports customization of numbers, currency, date and time formats, and measurement systems.
Keyboard Layout	Allows you to set up different national keyboard layouts, along with shortcut functions associated with Alt, Ctrl, Shift, Caps Lock, and other control keys.
Keyboard Shortcuts	Supports configuration of keyboard shortcut combinations for a wide variety of actions.

Security & Privacy

The Security & Privacy section allows you to configure encryption and password settings. The KDE Control Center view of this section is shown in Figure 17.27.

With the Crypto applet, you can configure SSL (Secure Socket Layer) encryption codes and certificates. Through the Passwords applet, you can set up what is echoed as you type in a password, along with a time period in which KDE remembers recently entered passwords.

FIGURE 17.27

KDE Security and
Privacy

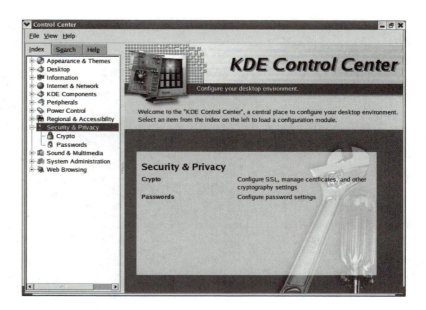

FIGURE 17.27

KDE Security and
Privacy

Sound & Multimedia

The Sound & Multimedia section lets you configure settings associated with your sound card. These settings include music files, default volumes, mixers, and input rates. On the more mundane side of sound, you can also configure the volume of system bells, as well as the sounds associated with various events. The KDE Control Center view of Sound & Multimedia is shown in Figure 17.28.

FIGURE 17.28

KDE Components

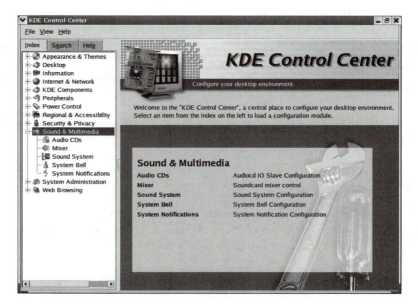

Audio CDs With the Audio CDs applet, you can configure several types of settings, as described in Table 17.5.

TABLE 17.5: AUDIO CDs APPLET CONFIGURATION

CATEGORY	DESCRIPTION
CDDA	With Compact Disk Digital Audio settings, you can configure CD device detect and error correction.
CDDB	Through the Compact Disk Data Base, you can set your CD players to find more information on your songs and CDs through CDDB servers such as those available through `freedb.org`.
MP3	The MP3 (MPEG audio layer 3) coding scheme compresses sound files without loss in quality; the associated options allow you to configure MP3 compression, filters, and encoding methods.
Ogg Vorbis	This is an open source alternate compression format to MP3 (the Ogg Vorbis name is derived from a video game maneuver and a character from a book).

Mixer The Mixer applet allows you to configure volumes, probed mixers, and devices per mixer.

Sound System The Sound System applet enables you to configure the KDE sound server, known as aRts, the analog real-time synthesizer. Four tabs are associated with this applet, as described in Table 17.6.

TABLE 17.6: SOUND SYSTEM TABS

TAB	DESCRIPTION
aRts	Lets you configure basic settings associated with the KDE sound server; you can set it with sound messages for various levels of server messages (`err`, `warn`, `info`, `debug`).
Sound I/O	Allows you to configure input/output, custom devices, quality, and buffer size.
Mixer	Sets the same information as the previously described Mixer applet.
MIDI	Lets you configure a synthesizer interface, based on the musical instrument digital interface.

System Bell With the System Bell applet, you can configure the volume, pitch, and duration of this warning device.

System Notifications You can configure sound and text messages in response to a wide variety of events. As shown in Figure 17.29, you can set different responses to various events in the categories described in Table 17.7. You can switch between these categories by clicking the drop-down text box at the top of the window.

FIGURE 17.29

KDE System Notifications

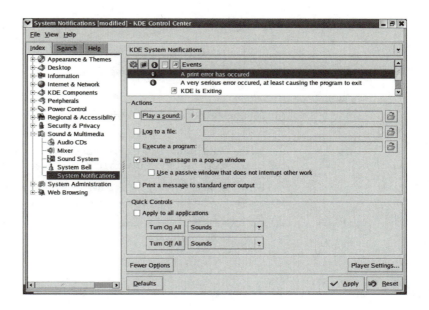

TABLE 17.7: APPLICATIONS WITH ASSIGNABLE SOUND EVENTS

APPLICATION	DESCRIPTION
AOL IM Client	Allows you to configure an instant messenger client such as Gaim to play sounds for different events; works when you configure Gaim with America Online's Instant Messenger plug-in.
Desktop Sharing	Permits configuration of sound events when connections are made between your computer and others on the network.
KDE Screen Ruler	Lets you configure a sound when you move the KDE Screen Ruler, accessible via K Menu ➢ Graphics ➢ More Graphics Applications ➢ Screen Ruler.
KDE System Guard	Supports sound settings associated with limits set in this utility, accessible via K Menu ➢ System Tools ➢ More System Tools ➢ KDE System Guard.
KDE System Notifications	Allows you to configure sounds associated with basic actions on the KDE desktop.
KInetD	Lets you set sounds when others connect to one of your xinetd servers.
KMail	Allows you to set a sound when new mail comes into your mail program.
KSirc	Supports sound events on the KSirc Internet Relay Chat application.
News Ticker	Similar to KMail; applies to monitored newsgroups.
The KDE Window Manager	Allows you to configure sounds associated with basic actions associated with KDE windows.

If you've installed the `kdegames-*` RPM package, you can also modify sound settings associated with some games.

System Administration

The System Administration applets enable you to configure a variety of administrative settings. The KDE Control Center view of System Administration is shown in Figure 17.30.

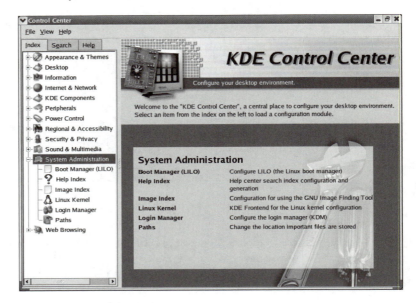

Boot Manager (LILO)   The default Red Hat boot manager is GRUB (Grand Unified Bootloader). However, if you're using LILO, you can use the Boot Manager (LILO) applet as a GUI front end to modify `/etc/lilo.conf`. Changes that you make are immediately reflected on the Expert Tab.

Help Index   You can configure and build the indexes associated with KDE help by using the Help Index applet.

Image Index   The Image Index applet allows you to configure GIFT (GNU Image Finding Tool) to search through image filenames and content.

Linux Kernel   If you've installed the `kernel-sources-*` RPM package for your kernel, you can actually use the Linux Kernel applet to do some reconfiguration.

LogIn Manager   You can configure the KDE display manager, `kdm`, through the LogIn Manager applet. Similar to the GDM setup utility, various tabs enable you to set up the basic appearance, language, font, background, sessions, permitted users, and auto-logins, as shown in Figure 17.31.

Paths   With the Paths applet, you can set up the directory paths to your desktop settings, trash folder, autostart configuration, and local documents. Normally, these should all be in your home directory (or a subdirectory thereof).

FIGURE 17.31

The KDE Login Manager

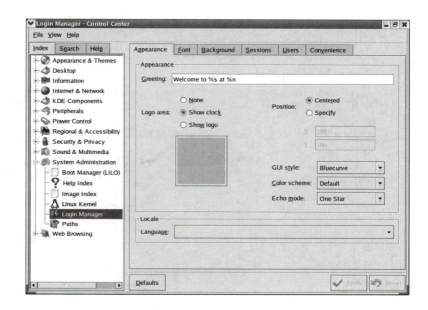

Web Browsing

The Web Browsing applets allow you to configure your KDE web browsing experience. The applets in this section are associated with the default KDE web browser, Konqueror. The KDE Control Center view of Web Browsing applets is shown in Figure 17.32; individual applets are described in Table 17.8.

FIGURE 17.32

Web Browsing configuration

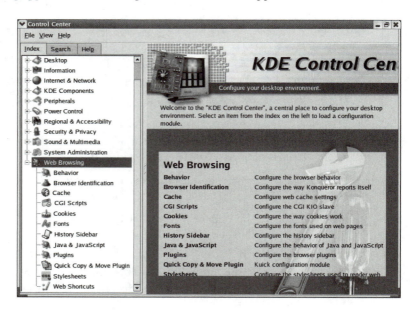

TABLE 17.8: WEB BROWSING APPLETS

APPLET	DESCRIPTION
Behavior	Sets the behavior of the browser for cursors, form completion, images, links, and more.
Browser Identification	Lets you customize the way your browser identifies itself; you can even identify Konqueror as a Microsoft Internet Explorer 6 browser for specific websites.
Cache	Allows you to set the disk cache for previously viewed web pages.
CGI Scripts	Supports access to CGI programs.
Cookies	Lets you configure acceptance policies for cookies from different websites.
Fonts	Allows you to set fonts associated with different site settings and languages.
History Sidebar	Supports the creation of a history of past links.
Java & JavaScript	Lets you enable Java executables by domain.
Plugins	Compiles a list of plug-ins associated with your browser.
Quick Copy & Move Plugin	Configures directory cache parameters.
Stylesheets	Supports Cascading Style Sheets, which supports a single look and feel for a website.
Web Shortcuts	Lists shortcut acronyms for major websites and search engines.

Learning About KDE Utilities

KDE comes with a number of bonus applications, accessible through the K Menu button. They fall into several categories: Accessories, Internet, Other, Preferences, Programming, Multimedia, and System Tools. This is not a comprehensive list of programs available through the K Menu button. GNOME utilities were covered in Chapter 16; we take a look at others in the following two chapters. While most of the utilities in this section are based on the work of the KDE project, we've included a few third-party utilities as well.

NOTE *The lists in this chapter may not reflect the options you see on your computer. Available menu options depend on the software that you have installed.*

Accessories

KDE includes a number of accessories that can help you with simple computing tasks. They're accessible through the K Menu ➢ Accessories submenu. Figure 17.33 shows the More Accessories submenu off the Accessories menu. Accessories that we do not cover here are primarily GNOME related and are addressed in Chapter 16.

Autorun The Autorun utility reads any currently installed CDs for autorun executable programs or audio CDs. They are run if found. If you want to allow regular users access to autorun programs, you'll need to add the `user,exec` options to the CD configuration line in `/etc/fstab`.

FIGURE 17.33

Accessories menus

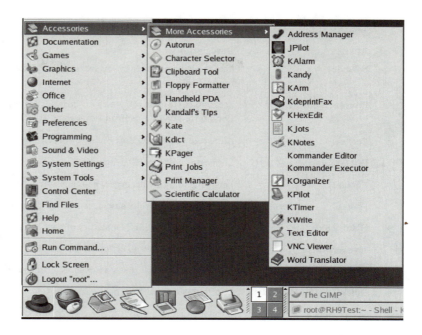

Character Selector   The Character Selector, also known as KCharSelect, allows you to work with a number of non-English languages that still use roman-style alphabets. As you can see in Figure 17.34, it provides an interface where you can include a number of special letters and accented characters in your documents.

FIGURE 17.34

The KDE Character Selector

Clipboard Tool   The Clipboard Tool opens the configuration options described earlier for the Klipper.

Floppy Formatter The Floppy Formatter (KFloppy) allows you to format standard floppy drives to the MS-DOS or ext2 filesystems. As shown in Figure 17.35, it has a straightforward interface that lets you customize the format.

FIGURE 17.35

Floppy Formatter

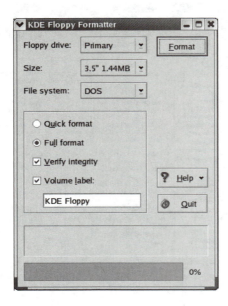

Handheld PDA The Handheld PDA utility starts GNOME Pilot, described in Chapter 16.

Kandalf's Tips The Kandalf's Tips utility opens the hints that you see when you first start KDE. An example is shown in Figure 17.36.

FIGURE 17.36

Kandalf's Tips

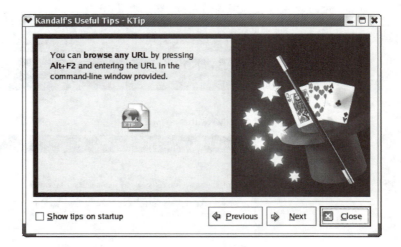

Kate   You can use Kate, the KDE advanced text editor, to edit various text files. As shown in Figure 17.37, Kate also provides you with a convenient window to the command-line interface.

FIGURE 17.37

Using Kate on /etc/inittab

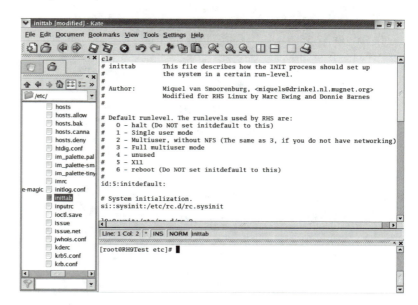

Kdict   The KDE dictionary (Kdict) provides access to the online dictionary server at dict.org. It uses TCP/IP port 2628; as long as you're connected to the Internet, it's easy to use to find the definitions that you need. An example is shown in Figure 17.38.

FIGURE 17.38

Online dictionary access

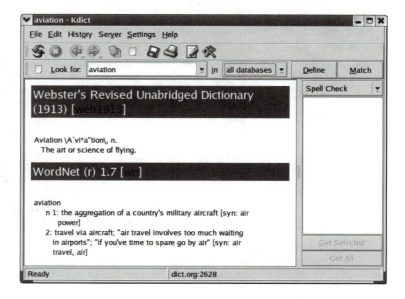

Kpager   The KDE pager (Kpager) opens a small window that displays open workspaces; it is functionally equivalent to the desktop workspace view described earlier within the KDE panel.

Print Jobs   The KJobViewer allows you to manage the current jobs in your print queue(s). Various functions allow you to hold, resume, delete, or move any current print jobs.

Print Manager   This opens the GNOME Print Manager utility described in Chapter 16.

Scientific Calculator   The KCalc utility is a configurable calculator that can be controlled through the numeric keypad. You can set it up in Trigonometric or Statistical modes, each with different functions.

More Accessories

The other KDE accessories are, for the most part, applets with minor functionality. We've described them briefly in Table 17.9.

TABLE 17.9: MORE KDE ACCESSORIES

ACCESSORY	DESCRIPTION
Address Manager	The KDE Address Book allows you to configure contact information for people in your address book.
JPilot	The JPilot utility is used for synchronizing data between KDE and handheld devices that conform to the PalmPilot and PalmOS standards; a sample view is shown in Figure 17.39.
KAlarm	With the KDE personal alarm message and command scheduler, you can set up reminders or administrative commands on a schedule.
Kandy	The Kandy utility allows you to synchronize the KDE address book with your mobile phone.
KArm	With the KArm utility, you can track the time that you spend on various tasks.
KdeprintFax	The KdeprintFax utility is an "add-on" to KDE Print; it allows you to view a file that you've printed to a fax device.
KHexEdit	The KHexEdit utility is a customizable hex editor that can display and help you edit data in hexadecimal, octal, and binary modes. (That corresponds to base 16, base 8, and base 2 for the math majors.) It can also show files in text mode.
KJots	The KJots utility lets you jot down short notes in an organized fashion. Any "books" that you create can be added to a hotlist.
KNotes	The KNotes utility allows you to add some short notes to a list that you can print or e-mail.
KOrganizer	The KOrganizer is a handy scheduling utility, shown in Figure 17.39.
KPilot	The KPilot utility uses the latest version of Desktop HotSync software; it is intended to substitute for Palm desktop software.
KTimer	KTimer allows you to start a command after a given delay; the default is 100 seconds.
KWrite	KWrite is a text editor suitable for programmers.

Continued on next page

TABLE 17.9: MORE KDE ACCESSORIES *(continued)*

ACCESSORY	DESCRIPTION
Text Editor	Text Editor is a more basic editor; KEdit is the default KDE text editor.
VNC Viewer	Covered in Chapter 16.
Word Translator	The Word Translator incorporates other dictionaries based on the server or that associated with Babylon (www.babylon.com). See Figure 17.40.

Once begun, a number of these utilities, such as KOrganizer, KNotes, and KAlarm, place icons on the panel, next to the system clock.

FIGURE 17.39

Syncing a handheld computer with JPilot

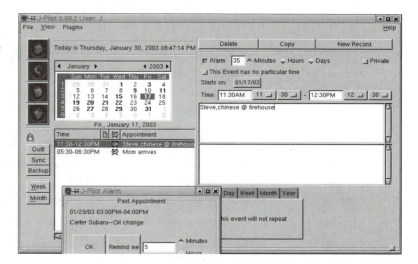

FIGURE 17.40

KDE Word Translator

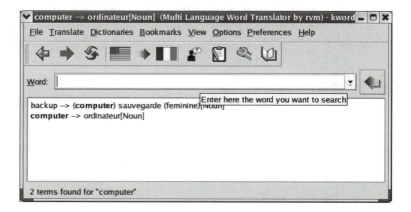

Internet

KDE includes several network utilities that can help you work your way through the Internet. They range from IRC clients to modem connection utilities. They're accessible through the K Menu ➢ Internet ➢ More Internet Applications submenu, shown in Figure 17.41. Several GNOME applications, including Mozilla, gFTP, Instant Messenger, Video Conferencing, Balsa, exmh, Galeon, IRC Client, Sylpheed, and Evolution, were addressed in Chapter 16. Ethereal is covered in Chapter 22.

FIGURE 17.41

The More Internet Applications submenu

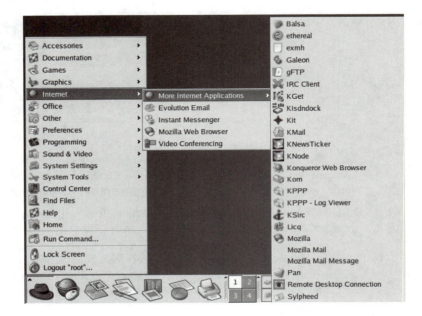

KGet   KGet is a KDE download manager also known as Caitoo. When integrated with the default KDE web browser, Konqueror, it lists and allows you to monitor, pause, and resume downloads. A sample download is shown in Figure 17.42.

Kisdndock   This applet allows you to configure any installed ISDN devices. ISDN, the Integrated Services Digital Network, is an option for digital Internet connections that works nominally at about twice the speed of a regular telephone modem. As ISDN is popular in Europe, it is not surprising that KDE, which is mostly developed in Europe, provides solid ISDN support.

If you haven't yet set up an ISDN device, you'll need to configure one first via `redhat-config-network-druid` as described in Chapter 21.

NOTE   The `redhat-config-network-druid` *utility was formerly known as* `internet-druid`.

FIGURE 17.42

KGet monitors downloads.

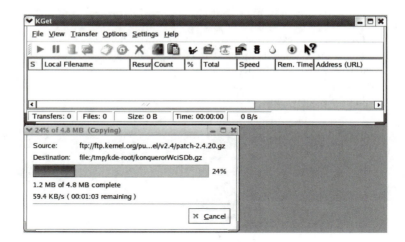

Kit   The Kit utility is currently the KDE Instant Messaging (IM) client for the AOL system. The first time you run Kit, you're taken through a wizard where you can set up an AOL IM account. Future versions of Kit may include support for other messaging systems.

KMail   KMail is the default KDE e-mail client. It is highly customizable; you can configure it with shortcuts and actions on the toolbar. Of course, you can also set up the e-mail accounts that you use.

For example, you can set it up with shortcuts for a number of functions, such as using e-mail filters and marking messages, replies, and more. Over 100 different shortcuts are possible. You can configure the main toolbar with the actions of your choice.

It is not difficult to configure a new e-mail account. In KMail, click Settings ➣ Configure KMail. Naturally, this opens the Configure KMail dialog box. In the left-hand pane, click Network; you'll be able to configure sending and receiving accounts in the tabs shown in Figure 17.43.

KNewsTicker   You can set up a news ticker in the panel. KNewsTicker can access a number of different sources. The process for adding KNewsTicker is a little different; you don't use the K Menu but need to add it directly to the panel.

To add KNewsTicker, right-click on an open area of the panel. In the menu that appears, select Add ➣ Applet ➣ KNewsTicker.

KNode   You can also use KNode as the default newsgroup reader. It's as straightforward to configure as KMail; once KNode is open, click Settings ➣ Configure KNode. This opens the Preferences - KNode dialog box. Click New to open up the New Account - KNode dialog box. As shown in Figure 17.44, KNode is highly configurable, and the entries for news accounts are straightforward.

FIGURE 17.43

Configuring KMail

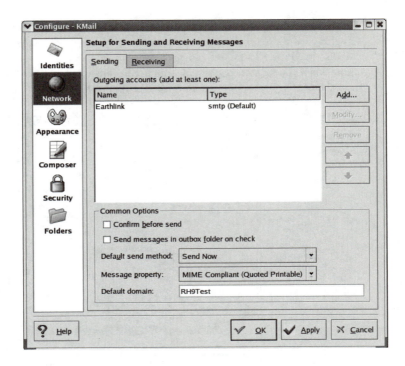

FIGURE 17.44

The KNode
newsreader

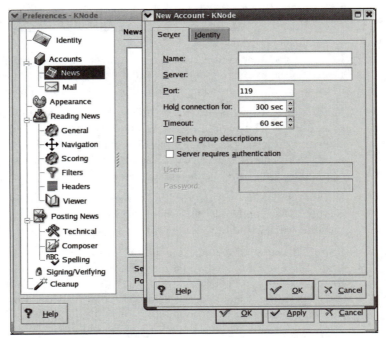

Konqueror Web Browser   Konqueror is the default KDE web browser. Like GNOME's Nautilus, it's also used to browse file folders. You've already seen the Konqueror configuration options when we discussed the KDE Control Panel earlier in this chapter. You can configure these settings and more when you select Settings ➤ Configure Konqueror. The basic browser is shown in Figure 17.45, and the configuration options are shown in Figure 17.46.

FIGURE 17.45

The Konqueror
Web Browser

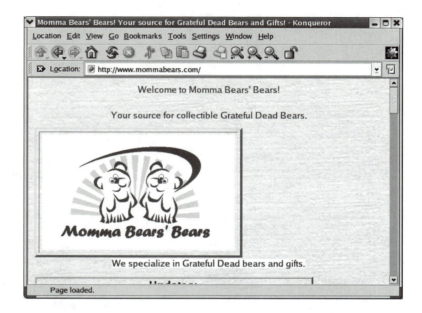

Korn   If you want a utility to monitor your mailbox, start Korn, the KDE mail checker. Once configured for the account of your choice (local, POP3, IMAP4, and more), start Korn. Once it's docked in the panel, it monitors configured mailboxes at fixed time intervals. The default is 5 minutes.

KPPP   One of my favorite Linux GUI applications is KPPP, which is primarily used to connect to an ISP over a telephone modem. It is highly configurable; you can set up the accounts of your choice for different ISPs or locations. If you're having trouble configuring a modem, KPPP makes it easy to experiment with different devices. KPPP also includes logs and terminal screens that can help you track the performance of your connection. The main KPPP screen is shown in Figure 17.47.

KPPP Log Viewer   The KPPP Log Viewer starts a connection log for the current month, which is especially useful if your connections incur costs per minute or byte. This is a common situation for some wireless and European telephone modem connections.

KSirc   If you want to connect to an IRC chat room, you can use the default KDE chat client, KSirc. Once KSirc is open, you can configure a new connection by selecting Connections ➤ New Server. As shown in Figure 17.48, you can select from available chat server groups, choose a server, enter a password if required, and then click Connect. If the connection is successful, you'll see a new window with your chat room.

Licq   Licq is another Internet chat client, with KDE support.

FIGURE 17.46

Configuring
Konqueror through
the KDE Control
Module

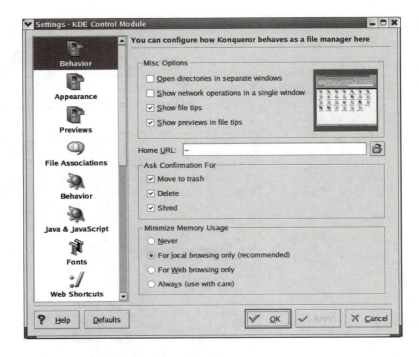

FIGURE 17.47

KPPP

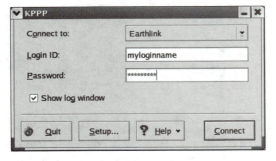

FIGURE 17.48

Configuring
KSirc for chat

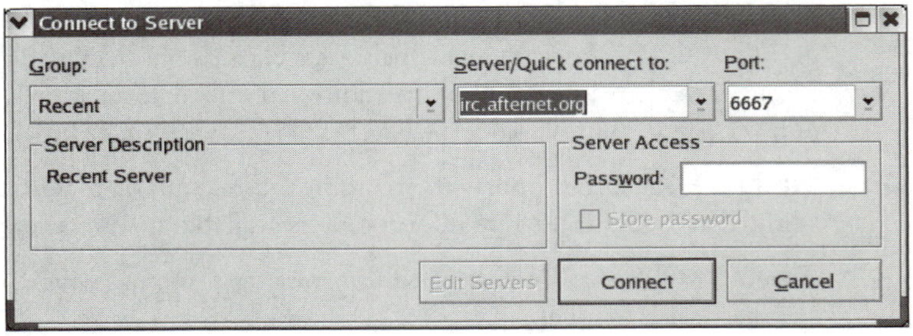

Other Utilities

KDE includes other utilities that generally do not easily fit into the other K Menu categories. Many of them can serve educational purposes. They range from Kalzium, which helps you learn the periodic table of the elements, to KVocTrain, which you use to enhance your vocabulary. These utilities are accessible through the K Menu ➤ Other submenu, shown in Figure 17.49. Some of the utilities in this menu that are not part of the KDE desktop are not covered in this chapter.

FIGURE 17.49

Other KDE utilities

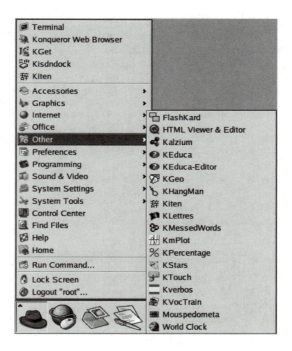

FlashKard FlashKard is a KDE vocabulary builder. Once a vocabulary list is loaded, you can quiz yourself on the meanings of the words in the list. A sample list in German is available in `sample-de.kvtml`, in the `/usr/share/apps/kvoctrain/examples` directory.

Kalzium Kalzium is a KDE utility that presents a periodic table of the first 103 elements, shown in Figure 17.50. Each element includes a clickable button, which provides more information about each element, and a link to additional information from the Chemistry department of the University of Split, Croatia (`www.ktf-split.hr/en/index.html`).

KEduca KEduca supports the creation and revision of form-based exams. You can add questions with KEduca-Editor. More information is available at `sourceforge.net/projects/keduca`.

KGeo KGeo is an interactive KDE geometry program, which helps math teachers illustrate basic geometrical principles.

KHangMan KHangMan is a KDE version of the hangman game for guessing words.

FIGURE 17.50

A KDE periodic table

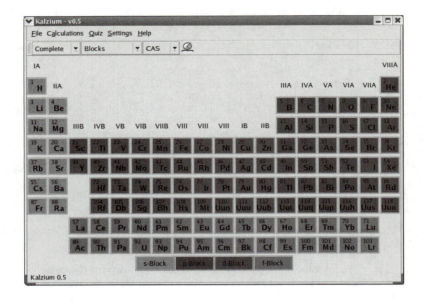

Kiten Kiten is another interactive dictionary; by default, it works with Japanese (Kanji) and English. An example translation is shown in Figure 17.51.

FIGURE 17.51

Kiten translating from English to Japanese

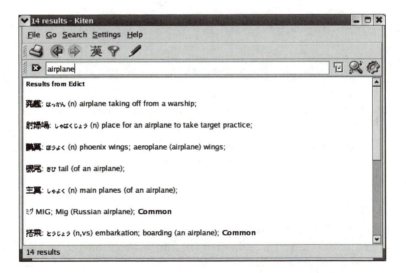

KLettres KLettres is a KDE utility that teaches the alphabet. It is currently configurable in Danish, Dutch, and French.

KMessedWords   KMessedWords is a KDE anagram game.

KmPlot   KmPlot is a KDE mathematical function plotter; it can help you graph various equations.

KPercentage   KPercentage is a KDE utility that quizzes students on calculating percentages.

KStars   KStars is a KDE planetarium utility that helps you identify different stars, based on a look at a clear night.

KTouch   KTouch is a KDE program that helps you learn to touch type.

Kverbos   You can use the Kverbos utility to learn different Spanish language verb forms.

KVocTrain   KVocTrain is another flash card utility, similar to FlashKard. It also uses `.kvtml` databases.

Mousepedometa   Also known as KOdometer, this utility tracks the mileage of your cursor across the desktop.

World Clock   The KDE World Clock can display the current time in different locations, along with a view of where the sun should be visible on a clear day.

Preferences

KDE includes several utilities in the Preferences submenu (K Menu ➤ Preferences). Just a few of the utilities shown in Figure 17.52 are KDE utilities; see Table 17.10 for a brief description.

NOTE   *Because none of the utilities in the More Preferences menu are based on KDE, we do not cover them here.*

TABLE 17.10: KDE UTILITIES IN THE PREFERENCES SUBMENU

UTILITY	DESCRIPTION
Configure Panel	This opens the Settings - KDE Control Module window, where you can set up the panel; described earlier in this chapter.
Desktop Settings Wizard	This wizard helps you configure KDE for your language, location, preferred system behavior, special effects, and style.

More Programming Tools

KDE includes several utilities in K Menu ➤ Programming ➤ More Programming Tools submenu. Just a few of the utilities shown in Figure 17.53 are KDE utilities; we describe them briefly in Table 17.11.

FIGURE 17.52

The Preferences menu

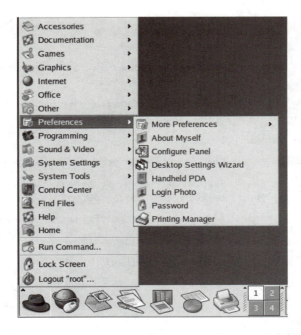

FIGURE 17.53

More Programming Tools

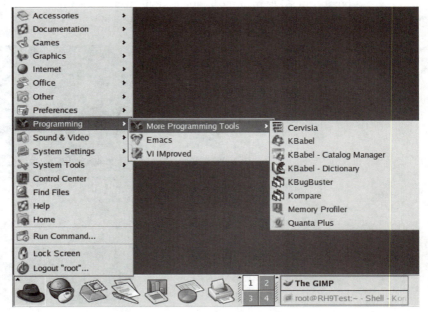

TABLE 17.11: KDE PROGRAMMING TOOLS

TOOL	DESCRIPTION
Cervista	A KDE tool for keeping track of different versions of source code, using CVS (Concurrent Versions System).
KBabel	Supports the use of other languages for comments and other guides in program code.
KBabel - Catalog Manager	Merges KBabel-based directories.
KBabel - Dictionary	Also known as PO Compendium; lists translation messages for a project.
KBugBuster	Supports bug management; by default, includes a connection to the KDE bug tracking system at bugs.kde.org.
Kompare	A KDE front end to the diff command for reviewing the differences between files.
Memory Profiler	For monitoring the memory behavior of programs , including leaks.
Quanta Plus	A web development tool for KDE.

Multimedia

A number of KDE multimedia applications are available when you click Main Menu ➢ Sound & Video. As shown in Figure 17.54, these include various audio and CD players and sound control utilities.

FIGURE 17.54

Multimedia Menus

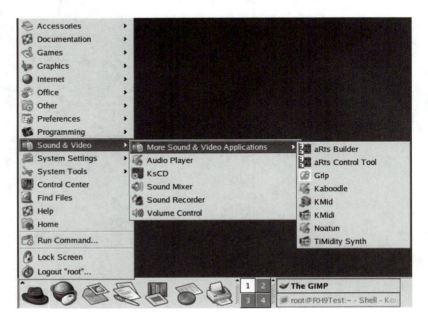

KsCD   The KDE small/simple CD Player is an easy-to-use player for audio CDs. As shown in Figure 17.55, it has the standard buttons that allow you to play and move between CD tracks. It also includes access to the compact disc database (CDDB) described earlier. If you click on the name of the song, you'll be able to select the song of your choice from the CD tracklist.

FIGURE 17.55

KDE CD Player

Sound Mixer   The KDE Sound Mixer, also known as KMix, allows you to regulate sound input from a number of different sources.

aRts Builder   As described earlier, aRts is the KDE sound server. aRts Builder is a graphical design tool that can help you configure connections for various sound characteristics.

aRts Control Tool   This is a tool for controlling different settings of the aRts sound server.

Kaboodle   Kaboodle is a media player for single files, such as those in .wav format.

KMid   The KDE MIDI/Karaoke file player allows you to play .mid and .kar files if your sound card has hardware support for raw MIDI files.

KMidi   KMidi is a front end to the TiMidity synthesizer (see Figure 17.56). If your sound card does not provide hardware MIDI support, you may be able to use KMidi to play .mid files. You'll also need an /etc/timidity.cfg configuration file; a sample is available in the /usr/share/apps/kmidi/config directory. If you see errors when you try to start KMidi, make sure you have the arts-devel-* RPM installed.

Noatun   The Noatun utility is a front end to the aRts sound server. When you start it, it may look like it's not working. In fact, it adds an icon to your panel. Right-click on the icon to open the basic Noatun menu. Similar to the XMMS audio player from Chapter 16, Noatun includes an equalizer and playlist menu.

TiMidity Synth   See KMidi.

System Tools

There are some KDE system tools that are not related to the redhat-config-* tools primarily covered in Chapter 19. The menus are shown in Figure 17.57. We cover a wide variety of administrative tools in this section.

FIGURE 17.56

KMidi at work

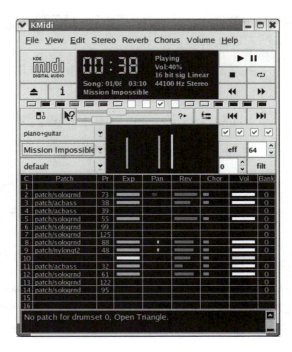

FIGURE 17.57

The More System Tools menu

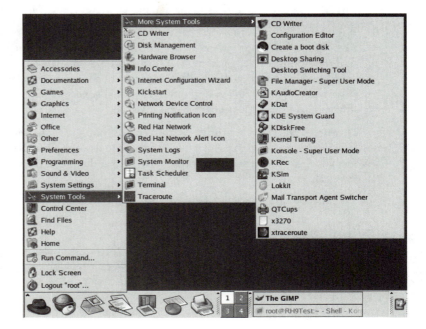

Create A Boot Disk   The Create A Boot Disk utility calls the `qmkbootdisk` command, which helps you create a boot disk for your installation on a 1.44MB floppy drive. For more information, see the discussion of `mkbootdisk` in Chapter 11. The interface is simple, as shown in Figure 17.58.

FIGURE 17.58

Making a boot disk

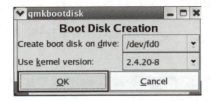

Desktop Sharing   Desktop Sharing, formerly known as `krfb`, supports management of `xinetd` servers.

File Manager   Opens the home directory for the current user in Konqueror.

KAudioCreator   This utility is somewhat out of place; it really belongs with the other multimedia applications in the Sound & Video menu. With KAudioCreator, you can copy tracks from audio CDs for writing to the CDs of your choice. It also supports CDDB access to help you find more information on each track.

KDat   KDat is a KDE tape archiver, based on the `tar` command.

KDE System Guard   The KDE task manager and performance monitor is known as the KDE System Guard, or `ksysguard` for short. By default, it presents graphical views of system loads based on the `top` command. You can also set up graphs to monitor a number of other systems. A basic view of this tool is shown in Figure 17.59.

FIGURE 17.59

KDE System Guard

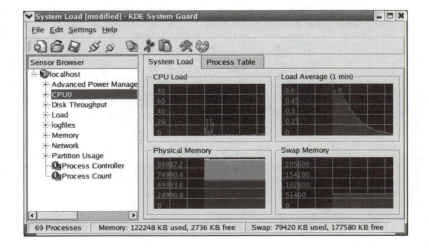

KDiskFree   The KDiskFree utility illustrates available free space on all mounted partitions; it is essentially an illustrated front end for the `df` command described in Chapter 7.

Kernel Tuning   You can modify some of the settings associated with your kernel, which are stored in the `/proc` directory, described in Chapter 11. For example, if your Linux computer is a gateway between networks, you'll want to enable IP Forwarding. One method is described in Chapter 21. Alternatively, you can set it up through the Kernel Tuning utility, shown in Figure 17.60.

FIGURE 17.60

Kernel Tuning

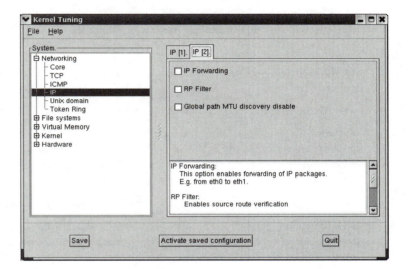

KRec   The KRec utility is a recording fron end to the KDE aRts sound server. It's a multimedia utility that actually belongs in the Sound & Video menu.

KSim   The KSim utility is a system monitor that is a simple front end to the `top` command. KSim commands are docked in the KDE panel; right-click on the KSim menu bar to open the KSim Configuration menu, shown in Figure 17.61. As you can see, KSim is highly customizable.

QTCups   As of this writing, QTCups is still part of the Red Hat More System Tools submenu. It is obsolete and superseded by the KDEPrint utility, which you can start from a command-line interface with the `kprinter` command. KDEPrint serves as an interface between KDE utilities and the active print daemon on your computer. As noted in Chapter 25, the default print service is CUPS.

FIGURE 17.61

Configuring KSim

Summary

In this chapter, we provided a basic introduction to the KDE desktop, the other major Linux GUI. It includes tools with much of the same functionality as you might find in Microsoft Windows—and more. In fact, you can distribute open applications on four or more different desktops. It's easy to configure the KDE desktop to your needs.

A substantial number of extras are available through KDE. This includes a wide variety of software that could easily cost you hundreds of dollars. KDE features the accessories that you need every day. The Internet applications include browsers, e-mail managers, and chat clients. The sound and video utilities allow you to manage, process, and record multimedia. And KDE includes a number of system tools that can help administrators manage their systems.

In the next chapter, we'll look at some of the more important Linux GUI applications, focused on office suites and graphics utilities.

Chapter 18

GUI Applications

RED HAT LINUX INCLUDES a number of bonus applications over and above what you would find on a Microsoft operating system. Perhaps the biggest bonuses are the fully featured office suites. These are programs included with Red Hat Linux that substitute for Microsoft Windows–based programs that can cost hundreds of dollars per computer.

The Linux office suites typically include a word processor, spreadsheet, graphics support, presentation manager, and a project scheduler. Some suites include more. You might need to download an application or two, but they are as freely available as the office suite applications that come with Linux. The three suites we'll cover in this chapter include OpenOffice, KOffice, and GNOME Office.

Red Hat Linux also features several graphical applications, including image viewers, scanning tools, screen-capture programs, and those that can view the same files as Adobe Acrobat Reader.

This chapter contains the briefest of introductions to each application. Many of these applications are quite substantial and could easily fill their own books. This chapter covers the following topics:

- Learning about OpenOffice
- Understanding GNOME Office
- Working with KOffice
- Taking advantage of graphical applications

Learning About OpenOffice

The default office suite for Red Hat Linux is OpenOffice, from www.openoffice.org. It was developed from the same code as Sun Microsystems' StarOffice. It includes several applications, which are briefly described in Table 18.1.

TABLE 18.1: OPENOFFICE APPLICATIONS

APPLICATION	DESCRIPTION
Calc	Spreadsheet
Draw	Diagram creator
Impress	Presentation manager
Math	Formula creator
Printer Setup	Administers a printer interface
Repair	Installation program
Writer	Word processor

You can open installed OpenOffice applications from the GUI of your choice. In GNOME, click Main Menu ➢ Office and then select the application of your choice from the menu that appears.

NOTE *If you're using KDE, the K Menu button corresponds to the GNOME Main Menu button. By default, both are located in the lower-left corner of the desktop, and both are associated with an icon of a Red Hat. In this chapter, directions are based on GNOME, the Red Hat default desktop; the instructions in KDE may vary slightly.*

Alternatively, you can start three OpenOffice applications directly from the panel at the bottom of the desktop. As we described in Chapters 16 and 17, you can start OpenOffice Writer by clicking on the icon of a pen and paper; you can start OpenOffice Impress by clicking on the icon of a bar graph and slide; and finally, you can start OpenOffice Calc by clicking the icon of a graph pie chart.

You can learn more about the OpenOffice.org project from their web page at `www.openoffice.org`.

OpenOffice Calc

Perhaps the first key business PC application was the spreadsheet. You can use a spreadsheet to define a range of numbers. With the equations of your choice, you can set up a spreadsheet to perform a variety of calculations in different scenarios. It's useful for everything from statistical analysis to business modeling and projections.

You can open OpenOffice Calc by selecting Main Menu ➢ Office ➢ OpenOffice.org Calc, or by running the `oocalc` command from a GUI terminal window. Figure 18.1 shows OpenOffice Calc and some basic data from the year 2000 U.S. census.

FIGURE 18.1

OpenOffice Calc and the census

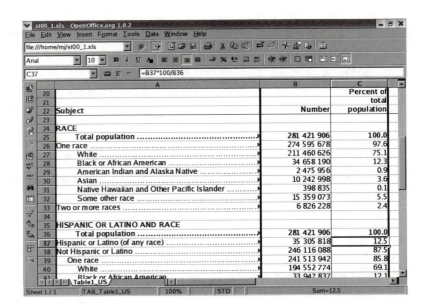

As you can see in the figure, OpenOffice Calc has the basic look and feel of a spreadsheet. Functionally similar to Microsoft Excel, Calc includes several toolbars, as described in Table 18.2.

TABLE 18.2: OPENOFFICE CALC TOOLBARS

TOOLBAR	DESCRIPTION
Formula	Reflects the cell location and any formulas associated with that cell
Function	Configures basic functions such as open, print, and undo
Hyperlink	Sets up access to web pages
Main	Allows the creation of charts with graphs; supports format and spell checks; permits sorting and grouping
Object	Supports formatting options, including fonts, justification, numbering systems, borders, and alignment

OpenOffice Calc works with many different types of spreadsheets, including the formats described in Table 18.3. As you can see, OpenOffice Calc can work with spreadsheets from a number of applications, including Microsoft Excel, StarOffice Calc, dBASE/FoxPro databases, and more. You can also set up OpenOffice Calc with text files in comma-separated format (see the accompanying sidebar).

TABLE 18.3: OPENOFFICE CALC FILE FORMATS

FORMAT	DESCRIPTION
.sxc	OpenOffice Spreadsheet
.stc	OpenOffice Spreadsheet template
.dif	Data Interchange Format
.dbf	dBASE/FoxPro database files
.xls	Microsoft Excel 97/2000/XP or Excel 95/5.0
.xlt	Microsoft Excel 97/2000/XP or Excel 95/5.0 template
.sdc	StarOffice Calc 5.0/4.0/3.0 (Sun StarOffice spreadsheet)
.vor	StarOffice Calc 5.0/4.0/3.0 template
.slk	Symbolic link format; includes formulas, and cell and file links
.wks	Lotus 1-2-3
.csv	Comma-separated format; a spreadsheet in a text file
.html	Web page

COMMA-SEPARATED FORMAT

Spreadsheets and other data tables are often represented in a text file in comma-separated format. In other words, each of the values in the following line can be imported into consecutive cells in a row in a spreadsheet:

```
height, 60, 61, 44, 78, 56, 66
```

OpenOffice Draw

You can use OpenOffice Draw to manage files in various graphics formats, from AutoCAD files to bitmaps. In other words, OpenOffice Draw is a design tool that can be used by everyone who works with graphics, from design engineers to graphics designers.

You can start OpenOffice Draw by selecting Main Menu ➢ Office ➢ OpenOffice.org Draw, or by running the **oodraw** command from a GUI terminal window. Figure 18.2 shows the GNOME desktop, ready for editing.

FIGURE 18.2

OpenOffice Draw
artwork

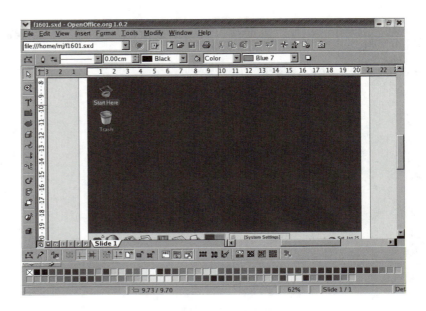

As you can see in the figure, OpenOffice Draw includes a wide variety of toolbars, some that allow you to manage color, as well as others that let you draw and add objects. The toolbars are described in Table 18.4.

TABLE 18.4: OPENOFFICE DRAW TOOLBARS

TOOLBAR	DESCRIPTION
Color	Allows selection from a variety of colors
Function	Configures basic functions such as open, print, and undo
Hyperlink	Sets up access to web pages
Main	Allows zoom; insertion of objects, such as text and geometric shapes; alignment of objects; and so on
Object	Configures grid creation, text editing, rotation, color, and so on.
Option	Supports editing and drawing options for lines, including thickness and color

OpenOffice Draw works with many types of drawings, including the formats described in Table 18.5. As you can see, OpenOffice drawings can work from a number of different applications, including Microsoft Excel, StarOffice Calc, dBASE/FoxPro databases, and more. You can also set up OpenOffice Draw with text files in comma-separated format.

TABLE 18.5: OPENOFFICE DRAW FILE FORMATS

FORMAT	DESCRIPTION
.sxd	OpenOffice drawing
.std	OpenOffice drawing template
.bmp	Microsoft Windows bitmap
.dxf	AutoCAD Interchange Format
.emf	Enhanced metafile
.eps	Encapsulated PostScript
.gif	Graphics Interchange Format
.jpg	Joint Photographic Experts Group
.met	OS/2 metafile
.pbm	Portable bitmap
.pcd	Photo CD (Kodak)
.pct	Macintosh Pict drawing
.pcx	Zsoft paintbrush
.pgm	Portable gray map
.png	Portable Network Graphic
.ppm	Portable pixel map
.psd	Adobe Photoshop
.ras	Sun raster image
.sda	StarOffice 5.0 Draw
.sdd	StarOffice 3.0 Draw
.sgf	StarWriter graphics
.sgv	StarDraw 2.0 graphics
.svm	StarView metafile
.tga	Truevision Targa
.tiff	Tagged Image File Format
.vor	StarOffice 5.0/3.0 Draw template
.wmf	Microsoft Windows metafile
.xbm	X bitmap
.xpm	X pixmap

OpenOffice Impress

When you create a presentation, you're essentially creating a slide show. Presentation applications are basically specialized word processors with graphics, and they support a slide show to a large audience in a room or online. You can use OpenOffice Impress to build the same types of presentations as you might with other applications, such as Microsoft PowerPoint or StarOffice Impress.

You can start OpenOffice Impress by selecting Main ➢ Office ➢ OpenOffice.org Impress, or by running the `ooimpress` command from a GUI terminal window. Figure 18.3 illustrates a typical presentation start screen, ready for your data.

FIGURE 18.3

OpenOffice Impress ready for a presentation

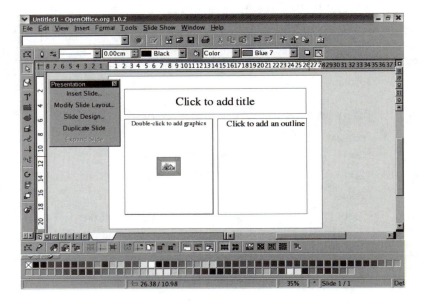

As you can see in the figure, OpenOffice Impress includes a wide variety of toolbars, some that allow you to manage color as well as others that allow you to draw, manage text, and add objects. Table 18.6 describes the toolbars.

TABLE 18.6: OPENOFFICE IMPRESS TOOLBARS

TOOLBAR	DESCRIPTION
Color	Allows selection from a variety of colors
Function	Configures basic functions such as open, print, and undo
Hyperlink	Sets up access to web pages
Main	Allows zoom; insertion of objects, such as text and geometric shapes; alignment of objects; and so on
Object	Configures grid creation, text editing, rotation, color, and so on.

Continued on next page

TABLE 18.6: OPENOFFICE IMPRESS TOOLBARS *(continued)*

TOOLBAR	DESCRIPTION
Option	Supports editing and drawing options for lines, including thickness and color
Presentation	Lets you manage the design of each slide

When you first start OpenOffice Impress, you'll see an AutoPilot Presentation wizard, which lets you start from a blank sheet, a presentation template, or an existing work. If you're creating a new presentation, OpenOffice Impress configures a slide design, output media, and basic presentation notes.

OpenOffice Impress works with other types of presentation formats, including those described in Table 18.7. As you can see, OpenOffice presentations can work with data from other applications, including Microsoft PowerPoint, StarDraw, StarImpress, and any application that can save in .cgm format.

TABLE 18.7: OPENOFFICE IMPRESS FILE FORMATS

FORMAT	DESCRIPTION
.sxi	OpenOffice Presentation
.sti	OpenOffice Presentation template
.sxd	OpenOffice drawing
.ppt	Microsoft PowerPoint 97/2000/XP
.pot	Microsoft PowerPoint 97/2000/XP template
.sda	StarDraw 5.0
.sdd	StarDraw 3.0/StarImpress 4.0/5.0
.vor	StarImpress 4.0/5.0 template

OpenOffice Writer

One of the banes of computing is dealing with the various word processing formats. You need converters to translate Microsoft Word documents to Corel WordPerfect documents to StarOffice Write documents. While converters are built into most word processing programs, including OpenOffice Writer, every word processing application includes special features that aren't always translated properly, if at all.

OpenOffice Writer does an excellent job. However, there are special features used by people in a number of industries—including publishing—that OpenOffice Writer does not handle properly. Nevertheless, OpenOffice Writer is good enough for most applications, businesses, and more.

You can start OpenOffice Writer by selecting Main Menu ➢ Office ➢ OpenOffice.org Writer, or by running the oowriter command from a GUI terminal window. New documents created in OpenOffice Writer can include all of the features that you might find in Microsoft Word. Figure 18.4 illustrates a typical document.

FIGURE 18.4

A Microsoft Word
document in
OpenOffice Writer

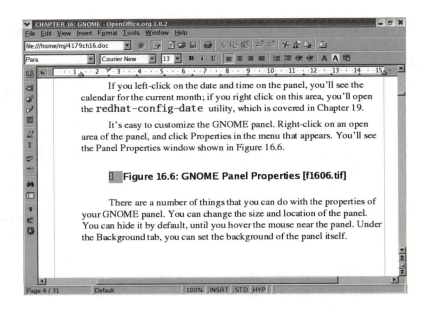

As you can see in the figure, OpenOffice Writer includes three basic toolbars, as described in Table 18.8.

TABLE 18.8: OPENOFFICE WRITER TOOLBARS

TOOLBAR	DESCRIPTION
Function	Configures basic functions such as open, print, and undo
Hyperlink	Sets up access to web pages
Main	Allows spell checking, zoom, insertion of objects such as text and geometric shapes, form creation, and so on
Object	Configures fonts, styles, formatting, highlighting, and color

OpenOffice Writer works with files from other word processors, including those described in Table 18.9.

TABLE 18.9: OPENOFFICE WRITER FILE FORMATS

FORMAT	DESCRIPTION
.sxw	OpenOffice "text" document; it's not really text format.
.stw	OpenOffice "text" document template.
.doc	Microsoft Word 97/2000/XP; an alternate .doc format for Microsoft Word 95 and 6.0 is also available.

Continued on next page

TABLE 18.9: OPENOFFICE WRITER FILE FORMATS *(continued)*

FORMAT	DESCRIPTION
.html	Hypertext markup language, suitable for a web page.
.rtf	Rich Text Format; a relatively universal format readable by several word processors.
.sdw	StarWriter 3.0/4.0/5.0.
.vor	StarWriter 3.0/4.0/5.0 template.
.txt	Regular text; an alternate .txt format with coding for line breaks is also available.

NOTE *When more experienced Linux users need desktop publishing, they use text-based tools. For example, tools such as TeX and LaTeX include text commands that format titles, italics, and more in a text file. This is not unprecedented; even WordPerfect set up similar text commands through version 5.2.*

Other OpenOffice Tools

Other OpenOffice tools of note are:

◆ OpenOffice Math allows users to create and document equations of varying complexity; it supports trigonometric functions, integrals, limits, exponents, and more. You can start it from the command line with the oomath command.

◆ OpenOffice Printer Setup allows you to configure a driver and print format for the other parts of the OpenOffice suite. You can start it from the command line with the oopadmin command.

◆ OpenOffice Repair lets you add, delete, or repair different components of the OpenOffice suite. You can start it from the command line with the oosetup command.

CROSSOVER OFFICE

If you want to move to Linux but absolutely need those Microsoft applications, one option is CodeWeavers' CrossOver Office. For $54.95 (retail), it uses some of the work of the WINE (WINE is not an emulator) project to let you run some of the most popular Microsoft Windows applications on your Linux computer. These applications include:

◆ Microsoft Word 97/2000 *

◆ Microsoft Excel 97/2000 *

◆ Microsoft Outlook 97/2000

◆ Microsoft PowerPoint 97/2000 *

◆ Microsoft Visio 2000

Continued on next page

CROSSOVER OFFICE *(continued)*

◆ Microsoft Internet Explorer 5.0/5.5

◆ Intuit Quicken 2002

◆ Lotus Notes R5

According to CodeWeavers, the applications noted with a * are "Gold Medal" applications that should run as you might expect in Microsoft Windows. Other applications may have significant bugs when you use CrossOver Office to run them under Linux. For details, navigate to www.codeweavers.com.

Understanding GNOME Office

There are a number of applications that are part of the GNOME Office suite. While they were not originally built as an integrated suite, they are integrated today. GNOME Office includes office applications developed by groups within the GNOME project. You can take a brief look at the list in Table 18.10.

TABLE 18.10: GNOME OFFICE APPLICATIONS

APPLICATION	DESCRIPTION
AbiWord	Word processor
Agnubis	Presentation manager; not currently available in RPM format, thus, not included with Red Hat Linux
Balsa	E-mail client
Dia	Diagramming program
Evolution	Personal information manager
Galeon	Web browser
GIMP	Image editing
GnuCash	Personal finance manager
Gnumeric	Spreadsheet
Guppi	Plotting; closely associated with Gnumeric
MrProject	Project management tool
Sketch	Vector drawing package; not included with Red Hat Linux
Sodipodi	Vector drawing package; not included with Red Hat Linux
Toutdoux	Project management tool; not included with Red Hat Linux

Not all of the tools are addressed here; for example, we covered Galeon and Evolution in Chapter 16, and we'll look at The GIMP later in this chapter. Not all of these tools are included with the Red Hat Linux 9 packages. For example, while the Agnubis presentation manager is part of the GNOME Office suite, it is still under development and has no official RPM package.

As of this writing, the GNOME website at `www.gnome.org/gnome-office` states that all of the OpenOffice applications will become part of GNOME Office. Yet development work on GNOME Office applications will continue.

NOTE *A number of GNOME Office applications are experimental and may not be ready for production uses. To see the status of your application, open it and then select Help ➢ About application. Generally, applications of version 1.0 and above are production ready; however, this does not preclude the problems. Most of these applications are developed and maintained by volunteers, and are under development even after version 1.0 is released.*

AbiWord

The GNOME word processor is known as AbiWord. It can open and close documents in many formats. Its capabilities are sufficient for most users and applications. Unfortunately, its support of Microsoft Word documents, in my opinion, is not as good as that of OpenOffice Writer. For example, Figure 18.5 illustrates a view of Chapter 16 that was formatted as a table.

FIGURE 18.5

AbiWord reads a Microsoft Word document.

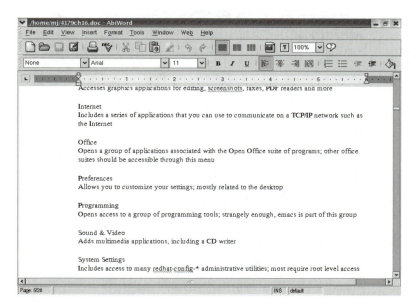

Unlike most OpenOffice applications, you need to select Main Menu ➢ Office ➢ More Office Applications before you can select AbiWord. Or you can start AbiWord with the `abiword` command in a GUI. This word processor supports a wide variety of formats, as shown in Table 18.11.

TABLE 18.11: ABIWORD DOCUMENT FORMATS

FORMAT	DESCRIPTION
.abw	AbiWord native format
.aw	Applix Words
.awt	AbiWord template
.dbk	DocBook
.doc	Microsoft Word
.fo	Extensible Stylesheet Language
.html, .htm	Hypertext Markup Language
.xhtml	Extensible Hypertext Markup Language
.isc, .iscii	Indian script code for information interchange
.kwd	KOffice word document
.latex	LaTeX; Lamport TeX tool to format text documents
.pdb	PalmDoc
.psitext, .psiword	Psion palm handheld computer document
.rtf	Rich Text Format
.txt, .text	Text; may also be encoded text
.nws	Newsgroup formatted text
.wml	Wireless Markup Language

Balsa

Balsa is a standard e-mail manager. Like the other e-mail applications we described in Chapters 16 and 17, it includes standard views of folders, as well as incoming and outgoing e-mail. Normally, it's set to the local account; Figure 18.6 illustrates incoming e-mail for the root user.

To start Balsa, select Main Menu ➤ Internet ➤ More Internet Applications ➤ Balsa. Alternately, you can start it from a command-line interface in the GUI with the `balsa` command.

The first time you run Balsa, you're prompted to set up incoming and outgoing settings for an e-mail account. You can configure it later with additional e-mail addresses from the Settings menu. All you need to do is configure a new identity for each account.

FIGURE 18.6

The Balsa e-mail
manager

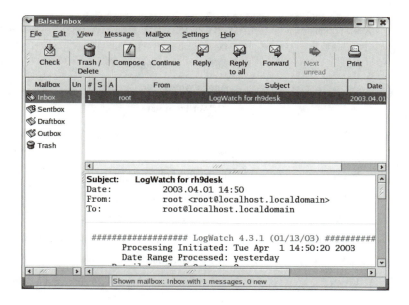

Dia

Dia, shown in Figure 18.7, is a diagram editor. As suggested by the name, it allows you to draw diagrams. As you can see in the figure, it supports the creation of different kinds of shapes in a diagram, similar to Microsoft Visio.

FIGURE 18.7

Dia, the diagram
editor

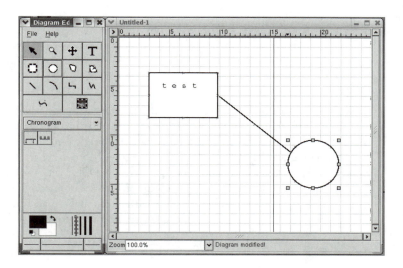

To start Dia, select Main Menu ➤ Office ➤ Dia Diagrams, or run the `dia` command from a GUI command-line interface.

GnuCash

GnuCash is an open source personal finance manager that can help you work with Quicken files.

To start GnuCash, select Main Menu ➤ Office ➤ More Office Applications ➤ GnuCash; or you can start it from a command-line interface in the GUI by using the gnucash command.

The first time you run GnuCash, you'll be prompted to set up a new account for your assets, liabilities, income, and expenses. You can also import files even from Quicken 2002; Figure 18.8 illustrates the import of a simple Quicken test file.

FIGURE 18.8

GnuCash imports a
Quicken file

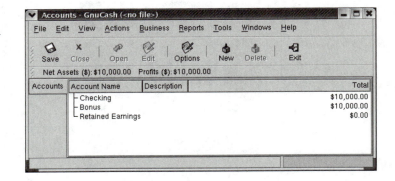

Gnumeric

The GNOME spreadsheet application, shown in Figure 18.9, is known as Gnumeric. As with AbiWord, you can start it by selecting Main Menu ➤ Office ➤ More Office Applications ➤ Gnumeric Spreadsheet. Or you can start it from a command-line interface in the GUI with the gnumeric command. This spreadsheet does support a wide variety of formats, as shown in Table 18.12.

TABLE 18.12: GNUMERIC FILE FORMATS

FORMAT	DESCRIPTION
.dif	Data Interchange Format
.dvi	From a groff text processor
.efs	Experimental
.po	Requires the GNOME glossary plug-in
.gnumeric	Gnumeric default XML format
.tex	LaTeX 2e file
.xls	Microsoft Excel format
.csv	Text export to a comma-separated format
.me	From a Troff text processor

FIGURE 18.9

Gnumeric

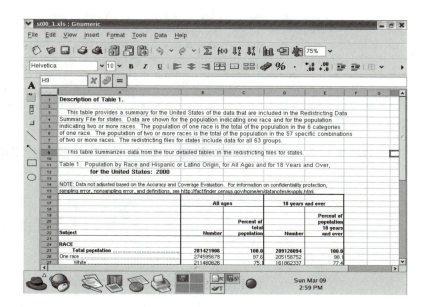

NOTE   *One component of a spreadsheet is a plotting program. The standard most closely associated with Gnumeric is known as Guppi. Unfortunately, the Guppi home page available at the time of this writing (*www.gnome.org/projects/guppi/*) recommends "other free plot programs" available at* www.gnome.org/projects/guppi/otherprogs.shtml

MrProject

The GNOME project management application is known as MrProject. You can start it by selecting Main Menu ➢ Office ➢ Project Management. Or you can start it from a command-line interface in the GUI with the `mrproject` command. It includes the basic tools of setting up a project: resource lists, Gantt charts, and task lists. However, it stands on its own; as of this writing, it does not import or export from other project management applications such as Microsoft Project.

Working with KOffice

There is a third major open source office suite, developed by the people behind KDE. While it's best to run KOffice applications in KDE, you can also run many of these applications in GNOME. The menu steps for starting each KOffice application are the same; they are accessible when you select Main Menu ➢ Office ➢ More Office Applications.

NOTE   *The Main Menu button in GNOME is also known as the K Menu button in KDE. In Red Hat Linux, both buttons normally have a Red Hat icon in the lower-left corner of the GUI desktop.*

The KOffice suite includes several applications, built mostly as a series of integrated applications. You can take a brief look at the list in Table 18.13.

NOTE *If you need to install KDE, use the* `redhat-config-packages` *utility described in Chapter 19. If you have installed KDE, you can make it your default GUI with the* `switchdesk` *utility described in Chapter 15.*

TABLE 18.13: KOFFICE APPLICATIONS

APPLICATION	DESCRIPTION
Karbon14	Lets you draw lines and shapes
KChart	Supports drawing graphs and charts
KFormula	Allows you to create and edit mathematical formulas
Kivio	Permits the creation of flow charts
KOffice Workspace	Opens a GUI front end to other KOffice applications
Kontour	Supports drawing lines and shapes; similar to Karbon14
KPresenter	Opens a presentation program
KSpread	Starts the KDE spreadsheet program
KThesaurus	Begins the KDE thesaurus
Kugar	Supports generation of business reports
KWord	Opens the KDE word processor

NOTE *Many KOffice applications are experimental and may not be ready for production use. To see the status of your application, open it and then select Help* ➢ *About application. Generally, applications of version 1.0 and above are production ready; however, this does not preclude the problems. Most of these applications are developed and maintained by volunteers, and are under development even after version 1.0 is released.*

Karbon14

One of the KDE drawing programs is known as Karbon14. It includes several basic drawing functions. You can start it by selecting Main Menu ➢ Office ➢ More Office Applications ➢ Karbon14, or by running the `karbon` command.

As of this writing, the version of Red Hat Linux 9 that I'm using includes Karbon14 version 0.0.1, and is thus not ready for production use. It is a work in progress. However, the potential is good, as you can see in Figure 18.10, which is from a later version of Karbon14. It will probably be available if you update the `koffice-*` RPM package from Red Hat in 2003.

FIGURE 18.10

Karbon14 at work

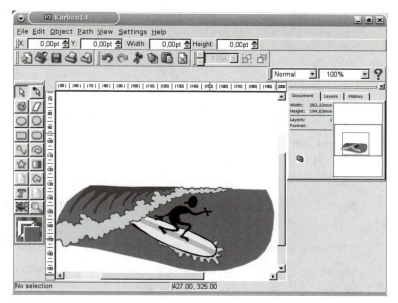

Figure 18.10 is courtesy of Rob Buis, one of the developers of Karbon14.

KChart

KChart is charting software that primarily is used with KSpread, the KDE spreadsheet application. You can start it by selecting Main Menu ➢ Office ➢ More Office Applications ➢ KChart, or by running the `kchart` command.

Once you've created a chart, it's easy to organize data in views such as a pie chart, a graph, or colored areas. Figure 18.11 illustrates a bar chart.

FIGURE 18.11

A bar chart in
KChart

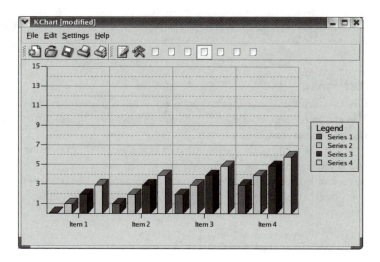

Kivio

Kivio is the KDE diagram editor. As you'd expect, it allows you to draw diagrams. It is similar to the GNOME Dia and Microsoft Visio programs. You can start it by selecting Main Menu ➤ Office ➤ More Office Applications ➤ Kivio, or by running the `kivio` command.

KPresenter

When you create a presentation, you're essentially creating a slide show. Presentation applications are basically specialized word processors with graphics, and they support a slide show to a large audience in a room or online. You can start KPresenter by selecting Main Menu ➤ Office ➤ More Office Applications ➤ KPresenter, or by running the `kpresenter` command.

You can use KPresenter to build the same types of presentations as you might with other applications, such as Microsoft PowerPoint or StarOffice Impress. Figure 18.12 illustrates a presentation imported from a Microsoft PowerPoint file.

FIGURE 18.12

A Microsoft Power-Point file open in KPresenter

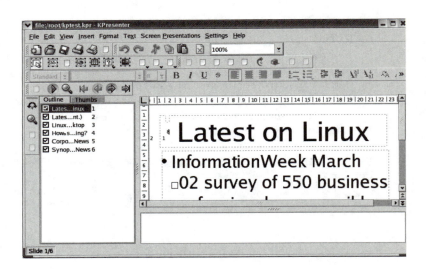

As you can see in the figure, KPresenter includes a wide variety of toolbars, some that allow you to manage color and others that let you draw, manage text, and add objects. The toolbars are described in Table 18.14.

TABLE 18.14: KPRESENTER TOOLBARS

TOOLBAR	DESCRIPTION
Edit	Includes edit and zoom functions
File	Adds basic file, print, and slideshow functions
Format	Includes functions to manage the look of lines and shapes

Continued on next page

TABLE 18.14: KPRESENTER TOOLBARS *(continued)*

TOOLBAR	DESCRIPTION
Insert	Supports adding text, tables, pictures, lines, and more
Presentation	Lets you manage the organization of your slides
Text	Supports management of text in the presentation
Tools	Adds zoom, rotate, and object management functions

When you first start KPresenter, you'll be able to select from different templates or existing documents. If neither choice works for you, KPresenter can start you with an empty document.

While KPresenter's ability to import files is limited to KPresenter, XML, and PowerPoint files, it can export presentations in a variety of formats, including KWord (.kwd), HTML, and RTF.

KSpread

A spreadsheet lets you define a range of numbers. With the equations of your choice, you can set up a spreadsheet to perform a variety of calculations in various scenarios. It's useful for everything from statistical analysis to business modeling and projections.

You can start it by selecting Main Menu ➤ Office ➤ More Office Applications ➤ KSpread, or by running the kspread command. Figure 18.13 illustrates KSpread and some basic population data from the year 2000 U.S. census.

FIGURE 18.13

KSpread and the census

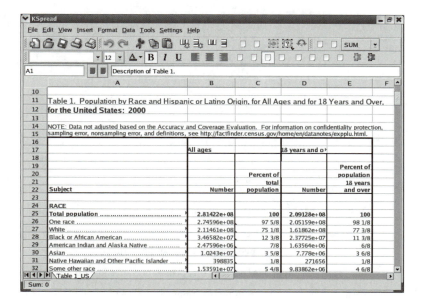

As you can see in the figure, KSpread has the basic look and feel of a spreadsheet. It includes several toolbars, described in Table 18.15.

TABLE 18.15: KSPREAD TOOLBARS

TOOLBAR	DESCRIPTION
Color/Border	Allows you to configure the look and feel of cell and table borders
Edit	Includes edit, sort, and chart functions
File	Adds basic file and print functions
Format	Supports basic formats for text and numbers in each cell
Math	Lets you configure basic math functions for a cell

KSpread works with many types of spreadsheets, including the formats described in Table 18.16. As you can see, KSpread works with spreadsheets from Microsoft Excel, Applix Spreadsheets, Gnumeric, and Quattro Pro, among others. You can also set up KSpread with text files in comma-separated format.

TABLE 18.16: KSPREAD FILE FORMATS

FORMAT	DESCRIPTION
.asa	Applix spreadsheet format
.csv	Comma-separated format; a spreadsheet in a text file
.gnumeric	Gnumeric spreadsheet format
.html	Web page
.ksp	Kspread spreadsheet
.wb2	Quattro Pro spreadsheet format
.xls	Microsoft Excel 97/2000/XP or Excel 95/5.0

KWord

One of the banes of computing is the different word processing formats. You need converters to translate Microsoft Word documents to Corel WordPerfect documents to AbiWord documents. While converters are built into most word processing programs, including KWord, every word processing application includes special features that aren't always translated.

There are a number of special features used by people in a number of areas that KWord does not handle properly. Nevertheless, KWord is good enough for most applications, businesses, and more. New documents created in KWord can include all of the features that you might find in most Microsoft Word documents.

You can start it by selecting Main Menu ➤ Office ➤ More Office Applications ➤ KWord, or by running the kword command. Figure 18.14 illustrates a typical document.

FIGURE 18.14

KWord showing a
Microsoft Word
document

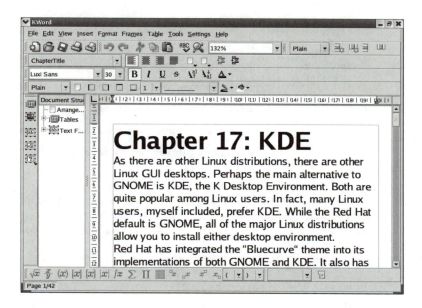

As you can see in the figure, KWord includes five default toolbars: File, Edit, Insert, Paragraph, and Format. KWord can accommodate up to eight different toolbars described in Table 18.17.

TABLE 18.17: KWORD TOOLBARS

TOOLBARS	DESCRIPTION
Borders	Allows you to configure the look and feel of borders
Edit	Includes edit, sort, zoom, and size functions
File	Adds basic file and print functions
Format	Supports basic formats for text and color
Formula	Includes math functions
Insert	Lets you add tables, pictures, and other objects
Paragraph	Supports styles, alignment, and bullets
Table	Allows you to set up a table in the document

KWord works with files from other word processors, including those listed in Table 18.18.

TABLE 18.18: KWord File Formats

FORMAT	DESCRIPTION
.kwd	KWord document
.doc	Microsoft Word
.html	Hypertext Markup Language, suitable for a web page
.rtf	Rich Text Format; a relatively universal format readable by several word processors
.sam	AmiPro document
.tex	TeX-formatted file
.txt	Regular text
.wpd	WordPerfect document

Other KOffice Tools

Other KOffice tools of note are accessible through the Main Menu ➤ Office ➤ More Office Applications submenu:

◆ KFormula allows you to create and document equations of varying complexity; it supports trigonometric functions, integrals, limits, exponents, and more. It is functionally similar to OpenOffice Math. You can start it with the `kformula` command.

◆ KOffice Workspace is a front end to other KOffice applications. You can start it with the `koshell` command.

◆ Kontour supports drawings; it can also take input from scanners. You can start it with the `kontour` command.

◆ KThesaurus lists comparable words in three categories: synonyms, more general words (hypernyms), and more specific words (hyponyms). You can start it with the `kthesaurus` command.

◆ Kugar is a report manager; the companion Kugar Designer is a report-creation tool; sample files are available in the `/usr/share/apps/kugar/templates` directory.

Taking Advantage of Graphical Applications

Linux is well suited for graphics. Several major motion picture studios produce animations and special effects on Linux computers. With that in mind, it's worth exploring some of the graphical applications available for Linux.

A number of graphical applications come with Red Hat Linux 9. They include PDF (Portable Document Format) readers, image viewers, and screen-capture programs. You can select most of these tools from the Main Menu ➤ Graphics and Main Menu ➤ Graphics ➤ More Graphics Applications submenus.

Graphical Document Readers

Three graphical document formats in Linux are PDF (Portable Document Format), PS (PostScript), and DVI (Device Independent).

While you can download Adobe Acrobat to read your PDF documents, Red Hat Linux includes two native PDF readers: xpdf and PS/PDF viewer. PostScript (PS) is a document format that you can also read with GNOME Ghostview (GGV). You can use the DVI Viewer, KViewShell, to read DVI documents.

NOTE *As strange as it sounds, the KDE Fax Viewer, KFax, is not used to send or receive faxes. It can only be used to view fax files. For more information on a Linux fax program, see* `www.cce.com/efax`.

XPDF

To start xpdf, select Main Menu ➤ Graphics ➤ PDF Viewer, or run the **xpdf** command. This opens a simple screen with no toolbar; you can click the right mouse button to access some basic commands. If you want to open a PDF document, type **o**; in the Open dialog box shown in Figure 18.15, you'll be able to access open PDF files.

FIGURE 18.15

Accessing a PDF file

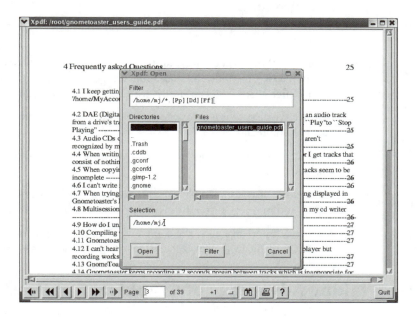

Once the file is open, you can use the arrow keys at the bottom of the screen to navigate through the document. Alternatively, you could use the basic commands listed in Table 18.19. Other commands are available; click the Question button for details.

TABLE 18.19: BASIC XPDF COMMANDS

COMMAND	DESCRIPTION
o	Opens a new file
f	Finds text
n	Goes to the following page
p	Moves to the previous page

THE PS/PDF VIEWER

The PS/PDF Viewer is also known as KGhostView. To start this application, select Main Menu ➢ Graphics ➢ More Graphics Applications ➢ PS/PDF Viewer, or run the `pdfviewer` command. This application provides a more intuitive interface for viewing both PDF and PS files, as shown in Figure 18.16.

FIGURE 18.16

Using KGhostView on a PDF file

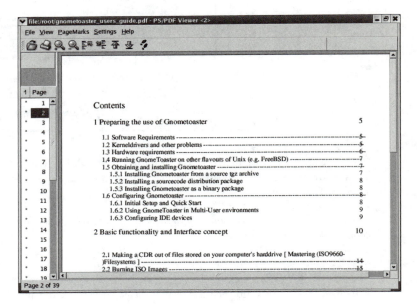

THE POSTSCRIPT VIEWER

The PostScript Viewer, also known as GNOME Ghostview (GGV), can also help you read PDF and PS files. To start this application, select Main Menu ➢ Graphics ➢ More Graphics Applications ➢ PostScript Viewer, or run the `ggv` command. It is similarly intuitive to KGhostView; the windows are similar.

THE DVI VIEWER

A number of Unix and Linux documents are processed from TeX to Device Independent (DVI) files. This DVI viewer is known as KGhostView. On the surface, it is similar to PDF, because it illustrates the GUI view of a typeset document.

To start this application, run the `kghostview` command. For full functionality, this application requires the `tetex-*` RPM packages. You can see it at work in Figure 18.17.

FIGURE 18.17

Viewing a DVI file

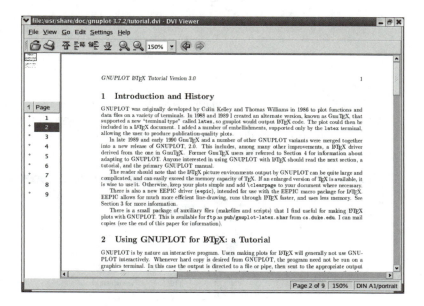

There are alternative DVI viewers. You can start KDVI by selecting Main Menu ➢ Graphics ➢ DVI viewer. You can start XDVI by selecting Main Menu ➢ Graphics ➢ More Graphics Applications ➢ DVI viewer

NOTE   *TeX and LaTeX are formatting languages common in Linux and Unix, and are used to set up text files in a format suitable for publication.*

Image Viewers

The Red Hat Linux GUI includes several image viewers. With some of these viewers, you can open, manipulate, and edit existing images. Each have different capabilities; viewers such as GQview help you create thumbnails; Kuickshow sets up an image browser; the Icon Editor helps you manage the look and feel of icons within various GUI applications.

GQVIEW

GQview is a graphics file viewer that lets you view a variety of images, set up slideshows, organize thumbnails, and more. To start this application, select Main Menu ➢ Graphics ➢ GQview Image Viewer, or run the `gqview` command. As you can see in Figure 18.18, the basic interface is fairly straightforward.

FIGURE 18.18

Using GQview to review images

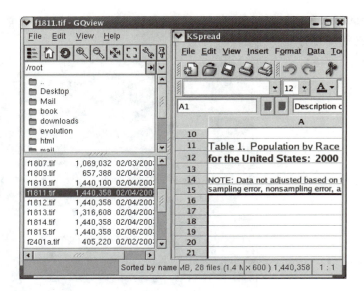

THE EYE OF GNOME

The Eye of GNOME is a graphics file viewer similar to GQview. It allows you to view images from a variety of file formats. Writing from this program is somewhat limited; by default you can write files only in JPEG and PNG formats.

To start this application, select Main Menu ➤ Graphics ➤ More Graphics Applications ➤ Eye of Gnome Image Viewer, or run the eog command. As shown in Figure 18.19, the commands for viewing the graphics file are fairly clear.

THE ICON EDITOR

The Icon Editor, KIconEdit, enables you to open and modify the look and feel of different icons. To start this application, select Main Menu ➤ Graphics ➤ More Graphics Applications ➤ Icon Editor, or run the kiconedit command.

THE IMAGE VIEWER

The Image Viewer, KView, is another graphics file viewer similar to GQview and the Eye of GNOME. It supports output in many different image formats. To start this application, select Main Menu ➤ Graphics ➤ More Graphics Applications ➤ Image Viewer, or run the kview command.

KUICKSHOW

Kuickshow is an image browser that lists available images in the directory of your choice. To start this application, select Main Menu ➤ Graphics ➤ More Graphics Applications ➤ Kuickshow, or run the kuickshow command.

When you double-click on an image file, Kuickshow opens the image in its own window. You can then right-click on the image to open a menu that lets you manipulate the look and feel of the image. The screens are shown in Figure 18.20.

FIGURE 18.19

Eye of GNOME

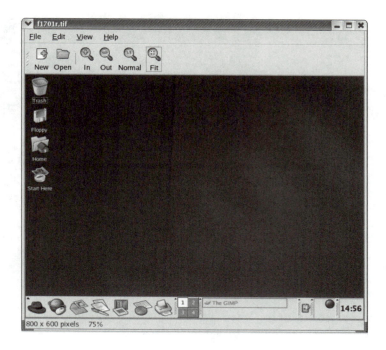

FIGURE 18.20

The Kuickshow
image manager

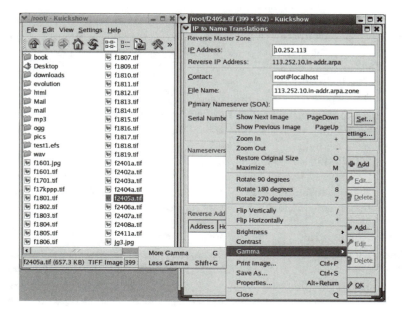

PAINT PROGRAM

The Paint Program, also known as KPaint, allows you to open, add to, and modify the images of your choice. To start this application, select Main Menu ➢ Graphics ➢ More Graphics Applications ➢ Paint Program, or run the `kpaint` command. For example, Figure 18.21 illustrates how I've added and cut some graphics from the first figure in Chapter 16.

FIGURE 18.21

Manipulating with KPaint

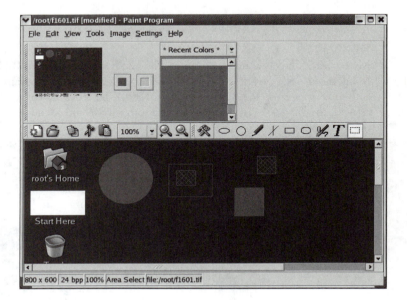

Screen-Capture Programs

Sometimes you'll want to record the settings on your screen. If you're describing a problem to someone, you can set up a picture that includes the look and feel of your desktop.

Some programs take their images from other hardware, such as digital cameras and scanners. Others take their images directly from a desktop screen or an active desktop window.

DIGITAL CAMERAS

There are several GUI digital camera front ends to the `gphoto2-*` RPM. The KDE package is Kamera; the standard Red Hat package is the Digital Camera Tool. To start this application, select Main Menu ➢ Graphics ➢ Digital Camera Tool, or run the `gtcam` command. The list of cameras that it can detect is not complete; more information is available from www.gphoto.org.

NOTE   There are a couple of specialty HOWTO documents at www.tldp.org *that may help: the Kodak-Digitalcam-HOWTO and the USB-Digital-Camera-HOWTO.*

SCANNING

The standard Red Hat GUI scanning program is known as xsane, which you can start by selecting Main Menu ➢ Graphics ➢ Scanning, or by running the **xsane** command. Not all scanners are detected by xsane; in that case, you're prompted with this information, and xsane does not open.

There is also a KDE scanning program, Kooka. It supports xsane and provides character-recognition functions. You start Kooka by selecting Main Menu ➢ Graphics ➢ More Graphics Applications ➢ Scan & OCR Program or by issuing the **kooka** command.

THE GIMP

My favorite Linux graphics program is The GIMP, which is the GNU Image Manipulation Program. Many Linux users prefer The GIMP to other high-end image programs, such as Adobe's Photoshop and Jasc's Paint Shop Pro. It's a part of the GNOME office suite. I've used it to configure most of the artwork for this book. To start this application, select Main Menu ➢ Graphics ➢ The GIMP, or run the **gimp** command.

For example, when I took a screenshot of KPPP in Chapter 17, I started The GIMP, then selected File ➢ Acquire ➢ Screen Shot. This opened the Screen Shot window. Once KPPP was ready, I clicked OK in the screenshot window; this turned the cursor into a plus sign (+). I used it to select the KPPP window. When I right-clicked the screenshot, it opened a menu that I used to save the image in the file of my choice. The various screens and result are shown in Figure 18.22.

FIGURE 18.22

The GIMP at work

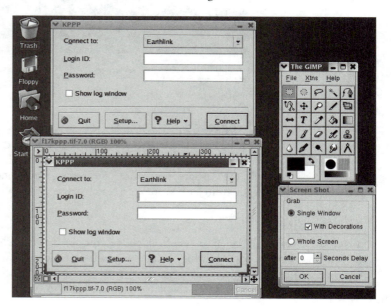

Another Graphical Program: Color Chooser

KColorChooser, also known as KColorEdit, allows you to edit color palettes. To start this application, select Main Menu ➢ Graphics ➢ More Graphics Applications ➢ Color Chooser, or run the **kcolor-chooser** command.

Figure 18.23 illustrates where DarkCyan fits in the standard color scheme. Note the relative levels of RGB (red, green, and blue); every color has different levels of red, green, and blue between 0 and 255.

FIGURE 18.23

Defining colors with KColorChooser

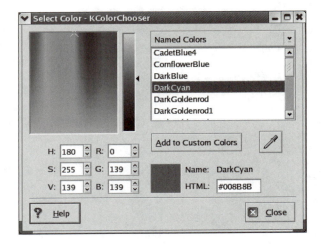

Summary

Red Hat Linux includes a wide variety of fully featured GUI applications. The Red Hat CDs include three office suites as well as several high-powered graphical applications.

The office suites included with Red Hat Linux are OpenOffice, GNOME Office, and KOffice. All three suites include word processors, spreadsheets, drawing programs, diagram creators, and presentation managers. Project management tools, mathematical formula managers, and personal finance programs are also available.

The graphical programs run the gamut from simple color managers (like GQview) to fully featured graphical programs (like The GIMP). GUI documentation viewers, such as PDF, DVI, and PS readers, fall into the same category.

In Chapter 19, we'll look at many of the GUI administrative tools created by Red Hat. We've referred to these tools by their utility names, which normally start with `redhat-config-*`. Most of these tools are available from the Main Menu ➢ System Settings submenu.

Chapter 19

Red Hat Graphical Front Ends

THIS CHAPTER FOCUSES THE graphical utilities developed by Red Hat that let you administer and configure Linux on your computer and network. The content of this chapter may be sacrilegious to more traditional Linux users—they prefer to work from the command-line interface.

Traditional Linux users do have a point: you can do more from the command line. The Red Hat graphical utilities are still a work in progress. In fact, they are just "front ends" for editing text configuration files. However, they help the newer Linux user make the transition to Linux.

We believe that you can use the Red Hat graphical utilities to configure hardware, local services, and network services, and administer your system on a basic level. If you analyze the resulting changes to the associated configuration files, you use these utilities to help you learn more about Linux.

However, keep in mind that these utilities are fairly new. Development work continues. You should check your configuration files after using a graphical utility to ensure that the changes reflect your intent.

To see the list of available utilities, go to a command-line interface. Type in **redhat-config-** and then press the Tab key twice. You'll see a whole list of utilities, as shown in Figure 19.1. Naturally, you can start these utilities with the commands you see. Some of these utilities are covered in more detail in other chapters.

FIGURE 19.1

redhat-config-*
graphical utilities

```
[root@RH9Desk root]# redhat-config-
redhat-config-bind              redhat-config-packages
redhat-config-bind-gui          redhat-config-printer
redhat-config-date              redhat-config-printer-gui
redhat-config-httpd             redhat-config-printer-tui
redhat-config-keyboard          redhat-config-proc
redhat-config-kickstart         redhat-config-rootpassword
redhat-config-language          redhat-config-samba
redhat-config-mouse             redhat-config-securitylevel
redhat-config-network           redhat-config-services
redhat-config-network-cmd       redhat-config-soundcard
redhat-config-network-druid     redhat-config-time
redhat-config-network-gui       redhat-config-users
redhat-config-network-tui       redhat-config-xfree86
redhat-config-nfs
[root@RH9Desk root]# redhat-config-
```

Most are also accessible in GNOME or KDE when you select Main ➤ System Tools or Main Menu ➤ System Settings. (If you're using KDE, the button still has a Red Hat; it's just called the K Menu button instead of the Main Menu button.) A number of these utilities require administrative privileges; if you're not logged in as the root (or otherwise privileged) user, you'll be prompted for the root password as required.

If you don't see a specific tool from a command line or the Main Menu, you may need to install it. In most cases, the RPM package name is the same as the command; for example, the Samba configuration tool is `redhat-config-samba`, which comes from the `redhat-config-samba-*` RPM.

Because there is no official category for any `redhat-config-*` utilities, I've classified them arbitrarily in this chapter. This chapter covers the following topics:

- ◆ Configuring with basic configuration utilities
- ◆ Connecting with network configuration utilities
- ◆ Using system administration utilities
- ◆ Working with service configuration utilities

Configuring with Basic Configuration Utilities

Several basic Red Hat graphical configuration utilities are available, and they are all accessible in GNOME when you select Main Menu ➤ System Settings. These utilities let you set the date and time, customize your keyboard, designate a default language, customize the functionality of your mouse, and set up your sound card, as summarized in Table 19.1.

TABLE 19.1: RED HAT BASIC ADMINISTRATION UTILITIES

UTILITY	FUNCTION
`redhat-config-date` `redhat-config-time`	Allows you to configure the date, time, and a connection to NTP server(s)
`redhat-config-keyboard`	Lets you set the default keyboard for your system
`redhat-config-language`	Permits you to change the default language associated with your graphical desktop
`redhat-config-mouse`	Allows you to configure the mouse or other pointing device that you're using
`redhat-config-soundcard`	Supports automatic detection and configuration of a sound card

Setting a Date and Time

Setting the right date and time for your computer can be important. If you're running an Internet store with servers in different time zones, you need to synchronize the time between the servers. Red Hat Linux is configured to use the Network Time Protocol (NTP), which is part of the TCP/IP protocol stack.

You can start the Red Hat Date/Time Properties tool by selecting Main Menu ➤ System Settings ➤ Date & Time, or you can run the `redhat-config-date` and `redhat-config-time` commands from a GUI command-line interface. This opens the Date/Time Properties window, shown in Figure 19.2.

FIGURE 19.2

Date/Time
Properties

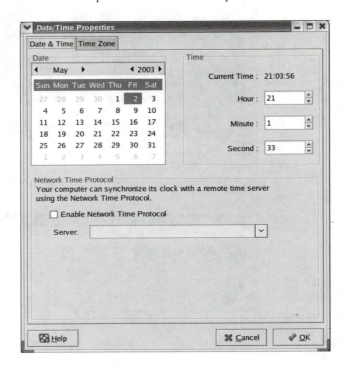

You can set the date and time yourself. Once you've accepted any changes, Linux changes the hardware clock on your computer. Alternatively, you can set your computer to synchronize its clock with a remote server. With NTP and a network connection, Linux can send a message to a central time server for the current date and time.

NOTE   *If you give up control of your system clock to an NTP server, the Date/Time Properties window does not allow you to set the time independently.*

In any case, Red Hat Linux also allows you to set the time zone associated with your computer. As you can see in Figure 19.3, you can set your computer to a wide range of different time zones. The default is the standard U.S. East Coast time zone, shown as America/New_York. You can set your system to any one of several hundred locations.

FIGURE 19.3

Setting your
time zone

Unless your computer is configured as a dual-boot with another operating system such as Microsoft Windows, you should activate the System Clock Uses UTC option. UTC is the French acronym for Coordinated Universal Time, which corresponds to Greenwich Mean Time. If you select UTC, Linux sets your hardware clock to this time and calculates the time zone difference to your location for the system clock.

Time zone changes are saved in /etc/sysconfig/clock; any NTP servers that you designate are recorded in /etc/ntp/ntpservers. Naturally, you can edit these files directly. Perhaps the authoritative website on the NTP server is located at the University of Delaware, at www.eecis.udel.edu/~ntp. It includes a link to a list of active NTP servers around the world.

The Red Hat Date/Time Properties tool automatically sets the Network Time Protocol daemon, ntpd, to start the next time you boot Linux in runlevels 3 and 5. You can verify this with the following command:

```
# chkconfig --list ntpd
```

If you've configured a firewall, the Date/Time Properties tool automatically creates firewall rules to allow your computer to receive data from an external NTP server. For example, if you list the rules in your firewall with the iptables -L command, you'll see the following rule in your firewall chain:

```
ACCEPT udp -- ns3.oit.unc.edu anywhere  udp spt:ntp dpt:ntp
```

where `ns3.oit.unc.edu` is the fully-qualified domain name of the time server. If you're using a different time server, substitute accordingly.

Configuring Your Keyboard

You can configure keyboards that correspond to a wide variety of languages and dialects or systems. You use the Red Hat keyboard utility to set the keyboard that most closely corresponds to your system.

Start this tool by selecting Main Menu ➤ System Settings ➤ Keyboard, or run the `redhat-config-keyboard` command from a GUI command-line interface. This opens the Keyboard window, shown in Figure 19.4.

FIGURE 19.4

Selecting a keyboard

As you can see in the figure, there can be more than one keyboard for different languages and national locations. If necessary, select the keyboard that most closely fits your hardware and click OK. Changes are reflected in `/etc/sysconfig/keyboard`.

TIP   *If you run* `redhat-config-keyboard` *from a text-mode console, this utility will give you the same choices (in a different order) in a blue text-mode, low-graphics screen.*

Selecting a Language

You can use the Red Hat language utility to select a graphical default from the languages that you have installed. Start this utility by selecting Main Menu ➤ System Settings ➤ Language, or run the `redhat-config-language` command from a GUI command-line interface. This opens the Language Selection window, shown in Figure 19.5. The window normally includes the languages that you included during the installation process.

FIGURE 19.5

Setting the default language

If you didn't remember to install the language that you need when you installed Red Hat Linux, you can adapt. Install the RPM packages associated with the desired languages. To find the appropriate list, open the `comps.xml` file. You can find it on the first Red Hat installation CD, in the `/RedHat/base` directory or the `/usr/share/comps/i386` directory. For example, if you want to install the packages associated with the Korean language, find the Korean Support section in that file. (For more information on `comps.xml`, including available languages, see Web Chapter 5, which can be found on the Sybex website at www.sybex.com.)

```
<packagelist>
    <packagereq type="mandatory">nvi-m17n</packagereq>
    <packagereq type="optional" requires="kdelibs">kde-i18n-Korean</packagereq>
    <packagereq type="optional" requires="man-pages">man-pages-ko</packagereq>
    <packagereq type="optional" requires="XFree86">ami</packagereq>
    <packagereq type="optional" requires="XFree86">hanterm-xf</packagereq>
    <packagereq type="mandatory">h2ps</packagereq>
    <packagereq type="mandatory">nhpf</packagereq>
    <packagereq type="mandatory">ttfonts-ko</packagereq>
</packagelist>
```

Install at least the mandatory RPM packages from this list. Next, open `/etc/sysconfig/i18n`. Modify the SUPPORTED variable for the appropriate locale. Different languages and character sets are listed in the `/usr/X11R6/lib/X11/locale` directory. For example, the associated language locale and character type for Korean in that directory is

```
ko_KR.UTF-8
```

Now open the `/etc/sysconfig/i18n` file. Add the desired locale to the SUPPORTED variable in the following format:

```
language_locale.chartype:language_locale:language
```

For the listed Korean language, locale, and character type, that is

    ko_KR.UTF-8:ko_KR:ko

You can see the result in Figure 19.6, which shows my /etc/sysconfig/i18n file. This file includes settings for Chinese, U.S. English, French, and Korean.

FIGURE 19.6

/etc/sysconfig/
i18n language
settings

```
LANG="en_US.UTF-8"
SUPPORTED="zh_CN.GB18030:zh_CN:zh:en_US.UTF-8:en_US:en:fr_FR.UTF-8:fr_FR:fr:ko_K
R.UTF-8:ko_KR:ko"
SYSFONT="latarcyrheb-sun16"
~
~
~
```

The Korean language option should now appear the next time you open the redhat-config-language utility window. When you select a different language, redhat-config-language tells you that the changes will take effect the next time you log in. Figure 19.7 illustrates the result, a Korean language version of the GNOME desktop.

FIGURE 19.7

The GNOME
desktop in Korean

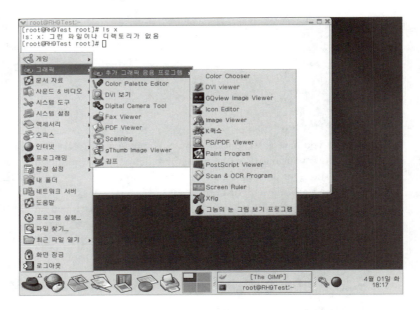

Some applications require their own language packages and settings, which is beyond the scope of redhat-config-language and this book. Several language-specific HOWTOs are available through the Linux Documentation Project (www.tldp.org) that may be able to help.

TIP   KDE includes its own language configuration applet in the KDE Control Center, as described in Chapter 17.

Configuring a Mouse

You can configure many kinds of pointing devices. The most common pointing device today is a mouse; the terms are used interchangeably during the configuration process. To configure the settings for your default pointing device, start the Red Hat mouse configuration utility.

Start this utility by selecting Main Menu ➤ System Settings ➤ Mouse, or run the `redhat-config-mouse` command from a GUI command-line interface. This opens the Mouse Configuration window, shown in Figure 19.8.

FIGURE 19.8

Configuring a mouse

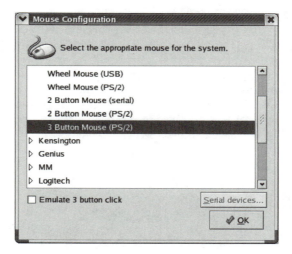

The default is based on your current `/etc/sysconfig/mouse` file. Any changes you make are written there. If you have a two-button mouse, you may want to activate the Emulate 3 Button Click option. This allows your mouse to simulate the functionality of a middle mouse button when you press both the left and right buttons simultaneously. As noted in Chapter 17, KDE uses the middle mouse button to open a pop-up menu of commands.

If you have a mouse that is connected to a serial port, you'll be able to select the Serial Devices button. This opens a menu where you can select the actual serial device in use. If you've used this computer on a Microsoft operating system before, you should set your mouse to the associated Microsoft COM port per Table 19.2.

TABLE 19.2: MOUSE SERIAL DEVICES

DEVICE FILE	DESCRIPTION
/dev/ttyS0	Corresponds to the Microsoft COM1 port
/dev/ttyS1	Corresponds to the Microsoft COM2 port
/dev/ttyS2	Corresponds to the Microsoft COM3 port
/dev/ttyS3	Corresponds to the Microsoft COM4 port

TIP   These serial devices also help you configure many telephone modems. If you've configured your modem in Microsoft Windows, pay attention to the COM port associated with the modem. If you run the `ls -l /dev/modem` *command, you may see a link to the corresponding device file shown in Table 19.2.*

If you've made a change and close `redhat-config-mouse`, Linux stops and restarts the mouse console.

TIP   You don't need a GUI to run `redhat-config-mouse`; *if you're in a text console, Red Hat automatically starts a text-mode version of this utility.*

Setting Up a Sound Card

Red Hat Linux lets you configure many kinds of sound cards. To set the settings for your default pointing device, start the Red Hat sound configuration utility.

Start this utility by selecting Main Menu ➤ System Settings ➤ Soundcard Detection, or run the `redhat-config-soundcard` command from a GUI command-line interface. This opens the Audio Devices window, shown in Figure 19.9.

FIGURE 19.9

Configuring a
sound card

If `redhat-config-soundcard` detects a sound card on your system, you'll see the make and model of the card in the Audio Devices window. You can test the result by clicking on the Play Test Sound option. Assuming that you have a sound card and have connected your speakers, you should hear a sound and get a confirmation window. Confirm the result. Then you click OK in the Audio Devices window; if Linux needs to install special kernel modules for your sound card, changes are written to `/etc/modules.conf`.

NOTE   As of this writing, if you install the `sndconfig-*` *RPM, you can use the* `sndconfig` *utility from the command line to configure your sound card. It is more flexible, since it allows you to set specific hardware addresses for your card. However, Red Hat has deprecated* `sndconfig`, *which means that they plan to delete it from a future release of Red Hat Linux. This is a sign of Red Hat's confidence in* `redhat-config-soundcard`.

Connecting with Network Configuration Utilities

Many graphical Red Hat utilities are available that help you connect your computer to a network. Some help you configure various network services. While these utilities are covered in detail in their respective chapters, let's take a brief look at each Red Hat network graphical tool.

This includes the utilities summarized in Table 19.3. Remember, this is an arbitrary list that summarizes the utilities in this section.

TABLE 19.3: RED HAT GRAPHICAL NETWORK CONFIGURATION UTILITIES

UTILITY	FUNCTION
redhat-config-network-druid	Helps you configure a network connection
redhat-config-network-tui	Helps you configure a network connection from a text console
redhat-config-network redhat-config-network-gui	Lists settings associated with configured network adapters
redhat-config-httpd	Lets you configure an Apache web server
redhat-config-bind	Allows you to set up a DNS server
redhat-config-nfs	Helps you configure an NFS server
redhat-config-samba	Lets you configure a Samba server
Samba Web Administration Tool	Allows you to configure a Samba server through a web-based interface

Basic Network Configuration

The two basic Red Hat graphical network configuration utilities are redhat-config-network and redhat-config-network-druid. These utilities control the configuration of network devices on your computer.

Start redhat-config-network-druid. Run that command from a graphical command-line interface, or select Main Menu ➢ System Tools ➢ Internet Configuration Wizard. This opens the Add New Device Type window, shown in Figure 19.10.

FIGURE 19.10

Adding a new
network device

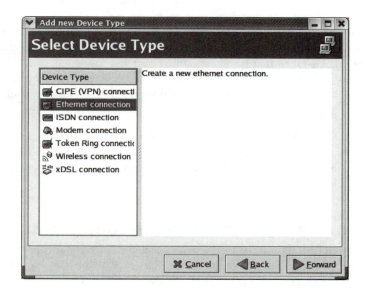

KUDZU

If Red Hat Linux did not detect your network card, try starting the Red Hat Hardware Discovery Utility, also known as kudzu. Sometimes kudzu can help you detect newly installed hardware, including network cards.

It runs automatically during the boot process. However, if you've just installed a new network card such as a PC Card in a laptop computer PCMCIA slot, you may need to run kudzu again. If it finds something new, it will offer to configure the hardware for you, as shown here.

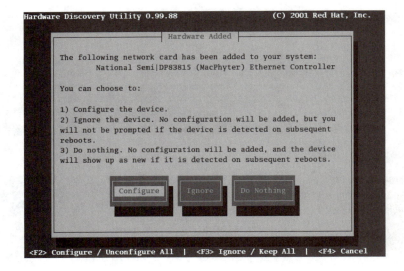

NOTE *See Chapter 21 for instructions for using* `redhat-config-network-druid` *to set up a telephone modem.*

   In this section, we'll use it to configure a second (undetected) Ethernet connection. Highlight Ethernet Connection in the window and click Forward to continue. This brings you to the window shown in Figure 19.11, where you can review the detected Ethernet card. If Linux has already detected your second network card, you should be home free. Figure 19.11 assumes that Linux did not detect this card. Select Other Ethernet Card and click Forward to continue.

   Now you can set up the device driver and hardware addresses associated with this second Ethernet card. Figure 19.12 allows you to specify the driver and hardware resources associated with the new card.

FIGURE 19.11

Selecting an
Ethernet Card

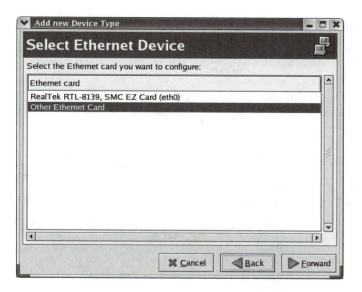

FIGURE 19.12

Specifying Ethernet
adapter resources

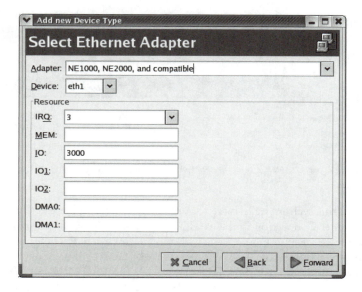

Finally, you can configure the network settings for the new card. As shown in Figure 19.13, you can use a DHCP or BOOTP server. (For more information on DHCP and BOOTP, see Chapter 24.) The Dialup option normally applies only if you're configuring a telephone modem, and is associated with a telephone modem connection to an ISP.

Alternatively, you can set up a static IP address. For more information on assigning IP addresses, see Chapter 20.

FIGURE 19.13

IP address settings

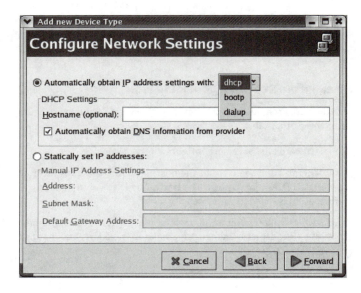

Once you've confirmed the changes, you're taken to the Network configuration window, shown in Figure 19.14. This is the `redhat-config-network` tool, which you can also access by selecting Main Menu ➤ System Settings ➤ Network.

FIGURE 19.14

Managing a network configuration

When a network card is first configured, it is not active. You may activate it through the boot process, or you can highlight it and click the Activate button, as shown in Figure 19.14. If the configuration that you set up is good, the displayed Status will change from Inactive to Active.

The configuration for each network card is saved in the `/etc/sysconfig/networking/devices` directory. The configuration file for an Ethernet network card is `ifcfg-eth`n, where *n* is the number associated with the card, usually 0 or 1.

SUPPLEMENTAL NETWORK CONFIGURATION

You can do more with the Network Configuration window shown in Figure 19.14. As you can see, the window contains three other tabs:

The Hardware tab lists each configured network device.

The DNS tab allows you to set the hostname for your computer, up to three different DNS servers, as well as a DNS search path. The hostname is saved in `/etc/sysconfig/network`; the DNS server information is saved in `/etc/resolv.conf`.

The Hosts tab allows you to set up your own database of hostnames or domain names and their corresponding IP addresses. Changes you make are saved in `/etc/hosts`.

Text-Mode Network Configuration

You can configure networking on your Linux computer from a text-mode console. Start with the `redhat-config-network-tui` command. As you can see in Figure 19.15, this allows you to set up Ethernet, telephone modem, or ISDN adapter network devices.

FIGURE 19.15

Text-mode network configuration

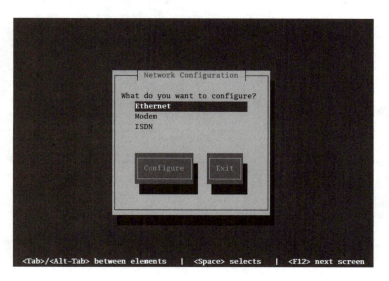

If you want to use this utility to set up an Ethernet connection, highlight that option, press the Tab key to highlight Configure, and then press Enter. This takes you to the Ethernet Configuration window, shown in Figure 19.16. For more information on DHCP, see Chapter 24; if you want to set a static IP address, see Chapter 20 for more information.

FIGURE 19.16

Configuring an Ethernet card in text mode

As with the graphical tool, changes are saved in the /etc/sysconfig/networking/devices directory. The configuration file is ifcfg-eth*n*, where *n* is the number associated with the card, usually 0 or 1.

If you want to use redhat-config-network-tui to set up a telephone modem, return to the screen shown in Figure 19.15. Highlight the Modem option, press the Tab key to highlight Configure, and then press Enter. This takes you to the Modem Configuration window, shown in Figure 19.17.

FIGURE 19.17

Configuring a modem connection

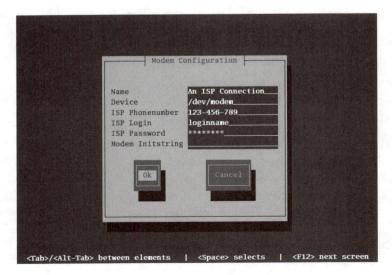

You can set the name of your choice. If your modem was properly detected, it should be linked to /dev/modem. You should get the remaining information from your ISP; you normally do not need to complete the Modem Initstring field.

For more information on each of these options, see Chapter 21. If your modem is working, changes are saved to the /etc/sysconfig/networking/devices directory. The configuration file is ifcfg-ppp*n*, where *n* is the number associated with the modem.

If you want to use redhat-config-network-tui to set up an ISDN adapter, return to the screen shown in Figure 19.15. Highlight the ISDN option, press the Tab key to highlight Configure, and then press Enter. This takes you to the ISDN Configuration window, shown in Figure 19.18.

FIGURE 19.18

Configuring an
ISDN adapter

Configure the adapter based on instructions from your ISP; this should include the Multiple Subscriber Number (MSN), normally provided by your ISP. If your ISDN adapter is working, changes are saved to the /etc/sysconfig/networking/devices directory. The configuration file is ifcfg-isdn*n*, where *n* is the number associated with the adapter.

NOTE   *ISDN stands for the Integrated Services Digital Network, an older digital standard for telephones. Consumer ISDN adapters are more popular in Europe; they normally support data transmission rates of 128 or 144Kbps, depending on the system.*

Apache

You can use the redhat-config-httpd utility to configure an Apache server on your computer. Start it from a GNOME desktop by selecting Main Menu ➢ System Settings ➢ Server Settings ➢ HTTP Server. This opens the Apache Configuration window, shown in Figure 19.19. For a detailed description of this utility, see Chapter 30.

FIGURE 19.19

The Apache configuration tool

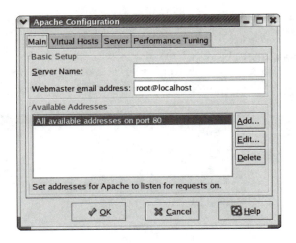

If you've already configured an Apache server, you'll be able to review the current configuration with this utility; it reads and writes key variables to and from the main Apache configuration file, `/etc/httpd/conf/httpd.conf`.

Domain Name Service (DNS)

You can use the `redhat-config-bind` utility to configure a Domain Name Service (DNS) server on your computer. Start it from a GNOME desktop by selecting Main Menu ➤ System Settings ➤ Server Settings ➤ Domain Name Service. This opens the Domain Name Service window, shown in Figure 19.20. For a detailed description of this utility, see Chapter 24.

FIGURE 19.20

The DNS configuration tool

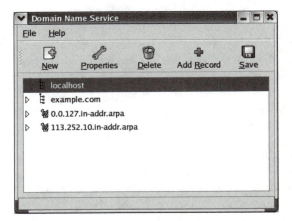

If you've already configured a DNS server, you'll be able to review the current configuration with this utility; it reads key variables from the main DNS configuration file, `/etc/named.conf`, as well as associated files in the `/etc` and `/var/named` directories.

Network File System (NFS)

You can use the `redhat-config-nfs` utility to configure a Network File System (NFS) server on your computer. Start it from a GNOME desktop by selecting Main Menu ➢ System Settings ➢ Server Settings ➢ NFS Server. This opens the NFS Server Configuration window, shown in Figure 19.21. For a detailed description of this utility, see Chapter 24.

FIGURE 19.21

NFS Server
Configuration

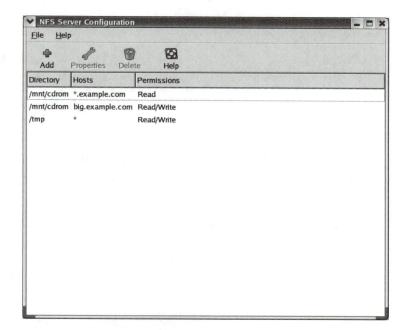

If you've already configured an NFS server, you'll be able to review the current configuration with this utility; it reads key variables from the main NFS configuration file, `/etc/exports`.

Samba

There are two different graphical Samba configuration utilities: `redhat-config-samba` and `samba-swat`. The first, `redhat-config-samba`, is a graphical Red Hat tool similar to the others, in this case, for configuring your Linux computer as a Samba server on a Microsoft Windows–based network. Start it from a GNOME or KDE desktop by selecting Main Menu ➢ System Settings ➢ Server Settings ➢ Samba Server. This opens the Samba Server Configuration window, shown in Figure 19.22.

The other tool, developed by the people behind Samba, is a web-based tool that can configure your Linux computer as a Samba server on a Microsoft Windows–based network in quite a bit of detail. Open the browser of your choice and navigate to `localhost: 901`. If the right services are active, this opens the Samba Web Administration Tool (SWAT) in the default browser, as shown in Figure 19.23.

FIGURE 19.22

Samba Server
Configuration

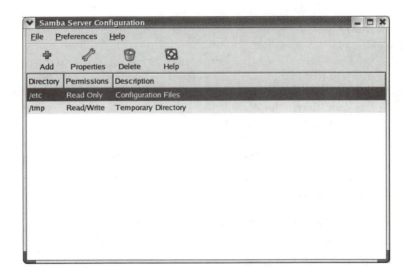

FIGURE 19.23

Samba Web
Administration Tool

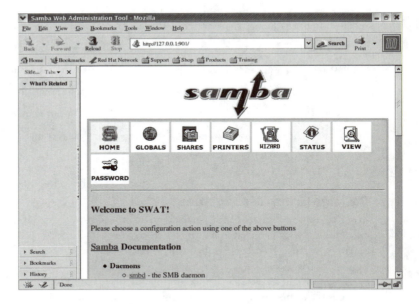

SWAT works only if you've installed the `samba-swat-*` RPM package and have enabled the service in the `/etc/xinted.d/swat` configuration file.

Both utilities are front ends that can help you configure the main Samba configuration file, `/etc/samba/smb.conf`, as well as other configuration files in the `/etc/samba` directory. For a detailed description of both utilities, see Chapter 29.

Using System Administration Utilities

Red Hat has developed a number of other graphical utilities that can help you with the day-to-day tasks of administering your Linux system. They are in various stages of development; expect improvements as Red Hat releases new packages and later versions of its distribution.

Table 19.4 summarizes the Red Hat graphical system administration utilities. Keep in mind that this is an arbitrary list of the utilities described in this section; you could also classify the other utilities in this chapter as system administration utilities.

TABLE 19.4: RED HAT GRAPHICAL SYSTEM ADMINISTRATION UTILITIES

UTILITY	FUNCTION
redhat-config-packages	Managing RPM package groups
redhat-config-rootpassword	Changing the root user's password
redhat-config-users	Adding and maintaining users
redhat-config-xfree86	Configuring the GUI
redhat-logviewer	Inspecting current log files
redhat-update-gnome-font-install redhat-update-gnome-font-install2	Updating fonts
redhat-config-kickstart	Building a Kickstart file for automated installation
redhat-config-securitylevel	Configuring a firewall
redhat-config-proc	Changing kernel settings in /proc
authconfig-gtk	Setting up authentication
authconfig	Using the text-mode version of authconfig-gtk

Package Group Management

You can use the redhat-config-packages utility to inspect, install, and remove the RPM packages currently on your Linux system. Start it from a GNOME desktop by selecting Main Menu ➢ System Settings ➢ Add/Remove Applications. This opens the Package Management window, shown in Figure 19.24.

If you installed Red Hat Linux graphically per Chapter 3, Figure 19.24 should look familiar. It includes the same organization of package groups that you used during the graphical installation process.

You can select *some* individual packages in each group for installation and removal. As an example, take a look at the packages associated with the KDE Desktop Environment. On the far right side of the associated entry, click Details. This opens the KDE Desktop Environment Package Details window, shown in Figure 19.25.

FIGURE 19.24

Package Management
by groups

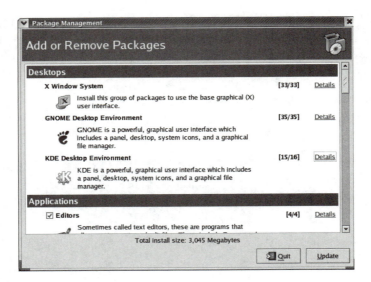

FIGURE 19.25

KDE Desktop
Environment
Package Details

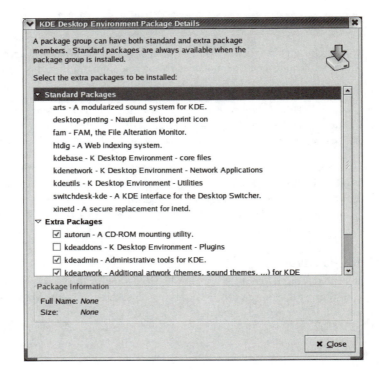

As you can see, there are two categories of packages: standard and extra. Standard packages correspond to the mandatory packages as defined in the `comps.xml` file described in Web Chapter 5. The extra packages are either default or optional packages as defined in `comps.xml`.

In this way, you can deselect the packages or package groups of your choice. Make any desired changes and click Close. When you click Update in the Package Management window, this utility makes sure that you don't have unsatisfied dependencies. You get a last chance to cancel (see Figure 19.26) before the deselected packages are removed from the system. Click Show Details to review the packages that are to be removed.

FIGURE 19.26

Before packages are removed

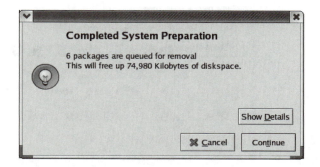

Adding new packages is a bit more complex, because it requires access to the installation RPMs. If you start `redhat-config-packages` from the command line, this utility will prompt you for CDs.

TIP   *If you have a network source for your Red Hat installation files, you don't need the installation CDs. For example, if the* `/RedHat/RPMS` *directory with your RPM packages is mounted on* `/mnt/source`, *run the* `redhat-config-packages --tree=/mnt/source` *command. As long as the RPMs are accessible over the network,* `redhat-config-packages` *starts and can use this source to install the packages that you specify.*

One more way to start `redhat-config-packages` is with the `redhat-cdinstall-helper --tree=/mnt/cdrom` command. You'll be prompted to insert the first Red Hat Installation CD before Red Hat takes you to the `redhat-config-packages` utility.

Linux logs the updated list of installed RPM packages each week in `/var/log/rpmpkgs`. The original list from when you installed Red Hat Linux is stored in `/root/install.log`.

Root Password

The `redhat-config-rootpassword` utility lets you change the password associated with the root user account. Start it from a GNOME desktop by selecting Main Menu ➢ System Settings ➢ Root Password. If you're not logged in as the root user, you're prompted for the root password, as shown in Figure 19.27.

FIGURE 19.27

You should have the root password before you can change it.

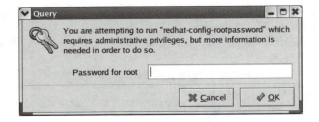

Assuming you enter the correct password (or are already logged into the root account), you'll see the Root Password dialog box, shown in Figure 19.28. The next time you want to log into the root account, you'll need this password.

FIGURE 19.28

Changing the root user password

Configuring Users

You can use the `redhat-config-users` utility to manage the users and groups with accounts on your Linux system. More information on the affected configuration files is available in Chapter 9.

Start it from a GNOME desktop by selecting Main Menu ➤ System Settings ➤ Users and Groups. This opens the Red Hat User Manager window, shown in Figure 19.29.

FIGURE 19.29

The Red Hat User Manager

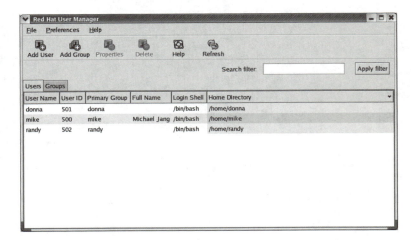

As you can see, this window includes two tabs. The Users tab lists current users on the system, from /etc/passwd. The categories should be familiar if you know this file. To add a user, click Add User. This opens the Create New User dialog box, shown in Figure 19.30.

FIGURE 19.30

Creating a new user

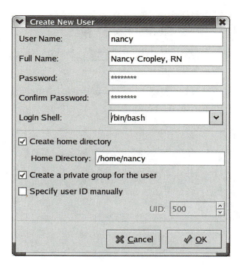

This dialog box allows you to enter the information associated with the new user, along with the password. Normally, the new user gets the next user ID available, in this case, 503. If you activate Specify User ID Manually, you can set the number of your choice.

You can add more account information for each user. Highlight a user and click Properties. This opens the User Properties dialog box, shown in Figure 19.31.

FIGURE 19.31

Changing user properties

There are four tabs of information within User Properties, which are described in Table 19.5.

TABLE 19.5: CONFIGURABLE USER PROPERTIES

TAB	DESCRIPTION
User Data	Lists basic data for the user, stored in /etc/passwd and /etc/shadow.
Account Info	Allows you to lock and/or set an expiration date for the account; the information is stored in /etc/shadow.
Password Info	Lets you set up password expiration parameters; the information is stored in /etc/shadow.
Groups	Permits you to set group membership for that user; the information is stored in /etc/group.

Click OK to return to the main Red Hat User Manager window. Next, select the Groups tab, which lists current groups from /etc/group. Click Add Group. This opens the Create New Group dialog box, shown in Figure 19.32. By default, each user is a member of his or her own group, with the same ID number. For example, user donna has a user ID of 501 and group donna has a group ID of 501. This is the User Private Group scheme described in Chapter 9.

FIGURE 19.32

Creating a new group

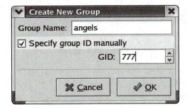

Whenever you create a special group, it's a good idea to give it a number in a different range from your users. I've created the group named angels. After selecting angels from the Groups tab, I clicked the Properties button, which opens the Group Properties dialog box. On the Group Users tab shown in Figure 19.33, you can add the users of your choice to this new group, in this case, nancy and randy.

FIGURE 19.33

Adding users to a group

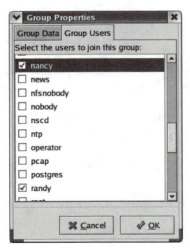

GUI Configuration

The Red Hat graphical configuration tool is `redhat-config-xfree86`, which is described in detail in Chapter 15. Start it from a GNOME desktop by selecting Main Menu ➤ System Settings ➤ Display. This opens the Display Settings window, shown in Figure 19.34.

FIGURE 19.34

Configuring the X Window

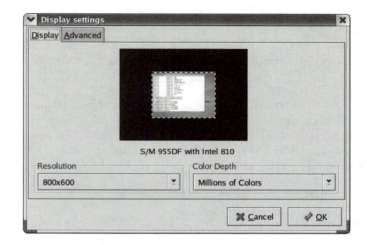

In most cases, you can run `redhat-config-xfree86` from a terminal window, even if you didn't choose to install graphical packages during the Red Hat Linux installation process. Once changes are made, you'll be able to see the results in `/etc/X11/XF86Config`. If you've used `redhat-config-xfree86` before, you'll probably see this comment at the top of that file:

```
# XFree86 4 configuration created by redhat-config-xfree86
```

Otherwise, if you've only configured the X Window during the Red Hat installation process, you'll see this comment instead:

```
# XFree86 4 configuration created by pyxf86config
```

Log Viewer

Red Hat includes a graphical viewer for standard log files, `redhat-logviewer`. Start it from a GNOME desktop by selecting Main Menu ➤ System Tools ➤ System Logs. This opens the System Logs window, shown in Figure 19.35.

Note the list of logs on the left and a view of the specific log file on the right. You can see right away, from the exclamation point (the alert icon) and "failed" messages that there might be some problem with `ntpd`, the Network Time Protocol daemon.

You can use this tool to search for specific messages; enter the search term of your choice and the `redhat-logviewer` isolates any messages with the search term. You might even realize that this search capability is a function of the `grep` command.

FIGURE 19.35

Reviewing
system logs

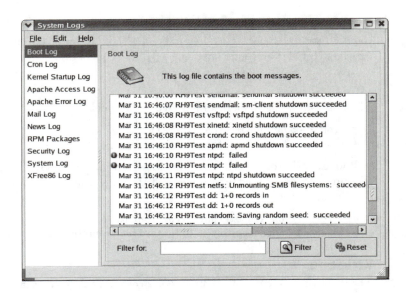

The `redhat-logviewer` is configured to review log files from standard locations. If you click Edit ➢ Preferences, that opens the Preferences dialog box, where you can change the file associated with a log, and specify the messages that set off the alert icon.

The standard locations for the `redhat-logviewer` log files are shown in Table 19.6.

TABLE 19.6: *REDHAT-LOGVIEWER* STANDARD LOG FILE LOCATIONS

LOG NAME	FILE LOCATION
Boot	`/var/log/boot.log`
Cron	`/var/log/cron`
Kernel Startup	`/var/log/dmesg`
Apache Access	`/var/log/httpd/access_log`
Apache Error	`/var/log/httpd/error_log`
Mail	`/var/log/maillog`
News	`/var/log/spooler`
RPM Packages	`/var/log/rpmpkgs`
Security	`/var/log/secure`
System	`/var/log/messages`
XFree86	`/var/log/XFree86.0.log`

If a log file is missing from the list, you may not have started the service before. For example, if you don't see an Apache Access Log in Figure 19.35, you probably haven't started or accessed the Apache web server on your computer.

Fonts

There are two similar-looking utilities related to fonts:

```
# redhat-update-gnome-font-install
# redhat-update-gnome-font-install2
```

Both can help you upload fonts that support printing from GNOME applications. The first utility generates a font map used in printing GNOME-based applications. They update the following font configuration files:

```
/etc/gnome/fonts/gnome-print-rpm.fontmap
/etc/gnome/libgnomeprint-2.0/fonts/libgnomeprint-rpm.fontmap
```

Kickstart

The Red Hat Kickstart configuration tool is `redhat-config-kickstart`, which is described in detail in Chapter 5. Start it from a GNOME desktop by selecting Main Menu ➤ System Tools ➤ Kickstart. This opens the Kickstart Configurator window, shown in Figure 19.36.

FIGURE 19.36

The Kickstart Configurator

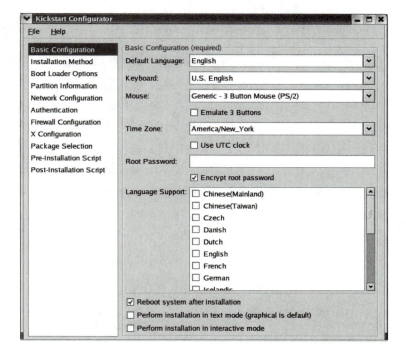

Normally, you should save Kickstart files to `ks.cfg`; a model Kickstart file based on how you installed Red Hat Linux on the local computer is available at `/root/anaconda-ks.cfg`.

Security Level

The Red Hat Firewall configuration tool is `redhat-config-securitylevel`, which is essentially the same tool that you used during the installation process in Chapter 3 or 4. Start it from a GNOME desktop by selecting Main Menu ➢ System Settings ➢ Security Level. This opens the Security Level Configuration window, shown in Figure 19.37.

FIGURE 19.37

Setting up a firewall

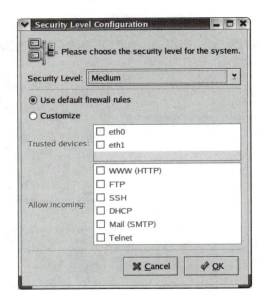

To summarize, you can configure three levels of firewall protection for your computer: high, medium, or none.

You can further customize the firewall. For example, if one of the network cards is connected only to the local network, you may want it to be a trusted device; firewall rules do not apply to traffic through trusted devices. In addition, you can customize the firewall to allow incoming data associated with the protocols shown in the Security Level Configuration window.

If you're using the default `iptables` firewall command, any changes that you make are written to `/etc/sysconfig/iptables`. For more information on firewalls and the `iptables` command, read Chapter 22.

The `redhat-config-securitylevel` utility is closely related to the GNOME `lokkit` firewall wizard, described in Chapter 16. Both can help you create an `iptables`-based firewall, using the same basic parameters.

Tuning the Kernel

The Red Hat kernel tuning tool is `redhat-config-proc`, which allows you to modify settings in the `/proc` directory. Some of the files in this directory are described in greater detail in Chapter 11. As of this writing, you can only start this utility from a GUI command-line interface; there is no entry in the GNOME Main Menu. Figure 19.38 displays the Kernel Tuning window.

WARNING *Be careful before you use* `redhat-config-proc`. *At the very least, back up your current* `/etc/sysctl.conf` *file first. Any changes you make can change the functionality of your kernel, which could easily stop Linux from working.*

FIGURE 19.38

Kernel Tuning

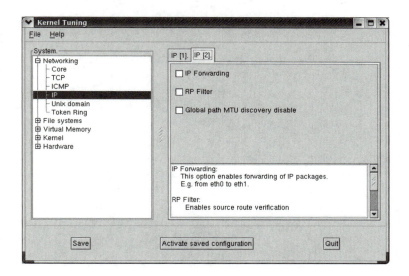

In the setting shown in Figure 19.38, you can enable IP Forwarding, which lets your Linux computer work as a gateway between two or more networks. Changes that you make are written to `/etc/sysctl.conf`.

Authentication

The Red Hat tool for setting up username and password databases is `authconfig-gtk`, which is essentially the same tool that you used during the installation process in Chapter 3 or 4. Start it from a GNOME desktop by selecting Main Menu ➢ System Settings ➢ Authentication. This opens the Authentication Configuration window, shown in Figure 19.39.

Depending on the type of installation, you may have already set this up during the Red Hat Linux installation process in Chapter 3 or 4. Since you may be seeing these options for the first time, we'll address them in detail here. First, the settings on the User Information tab are described in Table 19.7.

FIGURE 19.39

Setting up user
information
databases

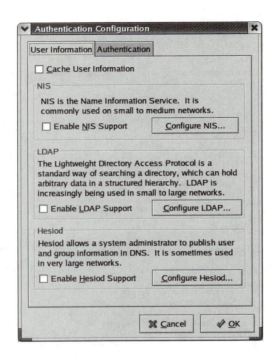

TABLE 19.7: AUTHENTICATION CONFIGURATION, USER INFORMATION TAB

SETTING	DESCRIPTION
Cache User Information	Sets the local server to store user settings.
Enable NIS Support	Configures authentication through an NIS Server.
Configure NIS	Opens a window where you can enter the name of the NIS domain and server.
Enable LDAP Support	Configures access to user information through the Lightweight Directory Assistance Protocol (LDAP).
Configure LDAP	Opens a window where you can enable Transmission Layer Security (TLS), which is the formal name of the Secure Socket Layer (SSL) protocol, along with an LDAP search database and server.
Hesiod	Configures authentication information and other configuration files in DNS; its functionally is similar to NIS.
Configure Hesiod	Opens a window where you can specify Hesiod LHS, which is the prefix for a DNS server name, and the Hesiod RHS, which is the suffix for a DNS server name. For example, if the address of a DNS server is nameserv.mommabears.com, the LHS is nameserv and the RHS is mommabears.com.

The settings found on the Authentication tab are shown in Figure 19.40; they include several other configuration options, described in Table 19.8.

FIGURE 19.40

Configuring additional username/password support

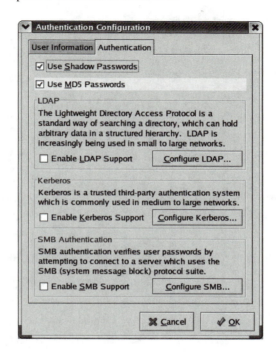

TABLE 19.8: AUTHENTICATION CONFIGURATION, AUTHENTICATION TAB

SETTING	DESCRIPTION
Enable LDAP Support	Configures user authentication through the Lightweight Directory Assistance Protocol (LDAP).
Configure LDAP	Opens a window where you can enable Transmission Layer Security (TLS), which is the formal name of the Secure Socket Layer (SSL) protocol, along with an LDAP search database and server.
Use Shadow Passwords	Enables the Shadow Password Suite, with passwords, account data, and group information protected in /etc/shadow and /etc/gshadow.
Use MD5 Passwords	Configures the use of the MD5 form of password encryption.
Enable Kerberos Support	Sets up strong encryption for checking user credentials, using this protocol developed at MIT.

Continued on next page

TABLE 19.8: AUTHENTICATION CONFIGURATION, AUTHENTICATION TAB *(continued)*

SETTING	DESCRIPTION
Configure Kerberos	Opens a window where you can set the Kerberos Realm—usually the name of the domain in upper case; the Kerberos Domain Controller (KDC), which is the name of the Kerberos server, using TCP/IP port 88; and any Kerberos administrative servers, using TCP/IP port 749.
Enable SMB Support	Sets up authentication using Microsoft Windows or Samba servers on a Microsoft Windows–based network.
Configure SMB	Opens a window where you can set the name of the workgroup or domain controller for the Microsoft Windows–based network.

Any changes you make are written to the `/etc/sysconfig/authconfig` configuration file.

TIP   If you want to configure Kerberos 5, you should configure your computers to a central NTP server, as described earlier with the `redhat-config-time` *utility.*

There is a text-mode version of the Authentication Configuration utility, which you start with the `authconfig` command. It includes two text-mode screens that allow you to enter the same information described in this section.

Working with Service Configuration Utilities

Red Hat has developed a number of other graphical utilities that help you with the day-to-day tasks of administering various Linux services, related to service runlevel management, printers, and mail servers, as summarized in Table 19.9.

TABLE 19.9: RED HAT SERVICE CONFIGURATION

UTILITY	FUNCTION
`redhat-config-service`	Allows you to manage service activation at different runlevels
`redhat-config-printer`	Starts the printer configuration utility; works with both CUPS and LPD daemons
`redhat-config-printer-tui`	A text-mode version of `redhat-config-printer`
`redhat-switch-printer`	Lets you switch between print daemons
`redhat-switch-printer-nox`	A text-mode version of `redhat-switch-printer`
`redhat-switch-mail`	Supports switches between mail servers, such as sendmail and Postfix
`switchdesk`	Allows you to switch the default GUI desktop

Setting Service Levels

The Red Hat Service configuration tool is `redhat-config-service`. It is essentially a way to run the `chkconfig` command as described in Chapter 13. Start it from a GNOME desktop by selecting Main Menu ➤ System Settings ➤ Server Settings ➤ Services. This opens the Service Configuration window, shown in Figure 19.41.

FIGURE 19.41

Setting service runlevels

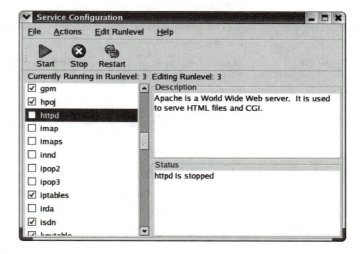

The service configuration window opens in the default runlevel as defined in `/etc/inittab`. Highlight the service of your choice, and you'll see a description of the associated daemon and its current status on the right side of the window.

In the Actions menu, you can start, stop, or restart a service; this corresponds to one of the following commands:

```
# service servicename stop
# service servicename start
# service servicename restart
```

In the Edit Runlevel menu, you can change the runlevel in work to 3, 4, or 5. Any changes you make are written to the `/etc/rc.d/rcn.d` directory, where *n* is the runlevel in question. Active daemons are associated with start scripts and dormant daemons are associated with kill scripts. The next time you boot Linux, it reads the start and kill scripts in each of these directories. For more information on runlevels and the scripts in each associated directory, see Chapter 13.

Configuring Printers

The Red Hat Printer configuration tool is `redhat-config-printer`. It is a front end to editing the configuration file for your active print daemon. As described in Chapter 25, this is either CUPS or LPD. Start it from a GNOME desktop by selecting Main Menu ➤ System Settings ➤ Printing. This opens the Printer Configuration window, shown in Figure 19.42.

FIGURE 19.42

Printer
Configuration

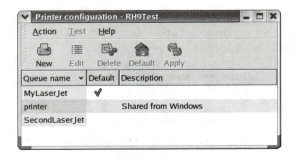

You can also start this utility with the `redhat-config-printer-gui` command. A text-mode console version is available by running the `redhat-config-printer-tui` command. For more information on this utility, see Chapter 25.

Switching Print Daemons

As discussed in Chapter 25, two major print daemons are available with Red Hat Linux 9: CUPS and LPD. The Red Hat Printer System Switcher is `redhat-switch-printer`. Assuming you have both systems installed, you can use it to switch the active print daemon. Start it from a GNOME desktop by selecting Main Menu ➤ System Settings ➤ More System Settings ➤ Printer System Switcher. This opens the Printer Configuration window shown in Figure 19.43.

FIGURE 19.43

Switching printer
systems

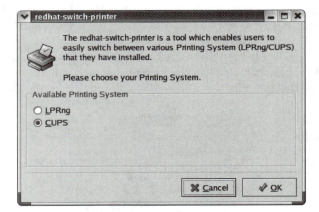

There is a text-mode console version available; you can get to it by running the `redhat-switch-printer-nox` command. Changes are made to the desired print daemons at the appropriate runlevels.

Switching Mail Agents

As discussed in Chapter 26, several mail server daemons are available with Red Hat Linux 9. The Red Hat Mail System Switcher is `redhat-switch-mail`. Assuming you have more than one mail system installed, you can use it to switch the active mail service daemon. As of this writing, you can only start this utility from a GUI command-line interface; there is no entry in the GNOME Main Menu. We display the resulting `redhat-switch-mail` window in Figure 19.44. Changes are made to the desired mail daemons at the appropriate runlevels.

FIGURE 19.44

Switching mail systems

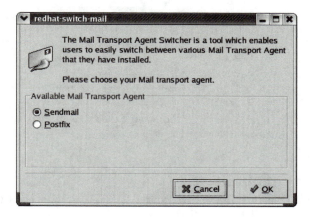

Switching Desktops

As discussed in Chapter 15, several GUI desktops are available with Red Hat Linux 9, including GNOME, KDE, and twm (which is shown as TWM in the window). The Red Hat Desktop Switcher is `switchdesk`. Assuming you have more than one GUI desktop installed, you can use it to switch your default GUI. Start it from a GNOME desktop by selecting Main Menu ➤ System Settings ➤ More System Settings ➤ Desktop Switching Tool. This opens the Desktop Switcher window, shown in Figure 19.45. The default desktop for each user is listed in his or her home directory, in the `~/.Xclients-default` file.

FIGURE 19.45

Switching default GUI desktops

Summary

In this chapter, we examined the graphical utilities created by Red Hat that can help you administer your Linux computer. You can start most of these utilities from a command-line interface within a graphical desktop. Most of the needed commands start with `redhat-config-`.

Remember, graphical utilities are front ends; in other words, they can help you make the changes that you need to various configuration files. They do not allow you to make all the changes that you could make in a text editor. They are fairly new, so you should check the results in the associated configuration files.

However, graphical utilities can be an aid and a learning tool for newer Linux administrators. Administrators can make changes in the graphical utility and study the results in the applicable configuration file.

We've arbitrarily classified these utilities in four categories. With the basic configuration utilities, you can configure basic settings related to the system clock, keyboard, language, mouse, and sound card. Using the network configuration utilities, you're able to set up new network cards, as well as the Apache, DNS, NFS, and Samba network servers.

The various graphical system administrative utilities enable you to install and remove RPM packages, manage the root password, set up users and groups, configure the GUI, examine log files, and install fonts. They also help you configure a Kickstart file for automated installations, set up a customized firewall, and tune the kernel. Finally, service configuration utilities support managing services at different runlevels, changing default printer and mail services, and switching default graphical desktop environments.

In the next chapter, we'll start to examine Linux and networking in detail. Chapter 20 starts with a somewhat theoretical look at the TCP/IP protocol stack and IP addressing. It also gives you the tools that you need to configure private IP addresses on your LAN. This prepares you for future chapters, where you'll learn to manage Linux on your LAN, secure your Linux network, and more.

## Part 5

Basic Linux Networking

In this Part, you will learn how to:

- ◆ Use TCP/IP
- ◆ Manage Linux on your LAN
- ◆ Secure your Linux network

Chapter 20

A TCP/IP Primer

Many of the same people who developed the Unix operating system also worked on the network that would eventually become the Internet. They designed TCP/IP as the standard group of network protocols for this purpose. Because Linux is a clone of Unix, it is also customized for TCP/IP. However, TCP/IP is only one of several *protocol stacks* associated with modern networking.

TCP/IP is named for two of its component protocols, the Transport Communications Protocol and the Internet Protocol. TCP/IP actually includes several hundred individual protocols. Officially, it is known as the TCP/IP Protocol Suite.

Before we dig into the details of TCP/IP, we'll step back and take a look at the fundamentals of computer networks, both small and large. We need a way to identify every computer on a network, and a standard method of transferring data. Several other protocol stacks are available, and in this chapter we'll address two of them: NetBEUI and IPX/SPX.

NetBEUI is the NetBIOS Enhanced User Interface, developed by Microsoft and IBM. IPX/SPX is also named for two of its component protocols, Internetwork Packet Exchange and Sequenced Packet Exchange. Like TCP/IP, IPX/SPX includes a substantial number of individual protocols.

To help software designers develop different protocols, they needed specifications for standard levels of communication. Their agreements are documented through the International Organization for Standardization (ISO) as the OSI model of networking, where OSI stands for Open Standards Interconnection

While the OSI model is often applied to TCP/IP, many designers subscribe to a conceptually similar four-level protocol stack. Many TCP/IP services would otherwise require software at several different OSI levels.

If you're not interested in all this theory, you can jump ahead to what you can do with TCP/IP, starting with IP addressing. Two versions of IP addresses are available. IP version 4 addressing is still in common use in the United States, but the newer IP version 6 addresses are coming into frequent use in other parts of the world. This chapter covers the following topics:

- ◆ Exploring network fundamentals
- ◆ Understanding protocol stacks
- ◆ Learning the basics of TCP/IP
- ◆ Using IP addressing

Exploring Network Fundamentals

A *network* consists of two or more computer systems set up to communicate with each other. To some extent, the "media" you use doesn't matter. You can set up a network using parallel cables, telephone modems, Ethernet cards, wireless adapters, or any other media that allow your computers to exchange information. If you can connect these computers directly or through a hub, you can set up a local area network (LAN). Each LAN typically has a special IP address known as a *network address*.

A LAN connects computers that are close to each other, such as within an office or a building. An internet consists of two or more connected LANs. Some internets are wide area networks (WAN). A WAN consists of two or more geographically separate networks. The biggest WAN is the Internet.

NOTE *Any network or group of networks that are managed by the same group is often known as a* domain. *For example, you could configure two separate networks,* linux.sybex.com *and* windows.sybex.com; *both would be part of the* sybex.com *domain.*

LANs and WANs

Linux LANs are usually configured to a standard known as IEEE 802.3, more popularly known as Ethernet. This type of network is much faster than a telephone modem. While standard Ethernet networks allow computers to communicate at speeds of 10 or 100Mbps (Ethernet and Fast Ethernet), Gigabit Ethernet (1000Mbps) is currently coming on line in many locations, and even faster networks (10Gbps Ethernet) are currently under development.

NOTE *Ethernet is actually a trade name. The proper name for this network is taken from the standard implemented by the Institute of Electrical and Electronics Engineers, IEEE 802.3. Fast Ethernet and Gigabit Ethernet are known by similar names, IEEE 802.3u and IEEE 802.3ae.*

But the distance between computers on an Ethernet is limited to a few hundred meters, depending on the type of connection. In essence, while the amount of area that a LAN can cover is limited, LANs are fast. In contrast, connections between LANs in a WAN can cover thousands of miles, but the speed of the connection is typically limited. Even "high-speed" WAN connections are typically limited to 1.4Mbps or less.

NOTE *This speed limit on WANs is based on cost. Internet WAN "backbones" can carry tens of gigabits of data and are expensive to build; consequently, the associated "bandwidth" is shared among the customers of this WAN.*

The Internet

Even if you've never set up a network, chances are good that you already know something about networking from your experience with the Internet. When connecting to the Internet, most users and many Linux administrators work through an Internet Service Provider (ISP). If you're responsible for a larger network, you may have your own direct connection to the Internet and thus act as your own ISP.

You connect to the Internet through your ISP's gateway, which is a computer that connects that ISP to the rest of the Internet. When you search for a domain name, such as www.mommabears.com, your computer has to find the appropriate computer address. On the Internet, this is known as an IP address, which is usually stored on a Domain Name Service (DNS) server.

Domains

When you installed Red Hat Linux, you may have entered a hostname, such as computer1, or a fully qualified domain name (FQDN), such as `linux1.mommabears.com`. Unless your computer serves information or otherwise directly connects to the Internet, the name you use does not matter. If you use a FQDN, make sure to use the same domain name when you install Linux on each of the computers on your network.

Alternatively, some ISPs may assign you a specific FQDN for your connection to the Internet. This is a common practice with higher speed connections such as cable modems or DSL (Digital Subscriber Line) adapters.

You can divide a domain into a number of subdomains. Each subdomain can represent a different LAN. For example, `linux.mommabears.com`, `windows.mommabears.com`, and `other.mommabears.com` can represent three different LANs.

Hostname

The alternative to an FQDN on a network is a hostname such as computer1. The FQDN of a computer includes the hostname and domain name, assembled together. For example, if your computer has a hostname of berkeley and your domain name is `california.now`, your fully qualified domain name is `berkeley.california.now`. Every hostname or FQDN is associated with a numeric address such as an IP address.

Hardware Address

Computers contact each other through the hardware address on their network cards. A hardware address might look like 00-60-08-8D-41-93. These are hexadecimal numbers, also known as base 16. Every network card built today is configured with a unique hexadecimal hardware address. When you configure a TCP/IP network, you associate an IP address with a hardware address.

NOTE   *In hexadecimal notation, there are 16 digits: 0, 1, 2, 3, 4, 5, 6, 7, 8, 9, a, b, c, d, e, and f.*

Understanding Protocol Stacks

Now you can see that computers on a network need different elements to communicate. They need domain names, numeric addresses, and hardware addresses. They also need connection managers and application protocols such as those related to mail, web pages, file servers, and more. These elements can be classified through a protocol stack.

A protocol stack is essentially a division of labor. Some protocols are associated with applications such as mail or DNS. Others cite domain names, IP addresses, and hardware addresses. Some can encrypt your data, manage the 1s and 0s of binary code, or govern a remote login session.

There are two major ways to divide this labor. One is known as the OSI model of networking. This section examines the basics of OSI, as well as a couple of the other major protocol stacks, NetBEUI and IPX/SPX. The other major model of networking is based on TCP/IP, and we discuss it later in this chapter.

TIP   *The arguments between supporters of the OSI and TCP/IP models of networking can be as vigorous as the arguments between the supporters of Linux and Microsoft Windows. While purists may object to the use of OSI to describe TCP/IP protocols, it is a useful learning exercise.*

OSI Levels

The OSI model of networking consists of seven levels. Before your computer sends a message over a network, your message is translated through these levels into the 1s and 0s that are actually sent over a network. The programs associated with each level perform different functions such as encryption, error checking, and routing.

The following is a brief description of each of these levels, from top to bottom, as shown in Figure 20.1. Pay attention to the numbers associated with each level.

FIGURE 20.1

The OSI model

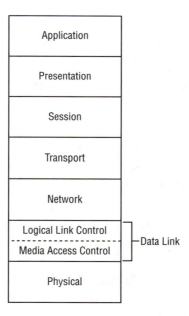

Application   Application-level (7) protocols start the translation process from the programs that you use. For example, HTTP is an Application-level protocol that translates data from web browsers such as Mozilla. Gateways are computers that can translate applications between networks.

Presentation   Presentation-level (6) protocols translate numbers and letters into lower-level computer code. One example is ASCII, which represents the numbers and characters on an English-language keyboard. Encryption protocols such as the Secure Sockets Layer (SSL) are also part of the Presentation level.

Session   Session-level (5) protocols manage the time you spend on a network. These protocols determine which computer is sending and receiving messages at any particular time. For example, Session-level software in your network card determines whether data moves one direction at a time (half-duplex) or both directions simultaneously (full-duplex).

Transport   Transport-level (4) protocols can resend your message until it gets a return receipt (a.k.a., an acknowledgment), or it can just send a message and make a best effort to get it to the destination computer. The two major TCP/IP Transport-level protocols are TCP and UDP. Transport protocols also begin breaking down messages into packets. TCP adds a request for acknowledgment to the start of the packet; UDP does not.

THE LIFE OF A PACKET

Unless your message is very small, computer networks don't send complete messages all at once. Starting at the Transport level, networks break messages down into packets. As you go further down OSI hierarchy, the packets may be further divided into smaller packets or even cells. Some protocols may send each packet or cell through a different route on the Internet; address information is included with each packet to make sure that your message gets reassembled at the right computer, in order.

For example, Ethernet packets, which are created at the Data-Link level, can contain up to 1518 bytes. This includes 1500 bytes of data and 18 bytes of address information (and more), to ensure that the packet gets to the right computer on a network.

The details of network design are rich and complex. Perhaps the standard reference for network design is *Computer Networks*, by Andrew Tanenbaum, Prentice Hall, 2002.

Network   Network-level (3) protocols actually move the data from computer to computer, and from network to network. IP is the quintessential Network-level protocol. Your messages need IP addresses to move between networks. Routers can manage traffic between networks at this level.

Data-Link   Data-Link-level (2) protocols are primarily used to make sure that your information gets to the destination computer correctly. This is often split into two sublevels: Logical Link Control (LLC) and Media Access Control (MAC). LLC protocols ensure that your messages reach the destination computer in order, without errors. This is also known as frame synchronization and error checking. MAC protocols help computers communicate with each other. That is why the hardware address of a network card is also known as a MAC address. Switches or bridges can manage traffic within a network at this level.

Physical   Physical-level (1) protocols translate data into the 1s and 0s of computer communication. They also govern the physical world of networking, such as the cables and connectors.

NOTE   *When you're shopping for network hardware, keep in mind that sales engineers often refer to components by a certain level. For example, standard switches work at level 2 and basic routers work at level 3. However, the boundaries are not rigid. For example, some switches include routing or transport functionality and are then advertised as "level 3" or "level 4" switches.*

NetBEUI

NetBEUI is the NetBIOS Extended User Interface. This is the set of protocols developed by Microsoft and IBM for networks. It is based on NetBIOS, the Network Basic Input Output System. NetBIOS includes a series of commands that allows a computer to send and receive data, as well as information on shared directories on other computers on that network.

The main drawback of NetBEUI and NetBIOS is that it is not routable. In other words, you can't connect a NetBEUI network to another network such as the Internet. A NetBEUI network is limited to 255 computers.

However, Microsoft has adapted NetBIOS commands to routable network protocol stacks such as TCP/IP and IPX/SPX. If you're an administrator of a network that includes Microsoft computers, you should know a few basic NetBIOS commands, such as `net view` and `net use`.

When you use Samba, you're taking advantage of the format associated with NetBIOS commands known as the Server Message Block (SMB). In Chapter 29, you'll learn about the commands that you can use on a Linux system. Since Samba is essentially the Linux/Unix implementation of NetBIOS, you should not be surprised to find Samba commands that correspond directly to NetBIOS commands such as `net view` and `net use`.

IPX/SPX

Like TCP/IP, IPX/SPX is actually a suite of protocols for network communication. It was developed by Novell, in support of its NetWare program, which is actually a network operating system.

Many older networks still use NetWare. However, NetWare also supports TCP/IP, so you probably do not need to adapt to IPX/SPX even if you're connecting to a NetWare-based network.

IPX/SPX is routable. In earlier versions of Microsoft Windows, IPX/SPX was the only choice available if you wanted to configure computers on multiple networks.

If you need to connect to an IPX/SPX network, you'll want the `mars-nwe-*`, `ipxutils-*` and `ncpfs-*` RPM packages. The first package allows your Linux computer to act as a file and print server on a NetWare network. The second package includes support for IPX/SPX. The final package includes the commands you need to act as a client on a NetWare network.

NOTE   *There are several other major protocol suites, including IBM's System Network Architecture (SNA), the Xerox Network System (XNS), and the Digital Equipment Corporation network (DECnet). DEC is now part of Hewlett-Packard.*

Learning the Basics of TCP/IP

TCP/IP is the dominant network protocol suite today. Even Novell has been using it for years on its NetWare servers, and Microsoft uses TCP/IP even though it developed the rival NetBIOS suite. TCP/IP is the language of the Internet, and is therefore generally the only protocol suite you need to know.

The TCP/IP Model

The TCP/IP model of networking includes four levels. The levels are roughly comparable to the OSI model. As shown in Figure 20.2, the TCP/IP Application level is somewhat functionally equivalent to the top three levels of the OSI model. The TCP/IP Link level is comparable to the bottom two levels of the OSI model.

FIGURE 20.2

The TCP/IP model of networking

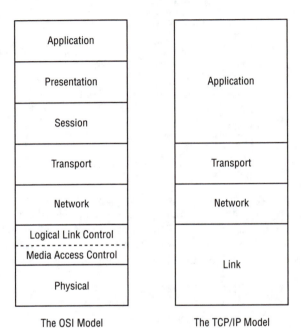

The OSI Model   The TCP/IP Model

Naturally, the TCP/IP levels are better suited to different TCP/IP protocols. For example, Chapter 27 describes secure versions of FTP that manage communications between a client and server, which is an OSI Session-level function. They translate data into ASCII or binary code, which is an OSI Presentation-level function. And they translate your FTP commands, which is an OSI Application-level function.

Major Protocols

There are hundreds of TCP/IP protocols. You've probably heard of many of them, such as FTP, HTTP, SMTP, SNMP, TCP, IP, just to name a few. Some of these protocols are detailed in the following sections.

TCP/IP APPLICATION-LEVEL PROTOCOLS

For a full list of TCP/IP Application-level protocols, see /etc/services. As shown in Figure 20.3, this file includes the name of a service, such as ftp, ssh, and smtp, the associated port number, and related comments.

FIGURE 20.3

/etc/services

```
# 21 is registered to ftp, but also used by fsp
ftp             21/tcp
ftp             21/udp          fsp fspd
ssh             22/tcp                          # SSH Remote Login Protocol
ssh             22/udp                          # SSH Remote Login Protocol
telnet          23/tcp
telnet          23/udp
# 24 - private mail system
smtp            25/tcp          mail
smtp            25/udp          mail
time            37/tcp          timserver
time            37/udp          timserver
rlp             39/tcp          resource        # resource location
rlp             39/udp          resource        # resource location
nameserver      42/tcp          name            # IEN 116
nameserver      42/udp          name            # IEN 116
nicname         43/tcp          whois
nicname         43/udp          whois
tacacs          49/tcp                          # Login Host Protocol (TACACS)
tacacs          49/udp                          # Login Host Protocol (TACACS)
re-mail-ck      50/tcp                          # Remote Mail Checking Protocol
re-mail-ck      50/udp                          # Remote Mail Checking Protocol
domain          53/tcp                          # name-domain server
```

TCP/IP has 65,536 available ports. Each port works conceptually like a TV channel. When you direct your Linux computer to the right port, you can receive the data associated with that port. The "well-known" ports are assigned by the Internet Assigned Numbers Authority (www.iana.org). Typical ports include 80 for HTTP (web pages), 21 for FTP communication, and 110 for POP3 e-mail.

Table 20.1 lists several important TCP/IP Application-level protocols and their associated ports.

TABLE 20.1: TCP/IP APPLICATION-LEVEL PROTOCOLS

PROTOCOL	PORT	DESCRIPTION
FTP	21	File Transfer Protocol; optimized for sending and receiving files
SSH	22	Secure Shell; encrypts communication between computers
Telnet	23	Connects in clear text to remote computers
SMTP	25	Simple mail transfer protocol for outgoing e-mail
HTTP	80	Hypertext Transfer Protocol for web pages
POP3	110	Post Office Protocol for receiving e-mail
SNMP	161	Simple Network Management Protocol for diagnosing networks
HTTPS	443	Secure HTTP
IPP	631	Internet Print Protocol, associated with the Common Unix Print System (CUPS)
SWAT	901	Samba web administration tool
NFS	2049	Network File Service for communication between Linux/Unix computers

TCP/IP TRANSPORT-LEVEL PROTOCOLS

By far, the two most important Transport-level protocols are TCP and UDP. Both take fully qualified domain names, such as www.sybex.com, and try to send your messages to those computers. TCP, also known as the Transmission Control Protocol, will keep sending a message until it gets an acknowledgment from the target computer. TCP is also known as a *connection-oriented* protocol.

On the other hand, UDP, also known as the User Datagram Protocol, does not need an acknowledgment. The assumption is that the network you're using is so reliable that any lost data doesn't really matter. UDP is also known as a *connectionless* protocol.

TCP/IP NETWORK-LEVEL PROTOCOLS

The key Network-layer protocol is IP, the Internet Protocol. This is most commonly associated with IP addresses such as 192.168.32.142. Both version 4 and version 6 IP addresses are discussed in detail toward the end of this chapter.

There is one other notable TCP/IP Network-layer protocol, the Internet Control Message Protocol (ICMP). This is most closely associated with the ping utility, which allows you to check the connection between your computer and every connected component on your network. You'll use ping and related utilities in Chapter 21.

NOTE   *The TCP/IP Network level is also known as the Internet level.*

TCP/IP LINK-LEVEL PROTOCOLS

The TCP/IP Link-level protocols are most closely associated with networking technologies such as Ethernet, Token Ring, and ATM. This is where network packets are organized. Once organized, they are grouped into a stream of bits (1s and 0s). Next, the bits are sent through the network cable or other transmission media.

While the focus of networks today is on Ethernet, you may encounter several other important networking technologies. This is just a short list of the available technologies:

Ethernet   Regular Ethernet follows the IEEE 802.3 standard. It allows for data transfer at a theoretical maximum speed of 10Mbps. Because Ethernet packets wait to avoid collisions on a busy network, actual speeds are often less than half the maximum.

Fast Ethernet   Fast Ethernet, which follows the IEEE 802.3u standard, allows for data transfer at a theoretical maximum speed of 100Mbps. It requires cables with a rating of Category 5 ("Cat 5") or better.

Gigabit Ethernet   Gigabit Ethernet, which follows the IEEE 802.3ae standard, allows for data transfer at a theoretical maximum speed of 1000Mbps. It requires transmission media such as fiber-optic cables.

Token Ring   Token Ring follows the IEEE 802.5 standard, which allows for data transfer at a theoretical maximum speed of 16Mbps. Since only the computer with the "token" is allowed to transmit data, it is more efficient than Ethernet, at least with respect to the maximum speed.

Asynchronous Transfer Mode (ATM)   ATM networks are a popular option for higher speed networks, because they can transfer data at 155Mbps or 622Mbps. While support for ATM is considered to be "experimental," ATM network cards are explicitly listed in the Linux Hardware-HOWTO. Developers are working on creating ATM networks with transfer speeds of over 2Gbps.

Point-to-Point Protocol (PPP)   No discussion of networking protocols can be complete without reference to the protocol that has served us so well through regular telephone modems. While speeds are still limited to 56Kbps (53Kbps in the United States), PPP has served us well. And for those of you with high-speed Internet access, please remember that as of this writing, fewer than 20 percent of U.S. Internet users use "high-speed" services such as cable modems or DSL adapters.

NOTE   *The TCP/IP Link level is also known as the Network Access level.*

Important Service Definitions

This section includes a basic list of major TCP/IP network services. If you are not too familiar with TCP/IP, this list can help you understand the services that are available. While you'll learn to configure some of these services in detail in later chapters, it can be useful to have a brief summary of each of the following services:

Domain Name System (DNS)   The Domain Name System is a database of fully qualified domain names, such as linux1.mommabears.com, and IP addresses, such as 192.168.1.231. When you connect to the Internet and search for a site such as www.redhat.com, your Linux computer looks for a DNS server. Once it has an IP address, this information is added to your requests. Your message can then be sent from network to network until it reaches the Red Hat website.

Dynamic Host Configuration Protocol (DHCP)   You can assign IP addresses to every computer on your network. But you need to be careful; if you accidentally assign the same IP address to two different computers, your network could fail. The Dynamic Host Configuration Protocol automates this process.

Address Resolution Protocol (ARP)   The Address Resolution Protocol associates IP addresses with the hardware address of a computer's network card. These hardware addresses are also known as MAC addresses. Computers on a network communicate with hardware addresses. Your network can have problems if the IP address is assigned to the wrong MAC address.

Using IP Addressing

Every computer on a TCP/IP network needs an IP address before it can communicate with others. You or your ISP can assign a permanent address, or IP addresses can be "leased" from a DHCP server. Your ISP assigns your computer a unique IP address whenever you're connected to the Internet.

To set up IP addresses for your network, you need a network address and a network mask. IP addresses that share the same network address and network mask are on the same LAN. Network addresses fall into one of five different address classes. Network masks define a range of IP addresses that you can assign with a specific network address.

Every network with a connection to other networks needs a gateway IP address for that connection. In Linux, you can limit access to and from your network with the `/etc/hosts.allow` and `/etc/hosts.deny` files, or through appropriate `iptables` or `ipchains` firewall commands.

IP Version 4

The IP address standard in use since the 1970s is IP version 4 (IPv4), which is a 32-bit address. With 32 bits, there are over 4 billion possible addresses (2^{32} = 4,294,967,296). That was more than enough addresses for the first years of the Internet. However, it isn't enough today. While the Internet is currently in transition to IP version 6 (IPv6), current IP version 4 (IPv4) addresses will still be usable after the transition is complete.

In fact, IPv4 addresses are easier to understand and easier to configure for many private LANs. I believe that IPv4 addresses will remain in common use for many years to come. In the next chapter, you'll learn how this allows you to configure private IP networks quickly and easily.

There are two ways to specify an IPv4 address: in binary notation, or in dotted decimal format. The following is a typical IPv4 private network address in binary notation:

11000000 10101000 00000001 00100000

Does this look confusing? Remember, this is the way computers read data. As humans, most of us are more familiar with the decimal system of numbers: 0, 1, 2, 3, 4, 5, 6, 7, 8, and 9. It's easy to convert bits into decimals: the above IPv4 address in dotted-decimal format is 192.168.1.32. But not everyone can make this conversion so easily. It's worth taking a bit of time to understand how to convert bits of an IPv4 address to dotted decimal notation.

THE BITS OF AN IPv4 ADDRESS

A bit is a binary digit. The binary system contains two possible numbers: 0 and 1. It's easy to represent a bit in a computer. All you need is a switch, or an electrical impulse or a pulse of light. When the switch is off, it's 0; when the switch is on, it's a 1.

By convention, there are 8 bits in a byte. In ASCII, every letter and number on an English language keyboard is associated with a unique byte. That is why a 32-bit IPv4 address is organized into four groups of 8 bits: there are 4 bytes in this address:

11000000 10101000 00000001 00100000

Now let's break down the bits in each byte. The first number in a byte, 00000001, equals 1 in decimal notation. That's followed by 00000010 = 2, 00000011 = 3 and so on. Several examples of this are shown in Table 20.2.

Now let's take the first byte in the given address, 11000000. That represents 10000000 = 128 and 01000000 = 64. Since 128 + 64 = 192, that's the first number in this IP address. The next number is 10101000, which is 128 + 32 + 8 = 168. Similarly, 00000001 = 1 and 00010000 = 32, which leads to an IPv4 address of 192.168.1.32, expressed in dotted-decimal notation.

Taken to its logical extreme, note that 11111111 in binary notation = 255 in our numbers.

TABLE 20.2: BYTES AND REGULAR NUMBERS

BYTE	REGULAR NUMBER
00000000	0
00000001	1
00000010	2
00000100	4
00001000	8
00010000	16
00100000	32
01000000	64
10000000	128

Address Classes

IPv4 addresses range from 0.0.0.0 to 255.255.255.255. These addresses are divided into five different address classes, A through E. You can assign IP addresses (when available) from Class A, B, or C. The range of addresses of each of the five different classes is shown in Table 20.3.

TABLE 20.3: IPv4 ADDRESS CLASSES

CLASS	RANGE	COMMENT
A	1.0.0.0 to 127.255.255.255	Allows networks of up to 16 million computers
B	128.0.0.0 to 191.255.255.255	Allows networks of up to 65,000 computers
C	192.0.0.0 to 223.255.255.255	Allows networks of up to 254 computers
D	224.0.0.0 to 239.255.255.255	Reserved for multicasts
E	240.0.0.0 to 255.255.255.255	Reserved for experiments

Not all of these IP addresses, even in classes A, B, and C, are usable. There are four types of addresses that you can't assign to a computer that is directly connected to the Internet:

◆ The first address in any network of IPv4 addresses is reserved as the network address.

◆ The last address in any network of IPv4 addresses is reserved as the broadcast address.

◆ The address 127.0.0.1 is reserved as the *loopback* address.

◆ There are groups of IPv4 addresses reserved as private addresses, suitable for private LANs that are connected to the Internet only through a firewall.

You'll learn about each of these addresses in detail in the next chapter, which will also cover the concepts of network and broadcast addresses, as well as network or subnet masks. These concepts will be covered in the context of a private IP network connected to the Internet.

IP Version 6

As strange as it sounds, 4 billion IPv4 addresses are not enough. All available IPv4 address groups have already been assigned. While you probably can get your own IPv4 address from your ISP (probably for an extra fee), work is under way to convert the Internet to IPv6.

There are 128 bits in an IPv6 address. That's over 340,000,000,000,000,000,000,000,000,000,000, 000,000,000 addresses. To ease the transition, a specific IPv6 address has been assigned to every IPv4 address. That leaves over 3.4×10^{38} addresses for all other uses. Your IPv4 address will work in an IPv6 world.

The way IPv6 is configured, it's easy to convert an IPv4 address to IPv6. For example, the IPv4 address

```
192.168.1.32
```

is identical to the following IPv6 address:

```
::192.168.1.32
```

However, IPv6 addresses are also shown in hexadecimal notation. This is also known as base 16, where the numbers are 0, 1, 2, 3, 4, 5, 6, 7, 8, 9, a, b, c, d, e, and f. One example of an IPv6 address is

```
4aed:0a21:3c53:7dab:0000:0000:0000:0451
```

It's easy to convert IPv4 addresses to hexadecimal notation. As an example, convert the previous IPv4 address to binary format:

```
11000000 10101000 00000001 00100000
```

Next, we know that $2^4 = 16$. In other words, there are 4 bits in every hexadecimal number. Therefore, you should regroup the IPv4 address into groups of 4 bits (which is incidentally known as a "nibble"...no kidding):

```
1100 0000 1010 1000 0000 0001 0010 0000
```

Now, converting these numbers one at a time to decimal format leads to

```
12 0 10 8 0 1 2 0
```

which equals the following in base 16 or hexadecimal format:

```
c0a8:0120
```

The corresponding IPv6 address is

```
0000:0000:0000:0000:0000:0000:c0a8:0120
```

Summary

Unix was developed concurrently with the network that would eventually become the Internet. TCP/IP was developed as the language of the Internet. As a Unix clone, Linux is well suited to communicating on the Internet.

A network includes two or more computers set up to communicate with each other. While a LAN connects computers that are physically close to each other, WANs connect two or more geographically distant LANs. The largest WAN is the Internet. LANs are generally faster than WANs due to cost. In either case, you need to configure FQDNs, hostnames, IP addresses, and hardware addresses to communicate on any network.

Network languages such as TCP/IP are also known as protocol stacks. Major protocol stacks such as NetBEUI and IPX/SPX include dozens of different protocols. Protocols are commonly classified in one of the seven levels associated with the OSI model of networking.

Because TCP/IP is the language of the Internet, it is the dominant network protocol suite. The TCP/IP model of networking includes four levels, which are better suited to describe the functionality of different TCP/IP protocols and services such as FTP, HTTP, SNMP, TCP, UDP, IP, Ethernet, and ATM. Other key TCP/IP network services include DNS, DHCP, and ARP.

Every computer that communicates on a TCP/IP network needs an IP address. The standard IP address system is IPv4. There are five IPv4 address classes. Since there aren't enough IPv4 addresses, we're currently in transition to IPv6. Nevertheless, IPv4 addresses are still in common use, especially since there is an IPv6 address available for every IPv4 address.

In the next chapter, you'll put these TCP/IP protocols and IP addresses to good use as you configure your computer and network. You'll also learn to connect your Linux LAN to the Internet.

Chapter 21

Managing Linux on Your LAN

NOW THAT YOU'VE LEARNED the networking theory in Chapter 20, you're ready to put that theory into practice on your Linux computer and network.

First you'll learn some of the basics of network hardware. Hubs connect the different computers in a LAN. Switches segment a LAN, which help you regulate traffic within your network. Routers serve as a junction between networks, directing traffic as needed.

Next, on a Linux computer, you need to configure your network card and make sure it's connected to the proper network card address by using the ifconfig and arp commands. Various commands are available to configure the hostname of your computer on a regular as well as a Network Information System (NIS)-based network. If you've set up Red Hat Linux correctly, the appropriate network settings should show in files such as /etc/hosts, /etc/host.conf, /etc/sysconfig/network, and /etc/resolv.conf.

As we continue, you'll learn to configure a LAN with IPv4 private addresses. One reason why IPv4 addresses are still in common use is that they allow you to easily configure a LAN. With the right routing configuration and one public IPv4 address, you can connect this LAN to the Internet.

Red Hat Linux includes some tools for connecting your computer to the Internet. While some are graphical, others require only the command-line interface. These tools include Red Hat's own Internet Configuration Wizard and minicom.

Finally, if you have problems with your network, commands are available to help you troubleshoot any problems that might arise. The netstat command lets you measure traffic through different TCP/IP ports. The ping command enables you to check connectivity. And finally, the traceroute command helps you visualize the route that your messages might take through diverse networks, especially the Internet. This chapter covers the following topics:

◆ Understanding routing, switching, and hubs

◆ Configuring your computer on a LAN

◆ Configuring private and public networks

◆ Creating Internet connections

◆ Troubleshooting your network

Understanding Network Hardware

Before getting into how you configure Linux for a network, let's take a step back. Think about the physical layout of your network. While this is a book on Linux, most network problems are actually physical. Loose wires, unconnected cables, dust in hubs or routers, and similar issues are the most common causes of network problems. Based on the OSI model discussed in Chapter 20, you need to consider five categories of hardware on a LAN:

- Physical-level transmission media
- Physical-level hubs
- Data-Link-level switches
- Network-level routers
- Application-level gateways

Transmission Media

Your computer sends your data as 1s and 0s over *transmission media*. The data may be electrical impulses through copper wires, light pulses through fiber-optic cables, or even radio waves through the air. Transmission media work at the Physical layer of the OSI model.

Whatever means you use to transmit signals, there is a range limit. For example, an Ethernet network may not work as well as you hope if the length of twisted-pair copper cable between a computer and a hub is greater than the specified maximum cable length of 328 feet (100 meters). Briefly, here are some things to watch out for with physical media such as copper wires or fiber-optic cables:

Connections Check your connections. Many networks fail because cables are not properly plugged in.

Length Networks have a range. The standard "Category 5" network cable may not allow your Fast Ethernet network to perform up to capacity if your cables are longer than 100 meters.

Installation Don't bend your cables too much. Severe bends can stretch parts of a cable, reducing their ability to carry data.

Hubs

A *hub* is the center of most modern LANs. Wired hubs are essentially boxes with sockets. With the right cable, you can connect a computer to each socket. When multiple computers are connected to a hub, the configuration looks like the spokes coming out of the center of a wheel, which is known as a *star* configuration. (I don't know why it isn't called a hub-and-spoke-configuration.)

Digital signals degrade with distance. A hub can rebuild a digital signal and retransmit it at its original strength. Because they just work with the 1s and 0s of computer communication, hubs also work at the Physical layer of the OSI model.

Switches

A *switch* is often used to split a larger LAN into two or more different logical network segments. Switches keep a database of hardware addresses on a LAN; in other words, they work at layer 2 of the OSI model.

Once first contact is made between two computers, they continue their conversation with their hardware addresses. Since switches know the hardware addresses on a LAN, they can retransmit every message (like a hub) and direct it toward the destination computer.

NOTE *Older switches are sometimes known as* bridges. *Both are designed at the Data-Link layer (2) of the OSI model.*

Routers

Routers transmit data between two or more LANs. A router has a network card on each of these LANs. In a TCP/IP network, each network card has an IP address. Thus, routers work at the Network layer of the OSI model.

In many cases, the gateway address that you configure in a file such as /etc/sysconfig/network should be the IP address of a router connected to your network.

Alternatively, you can configure a Linux computer as a router. First you need two or more network cards, connected to different networks. Then you must enable IP Forwarding in the kernel. It's easy to do with an IPv4 configuration by changing a setting in the /proc directory:

```
# echo 1 > /proc/sys/net/ipv4/ip_forward
```

You can configure a router within a LAN, if needed, and it will perform the same functions as a switch or even a hub. To make sure this change is still there the next time you boot Linux, open the /etc/sysctl.conf file and verify that the following variable is set to 1:

```
net.ipv4.ip_forward = 1
```

Gateways

For most purposes, Linux assumes that routers and gateways are functionally equivalent. For example, if your network is connected to an outside network though an Ethernet network card eth0 via a router, you can specify its connection to your LAN in the ifcfg-eth0 file in the /etc/sysconfig/networking/devices directory as your GATEWAY IP address.

However, a *gateway* serves a different purpose, because it can connect LANs using different protocol stacks such as TCP/IP and IPX/SPX. It works at the OSI Application layer.

Configuring Your Computer on a LAN

While Red Hat Linux usually configures your computer to connect to a LAN, you may want to change your configuration for various reasons. Say you have Linux on a laptop computer that you want to connect to another network. Or suppose you've acquired some computers from a different department. Or you're installing a second network card on your computer and need to make sure the configuration of each network card is correct. Or perhaps Red Hat Linux does not detect your network card.

Red Hat Linux normally configures your network cards during the installation process. All you need is a detectable network card with a Linux driver and a Dynamic Host Configuration Protocol (DHCP) server. Alternatively, you can enter IP address and hostname information manually. If you're connecting to an NIS network, you may need to enter the appropriate names during the installation process. Chapter 28 covers NIS in more detail.

But when problems arise, it's important to know where to look to solve network configuration problems for your Linux computer. Some basic commands include `ifconfig` and `arp` (for configuring your network card) and various commands related to the hostname.

It's also useful to understand the basic network configuration files. The `/etc/sysconfig/network` file is just the start of a series of important Linux network configuration files.

Configuring with *ifconfig*

Perhaps the key Linux network configuration command is `ifconfig`, in the `/sbin` directory. With the right options, you can use this command to assign IP addresses, hardware ports, and network masks, as well as activate or deactivate a network card. It's easy to check your current network configuration. As shown in Figure 21.1, there are two active network components on my computer: an Ethernet card (`eth0`) and a loopback device (`lo`). As you can see, `eth0` includes connection information presumably for the LAN. The loopback device helps you make sure that Linux is properly connected to the TCP/IP protocol stack.

FIGURE 21.1

`ifconfig` output

```
[root@RH9Test root]# ifconfig
eth0      Link encap:Ethernet  HWaddr 00:40:F4:3C:05:58
          inet addr:10.252.113.3  Bcast:10.252.113.255  Mask:255.255.255.0
          UP BROADCAST RUNNING MULTICAST  MTU:1500  Metric:1
          RX packets:9 errors:0 dropped:0 overruns:0 frame:0
          TX packets:8 errors:0 dropped:0 overruns:0 carrier:0
          collisions:0 txqueuelen:100
          RX bytes:1640 (1.6 Kb)  TX bytes:1632 (1.5 Kb)
          Interrupt:5 Base address:0x8000

lo        Link encap:Local Loopback
          UP LOOPBACK RUNNING  MTU:16436  Metric:1
          RX packets:67692 errors:0 dropped:0 overruns:0 frame:0
          TX packets:67692 errors:0 dropped:0 overruns:0 carrier:0
          collisions:0 txqueuelen:0
          RX bytes:4624266 (4.4 Mb)  TX bytes:4624266 (4.4 Mb)

[root@RH9Test root]# []
```

It's easy to assign a new IP address to your network card. The following command assigns a new IPv4 address to `eth1`:

```
# ifconfig eth1 10.122.238.3
```

As discussed later in this chapter, the standard network mask for this IP address is 255.0.0.0. You can also specify a different network mask with the new IP address:

```
# ifconfig eth1 netmask 255.255.255.0 10.122.238.3
```

Red Hat Linux has had problems in the past with assigning IRQ ports or I/O addresses to a *second* (or later) network card. You can assign different hardware addresses to a network card. For example, the following commands assign IRQ 9 and I/O address 0x300 to the third Ethernet card on your computer:

```
# ifconfig eth1 irq 9
# ifconfig eth1 io_addr 0x300
```

As you can see in Figure 21.1, these settings correspond to the `Interrupt` and `Base address` settings in the output from `ifconfig`. If you see an error, the interrupt or address may already be assigned or reserved for plug-and-play. .

You can use this command to activate or deactivate your network adapter. For example, the following commands deactivate and activate the `eth0` network adapter:

```
# ifconfig eth0 down
# ifconfig eth0 up
```

Configuring with *arp*

The Address Resolution Protocol (ARP) associates IP addresses with hardware addresses on a network card. Once your computer has made contact with another computer on your network, they exchange hardware addresses, which are then stored in an ARP database. Not surprisingly, you can find this database on your own computer by issuing the `arp` command (which identifies a problem):

```
# arp
Address        HWtype HWaddress          Flags Mask  Iface
192.168.7.2    ether  00:12:B5:64:3B:B2  C           eth0
RH9laptop      ether  00:60:0B:8A:41:93  C           eth0
192.168.7.2    ether  52:A5:CB:32:52:A2  C           eth0
experimental   ether  00:20:78:09:D3:6A  C           eth0
```

Depending on how contact was made, the Address column lists either the IP address or the name of the remote computer. The computer name is taken from `/etc/hosts` for your convenience. The HWtype column shows the type of network adapter. The HWaddress column lists the hardware address of the adapter, in hexadecimal notation.

This output shows a duplicate IP address, which can stop communication on your network. You can remove the associated computer's entry in your ARP table by using the `arp -d` *computername* command. Be sure to substitute the name or IP address of the offending computer for *computername*.

The Hostname Commands

Several commands are available for defining or listing the name of your computer on various networks. These commands are illustrated in Table 21.1. With all but the `dnsdomainname` command, you can set the name of your computer. For example, the `hostname ilovehackers` command sets the name of your computer to `ilovehackers`.

TABLE 21.1: HOSTNAME COMMANDS

COMMAND	FUNCTION
hostname	Lists or sets the hostname for the local computer
domainname	Lists or sets the NIS domain name
dnsdomainname	Lists the FQDN for the DNS server for your network
nisdomainname	See domainname
ypdomainname	See domainname

Network Configuration Files

Red Hat Linux contains many important network configuration files. These include basic configuration files commonly used on other Linux distributions, such as `/etc/hosts`, `/etc/resolv.conf`, and `/etc/host.conf`. Red Hat Linux also includes some newer configuration files that determine basic network settings in the `/etc/sysconfig` directory.

TIP   *Red Hat is working toward consolidating configuration data, especially related to network settings, in the `/etc/sysconfig` directory. If you're not sure where to look for configuration data, this directory is a good place to start.*

STATIC HOSTNAMES—*/ETC/HOSTS*

In the first days of the ARPAnet, only a handful of computers ran on this worldwide network. Those computers that were running Unix used the `/etc/hosts` file as a static database of computer names and IP addresses. Whenever a new university would join this network, it was relatively easy to change `/etc/hosts` and share a copy of this file with all computers.

While it is no longer practical to use `/etc/hosts` for the Internet, it is still a viable option for smaller networks. As long as you make sure that every computer on your LAN has the same copy of this file, it can serve your network well.

This file is fairly simple; each line includes an IP address, a fully qualified domain name (FQDN), and/or a hostname:

```
192.168.23.121    linux1.mommabears.com    linux1
```

DNS SERVERS—*/ETC/RESOLV.CONF*

The alternative to `/etc/hosts` is a Domain Name Service (DNS) server. In Linux, DNS is implemented through the Berkeley Internet Name Domain (`bind`), using the `named` daemon. (DNS is covered in detail in Chapter 24.) If you have IP addresses for your DNS servers, you can enter them in the `/etc/resolv.conf` configuration file.

This is a simple file; every DNS server is known as a `nameserver`; this file associates it with an IP address. If you're connecting your network to an ISP, you might add the IP addresses of your ISP's DNS server to your file, in lines similar to this one:

```
nameserver 207.217.126.81
```

SEARCH ORDER—*/ETC/HOST.CONF*

There are two databases of hostnames and IP addresses: `/etc/hosts` and DNS servers. The order is determined by `/etc/host.conf`. Normally, this file contains only one line:

```
order hosts,bind
```

This line configures your Linux computer to search for the right IP address in your `/etc/hosts` file, before checking `bind`, which, as described in the last section, is the Linux name for a DNS server. You could even include an NIS server in this list; see the discussion on `/etc/nsswitch.conf` in Chapter 28 for more information.

BASIC NETWORK SETTINGS—/*ETC/SYSCONFIG/NETWORK*

Basic network configuration data is listed in /etc/sysconfig/network. If you're having problems with your network, this is a good place to look. You should see the NETWORKING=yes line at the start of this file. Other variables are shown in Table 21.2. Not all of these variables are required in this configuration file; some are unneeded if you use a DHCP server. Others may be located in network-adapter specific files in the /etc/sysconfig/networking/devices directory.

TABLE 21.2: /*ETC/SYSCONFIG/NETWORK* VARIABLES

VARIABLE	DESCRIPTION
NETWORKING	This is yes or no; yes is required to let Red Hat Linux run networking.
HOSTNAME	The hostname name of your computer.
GATEWAY	The Gateway IP address of your computer.
GATEWAYDEV	The network device, such as eth1, that is connected to the network with the gateway; needed if you have more than one network card on the computer.
NISDOMAIN	The domain name of your NIS system, if available.

Configuring Private and Public Networks

In Chapter 20, you learned some of the basics of IPv4 addresses. Now you'll see how to make IPv4 addressing work in configuring a LAN that is connected to the Internet.

When you configure a network that's connected to the Internet, you can't select just any IP address. There are a number of *private* IP addresses that you can freely use on your internal network. However, for your connection to the Internet, you need at least one *public* IP address. Each of the computers on your network can access the Internet simultaneously using your public IP address.

Unfortunately, most public IP addresses are taken. Those that are still available are generally assigned by ISPs.

NOTE *Public IP addresses are used for communication between computers and networks on the Internet. On the other hand, the same private IP addresses can be used on independent private networks. To avoid confusion, private IP addresses are not valid for communication through the Internet.*

You can configure your LAN with private IP addresses, with one public IP address on a gateway computer for connecting your LAN to the Internet. To get a public IP address on the Internet, talk to your ISP. You'll get either a static IP address with a subnet or network mask, or instructions to get your address from a DHCP server.

NETWORK DEFINITIONS

Several basic definitions are used to define IP addresses on a LAN.

Network address   Every IP address includes two parts: the network address and the numbers associated with a particular host. A network address such as 192.168.22.0 uniquely identifies a specific network. Assuming it is a Class C address, it identifies a network with a range of IP addresses between 192.168.22.1 and 192.168.22.254.

Network mask   This special IP address (also known as a *subnetwork mask* or a *subnet mask*) lets you define a range of available IP addresses on a LAN. The three "standard" network masks are 255.0.0.0, 255.255.0.0, and 255.255.255.0.

Broadcast address   This is a special IP address used to communicate with all computers on that network. It is the last available IP address on a network. For example, if you have a network address of 192.168.22.0 and a network mask of 255.255.255.0, the broadcast address is 192.168.22.255.

Private IP address   This is an IP address that is dedicated for private LANs. You can use a private IP address on a LAN that is connected to the Internet through a computer with a public IP address. The same private IP addresses are often used on different LANs. However, you aren't allowed to use a private IP address to connect directly to the Internet.

Public IP address   This is an IP address that is used to communicate directly to the Internet.

Classless Inter-Domain Routing (CIDR)   CIDR is a method of specifying nonstandard network masks. This allows you to subdivide or combine standard IP address ranges.

Private IP Networks

To set up the computers inside your network with private IP addresses, you need a network address and a network mask. These two parameters define a range of IP addresses. As described in Chapter 20, three standard ranges of private IP addresses are available, as shown in Table 21.3.

TABLE 21.3: PRIVATE IP ADDRESS RANGES

RANGE	CLASS	DESCRIPTION
10.0.0.1–10.255.255.254	A	Can accommodate about 16 million computers in one domain
172.168.0.1–172.168.255.254	B	Can accommodate about 65,000 computers in one domain
192.168.0.1–192.168.255.254	C	Can accommodate up to 254 computers in one domain

When you choose a network address and network mask, you typically choose a subset of one of the IP address groups shown in Table 21.3. For example, if you have a network address of 10.0.0.0 and a network mask of 255.255.255.0, the range of possible addresses is 10.0.0.0 through 10.0.0.255, which consists of 256 different addresses. These addresses compose a subnetwork, also known as a *subnet*.

But as you may remember from Chapter 20, the first address in this subnet, 10.0.0.0, is reserved as the network address. And the last address in this subnet, 10.0.0.255, is reserved as the broadcast address. You can't assign either address to a specific computer. That leaves 254 addresses on this subnet that you can assign to actual computers.

NETWORK MASK

A network mask allows you to determine if a specific IP address is on the same LAN. It also enables you to differentiate network addresses from host addresses. When you put the network address together with the network mask, you can define the range of host addresses that you can assign to your computers.

Table 21.4 shows several examples of network addresses, host addresses, and network masks. The Available Host Addresses column defines the IP addresses that you can assign on your internal network.

TABLE 21.4: SAMPLE NETWORK ADDRESSES AND NETWORK MASKS

NETWORK ADDRESS	NETWORK MASK	AVAILABLE HOST ADDRESSES	NUMBER OF ASSIGNABLE IP ADDRESSES
10.0.0.0	255.0.0.0	10.0.0.1–10.255.255.254	16,777,214
10.21.92.0	255.255.255.0	10.21.92.1–10.21.92.254	254
10.182.0.0	255.255.0.0	10.182.0.1–10.182.255.254	65,534
172.168.78.0	255.255.255.0	172.168.78.1–172.168.78.254	254
172.168.0.0	255.255.0.0	172.168.0.1–172.168.255.254	65,534
192.168.3.0	255.255.255.0	192.168.3.1–192.168.3.254	254

From this information, you can derive the following "rules" for IP addressing:

◆ A network IP address is never used as a host address for a specific computer. This address comes just before the range of available host addresses.

◆ The 255s in a network mask normally correspond to the network address. For example, if your IP address is 10.162.4.23 and your network mask is 255.255.255.0, the network address is 10.162.4.0. The "host" part of the IP address is 23. See the section "Classless Inter-Domain Routing (CIDR)" for exceptions to this rule.

◆ The last address in an IP address range is reserved as the broadcast address. For example, for the last example in Table 21.4, the broadcast address is 192.168.3.255.

◆ Standard network masks are 255.0.0.0, 255.255.0.0, and 255.255.255.0. Other network masks are described in the section "Classless Inter-Domain Routing (CIDR)."

Configuring a Network

Before you set up TCP/IP on a LAN, you need to select a set of addresses. Based on the information in the previous sections, select a private network address and network mask. When you put the two addresses together, you get a range of IP addresses that you can assign to each computer on your LAN.

Perhaps the most common network mask is 255.255.255.0. As discussed earlier, this network mask allows you to choose from 254 IP addresses. In other words, if your network address is 10.168.0.0, this network mask allows you to assign 10.168.0.1, 10.168.0.2, 10.168.0.3, and so on through 10.168.0.254 to different computers on your network.

Remember, the first address in the network range, in this case 10.168.0.0, is reserved as the network address. The last address in this range, 10.168.0.255, is reserved as the broadcast address.

You have two choices with the assignable IP addresses. You can assign them to individual computers yourself, with commands such as `ifconfig` as described earlier. This means you also need to manually add the IP addresses for the DNS server and the default gateway. Alternatively, you can set up the range of available IP addresses on a DHCP server. As discussed in Chapter 24, DHCP servers can be configured to "lease" IP addresses to each computer on your network. That server can also pass along information related to the DNS server and gateway address for your network.

THE GATEWAY COMPUTER

On a network, the gateway computer is connected to your LAN and another network, such as the Internet. On a typical LAN, only one computer is directly connected to another network. That computer has two or more network cards: one is connected to the LAN, and the other is connected to the other network. One IP address is assigned to each network card. The gateway address is the IP address of the network card on the LAN.

To illustrate this configuration, look at Figure 21.2, which shows a LAN of five computers. The computer that is shown between the hub and the Internet is the gateway computer. The gateway address for all the other computers on this LAN is 10.190.18.3, which is the address that the gateway computer uses on the LAN.

FIGURE 21.2

Assigning IP addresses

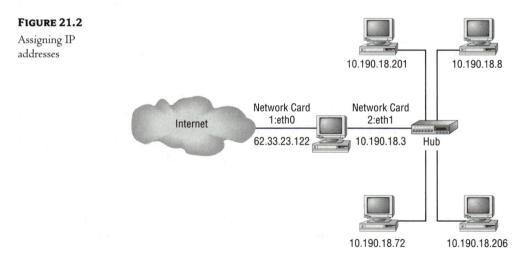

The other network card on the gateway computer gets the public IP address on the Internet, in this case, 62.33.23.122.

Classless Inter-Domain Routing (CIDR)

Classless Inter-Domain Routing (CIDR) is not the easiest topic for speed-readers. However, if you take these explanations step by step, you'll be a CIDR master in no time at all.

In most cases, the only network masks that you need on an IPv4 network are 255.0.0.0, 255.255.0.0, and 255.255.255.0. These network masks are most closely associated with Class A, B, and C addresses, respectively.

Those three network masks make it easy to differentiate network addresses from the host address. For example, if one of the computers on a distant network has an IP address of 192.168.38.48, with a network mask of 255.255.255.0, you know the network address is 192.168.38.0. The other computers on that LAN can have IP addresses between 192.168.38.1 and 192.168.38.254.

BITS AND BYTES

To understand CIDR, you need to understand the bits and bytes in an IPv4 address. There are 32 bits in an IPv4 address. They are organized into 4 different numbers between 0 and 255, which correspond to 4 bytes. There are 8 bits in a byte. Each bit represents a different number. The top row represents the bits in a byte; the bottom row represents their decimal equivalent.

1	1	1	1	1	1	1	1
128	64	32	16	8	4	2	1

For example, if you have a byte of 10000000, the corresponding number is 128. If you have a byte of 00010000, the corresponding number is 16. If your byte is 11111111, the corresponding number is $128 + 64 + 32 + 16 + 8 + 4 + 2 + 1 = 255$.

As an example, assume that you're setting up a Class C network, using the 192.168.38.0 network address. You may not even need 254 different IP addresses for your LAN; however, CIDR is useful if you're responsible for two LANs in separate buildings. In this case, you can use CIDR to subdivide IP addresses in a different way.

To understand how this works, let's take a step back and return to the bits. The following two IP addresses represent 192.168.38.48 and 255.255.255.0 in binary notation:

```
11000000 10101000 00100110 00110000
11111111 11111111 11111111 00000000
```

As discussed earlier, the 255s in a network mask correspond to the network IP address, in this case, 192.168.38.0. When expressed in bits, the 1s in a network mask correspond to the network address as shown:

```
11000000 10101000 00100110 00000000
```

NOTE *Note how 255.255.255.0 corresponds to 24 bits of an IPv4 address. In CIDR notation, this network address and mask can be shown as 192.168.38.0/24.*

The last 8 bits are not "covered," which gives us a range of $2^8 = 256$ host addresses, starting with 0. The 0 is assigned as the end of the host network address; 255 is assigned as the host broadcast address.

Neither of these addresses can be assigned to a specific computer; therefore, you have 254 addresses available on this LAN. Look at what happens when you add one more bit to the network mask:

```
11000000 10101000 00100110 00110000
11111111 11111111 11111111 10000000
```

The area "covered" by the 1s in the network mask represents the network address of 192.168.38.0. However, only the last 7 bits are not "covered," which gives us a theoretical range of $2^7 = 128$ host addresses, starting with 0 and ending with 127. Therefore, this particular network has an address of 192.168.38.0 and a broadcast address of 192.168.38.127. The network mask is 255.255.255.128.

NOTE   *See how 255.255.255.128 corresponds to 25 bits of an IPv4 address. In CIDR notation, this network, with this network mask, can be represented by 192.168.38.0/25.*

Alternatively, look at the same network mask for an IP address of 192.168.38.166:

```
11000000 10101000 00100110 10110000
11111111 11111111 11111111 10000000
```

Using the same rationale, this particular network has an address of 192.168.38.128, and a broadcast address of 192.168.38.255. Remember, neither of these addresses can be used on a specific computer. Thus, there are only 126 available host addresses.

With a standard Class C network mask of 255.255.255.0, you can configure 254 computers on the 192.168.38.0 network. With a slightly different network mask (255.255.255.128), you can configure two different LANs with 126 available host addresses.

Creating Internet Connections

Despite the hype surrounding high-speed Internet connections, the vast majority of home users still connect to the Internet with a 56Kbps telephone modem. However, the cost of higher-speed connections has come down to the point where it is cost-effective for small businesses who need Internet access. High-speed Internet connections are also known as *broadband*.

Several broadband connection services are available, including satellite, infrared, wireless, cable modems, and DSL (Digital Subscriber Line) services. These services transmit and receive data at 144Kbps and higher speeds. Because of this competition, many telephone companies have reduced the cost of "traditional" broadband services such as T1 lines (1.544Mbps) and ISDN (Integrated Services Digital Network, at 128Kbps and higher).

In most cases, connections to a broadband service are no different from connecting your computer to a router. The broadband provider gives or sells you a router. Either you connect to its DHCP server using the techniques described in Chapter 24, or you may be given the IP address for your gateway and DNS servers.

Perhaps the best representative of a Linux text-based telephone modem interface is `minicom`. Red Hat has developed its Internet Configuration Wizard to guide you when you're creating a telephone modem or broadband connection.

The Internet Configuration Wizard

The Red Hat Internet Configuration Wizard is different from the Microsoft tool of a similar name. You can start it with a console command in GNOME or KDE by issuing the `redhat-config-network-druid` command. As you can see in Figure 21.3, this opens the Add New Device Type window, with options that let you configure a variety of different network devices. While the focus of this section is on regular telephone modems, let's take a brief look at the other options:

FIGURE 21.3

Internet
Configuration
Wizard

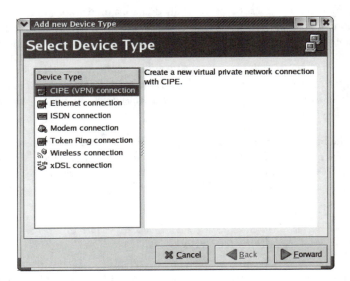

CIPE (VPN) Connection   Crypto IP Encapsulation (CIPE) is more commonly known as Virtual Private Networking (VPN), which involves building a secure network connection through a public network such as the Internet. This option allows you to set an IP address for each end of the connection as well as an appropriate encryption key.

Ethernet Connection   This allows you to specify a driver, a device name such as `eth1`, and resources such as an IRQ port, I/O address, and DMA channels appropriate for this network adapter. These settings use the `ifconfig` command to help Linux detect and communicate with this adapter. You can also set the network adapter to get IP addressing information from a DHCP server, or configure these settings yourself. If the DHCP server is on a remote network, you'll typically need to specify the BOOTP protocol.

ISDN Connection   As with Ethernet connections, this option allows you to specify a driver and resources for an ISDN adapter. Because ISDN is most popular in Europe, the settings are customized for several different nation-states on that continent.

Token Ring Connection   This is a front end similar to the Ethernet configuration option.

Wireless Connection   This is a front end similar to the Ethernet configuration option. Extra settings allow you to set the appropriate wireless channel and/or encryption key for your network.

xDSL Connection   Several types of DSL connections are available, which vary in upload and download speeds. In any case, this utility enables you to configure the connection for an Ethernet adapter, with a username and password for the broadband ISP. This should also work for most cable modem connections.

Now let us move on to configuring a modem with the Internet Configuration Wizard. In the Device Type window, select Modem Connection and click Forward. The wizard should try to detect your modem. If it doesn't and you really do have a modem on your computer, refer to the discussion in Chapter 2 on Winmodems. Whatever the result, it will take you to the Select Modem window, shown in Figure 21.4, where you can configure the device, baud rate, and other options for the modem.

NOTE   *Linux modem devices can often be translated to Microsoft COM ports: for example, /dev/tty0=COM1, /dev/tty1=COM2, and so on. The modem detected in Figure 21.4 is detected on the device file associated with COM3. So if your modem worked as part of a Microsoft operating system, you may be able to find its COM port and use the corresponding Linux device.*

The baud rate should generally be two or four times the connection speed of your modem; for a 56Kbps modem (53Kbps in the United States), you should normally select a baud rate of 115200 or 230400bps. Your modem will compress this data stream. In the Flow Control text box, you should generally leave the default, Hardware (CRTSCTS). When you're satisfied with the settings, click Forward.

TIP   *To check the device associated with a detected modem, run the* `ls -l /dev/modem` *command. It should be linked to the actual modem device file,* `/dev/ttyx`.

FIGURE 21.4

Configuring a modem

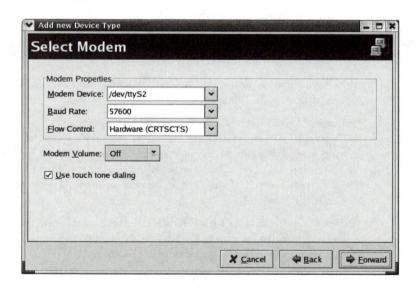

In the next window, you can add the access number, login name, and password for your ISP as shown in Figure 21.5. As long as you have this information, don't be concerned that your country is not on the Internet Provider list. (If you have a T-Online Account in Europe, click the T-Online Account Setup button, and then fill in the prompts provided by T-Online.)

FIGURE 21.5

Specifying an ISP

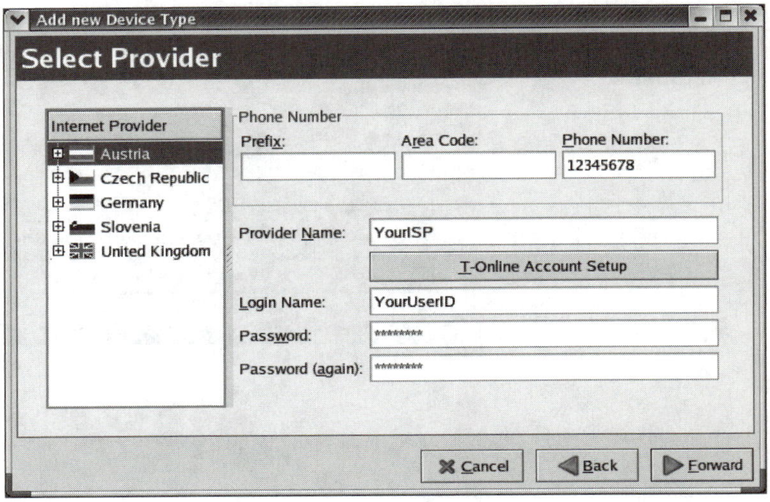

Click Forward again. The next window is the IP Settings dialog box shown in Figure 21.6. Normally, ISPs automatically provide IP address settings for a dial-up telephone modem connection. If your ISP has assigned you a static IP address, make sure you also have your assigned Subnet Mask and Gateway Address, and enter them here.

FIGURE 21.6

Specifying IP settings

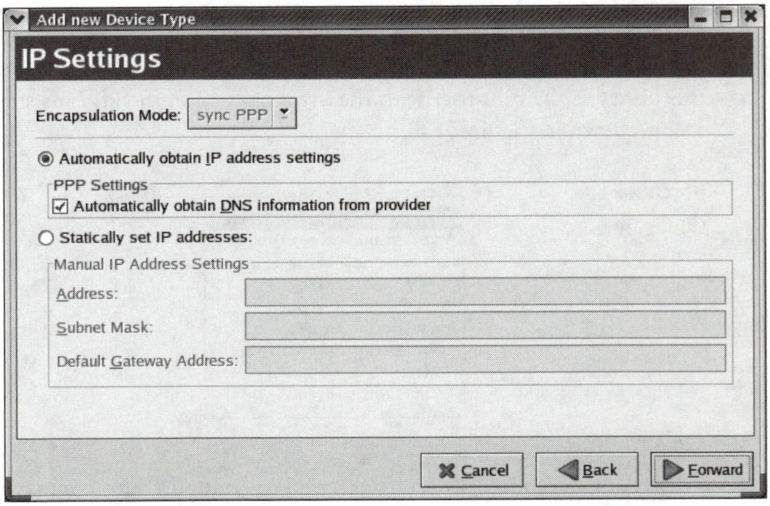

Click Forward, and in the next window, click Apply. You should see the Network Configuration window, with settings for your network adapters. While the **ppp0** device shown in Figure 21.7 is "Inactive," all that means is that your modem isn't yet connected. Highlight your modem and click Activate. If you enabled sound for your modem, you should hear it dialing your ISP.

FIGURE 21.7

Activating your modem

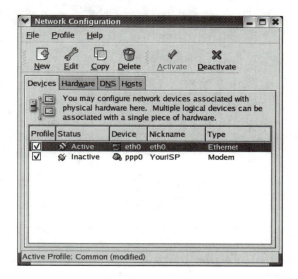

When you're ready to drop your modem connection, return to the Network Configuration window, highlight your modem, and click Deactivate.

Using *minicom*

One traditional command-line tool for modem connections is `minicom`. You can start by configuring this utility as the root user with the `minicom -s` command. This starts the `minicom` Configuration menu, shown in Figure 21.8.

FIGURE 21.8

Configuring `minicom`

Before you can use `minicom`, you need to configure it to connect to your modem. Select the Serial Port Setup menu and press Enter. You should see the menu shown in Figure 21.9. Depending on the modem, you may need to change the following settings:

FIGURE 21.9

Configuring the
serial port

```
A -     Serial Device      : /dev/ttyS1
B - Lockfile Location      : /var/lock
C -    Callin Program      :
D -   Callout Program      :
E -       Bps/Par/Bits     : 38400 8N1
F - Hardware Flow Control : Yes
G - Software Flow Control : No

    Change which setting?
```

```
    Screen and keyboard
    Save setup as dfl
    Save setup as..
    Exit
    Exit from Minicom
```

Serial Device   The device associated with your modem. If an `ls -l /dev/modem` command reveals a link to a device such as `/dev/ttyS0`, use that device. Otherwise, some trial and error may be required.

Bps/Par/Bits   Data settings for your modem. The bits per second (Bps) data rate should be two to four times the speed of your modem, because current modems compress data. Unless you have an older modem, the parity (Par) and stop bit (Bits) should match the default, 8N1.

Check your modem's documentation for any other settings, such as bps or hardware flow control, that you may need to change. Once configuration is complete, be sure to select Save Setup As dfl from the original menu. To start troubleshooting your modem, select Exit (not Exit from Minicom). This initializes your modem and brings you to a main `minicom` screen.

The most straightforward test is to try to dial your ISP. To do so, just enter the `atdt` command followed by the number of your ISP. For an example of this process, see Figure 21.10.

FIGURE 21.10

Connecting with
`minicom`

```
Welcome to minicom 2.00.0

OPTIONS: History Buffer, F-key Macros, Search History Buffer, I18n
Compiled on Jun 23 2003, 16:41:20.

Press CTRL-A Z for help on special keys

AT S7=45 S0=0 L1 V1 X4 &c1 E1 Q0
OK
atdt2611085
CARRIER 33600

PROTOCOL: LAP-M

CONNECT 9600
Authorized Use Only - Unauthorized Use is Prohibited - Sprint-ip


sdn-ar-008nctarb003t slot:10/mod:2


User Access verification

Login:/Username: █

 CTRL-A Z for help |230400 8N1 | NOR | Minicom 2.00.0 | VT102 | Online 00:00
```

NOTE *The* minicom *utility uses common commands associated with terminal modem software. For example,* atdt *is short for "Attention, use Touch-Tone dialing."*

Troubleshooting Your Network

We've discussed troubleshooting techniques throughout this book. Troubleshooting a network is no different. If you have a problem, collect data, identify and isolate the cause, research the symptoms with others, and if none of this works, apply the scientific method.

As noted earlier, the number one cause of network problems is physical: bad connections, cables, power, and so on. Once you've checked the physical problems, Linux has a number of troubleshooting commands that can help. While the netstat command allows you to collect data, the ping and traceroute commands help you isolate the problem.

Checking Network Status

There are two things you should do to check the status of your network. First, run the ifconfig command to make sure that your network card is still active. As discussed earlier, you can run the ifconfig eth0 up command to activate the eth0 network card. If your network card is working, the next step is to check the status of your network with the netstat command.

This command displays routing tables, proxy connections to outside networks, interface statistics, and more. For example, the netstat -a command displays all available connections. As shown in Figure 21.11, the Local Address column displays names and numbers, which correspond to TCP/IP ports described in earlier chapters. In the Foreign Address column, you can see telnet, http, and ssh connections that are established between the local computer and two others.

FIGURE 21.11

netstat -a output

```
[root@RH9Test root]# netstat -a | more
Active Internet connections (servers and established)
Proto Recv-Q Send-Q Local Address            Foreign Address         State
tcp        0      0 *:1024                    *:*                     LISTEN
tcp        0      0 RH9Test:1025              *:*                     LISTEN
tcp        0      0 RH9Test:783               *:*                     LISTEN
tcp        0      0 *:sunrpc                  *:*                     LISTEN
tcp        0      0 *:x11                     *:*                     LISTEN
tcp        0      0 *:ssh                     *:*                     LISTEN
tcp        0      0 RH9Test:ipp               *:*                     LISTEN
tcp        0      0 RH9Test:smtp              *:*                     LISTEN
tcp        0      1 10.252.113.3:2836         RH9Test:ipp             SYN_SENT
tcp        0      0 10.252.113.3:2831         laptop2:netbios-ssn     ESTABLISHED
udp        0      0 *:1024                    *:*
udp        0      0 *:687                     *:*
udp        0      0 *:bootpc                  *:*
udp        0      0 *:bootpc                  *:*
udp        0      0 *:sunrpc                  *:*
udp        0      0 *:631                     *:*
udp        0      0 10.252.113.1:ntp          *:*
udp        0      0 RH9Test:ntp               *:*
udp        0      0 *:ntp                     *:*
Active UNIX domain sockets (servers and established)
--More--
```

A routing table lists currently configured paths from your computer to another computer on or outside your network. Linux uses these paths to find the computers to which you want to connect. A variation of `netstat` enables you to inspect your routing tables. We've shown a fairly simple routing table in Figure 21.12. It includes three different types of IP addresses, as described in Table 21.5.

FIGURE 21.12

A routing table

```
[root@RH9Test root]# netstat -nr
Kernel IP routing table
Destination     Gateway          Genmask         Flags  MSS Window  irtt Iface
10.252.113.0    0.0.0.0          255.255.255.0   U      0 0            0 eth0
127.0.0.0       0.0.0.0          255.0.0.0       U      0 0            0 lo
0.0.0.0         10.252.113.113   0.0.0.0         UG     0 0            0 eth0
[root@RH9Test root]# []
```

TABLE 21.5: A ROUTING TABLE

DESTINATION	COMMENT
192.168.0.0	No gateway is required for addresses on this network, since it is on the current LAN.
127.0.0.0	No gateway is required for the loopback address, since it is on the local computer.
0.0.0.0	Use 192.168.0.113 as the default gateway for all IP addresses not specified earlier in this routing table. (You may see `default` in place of `0.0.0.0` in the Destination column.)

If needed, you can use the `route` command to add to your routing table. For example, assume you just added another LAN, with a network address of 10.0.0.0 and a network mask of 255.255.0.0, and connected it to a different network adapter, `eth1`. Add it to your routing table with the following command:

```
# route add -net 10.0.0.0 netmask 255.255.0.0 dev eth1
```

Checking Connections with *ping* and *traceroute*

If you have a specific problem on your network, such as a user who no longer has web or e-mail access, start by talking to the user. Based on your knowledge of browsers and e-mail managers, make sure the user knows how to access the desired service. You may also be able to log onto that user's computer through `ssh` or `telnet` and check the user's computer for yourself.

Linux includes a number of tools that allow you to work from the most basic network connection all the way to the connections required for the application. These command tools are based on the `ping` and `traceroute` commands. When diagnosing network connections, try the following commands. If they work, you'll need to press Ctrl+C to stop the response:

1. `ping 127.0.0.1`: This checks connectivity to the loopback address. If you see a continuous response such as `64 bytes from 127.0.0.1`... TCP/IP is properly installed on your computer.

TIP *One alternative to a continuous ping is the* `ping -c 4 ip_address` *command, which sends four ping packets to the destination computer and then stops automatically. You can even set* `alias ping='ping -c 4';` *for more information on the* `alias` *command, see Chapter 8.*

2. `ping your_ip_address`: Substitute the IP address defined for your network card for `your_ip_address`, based on the output from the `ifconfig` command. If you see a similar continuous response, your network card is properly configured.

3. `ping your_host_name`: Substitute the hostname for your computer, which usually can be found in `/etc/sysconfig/network`. If you see the same response as with the previous command, hostnames are properly configured on your computer.

4. `ping another_ip_address`: Substitute the IP address of another computer on your LAN for `another_ip_address`. You can use `ifconfig` to find IP addresses on Linux computers. (The corresponding Microsoft Windows command is `IPCONFIG`.) If you see a similar continuous response, communication is working on your LAN. You've at least configured those two computers with at least the same network address and netmask. As a follow-up, try the IP address for the default gateway on your LAN.

5. `ping another_hostname`: Substitute the name of a computer on a connected network for `another_hostname`. If you're connected to the Internet, one example is `ping www.Sybex.com`. If this works, your LAN's gateway or router is properly configured, and communication is possible to and from your LAN.

6. `traceroute another_hostname`: Use another name on a connected network. If you're connected to the Internet, run the `traceroute www.Sybex.com` command. Watch as you see the path your messages take from your computer to the Sybex website. If you're diagnosing a problem on interconnected networks, this command stops either at the destination or at the router or gateway that is having a problem.

For example, if you're having trouble with the `ping` command for the IP address of the router or gateway on your LAN, check the IP address of some other computer on your network. If you cannot connect to other computers on your LAN, there may be a problem with the cables or connections. Otherwise, it may be a problem with the hardware on the router computer.

Summary

In this chapter, you learned some of the basic steps required to configure a LAN with Linux. There are basic hardware components that you can use on a LAN. Transmission media usually involves copper wires or fiber-optic cables. Hubs connect computers on a LAN. Switches are often used to separate a LAN into segments. Routers can transmit data between two or more LANs. Gateways can even translate between different protocol stacks, such as TCP/IP and IPX/SPX.

For several reasons, you may need to change the network configuration that you set up during the Linux installation. Perhaps the key command to configure network cards is `ifconfig`. You can use `ifconfig` to assign hardware ports and IP address information. You can even use it to activate or deactivate a network adapter. The `arp` command lets you check for duplicate IP addresses. The hostname commands allows you to set the name of your computer as seen by various network services. Some of the key network configuration files are `/etc/hosts`, `/etc/resolv.conf`, `/etc/host.conf`, and `/etc/sysconfig/network`.

You can work with IPv4 addresses on your LAN. Just assign one of the private IP address ranges for the computers on your LAN. With the right network mask, you can choose from private IP address ranges in Class A, Class B, and Class C. Then all you need is one public IP address to connect your LAN to the Internet. You can use CIDR to configure IP networks with nonstandard network masks.

While broadband connections are often a more cost-effective option for business, most Internet users still connect with a telephone modem. Red Hat has developed an Internet Configuration Wizard to help you connect to several types of network adapters, including telephone modems. Alternatively, the `minicom` utility can help you configure an Internet connection from the command-line interface.

When you troubleshoot a network, first remember that most network problems are physical. Check your cables and connections. If that doesn't solve your problems, start collecting data. Work toward identifying the cause of the problem. Research the symptoms.

If none of these approaches help, step back, take the data that you have, and use the scientific method. Linux includes a number of commands that help you collect data and identify the cause of the problem, including `ifconfig`, `netstat`, `ping`, and `traceroute`. The `ifconfig` command helps you make sure that your network adapter is active. The `netstat` command lets you check current network connections and routing tables. The `ping` and `traceroute` commands allow you to check the connectivity within the network.

Now that you know the basics of network configuration, you're ready for Chapter 22, where you'll learn the best practices to secure your network. Red Hat Linux includes two key security systems: Pluggable Authentication Modules (PAM) and firewalls.

Chapter 22

Securing Your Linux Network

SECURITY IS IMPORTANT ON any computer network. All types of crackers are out there searching for vulnerable networks. Some look "just for fun," while others break into networks with criminal purposes in mind.

This chapter starts with a general overview of the best practices associated with network security. Some of these practices require good skills with Linux, which you can learn in this book. This chapter covers encryption, firewalls, and passwords and addresses the concepts of physical security. Other important skills require good judgment, which may come only with experience.

Red Hat Linux requires authentication, not only when users log into their accounts, but also when they try to use certain commands or services. The Pluggable Authentication Module (PAM) system is dynamically configurable for any number of situations.

The firewalls that you can configure with `iptables` help you customize your system for every service, on every TCP/IP channel. These commands are not difficult to understand, once you know how to break them down into their component parts. And once you understand `iptables`, you can create the firewalls that you need—that will protect you without denying needed services to your users.

Closely related to firewalls is *masquerading*, which hides the true identity of the computers on your LAN from others on the Internet. Masquerading is also a function of `iptables`.

Because no security system is perfect, you'll need to check for break-ins on a regular basis. Tools such as Ethereal let you check what you can see in clear text on the network. You can view log files, such as `wtmp`, to spot unauthorized users. Other tools, such as Tripwire, help you detect changes to critical files.

Yet it is possible to have too much security. If your users aren't following your password policies, those policies may be too difficult. If your users can't get to needed services, perhaps your firewall is too strong. Several other chapters in this book also address detailed requirements for security, from encryption to appropriate configuration of network services. This chapter covers the following topics:

◆ Understanding best practices

◆ Using Pluggable Authentication Modules

◆ Creating firewalls

◆ Setting up IP masquerading

◆ Detecting break-ins

◆ Troubleshooting access issues

Understanding Best Practices

There are a number of steps you can take to secure your network. Some basic practices require more common sense than computer savvy. The way you configure your computers can promote security. Encryption protects data traveling over the network. Good passwords in the right locations protect user accounts and computers. Firewalls also help you provide various degrees of network protection.

Physical Setup

The way you protect your computers and network hardware depends on their value, and on the risks in your environment.

In a home network, it is best to keep hubs and routers out of the reach of toddlers, and in locations where you won't spill coffee. Generally, you aren't worried about people who are trying to physically break into a home network.

In a corporate network, you'll want to secure your computers from sabotage, whether accidental or intentional. Depending on need, you may want to keep your servers, as well as your routers, switches, and hubs, in locked rooms. Secure rooms are also good locations for backup media. Just be sure that these locations have proper environmental controls such as air conditioning to maximize the life of your systems.

TIP   It's important to keep notes on your configuration, just in case you need to reinstall Linux from scratch.

In a military or other very secure setting, you'll probably be required to take stronger measures, such as removing or locking floppy drives and ports to which you can attach recording hardware. Depending on need, you can configure different levels of physical security for servers, network hardware, and workstations. In addition, you can keep internal networks more secure by isolating them from the Internet.

In any secure setting, consider the use of other basic security systems such as alarms, guards, cameras, ID systems, and similar devices.

Encryption

Encrypting sensitive data that you send over a network is a must. In most cases, this means that you use a private key to scramble the data that you send. On the other end of the connection, you then supply your users with a public key that they use to unscramble your data.

It is possible to activate different levels of security for your passwords, for various services, and other systems when you installed Red Hat Linux. The types of encryption that you can add to your system include the following:

MD5 passwords   Linux supports long passwords of up to 256 characters.

Shadow Password Suite   This type involves encrypting passwords in /etc/shadow, which is normally accessible only to the root user. The suite is active by default (see Chapter 9 for a detailed description).

Kerberos   This encryption system eliminates the need to send passwords over a network. With this system, both the client and the server are authorized by a ticket-granting service (TGS). Kerberos is a fully functional encryption system that does not work with the Shadow Password Suite, and is only partially compatible with the PAM system discussed later in this chapter. Kerberos was developed by the Massachusetts Institute of Technology.

GNU Privacy Guard   This is commonly used to encrypt e-mail, using the Linux version of the Pretty Good Privacy (PGP) system. GNU Privacy Guard is also used to verify the authenticity of downloads, such as RPMs. See Chapter 10 for more information.

RSA and DSA   Digital signature algorithms (DSA) are associated with Secure Shell (SSH) network access. For more information on using SSH with these algorithms, see Chapter 23.

Password Security

At least three levels of password security exist: on the computer, on the bootloader, and when logging into Linux. At each of these levels, you must decide whether you need a password, what type of password you want, and how often you should change that password. Chapter 9 covers the issues and options associated with user passwords.

PASSWORDS ON THE COMPUTER

Modern PC BIOSes include an option for adding a password for access to the BIOS menu. A BIOS can include a wide variety of options, including a network boot to a computer that might just record passwords that are typed in. Other changes to a BIOS could sabotage the data on your system.

However, modifying a BIOS, at least on standard PCs, requires physical access to the computer. In other words, if your system is physically secure, you might not need a password on your BIOS.

PASSWORDS ON THE BOOTLOADER

As we've mentioned before, two basic bootloaders are available: GRUB and LILO. Many users prefer GRUB, because they can protect it with a password. Otherwise, users can change the bootloader configuration file, change the root password by booting Linux in single-user mode, or even access other operating systems, such as Microsoft Windows, that may be accessible in a dual-boot configuration. For more basic information on GRUB, the default Red Hat Linux bootloader, see Chapter 11. Using the techniques discussed in Chapter 11, you can password-protect access to other operating systems. For example, if your computer includes a dual-boot configuration with Microsoft Windows, you can add a password to the appropriate stanza in the GRUB configuration file, `/boot/grub/grub.conf`, as shown here:

```
title DOS
    lock
    password --md5 sf934^(^$asjl
    rootnoverify (hd0,0)
    chainloader +1
```

The `lock` command keeps anyone from booting the associated operating system; attempts result in a `must be authenticated` error message. With this additional code, you first need to enter the password to edit GRUB, select the DOS option, and then enter the MD5 password you created to boot this operating system.

Firewalls and DMZs

Three basic types of firewalls are available. One can look at every packet of data that comes into your network and make decisions based on the type of data. Another is based on services such as Samba, NFS, and Apache; as we discuss in their respective chapters, various services have their own form of access control that can also serve as a firewall. The third basic type of firewall is based on the services associated with the `xinetd` daemon, as discussed in Chapter 23.

The main Red Hat Linux firewall tool is `iptables`. As you'll see later in this chapter, it lets you block just the traffic you identify. Alternatively, you can configure it to block all traffic, with exceptions for just the services that you need. When you configure a firewall on a gateway computer, it acts as a *bastion host*.

You can set different levels of firewall protection for different computers. For example, if you have a web server, you might configure two different firewalls, as shown in Figure 22.1. For Firewall I, you might configure a minimal level of protection, including commands that help you avoid typical problems associated with web servers, such as the so-called "ping of death." For Firewall II, you might include full protection, to help secure your network from the Internet. More information on securing your network from the ping of death and other issues is available later in this chapter.

FIGURE 22.1

Two firewalls

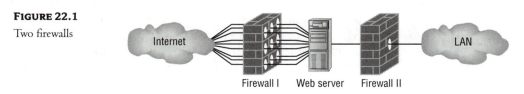

Internet   Firewall I   Web server   Firewall II   LAN

NOTE *The ping of death is a denial-of-service attack; so much data is sent by a* `ping` *command that no other network messages can get through to the target server.*

Using Pluggable Authentication Modules

Another level of security is based on Pluggable Authentication Modules (PAM). These modules are typically used to limit access to specific applications, such as `halt` or `redhat-config-network`, to the root user. Different modules let you regulate access by user, password, or access location. Control flags determine whether passing a PAM command line is enough to qualify the user to access the subject application.

NOTE *The definitions associated with PAM often overlap. For the purpose of this chapter, the commands that call PAM modules are "applications," and commands in PAM module files are "command lines."*

Basic Configuration

PAM includes a series of dynamically loadable modules that can be customized for specific applications. PAM configuration files are stored in the `/etc/pam.d` directory. Individual modules are stored in the `/lib/security` directory and are documented in the `/usr/share/doc/pam-`*version*`/txts` directory.

PAM command lines are all organized in the following format:

```
module_type    control_flag    module_location    arguments
```

In the sections that follow, we examine modules and control flags. The module location is simply the location of the file, normally in `/lib/security`. Arguments are associated with each module.

Module Types

There are four different types of PAM modules, each related to user authentication:

Password   Linux login consoles don't allow users to try to log in again and again, at least not easily. This is because of a PAM password module that sets limits for the number of attempted logins and password length.

Session   This type of module creates settings for an application. For example, PAM session modules can limit the number of times any specific user can log into a Linux server.

Account   This type of module manages access based on policies. For example, PAM account modules can allow or deny access based on a user list, time, or password expiration.

Auth   Short for authentication, an auth module checks the identity of a user. For example, PAM authentication modules can prompt for a username and password.

A common argument for each module is `service=system-auth`, which calls the `system-auth` PAM module for username and password requirements.

Control Flags

There are four possible control flags for each PAM command line. These flags, shown in Table 22.1, determine the action of the application when the module command succeeds or fails.

TABLE 22.1: CONTROL FLAGS IN PAM

CONTROL FLAG	DESCRIPTION
`optional`	The module doesn't really matter, unless all other modules also have the `optional` control flag.
`required`	If the module fails, the application associated with this file also fails.
`requisite`	If the module fails, immediately stop the authentication process and don't allow use of the command; later commands in the PAM file are ignored.
`sufficient`	If the module succeeds, immediately stop the authentication process, and OK the use of the command; later commands in the PAM file are ignored.

A PAM Example

To understand how PAM modules work, it is helpful to analyze a PAM configuration file, line by line. All PAM configuration files are located by default in `/etc/pam.d`. The following code example is based on the `redhat-config-xfree86` file in this directory. Note how this configuration file has the same name as the configuration utility discussed in Chapter 15. Let's take this file, line by line:

```
auth    sufficient  pam_rootok.so
```

The `auth` module type tells you that this command line is going to check the identity of a user. The `sufficient` control flag lets the application run if this command line succeeds. The `pam_rootok.so` module in the `/lib/security` dierectory returns PAM_SUCCESS if the user is root. In other words, if the root user runs `redhat-config-xfree86`, no other command lines in this file are run, and the application starts.

```
auth    sufficient  pam_timestamp.so
```

This command also uses the auth module type with a `sufficient` control flag. The `pam_timestamp.so` module normally returns PAM_SUCCESS for regular users who have run `sudo` in the past 5 minutes.

```
auth    required    pam_stack.so service=system-auth
```

This command uses the auth module type with a `required` control flag. The `pam_stack.so` module returns PAM_SUCCESS if the `service=system-auth` argument is satisfied. The `system-auth` module requires the user to enter the root password.

```
session required  pam_permit.so
```

This command uses the session module type with a `required` control flag. The `pam_permit.so` module always returns PAM_SUCCESS, so proceed to the next line.

```
session optional  pam_xauth.so
```

This command uses the session module type with an `optional` control flag. The `pam_xauth.so` module does not return success or failure. The `optional` flag makes this command line trivial with respect to this file. However, you can add a `debug` argument to log access requests in `/var/log/ messages`.

```
session optional  pam_timestamp.so
```

This command also uses the session module type with an `optional` control flag. The `pam_ timestamp.so` module updates any available timestamp file, normally located in the `/var/run/sudo` directory. There's one more command in this file:

```
account required  pam_permit.so
```

This command uses the account module type with a `required` control flag. The `pam_permit.so` module always returns PAM_SUCCESS.

Creating Firewalls

Any command or configuration file that is configured to block data from coming into your system or LAN is a *firewall*. Some of these commands and configuration files are covered in other chapters. The main Linux firewall tool is `iptables`. Various `iptables` commands can be connected in chains. Each of these commands can be used to block or allow data associated with specific protocols.

OTHER FIREWALL COMMANDS

The two legacy alternatives to `iptables` are `ipfwadm` and `ipchains`. The `ipfwadm` command is associated with the Linux kernel 2.0.x and is now obsolete. The `ipchains` command is associated with the Linux kernel 2.2.x and is still supported in the current Linux 2.4.x kernel.

Many good firewalls are available based on `ipchains`. If you want to use one of them, you'll need to do the following:

1. Turn off the `iptables` service with the `service iptables stop` command.

2. Use the `rmmod` command to remove the `ip_tables` (and dependent) modules.

3. Install the `ipchains-*` RPM.

4. Use `insmod` to activate the `ipchains.o` module.

You can then start adding `ipchains` rules to `/etc/sysconfig/ipchains`, and activate them with the `service ipchains start` command. Make sure that `ipchains` and not `iptables` is activated the next time you boot Linux with the appropriate `chkconfig` commands.

Data Directions and *iptables*

The `iptables` command is based on regulating data traffic in three directions: in, out, and through. In other words, you can configure `iptables` to stop data from coming in from an outside network. You can configure `iptables` to stop data from leaving your computer. And you can configure `iptables` to regulate data that travels forward through your computer: that is, between a LAN and another network such as the Internet.

Firewalls as Chains

No magic `iptables` command is available that works for everyone. Most firewalls are based on a series of `iptables` commands that are connected as chains. Let's take a look at a fairly simple firewall, based on a high-security firewall created during the installation of Red Hat Linux. The entries shown in Figure 22.2 are from `/etc/sysconfig/iptables`, where Red Hat Linux saves firewall commands.

For the moment, just note that four different chains are shown in this file: `INPUT`, `FORWARD`, `OUTPUT`, and `RH-Lokkit-0-50-INPUT`. The first three chains are default chains that allow all traffic to flow through the firewall. All of the commands that follow the `-A` are appended to the end of the RH-Lokkit chain. In the following sections, we explain `iptables` commands and options in more detail.

FIGURE 22.2

An `iptables` firewall

```
# Firewall configuration written by lokkit
# Manual customization of this file is not recommended.
# Note: ifup-post will punch the current nameservers through the
#        firewall; such entries will *not* be listed here.
*filter
:INPUT ACCEPT [0:0]
:FORWARD ACCEPT [0:0]
:OUTPUT ACCEPT [0:0]
:RH-Lokkit-0-50-INPUT - [0:0]
-A INPUT -j RH-Lokkit-0-50-INPUT
-A RH-Lokkit-0-50-INPUT -i lo -j ACCEPT
-A RH-Lokkit-0-50-INPUT -p udp -m udp -s 207.217.126.81 --sport 53 -d 0/0 -j ACCEPT
-A RH-Lokkit-0-50-INPUT -p udp -m udp -s 207.217.120.83 --sport 53 -d 0/0 -j ACCEPT
-A RH-Lokkit-0-50-INPUT -p tcp -m tcp --syn -j REJECT
-A RH-Lokkit-0-50-INPUT -p udp -m udp -j REJECT
COMMIT
~
~
~
~
~
~
~
```

Format of *iptables*

Let's analyze the `iptables` command in detail. This is a rich command; entire books are available that explore the various associated options. While we describe the masquerading options later in this chapter, let's look at a few important options now. The `iptables` command has a very specific format:

```
iptables -t table option pattern -j target
```

The first option here is based on the `-t table` option. Two basic tables are available: `filter` and `nat`. The `nat` table supports the Network Address Translation associated with masquerading. The `filter` table allows you to block or allow specific types of network traffic. Because `-t filter` is the default, this option is usually not specified in a firewall configuration file.

Options for *iptables*

Remember, there are three default chains: INPUT, OUTPUT, and FORWARD. Four main options are associated with `iptables`: you can list (`-L`), append (`-A`), or delete (`-D`) a specific rule, or flush (`-F`) all of the rules in a chain.

The `iptables -L` command lists all of the current rules on all chains. If your firewall is complex, you may want to list the rules on a specific chain. For example, the `iptables -L INPUT` command lists all firewall rules related to data coming into your computer. A sample list of current firewall rules is shown in Figure 22.3.

To add a new rule, you'll generally append it to the end of one of the chains. For example, the following command appends a limit of a packet every second to the `ping` command to data that is forwarded through your computer, thus preventing the so-called ping of death:

```
# iptables -A FORWARD -p icmp --icmp-type echo-request -m limit --limit 1/s -j ACCEPT
```

To delete an existing rule, first identify the chain and the location of the rule within the chain. For example, if you want to delete the rule related to rns3.earthlink.net in Figure 22.3, note that it's the third rule in the RH-Lokkit-0-50-INPUT chain. The appropriate command is

```
# iptables -D RH-Lokkit-0-50-INPUT 3
```

FIGURE 22.3

Current iptables rules

```
[root@RH9Test root]# iptables -L
Chain INPUT (policy ACCEPT)
target     prot opt source               destination
RH-Lokkit-0-50-INPUT  all --  anywhere              anywhere

Chain FORWARD (policy ACCEPT)
target     prot opt source               destination
RH-Lokkit-0-50-INPUT  all --  anywhere              anywhere

Chain OUTPUT (policy ACCEPT)
target     prot opt source               destination

Chain RH-Lokkit-0-50-INPUT (2 references)
target     prot opt source               destination
ACCEPT     all --  anywhere              anywhere
ACCEPT     udp --  rns1.earthlink.net    anywhere          udp spt:domain
ACCEPT     udp --  rns3.earthlink.net    anywhere          udp spt:domain
REJECT     tcp --  anywhere              anywhere          tcp flags:SYN,RST,ACK/
SYN reject-with icmp-port-unreachable
REJECT     udp --  anywhere              anywhere          udp reject-with icmp-p
ort-unreachable
[root@RH9Test root]# []
```

If you're a bit frustrated, you can start over. For example, if you had a series of rules in the FORWARD chain that you wanted to delete, run the following command:

```
# iptables -F FORWARD
```

This command can be a bit dangerous; if you ran the iptables -F command without specifying a chain, you would delete every rule in every chain. Basic iptables options are shown in Table 22.2.

TIP *If you accidentally flush your* iptables *chains, the original chains should still be available in* /etc/sysconfig/ iptables. *You can make Linux reread these rules with the* service iptables reload *command.*

TABLE 22.2: OPTIONS FOR *IPTABLES*

OPTION	FUNCTION
-A *chain rule*	Appends a rule to the end of a *chain*
-D *chain number*	Deletes the rule number from the specified *chain*
-F *chain*	Flushes, or deletes, all rules from the specified *chain*
-I *chain number rule*	Inserts a rule as the specified rule number in the noted *chain*
-L *chain*	Lists the current rules in the specified *chain*
-N *chain*	Starts a new nonstandard *chain*
-X *chain*	Deletes a user-defined *chain*

Patterns for *iptables*

Now it's time to examine the next step in the `iptables` command. Previously, you've identified the action to take on a chain. Next, you need to specify a pattern to match in the chain. Patterns can match the IP address of the message sender or source, the TCP/IP port, and or the protocol.

IP ADDRESS PATTERNS

Take the previous command that prevents the ping of death. For some reason, say you want to regulate the `ping` command solely from IP address 199.88.77.66. You could do so with the following command:

```
# iptables -A FORWARD -s 199.88.77.66 -p icmp --icmp-type
➡ echo-request -m limit --limit 1/s -j ACCEPT
```

Note the use of the `-s` option, which prepares the way for the source IP address. You could reverse the effect and regulate the `ping` command from every other address, by using an exclamation point:

```
# iptables -A FORWARD -s !199.88.77.66 -p icmp --icmp-type
➡ echo-request -m limit --limit 1/s -j ACCEPT
```

The exclamation point (!) tells `iptables` to treat whatever follows as an exception. In other words, this command is applied to every computer on the Internet unless it has the noted IP address.

It helps to specify a range of IP addresses such as a LAN. The following commands combine a network IP address with a subnet mask in regular and CIDR notation. (See Chapter 21 for a description of CIDR, which is short for Classless Inter-Domain Routing.)

```
# iptables -A FORWARD -s 199.88.77.0/255.255.255.0 -p
➡ icmp --icmp-type echo-request -m limit --limit 1/s -j ACCEPT
# iptables -A FORWARD -s 199.88.77.0/24 -p icmp --icmp-type
➡ echo-request -m limit --limit 1/s -j ACCEPT
```

Some of the other switches associated with `iptables` are shown in Table 22.3.

TABLE 22.3: SWITCHES FOR *IPTABLES*

SWITCH	FUNCTION
`--dport` *port*	Specifies the destination TCP/IP port number.
`--icmp-type` *message*	Allows you to specify the type of ICMP message; `echo-request` corresponds to the messages sent by a `ping` command.
`-j` *action*	Notes an action to be taken if the requirements of the command are satisfied; normally ACCEPT, DROP, REJECT, or LOG.
`--limit` *time*	Sets an allowable rate for a specific message; can be in seconds, minutes, hours, or days; e.g., 2/s = 2 per second.

Continued on next page

TABLE 22.3: SWITCHES FOR *IPTABLES* (*continued*)

SWITCH	FUNCTION
-m *condition*	Looks at the data for a match; may be a protocol, such as tcp or udp, or a condition, such as a limit.
-p *protocol*	Checks the data for a specific protocol, such as tcp or udp.
-s *ip_address*	Specifies a source IP address.
--sport *port*	Sets a source TCP/IP port.
--tcp-flags *fl1,...*	Looks for flags in a TCP packet:
	SYN (synchronize) packets are sent from a client and expect a reply.
	ACK (acknowledgment) packets acknowledge SYN requests.
	A FIN (finish) packet is the final one in a communication.
	RST (reset) packets tell a client that a request has been rejected.
	Example: --tcp-flags SYN,RST,ACK SYN looks for SYN, RST, and ACK packets, but passes only packets that have the SYN flag.

TCP/IP PROTOCOL PATTERNS

The iptables command looks at every data packet that comes in, goes out, or forwards through your computer. You can tell the command to look for a specific protocol. The most common protocol patterns are based on TCP, UDP, and ICMP. The key is the -p option, which specifies the protocol. For example, the earlier command that prevents the ping of death uses the -p icmp option, since ping is associated with ICMP. (For more information on ICMP, see Chapter 20.)

TCP/IP PORT PATTERNS

As noted in Chapter 20, over 65,000 TCP/IP ports are available. Many of these ports are dedicated to standard services. For example, the following command stops any attempt to connect from the 199.88.77.0/24 network with TCP packets to port 21, which is associated with FTP:

```
# iptables -A FORWARD -s 199.88.77.0/24 -p tcp --dport 21 -j REJECT
```

Actions for *iptables*

Say you've created an iptables command that looks for some pattern in the data that goes into, out of, or through your computer. But if it finds a match, you need to tell iptables what to do with that packet of data.

When iptables finds a match, the -j command tells the chain to jump to one of four conclusions: ACCEPT, DROP, REJECT, or LOG. These actions are explained in Table 22.4.

TABLE 22.4: ACTIONS FOR *IPTABLES*

ACTION	EXPLANATION
-j ACCEPT	Allows packets that match the specified characteristics into, out of, or through your computer.
-j DROP	Stops packets that match the specified characteristics into, out of, or through your computer.
-j REJECT	Stops packets that match the specified characteristics into, out of, or through your computer; a message is sent to the computer that sent the message.
-j LOG	Logs a record of matching packets in /var/log/messages.

Putting It All Together

Now that we've broken down the iptables command, you can create the firewall rules that you need. While tools such as redhat-config-firewall as described in Chapter 19 can help, GUI tools do not give you the degree of control that you may need. You need to know at least how to add and delete rules from a firewall chain.

STARTING WITHOUT A FIREWALL

As an experiment, let's start with a computer without a firewall. This assumes that you have a LAN of two or more computers. If you have firewall rules in /etc/sysconfig/iptables that you want to save, back them up. Append the rule discussed earlier on the ping of death. Revise it so it drops any ping requests from within your LAN.

The following steps assume a LAN with an address of 192.168.0.0/24; if your LAN has a different address and network mask, substitute accordingly.

1. Back up any current firewall. Copy /etc/sysconfig/iptables to a file in your home directory.

2. Flush any rules in your current firewall with the iptables -F command.

3. Append the ping of death rule as shown. This stops any pings to your computer (INPUT) from the cited network:

   ```
   # iptables -A INPUT -s 192.168.0.0/24 -p icmp --icmp-type echo-request -j DROP
   ```

4. Try the ping 127.0.0.1 command on the local computer. It should still work.

5. Go to another computer on your LAN. Try to ping the IP address of the first computer. You should see one ping message before everything stops.

6. If necessary, restore the original /etc/sysconfig/iptables file.

If you're in a mood for experiments, try these steps again, this time with a -j REJECT option at the end of the iptables command. Note the difference when you run the ping command from the other computer on your LAN.

INSERTING A FIREWALL RULE

Return to the high-security firewall described earlier, depicted in Figure 22.3. If you install a web server on your computer in the future, you'll want to revise your firewall a bit. The current firewall includes rules as follows:

```
Chain RH-Lokkit-0-50-INPUT (1 references)
target     prot opt source                destination
ACCEPT     all  --  anywhere              anywhere
ACCEPT     udp  --  rns1.earthlink.net    anywhere udp spt:domain
ACCEPT     udp  --  rns3.earthlink.net    anywhere udp spt:domain
REJECT     tcp  --  anywhere              anywhere tcp flags:SYN,RST,ACK/SYN reject-
➡ with icmp-port-unreachable
REJECT     udp  --  anywhere              anywhere udp reject-with icmp-port-
➡ unreachable
```

You need to insert an `iptables` rule that accepts data through TCP/IP port 80. Based on the conditions described earlier:

◆ We're inserting a rule in the chain named `RH-Lokkit-0-50-INPUT`. Make it the second rule in the chain (`-I RH-Lokkit-0-50-INPUT 2`).

◆ Since connections to a website need a reply, they require TCP packets (`-p tcp`).

◆ We know from `/etc/services` that connections to a website work through port 80 (`-m tcp --dport 80`).

◆ Requests to websites come from clients and should have SYN flags. They should be checked for and RST and ACK flags to make sure they're not coming from other computers acting as servers (`--tcp-flags SYN,RST,ACK SYN`).

◆ Finally, packets that meet all of these conditions should be accepted (`-j ACCEPT`).

Putting this all together, we end up with the following command:

```
# iptables -I RH-Lokkit-0-50-INPUT 2 -p tcp -m tcp
➡ --dport 80 --tcp-flags SYN,RST,ACK SYN -j ACCEPT
```

Once you add the command, you can see the following result in the `iptables` chain:

```
Chain RH-Lokkit-0-50-INPUT (1 references)
target     prot opt source                destination
ACCEPT     all  --  anywhere              anywhere
ACCEPT     tcp  --  anywhere              anywhere
➡ tcp dpt:http flags:SYN,RST,ACK/SYN
ACCEPT     udp  --  rns1.earthlink.net    anywhere udp spt:domain
ACCEPT     udp  --  rns3.earthlink.net    anywhere udp spt:domain
```

```
REJECT      tcp  --  anywhere          anywhere
➥ tcp flags:SYN,RST,ACK/SYN reject-with icmp-port-unreachable
REJECT      udp  --  anywhere          anywhere
➥ udp reject-with icmp-port-unreachable
```

If this is what you want to do, remember to save your configuration changes.

SAVING CONFIGURATION CHANGES

You can save configuration changes to `/etc/sysconfig/iptables` with the `service iptables save` command.

While `iptables` is the default for Red Hat Linux 9, it is always a good idea to check the service status of your firewall. You can do with the `chkconfig` command. For example, the following command should show the runlevels where Linux starts the `iptables` service:

```
# chkconfig --list iptables
iptables    0:off  1:off  2:on  3:on  4:on  5:on  6:off
```

If you see that the `iptables` service is not activated (and at the right runlevels), you can activate it. For example, the following command activates `iptables` the next time you start in runlevel 2, 3, or 5:

```
# chkconfig --level 235 iptables
```

NOTE   Remember, Red Hat Linux does not normally use runlevel 4. For details, see Chapter 11.

Setting Up IP Masquerading

IP masquerading allows you to hide the IP addresses of the computers on your LAN. It replaces these IP addresses with the public IP address on your gateway computer. This helps to protect the computers within your LAN from direct attack.

NOTE   IP masquerading is a form of Network Address Translation (NAT). Another way to implement NAT is with a proxy server.

IP masquerading and firewalls are commonly configured on the same computer on a LAN, the gateway between that LAN and an external network such as the Internet. Therefore, the developers of `iptables` have included options to use that command to configure masquerading.

Functionality

As described in Chapter 21, you can configure a gateway computer to connect to your LAN and another network such as the Internet. Assuming that you're connecting to the Internet, you can use private IP addresses within your LAN, and use a public IP address on the network card that is connected to the Internet.

Then to complete the connection, you must configure IP Forwarding on the gateway computer as described in Chapter 21. And then, you need to add an appropriate `iptables` command to your firewall.

Once you've set up masquerading, anyone who connects to the Internet from inside your LAN sends data packets through your gateway computer. For example, assume one of your users is looking for a website. The source address—that is, the IP address of the computer on your LAN—is replaced with the public IP address of your gateway computer. The `iptables` command assigns a nonstandard TCP/IP port to the packet. The gateway computer then caches the source IP address and the assigned TCP/IP port.

When the firewall receives the data for the website, the process is reversed. The assigned port is matched to the cache. The IP address of the source computer is taken from the cache and added to the data for the website. The gateway computer can then send the packets to the source computer.

IP Masquerading Commands

Let's take another look at the format of the `iptables` command. As discussed earlier, the default table is a filter, which is the firewall function associated with `iptables`:

```
iptables -t table option pattern -j target
```

However, a `-t nat` option is available that allows you to use `iptables` to configure masquerading. For example, the following command assumes that your network has an address of 10.0.0.0/24 and that the network card on your gateway that's directly connected to the Internet is eth2:

```
# iptables -t nat -A POSTROUTING -s 10.0.0.0/24 -o eth2 -j MASQUERADE
```

This command changes the IP address of the packets that are going out to the Internet (`-A POSTROUTING`), and the changes are only good for the private IP addresses on your LAN (`-j MASQUERADE`).

Detecting Break-ins

There are two standard ways to see if a cracker has broken into your system. One is to check logins as documented in the `/var/log/wtmp` file. The other is to check log file activity to see when the traffic on your Linux systems should be at a minimum.

But one of the ways people break into a system is by reading the clear-text passwords that a user might send over the network. One useful tool for looking at network traffic is Ethereal, a protocol analyzer that is available for Linux/Unix and Microsoft Windows. It's included with Red Hat Linux in the `ethereal-*` RPM packages.

Sniffing with Ethereal

A more descriptive but colloquial name for a protocol analyzer is a *sniffer*. Protocol analyzers such as Ethereal record, or "sniff," the traffic on a network. If you're on an Ethernet network, you can record all communication between all computers on the LAN.

If a message is transmitted in clear text, Ethereal converts it into a readable format. For example, take Figure 22.4, which shows an Ethereal view of various network packets. Note the highlighted packet number 19 carefully.

FIGURE 22.4

Ethereal reveals a password.

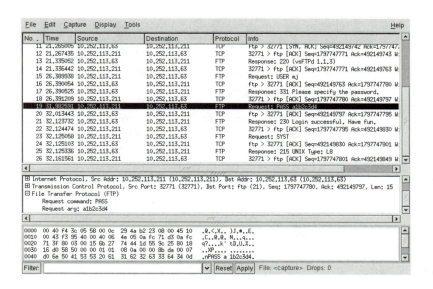

As you can see, packet 19 shows the password that user mj entered to connect to the local FTP server: `a1b2c3d4`.

This illustrates one reason why physical security on a network is so important: if crackers can gain physical access to a LAN, they can connect a computer with Ethereal and find the password of anyone who uses a clear-text server on that LAN.

Ethereal is far from the most sophisticated tool that a cracker can use. If you can detect a clear-text password with Ethereal, you know that a cracker could read that password as well.

Once you have installed the `ethereal-*` RPM packages, you can start this tool with the `ethereal` command.

Checking Logins

It's a good idea to inspect your log files for suspicious activity. For example, login records are available in the `/var/log/wtmp` file. Because this is a binary file, you need a binary reader, `utmpdump`, for this purpose. Read the records of this file by issuing the `utmpdump /var/log/wtmp` command. An excerpt from my output is shown in Figure 22.5.

Note the second-to-last entry in Figure 22.5. As you can see, the originating IP address is 128.99.1.64. If that does not belong to an authorized computer or network, you should be concerned. Someone might be trying to break into your system. You might then consider adding `iptables` firewall commands that would block access from this IP address or the associated IP network.

FIGURE 22.5

Reviewing login
activity

```
           ] [Fri Mar 28 10:21:34 2003 EST]
    [5] [02082] [5   ] [          ] [        ] [2.4.20-8       ] [0.0.0.0
           ] [Fri Mar 28 10:21:34 2003 EST]
    [5] [02083] [6   ] [          ] [        ] [2.4.20-8       ] [0.0.0.0
           ] [Fri Mar 28 10:21:34 2003 EST]
    [5] [02084] [x   ] [          ] [        ] [2.4.20-8       ] [0.0.0.0
           ] [Fri Mar 28 10:21:34 2003 EST]
    [6] [02078] [1   ] [LOGIN   ] [tty1   ] [               ] [0.0.0.0
           ] [Fri Mar 28 10:21:34 2003 EST]
    [6] [02079] [2   ] [LOGIN   ] [tty2   ] [               ] [0.0.0.0
           ] [Fri Mar 28 10:21:34 2003 EST]
    [6] [02080] [3   ] [LOGIN   ] [tty3   ] [               ] [0.0.0.0
           ] [Fri Mar 28 10:21:34 2003 EST]
    [6] [02081] [4   ] [LOGIN   ] [tty4   ] [               ] [0.0.0.0
           ] [Fri Mar 28 10:21:34 2003 EST]
    [6] [02082] [5   ] [LOGIN   ] [tty5   ] [               ] [0.0.0.0
           ] [Fri Mar 28 10:21:34 2003 EST]
    [6] [02083] [6   ] [LOGIN   ] [tty6   ] [               ] [0.0.0.0
           ] [Fri Mar 28 10:21:34 2003 EST]
    [7] [02138] [:0  ] [root    ] [:0     ] [               ] [128.99.1.64
           ] [Fri Mar 28 10:21:51 2003 EST]
    [7] [02246] [/0  ] [root    ] [pts/0  ] [:0.0   ] [       ] [0.0.0.0
           ] [Fri Mar 28 10:22:25 2003 EST]
--More--
```

Tripwire and Suspicious Activity

You learned about how log files are configured through /etc/syslog.conf in Chapter 13. Most log files are stored in the /var/log directory; log entries are stamped with a time of day. You can view different log files periodically, to check for suspicious activity at times when there should be no activity on your system or your network.

Unfortunately, a skilled cracker will try to fool you into believing that everything is all right on your system. For example, a cracker with root access could replace the files in your /var/log directory.

One important tool for checking the integrity of your files is Tripwire. As of this writing, there is both an open source and a commercial version of this software. The open source version is included with the Red Hat Installation RPMs and is documented at www.tripwire.org; the commercial version is available as part of the TriSentry suite from Psionic Technologies (www.psionic.com).

Tripwire is designed to check the integrity of key configuration files on your system. In order for the tool to be effective, you should install it as soon as possible; it can't detect unwanted changes after a cracker has broken into and changed key files on your system.

Once you've installed Tripwire, you need to set it up and create a basic database. Then the cron job that comes with the Tripwire RPM can check your files on a daily basis.

SETTING UP TRIPWIRE

It's easy to set up Tripwire. Just run the installation script, `/etc/tripwire/twinstall.sh`. The script is in text format; you can even use a text editor to modify the locations of installation files. It includes a copy of the Tripwire license, the GPL.

When you run the default script, you're prompted to add local and site *passphrases*, which are passwords used to encrypt access to Tripwire. During the setup process, the `twinstall.sh` script also creates a configuration and policy file in the `/etc/tripwire` directory.

Next, initialize the Tripwire database with the `tripwire --init` command. This command may take a few minutes as it uses its policy file, `tw.pol`, to build an initial database. It may cite a few errors as it searches for files that you may not have installed.

You can update the Tripwire policy file by editing `/etc/tripwire/twpol.txt`. For example, if you haven't installed the "Z" shell, you could delete the reference to `/bin/zsh`. Once your changes are complete, you can update Tripwire policies with the following command:

```
# tripwire --update-policy /etc/tripwire/twpol.txt
```

TIP *Once you install it, Tripwire is an important tool for defending your system. A cracker may try to hide his or her tracks by changing various tripwire files. You can prevent this by using some secure or read-only media; for example, some administrators write Tripwire files to a read-only CD.*

TRIPWIRE IN ACTION

Assuming you installed Tripwire from the Red Hat Linux RPM package, the database is checked daily. In fact, there is a `tripwire-check` script in the `/etc/cron.daily` directory. As discussed in Chapter 13, this script is run by default, at 4:02 A.M. every morning, through `/etc/crontab`.

You may want to edit this file to save the output; for example, you might direct the output from the `tripwire` command to a log file:

```
/usr/sbin/tripwire --check >> /var/log/tripwire
```

The resulting output is interesting. For the purpose of this book, I temporarily deleted the `/sbin/poweroff` file before running the `tripwire-check` script. In `/var/log/tripwire`, this led to the following output:

```
-------------------------------
Rule Name: Critical Utility Sym-Links (/sbin/poweroff)
Security Level: 100
-------------------------------


Removed:
"/sbin/poweroff"
```

While this warning seems subtle, it tells you that someone has deleted the `poweroff` command from your Linux system.

Troubleshooting Access Issues

It is possible to have too much security. Any security measure that is keeping users from needed services is probably doing more harm than good.

If your users need a service and your security measures block the use of that service, you need to make a choice. You can either provide an acceptable substitute, or you can relax your security measures in some way.

Sometimes, users may tell you that something is not working when it is really an issue with your security. For example, the `iptables DROP` option can lead to output that is confusing to users.

Too Much Security

Security is not helpful if it keeps users from getting their work done. However, some services are sufficiently dangerous that you need to provide your users with alternatives.

For example, if a user wants to connect to a remote computer via Telnet, it's probably in your best interest to help that user learn about the Secure Shell utilities described in Chapter 23. You generally don't want users sending their user passwords in clear text over the network.

Another example is with the Network File System (NFS), which is detailed in Chapter 28. NFS requires access to several different TCP/IP services: `nfs`, `portmap`, `rpc.mountd`, and `rpc.nfsd`. While NFS uses TCP/IP port 2049, standard Red Hat Linux firewalls also block port 111, which is associated with the RPC daemon.

Denial or Rejection

When users try to access a prohibited service, what they see depends on `iptables`, specifically the `DROP` or the `REJECT` option. For example, you could implement either of the following chains to stop users on the 192.168.0.0/24 network from connecting via Telnet:

```
# iptables -A INPUT -s 192.168.0.0/24 -p tcp -dport 23 -j DROP
# iptables -A INPUT -s 192.168.0.0/24 -p tcp -dport 23 -j REJECT
```

TIP   *Port 23 is the TCP/IP port for Telnet service. You can look up standard TCP/IP ports in* `/etc/services`.

Now compare what a user on the 192.168.0.0/24 network sees when she tries to connect via Telnet to a server that is set to `DROP` a request:

```
# telnet RHL9
Trying 192.168.0.34
```

A user who sees this output may complain to you that Telnet is not working. Now contrast that with the output for someone who is trying to connect to a server that is set to `REJECT` a request:

```
# telnet RHL9
Trying 192.168.0.34
telnet: connect to address 192.168.0.34: Connection refused
```

A user who sees this is more likely to understand that Telnet connections aren't allowed on server RHL9. When the user asks you why, you have an opportunity to educate your user about alternatives such as SSH.

Summary

You may be lucky. You may be administering a network that isn't connected to any other network, especially the Internet. Your servers and network components could be secure in locked rooms. And you may be able to trust your users. In this case, you might not need to secure your Linux network.

However, most LANs are connected to other networks. Many users need Internet connections to be productive. Unfortunately, any Internet access can expose your LAN to crackers who want to break into your systems.

There are best practices associated with network security, such as providing various levels of physical security for your computers and network components; configuring different levels of firewalls for your web server and internal LAN; encrypting communications with various protocols such as Kerberos and GPG; encrypting your passwords using MD5 and shadow passwords; and providing different levels of password security on your BIOS and Linux bootloader.

Pluggable Authentication Modules (PAM) let you limit access to specific applications, as defined in the `/etc/pam.d` directory. The files in this directory are associated with different applications. The four types of PAM modules are password, session, account, and auth. Each module is associated with one of four control flags: `optional`, `required`, `requisite`, and `sufficient`. These control flags drive the response to the module.

The main Red Hat Linux firewall utility is `iptables`. Various `iptables` commands can be connected in chains for data in three directions: `INPUT`, `OUTPUT`, and `FORWARD`. You can configure `iptables` to match different patterns: IP addresses, TCP/IP ports, even patterns that can prevent the ping of death. When a firewall command matches a pattern, you can set `iptables` to `ACCEPT`, `DROP`, `REJECT`, or `LOG` the occurrence.

You can also configure `iptables` for IP Masquerading. This is a form of Network Address Translation that hides the address of the computers on your LAN requesting access to an outside network such as the Internet. Each outgoing packet is associated with an unused port number; when the LAN gets an answer, that number is used to identify the requesting computer.

There are a number of ways to detect attempted break-ins to your Linux computer. One is to check logins to `/var/log/wtmp`. Another is to use the Tripwire RPM package. It's also useful to check your traffic with Ethereal; it tells you if users are sending their passwords over the network in clear text.

Of course, it is possible to have too much security. Any measure that keeps your users from needed services may be too strong. The way you configure `iptables` can confuse your users.

In the next chapter, we'll examine other ways to access computers through the network. Some are not secure such as the Remote Shell and Telnet. On the other hand, the Secure Shell is quite secure, because it encrypts communication with passphrases and more. You can also help protect even insecure services using the `tcp_wrappers` access control files.

Part 6

Linux Network Services

In this Part, you will learn how to:
◆ Work with remote access and xinetd services
◆ Use DNS and DHCP
◆ Manage printing with CUPS and LPD
◆ Operate mail services

Chapter 23

Remote Access and xinetd Services

NETWORKS ARE EFFECTIVE WHEN users are able to read their files and run their programs from remote locations. If you have users who often need remote access, you should consider configuring some Linux remote access services.

There are a number of different ways to access a Linux computer from a remote location. Several remote access services are controlled by the Extended Internet Services Daemon, xinetd. This daemon listens to ports such as those associated with the FTP and Telnet services. If you have the appropriate servers installed, xinetd starts these services upon request.

The xinetd daemon controls the operation of a number of remote access services, including the Remote Shell (RSH), Telnet, FTP, and POP3. Once installed, each of these services includes configuration files in the /etc/xinetd.d directory. You activate each service through these files; in many cases, you can also create a service-specific firewall.

Using the TCP Wrappers system, you can configure a detailed firewall for xinetd services. To regulate access to individual or all xinetd services, you customize /etc/hosts.allow and /etc/hosts.deny. You can still regulate access with an iptables firewall as described in Chapter 22.

A number of xinetd services send messages in clear text. In Chapter 22, you've seen how this can put even your passwords at risk. One alternative for remote access to a Linux computer is the Secure Shell (SSH). The SSH daemon can be configured with private and public keys to encrypt messages over a network.

With all of these levels of security, it isn't always easy to diagnose a service problem. If users are having trouble accessing a server, you may need to check the available firewalls, one at a time. Other possibilities are that services are not active, or that various iptables commands or TCP Wrappers are blocking access. This chapter covers the following topics:

◆ Using typical extended services

◆ Controlling access with TCP Wrappers

◆ Understanding the Secure Shell

◆ Troubleshooting access issues

Using Typical Extended Services

Several basic services are controlled by xinted. These services include RSH, Telnet, POP3, and FTP, among others. For a list of currently installed xinetd services, review your /etc/xinetd.d directory.

The xinetd daemon includes two levels of configuration files. The first is /etc/xinetd.conf, which sets basic parameters. By default, it refers to configuration files in /etc/xinetd.d for service-specific parameters.

Many of the xinetd services are not encrypted. However, they do have their own levels of security. If you use the security measures associated with each service to limit their use to trusted users and computers, you limit the risks. As a Linux administrator, you need to make a judgment whether this is good enough for you and your organization.

The *xinetd* Configuration File

The first Extended Internet Services Daemon configuration file is /etc/xinetd.conf. The settings in this file set basic parameters for all services managed by xinetd. The default Red Hat Linux configuration file is fairly straightforward, as shown in Figure 23.1.

FIGURE 23.1

/etc/xinetd.conf

```
#
# Simple configuration file for xinetd
#
# Some defaults, and include /etc/xinetd.d/

defaults
{
        instances               = 60
        log_type                = SYSLOG authpriv
        log_on_success          = HOST PID
        log_on_failure          = HOST
        cps                     = 25 30
}

includedir /etc/xinetd.d


~
~
~
~
~
~
~
"/etc/xinetd.conf" 16L, 289C
```

Table 23.1 explains the parameters shown in this file. As you can see, this file uses instances to regulate the load on xinetd, specifies logging parameters, stops excessive connections, and includes the files in /etc/xinetd.d.

You can configure any of these parameters in other configuration files in the /etc/xinetd.d directory. When IP addresses are required, use regular or CIDR notation.

TABLE 23.1: *XINETD.CONF* PARAMETERS

COMMAND	DESCRIPTION
instances	Maximum number of active xinetd servers.
log_type	Specifies logging; SYSLOG authpriv specifies logging per /etc/syslog.conf, per Chapter 13.
log_on_success	Specifies logging information when a service starts and stops; useful parameters include PID, HOST, and USERID.
log_on_failure	Specifies logging information when a user requests a service that can't start; useful parameters include HOST and USERID.
cps	Regulates the rate of incoming connections; if connections exceed 25/sec, xinetd is disabled for 30 seconds, which can slow attempts to crack an xinetd service.
includedir	Every file in the specified directory is read as an xinetd configuration file.
only_from	Notes the IP addresses allowed to access the service.
no_access	Service is not allowed to computers with these IP addresses.
access_times	Specifies the times that access to the service is allowed; e.g., access_times = 08:00-23:00 means service is allowed between 8:00 A.M. and 11:00 P.M.

Activating *xinetd* Services

You activate an xinetd service in one of two ways: Either you directly edit the appropriate configuration file, or you activate it with the appropriate chkconfig command. For example, if you've installed the telnet-server-* RPM package, open the telnet configuration file from the /etc/xinetd.d directory in a text editor. This and other xinetd configuration files contain a key parameter:

```
disable = yes
```

In other words, the service is disabled by default. You can enable it by changing this to

```
disable = no
```

You can make this change by editing this file directly in a text editor, or by using the following command, where *service_name* is the name of the service (such as Telnet) that you want to activate:

```
# chkconfig service_name on
```

Of course, you can reverse the process with the following command:

```
# chkconfig service_name off
```

After making a change, you need to make xinetd reread the appropriate configuration file with the following command:

```
# service xinetd reload
```

Alternatively, you could reboot Linux, which would restart xinetd and make it reread the /etc/xinetd.d configuration files. But as you've probably noticed, rebooting Linux is rarely required.

TIP *The* `service` *command runs any of the scripts in the* `/etc/rc.d/init.d` *directory. For example, the* `service xinetd reload` *command is functionally equivalent to* `/etc/rc.d/init.d/xinetd reload`.

The Remote Shell

If you have the same account on multiple computers, the Remote Shell (RSH) is an easy way to connect to different accounts on the computer of your choice. For example, once you've enabled and properly configured RSH, you can access different accounts on different Linux computers. RSH requires the `rsh-*` RPM package on clients and the `rsh-server-*` RPM package on a server.

There are four RSH commands, also known as the "r" commands: `rsh`, `rlogin`, `rexec`, and `rcp`. Once the RSH server is installed, the first three of these commands have their own configuration files in `/etc/xinetd.d`. Activate the "r" commands that you want by using the techniques we described earlier. Don't forget to reload the `xinetd` service. The following command allows user mj to open his account on the computer named RHL9:

```
[mj] $ rlogin RHL9
Password:
Last login: Tue Mar 17 10:27:43 from tty2
```

In this case, user mj needs to enter his password. But that isn't even necessary; he can create a `.rhosts` file on his home directory on each computer. As long as it includes the names of both the client and server computers, a password isn't even required. Alternatively, a Linux administrator can include the same information in `/etc/hosts.equiv`, and every user with an account on both computers wouldn't need a password to check files on the other computer.

It's almost as easy to access a different account on a remote computer; the following sequence accesses the account of user lula on RHL9:

```
[mj] $ rlogin -l lula RHL9
Password:
Last login: Tue Mar 17 10:29:26 from tty2
```

In other words, if a cracker knows the accounts on your Linux server, and can overwrite the `.rhosts` or `/etc/hosts.equiv` file on that computer, she can access the files of her choice.

If you need to create `.rhosts` or `/etc/hosts.equiv` files, set their immutable flags. Once you do, these files can't be deleted. You can do this with the `chattr +i` *filename* command, as follows:

```
# chattr +i .rhosts
# chattr +i /etc/hosts.equiv
```

Unfortunately, a cracker who gains root user access can unset the immutable flag with the `chattr -i /etc/hosts.equiv` command.

Telnet

The Telnet service is a simple way to connect to a remote computer. Many users are familiar with this service, and it is fairly easy to use. Telnet lets you quickly configure a number of different Linux terminals. In addition, you can practice configuring other `xinetd` services by using Telnet. Unfortunately, it also sends messages, including passwords, in clear text. Therefore, your use of Telnet should be limited to networks that are already secure.

In Red Hat Linux, there are separate Telnet client and server RPM packages: `telnet-*` and `telnet-server-*`.

Once the network connection is made, Telnet is just like any other Linux command-line interface. One advantage is that Telnet is available on a variety of operating systems; Figure 23.2 shows an example of a Telnet connection to a Linux computer from a Windows XP operating system.

FIGURE 23.2

Telnet connection
from a Microsoft
computer

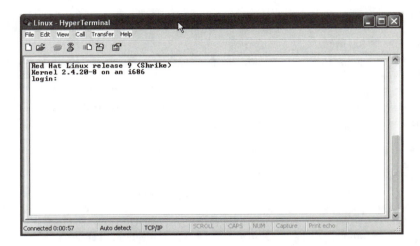

If you're having trouble with a Telnet connection or terminal, your Telnet client may be having a problem with the terminal messages sent from the Linux server that you're administering. One command that sets the environment variable to an older but standard terminal program is

```
TERM=vt100
```

As with other `xinetd` services, you need to activate it through the `/etc/xinetd.d/telnet` configuration file and reload `xinetd` before the Telnet server is active. Then you can access it from other computers with the `telnet` *hostname* command.

FTP Servers

The File Transfer Protocol, FTP, is one of the oldest protocols in the TCP/IP protocol suite. Because it is built for transferring files, it is still more efficient than newer protocols such as HTTP that can also transfer files. When I download the files to create Red Hat Linux CDs, I use an FTP server.

We cover FTP servers in detail in Chapter 27, so we'll look at only the activation requirements here. One of the most common FTP servers is WU-FTP, maintained by Washington University in St. Louis. It's no longer included with Red Hat Linux; but you can download it from the FTP site at `ftp.wu-ftpd.org` or the SpeakEasy RPM library at `www.rpmfind.net`. As you'd expect, when you install the `wu-ftpd-*` RPM, it installs a `wu-ftpd` configuration file in the `/etc/xinetd.d` directory.

As with other `xinetd` services, you need to activate it by setting `disable = yes` in the `wu-ftpd` configuration file.

Other Super Server Services

A number of other xinetd servers are available. They range from `finger`, which can give you more information about a specific user, to `pop3s` and `imaps`, which allow remote users to access their e-mail securely through your server. Some basic xinetd services are listed in Table 23.2. The list is not comprehensive.

TABLE 23.2: BASIC *XINETD* SERVICES

SERVICE	FUNCTION
amanda	Configures the advanced Maryland automatic network disk archiver for backups
finger	More information for a user, specified via `chfn`, stored in /etc/passwd
imap	Supports remote access to an IMAP4 mail server
ipop3	Supports remote access to a POP3 mail server
rlogin	Allows use of the `rlogin` command
rsh	Configures the RSH server
swat	Supports the Samba Web Administration Tool; see Chapter 29
telnet	Sets up the Telnet server
wu-ftpd	Configures the WU-FTP server; see Chapter 27

Controlling Access with TCP Wrappers

The best way to protect your system from crackers is to disable or uninstall as many services as possible. For example, a cracker can't use the `telnet` command to break into your computer if you don't have the Telnet server RPM installed.

If don't need an xinetd service immediately, one option is to deactivate it in the /etc/xinetd.d directory. In most cases, it's sufficient to leave all but required services disabled in the associated configuration files.

But some users need to get to their e-mail when they're in remote locations, and some need Telnet. For those who need access to larger files from remote locations, FTP servers are still the most effective way to transfer files over the Internet.

You can configure access control to all of these services using TCP Wrappers.

Regulating Access

You can minimize risks to your Linux computer in two different ways. First, you can regulate users and/or computers allowed to access a service through its configuration files, some of which are located in the /etc/xinetd.d directory. Other files are associated with different services and we address them in later chapters. Alternatively, you can use TCP Wrappers to regulate computer access through the /etc/hosts.allow and /etc/hosts.deny files.

You can add various rules to these files. These rules are read in the following order:

1. TCP Wrappers reads the /etc/hosts.allow file. If access is explicitly allowed, access is granted.

2. TCP Wrappers reads the /etc/hosts.deny file. If access is explicitly denied, users from the specified computer are not allowed to start the service.

3. If the computer or IP address is not found in either file, access is automatically granted, and xinetd starts the service.

4. If the computer or IP address is found in both files, the rule in /etc/hosts.allow comes first.

For example, if you configure rules that explicitly open a service to computer A in /etc/hosts .allow and then denies it in /etc/hosts.deny, computer A gets access.

In addition, any changes that you save to either file take effect immediately. You don't need to restart or reload the xinetd daemon.

The *xinetd* Firewall

A specific type of syntax is associated with /etc/hosts.allow and /etc/hosts.deny. First, as with other scripts, blank lines and comments that start with a # are not read. Each command line in these files should follow this configuration:

```
daemon: client: spawn command
```

In other words, when you specify a server daemon, you can associate it with a group of hostnames or IP addresses. When there is a match, you can also trigger a command, such as a message to the user or a log entry.

The simplest version of this command line is

```
ALL: ALL
```

which applies to all xinetd daemons and all computers. The options are complex, so it's easiest to examine the options one at a time.

TCP WRAPPER DAEMONS

You can specify individual daemons, but keep in mind that the name of the daemon may not be what you expect. For example, the name of the Telnet daemon is in.telnetd.

If you want to specify multiple daemons, just cite them together and separate the names of the daemons with a space. For example, the following line in /etc/hosts.deny blocks access to local Telnet and RSH servers to all users:

```
in.telnetd in.rshd: ALL
```

If in doubt on daemon names, refer to the configuration file in the /etc/xinetd.d directory. Each of these files includes the name of the daemon as the server variable.

TCP WRAPPER CLIENTS

You specify the names of different computers, or client names, in TCP Wrappers commands by host or by IP address. Several wildcard parameters are available as well.

There are several ways to specify hostnames. You can specify them one at a time; for example, the following command prevents access to local RSH and Telnet servers from the computers named sugaree and delilah:

```
in.rshd in.telnetd: sugaree delilah
```

Or you can specify the fully qualified domain name (FQDN) of a computer, such as `sugaree` `.mommabears.com`. Wildcards are allowed with FQDNs; for example, just include the leading dot in `.mommabears.com` to apply the rule to all computers on the mommabears.com network.

It's possible to specify different computers; for example, the following line applies the rule to all computers on the `mommabears.com` network except `delilah.mommabears.com`:

```
in.rshd: .mommabears.com EXCEPT delilah.mommabears.com
```

You can apply these principles to IP addresses; for example, the following line applies the rule to all computers on the 192.168.0.0 network except 192.168.0.102. Note the trailing dot in 192.168.0.; it applies to all computers with IP addresses between 192.168.0.0 and 192.168.0.255:

```
in.rshd: 192.168.0. EXCEPT 192.168.0.102
```

NOTE *CIDR notation such as 192.168.0.0/24 does not work in the* `/etc/hosts.allow` *or* `/etc/hosts` `.deny` *files.*

Table 23.3 lists the wildcards that can be used in place of hostnames, FQDN, or IP addresses. They are fairly self-explanatory.

TABLE 23.3: TCP WRAPPER WILDCARDS

WILDCARD	APPLICATION
ALL	All computers, including the localhost.
EXCEPT	Exceptions to the rule.
KNOWN	Known computers—e.g., from DNS or `/etc/hosts`.
LOCAL	Computers with a single hostname; the name can't include a dot.
PARANOID	Computers where the hostname or FQDN does not match the IP address.
UNKNOWN	Computers not in the `/etc/hosts` or DNS databases.

TCP WRAPPERS COMMANDS

Normally, all attempts to start an `xinetd` service are automatically added to `/var/log/messages`. You can use the `spawn` command to run another shell command as well. For example, use the following command to send an alert e-mail to the noted address:

```
in.telnetd: ALL: spawn /bin/mail -s "Telnet security alert" mj@example.com
```

Another common use is to send a special message to a log file in `/var/log` that identifies the date and time when someone tried to access the service.

Understanding the Secure Shell (SSH)

If you're concerned about someone intercepting your clear-text network communications, consider installing the Secure Shell. Because it encrypts your communications over any network, it's a viable alternative to the RSH commands as well as Telnet.

SSH Installation

The SSH includes several component RPM packages, as shown in Table 23.4. Use the `rpm` commands discussed in Chapter 10 to install them as required.

TABLE 23.4: SECURE SHELL (SSH) PACKAGES

PACKAGE	FUNCTION
`openssh-*`	Core files for SSH client and server
`openssh-askpass-gnome-*`	Files that support passphrase management inside GNOME
`openssh-askpass-*`	Files that support GUI management of SSH passphrases
`openssh-clients-*`	Client files for connecting to SSH servers
`openssh-server-*`	SSH servers

TIP   You can even use SSH on Microsoft Windows computers. As of this writing, a free version of the Open SSH package is available for download from Network Simplicity at `www.networksimplicity.com`. *Once installed and configured, it works just like the Linux version of SSH.*

SSH Configuration

The main SSH configuration file is `/etc/ssh/sshd_config`. While the default file works in most cases, you can adjust the settings in this file for special TCP/IP ports—for example, to limit access to different IP addresses, to adjust the size of encryption keys, to override RSH authentication, and to enable the use of Kerberos.

Once you have the appropriate packages installed, the next step is to create private and public encryption keys. You keep the private key secure on your Linux server. Public encryption keys allow others to scramble the messages that they send to you. Alternatively, messages that you send are encrypted with the private key. They include the public key, which is used to unscramble the message only on the destination computer. These keys are based on random numbers so large (512 bits and more) that it would take weeks for a cracker with a personal computer to find.

Two basic SSH commands allow you to create private and public keys: `ssh-keygen -t rsa` and `ssh-keygen -t dsa`. These commands let you create keys based on the algorithm created by RSA Security or the Digital Secure Algorithm.

Both commands create the private and public keys, by default, in the `ssh` subdirectory of the user's home directory; thus `~/.ssh`, as listed in Table 23.5. When prompted, create a passphrase. If you don't set a passphrase, a cracker could steal your SSH private key. In some cases, this would allow the cracker to use your digital identity to use your credit cards or sign contracts in your name.

TABLE 23.5: DEFAULT SSH KEY FILES

ALGORITHM	PRIVATE	PUBLIC
DSA	`~/.ssh/id_dsa`	`~/.ssh/id_dsa.pub`
RSA	`~/.ssh/id_rsa`	`~/.ssh/id_rsa.pub`

Sample Session

Once you've installed the right RPMs on clients and servers and created the appropriate SSH keys, you're ready to begin using the Secure Shell. If desired, you can check to make sure the SSH server is running by issuing the `service sshd status` command.

Now you can connect directly to your account on another computer. For example, assume you are a user named tblair and have an account on both computers. Run the `ssh sugaree.mommabears.com` command to connect to that computer. Be sure to substitute the computer name or IP address of your choice for `sugaree.mommabears.com`.

The first time you try to connect with `ssh` (or related commands), you'll see a message like the following:

```
The authenticity of host 'sugaree.mommabears.com' can't be
➥ established. RSA key fingerprint is
➥ 34:21:d2:3c:34:83:40:23:d2:c2:9f:34:90:e3:a3. Are
➥ you sure you want to continue connecting (yes/no)?
```

Select yes, and enter your password on the remote computer to complete the connection. You'll be able to work on the remote computer, and messages between your computers will be encrypted. Alternatively, you could log into a different account, say vputin, as follows:

```
# ssh vputin@sugaree.mommabears.com
```

Alternatively, you could use the secure FTP service associated with SSH. If user vputin has a group of RPMs on his account and you have his password, you could use the secure FTP service to download files from his home directory on the remote computer. For example, the following commands log into that account and then download the source code for a new GNU C compiler to the local `/tmp` directory:

```
# sftp vputin@sugaree.mommabears.com
sftp> get gcc-3.9-8.src.rpm /tmp
```

Troubleshooting Access Issues

With all of these layers of protection, understanding an access problem can take some detective work. Here are some steps to follow if your users are having trouble accessing a service on your computer:

- Make sure the service is installed.
- Check to see that the service is active.
- Inspect security-related configuration files for the service.
- If it is an `xinetd` service, inspect the `/etc/hosts.allow` and `/etc/hosts.deny` files.
- Check the `iptables` firewall chains with the `iptables -L` command.

Check That the Service Is Installed

Checking for an installed service is fairly straightforward; as described in Chapter 10, you check the installation of an RPM package with the `rpm -q` *packagename* command.

Remember, it's common to organize services in separate client and server RPM packages. For example, there are separate client and server packages for Telnet, FTP, and SSH.

Verify That the Service Is Active

It's easy to use the scripts in the `/etc/rc.d/init.d` directory. As discussed in Chapter 13, every service daemon includes a script in this directory, which you can check with the `/etc/rc.d/init.d/`*script* `status` command. Alternatively, you could use the `service` *script* `status` command.

If you're wondering about an `xinetd` service, check the associated configuration file in the `/etc/xinetd.d` directory. By default, these services are set with `disable = yes`, which keeps a service closed.

And don't forget to use a tool such as `chkconfig` to make sure the service is active the next time you reboot Linux. For example, the following command verifies that `httpd` is active at runlevels 2, 3, and 5 when Linux starts:

```
# chkconfig --list 235 httpd on
```

The syntax for an `xinetd` service is slightly different, since these services are active at every runlevel where `xinetd` is active:

```
# chkconfig swat on
```

Inspect the Service-Specific Security Files

Many services include their own configuration files, which can limit or regulate access. Services such as Apache and Samba can be configured to limit access to different users and computers in their main configuration files. There are also `xinetd` services such as WU-FTP that have their own security files, such as `/etc/ftpaccess`. Service-specific security files are described in more detail in the chapters associated with each service.

Inspect the Extended *xinetd* Security Files

You've already learned how access can be limited through `/etc/hosts.allow` and `/etc/hosts.deny`. Just remember that similar commands can be used to limit access through the `/etc/xinetd.d` configuration files.

Check the Firewall *iptables* Chains

You can configure a firewall during or after the Red Hat Linux installation process. After installation, you can use the `lokkit` or `redhat-config-securitylevel` utilities. Each of these Red Hat Linux–specific tools offer default High and Medium security options, which lead to the same `iptables` chains.

NOTE   *Of course, you can configure your firewall with your own* `iptables` *commands, using the techniques described in Chapter 22.*

The rules associated with both firewalls block access to your computer for most major TCP/IP ports. For example, to allow access to an Apache server on your computer either set the appropriate `iptables` command, as described in Chapter 22, or use `lokkit` or `redhat-config-securitylevel` to customize the firewall to accept data to the appropriate TCP/IP port. (In this case, the right port is 80; you can look up different TCP/IP ports in `/etc/services`.)

Summary

Users often need to get their files from remote locations. The files that an engineer has on his laptop may not be the configuration files he needs to solve a client's problem. Linux provides a selection of different remote access services. Many of them are part of the Extended Internet Services Daemon, `xinetd`.

The `xinetd` daemon controls access to and starts various services on demand. Access is controlled through `/etc/xinetd.conf` and individual service files in the `/etc/xinetd.d` directory. New `xinetd` services are disabled by default. Three major `xinetd` remote access services are FTP, Telnet, and RSH.

Access to `xinetd` services is controlled through TCP Wrappers, which depends on configuration commands in `/etc/hosts.allow` and `/etc/hosts.deny`. You can configure commands for specific services, addressing specific computers or networks. When there is a match, you can also set these commands to run shell commands that might send you a warning or send the information to a log file.

One alternative service that encrypts remote communication is the Secure Shell (SSH). The various `openssh-*` RPM packages allow you to use RSA or DSA encryption for network communication. With this type of public/private key system, it is important for you to protect your private key with a passphrase. You can use SSH commands to open your account on remote computers, or even connect securely to a SSH-enabled FTP server.

Troubleshooting remote access issues can be problematic, because there is a wide range of available firewalls. A service might not be installed or active. Many services have their own security-related configuration files, and you'll need to check those files. You can protect `xinetd` services through `/etc/hosts.allow` and `/etc/hosts.deny`. And of course, you can configure firewalls with `iptables`.

In Chapter 24, we'll look at detailed configuration requirements for two major Linux servers and their clients: the Domain Name Service (DNS) and the Dynamic Host Configuration Protocol (DHCP).

Chapter 24

DNS and DHCP

TWO KEY SERVICES CAN help every Linux computer manage hostnames and IP addresses. The Domain Name Service (DNS) is typically configured as a database of hostnames or domain names and IP addresses. The Dynamic Host Configuration Protocol (DHCP) enables you to ration IP addresses by leasing them to different computers on your LAN. As with most other Linux services, both DNS and DHCP include a client and a server.

The Linux DNS server is based on Berkeley Internet Name Domain (BIND) software, and can be configured through a series of files in /etc and /var/named. It is also known as a nameserver, using the named daemon. Any Linux computer that is configured to use TCP/IP is by default configured as a DNS client. When you look for a website, your computer acts as a DNS client. It looks to the DNS server for the associated IP address so it knows where to send its message on the Internet.

A DHCP server can lease IP addresses and provide other key information that allows your computer to define itself on your LAN. DHCP servers can be configured with information that enables your computer to access external networks, find other important servers, and more. Red Hat Linux has changed the name of its DHCP client a number of times in recent years, but the functionality is still the same. It gets IP addresses from a DHCP server, and it collects any other information available from that server. This chapter covers the following topics:

- ◆ Configuring a DNS server
- ◆ Using DNS clients
- ◆ Setting up a DHCP server
- ◆ Working with DHCP and BOOTP clients

Configuring a DNS Server

A Domain Name Service (DNS) server is a flexible database of fully qualified domain names (FQDN), such as www.sybex.com, and IP addresses, such as 63.99.198.12. The Linux version of DNS is based on BIND, which powers most of the DNS servers on the Internet.

No one DNS server can hold all of the FQDNs and IPv4 addresses on the Internet. If a DNS server does not have a FQDN in its database, it can refer to other DNS servers. Once the server finds the right IP address, it adds the FQDN and IP address to its database.

DNS is configured through the basic configuration files /etc/named.conf and /etc/named.custom, as well as through detailed configuration files in the /var/named directory. It is still best to edit these files directly to configure DNS.

However, as of this writing, Red Hat encourages the use of redhat-config-bind to configure your DNS server. Configuring DNS is not easy; redhat-config-bind is probably a better option for less experienced Linux administrators. This tool requires a GUI such as GNOME or KDE.

Packages

Not all of the RPM packages that you need for DNS are installed by default. The required packages are listed in Table 24.1; as you might remember from Chapter 10, you can use the rpm -q *packagename* command to see if they're installed. Once the packages are installed, you can use the rpm -ql *packagename* command to see the associated files.

TABLE 24.1: DNS RPM PACKAGES

PACKAGE	FUNCTION
bind-*	The DNS name server software
bind-devel-*	DNS development tools; not required
bind-utils-*	DNS tools such as dig and host
caching-nameserver-*	Basic configuration files for a caching DNS server; includes sample /etc/named.conf and /var/named/localhost.zone files
redhat-config-bind-*	The Red Hat GUI DNS configuration tool; required

DNS Concepts

As we mentioned earlier, no single DNS server can contain the database of FQDN and IP addresses for the entire Internet. Because of the volume of associated data, it isn't practical to centralize DNS information. Therefore, DNS servers are organized in *zones*. Each DNS server has its *zone of responsibility*. DNS zones are based on the way FQDNs are organized.

Start with a basic FQDN, www.mommabears.com.. This includes a root zone, which is not the .com, but the period to the right of the .com.

NOTE   *The root DNS servers are listed in* /var/named/named.ca, *which is part of the* caching-nameserver-* *RPM package.*

The next phrase may be .com, .net, .org, and so on; these are known as *top-level domains*. In this case, mommabears is a subdomain of .com, and www is the name (or more likely the alias) of a computer with the Momma Bears' web server.

A master DNS server on the `mommabears.com.` network would be the authoritative server for that zone. Conversely, `mommabears.com.` is the Forward (or Primary) Master Zone for that DNS server.

These database zones aren't complete unless you can reverse the process. In other words, you should be able to find an IP address from a FQDN—and you should be able to reverse the process by finding a FQDN from an IP address. The reverse database is known as a Reverse Master Zone.

You can configure four different types of DNS servers. As you'll recall from Chapter 21, the IP address of any DNS server that you use should be listed in `/etc/resolv.conf`.

Master   A master DNS server is the authoritative server for a specific zone, such as `sybex.com`. Queries for IP addresses from computers on the `sybex.com` network normally go to this server. Other DNS servers refer to this master for addresses of other networks and computers within `sybex.com`.

Slave   Queries for IP addresses from within `sybex.com` can go to this server; it gets its FQDN/IP address database from a master DNS server.

Caching-only   A caching-only DNS server stores recent requests for IP addresses. If you have a caching-only DNS server on your LAN and your DNS server is on a remote network, your computers can often get quicker answers by using the caching-only DNS server.

Forwarding   A forwarding DNS server does not store any FQDN/IP address information. It does store the IP addresses of other DNS servers in `/etc/named.conf`.

Initial DNS Configuration

Normally, I encourage users to configure Linux services at the command-line interface. If you do so, you learn more about the service and can better customize the service for the network.

However, Red Hat has reconfigured the DNS configuration files to encourage users to use the Red Hat GUI DNS configuration tool, `redhat-config-bind`. Even trivial errors in the main DNS configuration file can keep you from running DNS. If you're fairly new at Linux, using `redhat-config-bind` to edit `/etc/named.conf` can keep these errors to a minimum. If you need to customize your DNS server further, include the additional information in the `/etc/named.custom` file. This format is similar to the LPD printer configuration files discussed in Chapter 25.

TIP   You don't have to use `redhat-config-bind`—you can still edit `/etc/named.conf` directly. However, any subsequent changes made through `redhat-config-bind` will overwrite anything that you've added to `/etc/named.conf`. If you prefer to edit `/etc/named.conf` directly, don't install the `redhat-config-bind-*` RPM. You can also skip to the next section, on DNS configuration files.

CONFIGURING A PRIMARY DNS SERVER

To configure a primary DNS server, start the GUI of your choice, open a text console window, and enter the `redhat-config-bind` command to open a Domain Name Service window similar to the one in Figure 24.1. When you first install DNS, the only entries are based on the local computer.

FIGURE 24.1

redhat-config-bind

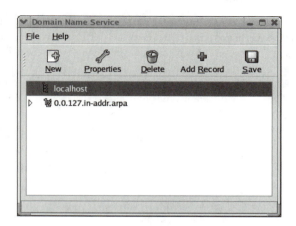

NOTE *Alternatively, in GNOME or KDE, you can select Main Menu (or K Menu) ➤ System Settings ➤ Server Settings ➤ Domain Name Service.*

When you configure a primary or master DNS server, you're configuring /etc/named.conf and various files in /var/named. In the Domain Name Service window, click New. In the Select a Zone Type window, click the Forward Master Zone option. Enter a domain name; if you don't have one, example.com is an official generic domain name that you can use, as shown in Figure 24.2.

FIGURE 24.2

Selecting a zone

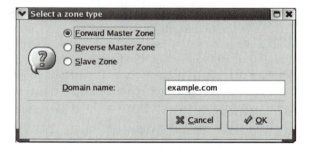

When you click OK, this opens the Name To IP Translations window shown in Figure 24.3. In this window, enter the hostname of your Primary Nameserver (SOA)—your DNS server. Remember to add a period at the end of the hostname.

FIGURE 24.3

Adding a DNS server

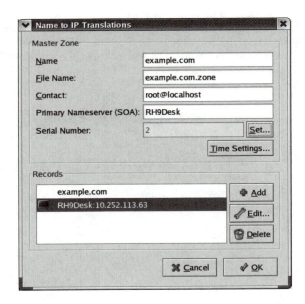

You also need to enter the IP address for your DNS server. When you click Add, the Add a Record window appears; click the Nameserver tab as shown in Figure 24.4. In the Domain Name text box, enter the hostname of your DNS server computer; note that the rest of the FQDN is already filled in. Also observe how your information is added by default to the reverse address table. In the Served By text box, enter the IP address of that computer. When you're done, click OK twice to return to the Domain Name Service window.

FIGURE 24.4

Adding the DNS server record

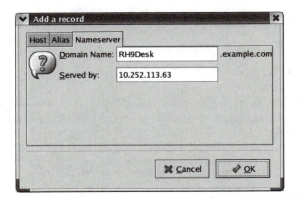

Now you'll add the Reverse Master Zone. Click New; this time, select Reverse Master Zone in the Select A Zone Type window. The text box now reads "IP Address (first 3 Octets)." IPv4 addresses include four numbers, also known as octets. For example, if your network IP address is 10.252.113.0, enter **10.252.113** in the text box and click OK. This opens a new IP To Name Translations window, as shown in Figure 24.5.

FIGURE 24.5

Configuring a reverse zone

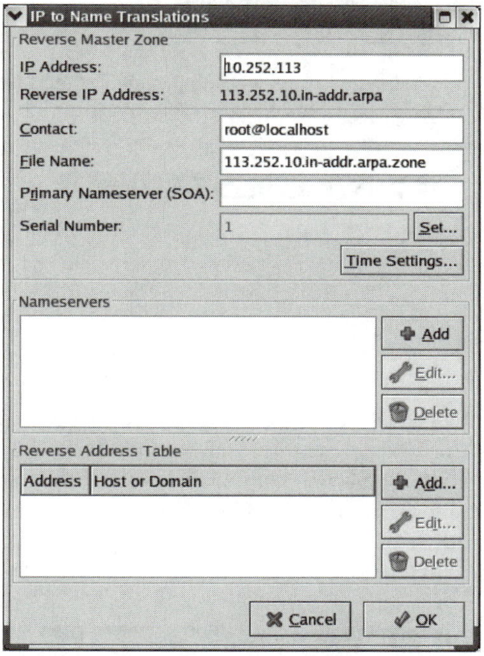

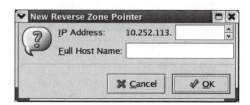

You need to reenter the information for your Primary Nameserver (SOA). You'll also need to click Add in the Nameservers section to add at least the IP address of that DNS server to the list. Click OK and repeat as needed.

Next, click Add in the Reverse Address Table section to open the New Reverse Zone Pointer window, shown in Figure 24.6. In this window, enter the IP address for a computer on your LAN and its hostname or FQDN.

FIGURE 24.6

Adding information to the reverse zone

Repeat the process until you've added all the computers on your LAN to the Reverse Address Table. Don't forget the computer on your network with the DNS server. Click OK to exit the IP to Name Translations window. Now you've created a master DNS server. To save the configuration, click the Save button. This saves your configuration in `/etc/named.conf` and in various `/var/named` files.

You can now start DNS using the instructions shown in the "Starting DNS" section later in this chapter. You can also configure a DNS slave server using `redhat-config-bind`, or configure all of your DNS servers by directly editing the appropriate configuration files.

A DNS Slave Server

You can also use `redhat-config-bind` to create a DNS slave server. Slave DNS servers are, by definition, on a different computer. They look to a master DNS server for database information.

Start `redhat-config-bind` on the second computer. Click New. When the Select A Zone Type window in Figure 24.2 appears, select Slave Zone, and enter the domain name for your network. Using the current example, that would be `example.com`. Click OK.

The Slave Zone Settings window should appear, as shown in Figure 24.7. The name of your domain and database filename should automatically appear in the Name and File Name text boxes. Enter the IP address for your primary DNS server in the Masters List text box, and then click Add.

FIGURE 24.7

Slave zone DNS
server settings

DNS Configuration Files

Several configuration files are required for a DNS server: `/etc/named.conf` and database files in the `/var/named` directory. You can use `redhat-config-bind` to create the settings for these files, or you can add them directly to these files with the text editor of your choice. It's helpful to examine each of these files in detail.

DNS /ETC/NAMED.CONF

The main DNS configuration file is `/etc/named.conf`. A working example of this file (built through `redhat-config-bind`) is shown in Figure 24.8. You can just as easily create this file in any text editor. However, if you use `redhat-config-bind`, be sure to add any additional parameters to `/etc/named.custom`.

FIGURE 24.8

/etc/named.conf

```
#
# Generated automatically by redhat-config-bind, alchemist et al.
# Any changes not supported by redhat-config-bind should be put
# in /etc/named.custom
#
controls {
        inet 127.0.0.1 allow { localhost; } keys { rndckey; };
};

include "/etc/named.custom";

include "/etc/rndc.key";

zone   "0.0.127.in-addr.arpa" {
        type master;
        file   "0.0.127.in-addr.arpa.zone";
};
zone   "113.252.10.in-addr.arpa" {
        type master;
        file   "113.252.10.in-addr.arpa.zone";
};

zone   "localhost" {
        type master;
        file   "localhost.zone";
};
zone   "example.com" {
        type master;
        file   "example.com.zone";
};
```

It's useful to break down this file, command by command. First, the following command allows only users on the local computer to use the **rndc** command to maintain this DNS server:

```
controls {
     inet 127.0.0.1 allow { localhost; } keys { rndckey; };
};
```

NOTE   *Most administrators use SSH (see Chapter 23) to connect to remote DNS servers. However, you could also set the* controls *line in* /etc/named.conf *to the IP address and name of another computer on your LAN. You could then use* **rdnc***, the name server control utility, to manage your DNS server remotely.*

Next, the include directive adds the contents of the stated files:

```
include "/etc/named.custom";
include "/etc/rndc.key";
```

The options directive specifies the directory with your DNS database files, usually /var/named:

```
options {
     directory "/var/named";
  };
```

NOTE   *If you used* redhat-config-bind, *you should find the* options *command entry in your* /etc/named.custom *file.*

This DNS server has basic zones of authority. The localhost computer, IP address 127.0.0.1, is by default a zone of authority. The domain of your LAN—in this case, `example.com`—is a second zone of authority. Inverse zones, as indicated by the `in-addr.arpa` statement, are also an important part of the DNS database. Because these are reverse IP addresses, the 0.168.192.in-addr.arpa zone is based on the 192.168.0.0 network address.

```
zone "0.0.127.in-addr.arpa" {
     type master;
     file "0.0.127.in-addr.arpa.zone"
};
zone "0.168.192.in-addr.arpa" {
     type master;
     file "0.168.192.in-addr.arpa.zone"
};
zone "localhost" {
     type master;
     file "localhost.zone"
};
zone "example.com" {
     type master;
     file "example.com.zone"
};
```

But this does not include the database for the entire Internet; it is important to give your DNS server a way to access that database. It's available as the `/var/named/named.ca` file from the `caching-nameserver-*` RPM. You should add the following stanza to your `/etc/named.conf` configuration file to refer other queries to the root servers for the Internet:

```
zone "." {
     type hint;
     file "named.ca"
};
```

NOTE *If you used* `redhat-config-bind`, *you should find this* `zone` *command in your* `/etc/named.custom` *file.*

If this were a secondary (slave) DNS server for the `example.com` network, you'd need to first get information from the master DNS server (if the IP address for your DNS server is different, substitute accordingly):

```
zone "example.com" {
     type slave;
     file "example.com.zone";
     masters {
             192.168.0.213
             }

};
```

Alternatively, if this is a forwarding-only DNS server, for all domains you might see a different options statement, where the forwarders are the IP addresses of other DNS servers, perhaps for your ISP:

```
options {
        directory "/var/named";
        forward only;
        forwarders {
                10.11.12.13;
                10.11.12.14;
                10.11.12.15;
        };
```

Finally, for a caching-only DNS, you'll need the `caching-nameserver-*` RPM package. It includes a version of `/etc/named.conf` that should work in most cases. The only question is whether there might be a firewall that blocks your requests to other DNS servers. If so, remove the two forward slashes from in front of this command, which serve as comment characters:

```
// query-source address * port 53
```

As you've seen in Chapter 22, even the default high-security Linux `iptables` firewall allows DNS requests through TCP/IP port 53. Without this command, requests to other DNS servers might be blocked since the latest versions of BIND often use other ports.

DNS DATABASE FILES

The database files that support a DNS server are by default located in `/var/named`. The files stored depend on the name of your domain, the IP address of your network, and whether you're supporting a regular or a caching-only DNS server. Some of the files you might see are listed in Table 24.2.

TABLE 24.2: DNS DATABASE FILES IN */VAR/NAMED*

FILE	FUNCTION
`0.0.127.in-addr.arpa.zone`	Specifies the reverse zone file for localhost.
`netaddr.in-addr.apra.zone`	Specifies the reverse zone file for the LAN, where *netaddr* is the first three octets of a network address, backwards; e.g., for the 192.168.4.0 network, this file would be `4.168.192.in-addr.arpa.zone`.
`domain.zone`	Specifies the zone file for the LAN, where an address such as `example.com` is substituted for *domain*.
`localhost.zone`	Specifies the zone file for localhost.
`named.ca`	Lists Internet root servers; from the `caching-nameserver-*` RPM.
`named.local`	Specifies the PTR, a reverse zone record for localhost.

Now let us examine a forward and a reverse zone database file. Start with Figure 24.9, which is a view of the zone file for the hypothetical example.com LAN.

FIGURE 24.9

/var/named/
example.com.zone

```
$TTL 86400
@       IN      SOA     RH9Desk.  root.localhost (
                        2 ; serial
                        28800 ; refresh
                        7200 ; retry
                        604800 ; expire
                        86400 ; ttl
                        )


        ⎕IN     NS      10.252.113.63

RH9Laptop       IN      A       10.252.113.55
RH9Test         IN      A       10.252.113.211
laptop2         IN      A       10.252.113.121
~
```

As you can see, this file contains a number of strange-looking commands. It essentially sets RH9 as the nameserver (ns) for the example.com domain, with three other computers on that network.

You may want to configure a couple of other types of servers on this network. For example, the following lines set up two different mail servers; the lowest number gets higher priority:

```
MX      10 mail.example.com ; Primary Email Server
MX      20 mail2.example.com ; Secondary Email Server
```

If you configure different servers on the same computer, you should set up aliases. For example, the following commands set up a news server and a web server on the same computer as an FTP server:

```
ftp     IN      A       192.168.0.34
www     IN      CNAME   ftp
news    IN      CNAME   ftp
```

Table 24.3 explains some of the commands in this zone file.

TABLE 24.3: DNS ZONE FILE COMMANDS

COMMAND	DESCRIPTION
$TTL	Specifies the time to live (TTL) on records on this database before deletion; normally in seconds; alternatively 3D = 3 days.
@	Sets a reference to the local computer.
IN	Assigns Internet class data.
SOA	Start of authority; specifies the DNS server for this zone.
root.localhost	Contains the e-mail address of the administrator for this DNS; reinterpreted as root@localhost.
serial	Specifies the serial number associated with this file; you should update it any time you've changed your DNS configuration, or other DNS servers might forget that your DNS server exists.

Continued on next page

TABLE 24.3: DNS ZONE FILE COMMANDS *(continued)*

COMMAND	DESCRIPTION
refresh	Notes the time between checks to the primary DNS server for this zone, in seconds.
retry	Sets a time to try to contact a DNS server if the first attempt fails. If a refresh attempt can't reach a DNS server, try again after this many seconds.
expire	Notes a stop time; If refresh and retry attempts don't reach a DNS server, stop activity on this zone after this much additional time; in seconds.
ttl	Sets the time to live for individual records in this DNS server.
NS	Specifies the name of the nameserver, a.k.a. the DNS server.
A	Contains an address record for this hostname and IP address.
CNAME	Specifies the canonical name; alias for a different hostname.
MX	Specifies a mail server.
PTR	Contains the pointer, or a reverse record, in a reverse zone file.

Now look at the reverse database file in Figure 24.10. As you can see, it includes the same basic commands as in a regular DNS database file. The PTR records may appear a bit strange.

FIGURE 24.10

A reverse zone file

```
$TTL 86400
@        IN      SOA     RH9Desk.example.com.    root.localhost (
                        3 ; serial
                        28800 ; refresh
                        7200 ; retry
                        604800 ; expire
                        86400 ; ttk
                        )


@        IN      NS      10.252.113.63.

121      IN      PTR     laptop2.example.com.
122      IN      PTR     laptop3.example.com.
63       IN      PTR     RH9Desk.example.com.
```

To find the IP address, you need the PTR record number as well as the name of the file. For example, the first PTR record line starts with the number 121, and the FQDN is laptop2.example.com. When correlated with the name of the file, 113.252.10.in-addr.arpa.zone, that means the IP address of laptop2.example.com. is 10.242.113.121

Starting DNS

Once you've configured DNS, you'll want to try out your new server. The easiest way to do this in Red Hat Linux is with the DNS service script. Remember, `named` is the daemon that runs the Linux DNS server:

```
# service named start
```

Next, you'll want to see if it works. As described in Chapter 21, the IP addresses of DNS servers are normally listed in /etc/resolv.conf. Once you've started your nameserver, you can see how it works. Try the `dig` command, the DNS lookup utility, to look up a specific FQDN on the Internet. Figure 24.11 shows how this works. Note the SERVER line near the bottom of the figure, which illustrates that this comes from a DNS server on a computer on my local network, with an IP address of 10.252.113.63.

FIGURE 24.11

The `dig` command

```
[root@RH9Desk root]# dig www.mommabears.com

; <<>> DiG 9.2.1 <<>> www.mommabears.com
;; global options:  printcmd
;; Got answer:
;; ->>HEADER<<- opcode: QUERY, status: NOERROR, id: 64701
;; flags: qr rd ra; QUERY: 1, ANSWER: 1, AUTHORITY: 3, ADDITIONAL: 0

;; QUESTION SECTION:
;www.mommabears.com.             IN      A

;; ANSWER SECTION:
www.mommabears.com.     1685    IN      A       66.36.97.32

;; AUTHORITY SECTION:
mommabears.com.         1685    IN      NS      ns3.hosting4u.net.
mommabears.com.         1685    IN      NS      ns.hosting4u.net.
mommabears.com.         1685    IN      NS      ns2.hosting4u.net.

;; Query time: 262 msec
;; SERVER: 10.252.113.63#53(10.252.113.63)
;; WHEN: Mon Mar  3 18:03:23 2003
;; MSG SIZE  rcvd: 118

[root@RH9Desk root]#
```

If you're satisfied with the result, remember to make sure `named` starts the next time you restart Linux. Use the `chkconfig --level 235 named` command to ensure this daemon starts at runlevels 2, 3, and 5.

TIP   When you start DNS during the boot process, you can also check startup messages in the /var/log/messages file. If there is a problem, such as a syntax error in /etc/named.custom, you'll see an indication here.

Using a DNS Client

If you've configured your computer to communicate on the Internet, you've already set it up as a DNS client. When you try to access another computer, you look for a database of hostnames and IP addresses.

As discussed in Chapter 21, there are two databases of hostnames and IP addresses: `/etc/hosts` and the DNS servers listed in `/etc/resolv.conf`. The database that your computer searches, and the order, is determined by your `/etc/host.conf` file, which normally includes one line: `order hosts,bind`. This means your computer first looks for IP addresses in `/etc/hosts` before searching any DNS servers listed in `/etc/resolv.conf`, which you can configure per the instructions in Chapter 21.

No additional configuration is required.

Setting up a DHCP Server

The Dynamic Host Configuration Protocol (DHCP) can automatically give all TCP/IP computers on your network the information that it needs to communicate. This includes the routers, the DNS servers, other name type servers, as well as basic IP addressing information.

To set up a computer as a DHCP server, you'll need to make sure that the network card can handle multicast requests. If you have older Microsoft Windows computers, you should also set up the broadcast address as a dedicated route. Then you can configure the DHCP configuration file, `/etc/dhcpd.conf`. If you want to use your DHCP server for remote networks, you'll also have to configure `dhcrelay` on the router/gateway between your LANs. The `dhcrelay` daemon supports the BOOTP protocol. But first, let's take a look at the RPM packages that you'll need.

Packages

Not all of the RPM packages that you need for DHCP are installed by default. The required packages are listed in Table 24.4; as you might remember from Chapter 10 and earlier in this chapter, you can use the `rpm -q` *packagename* command to see if they're installed. After you confirm this, you can use the `rpm -ql` *packagename* command to see the associated files.

TABLE 24.4: DHCP RPM PACKAGES

PACKAGE	FUNCTION
dhcp-*	DHCP server software
dhcp-devel-*	DHCP development tools; not required
dhclient-*	DHCP client software

Basic Configuration

A Linux computer configured as a DHCP server requires multicast support on the network card and the "all ones" broadcast address enabled.

Multicast support is probably already built into your network card and kernel. To check, run the `ifconfig` command. You should see output for your network card(s). Just under the entries for the associated IP addresses, you should see the following:

```
UP BROADCAST RUNNING MULTICAST  MTU:1500  METRIC:1
```

If you don't see `MULTICAST` in this line, you'll need to reconfigure network support for `MULTICAST` in the kernel. Refer to Chapter 12 for details.

You may also need to configure the route to the "all ones" broadcast address, which is 255.255.255.255. Older clients, such as Microsoft Windows 95, need to hear this broadcast address; otherwise, they won't even know that your DHCP server is there. If your DHCP server will be used for older clients on your network, run the following command:

```
# route add -host 255.255.255.255 dev eth0
```

The Configuration File: */etc/dhcpd.conf*

Now you can configure the main DHCP server configuration file, `/etc/dhcpd.conf`. Let's start with a sample file from the `dhcp-*` RPM, `dhcp.conf.sample` in the `/usr/share/doc/dhcp-versnum` directory. This sample lists a number of IP addresses, which you'll want to change to match the settings for your own network.

To learn more about DHCP servers, you may find it helpful to analyze the file in detail. The following is based on a line-by-line excerpt from the sample file. The first line allows Dynamic DNS updates to the latest available "interim" standard. A number of IP addresses are shown. If the applicable IP addresses for your network are different, substitute accordingly:

```
ddns-update-style interim;
```

You may not want individual users to update their hostname or IP address entries in the DNS server, so you use this command:

```
ignore client-updates;
```

Alternatively, you can use the command `allow client-updates`, which permits users to update their hostname or IP address entries.

The following line sets the default range of allowable IP addresses. Some of these addresses may be reserved for specific computers by later commands:

```
subnet 192.168.0.0 netmask 255.255.255.0 {
```

If your LAN is connected to another LAN, there should be a gateway IP address on a router that connects your LAN to the other. The following command specifies that gateway IP address:

```
option routers 192.168.0.1;
```

The following command is straightforward; it specifies the subnet mask, also known as the network mask, for the network:

```
option subnet-mask 255.255.255.0;
```

If you configure an NIS authorization database for your network, you can specify its domain (substitute it for `domain.org` in this command). For more information on NIS, see Chapter 28.

```
option nis-domain "domain.org";
```

Naturally, you probably have a domain name for your network. Based on the examples earlier in this chapter, it might be something like example.com. In this command, substitute the domain name for your LAN for `domain.org`:

```
option domain-name "domain.org";
```

If you've set up a DNS server on your LAN, list its address here. It can help this DHCP server find your DNS server for updates as required. You can use similar lines to identify the servers for incoming or outgoing e-mail (`option pop-server` or `smtp-server`), a web server (`option www-server`), or even a server dedicated to log files (`option log-server`):

```
option domain-name-servers 192.168.1.1;
```

The next statement helps you keep your network synchronized. The time is shown in seconds, relative to Greenwich Mean Time (GMT). In other words, U.S. Eastern Standard Time is 18000 seconds, or 5 hours, behind GMT. If you are in a different time zone, substitute accordingly.

```
option time-offset -18000; # Eastern Standard Time
```

Some computer clocks are faster than others. Computer clocks can slow down if a battery is low. If you have several computers running the same process, such as a web server, it can be important to synchronize their clocks. This is possible with a Network Time Protocol (NTP) server, which you may have configured in Chapter 19 with the `redhat-config-time` utility. This statement allows you to call the NTP server of your choice:

```
option ntp-servers 192.168.1.1;
```

Some Linux computers are configured as part of a Microsoft Windows–based network. One of the Microsoft name services for different computers is based on NetBIOS names. This is known as the Windows Internet Naming Service (WINS):

```
option netbios-name-servers 192.168.1.1;
```

It is possible to configure the DHCP server as a "p-node" computer; in other words, it looks for a WINS server and possibly a LMHOSTS file for name resolution:

```
option netbios-node-type 2;
```

You can configure a range of IP addresses that this DHCP server can assign to computers on remote networks. These addresses must fit within the range of defined network addresses.

```
range dynamic-bootp 192.168.0.128 192.168.0.254
```

DHCP servers assign IP addresses on a temporary basis. The first time an IP address may be renewed is the `default-lease-time`, in seconds:

```
default-lease-time 21600
```

An IP address should be renewed by the `max-lease-time`, in seconds:

```
max-lease-time 43200
```

You can assign a fixed IP address, based on the hardware address of a specific computer's network card. The `next-server` variable in this case refers to the alternate DNS server (`host ns`):

```
host ns {
    next-server marvin.redhat.com
    hardware ethernet 12:23:34:45:AB:CD
    fixed-address 207.175.42.254
}
```

Once you've customized this file for your LAN, save it as `/etc/dhcpd.conf`.

Starting the DHCP Server

To run the Linux DHCP server, you need a network card that already has an IP address. If necessary, use the `ifconfig` command to assign an IP address, as discussed in Chapter 21.

Starting the DHCP service is easy. Just run the `dhcpd` script with a command such as `service dhcpd start`. Remember to use a command such as `chkconfig` to make sure that your DHCP server starts the next time you boot Linux.

DHCP Servers and Remote Networks

When you can configure a DHCP server to reserve a series of IP addresses for remote networks (see the range `dynamic-bootp` variable in the previous section), a DHCP server needs help. Normally, gateways or routers that sit between networks block DHCP messages. That is where you should implement the BOOTP protocol, which opens up a path through a router or gateway for DHCP communication between your LANs.

To set up BOOTP, install the `dhcrelay` daemon (from the `dhcp-*` RPM package) on the gateway or router computer. Then you can configure command options in the `/etc/sysconfig/dhcrelay` configuration file. For example, the following commands in that file let `dhcrelay` listen on both the `eth0` and `eth1` network cards. The `DHCPSERVERS` should be connected to at least one of these network cards. You can then specify any network cards connected to networks that need remote DHCP service.

```
INTERFACES="eth0 eth1"
DHCPSERVERS="192.168.0.213"
```

Remember to start the `dhcrelay` script and use `chkconfig` to make sure that `dhcrelay` is active the next time you boot Linux.

TIP   One common mistake is to specify only the network adapters that are connected to the LANs that need remote DHCP service. Remember to include the adapter that is connected to the LAN with the DHCP server.

A Lease Database

Once computers on your networks start getting addressing information from your DHCP server, the results will be documented in `/var/lib/dhcp/dhcpd.leases`. An example of this file is shown in Figure 24.12, which displays IP address assignments to the hardware address of different network cards on your LAN.

FIGURE 24.12

dhcpd.leases

```
# All times in this file are in UTC (GMT), not your local timezone.   This is
# not a bug, so please don't ask about it.    There is no portable way to
# store leases in the local timezone, so please don't request this as a
# feature.    If this is inconvenient or confusing to you, we sincerely
# apologize.    Seriously, though - don't ask.
# The format of this file is documented in the dhcpd.leases(5) manual page.
# This lease file was written by isc-dhcp-V3.0pl1

lease 192.168.0.254 {
  starts 1 2002/10/14 14:35:09;
  ends 1 2002/10/14 20:35:09;
  binding state active;
  next binding state free;
  hardware ethernet 00:60:08:8d:41:93;
}
lease 192.168.0.253 {
  starts 1 2002/10/14 14:37:59;
  ends 1 2002/10/14 20:37:59;
  binding state active;
  next binding state free;
  hardware ethernet 00:10:b5:64:3b:b2;
}
~
```

Working with DHCP and BOOTP Clients

Configuring a DHCP client is fairly easy. Once networking is configured, you need to point the startup script for your network card to look for a DHCP server. Once configured, your computer broadcasts a request looking for a DHCP server the next time it boots.

Naturally, you need to make sure that networking is enabled. Check your /etc/sysconfig/network file. It should include the following entry:

NETWORKING=yes

Now revise your network card configuration file. It's usually in the /etc/sysconfig/network-scripts directory. If the network card is eth0, the filename is ifcfg-eth0, and the file should contain the following:

DEVICE=eth0
BOOTPROTO=dhcp
ONBOOT=yes

There are two alternatives for the BOOTPROTO variable: bootp and dialup. These alternatives are almost self-explanatory; bootp assumes the DHCP server is on a remote network; dialup configures the device for a dial-up connection, such as to an ISP on the Internet.

Once the configuration files are changed, the easiest way to start your computer as a new DHCP client is with the dhclient command. The result should resemble that shown in Figure 24.13.

NOTE   *Red Hat has changed the name of its DHCP client a number of times in the past couple of years; previous names included* dhcpcd *and* pump.

FIGURE 24.13

Leasing an IP
address

```
[root@RH9Test root]# dhclient
Internet Software Consortium DHCP Client V3.0pl1
Copyright 1995-2001 Internet Software Consortium.
All rights reserved.
For info, please visit http://www.isc.org/products/DHCP

Listening on LPF/eth1/00:10:b5:64:3b:b2
Sending on   LPF/eth1/00:10:b5:64:3b:b2
Listening on LPF/lo/
Sending on   LPF/lo/
Listening on LPF/eth0/00:40:f4:3c:05:58
Sending on   LPF/eth0/00:40:f4:3c:05:58
Sending on   Socket/fallback
DHCPDISCOVER on eth1 to 255.255.255.255 port 67 interval 7
DHCPDISCOVER on eth0 to 255.255.255.255 port 67 interval 5
DHCPOFFER from 10.252.113.113
DHCPREQUEST on eth0 to 255.255.255.255 port 67
DHCPACK from 10.252.113.113
bound to 10.252.113.3 -- renewal in 125720 seconds.
[root@RH9Test root]#
```

Summary

There are two key services that help your Linux computer communicate on a TCP/IP network such
as the Internet: DNS and DHCP. This chapter showed you how to configure clients and servers for
each service.

A DNS server is a database of FQDN and IP addresses. You can configure master, slave, caching-
only, or forwarding DNS servers. Red Hat encourages the use of `redhat-config-bind` to configure
the main DNS configuration files, `/etc/named.conf` and several files in `/var/named`. If you use this
tool, add special configuration options to `/etc/named.custom`. Once you've configured the server,
you can start the `named` daemon, which controls DNS, with the `service named start` command.

Generally, no special configuration is required to set up a DNS client. Normally, a DNS client
will search through `/etc/hosts` before moving to the DNS servers identified in `/etc/resolv.conf`.

A DHCP server enables you to manage the IP addresses on your network. You can also set up
other basic network information in the `/etc/dhcpd.conf` configuration file, such as gateways, DNS
servers, NIS servers, and even SMTP servers. As long as the DHCP server computer has a network
card with an IP address, you can start the DHCP server with the `service named dhcpd` command.
Configuring a gateway computer to transfer DHCP messages between networks is possible with the
`dhcrelay` daemon. Once you've set up a DHCP server, you can lease an address with the `dhclient`
command. Leased addresses are stored in a `/var/lib/dhcp/dhcpd.leases` database.

Configuring DHCP clients is fairly easy; the key file is the configuration file for your network
card in the `/etc/sysconfig/network-scripts` directory. If there is a DHCP server for your LAN,
you can get your IP addressing information for it immediately with the `dhclient` command.

In the next chapter, we'll look at the two major print systems for Linux: the Common Unix Print
System (CUPS) and the Line Print Daemon (LPD).

Chapter 25

Printing with CUPS and LPD

WHEN YOU INSTALL RED Hat Linux, it does not automatically detect printers. Therefore, all administrators need to know some of the arcane details of printer configuration.

Two major print systems are available for Red Hat Linux. The Common Unix Print System (CUPS) is now the default print service. The Line Print Daemon (LPD) was the default through Red Hat 8.0; Red Hat includes software that accommodates LPD commands and applications in the CUPS system.

CUPS, which is based on the Internet Print Protocol (IPP) version 1.1, allows administrators to organize networked printers in groups. The CUPS technical term for a group of printers is a *class*. CUPS includes a web-based configuration interface. It also works well with single local printers.

You can also organize large numbers of printers through the web interface. But to comprehend the implications for your network, you should also understand the contents of the associated configuration files. While the language in the `/etc/cups` configuration files may seemancient, it is quite similar to the language associated with the Apache web server configuration file in Chapter 30.

In contrast, LPD was adapted from the BSD operating system, and works well with single printers on small networks. Red Hat has *deprecated* LPD, which means that it will remove LPD from a future release of Red Hat Linux.

NOTE *The BSD operating system is also known as the Berkeley Standard Distribution. Like Linux, it too is a clone of Unix.*

With CUPS, you do not have to give up any applications that are built for LPD. If you're more familiar with LPD, you can still use CUPS. It includes an `xinetd` service that lets you use standard LPD commands such as `lpr` and `lpq`. Once you've selected your preferred print server, you should install and activate the appropriate packages. If you choose CUPS as your print daemon, you can also activate the `cups-lpd` daemon for applications that need LPD-style commands. This chapter covers the following topics:

◆ Using the Internet Print Protocol (IPP)

◆ Configuring the Common Unix Print System (CUPS)

◆ Using the Line Print Daemon (LPD)

Using the Internet Print Protocol

In the past, Unix and allied systems such as Linux did not do a very consistent job with printer interfaces. As companies such as AT&T, HP, and Sun created their own versions of Unix, they also created proprietary print interfaces. While Linux did well to adapt the LPD packages, the evolving industry standard is based on the Internet Print Protocol (IPP).

CUPS is the Linux and Unix way of working with IPP. It was developed by Novell and Xerox with four goals in mind—to enable users to:

◆ Find available printers on a network

◆ Send print jobs to an IPP-configured printer

◆ Read the status of their print jobs

◆ Cancel any print jobs they may have created

CUPS allows you to send print jobs to a specific URI, such as `parallel:/dev/lp0`.

NOTE *A URI is a Uniform Resource Identifier. You're probably more familiar with URLs (Uniform Resource Locators), which are a subset of URIs. As you know, a URL is used in web browsers to point to sites such as* `ftp://ftp.redhat.com` *or* `http://www.sybex.com`. *A URI can point to more things, such as* `mailto:abc@def.ghi`, `smb://comp1/printername`, *or* `parallel:/dev/lp1`.

CUPS implements IPP in a number of different ways. Several of the standards, as shown in Table 25.1, probably seem familiar to those of you who know LPD. The standard actions shown are far from a comprehensive list. More detailed information is available from the developers of CUPS, Easy Software Products, at `www.easysw.com`.

TABLE 25.1: CUPS FUNCTIONALITY

ACTION	DESCRIPTION
Print	Sends a file to a printer at a specific URI
Validate	Makes sure that a job has the right priority, printer, etc.
Create	Sets up an empty print job
Send	Sends a file for processing as a print job
Cancel	Cancels a print job
Pause	Stops action by a printer
Resume	Resumes action by a printer
Purge	Clears jobs from a printer's spool

In addition, CUPS includes a number of administrative functions over and above the standard LPD system. Some of these functions are shown in Table 25.2. Once again, this is not a comprehensive list.

TABLE 25.2: SPECIAL CUPS FUNCTIONS

ACTION	DESCRIPTION
CUPS-Get-Default	Finds the URI for the default printer
CUPS-Get-Printers	Finds the URIs for all printers configured on the network with CUPS
CUPS-Add-Modify-Printers	Adds or modifies a printer through CUPS
CUPS-Delete-Printer	Deletes a printer from a CUPS class
CUPS-Get-Classes	Finds the types of printers available in each CUPS class
CUPS-Add-Modify-Class	Adds a new printer class, or modifies an existing CUPS printer class
CUPS-Delete-Class	Deletes an existing class of CUPS printers
CUPS-Accept-Jobs	Sets a specific printer or print class to start accepting print jobs
CUPS-Reject-Jobs	Sets a specific printer or print class to start rejecting print jobs

With these basic concepts in mind, you're ready to learn how to configure CUPS on your computer and network.

Configuring the Common Unix Print System

In many cases, configuring the Common Unix Print System (CUPS) is easy. Since CUPS is the default, if the right packages are installed CUPS may already be activated on your computer. Many LPD commands can be used on CUPS printers; all you need to do is activate the `xinetd`-managed daemon, `cups-lpd`.

You can configure many CUPS printers through a web-based interface on TCP/IP port 631, which is the communications channel for IPP. However, if you're configuring a group of CUPS printers, you need to know how to directly edit the CUPS configuration files in the `/etc/cups` directory.

Check your current CUPS RPM packages. Install them if they're not already on your computer. These packages are summarized in Table 25.3.

TABLE 25.3: CUPS RPM PACKAGES

PACKAGE	DESCRIPTION
`cups-*`	The main CUPS package, which includes basic commands and default configuration files.
`cups-libs-*`	A package that allows you to use access CUPS commands without having to use LPD commands such as `lpr`.
`cups-devel-*`	The CUPS development libraries.
`cups-drivers-*`	Drivers for CUPS-based printers. You may need to download these from a third-party source such as `www.rpmfind.net`; alternatively, the `redhat-config-printer-*` package and command includes a broad list of printer drivers.

Continued on next page

TABLE 25.3: CUPS RPM PACKAGES *(continued)*

PACKAGE	DESCRIPTION
`foomatic-*`	A spooler independent database of printers; supports `redhat-config-printer`.
`hpijs-*`	Print drivers optimized for HP printers.

In the sections that follow, we start with the web-based interface, and then offer a detailed look at each of the CUPS configuration files in /etc/cups. Finally, we look at some basic CUPS commands and the `cups-lpd` service that lets you use LPD commands.

NOTE The names of the CUPS files, daemons, and scripts may be a bit confusing. The CUPS daemon is cupsd, *in the* /usr/sbin *directory. However, Red Hat Linux lets you start and stop CUPS with a* cups *script in the* /etc/rc.d/init.d *directory. Finally, the main CUPS configuration file is* cupsd.conf, *in the* /etc/cups *directory.*

Graphical Configuration

You can set up CUPS printers on the web browser of your choice. It's quite possible that the CUPS RPM packages are installed and the `cups` daemon is active. In that case, all you need to do is open the local browser of your choice on TCP/IP port 631.

NOTE You can run the CUPS configuration program from a web browser on a remote computer. However, this requires you to have no firewall between those two computers—at least none that block port 631. While we don't encourage this practice, you may find the risks acceptable if you're on a LAN protected from outside networks with a firewall.

FOR UPGRADERS: CONVERTING FROM LPD TO CUPS

If you're using Red Hat 8.0 or earlier, your default print server is probably LPD. If you upgrade to Red Hat 9, Red Hat is not supposed to automatically change your print server; LPD remains active on your computer.

Assuming you've made the decision to move to CUPS, you'll want to make sure that the lpd daemon is no longer active when you start Linux. Then you can make sure that the cupsd daemon (from the /usr/sbin directory) is activated at the appropriate runlevels. The following commands should work:

```
# chkconfig --level 2345 lpd off
# chkconfig --level 2345 cups on
```

Before you actually use a CUPS printer, you'll need to run redhat-switch-printer to let you switch from LPD and CUPS. (LPD is sometimes known by the name of its RPM package, LPRng, or Line Print Request, next generation.)

Naturally, if you've just installed Red Hat Linux 9 and want to use LPD instead, you can reverse these steps.

Now open the browser of your choice, and direct it to `http://localhost:631`. Figure 25.1 shows the result in the Mozilla web browser.

FIGURE 25.1

The CUPS printer configurator

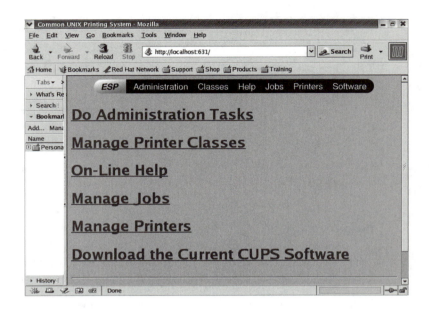

TIP *You may see the following message in your browser: "The connection was refused when attempting to contact server-name:631." If you do, you haven't activated the* **cupsd** *daemon, or you have a firewall that's blocking access to port 631.*

As you can see, there are six different command options; the ESP link at the top of the web page is a link to the people behind CUPS, Easy Software Products at www.easysw.com. The other options are fairly straightforward and are summarized in Table 25.4.

TABLE 25.4: CUPS CONFIGURATION MENU OPTIONS

OPTION	DESCRIPTION
ESP	Navigates to www.easysw.com
Administration: Do Administration Tasks	Allows you to add or manage printers, classes, and print jobs
Classes: Manage Printer Classes	Lets you add or manage a group of printers as a class
Help: On-Line Help	Includes HTML and PDF manuals related to CUPS
Jobs: Manage Jobs	Allows you to manage current print jobs in the CUPS system
Printers: Manage Printers	Lets you add or manage an individual printer
Software: Download The Current CUPS Software	Navigates to www.cups.org for the latest available CUPS packages

Since the Administration link provides an "all-in-one" configuration interface, we'll examine these options (except ESP) in reverse order.

TIP   *Before you continue, back up the files in your* /etc/cups *directory. The original format of these files will be used later in this chapter.*

You can use the redhat-config-printer tool described later in this chapter to configure or edit the printers of your choice. It works with either CUPS or LPD, as long as only one of these (not both) daemons is active. It's in the Red Hat's Printer GUI Tool section.

TIP   *The* redhat-config-printer *tool provides easy access to a wide variety of print drivers, customized by manufacturer and model.*

DOWNLOADING CUPS

If you want to download the latest version of CUPS, it's available from the CUPS website at www.cups .org; see Figure 25.2. As of this writing, downloadable versions from www.cups.org are available only in tarball-style formats and may not be customized for Red Hat Linux.

NOTE   *The* www.cups.org *website is maintained by Easy Software Products; their home page is* www.easysw.com. *But remember, CUPS is open-source software licensed under the GPL.*

Therefore, it's usually best to download the latest version of CUPS from a Red Hat FTP server. As described in Chapter 10, there are two basic paths to the latest Red Hat–customized CUPS software: download from a Rawhide directory or use the up2date utility.

FIGURE 25.2

The CUPS
home page

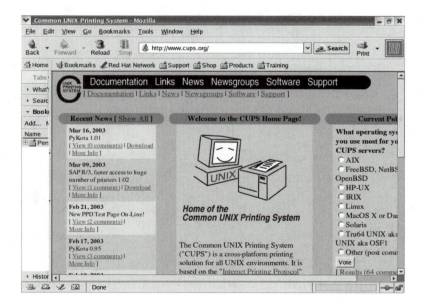

MANAGING PRINTERS

At this point, click on the Printers or Manage Printers link. The CUPS configuration tool takes you to a list of currently configured printers. Click Add Printer. Even if you're logged in as the root user, CUPS should prompt you for your administrative account, as shown in Figure 25.3.

FIGURE 25.3

Authorized access

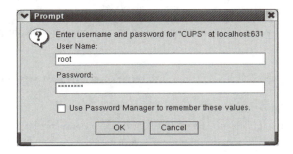

Once you've entered the appropriate username (usually root) and password, you're taken to the Add New Printer screen shown in Figure 25.4.

FIGURE 25.4

The Add New Printer screen

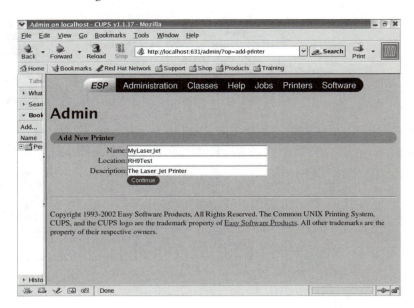

In this screen, you'll need to enter the name, location, and description of the printer, as defined in Table 25.5.

TABLE 25.5: ADDING A NEW PRINTER

ENTRY	DESCRIPTION
Name	A basic name for your printer such as MyLaserJet or HPLaserJet.
Location	The hostname or domain name associated with the printer, such as RH81Test or HPLaser.mommabears.com.
Description	A descriptive name of your choice; you could include the physical location of the printer.

Make your entries, click Continue, and move on to the next section.

Specifying a Print Device

As you can see in Figure 25.5, a variety of print devices are available. CUPS can administer printers connected to various physical ports as well as print servers. Some of these options are described in Table 25.6.

FIGURE 25.5

Specifying a print device

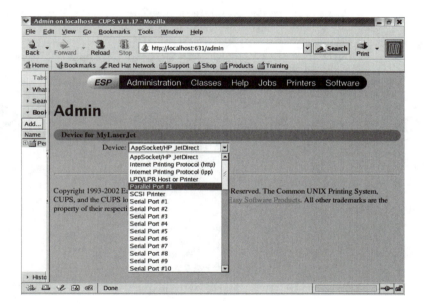

TABLE 25.6: CUPS PRINT DEVICE TYPES

DEVICE	DESCRIPTION
AppSocket/HP JetDirect	For printers connected to a Hewlett-Packard JetDirect print server.
Internet Printing Protocol (http)	If you're setting CUPS to communicate on port 80, you can set the address of your printer as http://printername.

Continued on next page

TABLE 25.6: CUPS Print Device Types *(continued)*

DEVICE	DESCRIPTION
Internet Printing Protocol (ipp)	Normally, CUPS uses IPP port 631, which corresponds to a URI of `ipp://printername`.
LPD/LPR Host Or Printer	For printers managed through an LPD print server.
Parallel Printer	For printers connected via a local parallel port.
SCSI Printer	For printers connected via a SCSI interface.
Serial Port #*x*	For printers connected to a local serial port.
USB Printer #*x*	For printers connected to a local USB port.
Windows Printer Via SAMBA	For shared printers connected via a Microsoft Windows computer; may also apply to Linux computers that connect to a network via Samba.

Make your selection, click Continue, and proceed to the next section.

Setting a URI

Next, you'll set the URI for the new printer. CUPS prompts you with the first letters of the URI, such as `lpd`, `smb`, `socket`, or `http`. In the previous step, we selected Internet Print Protocol (IPP) as the print device. In the example shown in Figure 25.6, the printer is connected to the computer named RH90, with the printer name of MyLaserJet.

FIGURE 25.6

Setting a
printer URI

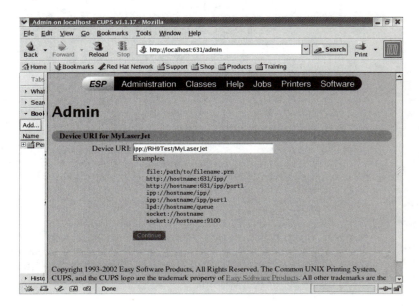

TIP   *If you selected a local physical printer port, no URI is required; CUPS skips this section.*

If your computer includes more than one print port, you can add the device name to the end of the URI:

```
ipp://RH9/MyLaserJet/dev/lp0
```

Alternatively, if you were configuring a shared Samba printer, the URI would start with `smb:` and end with the share name. For example, a shared Samba printer named myprint on a computer named printserv would have the following URI:

```
smb://printserv/myprint
```

Enter the appropriate URI, click Continue, and proceed to the next section.

Selecting a Print Model

This section is fairly straightforward. You're telling CUPS what print filter to use for your printer. In this section, you should select the make of your printer, as shown in Figure 25.7. If the make of your computer is not shown, it may be a PostScript printer. Alternatively, your printer may not need a filter; in other words, it can handle "raw" output. Raw and PostScript options are available here as well.

FIGURE 25.7

Selecting a print model

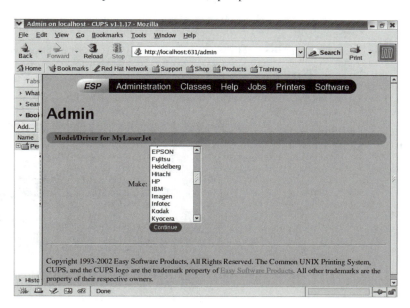

If you see only a small list of print models and drivers, that's because Red Hat is focusing more on configuration via `redhat-config-printer`, which has an extensive collection of print drivers, courtesy of the `foomatic-*` RPM. Other versions of Linux include additional print drivers with the `cups-drivers-*` RPM package. This RPM was also a part of Red Hat 8.0. Select your print model, click Continue, and then proceed to the next section.

Selecting a Print Driver

Now you can select a print driver. Depending on the make of your printer, the options can be extensive. If you see more than one driver for your printer in Figure 25.8, some trial and error may be appropriate

FIGURE 25.8

Selecting a print driver

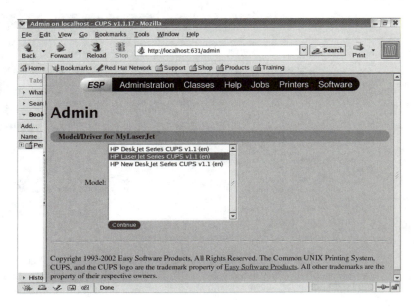

Select your print model and click Continue. You should see a message like the following:

`Printer MyLaserJet has been added successfully.`

The name that you set for the printer should now be a link in the browser (indicated by the underline). You can click on the link to see the current status of your newly configured CUPS printer.

Now navigate to `http://localhost:631` to return to the main CUPS menu.

MANAGING JOBS

It is easy to check the current queue of print jobs. Click the Jobs or Manage Jobs link, and you'll see a current list of jobs in the queue. These jobs are stored in files in the `/var/spool/cups` directory. If there are pending jobs, you'll see them in a format similar to what is shown in Figure 25.9.

As shown in the figure, it's easy to Hold or Cancel pending print jobs. Any job that is held is stored in `/var/spool/cups`; other jobs are processed first. You can then release the job to the queue as desired. More details on each job are available by clicking the associated ID.

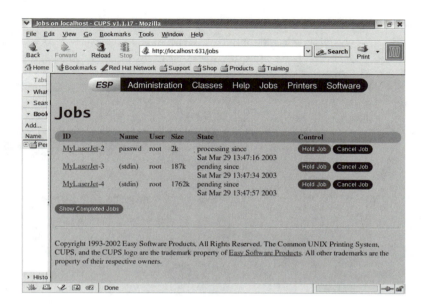

One useful CUPS feature is a history of completed jobs. Click the Show Completed Jobs button to inspect your completed jobs, similar to what's shown in Figure 25.10. You can use this feature to monitor the activity of your printers to see if a print job is complete.

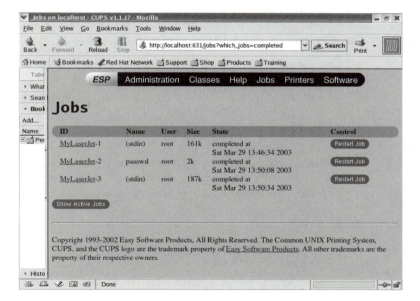

TIP   *If you're having trouble printing from a CUPS configured printer, you might have accidentally switched to LPD.*

ACCESSING ONLINE HELP

Considerable online help is available for CUPS. All you need to do is click Help or On-Line Help. Either link opens the CUPS documents that are installed with the `cups-*` RPM in your local computer. Briefly, they include the documents shown in Table 25.7. Additional manuals are available for CUPS developers.

TABLE 25.7: CUPS ONLINE DOCUMENTS

DOCUMENT	DESCRIPTION
An overview of the Common Unix Printing System	Describes the basic structure of CUPS, how it works with IPP 1.1, and compatibility with LPD commands
Software Users Manual	Includes a detailed description of the way you can customize printing with the right CUPS commands
Software Administrators Manual	Includes a detailed description of the CUPS installation and the language of the `/etc/cups` configuration files
CUPS Implementation of IPP	Compares CUPS functionality to IPP requirements

Now navigate to `http://localhost:631` to return to the main CUPS menu.

MANAGING PRINTER CLASSES

The strength of CUPS is how it allows you to organize groups of printers. Once you've configured your printers, you can group them into CUPS classes. When you send a print job to a class, the job is processed by the first available printer in that class. Users no longer need to wait until an available printer is free.

In the CUPS menu, click Classes. CUPS takes you to a screen with currently configured printer classes. Click Add Class to open the Add New Class screen, shown in Figure 25.11. In this case, the new class name is HPLasers, which is different from any existing printer name. The Location and Description fields are essentially the same as when you added a new CUPS printer; Location corresponds to the hostname or domain name associated with the print server, and Description gives you a chance to add a descriptive comment about the new printer class.

Click Continue; CUPS now takes you to the Members For *PrintClassName* screen. All configured CUPS printers are included in this screen, even if they're already assigned to a different class. To add the printers shown in Figure 25.12 to the new HPLasers class, highlight them and click Continue. CUPS displays a message that the HPLasers class has been added successfully. Now you can print to HPLasers, and CUPS will send the job to the first available printer in that class.

FIGURE 25.11

Adding a new printer class

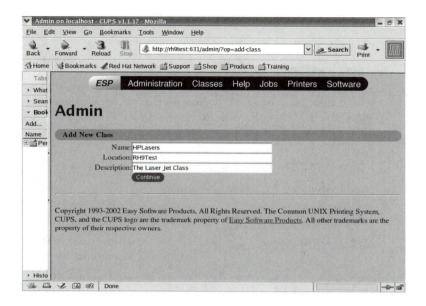

FIGURE 25.12

Adding printers to the new class

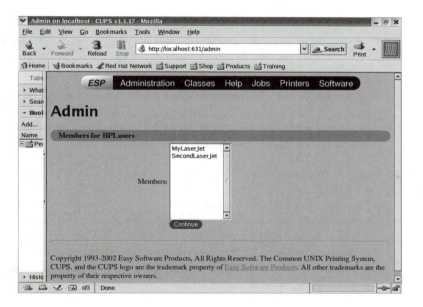

Click Classes again, and you'll see a screen with your configured printer classes. Figure 25.13 illustrates the class that we created, with the members MyLaserJet and SecondLaserJet1.

Now navigate to `http://localhost:631` to return to the main CUPS menu.

FIGURE 25.13

A defined
printer class

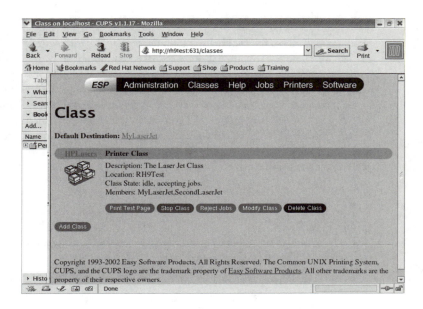

ADMINISTRATIVE TASKS

When you click Administration or Do Administration Tasks, you're taken to a menu where you can manage printer classes, print jobs, and printers. As shown in Figure 25.14, this is close to an "all-in-one" CUPS administration menu.

FIGURE 25.14

The CUPS
Administration menu

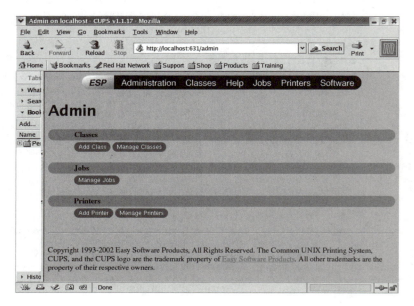

The *lpadmin* Command

While it's common for expert Linux administrators to administer from the command-line interface, many have come to trust the CUPS web-based configurator. Many don't trust the extra layer associated with a GUI interface; there is more that can go wrong. Not surprisingly, it's still possible to administer CUPS printers from the command line by using the `lpadmin` command. So many printer types and models are available, however, that this command becomes impractical.

But you can administer from the command line. One key function is to set up a user-based quota for your printer. This can help you track usage. For example, you can set quotas on a specific printer using the `lpadmin` command. The following command specifies that all users are limited to 10 pages per day on the printer named MyLaserJet:

```
# lpadmin -p MyLaserJet -o job-quota-period=86400 -o job-page-limit=10
```

Alternatively, you could use the `-o job-k-limit` switch to limit the amount of data sent to the printer in kilobytes.

You can also limit access to a specified printer. For example, the following command limits access to printer MyLaserJet to user ez and tblair:

```
# lpadmin -p MyLaserJet -u allow:ez,tblair
```

Alternatively, this command prohibits access to printer MyLaserJet for user mj:

```
# lpadmin -p MyLaserJet -u deny:mj
```

The `lpadmin` command affects the data in `/etc/cups/printers.conf`.

The *lpstat* Command

You can check the status of your printers and classes with the `lpstat` command. It's fairly straightforward; the `-c class` option lists members of the specified class; the `-v printer` option lists the device or address for the specified printer.

Configuration Files

The CUPS configuration files are stored in the `/etc/cups` directory. If you're familiar with the Apache web server described in Chapter 30, you should be comfortable with CUPS.

The language is similar. Remember, CUPS lists printers by their URIs, such as `ipp://RH9/MyLaserJet`. As you know, URLs list locations with addresses such as `http://www.sybex.com`. The standard configuration files are listed in Table 25.8; we examine `/etc/cups/cupsd.conf` in detail in the following section.

TABLE 25.8: CUPS CONFIGURATION FILES (IN */ETC/CUPS*)

FILE	DESCRIPTION
`classes.conf`	Specifies different groups of printers; when you create a new printer class with the CUPS web-based tool, the details are written here.
`client.conf`	Points to a default CUPS server; you may specify encryption requirements.
`cupsd.conf`	The main CUPS configuration file.

Continued on next page

TABLE 25.8: CUPS CONFIGURATION FILES *(continued)*

FILE	DESCRIPTION
`mime.convs`	Lists filters for various file formats, such as documents and images.
`mime.types`	Lists file types that can be processed through CUPS printers.
`printers.conf`	The configuration file changed by the CUPS web-based tool; the details are written here.
`pstoraster.convs`	Contains a conversion filter for Ghostscript files, the way GNU works with PostScript printers.

/etc/cups/cupsd.conf

While you can set up CUPS printers and classes with the web-based tool, to administer a group of printers you need to understand the main CUPS configuration file, `/etc/cups/cupsd.conf`. This section explains the default version of this file in detail; as you'll see, a number of variables are commented out that you can activate for your network of printers.

The variables listed in this section don't exactly match the order shown in the default `/etc/cups/cupsd.conf` configuration file; for example, variables related to log files are grouped together in their own section.

Other variables are available for `cupsd.conf`; for more information see the CUPS Software Administrator's Manual, available in the On-Line Help section of the CUPS GUI configuration program.

NOTE *Remember, the # is a comment code; you need to remove it to activate the command. In some cases, the command shown as a comment is the default.*

SERVER VARIABLES

The `ServerName` variable is straightforward; it lists the visible name of your CUPS print server computer. By default, it is set to the hostname of the local computer:

```
#ServerName myhost.domain.com
```

This name should match the `ServerName` variable on CUPS client computers in `/etc/cups/client.conf`. Next, the `ServerAdmin` variable is essentially set to the e-mail address of the "webmaster" of the CUPS server:

```
#ServerAdmin root@your.domain.com
```

STANDARD DIRECTORIES

Several files are listed in `cupsd.conf`; if listed with the relative path, they are relative to the directory listed as `ServerRoot`; by default, this is set to `/etc/cups`:

```
#ServerRoot /etc/cups
```

By default, the CUPS RPM packages store standard print data in the `/usr/share/cups` directory. This includes classifications, fonts, character sets, the help documents, and more. You can change where CUPS looks for this directory by changing the following variable:

```
#DataDir /usr/share/cups
```

When you send a print job, it is processed into a file that is stored on a spool. Normally, the file stays in the spool directory until the printer physically processes the job. The standard directory is specified with the `RequestRoot` variable. By default, it's `/var/spool/cups`:

```
# RequestRoot /var/spool/cups
```

CUPS also needs a temporary directory writeable by all users. Filters may be stored in this directory while a print job is being processed. While the default is `/var/tmp`, Red Hat Linux configures this in the `/var/spool/cups/tmp` directory, as shown here:

```
#TempDir /var/spool/cups/tmp
```

If you create your own temporary CUPS directory as root, you can set the appropriate permissions with this command:

```
# chmod a+t /tempdir
```

To help you visualize the result, here is the output from an `ls -l /var/spool/cups` command:

```
drwx------T   2 lp    sys    4096 Mar 3 12:48 tmp
```

LOG FILE VARIABLES

As described in Chapter 13, most log files are stored in the `/var/log` directory. CUPS log files are no exception; they are stored in the `/var/log/cups` directory. The standard log file lines are as follows:

```
#AccessLog /var/log/cups/access_log
#ErrorLog /var/log/cups/error_log
#PageLog /var/log/cups/page_log
```

These variables are set to default values. Of course, you can redirect these log files to the directory of your choice. These logs collect data as described in Table 25.9.

TABLE 25.9: CUPS LOG FILES

FILE	DESCRIPTION
access_log	Lists HTTP files accessed through the CUPS web management tool
error_log	Includes more than just error messages; in standard log format, includes err, warn, info, and debug messages
page_log	Notes each page that is sent to a printer

Chapter 13 describes how log files are rotated on a weekly basis. The MaxLogSize variable also forces the aforementioned logs to be rotated once the log file reaches a certain size. If the variable is not set, the default is 1MB; if it's set to 0, logs aren't rotated unless specified by another job such as those listed in the /etc/cron.daily directory:

```
MaxLogSize 0
```

Chapter 13 also describes how logs collect data based on settings in the /etc/syslog.conf configuration file. The available levels for CUPS, which are slightly different, appear in Table 25.10. By default, LogLevel is set to info:

```
LogLevel info
```

TABLE 25.10: CUPS LOG LEVELS

LEVEL	DESCRIPTION
emerg	Conditions that prevent CUPS from working
alert	Items that must be addressed immediately
crit	Critical errors that might not prevent CUPS from working
error	General errors
warn	Warning messages
notice	Temporary errors
info	All requests
debug	Basic debug information
debug2	All debugging information

SECURITY PRINTOUTS

You can set a header on each printed page. If security requirements are associated with printouts on your network, you can uncomment one of the following commands:

```
#Classification classified
#Classification confidential
#Classification secret
#Classification topsecret
#Classification unclassified
```

By default, there is no Classification. But if there is one, the ClassifyOverride variable may apply. If you set this variable to on, it allows users to change the classification associated with a specific print job. The default is off, as shown here:

```
#ClassifyOverride Off
```

The standard font used by the CUPS web-based configuration tool is set by the `DefaultCharset` variable. Common options include `iso-8859-1` and `windows-1251`. But this does not apply if a `DefaultLanguage` variable is present, or if the CUPS client sets a different `DefaultCharset`:

```
#DefaultCharset utf-8
```

The `DefaultLanguage` specifies the language used for connections to the CUPS web browser tool. By default, it's English (en); alternatives include German (de), Spanish (es), French (fr), and Italian (it):

```
#DefaultLanguage en
```

As with Apache, the `DocumentRoot` variable specifies the base directory for different HTML pages. In this case, these HTML pages are associated with the CUPS web browser tool. By default, it's set to the `/usr/share/doc/cups-versionnumber` directory.

```
#DocumentRoot /usr/share/doc/cups-versionnumber
```

Linux generally implements PostScript files using Ghostscript. When such files are sent to a printer, they need the fonts as currently specified by the `FontPath` variable. By default, this variable is set as:

```
#FontPath /usr/share/cups/fonts
```

PRINT JOB MANAGEMENT

There are four basic variables related to how print jobs are managed. For example, you can configure your CUPS print server to keep a record of past jobs, or even the spool files. The `PreserveJobHistory` variable, which is set to yes by default, keeps a record of past jobs:

```
#PreserveJobHistory Yes
```

You can keep a history of past job spool files. If this variable is set to yes, you can reprint previous jobs until you purge them. However, the `PreserveJobFiles` variable by default is set to no:

```
#PreserveJobFiles No
```

You may not have unlimited hard disk space. The `MaxJobs` variable sets a limit on the number of previous print jobs that you might preserve. The default is 500:

```
#MaxJobs 500
```

Naturally, this goes hand-in-hand with a limit on copies, as defined by the `MaxCopies` variable:

```
#MaxCopies 100
```

Normally, it's a good idea to set quotas to track usage of your CUPS printers, as described earlier with the `lpadmin` command. Print jobs are normally not purged, so data associated with printer usage remains on your system.

Conversely, if you have not set quotas, you have no need to keep track of the number of print jobs run by any user.

You can then activate the `AutoPurgeJobs` variable, which automatically deletes print jobs from the system.:

```
#AutoPurgeJobs No
```

You can configure a list of available printers in a standard file such as `/etc/printcap` with a straightforward command:

```
#Printcap /etc/printcap
```

Normally, `/etc/printcap` is based on the LPD system, developed for BSD. However, a similar format is available for the Solaris operating system. While the BSD-style system is the default, you can activate either with one of the following commands:

```
#PrintcapFormat BSD
#PrintcapFormat Solaris
```

NOTE *Don't worry about the* `PrintcapGUI` *variable; it's used for printer control only for the SGI IRIX operating system.*

Some print jobs need help from a program; these programs are normally stored in executable format in `/usr/lib/cups`, as specified by the `ServerBin` variable:

```
#ServerBin /usr/lib/cups
```

Most printers are configured to print graphics in "Raster" mode, dot by dot. However, the Raster Image Processing Cache variable, `RIPCache`, is used by specialized print filters such as imagetoraster and pstoraster. By default, the cache is 8MB; you can set caches in kilobytes and gigabytes with values such as 100k or 1g.

```
#RIPCache 8m
```

NOTE *In this case, RIP has nothing to do with the TCP/IP Routing Information Protocol.*

If you find that the print jobs are taxing the capacity of your server, you may want to set a `FilterLimit`. Normally, this variable is set to 0, which corresponds to no limit:

```
#FilterLimit 0
```

The number that you use will be based on trial and error; a couple of guidelines are available. If you want to print to a regular printer, you should set this value to 200; if you have several regular printers, set this value higher. If you set this value lower than 200, you effectively limit CUPS to processing one job at a time.

ENCRYPTION SUPPORT

Sometimes network communication is encrypted. You can configure CUPS to read encrypted print requests. The SSL certificate and key are defined by the following variables:

```
#ServerCertificate /etc/cups/ssl/server.crt
#ServerKey /etc/cups/ssl/server.key
```

And these certificates must be refreshed over a network periodically, as driven by the `RootCertDuration` variable, in seconds:

```
#RootCertDuration 300
```

CUPS ACCOUNTS

While CUPS is started by the root user, CUPS jobs are normally run by other users with less access. And when you access CUPS from a different computer, CUPS assigns you a different username, remroot, as specified by the RemoteRoot variable:

```
#RemoteRoot remroot
```

The standard CUPS user is lp and the standard group is sys, as defined by the User and Group variables. You can supersede these with the RunAsUser Yes command:

```
#User lp
#Group sys
```

BASIC NETWORK SETTINGS

CUPS was developed for TCP/IP networks. When you configure CUPS, you can set it to listen for specific computers and/or IP addresses on specific ports. For example, the following commands set CUPS to listen on Port 631, for requests from the computer named linux.mommabears.com, for requests from the 192.168.22.0 network:

```
Port 631
Listen linux.mommabears.com
Listen 192.168.22.0
```

If you want to listen for a specific hostname, you need to set the HostNameLookups variable to on. You can even combine some of these settings; for example, the following commands set CUPS to listen for requests from the 10.11.12.0 network, on port 80:

```
Listen 10.11.12.0:80
```

NOTE   In Apache 2.0.x, the Listen *directive has replaced the* Port *directive. See Chapter 30 for more information.*

Normally, you should stick with IP addresses in the cupsd.conf configuration file. Looking up domain names in a DNS server can take time and slow down your CUPS print server. If you want, you can set the HostNameLookup variable to direct CUPS to look for the IP address associated with a domain name. Naturally, the default is off; however, the following commented line is included in the default Red Hat Linux cupsd.conf file:

```
# HostNameLookups On
```

CUPS normally keeps open connections with web browsers, courtesy of the KeepAlive On variable. However, if you're administering CUPS through an older web browser such as Netscape 2.x, KeepAlive doesn't work. In that case, you need to set a time that CUPS will wait for data from the web-based tool. That's defined by the KeepAliveTimeout setting, which keeps the connection open for the noted period of time, in seconds:

```
#KeepAlive On
#KeepAliveTimeout 60
```

USER LIMITS

When you set up a print server on a network, any user may request access at any time. The MaxClients variable limits the number of users that connect to your CUPS print server; the default limit is 100 users:

```
#MaxClients 100
```

You can log into a single host computer multiple time; by default, that's ⅒oth the value of MaxClients.

You may also want to regulate the size of jobs sent through your CUPS print server. You might want very large jobs to be sent to other servers. You can set a limit with the MaxRequestSize variable in bytes or megabytes. However, the default is to avoid a limit by using the following command:

```
#MaxRequestSize 0
```

Related variables include MaxJobsPerPrinter and MaxJobsPerUser. If you want to set job limits on your CUPS printers or users, these variables are easy to understand.

Sometimes, a user will try to send a print job, but her program doesn't comply. A standard Timeout variable is set to close the CUPS connection; the default is 300 seconds:

```
#Timeout 300
```

NETWORK BROWSING

The browse parameters in CUPS relate to whether other computers on your network (or even other networks) can see the printers that you've configured with your CUPS server. By default, Browsing is on; other parameters determine how other computers see your CUPS printers.

There are two protocols that you can configure for CUPS browsing: CUPS and SLPv2. CUPS broadcasts printer information; SLPv2 is the second version of the Service Location Protocol (SLP), which allows other computers to find available services.

Either protocol can be configured to collect and distribute information on shared printers on the network. The default is CUPS; if you want to use SLPv2, your network needs access to at least one SLPv2 directory agent. While CUPS is the default protocol, you can configure either or both with one of the following commands:

```
#BrowseProtocols cups
#BrowseProtocols slp
#BrowseProtocols all
```

When your CUPS server broadcasts data on your shared printers, it needs a broadcast address. This is usually the broadcast IP address for your network, and is designated as BrowseAddress. If your network includes a dial-up connection, you can set BrowseAddress to @LOCAL; or, if you want browsing only on the network connected to your eth2 network card, use @IF(eth2). You can use as many BrowseAddress commands as you need. Here are some examples:

```
#BrowseAddress 192.168.99.255
#BrowseAddress 10.255.255.255
#BrowseAddress @IF(eth1)
```

If your printer names are self-explanatory (`hplaser@joescomp`, for example), you don't have to specify the full location of the printer. CUPS assumes that you have some skill in this area, so the `BrowseShortNames` variable is set to yes. If you're in a big organization with large numbers of printers, and you want extended data on each printer, set it to `No.`, as shown here:

```
#BrowseShortNames Yes
```

Whenever you add or share a new CUPS printer, CUPS needs to update the list of available printers. This is controlled through the `BrowseInterval` variable, which is set to 30 seconds by default:

```
#BrowseInterval 30
```

Alternatively, you could set `BrowseInterval` to 0, which means that information on new CUPS printers will not be sent automatically to other computers. However, you can configure another CUPS server to find your printer browse list. For example, the following command gets the list of printers from a CUPS server at 192.168.0.222 on port 631:

```
#BrowsePoll 192.168.0.222:631
```

Whatever you do, don't set `BrowseTimeout` to a value lower than `BrowseInterval`. If you do, printers are removed from your list before they're shared with the rest of the network. The default is 300 seconds:

```
#BrowseTimeout 300
```

If you want to provide access to other networks, use the `BrowseRelay` variable. The following are examples of commands you'd use to send the list of your shared CUPS printers to computers on other networks. The first address or interface must be on the local network. If you're using IP addresses, the second address can be a broadcast address for the other network.

```
#BrowseRelay 192.168.0.222 10.12.15.255
#BrowseRelay 192.168.0.0/24 10.12.15.255
```

The default port for CUPS broadcasts is the standard TCP/IP port for the Internet Print Protocol (IPP), 631. You could make your system a bit more secure by specifying a different port, but you'd have to make sure that all other computers on your network are looking for printers on that different port by using the `BrowsePort` variable:

```
#BrowsePort 631
```

BROWSE SECURITY

You can limit the computers that are allowed to browse your list of CUPS printers. By default, `BrowseAllow` accepts data from all addresses and `BrowseDeny` does not deny access to any computer. You can specify networks by their IP address, network address, or domain name in a number of ways. Here are examples of valid commands:

```
# BrowseAllow 10.12.0.0/24
# BrowseAllow 10.12.0.0/255.255.0.0
# BrowseAllow all
# BrowseDeny *.example.com
```

```
# BrowseDeny none
# BrowseDeny @IF(eth1)
```

But what comes first, Allow or Deny? That's determined by the **BrowseOrder** variable. If it's set to

```
#BrowseOrder allow,deny
```

computers are allowed to see your list of shared printers, unless specifically listed in a **BrowseDeny** command. Conversely, the following command allows access only if the computer is listed in a **BrowseAllow** command:

```
#BrowseOrder deny,allow
```

*NOTE   Naturally, if you want to specify a domain or a hostname, you need to set **HostNameLookups** to **On**.*

SYSTEM SECURITY

The area of security is where **cupsd.conf** looks most like an Apache configuration file. While the default CUPS user is sys, as defined by the **SystemGroup** variable

```
#SystemGroup sys
```

you can configure **<Location />** containers to regulate access IP addresses, classes, jobs, encryption, and more. The standard Red Hat configuration allows access to the CUPS server only from the local computer:

```
<Location />
Order Deny,Allow
Deny from All
Allow From 127.0.0.1
</Location>
```

You can specify other IP addresses in regular or CIDR notation. If you have **HostNameLookups** set to on (not recommended), you can even use host or domain names. As shown here, you can limit access by class (the first example limits access to a class named **AnyPrinter**) or by printer (the second example limits access to a specific printer named HPLaserJet):

```
<Location /AnyPrinter>
Order Deny,Allow
Deny from All
Allow From 127.0.0.1
</Location>

<Location /AnyPrinter/HPLaserJet>
Order Deny,Allow
Deny from All
Allow From 127.0.0.1
</Location>
```

Other containers allow you to regulate administrative operations, as shown in Table 25.11.

TABLE 25.11: LOCATION CONTAINER OPTIONS

CONTAINER	DESCRIPTION
`<Location />`	Associated with all CUPS print operations.
`<Location /admin>`	Associated with CUPS administrative operations; it may be a good idea to limit administrative access to CUPS.
`<Location /classes>`	Associated with limits on all configured CUPS printer classes.
`<Location /classes/classname>`	Associated with limits on the CUPS printer class named *classname*.
`<Location /jobs>`	Associated with limits on print job management.
`<Location /printers>`	Associated with limits administrative access on managing all printers.
`<Location /printers/printname>`	Associated with limits administrative access on managing the printer named *printname*.

Don't forget to end your containers with the `</Location>` command. Besides `Order`, `Deny`, and `Allow`, there are other commands that you can add to a `<Location />` container. They are described in Table 25.12.

TABLE 25.12: LOCATION DIRECTIVE COMMANDS/DEFINITIONS

COMMAND	DESCRIPTION
`Allow`	Used for computers or interfaces allowed to access the specified printer or class.
`Anonymous`	Indicates that no username or password is required; generally the default.
`AuthClass`	Specifies required authentication; options include `Anonymous`, `User`, `System`, and `Group`.
`AuthGroupName`	Sets the name of the group associated with a `Group` `AuthClass`.
`AuthType`	Defines the type of required usernames and passwords; options include `None`, `Basic` using `/etc/passwd`, `Digest` and `Basic Digest` using `/etc/cups/passwd.md5`.
`Deny`	Used for computers or interfaces not allowed to access the specified printer or class.
`Encryption`	Specifies whether encryption is required for usernames and passwords; options include `Never`, `IfRequested`, `Required`, and `Always`.
`Limit`	Specifies allowed CUPS request commands.
`LimitExcept`	Specifies prohibited CUPS request commands.
`Order`	Specifies how CUPS reads the `Deny` and `Allow` commands.
`Require`	Limits access to a group, a user, or all users with `valid-user`.

PRINTER CLASSES

You don't have to configure a class for each CUPS printer. You can set up `ImplicitClasses` for different printers with the same name, such as HPLaserJet. Print jobs to an Implicit Class are sent to the printer with the first available queue. `ImplicitClasses` is on by default:

```
#ImplicitClasses On
```

You can set the Implicit Class name to `AnyPrinter` by setting `ImplicitAnyClasses` to on. It is off by default:

```
#ImplicitAnyClasses Off
```

If you're using `ImplicitClasses`, your users don't really need to know about individual printers in a class. If `ImplicitClasses` is on, the `HideImplicitMembers` variable is on by default.

```
#HideImplicitMembers On
```

Printer Management

Once you've configured CUPS, you can use the CUPS GUI tool to manage current print jobs. You can also set up the `cups-lpd` service to allow you to use most standard LPD commands, including `lpr`, `lpq`, and `lprm`. These commands are covered later in this chapter. Finally, you can monitor the CUPS log files in the `/var/log/cups` directory for status, errors, and suspicious access attempts.

JOB MANAGEMENT

It's easy to manage active CUPS print jobs. The CUPS Jobs screen in Figure 25.15 shows two different print jobs. If you need to print job MyLaserJet-8 first, you click MyLaserJet-7's Hold Job button. CUPS displays a message that "Job 7 has been held from printing," and Job MyLaserJet-8 starts automatically.

FIGURE 25.15

Managing CUPS print jobs

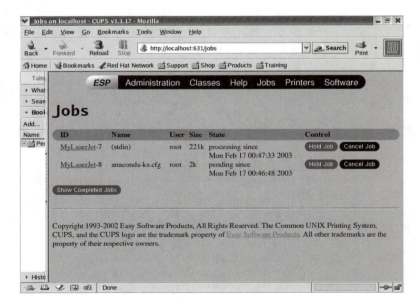

Job MyLaserJet-7 is held in the print queue until you return to the Jobs menu and click the Release Job button.

ACTIVATING LPD COMMANDS

To activate LPD-style commands for a CUPS server, you need to activate the `cups-lpd` service in the `/etc/xinetd.d` directory. You can activate this service with the `chkconfig service cups-lpd on` command. More information on managing `xinetd` services is available in Chapter 23.

You may need to activate `cups-lpd` for some applications that were originally designed for an LPD-style interface.

CUPS LOG FILES

CUPS log files, which we briefly described earlier in this chapter, are normally stored in the `/var/log/cups` directory. The `access_log` file lists the computer along with the date and time of access to the CUPS server. The example shown in Figure 25.16 lists access from only the default local computer, localhost.

FIGURE 25.16

CUPS `access_log` file

```
localhost - root [29/Mar/2003:13:57:21 -0500] "POST /admin/ HTTP/1.1" 200 342
localhost - root [29/Mar/2003:13:57:18 -0500] "POST /admin HTTP/1.1" 200 1780
localhost - - [29/Mar/2003:13:57:24 -0500] "POST / HTTP/1.1" 200 220
localhost - - [29/Mar/2003:13:57:25 -0500] "GET /classes/HPLasers HTTP/1.1" 200
0
localhost - - [29/Mar/2003:13:57:25 -0500] "POST / HTTP/1.1" 200 77
localhost - - [29/Mar/2003:13:57:28 -0500] "POST / HTTP/1.1" 200 125
localhost - - [29/Mar/2003:13:57:28 -0500] "POST / HTTP/1.1" 200 125
localhost - - [29/Mar/2003:13:57:25 -0500] "GET /classes/HPLasers HTTP/1.1" 200
3170
localhost - - [29/Mar/2003:13:57:29 -0500] "GET /images/classes.gif HTTP/1.1" 20
0 591
localhost - - [29/Mar/2003:13:57:29 -0500] "GET /images/stop-class.gif HTTP/1.1"
 200 245
localhost - - [29/Mar/2003:13:57:29 -0500] "GET /images/delete-class.gif HTTP/1.
1" 200 259
localhost - - [29/Mar/2003:13:57:29 -0500] "GET /images/modify-class.gif HTTP/1.
1" 200 267
localhost - - [29/Mar/2003:13:57:29 -0500] "POST / HTTP/1.1" 200 220
localhost - - [29/Mar/2003:13:57:31 -0500] "GET /classes HTTP/1.1" 200 0
localhost - - [29/Mar/2003:13:57:31 -0500] "POST / HTTP/1.1" 200 77
localhost - - [29/Mar/2003:13:57:32 -0500] "POST / HTTP/1.1" 200 77
localhost - - [29/Mar/2003:13:57:31 -0500] "GET /classes HTTP/1.1" 200 3010
```

The `error_log` file lists more than just standard errors; as shown in Figure 25.17, it also lists basic activity of the CUPS server, including on the first line, the print job that was held in the previous section.

Finally, the `page_log` file lists any job that's been sent to the queue, even if it was cancelled. An example of this file is shown in Figure 25.18.

FIGURE 25.17

CUPS `error_log` lists more than just errors.

```
I [29/Mar/2003:13:54:11 -0500] Started "/usr/lib/cups/cgi-bin/jobs.cgi" (pid=240
9)
E [29/Mar/2003:13:54:11 -0500] cancel_job: "" not authorized to delete job id 4
owned by "root"!
I [29/Mar/2003:13:54:14 -0500] Started "/usr/lib/cups/cgi-bin/jobs.cgi" (pid=241
0)
I [29/Mar/2003:13:54:28 -0500] Started "/usr/lib/cups/cgi-bin/printers.cgi" (pid
=2411)
I [29/Mar/2003:13:54:33 -0500] Started "/usr/lib/cups/cgi-bin/admin.cgi" (pid=24
12)
I [29/Mar/2003:13:55:07 -0500] Started "/usr/lib/cups/cgi-bin/admin.cgi" (pid=24
15)
I [29/Mar/2003:13:55:15 -0500] Started "/usr/lib/cups/cgi-bin/admin.cgi" (pid=24
16)
I [29/Mar/2003:13:55:20 -0500] Started "/usr/lib/cups/cgi-bin/admin.cgi" (pid=24
17)
I [29/Mar/2003:13:55:23 -0500] Started "/usr/lib/cups/cgi-bin/admin.cgi" (pid=24
18)
I [29/Mar/2003:13:55:25 -0500] Setting SecondLaserJet device-uri to "parallel:/d
ev/lp0" (was "".)
I [29/Mar/2003:13:55:25 -0500] Setting SecondLaserJet printer-is-accepting-jobs
to 1 (was 0.)
```

FIGURE 25.18

CUPS `page_log` lists print jobs.

```
MyLaserJet root 1 [29/Mar/2003:13:46:32 -0500] 1 1
MyLaserJet root 2 [29/Mar/2003:13:47:18 -0500] 1 1
MyLaserJet root 3 [29/Mar/2003:13:50:10 -0500] 1 1
MyLaserJet root 4 [29/Mar/2003:13:50:34 -0500] 1 1
~
~
~
~
~
~
~
~
~
~
~
~
~
~
~
~
~
"/var/log/cups/page_log" 4L, 208C
```

Using the Line Print Daemon

The default print server for Red Hat Linux is CUPS. Since CUPS took over as the default for the first time on Red Hat Linux 9, I assume that many of you still prefer to use the Line Print Daemon (LPD). While LPD has served Linux well, it does not have the capabilities of CUPS with respect to print groups or classes. CUPS allows you to work with IPP, which is the evolving standard for print servers on most operating systems.

The LPD system includes only one RPM package, `LPRng-*`. If you want to use LPD, install this package. The key LPD configuration file is `/etc/printcap`, which is part of the basic `setup-*` RPM package. You can edit this directly or use the `redhat-config-printer` utility. Once you've configured a printer, you can maintain that printer directly from the command-line interface with commands such as `lpr`, `lpq`, `lpc`, and `lprm`.

SETTING LPD AS THE DEFAULT

The `cupsd` daemon is active by default in Red Hat Linux 9. If you prefer LPD, you'll need to deactivate `cupsd` and activate `lpd` with the `service cups stop` and `service lpd start` commands. Next, deactivate the `cups-lpd` daemon with the `chkconfig cups-lpd off` command. Then, switch the print service with the `redhat-switch-printer` utility.

If you want to make the change permanent, make sure that Linux is set to start `lpd` at the desired runlevels by using the `chkconfig` command. See Chapter 13 for more information on `chkconfig`.

The LPD Configuration Files

While veteran Linux users often edit basic configuration files directly in a text editor, LPD uses fairly obscure commands, as shown in Figure 25.19.

FIGURE 25.19

A sample LPD configuration file (`/etc/printcap`)

```
HPLaser:\
        :ml#0:\
        :mx#0:\
        :sd=/var/spool/lpd/HPLaser:\
        :af=/var/spool/lpd/HPLaser/HPLaser.acct:\
        :sh:\
        :lp=/dev/lp0:\
        :lpd_bounce=true:\
        :if=/usr/share/printconf/util/mf_wrapper:

printer:\
        :ml#0:\
        :mx#0:\
        :sd=/var/spool/lpd/printer:\
        :af=/var/spool/lpd/printer/printer.acct:\
        :sh:\
        :lp=/dev/lp0:\
        :lpd_bounce=true:\
        :if=/usr/share/printconf/util/mf_wrapper:

printer1:\
        :ml#0:\
        :mx#0:\
```

Red Hat actually includes two configuration files for LPD printers: `/etc/printcap` and `/etc/printcap.local`. If you use `redhat-config-printers`, the results are written directly to (and over-writes anything in) `/etc/printcap`.

If you also want to configure printers by directly editing a configuration file, you should type the needed commands into `/etc/printcap.local`. The contents of this file are included in `/etc/printcap` when you restart the `lpd` daemon.

There are a number of programming codes in a typical `/etc/printcap` file. Some of them are shown in Table 25.13.

TABLE 25.13: *`/ETC/PRINTCAP`* PROGRAMMING CODES

CODE	DESCRIPTION
:	Divides code lines in an `/etc/printcap` command.
\	Connects two lines together; it "escapes" the effect of a new line.
af	Associated with an accounting filter (`af`).
if	Uses an input filter (`if`) for a specific printer.
lp	Indicates the line print (`lp`) device associated with the printer.
lpd_bounce	Sends print jobs through a filter if set to true.
ml	Checks for non-printable characters; if set to a value other than 0, it will prevent printing of most binary files.
mx	Specifies the maximum file size; if set to 0, there's no limit.
sd	Indicates the spool directory.
sh	Suppresses headers.
pl	Specifies the page length, in lines.
pw	Specifies the page width, in characters.

In other words, there are three command lines in Figure 25.18; the backslash is used to continue a command from one line to another. For example, the following commands are read as if they were on the same line:

```
printer:\
       :ml#0
```

There are two other major LPD configuration files. The default versions of these files are good for most purposes. In most cases, you can change what you need in `/etc/printcap` or in the application that you're using. Since these files are rarely edited, we'll just mention their purpose. The `/etc/lpd.conf` file notes the default settings for printers. The `/etc/lpd.perms` file sets permissions for the LPD spooler.

NOTE *If you're using CUPS, `/etc/printcap` includes a simple list of configured printers and printer classes.*

Printer Management

Four basic commands are associated with the LPD: the Line Printer Request, `lpr`; the Line Printer Query, `lpq`; the Line Printer Remove, `lprm`; and the Line Printer Control, `lpc`. These are sometimes known as the lp commands.

NOTE   *If you're using CUPS and have activated the* `cups-lpd` *service in* `/etc/xinetd.d`*, these commands don't work quite the same, but should give you a similar result.*

LPR

When you have Linux read the contents of a file with the `cat` command, the shell sends the result to standard output, which normally means that you see the result on your screen. In contrast, when you use `lpr`, the shell sends the result to a spool file on the local computer, then on to a print server computer, and finally to the printer. The `lpr` command is effectively a client. When it produces a spool file, the result is processed by the `lpd` server on a local or remote network.

Therefore, when you run a command such as `lpr file`, the shell sends the result to the default printer as configured in `/etc/printcap`. Alternatively, you can send the print job to a different printer. For example, if colorprinter is configured in `/etc/printcap`, the following command sends the job to that printer:

```
# lpr -Pcolorprinter file1
```

NOTE   *When using the* `lpr` *command to specify a printer, there's no space between the* `-P` *and the name of the printer.*

Other variations on the `lpr` command are shown in Table 25.14.

TABLE 25.14: *LPR* COMMANDS

COMMAND	RESULT
`lpr -h file1`	Prints `file1` without a job control page, which normally contains the user account and hostname of the source computer. The job control page is also known as the *burst* page.
`lpr -Pother file1`	Prints `file1` to the printer named *other*, as defined in the `/etc/printcap` file.
`lpr -s file1`	Creates a symbolic link to `file1`, which avoids creating a spool file. This was required for larger (>1MB) files on the Berkeley Standard Distribution version of `lpr`. Red Hat Linux 9 uses the LPRng program, which makes this unnecessary.

LPQ

The `lpq` command gives you the current print queue. There are three basic options, as shown in Table 25.15. This command also includes a list of job numbers, which you might need for the `lprm` command.

TABLE 25.15: *LPQ* COMMAND EXAMPLES

COMMAND	RESULT
`lpq`	Returns the current print queue for the default printer, as defined in your `/etc/printcap` file.
`lpq -P` *`printer`*	Returns the print queue for the named *printer*. Uses the name as defined in your `/etc/printcap` file.

LPRM

If a print job isn't already in your printer's memory, the `lprm` command can delete print jobs currently in your queue. With `lprm`, you can remove a print job in one of three ways: by print job number, by user, or by printer. Table 25.16 shows examples of this command.

TABLE 25.16: *LPRM* COMMAND EXAMPLES

COMMAND	RESULT
`lprm 188`	Removes print job 188, as defined in the output to the `lpq` command
`lprm -P hp2 mj`	Removes print jobs of user mj from the printer labeled hp2 in your `/etc/printcap` file

LPC

The `lpc` command allows you to control a number of characteristics of each printer. As shown in Table 25.17, this command lets you check printer status, kill active print jobs, or even redirect jobs to a different printer.

TABLE 25.17: *LPC* COMMAND EXAMPLES

COMMAND	RESULT
`lpc -P canon1 status`	Displays the status of the printer named *canon1*. In other words, the output tells you whether you can send print jobs to a queue, the number of jobs in the queue, whether the printer will accept jobs, and communication status with the printer.
`lpc disable`	Disables sending jobs ("spooling") to a print queue for the default printer. Opposite of `lpc enable`.
`lpc start`	Restarts transfers from the print queue.
`lpc stop`	Stops communication between the print queue and your printer.

Red Hat's Printer Tool

Because the commands associated with /etc/cups/cupsd.conf and /etc/printcap is so obscure, the more popular option for configuring CUPS or LPD printers is a graphical tool. Red Hat's tool is based on redhat-config-printer (and redhat-config-printer-gui) available through the RPM of the same name. You can run this command from a text or a GUI command-line console. While the look and feel are different (see Figures 25.20 and 25.21), the information is the same.

TIP   The print system configured by redhat-config-printer is based on the active print daemon, which can be changed through the redhat-switch-printer utility.

FIGURE 25.20

redhat-config-printer, command-line version

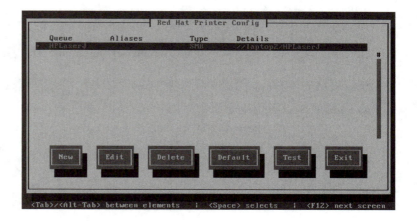

FIGURE 25.21

redhat-config-printer, GUI version

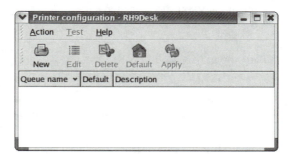

It's easy to use redhat-config-printer to set up a new printer. The following steps are based on the GUI version of this tool, which starts in a Printer Configuration window:

1. Click New; when you see the Add A New Print Queue dialog box, click Forward to continue.

2. In the Queue Name dialog box, enter a short name for your printer and a description, similar to what is shown in Figure 25.22. When you're ready, click Forward to continue.

FIGURE 25.22

Adding a printer queue

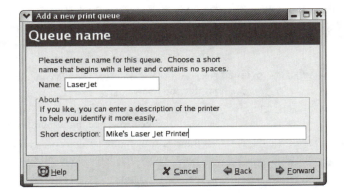

3. In the Queue Type dialog box, you'll see available printer ports, similar to what's shown in Figure 25.23. For example, /dev/lp0 corresponds to the first parallel port. If you're configuring a local printer, select the available port of your choice and then click Forward. If that does not meet your needs, try one of the following alternatives:

FIGURE 25.23

Selecting a queue type

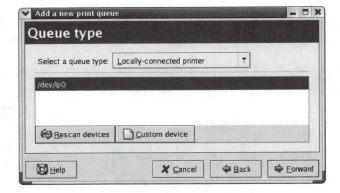

◆ If you don't see your port, first try the Rescan Devices option.

◆ If that does not work, you can click Custom Device and enter the device associated with your printer port.

◆ If you want to select a network printer, click the Select A Queue Type drop-down text box. Available choices are listed in Table 25.18.

TABLE 25.18: NETWORK QUEUE TYPES

TYPE	DESCRIPTION
Networked CUPS (IPP)	For printers on a remote CUPS server; requires the server host or domain name and IPP path.
Networked Unix (LPD)	For printers on a remote LPD server; requires the server host or domain name as well as the name of the remote queue.
Networked Windows (SMB)	For printers on a remote Microsoft Windows print server; should detect shared printers automatically.
Networked Novell (NCP)	For printers on a remote Novell print server; requires the server host or domain name, the queue name, and the authorized username and password.
Networked JetDirect	For printers on a remote JetDirect print server that's directly connected to the network; requires the name of the JetDirect printer.

4. In the Printer Model dialog box, select the make and manufacturer for your printer. Select the driver best suited to your printer, using these guidelines, and then click Forward to continue:

   ◆ Some printers work with the PostScript print driver; printers that process raw print data can use the Raw Print Queue driver; generic drivers are also available for text and various dot-matrix printers.

   ◆ To select a specific model, click on the Generic (Click To Select Manufacturer) text box; a series of manufacturers are shown, similar to Figure 25.24. Once you make your selection, you'll be able to select a print model that most closely matches your printer.

FIGURE 25.24

Selecting a printer manufacturer

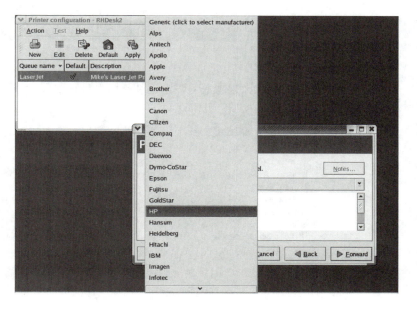

5. You'll now see the Finish, And Create The New Print Queue dialog box. It will include a summary of your selections, similar to Figure 25.25. If you're satisfied with your selections, click Apply.

FIGURE 25.25

Print configuration summary

6. You're given an opportunity to print a test page. It's a good idea; if you're connected to your printer, click Yes.

You're taken back to the Printer Configuration dialog box. You should now see an entry for your new printer. You can edit the settings; simply highlight the printer and click Edit. This opens the Edit A Print Queue dialog box for the printer that you just configured. The five tabs in this dialog box are summarized in Table 25.19.

TABLE 25.19: EDITING PRINTER SETTINGS

TAB	DESCRIPTION
Queue Name	Lets you specify the name of the print queue
Queue Type	Allows you to revise the device, even to a networked printer
Queue Options	Lets you configure basic settings for banner pages, margins, and the filter
Printer Driver	Lets you change the driver
Driver Options	Allows you to specify more driver settings

Before leaving `redhat-config-printer`, be sure to click Apply. This action writes your changes to `/etc/cups/cupsd.conf` for CUPS or `/etc/printcap` for LPD and then restarts the appropriate print daemon.

Summary

In this chapter, we examined the two major options for print servers, CUPS and LPD. CUPS is the new default Red Hat Linux print server. LPD, which has been the default for years, will be removed in a future release of Red Hat Linux, so it is important for you to learn about CUPS.

CUPS is short for the Common Unix Print System. It provides a common way for Linux and other Unix-type operating systems to work with the Internet Print Protocol (IPP). IPP is becoming the standard print server for a wide variety of operating systems, so it makes sense to move to CUPS.

CUPS includes a graphical browser-based tool available on port 631. With the CUPS tool, you can configure printers, classes of different printers, and print jobs. Print devices and drivers are available for a number of different connections and protocols. You can even configure a group of printers as a class; print jobs are automatically sent to the first available printer in that class.

CUPS configuration files are stored in the `/etc/cups` directory. While the main CUPS configuration file, `cupsd.conf`, is long, it is based on the same format as Apache configuration files. A substantial number of settings are available for everything from job size to logs to security.

Once you've configured printers and print classes, it's easy to use the CUPS web-based configuration tool to manage printers and print jobs. For example, in the Jobs section, you can hold a print job to allow a higher priority job through. Alternatively, you can use `redhat-config-printer`. That all depends on the daemon setting shown in `redhat-switch-printer`. You can also check the status of current printers with the `lpstat` and `lpadmin` commands. If you activate the `cups-lpd` daemon, you can also use several basic LPD-style commands.

The Line Print Daemon is based on the `LPRng-*` RPM. You can configure printers by directly editing `/etc/printcap.local`, or you can use `redhat-config-printer` to write printer commands directly to `/etc/printcap`. You can manage the printers and queues with several basic commands, including `lpr`, `lpq`, `lprm`, and `lpc`.

In Chapter 26, we'll look at mail servers and clients, with a focus on configuring sendmail for your network.

Chapter 26

Mail Services

IN THIS CHAPTER, WE'LL look at one of the essential applications for any computer that is connected to a network: e-mail. Various server services are used to send and to receive e-mail, and each server is associated with one or more protocols. While e-mail clients are relatively straightforward to configure, e-mail servers have a number of rich and complex options.

There are several basic TCP/IP protocols related to e-mail. The two most common protocols for receiving e-mail are the Post Office Protocol (POP) and the Internet Message Access Protocol (IMAP). The Simple Mail Transfer Protocol (SMTP) is an important protocol for sending mail from your network.

The most common SMTP e-mail server on the Internet is sendmail. While the basic sendmail configuration file is complex, Red Hat Linux includes a macro file that is easy to customize based on what you need. You can edit this file and then use a macro processor to generate a custom configuration file for sendmail. This configuration file also helps you address security needs by setting up responses for FQDN that you can't verify and domains where you don't want to send mail.

There are two basic servers for incoming e-mail, based on the IMAP4 and POP3 protocols. You can create your own incoming e-mail server, or you can set up your e-mail clients to use incoming e-mail servers from an outside e-mail provider. Red Hat Linux includes both of these servers, in regular and secure versions, in one RPM package.

Most computer users are familiar with at least one e-mail client. The principles behind them are the same. They take the e-mail data and format it in a fashion to which you can easily read and reply. Linux includes both text and graphical e-mail clients. This chapter covers the following topics:

◆ Examining general mail services

◆ Configuring sendmail

◆ Using incoming e-mail servers

◆ Configuring mail clients

Examining General Mail Services

Three kinds of mail services are available: Message Transfer Agents (MTA), Mail Delivery Agents (MDA), and Mail User Agents (MUA).

An MTA is a server that sends e-mail through a network. Linux uses MTA agents such as sendmail, which uses the SMTP protocol to send e-mail over a TCP/IP network like the Internet.

An MDA is a mail processor. It takes messages from the Internet and stores them in servers or spools where mail readers (a.k.a MUAs)—such as pine, Mozilla Mail, KMail, and Evolution—can read them. The most common example of an MDA is procmail. While the `procmail-*` RPM is installed by default, it works seamlessly with a properly configured sendmail (and other outgoing e-mail server) package.

An MUA is an application that helps you send and receive e-mail through these servers. Most users are familiar with at least one MUA, like those listed, or Lotus Notes, Netscape, or pine. When you prepare and send an e-mail message, you're using an MUA to send a message to an MTA such as sendmail.

The two major protocols for receiving e-mail are POP3 and IMAP4. Mail servers configured to either protocol are simply one step in the MDA process.

NOTE   *All you need to do to configure POP3 or IMAP4 is enable their respective configuration files (`pop3s` and `imaps`) in the `/etc/xinted.d` directory. See Chapter 23 for more information.*

Key Protocols

A substantial number of TCP/IP protocols are involved in sending an e-mail message from one user to another. We've mentioned three of them: SMTP, POP3, and IMAP4.

As a Linux administrator, you've probably set up an e-mail server at some point in time. While sendmail is the most important of the SMTP servers, several alternatives are available, including Exim, Postfix, and Qmail.

As a Linux administrator, you may also help users configure their e-mail clients. Generally, you'll need to know the names of any incoming e-mail servers on your network or with your ISP. This may include the name of the mail exchanger (`MX`) record that you created in your DNS server in Chapter 24. But this chapter is focused on outgoing mail.

Older mail servers used the Unix-to-Unix Copy Protocol (UUCP), which sent messages directly from computer to computer. If the message had to go to a different network, you would have to specify each computer on the path. Needless to say, this has become unwieldy with the expansion of the Internet.

Alternate Mail Servers

While the rest of this chapter is focused on sendmail, there are alternatives, based on the search for the easy-to-configure e-mail server. Packages for each of these systems (except the commercial version of sendmail, which is Sendmail) are available from sources such as `www.rpmfind.net`.

Commercial Sendmail   Unlike the version included with Red Hat Linux, the commercial version of Sendmail is designed for the enterprise. In other words, it can help you serve many thousands of users. It is even configurable for mobile clients. More information is available at `www.sendmail.com`.

Exim   The Exim MTA was developed at Cambridge (U.K.) and is licensed under the GPL. While based on an older MTA known as Smail, it can also help you verify user addresses and refuse e-mail.

This helps you minimize spam sent to users on your system. More information is available at `www.exim.org`.

Postfix   The Postfix MTA is an alternative to sendmail that is probably already installed on your Red Hat Linux system. It is the successor to the VMailer and IBM Secure Mailer systems. As described in Chapter 19, you can use `redhat-switchmail` to switch between these servers. You can find more information at `www.postfix.org`.

Qmail   The Qmail MTA is another alternative to sendmail. According to `www.qmail.org`, Qmail is used by an impressive list of Internet sites. The developer, D. J. Bernstein, has offered a cash reward for the first person to find a security hole in this system (`cr.yp.to/qmail/guarantee.html`).

Smail   The Smail MTA is reportedly easier to configure than sendmail. It also includes support for blocking messages. In addition, it helps you protect yourself from "spoofed" messages that try to mask themselves as coming from trusted sites. While no official website exists for this MTA, the developers can be found at `www.planix.com`.

Configuring sendmail

As with most complex Linux services, sendmail components can be installed from a number of RPM packages. There are many key configuration files, over and above the `sendmail.cf` configuration file and `sendmail.mc` macro.

With the latest version of sendmail, the configuration files are now split into two parts. When sendmail receives e-mail, it uses `sendmail.cf`. When sendmail sends e-mail, it uses `submit.cf`.

Once you get sendmail up and running, you can modify various configuration files to promote security.

NOTE   *This is far from a comprehensive discussion on sendmail; there are 1000-page books available just on this service. One good reference is* Linux Sendmail Administration, *by Craig Hunt (Sybex, 2001).*

Packages

The only RPM that you need for a working sendmail configuration is the `sendmail-*` RPM, whose packages are installed by default. Available sendmail packages are listed in Table 26.1; as you might remember from Chapter 10, you can use the `rpm -q` *packagename* command to see if they're installed. Once they're installed, you can use the `rpm -ql` *packagename* command to see the associated files.

TABLE 26.1: SENDMAIL RPM PACKAGES

PACKAGE	FUNCTION
`sendmail-*`	The sendmail MTA software
`sendmail-cf-*`	Tools and templates for creating a wide variety of sendmail configuration files
`sendmail-devel-*`	Development libraries for sendmail
`sendmail-doc-*`	Release notes, FAQ, and other sendmail documentation

Basic Configuration Files

There is more to sendmail than just the basic configuration file, `sendmail.cf`, and the macro file, `sendmail.mc`. As with many other daemons, sendmail has a control file in `/etc/sysconfig`. You can set it to forward e-mail to a different user through `/etc/aliases`. Many other configuration files are stored in `/etc/mail`.

BASIC */ETC/SYSCONFIG/SENDMAIL*

The `/etc/sysconfig/sendmail` file is fairly simple:

```
DAEMON=yes
QUEUE=1h
```

The `DAEMON=yes` entry sets sendmail to listen for messages on TCP/IP port 25, which is associated with SMTP. The `QUEUE=1h` entry tells sendmail to try to deliver queued mail every hour.

SENDMAIL ALIASES

The `/etc/aliases` file is also simple. It specifies the users that should really receive e-mail. For example, if you try to send mail to a service such as `ftp@localhost`, the following entry redirects that mail to `root@localhost`:

```
ftp:      root
```

Or, you can redirect e-mail from a former to a current employee:

```
byeltsin:    vputin
```

SENDMAIL */ETC/MAIL* CONFIGURATION FILES

There are a number of files in `/etc/mail` that you can use to configure sendmail or to set up databases to regulate how sendmail works. If you want to enable these configuration files, you generally need an entry in the `sendmail.mc` macro file. If there is a `.db` file, you can in most cases convert a text file such as `access` to `access.db` by using the `makemap` command.

access and access.db   Configures domains or e-mail addresses; e-mail from these sources can be dropped (`DISCARD`), rejected with an error message (`REJECT`), or sent to the specified address (`RELAY`). You can minimize unwanted e-mail by dropping or rejecting it from specific domains or e-mail addresses. Look at the `/etc/mail/access` file for examples.

domaintable and domaintable.db   Maps two different domains. These files are useful if you've converted your domain name and others are still sending e-mail to your users' old e-mail addresses. If you've just converted your domain name from `dictatorsrus.com` to `democracyisus.com`, you could add the following line to your `domaintable` file:

```
dictatorsrus.com     democracyisus.com
```

helpfile   Provides help for commands available at the sendmail prompt. You can get to the sendmail prompt with the `telnet localhost 25` command.

local-host-names   Contains aliases or other hostnames for your sendmail server. Just enter other names for your sendmail server computer on individual lines in this file.

mailertable and **mailertable.db**   Lets you specify an unusual e-mail server type for a specific address; rarely used.

Makefile   Lets you compile different options; an alternate to the sendmail macro processor.

sendmail.cf and **sendmail.mc**   Allows you to configure sendmail; **sendmail.cf** is the configuration file; **sendmail.mc** is a macro file that can be processed into the configuration file. More information on these files is available later in this chapter.

statistics   Contains statistics for sendmail usage. Run the **mailstats** command to read this file.

submit.cf and **submit.mc**   Allows you to limit sendmail usage to specific groups. The syntax in the default **submit.mc** file is the same as in **sendmail.mc**. More information on **submit.mc** is available later in this chapter.

trusted-users   Lets you list users who can send e-mail on behalf of your other users. Rarely used; would you ever want to give anyone this kind of power?

virtualusertable and **virtualusertable.db**   Supports e-mail forwarding; similar to the `/etc/aliases` file, for external users.

Understanding *sendmail.mc*

The `/etc/mail/sendmail.cf` configuration file can be intimidating—it is on the order of 2000 lines long! By comparison, the `/etc/mail/sendmail.mc` file, at about 70 lines, is easy to read and understand. Once you've configured this file to your liking, you can use an appropriate make command or the m4 macro processor to generate the custom `sendmail.cf` file that you need. Take a look at this file; I've included additional comments where appropriate. As you probably won't need to modify most of this file, my comments are limited. As sendmail is a complex topic, please refer to *Linux Sendmail Administration*, by Craig Hunt, for more information.

NOTE   *The quote marks inside the parenthesis in* sendmail.mc *may not be what you expect: they start with a back quote (`) and end with a single quote (') mark. The back quote is the character above the Tab key on a U.S. keyboard.*

The `divert(-1)` command is a standard way to start the `sendmail.mc` file; if paired with `divert(0)`, all lines between these commands are ignored as comments.

```
divert(-1)dnl
```

All lines that start with `dnl` are comments; these particular comments include one way to process the `sendmail.mc` file; alternatively, you can still regenerate `/etc/mail/sendmail.cf` with the m4 `sendmail.mc > sendmail.cf` command.

```
dnl #
dnl # This is the sendmail macro config file for m4. If you make changes to
dnl # /etc/mail/sendmail.mc, you will need to regenerate the
dnl # /etc/mail/sendmail.cf file by confirming that the sendmail-cf package is
dnl # installed and then performing a
dnl #
dnl #     make -C /etc/mail
dnl #
```

The following `include` command adds the `cf.m4` command as a macro processing prototype; by default, it requires installation of the `sendmail-cf-*` RPM

```
include(`/usr/share/sendmail-cf/m4/cf.m4')dnl
```

The `VERSIONID` is the label associated with each sendmail configuration file

```
VERSIONID(`setup for Red Hat Linux ')dnl
```

Naturally, any `OSTYPE` command specifies the operating system, in this case, `linux`.

```
OSTYPE(`linux')dnl
```

The `define` command shown below coordinates your sendmail server with an outgoing e-mail server, presumably outside your network. If you want to activate this command, delete the `dnl` in front of `define` and replace `smtp.your.provider` with the outgoing (SMTP) e-mail server address of your ISP.

```
dnl #
dnl # Uncomment and edit the following line if your outgoing mail needs to
dnl # be sent out through an external mail server:
dnl #
dnl define(`SMART_HOST', `smtp.your.provider')
dnl #
```

Generally, no changes are required to the commands shown below; see *Linux Sendmail Administration* for more information.

```
define(`confDEF_USER_ID', ``8:12'')dnl
define(`confTRUSTED_USER', `smmsp')dnl
dnl define(`confAUTO_REBUILD')dnl
define(`confTO_CONNECT', `1m')dnl
define(`confTRY_NULL_MX_LIST',true)dnl
define(`confDONT_PROBE_INTERFACES',true)dnl
define(`PROCMAIL_MAILER_PATH',`/usr/bin/procmail')dnl
define(`ALIAS_FILE', `/etc/aliases')dnl
dnl define(`STATUS_FILE', `/etc/mail/statistics')dnl
define(`UUCP_MAILER_MAX', `2000000')dnl
define(`confUSERDB_SPEC', `/etc/mail/userdb.db')dnl
define(`confPRIVACY_FLAGS', `authwarnings,novrfy,noexpn,restrictqrun')dnl
```

The two commands shown below that start with `define(`confAUTH_OPTIONS'` are mutually exclusive. TLS is Transport Layer Security, which is the successor to SSL, the Secure Socket Layer.

```
define(`confAUTH_OPTIONS', `A')dnl
dnl #
dnl # The following allows relaying if the user authenticates, and disallows
dnl # plaintext authentication (PLAIN/LOGIN) on non-TLS links
dnl #
dnl define(`confAUTH_OPTIONS', `A p')dnl
dnl #
dnl # PLAIN is the preferred plaintext authentication method and used by
```

```
dnl # Mozilla Mail and Evolution, though Outlook Express and other MUAs do
dnl # use LOGIN. Other mechanisms should be used if the connection is not
dnl # guaranteed secure.
dnl #
```

If you need to prevent plain-text logins to your sendmail server, change these two commands so they read:

```
dnl define(`confAUTH_OPTIONS', `A')dnl
define(`confAUTH_OPTIONS', `A p')dnl
```

Now let's continue on with the default `sendmail.mc` file. The following two commands relate to authorization methods:

```
dnl TRUST_AUTH_MECH(`EXTERNAL DIGEST-MD5 CRAM-MD5 LOGIN PLAIN')dnl
dnl define(`confAUTH_MECHANISMS', `EXTERNAL GSSAPI DIGEST- MD5 CRAM-MD5 LOGIN
➥ PLAIN')dnl
```

The following commands allow you to use any SSL certificates on your system with sendmail. For more information on SSL certificates, see Chapter 30. The certificates that you can create in that chapter for Apache can also apply here.

```
dnl #
dnl # Rudimentary information on creating certificates for sendmail TLS:
dnl #     make -C /usr/share/ssl/certs usage
dnl #
dnl define(`confCACERT_PATH',`/usr/share/ssl/certs')
dnl define(`confCACERT',`/usr/share/ssl/certs/ca-bundle.crt')
dnl define(`confSERVER_CERT',`/usr/share/ssl/certs/sendmail.pem')
dnl define(`confSERVER_KEY', `/usr/share/ssl/certs/sendmail.pem')
dnl #
```

The following `define` command supports integration with the Lightweight Directory Assistance Protocol (LDAP), which provides detailed user information and can therefore replace the `/etc/aliases` and the `/etc/mail/virtusertable.db` files shown below. Integration of sendmail and LDAP is a complex topic beyond the scope of this book.

```
dnl # This allows sendmail to use a keyfile that is shared with OpenLDAP's
dnl # slapd, which requires the file to be readble by group ldap
dnl #
dnl define(`confDONT_BLAME_SENDMAIL',`groupreadablekeyfile')dnl
dnl #
```

The following commands specify actions associated with e-mail that can't find the destination.

```
dnl define(`confTO_QUEUEWARN', `4h')dnl
dnl define(`confTO_QUEUERETURN', `5d')dnl
dnl define(`confQUEUE_LA', `12')dnl
dnl define(`confREFUSE_LA', `18')dnl
define(`confTO_IDENT', `0')dnl
dnl FEATURE(delay_checks)dnl
FEATURE(`no_default_msa',`dnl')dnl
```

This FEATURE command sets the default sendmail shell, smrsh. The mailertable.db associates different domain names.

```
FEATURE(`smrsh', `/usr/sbin/smrsh')dnl
FEATURE(`mailertable', `hash -o/etc/mail/mailertable.db')dnl
FEATURE(`virtusertable', `hash -o/etc/mail/virtusertable.db')dnl
FEATURE(redirect)dnl
FEATURE(always_add_domain)dnl
FEATURE(use_cw_file)dnl
FEATURE(use_ct_file)dnl
dnl #
dnl # The -t option will retry delivery if e.g. the user runs over his quota.
dnl #
FEATURE(local_procmail,`',`procmail -t -Y -a $h -d $u')dnl
FEATURE(`access_db', `hash -T<TMPF> -o/etc/mail/access.db')dnl
FEATURE(`blacklist_recipients')dnl
```

If the root user tries to log in; the EXPOSED_USER command requires the full e-mail address.

```
EXPOSED_USER(`root')dnl
dnl #
dnl # The following causes sendmail to only listen on the IPv4 loopback address
dnl # 127.0.0.1 and not on any other network devices. Remove the loopback
dnl # address restriction to accept email from the internet or intranet.
dnl #
```

By default, sendmail listens for and processes e-mail only from the local computer. If you want this sendmail server to work for other computers on your network, add a dnl in front of this command and remove it from one of the following commands.

```
DAEMON_OPTIONS(`Port=smtp,Addr=127.0.0.1, Name=MTA')dnl
dnl #
dnl # The following causes sendmail to additionally listen to port 587 for
dnl # mail from MUAs that authenticate. Roaming users who can't reach their
dnl # preferred sendmail daemon due to port 25 being blocked or redirected find
dnl # this useful.
dnl #
```

If you activate the following DAEMON_OPTIONS command, sendmail will listen for e-mail from e-mail users who send their accounts and passwords; that is, whose e-mail mangers authenticate. This process works through TCP/IP port 587.

```
dnl DAEMON_OPTIONS(`Port=submission, Name=MSA, M=Ea')dnl
dnl #
dnl # The following causes sendmail to additionally listen to port 465, but
dnl # starting immediately in TLS mode upon connecting. Port 25 or 587 followed
dnl # by STARTTLS is preferred, but roaming clients using Outlook Express can't
dnl # do STARTTLS on ports other than 25. Mozilla Mail can ONLY use STARTTLS
dnl # and doesn't support the deprecated smtps; Evolution <1.1.1 uses smtps
```

```
dnl # when SSL is enabled-- STARTTLS support is available in version 1.1.1.
dnl #
dnl # For this to work your OpenSSL certificates must be configured.
dnl #
```

If you want to require secure connections to your sendmail server, you could activate this command, which requires the use of TLS. However, as noted in the comments, you should not activate this command if your users work with Microsoft Outlook Express or Evolution below version 1.1.1.

```
dnl DAEMON_OPTIONS(`Port=smtps, Name=TLSMTA, M=s')dnl
dnl #
dnl # The following causes sendmail to additionally listen on the IPv6 loopback
dnl # device. Remove the loopback address restriction listen to the network.
dnl #
dnl # NOTE: binding both IPv4 and IPv6 daemon to the same port requires
dnl #        a kernel patch
dnl #
```

Activate the command shown below if you've configured your network to use IPv6, as described in Chapter 20. This is the IPv6 equivalent of the default command noted earlier that accepts e-mail only from the local computer.

```
dnl DAEMON_OPTIONS(`port=smtp,Addr=::1, Name=MTA-v6, Family=inet6')dnl
dnl #
dnl # We strongly recommend not accepting unresolvable domains if you want to
dnl # protect yourself from spam. However, the laptop and users on computers
dnl # that do not have 24x7 DNS do need this.
dnl #
```

This FEATURE command means that sendmail doesn't do a reverse DNS lookup on an e-mail. Unless you have reliable access to a DNS server and can accept the extra traffic, keep the command as is.

```
FEATURE(`accept_unresolvable_domains')dnl
dnl #
```

This FEATURE command allows the use of the MX records for a mail server as specified in a DNS database. See Chapter 24 for more information on DNS.

```
dnl FEATURE(`relay_based_on_MX')dnl
dnl #
dnl # Also accept email sent to "localhost.localdomain" as local email.
dnl #
```

The LOCAL_DOMAIN command specifies an alias for the local computer; localhost.localdomain is a default alias in /etc/hosts.

```
LOCAL_DOMAIN(`localhost.localdomain')dnl
dnl #
dnl # The following example makes mail from this host andany additional
dnl # specified domains appear to be sent from mydomain.com
dnl #
```

This MASQUERADE_AS command changes the label that sendmail attaches to your outgoing e-mail. If you activate this command, change mydomain.com to the label you desire; typically used to specify e-mail from a subdomain. For example, if I'm on the mommabears.com network, I could set MASQUERADE_AS to linux.mommabears.com.

```
dnl MASQUERADE_AS(`mydomain.com')dnl
dnl #
dnl # masquerade not just the headers, but the envelope as well
dnl #
dnl FEATURE(masquerade_envelope)dnl
dnl #
dnl # masquerade not just @mydomainalias.com, but @*.mydomainalias.com as well
dnl #
dnl FEATURE(masquerade_entire_domain)dnl
dnl #
```

With the MASQUERADE_DOMAIN command, you can tell sendmail to handle e-mail addresses from other domains in the same way. For example, these commands, if active, set e-mail from these subdomains (localhost, localhost.localdomain, mydomainalias.com, and mydomain.lan) to the domain specified earlier with the MASQUERADE_AS command.

```
dnl MASQUERADE_DOMAIN(localhost)dnl
dnl MASQUERADE_DOMAIN(localhost.localdomain)dnl
dnl MASQUERADE_DOMAIN(mydomainalias.com)dnl
dnl MASQUERADE_DOMAIN(mydomain.lan)dnl
```

The following MAILER commands specify the type of server that actually sends out the e-mail.

```
MAILER(smtp)dnl
MAILER(procmail)dnl
```

Revising *sendmail.mc*

Before you start, it's a good idea to make backups of your sendmail.cf and sendmail.mc files in your /etc/mail directory.

There are a couple of lines that you should change in the default sendmail.mc configuration file. First, this line limits the sendmail server to sending e-mail only to the specified address; 127.0.0.1 is the loopback address for the local computer:

```
DAEMON_OPTIONS(`Port=smtp,Addr=127.0.0.1, Name=MTA')
```

If you have reliable DNS access and high-speed Internet access, comment out this next line. It keeps sendmail from checking the domain associated with incoming e-mail addresses. You can comment out the line by putting dnl in front; when you restart the sendmail service, sendmail automatically starts checking domains:

```
FEATURE(`accept_unresolvable_domains')dnl
```

Understanding *submit.mc*

The `submit.mc` is the macro file used to create `submit.cf`, the sendmail configuration file for outgoing e-mail. It is processed in the same way as `sendmail.mc`; fortunately, this file is simpler. Generally, you don't need to make any changes to this file—but it's helpful to understand this file to know what other files to configure.

These first commands are essentially the same as the first commands in `sendmail.mc` and are explained in that section of this chapter.

```
divert(-1)dnl
divert(0)dnl
include(`/usr/share/sendmail-cf/m4/cf.m4')
VERSIONID(`linux setup for Red Hat Linux')dnl
```

The `confCF_Version` command simply adds to the version name.

```
define(`confCF_VERSION', `Submit')dnl
```

This adds an operating system type, similar to the `OSTYPE(`linux')dnl` command in `sendmail.mc`.

```
define(`__OSTYPE__',`')dnl dirty hack to keep proto.m4 from complaining
```

`DECNET` is a network type common on older mainframe and microcomputers.

```
define(`_USE_DECNET_SYNTAX_', `1')dnl support DECnet
```

The `confTIME_ZONE` variable adds a time stamp.

```
define(`confTIME_ZONE', `USE_TZ')dnl
```

This setting avoids looking through any NIS list for users and passwords; the alternative source of usernames and passwords is `/etc/passwd`.

```
define(`confDONT_INIT_GROUPS', `True')dnl
```

This sets the location of the process identifier (PID) file.

```
define(`confPID_FILE', `/var/run/sm-client.pid')dnl
```

The `confDIRECT_SUBMISSION_MODIFIERS` variable assumes standard "canonical" host names.

```
dnl define(`confDIRECT_SUBMISSION_MODIFIERS',`C')
```

The `use_ct_file` FEATURE reads `/etc/mail/trusted-users` for standard users.

```
FEATURE(`use_ct_file')dnl
dnl
dnl If you use IPv6 only, change [127.0.0.1] to [IPv6:::1]
```

This notes the message submission program (`msp`) on the local computer (127.0.0.1).

```
FEATURE(`msp', `[127.0.0.1]')dnl
```

In most cases, you don't need to change anything in this file; if you do, please remember to back it up first! If you've installed the `sendmail-doc-*` RPM, more information on this file is available in `README.cf`, in the `/usr/share/doc/sendmail` directory.

Processing and Reactivating sendmail

If you haven't already done so, now is a good time to back up your current `sendmail.cf` configuration file. Once you've made the desired changes, you'll want to use the `m4` macro processor or the `make -C /etc/mail` command to create a new `sendmail.cf` file. Then, restart the `sendmail` daemon with the following commands.

```
# m4 /etc/mail/submit.mc > /etc/mail/submit.cf
# service sendmail restart
```

These commands won't work unless you've installed the `sendmail-cf-*` RPM.

Using Incoming E-mail Servers

Two basic incoming e-mail servers are in common use today. These servers correspond to the two major incoming e-mail protocols: POP3 and IMAP4. In Red Hat Linux, both servers are available as part of the `imap-*` RPM package, and are installed as an `xinetd` service (see Chapter 23).

You don't need to create your own e-mail server. You can set up yourself or your clients to use an e-mail server from a provider such as `mail.com` or `yahoo.com`. If you want to create your own e-mail server, install the `imap-*` RPM. Remember to activate its `xinetd` configuration with the `service servername on` command, and then run `service xinetd reload` to make sure `xinetd` rereads the appropriate configuration file.

If you have a DNS server on your LAN, you can also configure it with an MX entry in the appropriate `/var/named` database file. For more information on DNS, see Chapter 24.

The POP3 protocol is still more popular on the Internet. When you connect from an e-mail client, a POP3 server automatically downloads your e-mail. With most clients, you can choose to keep an original copy of the e-mail on the server.

In contrast, the IMAP4 protocol is more flexible. If you're using an IMAP4 server, you can organize your e-mail on folders on the server. You can search through different messages for keywords, and you can download the messages you want. This is useful for users with multiple computers who need a central database for their e-mail.

The POP3 E-mail Server

Once you've activated a POP3 server, you'll need to create accounts. Anyone who wants to use your POP3 server will require an account on your system. However, those users do not need a home directory.

As you might recall from Chapter 9, the `useradd username` command automatically creates a home directory for a new user. However, if you add a new user by directly editing `/etc/passwd`, you don't have to add a home directory. Then the `passwd username` command allows you to assign a new password.

Once you've created a user account, you'll need to tell your user to add the username and the FQDN of the computer that you've configured as the e-mail server to his or her e-mail client. The latter part of this chapter includes details on how to do so with various e-mail clients.

The IMAP4 E-mail Server

After you've activated an IMAP4 server, you'll need to create accounts (the same as you would with a POP3 server). If somebody wants to use your IMAP4 server, that person will need an account on your system. Unlike for a POP3 server, users on an IMAP4 server do need home directories on your system.

The `useradd` *username* command automatically creates a home directory for a new user, as detailed in Chapter 9. Then the `passwd` *username* command allows you to assign a new password.

When you've created the account, as you would with the POP3 server, you'll need to tell your user to add the username and the FQDN of the computer that you've configured as the e-mail server to his or her e-mail client.

Configuring Mail Clients

Most people use graphical e-mail clients, such as Evolution and Netscape. However, text-based e-mail clients are still popular in the worlds of Linux and Unix. Just as experienced Linux administrators prefer to work from the command-line interface, they often prefer to work with e-mail clients in text mode. While graphical e-mail can be pretty, a graphical e-mail to a large group of users can easily consume the capacity of many e-mail servers.

You may also need to help users configure their own e-mail clients; this should be an easier process.

Text-Based Clients

By default, you can use the `mail` program to send and receive e-mail. People who are newer to computers tend to use graphical e-mail clients. However, many users, especially in university and scientific settings, still use text-based e-mail clients. Perhaps the two most common text-based clients are `pine` and `elm`. Although Red Hat plans to delete it from a future release, `pine` (Program for Internet News and E-mail) is the more user-friendly of the text-based clients; therefore, it is what I cover here.

The `pine` client may not be installed on your installation of Red Hat Linux. It is easy to install from the `pine-*` RPM. Starting this e-mail client is easy with the `pine` command. Unfortunately, Red Hat has deprecated `pine`, which means you may need to convert to a different e-mail client in future versions of Red Hat Linux. Graphical e-mail clients are described in the next section; one good alternative text-based e-mail client is `mutt`.

The first time you run `pine`, you'll see an introduction followed by the main menu displayed in Figure 26.1. Examine the commands in the main part of the screen (?, C, I, L, A, S, and Q) as well as the command options at the bottom of the screen (?, P, R, O, >, N, and K).

NOTE   *The `pine` command menu is one place in Linux where case does not matter; for example,* **P** *works as well as* **p**.

As you can see, you can type **C** to start an e-mail message, **I** to view current messages, **L** to list current folders, and more. But the first step is to set up `pine` to read your e-mail. Type the **S** command. You'll see the Setup screen. Next, type **C** to begin basic configuration. You'll see a screen similar to Figure 26.2.

FIGURE 26.1

The pine
main menu

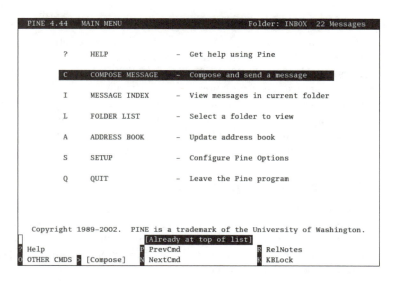

FIGURE 26.2

Basic pine
configuration

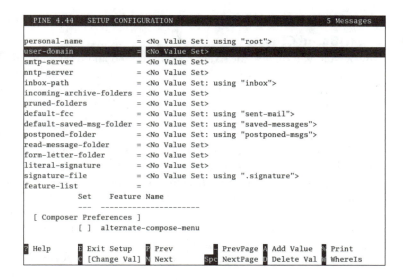

While the pine setup section includes a large number of configuration options, you'll need to set three things to start receiving your e-mail. These tips assume that your e-mail address is abcd@example.com and the incoming e-mail server is mail.example.com. Substitute according to your needs.

◆ Set the personal-name to what you want your e-mail recipients to see.

◆ Add the domain name associated with your e-mail address to user-domain. For example, if your e-mail address is abcd@example.com, add **example.com** to the user-domain field.

◆ Set the `inbox-path`. Based on this example, if `mail.example.com` is a POP3 server, enter `{mail.example.com/pop3/user=abcd}INBOX`. If it's an IMAP4 server, enter **{mail.example.com/user=abcd}**.

TIP *Some e-mail servers have special requirements. For example, some domains require the full e-mail address, such as* abcd@example.com, *as the username in the* `inbox-path`. *They may also require a different domain name for the incoming mail server, the* `user-domain`. *If in doubt, consult your e-mail provider for details.*

If you use an external SMTP server, such as the one associated with your ISP, you can also enter it here. Press the Page Down key a few times. Take a look at the rich variety of options available for `pine`.

NOTE *Before version 4.x,* `pine` *could not handle POP3 e-mail.*

When you're through making changes, type **E** to exit the Setup Configuration screen. Assuming you're satisfied with the changes, type **Y** to confirm when prompted; you'll be taken back to the main menu shown in Figure 26.1. In the main menu, type **L**, highlight INBOX, and press Enter. The first time you do this, you should be prompted for your e-mail password.

Next, `pine` will go to your e-mail server, get your latest messages, and show them to you in a message index similar to Figure 26.3 (I've masked the identity of my e-mails). From here, everything is fairly intuitive, and you can use the command options shown at the bottom of the screen. To read a message, highlight it and press Enter.

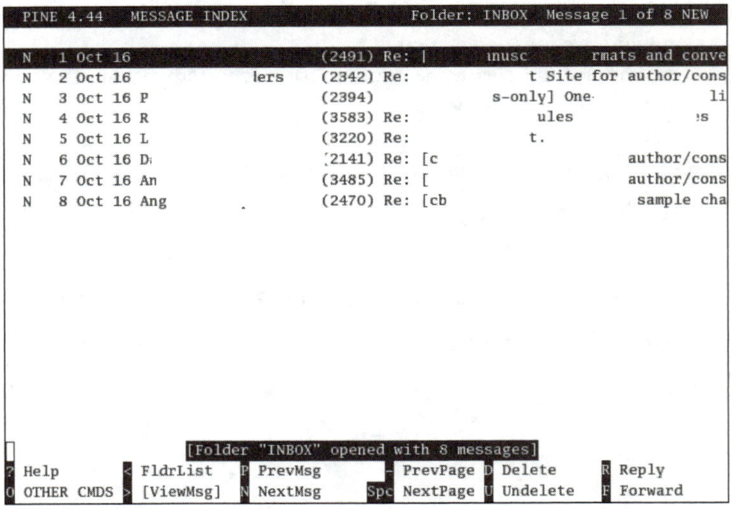

FIGURE 26.3

The `pine` message index

Creating a new message is easy. Return to the main menu as shown in Figure 26.1; then type **C** to start composing a new message. If you've ever used e-mail before, the format shown in Figure 26.4 should be quite familiar. The commands at the bottom are Control characters; for example, when you're done with a message, the Ctrl+X command sends your message (after you type **Y** to confirm). If you've configured an SMTP server or your sendmail service is working, `pine` should send your message automatically.

FIGURE 26.4

Creating pine
e-mail

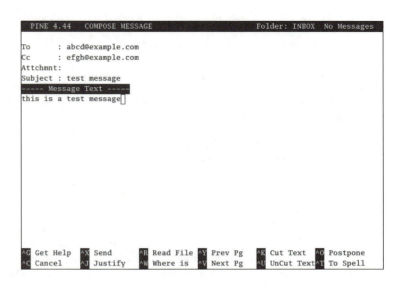

Graphical Clients

Three basic graphical e-mail clients are available in Linux: Evolution, Mozilla Mail, and KMail. We discussed the basic operation of these clients in Part IV. In this section, we'll look at the configuration windows for these clients.

For any e-mail client, the configuration requirements are the same. As you may have done with the pine text e-mail client, you'll need at least the information described in Table 26.2.

TABLE 26.2: DATA NEEDED FOR E-MAIL CLIENTS

DATA	DESCRIPTION
Name	The name you want other users to see
Domain Name	The information after the @ in your e-mail address
Inbox Server	The FQDN of your incoming e-mail server; sometimes listed as "Host" or "Server Name"
Username	Your username or login on the e-mail server; normally just the part before the @ in your e-mail address

CONFIGURING EVOLUTION

If you're using Evolution, which we introduced in Chapter 18, open it in your favorite GUI. From the menu bar, click Tools ➤ Settings. This opens an Evolution Settings window shown in Figure 26.5.

FIGURE 26.5

Evolution Settings

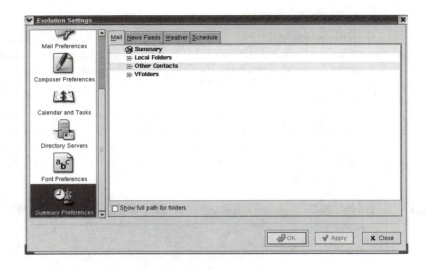

In the left-hand pane, scroll up until you can click the Mail Accounts icon; then click Add to create a new account, or highlight an existing account and click Edit. This should bring you to the Evolution Account Editor. Enter your basic account information on the Identity tab, and then click the Receiving Mail tab shown in Figure 26.6. Select a Server Type if required, enter the FQDN for your inbound e-mail server in the Host text box, and enter your username on that server in the User-name text box.

FIGURE 26.6

Configuring an Evolution e-mail account

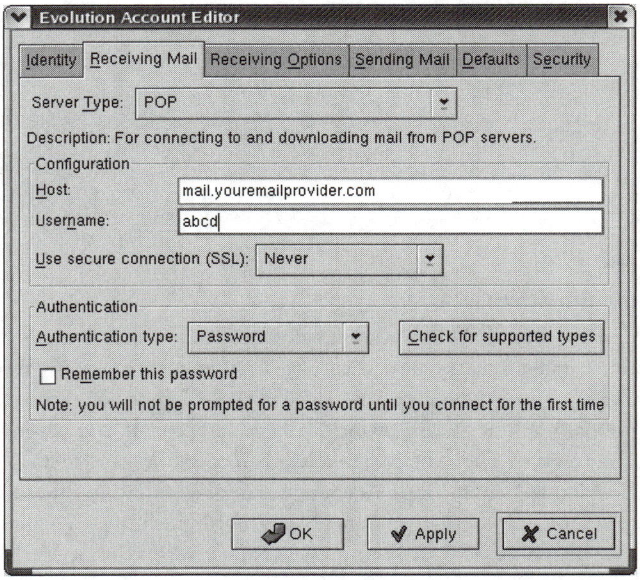

CONFIGURING KMAIL

If you're using KMail, which we looked at in Chapter 17, open it in your favorite GUI. From the menu bar, click Settings ➤ Configure KMail. In the Configure window that appears (see Figure 26.7), click Network in the left-hand pane, then click on the Receiving tab. Click Add to create a new account and select an account type (local, POP3, IMAP, or Maildir). Alternatively, highlight an existing account and click Modify.

This will bring you to an Add Account - KMail or a Modify Account - KMail window. The only difference between the two windows is in the title. An example is shown in Figure 26.8. Enter the name you want others to see when they receive your e-mail and specify a password if desired. Next, enter the FQDN for your inbound e-mail server in the Host text box, and type your username on that server in the Login text box.

FIGURE 26.7

Configuring KMail

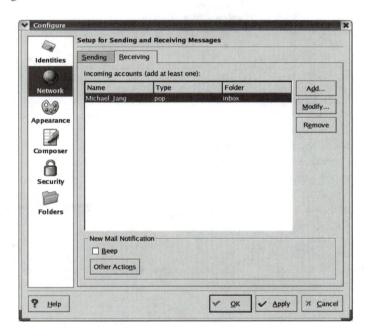

CONFIGURING MOZILLA MAIL

If you're using Mozilla Mail, you may notice striking similarities to the Netscape 6.*x* mail client. This is possible, since Netscape now uses a GPL-style license (see the note). Open Mozilla Mail in your favorite GUI. From the menu bar, click Edit ➤ Mail & Newsgroups Account Settings. The Mail & Newsgroups Account Settings window should appear. If you haven't created an e-mail account before, you'll have to go through the Mozilla Mail Account Wizard first.

In the Mail & Newsgroups Account Settings window, highlight the name of your account; you can enter identity information here. Next, highlight Server Settings, as shown in Figure 26.9. You should see the name of your incoming e-mail server in the Server Name text box. For more information on Mozilla Mail, see Chapter 16.

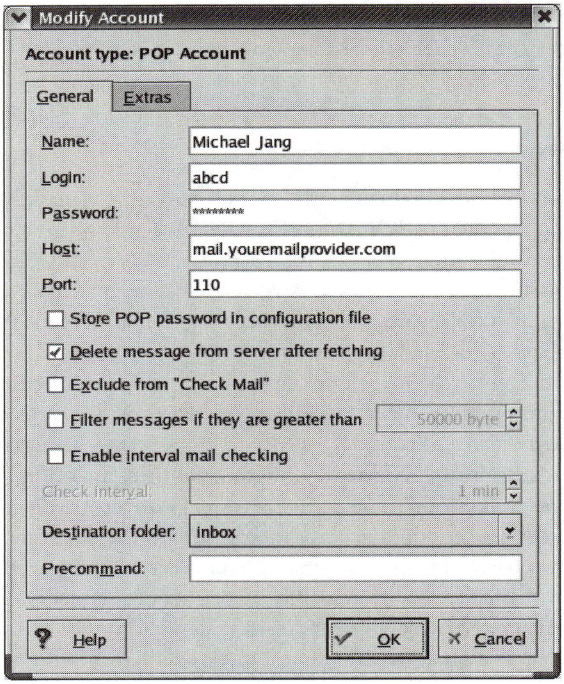

FIGURE 26.8

Modifying a KMail e-mail account

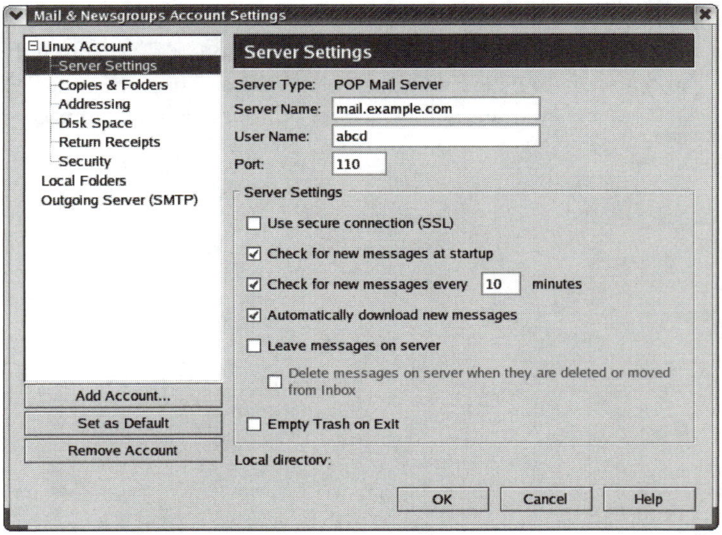

FIGURE 26.9

The Mail & Newsgroups Account Settings window

NOTE *Not everyone in the open source/FSF community is happy with the Netscape license. For a sample of the reasons, read* www.gnu.org/philosophy/netscape-npl.html.

Summary

There are servers that send e-mail, and servers that receive e-mail. Modern versions use some basic TCP/IP protocols: SMTP, POP3, and IMAP4. To send and receive e-mail through these protocols, you can choose among three types of mail services: MTA, MDA, and MUA. An MTA such as sendmail sends e-mail through a network. An MDA such as procmail takes messages from the Internet and stores them in spools, sometimes on incoming e-mail servers. An MUA is an e-mail client such as pine, KMail, Mozilla Mail, or Evolution.

sendmail is currently the most popular outgoing e-mail server on the Internet. Since editing the sendmail.cf configuration file is difficult, Red Hat provides a macro file, sendmail.mc, which can be more easily understood and edited. It is easy to convert into sendmail.cf with the m4 macro processor. There are other important sendmail configuration files, including /etc/sysconfig/sendmail and /etc/aliases, as well as other files in the /etc/mail directory. Once you have your new sendmail.cf file, you can make the sendmail daemon reread it with the service sendmail restart command.

There are two basic options for e-mail servers that conform to the POP3 and IMAP4 protocols. Secure versions of each server are available. All are xinetd services that can be installed from the imap-* RPM package. Once these services are installed and activated, your users will need a username and the FQDN of the e-mail server. If it's an IMAP4 server, they'll also need a home directory for their e-mail files.

Both text and graphical e-mail clients are available. One useful highly configurable text-based client is pine. Graphical e-mail clients are available in a number of forms, including Evolution, Mozilla Mail, and KMail.

In the next chapter, we'll take a look at various FTP clients and servers. The FTP client is flexible; you can even use FTP commands to connect and upgrade your RPMs. You can install anonymous, standard, and even secure FTP servers on your Red Hat Linux computer.

Part 7

Linux File-Sharing Services

In this Part, you will learn how to:
- ◆ Use FTP clients and servers
- ◆ Manage NFS and NIS
- ◆ Configure Samba
- ◆ Set up Web Services

Chapter 27

FTP Clients and Servers

THE FILE TRANSFER PROTOCOL (FTP) is one of the oldest members of the TCP/IP protocol stack, yet it is still in common use today. As the name suggests, it is optimized for transferring files. While you can also download a file through an alternative protocol (such as HTTP) or an encrypted service (such as SFTP), FTP is faster. I use FTP to download the CD files whenever Red Hat releases a new version of their Linux distribution; for me, with my DSL connection, the FTP download speeds over the same transmission media are twice as fast as with HTTP.

As with other services, there are FTP clients and FTP servers. A rich variety of commands are associated with FTP clients; you can even upgrade RPMs directly with the right `ftp` command. And of course, GUI FTP clients exist that work just as well.

Many FTP servers are available for Linux, and in this chapter we cover two of them: very secure FTP (vsFTP) and Washington University's (St. Louis) WU-FTP. Both servers can be configured to allow anonymous users. vsFTP is now the default; WU-FTP was the default FTP server through Red Hat Linux 8.0 (but is not included with Red Hat Linux 9). While neither server is truly secure, each has its own configuration file to control users and computers that are allowed access. Both have ways of protecting the other files and directories on your system. This chapter covers the following topics:

◆ Using FTP as a client

◆ Configuring the secure FTP server

◆ Creating an anonymous FTP server

◆ Using FTP servers with real users

Using FTP as a Client

The FTP service has a long history, with commands that predate shells such as bash. You should learn how to use FTP as a client, at least because key Red Hat RPMs are updated on FTP servers. As with other Linux clients, GUI FTP clients such as gFTP (GNOME FTP) are simply "front ends" for the commands that you can run at the text console.

The following sections describe a connection from an FTP client to Red Hat's main FTP site, `ftp.redhat.com`. This site is often quite busy, especially during the workday in the United States.

Red Hat has a list of a large number of FTP mirror sites (`www.redhat.com/download/mirror.html`) that should include files that are nearly as up-to-date as those you'll find at `ftp.redhat.com`. If you have problems accessing `ftp.redhat.com`, try one of the mirror sites.

Basic Commands

As you can see in Figure 27.1, a substantial number of commands are associated with the FTP client. Only an essential few FTP commands are covered here; data on even rarely used FTP commands is available through the FTP manual you can find with the `man ftp` command. You can view a simple description of a command from the `ftp>` prompt by entering `help command`.

FIGURE 27.1

FTP client commands

```
Commands may be abbreviated.  Commands are:

!               debug           mdir            sendport        site
$               dir             mget            put             size
account         disconnect      mkdir           pwd             status
append          exit            mls             quit            struct
ascii           form            mode            quote           system
bell            get             modtime         recv            sunique
binary          glob            mput            reget           tenex
bye             hash            newer           rstatus         tick
case            help            nmap            rhelp           trace
cd              idle            nlist           rename          type
cdup            image           ntrans          reset           user
chmod           lcd             open            restart         umask
close           ls              prompt          rmdir           verbose
cr              macdef          passive         runique         ?
delete          mdelete         proxy           send
ftp> help rmdir
rmdir           remove directory on the remote machine
ftp> help open
open            connect to remote ftp
ftp> help close
close           terminate ftp session
ftp>
```

Table 27.1 describes some important FTP commands. You may note similarities between a number of these commands and those you know in the bash shell.

TABLE 27.1: BASIC FTP CLIENT COMMANDS

COMMAND	DESCRIPTION
`!command`	Runs a shell command on the local computer, in the local directory.
`ascii`	Sets file transfer to ASCII mode; best for text files.
`binary`	Sets file transfer to Binary mode; best for executables and compressed files.
`bye`	Exits from the current FTP session; synonym for `exit`.
`cd`	Changes the directory; similar to the Linux version of this command.
`dir`	Equivalent to the `ls -l` shell command.

Continued on next page

TABLE 27.1: BASIC FTP CLIENT COMMANDS *(continued)*

COMMAND	DESCRIPTION
get *ftpfile localfile*	Copies the *ftpfile* from the FTP server to *localfile* on the local computer; mget allows you to use wildcards, which is also known as *globbing*.
ls	See dir.
put *localfile ftpfile*	Copies the *localfile* from the local computer to *ftpfile* on the FTP server; mput allows you to use wildcards/globbing.
pwd	Lists the present working directory on the FTP server; if you've configured FTP securely, the root directory that you see on the FTP server will be the main directory for FTP files, usually /var/ftp.
user	Allows you to enter a username; prompts for a password.

Connecting to *ftp.redhat.com*

Now let's get some practice with using the command-line FTP client. Assuming your Linux computer is connected to the Internet, run the `ftp ftp.redhat.com` command. The Red Hat FTP site allows only anonymous connections. While the commands shown in Figure 27.2 seem to require a password, no special password is needed. By custom, when you connect to an FTP server anonymously, you're supposed to enter your e-mail address when prompted for a password.

NOTE You can set up an FTP connection on your own network. Read ahead and create one of the servers discussed in the section "Creating an Anonymous FTP Server" later in this chapter. Once the server is active, you can connect to it from the local computer with the `ftp localhost` command.

FIGURE 27.2

Connecting to an FTP server

```
[root@RH9Desk root]# ftp ftp.redhat.com
Trying 66.77.185.6...
Connected to ftp.redhat.com (66.77.185.6).
220 Red Hat FTP server ready. All transfers are logged.
Name (ftp.redhat.com:root): anonymous
331 Please specify the password.
Password:
230 Login successful. Have fun.
Remote system type is UNIX.
Using binary mode to transfer files.
ftp> 
```

At the `ftp>` prompt, enter the commands you need. Try out some of the commands shown in the previous section. You may note that commands such as `put` do not work; anonymous users aren't allowed to write to standard Red Hat FTP servers.

NOTE By default, the root user is not allowed to access any FTP server. If you try to log in through FTP as root, even a correct password will be rejected.

As an example, navigate to the directory with i386 Rawhide RPMs. As of this writing, they are located in the `/pub/redhat/linux/rawhide/i386/RedHat/RPMS` directory. You should find a long list of RPMs here.

NOTE *While there are RPMs for other CPUs, those created for the i386 are most common. Although i386 RPMs are not optimized for other Intel CPUs, they do work. We discuss this topic in greater detail in Chapter 10.*

Rawhide is the Red Hat storage area for the latest RPM packages. If **up2date** (discussed in Chapter 10) is not your style, you can update RPM packages directly. Download the packages from the current Rawhide database, using commands similar to those shown in Figure 27.3. You can then install or upgrade these packages at your leisure.

FIGURE 27.3

Downloading a
Rawhide RPM

```
ftp> cd RPMS
250 CWD command successful.
ftp> ls z*
227 Entering Passive Mode (10,252,113,155,11,207).
125 Data connection already open; Transfer starting.
-rwxrwxrwx   1 owner     group         1011615 Feb 25 13:42 zebra-0.93b-1.i386.rp
m
-rwxrwxrwx   1 owner     group          113724 Feb 24  0:40 zip-2.3-16.i386.rpm
-rwxrwxrwx   1 owner     group           15425 Feb 24  0:40 zisofs-tools-1.0.4-2.
i386.rpm
-rwxrwxrwx   1 owner     group           33793 Feb 24 13:47 zlib-1.1.4-8.i386.rpm
-rwxrwxrwx   1 owner     group           70750 Feb 24 13:47 zlib-devel-1.1.4-8.i3
86.rpm
-rwxrwxrwx   1 owner     group         1407003 Feb 24  0:41 zsh-4.0.6-5.i386.rpm
226 Transfer complete.
ftp> mget zip*
mget zip-2.3-16.i386.rpm? y
227 Entering Passive Mode (10,252,113,155,11,209).
125 Data connection already open; Transfer starting.
WARNING! 385 bare linefeeds received in ASCII mode
File may not have transferred correctly.
226 Transfer complete.
113724 bytes received in 2.02 secs (55 Kbytes/sec)
ftp> bye
221
[root@RH9Desk root]#
```

Alternatively, you don't have to bother with this process. As described in Chapter 10, you can use a one-line `rpm` command to directly connect and install the latest RPM package on the FTP server of your choice.

The GUI FTP Client

Of course, there are graphical versions of the FTP client. One common graphical FTP client is gFTP, which you can start by entering **gftp** in a command-line interface in your favorite GUI. This opens the gFTP client, shown in Figure 27.4.

NOTE *You can run **gftp** from a regular virtual console; it's part of the gFTP package and opens a text-mode FTP client similar to **ftp**.*

The gFTP client is convenient; it has several common sites preconfigured in the Bookmarks menu. However, the sites, such as what you might open when you select Bookmarks ➢ RedHat Sites ➢ RH Rawhide, aren't always kept up-to-date. Nevertheless, it is a convenient way to make an FTP connection. For example, try Bookmarks ➤ RedHat Sites ➤ RH Main. If the Red Hat FTP server is not overloaded, it should bring you to the base Red Hat FTP directory shown in Figure 27.5.

FIGURE 27.4

The gFTP Client

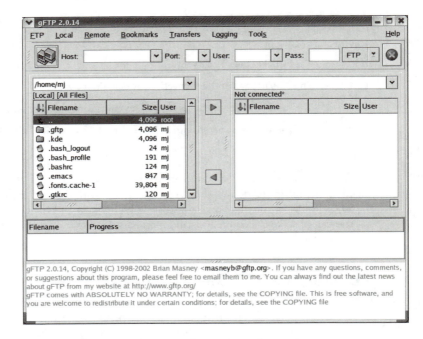

FIGURE 27.5

gFTP in action

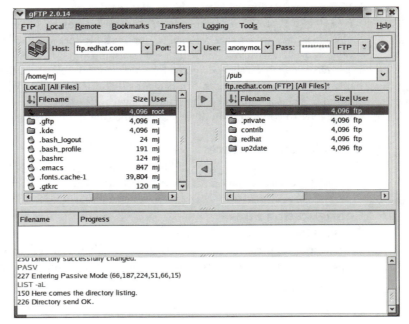

Compare the differences between Figure 27.4 and Figure 27.5. When you select a gFTP bookmark, it fills in a number of entries (described in Table 27.2) in various text boxes.

TABLE 27.2: ENTRIES FOR CONNECTING A GFTP CLIENT

ENTRY	FUNCTION
Host	The FQDN of the FTP server.
Port	The TCP/IP port for the connection; by default, it's 21.
User	The username for the connection; anonymous is common for an anonymous FTP server.
Pass	The password associated with the username. By convention, it's supposed to be your e-mail address.

You may want to go to a subdirectory on an FTP server. To navigate to the desired directory, double-click it. Remember, the double-dot (..) is associated with the next higher-level directory. Once you've found the folder or file that you want to copy, highlight it and click the arrow button.

You can observe the commands and messages that are transmitted in the bottom part of the gFTP window.

The Secure FTP Server

One of the big drawbacks of a regular FTP server is security. You can configure a secure FTP server as discussed in Chapter 23, but encryption can hurt performance. And the sftp commands are not standard.

One compromise is the Very Secure FTP server, vsFTP. Red Hat has made it the default and only FTP server for Red Hat Linux 9. I've included references to the former Red Hat Linux default FTP server, WU-FTP, for those familiar with older versions of Red Hat.

While it does not encrypt communications, vsFTP does avoid some of the security problems commonly associated with WU-FTP. It's used as a standard FTP server for a number of sites, including ftp.redhat.com. It can be configured for anonymous or real users. In fact, the home page for this server (http://vsftpd.beasts.org) suggests that it is faster than WU-FTP.

vsFTP shares a number of characteristics with WU-FTP. Where possible, in the sections that follow we refer to configuration files we'll examine later in our discussion of WU-FTP.

Basic Security Features

The commands associated with vsFTP are normally configured with minimal privileges; this reduces the risk of a cracker using one of these commands to gain root access to your system.

Configuration Files

The vsFTP package includes configuration files in the /etc directory. Two of these files, vsftpd
.ftpusers and vsftpd.user_list, essentially disallow access from privileged users. This list is simple; it includes a list of users, such as root, bin, and adm. The main configuration file is

/etc/vsftpd/vsftpd.conf. The following is a line-by-line analysis of the default configuration file, which includes several options. More details are available via the man vsftpd.conf command.

I've included the entire file with my own comments to help you understand each command.

```
# Example config file /etc/vsftpd.conf
#
# The default compiled in settings are very paranoid. This sample file
# loosens things up a bit, to make the ftp daemon more usable.
#
# Allow anonymous FTP?
anonymous_enable=YES
```

The first notes, starting with the #, are comments. You may have noticed that the first comment line is wrong; it reflects the old location of the vsftpd.conf file. By default, vsFTP allows anonymous access with the previous command. Users can log anonymously as user anonymous or ftp.

```
# Uncomment this to allow local users to log in.
local_enable=YES
```

The default Red Hat configuration local-enable variable allows users with a regular account on the FTP server to log in as real users.

```
# Uncomment this to enable any form of FTP write command.
write_enable=YES
```

These users have access to all directories on the FTP server, including the root (/) directory. You may want to comment out the write_enable command; otherwise, logged in users have a dangerous level of access to your system. You can also configure all access to an unprivileged user, as described later with the nopriv_user variable.

To minimize the problem, you could add the chroot_local_user=YES command, which prevents users from accessing the root (/) directory on the FTP server. However, users who are allowed to upload to their home directories could then upload executable files that compromise the security of the server.

The default Red Hat configuration allows real users to delete files in their home directories. It does not allow anonymous users to delete files.

```
# Default umask for local users is 077. You may wish to change this to 022,
# if your users expect that (022 is used by most other ftpd's)
local_umask=022
```

Without this umask command (see Chapter 6), uploaded files have read and write permissions, limited to the owner of the file. With this command, all users have at least read permissions to uploaded files.

```
# Uncomment this to allow the anonymous FTP user to upload files. This only
# has an effect if the above global write enable is activated. Also, you will
# obviously need to create a directory writable by the FTP user.
#anon_upload_enable=YES
```

Sometimes, you want to allow anonymous users to upload to your FTP server. While you risk having users overload the partition with the /var filesystem, you can limit this risk by mounting /var on a separate partition, as discussed in Chapter 7. As we describe later in our discussion of anonymous servers, you'll need to set appropriate permissions for the directory where you accept uploads, such as /var/ftp/pub. Note that this setting is disabled in the default vsftpd.conf configuration file.

```
# Uncomment this if you want the anonymous FTP user to be able to create
# new directories.
#anon_mkdir_write_enable=YES
```

You can also let anonymous users create new directories wherever they have write permissions. Note the comment mark (#) in front of the command, which disables the setting; you'd also need to add an anon_other_write_enable=YES line to let users actually write files to the new directories.

```
# Activate directory messages - messages given to remote users when they
# go into a certain directory.
dirmessage_enable=YES
```

By default, users are allowed to see messages in a .message file in different directories. When the user changes to that directory, the contents of the relevant .message file (or a filename specified by the message_file=*filename* command) are shown.

```
# Activate logging of uploads/downloads.
xferlog_enable=YES
```

Normally, a record of uploads and downloads are stored in /var/log/vsftpd.log. You can specify a different file with the xferlog_file=*filename* command.

```
# Make sure PORT transfer connections originate from port 20 (ftp-data).
connect_from_port_20=YES
```

Some FTP clients may require the previous command. Port 20 is one of the TCP/IP ports shown in /etc/services.

```
# If you want, you can arrange for uploaded anonymous files to be owned by
# a different user. Note! Using "root" for uploaded files is not
# recommended!
#chown_uploads=YES
#chown_username=whoever
```

The user who uploads a file does not have to own that file. For example, the following commands, slightly different from what you see in the vsftpd.conf file, would change ownership of any uploaded files to user mj:

```
chown_uploads=YES
chown_username=mj
```

Next, we look at the standard log file location:

```
# You may override where the log file goes if you like. The default is shown
# below.
#xferlog_file=/var/log/vsftpd.log
```

Normally, vsFTP log files are stored in /var/log/vsftpd.log. You can change this to the location of your choice.

```
# If you want, you can have your log file in standard ftpd xferlog format
xferlog_std_format=YES
```

This command enables the standard format for logging uploads and downloads to the FTP server, as used for WU-FTP. Try disabling this command by adding a # in front. Write this file, then set up a transfer from an FTP connection. Read the results in the /var/log/vsftpd.log file. The nonstandard vsFTP log format is more descriptive.

```
# You may change the default value for timing out an idle session.
#idle_session_timeout=600
```

The vsFTP server regulates how long a user can sit idle while logged on. By default, it's 300 seconds. The previous command, if active, changes this period to 10 minutes.

```
# You may change the default value for timing out a data connection.
#data_connection_timeout=120
```

Sometimes there are errors during a file transfer. If there is an error, the FTP client will try to reconnect. But there comes a point where it is better to restart the connection. The default period is 300 seconds; the previous command, if active, changes that to two minutes.

```
# It is recommended that you define on your system a unique user which the
# ftp server can use as a totally isolated and unprivileged user.
#nopriv_user=ftpsecure
```

You can set up a special unprivileged user, *ftpsecure*, by enabling the previous command. If you do, make sure the user exits in /etc/passwd.

SETTING UP SPECIAL FTP USERS

You should set up *ftpsecure* almost as a "guest" type user. Once configured, all users that connect to your FTP server get the ftpsecure username. If you don't want users to log in directly to your computer, you can change the associated entry in /etc/password to set up /sbin/nologin as the default shell:

```
ftpsecure:x:601:601::/home/ftpsecure:/sbin/nologin
```

The following command allows less capable FTP clients to cancel a download without hanging.

```
# Enable this and the server will recognise asynchronous ABOR requests. Not
# recommended for security (the code is non-trivial). Not enabling it,
# however, may confuse older FTP clients.
#async_abor_enable=YES
```

However, this setting is not needed for the regular command-line FTP client described earlier in this chapter.

```
# By default the server will pretend to allow ASCII mode but in fact ignore
```

```
# the request. Turn on the below options to have the server actually do ASCII
# mangling on files when in ASCII mode.
# Beware that turning on ascii_download_enable enables malicious remote parties
# to consume your I/O resources, by issuing the command "SIZE /big/file" in
# ASCII mode.
# These ASCII options are split into upload and download because you may wish
# to enable ASCII uploads (to prevent uploaded scripts etc. from breaking),
# without the DoS risk of SIZE and ASCII downloads. ASCII mangling should be
# on the client anyway..
#ascii_upload_enable=YES
#ascii_download_enable=YES
```

If you need to transfer files in ASCII mode, enable one or both of the previous "ascii" commands. It should rarely be necessary, even for text files, unless you need to preserve certain types of formatting.

```
# You may fully customise the login banner string:
#ftpd_banner=Welcome to blah FTP service.
```

You can configure the previous ftpd_banner message for users before they log in. For example, you might change the message as follows if you only want anonymous logins:

```
# ftp_banner=Welcome. Type ftp at the prompt for an anonymous login.
```

Sometimes crackers will attempt something similar to the "ping of death" described in Chapter 22 on your FTP server.

```
# You may specify a file of disallowed anonymous e-mail addresses. Apparently
# useful for combatting certain DoS attacks.
#deny_email_enable=YES
# (default follows)
#banned_email_file=/etc/vsftpd.banned_emails
```

If you enable both of the previous commands, you can create a list of anonymous passwords in /etc/vsftpd.banned_emails that aren't allowed access. This can deny access to crackers who use automated tools to try to bring down your FTP server.

```
# You may specify an explicit list of local users to chroot() to their home
# directory. If chroot_local_user is YES, then this list becomes a list of
# users to NOT chroot().
#chroot_list_enable=YES
# (default follows)
#chroot_list_file=/etc/vsftpd.chroot_list
```

If you activated chroot_list_enable=YES, you can configure a group of users who see their home directory as the root (/) directory in /etc/vsftpd.chroot_list. If you also configure chroot_local_user=YES, the effect of the list in /etc/vsftpd.chroot_list is reversed.

```
# You may activate the "-R" option to the builtin ls. This is disabled by
# default to avoid remote users being able to cause excessive I/O on large
# sites. However, some broken FTP clients such as "ncftp" and "mirror" assume
# the presence of the "-R" option, so there is a strong case for enabling it.
#ls_recurse_enable=YES
```

If you activate the previous command, FTP clients can run the `ls -R` command on any available directory, which allows users to see the contents of subdirectories. However, this is disabled by default; a user who is logged into an FTP server multiple times could create a large load by running `ls -R` on all sessions.

```
pam_service_name=vsftpd
```

The `pam_service_name` lists the Pluggable Authentication Module (PAM) file associated with vsFTP. For more information on PAM, see Chapter 22.

```
userlist_enable=YES
```

This command makes vsFTP check for prohibited usernames in the `/etc/vsftpd.user_list` file.

```
#enable for standalone mode
listen=YES
```

This allows vsFTP to be run as its own daemon, supported by the `vsftpd` script in the `/etc/rc.d/init.d` directory. Otherwise, you could run vsFTP as a `xinetd` script described in Chapter 23.

Creating an Anonymous FTP Server

It is not difficult to create an anonymous FTP server. However, there are details involved in securing that server. When the server is properly configured, users won't be able to get above the base FTP directory, `/var/ftp`, and certainly not to the root (`/`) directory. The default Red Hat FTP configuration is based on the vsFTP server.

This section shows you how to create a basic anonymous-only FTP server. It can work with vsFTP or the WU-FTP servers. You can customize the configuration further using many of the settings described later in this chapter.

Configuring vsFTP

Once the appropriate packages are installed, you'll need to activate the service. Assuming you're using vsFTP, you'd run the `service vsftpd start` command. Remember to use the appropriate `chkconfig` command (see Chapter 13) to make sure vsFTP is active the next time you start Linux.

As discussed earlier, the vsFTP configuration file, `vsftpd.conf`, allows anonymous access by default.

The key command in the vsFTP configuration file which supports an anonymous server was described in the first part of this chapter: refer to the `anonymous_enable` command in `/etc/vsftpd/vsftpd`. What follows is a description of what you would need to do to WU-FTP server configuration files.

Configuring WU-FTP

If you've installed the WU-FTP server, you'll need to work with several `/etc/ftp*` configuration files, as described in the following sections. The next major section, "Configuring WU-FTP with Real Users," describes each configuration file in more detail.

NOTE   *WU-FTP is no longer included with Red Hat Linux; but you can download it from the FTP site at* `ftp.wu-ftpd.org` *or the SpeakEasy RPM library at* `www.rpmfind.net`.

Anonymous Directories

You can set up a basic anonymous FTP connection on WU-FTP. You'll need the `anonftp-*` RPM to install several subdirectories in `/var/ftp` for the files and commands that an FTP user needs to navigate in that directory and its subdirectories. These subdirectories are listed in Table 27.3.

TABLE 27.3: ANONYMOUS FTP DIRECTORIES

DIRECTORY	DESCRIPTION
`/var/ftp/bin`	Executable shell commands; available commands are limited.
`/var/ftp/etc`	Configuration files; by default includes abbreviated versions of `passwd` and `group`.
`/var/ftp/lib`	Program libraries.
`/var/ftp/pub`	Files for users; permissions can be configured for uploads.

You need to know that WU-FTP is an `xinetd` service; the techniques described in Chapter 23 apply. Make sure that the service is not disabled in the `/etc/xinetd.d/wu-ftpd` file and that it isn't blocked in `/etc/hosts.deny` (as well as by any `iptables` firewall that might be active).

RESTRICTING ACCESS

It's easy to limit access to an FTP server to anonymous users. First, open the `/etc/ftpaccess` configuration file. By default, it should include the following entry:

```
# User classes . . .
class    all    real,guest,anonymous    *
```

This FTP access `class` allows access to real, guest, and anonymous users from all addresses. Limit access to anonymous users from the 192.168.0.0/24 network by changing this line as follows:

```
class    all    anonymous    192.168.0.0/24
```

ANONYMOUS FTP SECURITY

There are several default measures that protect an anonymous FTP website created with the WU-FTP server. In this section, we examine those measures.

Limiting Access

By default, all logins are directed to the `/var/ftp` directory. You can change that in `/etc/ftpaccess` by activating the following line for desired users:

```
# realuser user1,user2
```

If you remove the comment mark (#) and change *user1* and *user2* to real users on your system, the FTP server sends these users to their home directories when they log in—and they have access to higher-level directories such as root (/).

If you want all users to access your FTP server starting in the `/var/ftp` directory, comment out this line in `/etc/ftpaccess`.

The chroot Jail

The concept that protects other directories on an FTP server is the *chroot jail*. By definition, there is no higher directory than root (/). The `chroot /abc/def` command changes the effective root directory to `/abc/def`.

On an anonymous FTP server, the `/var/ftp` directory looks like the root (/) directory. The configuration for the anonymous FTP server applies the `chroot /var/ftp` command to all users who log into that server. If an anonymous user tries to run a command such as `cd /var` or `cd /etc`, it won't work, because higher-level directories are protected by the chroot jail.

Command Limits

Access to dangerous commands can also be limited. By default, `/etc/ftpaccess` limits access to four commands, as shown. You may wish to add other commands to the list. For example, if you make a command executable by an authorized user, you can add it to this list to prevent access by anonymous users:

```
chmod        no    guest,anonymous
delete       no    anonymous
overwrite    no    anonymous
rename       no    anonymous
```

Configuring WU-FTP with Real Users

The information in this and the previous section is based on the WU-FTP server package, which must now be loaded from a third-party site such as those described earlier. We've already described how to enable anonymous user access. In this section, you'll learn about the configuration files associated with WU-FTP and how to apply them to regular users on your system.

Configuration Files

Several configuration files are associated with the WU-FTP package, all in the `/etc` directory: `ftpaccess`, `ftpconversions`, `ftpgroups`, `ftphosts`, and `ftpusers`.

Of these files, `ftpusers` is now obsolete and `ftpgroups` is rarely used; the functionality of these files is now part of `ftpaccess`. In this section, we describe the other configuration files in detail.

Alternate examples of each of these configuration files are available in the WU-FTP documentation, in the `/usr/share/doc/wu-ftpd-`*versionnumber*`/examples` directory.

/ETC/FTPACCESS

We examined a couple of characteristics of the default `/etc/ftpaccess` file earlier in this chapter. Now it is time to examine this file line by line. The first lines take the functionality of `/etc/ftpusers`:

```
deny-uid %-99 %65534-
deny-gid %-99 %65534-
allow-uid ftp
allow-uid ftp
```

These lines deny access to User and Group IDs less than 99 and greater than 65534, except user ftp. If you examine your /etc/passwd and /etc/group files, you'll see that these ID numbers are associated with administrative accounts. You can limit access to all users except ftp with a simple change:

```
deny-uid *
deny-gid *
allow-uid ftp
allow-uid ftp
```

The following line sets up the chroot jail. All users are classified as guest users, and they're limited to their home directories. For example, if user mj logs in, he is sent to /home/mj:

```
guestuser *
```

We discussed the next line in the previous section; user mj isn't allowed to navigate to the /home or root (/) directory unless the following line is activated:

```
# realuser user1,user2
```

Remember, the hashmark (#) makes Linux ignore the information that follows; if you remove the #, *user1* and *user2* gain full user privileges on that FTP server. The following line can be used to limit the users on the realuser list. For example, if the previous line was realuser *, you can add the ftpchroot group to /etc/group. Members of the ftpchroot group would not be allowed to navigate above their respective home directories:

```
# guestgroup ftpchroot
```

NOTE *The management of user and group configuration files such as /etc/passwd and /etc/group is discussed in Chapter 9.*

As described earlier, the first line that follows allows access from real, guest, and anonymous users. The next line, if active, limits access to real users who log in from the 192.168.0.0/24 network. Anonymous access is not allowed; users need to enter their passwords. One obvious drawback is that real user passwords are sent over your LAN in clear text:

```
class   all    real,guest,anonymous   *
# class   all    real    192.168.0.0/24
```

If you comment out the previous guestuser * line, you can substitute *real* for *guest*:

```
class   all    guest   192.168.0.0/24
```

If you're the administrator for your server, you'll want to substitute your e-mail address here:

```
email root@localhost
```

The following command limits the number of attempted logins. In this case, after five login attempts this FTP server closes the connection:

```
loginfails 5
```

In the Linux and Unix worlds, README* files are commonly used for instructions or to supply more information about the packages contained in a specific directory. The following lines return a

`Please read the file README` message whenever a user logs into and changes to a directory with a README file:

```
readme     README*    login
readme     README*    cwd=*
```

As the administrator of the FTP server, you may want to send other messages to your users. The following lines allow you to add a welcome message to the `welcome.msg` file in the opening directory. You can also add `.message` files to send additional messages to users who use the `cd` command to navigate to those directories:

```
message    /welcome.msg    login
message    .message        cwd=*
```

You can see what happens when I added a README file to the `/var/ftp` directory as well as information to various message files in Figure 27.6.

FIGURE 27.6

FTP login messages

```
Connected to RH9Test (10.252.113.63).
220 RH9Test FTP Server (Version wu-2.6.2-8) ready.
Name (RH9Test:root): anonymous
331 Guest login ok, send your complete e-mail address as password.
Password:
230-This is a test message welcoming users to a new FTP server
230-
230-You can add the rules or requests of your choice to the welcome.msg.
230-
230-Using this file makes sense for an Anonymous FTP server; otherwise, you'd ha
ve to add welcome messages to each user's home directory.
230-
230-Please read the file README
230-  it was last modified on Sat Apr 5 15:34:29 2003 - 0 days ago
230 Guest login ok, access restrictions apply.
Remote system type is UNIX.
Using binary mode to transfer files.
ftp> cd etc/
250-This is a test message warning about the embedded /var/ftp/etc directory
250-
250-Please be careful about anything you might add to this directory.
250-
250 CWD command successful.
ftp> █
```

It's useful to store packages in compressed format on an FTP server. The following commands allow users who access such packages to have them uncompressed or unpackaged automatically, per the commands in `/etc/ftpconversions`, which is described in a later section, "*/etc/ftpconversions*":

```
compress   yes    all
tar        yes    all
```

You'll recognize the following commands from an earlier section. If you keep the `guestuser *` line, with slight modifications to `/etc/ftpaccess` (shown in bold), you can prevent all users from using these commands.

```
chmod      no     guest,anonymous
delete     no     guest,anonymous
```

```
overwrite   no    guest,anonymous
rename      no    guest,anonymous
```

While logins to the FTP server are normally stored in `/var/log/messages`, file transfers to and from the server are logged to `/var/log/xferlog`:

```
log transfers anonymous,guest,real inbound,outbound
```

If you run the `ftpshut` command, it creates a temporary `/etc/shutmsg` file. This command refuses additional logins if a shutdown of the FTP server is imminent:

```
shutdown /etc/shutmsg
```

Anonymous users are supposed to enter their e-mail address as the password. If they do, you can see their password in `/var/log/messages`. The following command sends a warning to users who connect to the FTP server without entering an e-mail address in proper format. As configured, users are still logged onto the server even with an invalid e-mail address.

```
passwd-check rfc822 warn
```

LIMITS IN */ETC/FTPACCESS*

If you're running an FTP server on the Internet, you may want to limit the number of simultaneous users connected to your server. This can help ration the speed at which your users can download their files. One simple way to create a limit in `/etc/ftpacess` is with the `limit` command. For example, the following command prevents more than 20 users from signing on to your FTP server at any one time. The `warning.msg` file is sent to users who try to log in when the limit is reached:

```
limit    all    20    Any    warning.msg
```

Perhaps you just want to limit access to users during the day (8 A.M.–5 P.M.), when your server may be busy with other tasks:

```
limit    all    20    Wk0800-1700    warning.msg
```

The syntax of time in this command is based on the UUCP remote host description file. The easiest way to find this file is by searching for `1.sys` in your favorite search engine.

TIP   *I like to search the newsgroups for answers to common Linux problems. Remember, Linux is under constant development by a worldwide community of users and developers; they often discuss their Linux issues through newsgroups and many other forums. It's easy to search through the newsgroups via* `groups.google.com`.

You can also limit the amount of data that a user can download from your FTP server. For example, the following command limits the amount of downloadable files to 100MB:

```
byte-limit    out    100000000    all
```

Alternatives to `out` (downloads) are `in` (uploads) and `total` (both directions).

/ETC/FTPCONVERSIONS

The /etc/ftpconversions file, shown in Figure 27.7, allows you to run selected commands during the upload or download process. For example, if you have a compressed file of pictures named pictures.gz on your FTP server, the third line in /etc/ftpconversions lets you download and uncompress the pictures directly with the following command at the ftp> prompt:

```
ftp> get pictures
```

Note how the .gz is left out of the request. The FTP server automatically refers to /etc/ ftpconversions for the needed command.

FIGURE 27.7

/etc/ ftpconversions

```
:.Z:  :   :/usr/bin/compress -d -c %s:T_REG|T_ASCII:O_UNCOMPRESS:UNCOMPRESS
   :  :.Z:/usr/bin/compress -c %s:T_REG:O_COMPRESS:COMPRESS
:.gz:  :   :/bin/gzip -cd %s:T_REG|T_ASCII:O_UNCOMPRESS:GUNZIP
   :  :.gz:/bin/gzip -9 -c %s:T_REG:O_COMPRESS:GZIP
   :  :.tar:/bin/tar -c -f - %s:T_REG|T_DIR:O_TAR:TAR
   :  :.tar.Z:/bin/tar -c -Z -f - %s:T_REG|T_DIR:O_COMPRESS|O_TAR:TAR+COMPRESS
   :  :.tar.gz:/bin/tar -c -z -f - %s:T_REG|T_DIR:O_COMPRESS|O_TAR:TAR+GZIP

~
~
~
~
~
~
~
~
~
~
~
~
~
"/etc/ftpconversions" 8L, 543C
```

/ETC/FTPHOSTS

The /etc/ftphosts file looks conceptually similar to the /etc/hosts.allow and /etc/hosts.deny files associated with xinetd services (see Chapter 23). You can allow and deny access to the FTP server from specific users. However, the functionality isn't quite what you might expect.

For example, the following line allows FTP access only from user hdean from the computer with the given IP address. No other users and no other computers are allowed access to this FTP server. You can substitute the FQDN for the IP address.

```
allow    hdean     192.168.0.32
```

Alternatively, the following line denies access to user glocke only from the noted computer:

```
deny     glocke    linux.example.com
```

Commands

FTP server commands let you regulate when FTP servers are active, and allow you to view a list of currently connected users. For example, the following command warns users at their next command that the FTP server will shut down in 15 minutes, or at 3:30 P.M.:

```
ftpshut +15 "The FTP Server will close in 15 minutes"
ftpshut 1530 "The FTP server will stop at 3:30 PM"
```

You can set this up as a `cron` script, as discussed in Chapter 13. This allows you to shut down the FTP server on a regular basis. Other FTP server–related commands are listed in Table 27.4.

TABLE 27.4: FTP SERVER COMMANDS

COMMAND	DESCRIPTION
ftpwho	Lists connected users and origin IP addresses
ftpcount	Lists number of connections
ftpshut	Allows you to shut down an FTP server now or at a specified time
ftprestart	Stops and restarts an FTP server

Anonymous Uploads

By default, anonymous users aren't allowed to write to any of the `/var/ftp` directories. In some cases, you may want to allow users to supply their files in a directory such as `/var/ftp/pub`.

To allow uploads, you'll need to modify the `/etc/ftpaccess` file and the permissions on the appropriate directory. For example, the following line allows uploads to the `/var/ftp/letter` directory:

```
upload    /var/ftp    /letter    yes    cindy    ywow    0660
```

On the FTP server, these files are owned by user cindy, group ywow, with 660 permissions that allow the user cindy and members of the ywow group to read and write to uploaded files.

You'll also need proper permissions on the upload directory. To write a file to a directory, you need at least write and execute permissions. In this case, the `chmod 733 /var/ftp/letter` command would meet these minimum requirements. Of course, if you want regular users on the server to read the files in that directory, you can provide less restrictive permissions with a command such as `chmod 733 /var/ftp/letter`. For more information on permissions, see Chapter 6.

Summary

The File Transfer Protocol, FTP, is still in common use today. FTP is optimized for sharing files. Download speed for files is as important as ever. For example, you want to keep the time it takes to download a 650MB+ file for a Red Hat Installation CD to a minimum.

There are text-based and graphical FTP clients. While graphical clients such as gFTP are pretty, they are essentially front ends for the command-line FTP client. A substantial number of commands are available at the `ftp>` command prompt. It's even easy to use the FTP client to connect to the Red Hat FTP site to download the latest RPMs. One advantage to a GUI client such as gFTP is convenience; for example, it provides preconfigured bookmarks that help you connect to commonly used FTP servers.

The default Red Hat FTP server is known as Very Secure FTP, or vsFTP. Its developers believe that it is more efficient than WU-FTP, the previous default Red Hat FTP server. While it still transmits data in clear text, which can endanger passwords, it avoids the WU-FTP risks of compromising the root account. vsFTPd does this by giving its commands unprivileged status. The key configuration file is `/etc/vsftpd.conf`. In this file, you can configure anonymous access, messages, logging, uploading, and more.

It's common to configure an anonymous FTP server. For this purpose, you also need the `anonftp-*` RPM package, which configures anonymous directories in `/var/ftp`. This works with vsFTP and WU-FTP. Anonymous users can't go above this directory because of the concept of the chroot jail. vsFTP can be configured for anonymous access. In WU-FTP, it's fairly easy to restrict access to anonymous users and critical commands in `/etc/ftpaccess`.

You can also set up WU-FTP with real users, based on the user accounts in the FTP server's `/etc/passwd` file. Key configuration files in the `/etc` directory include `ftpaccess`, `ftpconversions`, and `ftphosts`. With the right changes, you can even configure user and time limits, as well as anonymous uploads on your FTP server. Several commands let you manage a WU-FTP server, including `ftpwho`, `ftpcount`, `ftpshut`, and `ftprestart`.

In the next chapter, we'll explore the services for a network of Linux and Unix computers. The Network File System (NFS) is optimized for sharing files between these computers. And the Network Information System (NIS) allows you to configure a single database of login and other configuration files for a network.

## Chapter 28

Linux Sharing Services: NFS and NIS

On a network with Linux and Unix computers, the two common sharing services are the Network File System (NFS) and the Network Information Service (NIS). NFS lets you mount remote directories seamlessly on your Linux computer. NIS allows you to keep a common database of key configuration files on your network.

When you mount an NFS directory, you may not be able to tell the difference from a directory on your own computer. For example, you could configure home directories for all of your users on a server and share it through NFS. Then you could configure client computers on your LAN to mount `/home` during the boot process. NFS may look a bit complex, because it uses up to six daemons, but the basic configuration files and commands are easy. If you're less familiar with NFS, the graphical `redhat-config-nfs` tool can help. And in this chapter, you'll learn to understand and manage the risks commonly associated with NFS.

Every Linux computer normally has its own basic configuration files for users, such as `/etc/passwd` and `/etc/group`. On many LANs, it would be easier to configure all users with the same username and password. Without NIS, that means making sure that all users have an account on each computer—and each account has the same UID and GID numbers. This can be a cumbersome process. With NIS, you can configure a single database of usernames, passwords, and a number of other configuration files. This chapter covers the following topics:

- ◆ Configuring NFS servers
- ◆ Working with NFS clients
- ◆ Setting up NIS servers
- ◆ Using NIS clients

Configuring Network File System Servers

The Network File System (NFS) is fundamental to Linux. In fact, one of the basic NFS configuration files is included in the same `setup-*` RPM package as `/etc/passwd` and `/etc/profile`. Yet managing NFS means that you need to pay attention to a number of different daemons.

Setting up exports from an NFS server is relatively easy. Basically, all you need to do is add a line for each shared directory to `/etc/exports` and share it with the network, and you're on your way. But pay attention to the syntax; the right commands help you secure the directories that you share through NFS.

One key to NFS is the remote procedure call (RPC), which allows you to seamlessly run commands on remotely mounted directories. All of the NFS daemons use RPC.

The GUI configuration tool for NFS, `redhat-config-nfs`, can help you configure simple shared directories. Remember, this GUI tool is just a front end for what you'll learn in this chapter about configuring NFS.

NFS Packages

The packages you need for NFS may already be installed. Some of these packages are fundamental to a smoothly running Linux system. Table 28.1 lists the packages associated with NFS. As we explained in Chapter 10, you can run the `rpm -qi packagename` command to learn more about each package.

TABLE 28.1: NFS-RELATED RPM PACKAGES

PACKAGE	FUNCTION
setup-*	Shared NFS directories are defined in /etc/exports.
initscripts-*	Includes the basic scripts for mounting network directories during the boot process.
nfs-utils-*	Includes basic NFS commands and daemons.
portmap-*	Supports secure NFS remote procedure call (RPC) connections.
quota-*	Includes rpc.rquotad for quotas on directories shared over a network; this package is not required.

Basic Daemons

At least five Linux services are required to run NFS smoothly. They each relate to different functions, from mounting to making sure that remote commands get to the right place. These services are started through the `nfs`, `nfslock`, and `portmap` scripts in the `/etc/rc.d/init.d` directory. Here's a brief description of each daemon:

The basic NFS   Naturally, there is an NFS server daemon, `rpc.nfsd`, that's started through the `nfs` script in the `/etc/rc.d/init.d` directory. The NFS daemon also starts the mount daemon (`rpc.mountd`) and exports shared directories. You can implement configuration changes by stopping and restarting the NFS service.

RPC mount While you can use the `mount` command to connect to local directories (such as from a floppy) or network directories (such as from a Samba server), there is a special daemon for mounting NFS directories: `rpc.mountd`.

The portmapper While the `portmap` daemon just directs RPC traffic, it is essential to NFS service. If `portmap` is not running, NFS clients can't find directories shared from NFS servers.

Reboots and `statd` There will be times when your connection to an NFS server goes down. You may have a scheduled reboot, or your server may just have crashed. The `rpc.statd` daemon works with `rpc.lockd` to help clients recover NFS connections after an NFS server reboots.

Locking When files are opened through a shared NFS directory, a lock is added. The lock prevents users from overwriting the same file with different changes. Locking is run through the `rpc.lockd` daemon, via the `nfslock` script.

Setting Up Exports

Shared NFS directories are listed in `/etc/exports`. As an example, assume you have one CD drive on your NFS server that you want to share with the other computers on your LAN. Normally, CDs are mounted on the `/mnt/cdrom` directory. You also want to share the `/tmp` directory to help share special packages. The format is simple:

```
sharedirectory     hosts(specs)
```

In other words, in `/etc/exports`, you specify the directory that you want to share, the computers that you want to share with, and the limits that you need. Let's look at a couple of examples of how you might do this:

```
/mnt/cdrom *.example.com(ro,sync) big.example.com(rw,sync)
/tmp  *(rw,insecure,sync,no_wdelay,anonuid=600)
```

The *shareddirectory* is self-explanatory. There are several ways to specify the computers that you want to share with; while you can use IP addresses, NFS does not recognize CIDR notation. Several examples are shown in Table 28.2.

TABLE 28.2: SPECIFYING HOSTS IN */ETC/EXPORTS*

EXAMPLE	EXPLANATION
`*.example.com`	All computers in the `example.com` domain
`newcomp`	The computer named newcomp
`10.11.12.13/255.255.255.0`	The network with the specified IP address and subnet mask

Finally, you must specify if and how you want to limit access to the shared directory. Do you want it shared as a read-only filesystem? Do you intend to share all subdirectories of a shared directory? Do you want to give the root user from a specific computer root-level access through the directory?

While the options shown in this section may be a bit cryptic, you can specify these parameters and more in /etc/exports, as described in Table 28.3.

Starting with Red Hat Linux 8.0, you now need to specify sync or async for any shared directory. In other words, you have to specify whether the shared NFS directory responds to a command before a file is written permanently, such as to a hard disk.

TABLE 28.3: /ETC/EXPORTS SHARED DIRECTORY SPECIFICATIONS

SPEC	EFFECT
ro	If a directory is mounted ro, users can only have read-only access to it (default).
rw	If a directory is mounted rw, users can read or write to it.
sync	All data is written to a share as requested.
async	NFS may respond to a request before writing data.
secure	NFS requests (default) are sent through a secure TCP/IP port below 1024; default medium- and high-security firewalls block these ports.
insecure	NFS requests are sent through TCP/IP ports above 1024.
wdelay	If more than one computer is about to write to a shared NFS directory, the writes are grouped together (default).
no_wdelay	If more than one computer is about to write to a shared NFS directory, the data is written immediately; if you've set async, this setting is not required.
hide	NFS by default shares directories, such as /home/mj, without sharing their subdirectories, such as /home/mj/.kde.
no_hide	When you share an NFS directory, this automatically also shares the subdirectories.
subtree_check	If you export a subdirectory such as /usr/sbin, this forces the NFS server to check lower-level directories (e.g., /usr) for permissions (default).
no_subtree_check	If you export a subdirectory, such as /home/mj, it does not check the higher-level directory, such as /home, for permissions.
insecure_locks	For older NFS clients, this does not check if a user has read access to a requested file; same as no_auth_nlm.
secure_locks	For older NFS clients, this checks for user permissions on a requested file (default); same as auth_nlm.
all_squash	The UID and GID of exported files are mapped to the user anonymous; good for public directories.
no_all_squash	The UID and GID of exported files are retained (default).
root_squash	All requests from the user root are translated or mapped as if they came from the user anonymous (default).

Continued on next page

TABLE 28.3: */ETC/EXPORTS* SHARED DIRECTORY SPECIFICATIONS *(continued)*

SPEC	EFFECT
no_root_squash	This allows the root user to have full administrative access through the shared directory.
anonuid=xyz	This specifies the UID of the anonymous user in the NFS server's /etc/passwd file.
anongid=xyz	This specifies the GID of the anonymous group in the NFS server's /etc/group file.

Now that you've seen what can go into an /etc/exports file, return to the earlier example. It should make sense to you now:

```
/mnt/cdrom *.example.com(ro,sync) big.example.com(rw,sync)
/tmp  *(rw,insecure,sync,no_wdelay,all_squash,anonuid=600)
```

The first line shares the /mnt/cdrom directory with all computers in the example.com domain. This directory is read-only, unless the connection is made from the computer named big.example.com. (Naturally, this works only if your CD is writeable.)

The next line shares the /tmp directory with all computers. Computers that connect to this share can read or write (rw) to /tmp. The requests can be sent through TCP/IP ports above 1024 (insecure). Requests are written to /tmp before anything else is done (sync). Data is written immediately to disk, even if other computers that are sharing this directory are also about to write a file (no_wdelay). When mounting this directory, all users are given permissions associated with UID 600 in the NFS server's /etc/passwd file.

Securing NFS

You can configure security for shared NFS directories at two levels: through the settings in /etc/exports and through a firewall. You've just looked at /etc/exports. When you want to block NFS shared directories to outside networks, you may want to use appropriate iptables commands or even appropriate commands in /etc/hosts.allow and/or /etc/hosts.deny.

But sometimes, you may want to let users get to shared NFS directories through a firewall. While allowing NFS connections through the Internet is strongly discouraged, allowing NFS connections between LANs internal to a company or organization is probably safe.

When thinking of NFS security and firewalls, you need to consider two TCP/IP ports: 111 and 2049. As you can see from /etc/services, port 111 is related to the portmap daemon, and port 2049 is the channel for NFS.

NFS AND AN *IPTABLES* FIREWALL

We discussed the basics of iptables in Chapter 22. As we discussed in Chapters 3 and 19, the Red Hat Linux firewall tools lokkit and redhat-config-securitylevel allow you to configure standard high or medium firewalls.

The default high-security firewall blocks all network communication, except responses from DNS servers. Naturally, the two TCP/IP ports required for NFS communication are also blocked.

The default medium-security firewall, as shown in Figure 28.1, blocks all communication on all ports between 0 and 1023, which includes the standard `portmap` port 111. It also explicitly rejects data moving on NFS port 2049.

NOTE *For more information on the format of* `iptables` *firewalls, see Chapter 22.*

FIGURE 28.1

A standard medium firewall

```
Chain INPUT (policy ACCEPT)
target       prot opt source              destination
RH-Lokkit-0-50-INPUT  all  --  anywhere              anywhere

Chain FORWARD (policy ACCEPT)
target       prot opt source              destination
RH-Lokkit-0-50-INPUT  all  --  anywhere              anywhere

Chain OUTPUT (policy ACCEPT)
target       prot opt source              destination

Chain RH-Lokkit-0-50-INPUT (2 references)
target       prot opt source              destination
ACCEPT       all  --  anywhere            anywhere
REJECT       tcp  --  anywhere            anywhere          tcp dpts:0:1023 flags:
SYN,RST,ACK/SYN reject-with icmp-port-unreachable
REJECT       tcp  --  anywhere            anywhere          tcp dpt:nfs flags:SYN,
RST,ACK/SYN reject-with icmp-port-unreachable
REJECT       udp  --  anywhere            anywhere          udp dpts:0:1023 reject
-with icmp-port-unreachable
REJECT       udp  --  anywhere            anywhere          udp dpt:nfs reject-wit
h icmp-port-unreachable
REJECT       tcp  --  anywhere            anywhere          tcp dpts:x11:6009 flag
s:SYN,RST,ACK/SYN reject-with icmp-port-unreachable
REJECT       tcp  --  anywhere            anywhere          tcp dpt:xfs flags:SYN,
RST,ACK/SYN reject-with icmp-port-unreachable
[root@RH9Test root]# []
```

First, delete the rules that REJECT NFS data. As you can see from Figure 28.1, these rules are third and fifth in sequence in the RH-Lokkit-0-50-INPUT firewall. Therefore, you'll want to run these commands:

```
# iptables -D RH-Lokkit-0-50-INPUT 5
# iptables -D RH-Lokkit-0-50-INPUT 3
```

Next, make sure that the firewall accepts input through port 111. As you may remember from Chapter 22, you can add rules with the -I switch. For example, the following commands accept TCP and UDP inputs through port 111 as the second and third commands in the firewall:

```
# iptables -I RH-Lokkit-0-50-INPUT 2 -p tcp -m tcp --dport 111 -j ACCEPT
# iptables -I RH-Lokkit-0-50-INPUT 3 -p udp -m udp --dport 111 -j ACCEPT
```

Once you're satisfied with the changes, save the firewall for the next time you boot Linux by issuing this command:

```
# iptables-save > /etc/sysconfig/iptables
```

Now you should be able to set up NFS connections through your firewall.

NOTE   As described in Chapter 22, you can also save new firewall rules in `/etc/sysconfig/iptables` *with the* `service iptables save` *command.*

NFS AND A TCP WRAPPERS FIREWALL

In Chapter 23, we discussed another Linux firewall related to `xinetd` services. With the wrong commands in `/etc/hosts.deny`, you can block the `portmap`, `rpc.mountd`, `rquotad`, `statd`, and `lockd` services. For example, the simplest firewall in `/etc/hosts.deny` blocks everything:

```
ALL:ALL
```

You might recall that `xinetd` reads `/etc/hosts.allow` first. So you can let the `portmap` through this firewall with a simple command. For example, you could add this command in `/etc/hosts.allow` to let `portmap` through for the given network IP address (192.168.0.0):

```
portmap: 192.168.0.0/255.255.255.0
```

Use the same techniques with the other NFS-related services. Remember, CIDR notation such as 192.168.0.0/24 is not allowed in either the `/etc/hosts.allow` or `/etc/hosts.deny` file.

Starting NFS

You've configured exports. You've customized any firewall you may have. Finally, you're ready to start NFS and export the directories that you plan to share.

Start with the `rpcinfo -p` command. If NFS is running properly, you should see entries for at least `portmap`, `nfs`, and `mountd`, similar to what is shown in Figure 28.2.

FIGURE 28.2

Checking NFS daemons

```
[root@RH9Test root]# rpcinfo -p
   program vers proto   port
    100000    2   tcp    111  portmapper
    100000    2   udp    111  portmapper
    100024    1   udp   1024  status
    100024    1   tcp   1024  status
    391002    2   tcp   1025  sgi_fam
    100011    1   udp    947  rquotad
    100011    2   udp    947  rquotad
    100011    1   tcp    950  rquotad
    100011    2   tcp    950  rquotad
    100003    2   udp   2049  nfs
    100003    3   udp   2049  nfs
    100021    1   udp   1026  nlockmgr
    100021    3   udp   1026  nlockmgr
    100021    4   udp   1026  nlockmgr
    100005    1   udp   1027  mountd
    100005    1   tcp   2068  mountd
    100005    2   udp   1027  mountd
    100005    2   tcp   2068  mountd
    100005    3   udp   1027  mountd
    100005    3   tcp   2068  mountd
[root@RH9Test root]# []
```

If you don't, NFS isn't ready, and you need to start these daemons. If necessary, you should be able to start the `rpc.mountd` and `nfs` daemons with the `service nfs start` command. You should also be able to start the `portmap` daemon with the `service portmap start` command.

Once the service is started, you can export the shared directories with the appropriate `exportfs` command. Some of the options are listed in Table 28.4.

TABLE 28.4: *EXPORTFS* COMMANDS

COMMAND	FUNCTION
`exportfs -a`	Exports all shared directories from /etc/exports
`exportfs -r`	Revises the list of shared directories after you've changed /etc/exports
`exportfs -u`	"Unexports" all directories
`exportfs -v`	Displays currently shared directories

Now you're ready to connect to a shared directory from an NFS client computer. But there's one thing left to do: make sure that the right services will start the next time you boot Linux. As discussed in Chapter 13, you can do this with the proper `chkconfig` command. The following commands check the runlevels at which the `nfs` and `portmap` daemons start:

```
# chkconfig --list nfs
# chkconfig --list portmap
```

And if necessary, the following commands make sure that these daemons start at the appropriate runlevels. When the `nfs` daemon starts, it also starts `rpc.mountd` and, if available, the `rpc.rquotad` daemon as well.

```
# chkconfig --level 235 portmap on
# chkconfig --level 235 nfs on
```

Configuring with *redhat-config-nfs*

You can also use `redhat-config-nfs` to configure your NFS server in a GUI. To start it, run this command, or in GNOME (or KDE), use the Main Menu (K Menu) ➤ System Settings ➤ Server Settings ➤ NFS Server command. This opens the NFS Server Configuration menu shown in Figure 28.3.

To start the configuration process, click the Add button. This opens the Add NFS Share window shown in Figure 28.4. We'll look at configuring the directories described earlier with `redhat-config-nfs`. For your reference, the previous commands from `/etc/exports` that we'll be emulating are:

```
/mnt/cdrom *.example.com(ro,sync) big.example.com(rw,sync)
/tmp   *(rw,insecure,sync,no_wdelay,all_squash,anonuid=600)
```

FIGURE 28.3

The NFS Server
Configuration menu

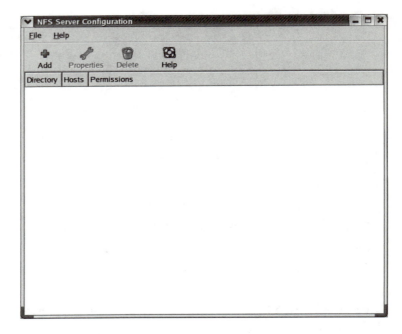

FIGURE 28.4

Adding a shared
NFS directory

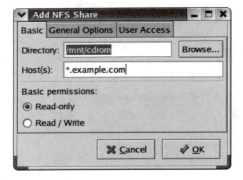

As shown in Figure 28.4, we've set up a share of the /mnt/cdrom directory, with read-only permissions for computers in the *.example.com domain. You can set up a separate share of /mnt/cdrom or /tmp to a specific computer such as big.example.com with read/write permissions.

Select the General Options tab, as shown in Figure 28.5. You can set up several of the options described in Table 28.5. By default, only Sync Write Operations On Request is active. Table 28.5 lists each option and its corresponding command.

FIGURE 28.5

The General
Options tab

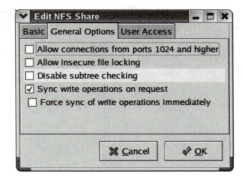

TABLE 28.5: ADD NFS SHARE GENERAL OPTIONS AND THEIR CORRESPONDING NFS */ETC/EXPORTS* COMMAND

OPTION	NFS COMMAND
Allow Connections From Ports 1024 And Higher	`insecure`
Allow Insecure File Locking	`insecure_locks`
Disable Subtree Checking	`no_subtree_check`
Sync Write Operations On Request	`sync`
Force Sync Of Write Operations Immediately	`no_wdelay`

Select the User Access tab, as shown in Figure 28.6. Table 28.6 lists each option and its corresponding command.

FIGURE 28.6

The User Access tab

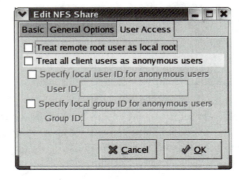

TABLE 28.6: ADD NFS SHARE USER ACCESS OPTIONS AND THE CORRESPONDING NFS */ETC/EXPORTS* COMMAND

OPTION	NFS COMMAND
Treat Remote Root User As Local Root	no_root_squash
Treat All Client Users As Anonymous Users	all_squash
Specify Local User ID For Anonymous Users	
UID	anonuid=*userid*
Specify Local Group ID For Anonymous Users	
Group ID	anongid=*groupid*

You'll note that the first two commands on this tab are mutually exclusive; in other words, you can't treat a remote user as root if you've configured all NFS clients as anonymous users.

The Specify Local User ID and Specify Local Group ID options aren't configured with a corresponding NFS command; they make no sense and are therefore not activated unless you've set a specific user or group ID. For more information on user and group ID concepts, see Chapter 9.

The resulting /etc/exports file is slightly different from before; separate lines are required for the read-only and read/write setups to the computer and network specified earlier:

```
/mnt/cdrom *.example.com(ro,sync)
/mnt/cdrom big.example.com(rw,sync)
/tmp    *(rw,insecure,sync,no_wdelay,all_squash,anonuid=600)
```

Remember, you can't configure NFS with redhat-config-nfs alone; for example, you still need to make sure that you don't have a firewall blocking NFS messages, as explained earlier in this chapter. You also should make sure that the nfs and portmap daemons are started at the appropriate runlevels the next time you boot Linux.

Working With NFS Clients

From a client computer, you need to know the available shared directories, the right way to mount these directories, and how to configure these directories to mount automatically the next time Linux boots on your computer.

Listing Shared Directories

It's easy to list the shared directories from an NFS server. All you need is the hostname or IP address of the server. The following command gives you the current list of shared directories from the computer named RHL9:

```
# showmount -e RHL9
Export list for RHL9:
/home/gb RHL9*
/tmp     *.example.com
```

TIP   *You can use the* `showmount -e` *command on the NFS server to make sure that it is actually exporting the directories that you want to share through* `/etc/exports`.

This command lists two shared directories, along with the computers that are allowed to connect to each directory. If the list is not accurate, or the command does not work, take the following steps:

Check the daemons on the server.   Are the `nfs`, `portmap`, and `mountd` daemons running?

Inspect the firewalls on both the server and the client.   Are any `iptables` commands blocking ports 111 and 2049? Are some of the NFS services blocked in `/etc/hosts.deny`?

Verify that you exported the directories in `/etc/exports`.   On the NFS server, run the `showmount -e` command. Remember, if you've just modified this file, you'll need to run the `exportfs -r` command on the server to refresh the export list.

If all else fails, refer to the discussion in Chapter 21 on network troubleshooting. While commands are available for testing network connectivity, the most common cause of network problems is the physical connections.

Mounting a Shared NFS Directory

Assuming everything is all right on the server, try the `showmount -e` *NFSserver* command again. Once you see the export list, you can mount one of these directories on your Linux computer. The following example mounts the `/tmp` directory from the computer named RHL9 on the local computer's `/tmp` directory:

```
# mount -t nfs RH81:/tmp /tmp
```

To translate, this mounts an NFS (`-t nfs`) filesystem, the `/tmp` directory from RHL9 on the local `/tmp` directory. But if there is a problem on the NFS server, or on the network connection, risks are involved. Suppose your connection "hangs," which locks up your console. Your computer will keep trying to connect, even if the NFS server has disappeared. Thus, a command with options (`-o`) like the following is preferred:

```
# mount -t nfs -o soft,intr,timeo=50 RH81:/tmp /tmp
```

This adds options to soft mount, interruptible by the NFS server, with a timeout (`timeo`) of 50 tenths of a second (which of course corresponds to 5 seconds). But as discussed in Chapter 7, this command can be simplified. You can enter mount information in `/etc/fstab`:

```
RHL9:/tmp    /tmp    nfs    soft,intr,timeo=50  0 0
```

Then all you would need to run to mount the shared `/tmp` directory is this command:

```
# mount /tmp
```

Setting Up Network Information Service Servers

The Network Information Service (NIS) is a distributed database service that uses one set of configuration files for multiple computers on a LAN.

All Linux computers come with the same basic configuration files. An NIS database of configuration files may be easier to maintain instead of different versions of the same file on different computers.

For example, you may want your users to be able to enter the same username and password at each of your computers. One approach is to copy the /etc/passwd and /etc/group files to every computer on your LAN. Alternatively, you can configure a central database on an NIS server. In NIS, these databases are also known as *maps*.

You may have a larger LAN and don't want to go to the trouble of creating a DNS server. While you could copy the /etc/hosts file to every computer on your LAN, this becomes more difficult as you add more computers to your LAN. Storing /etc/hosts on a central NIS server map is an excellent option.

NOTE *While creating a DNS server is not difficult, it does mean running another service. Many administrators try to keep their services to a minimum. One way to do this is by avoiding the use of DNS on a local network, relying on /etc/hosts shared via NIS and on the DNS servers of an ISP for the Internet.*

Red Hat Linux 9 comes with the packages needed to support a regular NIS version 2.2 server. In this chapter, you'll notice a couple of references to nisplus, which is based on the NIS version 3.*x* server (reportedly troubled by bugs).

In the following sections, we'll examine the required RPM packages, define the domain, define what we're going to share, start the NIS services, and generate the database maps that we'll need.

NOTE *The drawback to NIS is security. If you have an NIS server, it should be on a LAN behind a firewall. You should not have a firewall between NIS servers and clients. While there are a number of things you can do with firewalls to help secure NIS on a LAN, it may be more trouble than it's worth. A simple web search for the terms NIS and security reveals many thousands of websites and messages detailing various security issues.*

NIS Packages

Four basic RPM packages are associated with NIS, as shown in Table 28.7. Notice that the portmap-* RPM used by NFS is included here as well. As described in Chapter 10, you can run the rpm -qi *packagename* command to learn more about each package.

TABLE 28.7: NIS RPM PACKAGES

PACKAGE	FUNCTION
portmap-*	Supports secure NIS remote procedure call (RPC) connections.
ypbind-*	The NIS client package; it binds a client to a server.
ypserv-*	The NIS server package.
yp-tools-*	Includes basic NIS commands.

Defining the NIS Domain

NIS clients and servers are organized in domains. Unfortunately, NIS domains are unrelated to the domains associated with computer names such as `linux.mommabears.com`, or even the domains associated with Microsoft networks.

First, your computer may already have an NIS domain name. To find out, run the `domainname` command. If it returns "(none)", your computer does not have an assigned NIS domain.

Assigning an NIS domain name is easy. For example, the following command defines a domain name of nistest for the local computer:

```
# domainname nistest
```

You'll also want to add a corresponding entry in `/etc/sysconfig/network` so it is known the next time you boot Linux. In this case, here's the line you need to add:

```
NISDOMAIN=nistest
```

Defining Shared Files

Once you've installed the required RPMs and set the NIS domain name, the next step is to configure the NIS server. This starts with the `Makefile` in the `/var/yp` directory. It is an extensive file; essentially, you get to set parameters, and the script at the bottom processes the files that you select into NIS database maps to be shared on the NIS domain. The variables we'll describe in this section are based on the default `Makefile` and are limited to that file.

You can configure NIS to look for computers that aren't in the NIS database. If you enable this command (by removing the #), it looks to your DNS servers for more information:

```
#B=-b
```

On larger LANs, you may have a backup NIS server. If you do, you'll want to change `true` to `false`. NIS then looks for the names of slave servers in `/var/yp/ypservers`:

```
NOPUSH=true
```

By default, regular users have user IDs and group IDs of 500 and above. Lower ID numbers include administrative users. The following commands exclude lower ID numbers from the appropriate NIS map database:

```
MINUID=500
MINGID=500
```

TIP   If you want to keep some "local-only" users, you can set higher ID numbers. For example, if you set MINUID and MINGID to 505, the first five users on all computers on the NIS domain will be local.

If you try to connect to an NFS server on an NIS domain as a root user, the following commands map the root user ID to a special user known as nobody, which has few privileges:

```
NFSNOBODYUID=65534
NFSNOBODYGID=65534
```

As you might remember from Chapter 9, passwords are normally kept in /etc/shadow and /etc/gshadow. If your Linux system is configured this way, these commands incorporate passwords into the NIS map database:

```
MERGE_PASSWD=true
MERGE_GROUP=true
```

The following source directories should be standard. Unless you've changed the location of basic files such as /etc/passwd, you should not have to change any of these settings:

```
YPSRCDIR = /etc
YPPWDDIR = /etc
YPBINDDIR = /usr/lib/yp
YPSBINDDIR = /usr/sbin
YPDIR = /var/yp
YPMAPDIR = $(YPDIR)/$(DOMAIN)
```

Many of the following settings are standard. For example, GROUP is associated with YPPWDDIR, which is the /etc directory. From the first line in this list, the group configuration file is /etc/group, which is the standard location. If you've changed the location of any of these configuration files, revise these lines accordingly:

```
GROUP       = $(YPPWDDIR)/group
PASSWD      = $(YPPWDDIR)/passwd
SHADOW      = $(YPPWDDIR)/shadow
GSHADOW     = $(YPPWDDIR)/gshadow
ADJUNCT     = $(YPPWDDIR)/passwd.adjunct
#ALIASES    = $(YPSRCDIR)/aliases  # could be in /etc/mail
ALIASES     = /etc/aliases
ETHERS      = $(YPSRCDIR)/ethers
BOOTPARAMS  = $(YPSRCDIR)/bootparams
HOSTS       = $(YPSRCDIR)/hosts
NETWORKS    = $(YPSRCDIR)/networks
PRINTCAP    = $(YPSRCDIR)/printcap
PROTOCOLS   = $(YPSRCDIR)/protocols
PUBLICKEYS  = $(YPSRCDIR)/publickey
RPC         = $(YPSRCDIR)/rpc
SERVICES    = $(YPSRCDIR)/services
NETGROUP    = $(YPSRCDIR)/netgroup
NETID       = $(YPSRCDIR)/netid
AMD_HOME    = $(YPSRCDIR)/amd.home
AUTO_MASTER= $(YPSRCDIR)/auto.master
AUTO_HOME   = $(YPSRCDIR)/auto.home
AUTO_LOCAL  = $(YPSRCDIR)/auto.local
TIMEZONE    = $(YPSRCDIR)/timezone
LOCALE      = $(YPSRCDIR)/locale
NETMASKS    = $(YPSRCDIR)/netmasks
YPSERVERS   = $(YPDIR)/ypservers
```

Next, you can select the files to share through your NIS server. The following list is from the default configuration file; you can add or subtract from the list by placing it in or removing it from the comment area (with the #):

```
all: passwd group hosts rpc services netid protocols mail \
    # netgrp shadow publickey networks ethers bootparams \
    # printcap amd.home auto.master auto.home auto.local \
    # passwd.adjunct timezone locale netmasks
```

The rest of the `Makefile` processes these settings. Because this is not a programming book, I won't cover any further configuration; the default script in the rest of this file is sufficient for most users.

Creating a Database Map

Once you've configured the `/var/yp/Makefile`, the next step is to start the NIS server. Since it's a standard Linux service, simply issue the following command:

```
# service ypserv start
```

NOTE   *The* ypserv *daemon won't work if you haven't defined an NIS domain name. As described earlier, you can do this with the* domainname *yourNISdomain* *command.*

Now you can process the `Makefile` into a database map. The `/usr/lib/yp/ypinit -m` command processes the `Makefile` to a `/var/yp/dommainname` subdirectory, where *domainname* is the name of the NIS domain. You might realize that the `/usr/lib/yp` directory is not a part of the PATH (see Chapter 8), so you'll need to run the `ypinit` command using the full directory path.

NOTE   *Don't forget to make sure that the NIS service starts the next time you boot Linux. The* chkconfig --level *345* ypserv on *command ensures that the NIS server starts automatically at runlevels 3, 4, and 5.*

When you run this command, you'll be prompted to enter the names of the computers that you want to add to your NIS domain. In the case shown, RHL9 is the name of the NIS server computer; you may have a computer with a name like `linux.example.com`. The computers that you add are included in `/var/yp/ypservers`, which means you can configure them as NIS slave servers.

```
# /usr/lib/yp/ypinit -m

At this point, we have to construct a list of the hosts which will run NIS servers.
RHL9 is in the list of NIS server hosts. Please continue to add the names for the
other hosts, one per line. When you are done with the list, type a <control D>
        next host to add: RHL9
        next host to add:
```

When you've finished adding computers to your NIS domain, you're asked to confirm your list. If you type **n**, you're prompted to start your list again. Otherwise, the `ypinit` command should start processing your `Makefile` with messages similar to those shown in Figure 28.7.

FIGURE 28.7

Processing the NIS database

```
The current list of NIS servers looks like this:

RHL9
RHL9laptop

Is this correct?  [y/n: y]  y
We need a few minutes to build the databases...
Building /var/yp/nistest/ypservers...
Running /var/yp/Makefile...
gmake[1]: Entering directory `/var/yp/nistest'
Updating passwd.byname...
Updating passwd.byuid...
Updating group.byname...
Updating group.bygid...
Updating hosts.byname...
Updating hosts.byaddr...
Updating rpc.byname...
Updating rpc.bynumber...
Updating services.byname...
Updating services.byservicename...
Updating netid.byname...
Updating protocols.bynumber...
Updating protocols.byname...
Updating mail.aliases...
gmake[1]: Leaving directory `/var/yp/nistest'

RHL9 has been set up as a NIS master server.

Now you can run ypinit -s RHL9 on all slave server.
[root@RHL9 root]# []
```

TIP   If you see an error starting with `failed to send 'clear' to local ypserv,` *you probably forgot to start the NIS server, the* `ypserv` *daemon.*

Updating the Database Map

If you need to update the NIS database, navigate to the /var/yp directory, and then run the make command. As you may remember from Chapter 12, a Linux Makefile can be typically processed in this fashion, for a kernel, for many packages, and yes, for the NIS database.

NIS Slave Servers

In larger networks, it's useful to have backups. The NIS slave server includes the information that the other computers on your network may need to keep going. To set up an NIS slave server, there are things you need to do on both the NIS master and the NIS slave computers.

CONFIGURING THE NIS MASTER

On the master, make sure that you've added both computers to the list of NIS computers on the NIS domain, in /var/yp/ypservers. You should have already done this when you ran the /usr/lib/yp/ ypinit -m command.

You also need to revise one line in the master NIS server's `/var/yp/Makefile` to show `NOPUSH=false`. This allows your NIS master server to copy its database to the NIS slave with the `yppush` command.

You'll also need to start the NIS map transfer server daemon, `ypxfrd`. Naturally, you can do this while Linux is running by using the `service ypxfrd start` command; to make sure it starts the next time you boot Linux, run the following command:

```
# chkconfig --level 345 ypxfrd on
```

CONFIGURING THE NIS SLAVE

Once the NIS master server is ready, there are just a few things that you need to check on the NIS slave. First, NIS slave servers should also be clients of both servers. For more information, read about NIS clients in the next section.

Make sure that your NIS slave computer is bound to the NIS master server. As long as you've assigned the NIS domain name on the slave computer, the `ypbind` command should do this automatically. The `ypserv` daemon should be running; you can check this with the `service ypserv status` command. Start these daemons as required. When you're ready, try the following command (substitute the hostname of your NIS master server for RHL9):

```
# /usr/lib/yp/ypinit -s RHL9
```

If the command is successful, you'll see a long series of messages, each of which transfers a configuration file from the NIS master to the NIS slave. One example is:

```
Transferring passwd.byname...
Trying ypxfrd ... success
```

If you need to troubleshoot, you should see some messages here (and from a `ypbind -debug` command). Besides checking the network, recheck the NIS master server configuration process. Also, check that you've set `NOPUSH=false` on the NIS master to accommodate the NIS slave server. Make sure the appropriate services are started on the local NIS slave computer.

NOTE   *By default, NIS does not use DNS servers, so it's important to have at least the NIS master server information in the NIS slave computer's* `/etc/hosts` *file.*

Using NIS Clients

Configuring your computer as an NIS client is easy; all you need to do is edit `/etc/yp.conf` and run the `ypbind` command. If you want to set up the computer as a permanent NIS client, just remember to run the `chkconfig --level 345 ypbind on` command to make sure that it starts at the appropriate runlevels.

There are a number of "yp" based commands that can help you test your connection. To make sure your NIS client computer actually uses some of the database map files, you must configure the `/etc/nsswitch.conf` file.

NIS Client Configuration in *yp.conf*

It's easy to configure an NIS client. Open /etc/yp.conf in a text editor. You'll see three basic commands:

```
domain NISDOMAIN server HOSTNAME
domain NISDOMAIN broadcast
ypserver HOSTNAME
```

The entries here are straightforward. Substitute the name of your NIS domain for *NISDOMAIN*. Substitute the name of the computer with the NIS server for *HOSTNAME*. If you also have a slave server, add the following command:

```
domain NISDOMAIN server NISSLAVEHOSTNAME
```

where *NISSLAVEHOSTNAME* is the hostname of the NIS slave server. Now you're ready to start the NIS client with the `service ypbind start` command.

TIP   *If* ypbind *is having problems communicating with the NIS server, check for a firewall on the NIS server—it may be blocking NIS communication. Generally, NIS should be run on a LAN protected only from outside networks by a firewall.*

NIS Client Commands

There are a number of commands that you can use as an NIS client. Conveniently, they all start with the letters "yp." They enable you to set passwords on the remote NIS server database, test the connection, read files from the NIS server database, and more. We take a look at these commands in the following sections.

YPCAT

The `ypcat` command reads files available from an NIS server database. Like the regular `cat` command, it just scrolls the information available from the file. However, what you see in an NIS client may vary slightly from the actual file on the server. For example, the following command just lists the /etc/passwd information for users with an UID >= 500 (unless you've changed the `MINUID` and `MINGID` variables in /var/yp/Makefile):

```
# ypcat passwd
```

YPCHFN

The `ypchfn` command changes the finger information on the NIS server database map. Like the `chfn` command, it normally applies to the current user. If you're in the root account, you run the `chfn username` command to change the finger information for the user of your choice.

As described in Chapter 23, you can store finger information, such as a user's full name and telephone number, in the fifth field of that user's entry in /etc/passwd.

Thus, the following command prompts you to change the finger information for user mj on the RHL9 NIS server. It also provides a series of prompts to help you revise user mj's finger information:

```
# ypchfn mj
Changing NIS account information for mj on RHL9.
Please enter root password:

Changing full name for mj on RHL9.
To accept the default, simply press return. To enter an empty field, type the word
"none".
Name [Michael Jang]:
```

YPCHSH

The ypchsh *username* command changes the default shell for a specific user in the NIS server's /etc/passwd file. It works in a similar way to ypchfn; this command prompts you for the NIS server root password, and then prompts you to change the shell.

YPMATCH

The ypmatch *username* passwd command is an easy way to search through the NIS database file for your LAN's username entry in the master NIS server's /etc/passwd file.

YPPASSWD

The yppasswd *username* command allows you to change the password for a user on the NIS server. The user will have to use the new password to log onto any NIS client computers. Like the ypchfn and ypchsh commands, you're prompted for the NIS server root password before you're prompted to enter the new password for the desired user.

YPPUSH

If you've recently changed the NIS database on the master server, the yppush command forces that master server to send a copy of the revised database maps to any NIS slave servers listed in the /var/yp/ypservers file.

Configuring */etc/nsswitch.conf*

If you have an NIS server on your network, you'll want to make sure that the /etc/nsswitch.conf file on the NIS client looks for an NIS server for any associated configuration files. It also can point your client computer to other sources, such as the local configuration files.

For example, if you don't have an NIS server, your /etc/nsswitch.conf should be simple, with commands like these:

```
passwd:  files
shadow:  files
group:   files
hosts:   files dns
```

Each of these commands specifies a search order. For example, the `hosts` line specifies a search through the local file (`/etc/hosts`) before moving on to a DNS server (which matches the configuration in (`/etc/host.conf`). However, if you have an NIS server, you should include it in the list. For example, the following lines look to a properly bound NIS server database first:

```
passwd:  nis files
shadow:  nis files
group:   nisfiles
```

The `nis` entry corresponds to the standard NIS server. If you're using NIS version 3.*x*, you'll want to replace that entry with `nisplus`.

If you want to use the central NIS server `/etc/hosts` database, add a corresponding entry in `/etc/host.conf`. For example, the following directs your computer to first search through the NIS `/etc/hosts` database, then search the local `/etc/hosts`, and then finally search any DNS servers in `/etc/resolv.conf`:

```
order nis,hosts,bind
```

Summary

If you're sharing files between Linux and Unix computers, the standard service is the Network File System (NFS). Running NFS requires starting several `/etc/rc.d/init.d` scripts, including `nfs`, `nfslock`, and `portmap`. NFS directories are shared through `/etc/exports` and posted with the `exportfs` command. NFS communication can be blocked through TCP/IP ports 111 and 2049 by `iptables` firewalls as well as TCP Wrappers rules in `/etc/hosts.allow` and `/etc/hosts.deny`.

Once you've shared a directory through NFS, you can mount it from an NFS client computer. The `showmount -e NFSserver` command lists shared directories. You mount an NFS server just like any other local or remote directory. Be sure to configure the mount in `/etc/fstab` in ways that do not "hang" when the NFS server is not available.

As NFS shares directories with other Linux and Unix computers, the Network Information Service (NIS) shares configuration files with Linux and Unix computers. For example, you can use NIS to create a single database of usernames and passwords by converting an `/etc/passwd` and `/etc/groups` file on a server into a single shared database. You need to define an NIS domain name and shared files in `/var/yp/Makefile`. Once your `Makefile` is ready, you can convert it to a database with `ypinit`; changes can be processed with the `make` command in the `/var/yp` directory. Slave servers can also be configured with `ypinit` and refreshed with `yppush`.

Configuring an NIS client is relatively easy; just `ypbind` it to the appropriate server. Alternatively, you can use the `authconfig` command Once you've connected, NIS client commands let you look through the available databases. Finally, `/etc/nsswitch.conf`, properly configured, points your NIS client computer to the appropriate database on your NIS server.

In the next chapter, we'll examine Samba, which allows you to share files and directories with Linux, Unix, and Microsoft Windows computers.

Chapter 29

Making Samba Work for You

WITH SAMBA, YOU CAN make your Linux computer a part of a Microsoft-based network. In this chapter, you'll learn how to configure Samba as a client and as a server on a network of Microsoft Windows computers.

Computers with various Microsoft operating systems can communicate with each other using the Server Message Block (SMB) protocol. When a Microsoft operating system shares files or printers on a TCP/IP network, it uses the Common Internet File System (CIFS). Samba is the way a Linux computer communicates with SMB and CIFS.

Samba is a heterogeneous service. Once you've configured Samba, other Microsoft Windows computers won't be able to tell the difference. Like CUPS from Chapter 25, Samba includes its own web-based configuration utility, SWAT.

You can use Samba packages to configure your Linux computer as a server or a client, and then connect to or share directories and printers. As a Samba client, you can also connect to a shared Microsoft directory in a terminal mode that looks like a text-based FTP connection.

The main Samba configuration file is /etc/samba/smb.conf. Many Linux administrators configure it directly in a text editor, and you can learn how to do the same to share directories and printers from your Linux computer. It's easy to test and troubleshoot the changes you make to smb.conf.

Samba features two GUI configuration tools. SWAT (Samba Web Administration Tool) is a full-featured, browser-based tool available through TCP/IP port 901. Although simpler, the redhat-config-samba tool can help you configure basic settings for your Samba server and shared directories. This chapter covers the following topics:

- Bridging the gap between Linux and Microsoft Windows
- Configuring Samba as a client
- Understanding the Samba configuration file
- Managing Samba users
- Using SWAT
- Exploring the redhat-config-samba alternative

Bridging the Gap between Linux and Windows

As a heterogeneous service, Samba bridges the gap between Linux and Microsoft Windows—which essentially means that it can communicate equally well with either operating system. In fact, you can configure Samba to share directories and printers in the same way as any other member of a Microsoft Windows network.

Functioning on a Microsoft Network

One of the advantages of Samba is that it allows you to configure a Linux or Unix computer to function in different ways on a Microsoft Windows network. When your configuration is complete, Microsoft users don't even need to know that they're communicating with a Linux computer. With Samba, you can configure your Linux computer to look like any of the following types of computers:

- Member of a Microsoft Windows workgroup
- Member of a Microsoft Windows domain
- Microsoft Windows member server
- Microsoft primary domain controller (PDC)

Samba 2.2.7 (included with Red Hat Linux 9) does not allow you to configure Linux as a BDC. However, the functionality is possible; see the Samba BDC HOWTO at `www.samba.org` for more information. The people behind Samba are working on incorporating explicit BDC support in Samba 3.0.

Samba was originally based on Microsoft's LAN Manager system, where client computers used NetBIOS names over a TCP/IP network, NBT (NetBIOS over TCP/IP); it does not need Microsoft's other networking system, NetBEUI. For more information on NetBIOS and NetBEUI, see Chapter 20.

Licensing

Don't let the title of this section make you panic. Samba is licensed under the GPL, and is freely available as a part of different Unix-style operating systems, including Red Hat Linux 9.

Samba makes it possible for you to set up Linux computers as part of a Microsoft network. It can reduce the number of Microsoft operating systems that you need to purchase for your network. As of this writing, you don't need to pay for any Microsoft license to use Samba.

NOTE *There is speculation that Microsoft is preparing legal action to stop free Samba connections to its networks. But I think a number of companies would oppose such efforts. In my opinion, as long as some of these companies back the people behind Samba, such legal action could take years, by which time other technologies could be available.*

Definitions

This chapter contains a few terms that are either exclusive to Samba or more closely related to the world of Microsoft networking. They include:

Primary domain controller (PDC) The computer that has the central database of usernames and passwords. It often also contains the central database of Microsoft Windows logon profiles.

Backup domain controller (BDC)   This computer gets its information from a PDC. *PDC* and *BDC* are Windows NT concepts.

Browse list   A list of shared resources on a network.

Browse master   A computer in charge of maintaining a browse list for a network.

Domain   A network with a centralized database of at least usernames and passwords. This concept is quite different from an Internet domain name.

Member Server   Any computer on a Microsoft Windows network that shares directories or printers and is not a PDC or a BDC.

Peer-to-peer   A group of computers on a LAN, each of which can act as a server; commonly associated with a workgroup.

Server   A computer that shares directories or printers.

Share   Any directory or printer that is shared on a network.

Workgroup   A LAN without a dedicated server. Each computer is responsible for its own usernames and passwords; each computer often shares directories and printers with the rest of the LAN.

NOTE   *In this chapter, the term "Microsoft server" on a network can refer to any Microsoft operating system that shares directories or printers. It can also refer to a Samba server on a Linux computer.*

Packages

Five basic packages are associated with Samba on Red Hat Linux. All you need to configure your computer as a Microsoft client is `samba-client-*` and `samba-common-*`. The other packages help you configure your computer as a server on a Microsoft-style network. These packages are summarized in Table 29.1

TABLE 29.1: SAMBA RPM PACKAGES

PACKAGE	DESCRIPTION
`samba-*`	The basic Samba server package, this includes commands for matching Linux and Microsoft usernames and passwords.
`samba-client-*`	This package allows you to set up your Linux computer to read shared Microsoft directories and print to shared Microsoft printers.
`samba-common-*`	This package includes files required to support Linux as a Samba client and as a Samba server.
`samba-swat-*`	This GUI tool lets you modify the main Samba configuration files, especially `smb.conf`; if you don't need fine-grained control, you may consider `redhat-config-samba` as an alternative.
`redhat-config-samba-*`	This is the alternative to `samba-swat`; it's simpler but less mature and allows less configuration control.

Configuring Samba as a Client

With the samba-client-* and samba-common-* RPM packages, you can see the directories and print-ers shared from a Microsoft computer. You can connect to a shared directory in two basic ways: by mounting a shared Microsoft Windows directory on a local Linux directory, or by connecting to the shared directory in terminal mode, as if you were connecting to an FTP server. In addition, you need to know how to connect to a shared printer connected to a Microsoft computer.

Shared Samba Directory

It is easy to connect to a shared directory from a Microsoft server. As shown in Figure 29.1, all you need is the smbclient command, along with the name or IP address of the server. The command is slightly unusual; note the backslashes associated with the smbclient command.

FIGURE 29.1

Reviewing the shares from a Microsoft server

```
[root@RH9Test root]# smbclient -L \\laptop2
added interface ip=10.252.113.63 bcast=10.252.113.255 nmask=255.255.255.0
Password:
Domain=[WORKGROUP] OS=[Windows 5.1] Server=[Windows 2000 LAN Manager]

        Sharename       Type        Comment
        ---------       ----        -------
        IPC$            IPC         Remote IPC
        D$              Disk        Default share
        SharedDocs      Disk
        print$          Disk        Printer Drivers
        ftproot         Disk
        Downloads       Disk
        HPLaserJ        Printer     Comment Test
        Temp            Disk
        RedHat          Disk
        OEDboot         Disk
        ADMIN$          Disk        Remote Admin
        C$              Disk        Default share
        Proposals       Disk
        ml3             Disk
        RedHatOld       Disk

        Server                      Comment
        ---------                   -------

        Workgroup                   Master
        ---------                   -------
[root@RH9Test root]# []
```

There are a number of interesting shares in this directory. If the appropriate permissions are set on the Microsoft server, you can mount any of these shared directories almost like an NFS directory. The difference is subtle. For example, the following command can mount the Downloads directory shared from the computer named laptop2 on the local directory /root/downloads. Linux follows up by requesting a password.

```
# mount '//laptop2/downloads' /root/downloads
Password:
```

The mount command actually serves as a "front end" to the `mount.smbfs` command, from the `samba-client` RPM package. You could also substitute the `smbclient` command.

NOTE   *Strictly speaking, you should specify the Samba file type for* mount *by using the* -t smbfs *switch; because* mount *is a "front end" for* mount.smbfs, *this is not required.*

Since there is no username, this mount command will work only with a Microsoft Workgroup–style shared directory. In other words, this requires a shared directory from a Windows 95/98/ME computer—or a shared directory where the user Everyone is allowed access—and you need just the password associated with the shared directory (if required). (Microsoft Windows NT/2000/XP computers can also be configured in this manner.)

However, most networks are more restrictive. On Microsoft Windows servers, you can limit access to specific users and or groups. In that case, you must have a username and password with appropriate privileges to that directory. The -o option allows you to enter usernames, passwords, and more when specifying a share. I personally prefer to specify just the username in the command line so I don't have to type the password in clear text in a terminal. Linux automatically prompts for a password.

```
# mount -o username=michael '//laptop2/downloads' /root/downloads
Password:
```

NOTE   *You can even provide variable levels of access; for example, you can configure read-only access for guest users, while providing full access to privileged users.*

The specifications for a Windows server can get more complex. Some of the other available Samba mount options are shown in Table 29.2.

TABLE 29.2: SAMBA *MOUNT -O* OPTIONS

OPTION	DESCRIPTION
username=*winuser*	Allows you to specify the Microsoft username of an authorized user on the Microsoft server.
password=*winpass*	Lets you specify the Microsoft password associated with the privileged Microsoft user; if you enter only a username, you're automatically prompted for a password.
credentials=*file*	Reads a username and password from a specified file, which you can protect, like /etc/shadow; useful for automatic mounting from files such as /etc/fstab. The syntax is: username=*winuser* password=*winpass*
uid=*linuser*	Allows you to set the Linux users who own the files on the mounted filesystem; can be a user ID number or a username.
workgroup=*winwork*	Lets you specify the workgroup with the shared directory.

NOTE *These commands assume that the name of the Microsoft Windows computer is listed in your DNS server or* /etc/hosts *file. You could substitute the IP address for the computer name.*

Samba Terminal Mode

With the name of the Microsoft Windows computer and share, you can connect directly to that shared directory as if it were an FTP server. Once connected, you can upload and download files as well. For example, the command shown in Figure 29.2 connects to the directory I used for this book. Note how I use double quotes with the **cd** command to navigate to a two-word Windows XP directory.

FIGURE 29.2

The direct Samba connection

```
[root@RH9Test root]# smbclient //laptop2/ml3 -U michael
added interface ip=10.252.113.63 bcast=10.252.113.255 nmask=255.255.255.0
Password:
Domain=[WORKGROUP] OS=[Windows 5.1] Server=[Windows 2000 LAN Manager]
smb: \> cd "Other Stuff"
smb: \Other Stuff\> dir
  .                                   D        0  Wed Apr  2 19:05:15 2003
  ..                                  D        0  Wed Apr  2 19:05:15 2003
  4179CoverCopy.doc                   A    24064  Tue Mar 11 09:57:36 2003
  4179CoverCopy_mj.doc                A    26624  Tue Mar 11 10:15:36 2003
  4179CoverCopy_mja.doc               A    28672  Tue Mar 11 13:57:46 2003
  4179EP1.doc                         A    52224  Mon Mar 31 16:09:49 2003
  4179EP4.doc                         A    51712  Mon Mar 31 16:09:08 2003

              45778 blocks of size 524288. 28963 blocks available
smb: \Other Stuff\> help
?               altname         archive         blocksize       cancel
cd              chmod           chown           del             dir
du              exit            get             help            history
lcd             link            lowercase       ls              mask
md              mget            mkdir           more            mput
newer           open            print           printmode       prompt
put             pwd             q               queue           quit
rd              recurse         rename          rm              rmdir
setmode         symlink         tar             tarmode         translate
!
smb: \Other Stuff\> []
```

Also note the list of available commands. Many of these commands should look familiar from Chapter 27. In fact, Samba implements the chroot jail features described in that chapter.

Connecting to a Printer

Shared printers from Microsoft Windows computers should be easy to configure in Linux. If the browse functionality of your Microsoft network is working, you'll be able to select the printer with the redhat-config-printer wizard, in the Queue Type screen, as described in Chapter 25.

But this is not always possible. Microsoft browsing may have trouble finding your printer on a timely basis. Or you might have forgotten to make your printer browsable. You can configure a standard local printer and change the settings later. For example, Figure 29.3 illustrates a standard printer that I configured locally.

FIGURE 29.3

A redhat-config-printer local printer

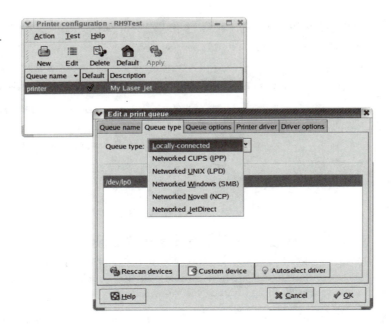

It's easy to change this to point to a remote printer; you simply click on the Queue Type drop-down box. From the resulting list, select Networked Windows (SMB) printer.

The format required to connect to a Samba printer is illustrated in Figure 29.4. Each entry is described in Table 29.3.

FIGURE 29.4

Configuring a Samba print queue

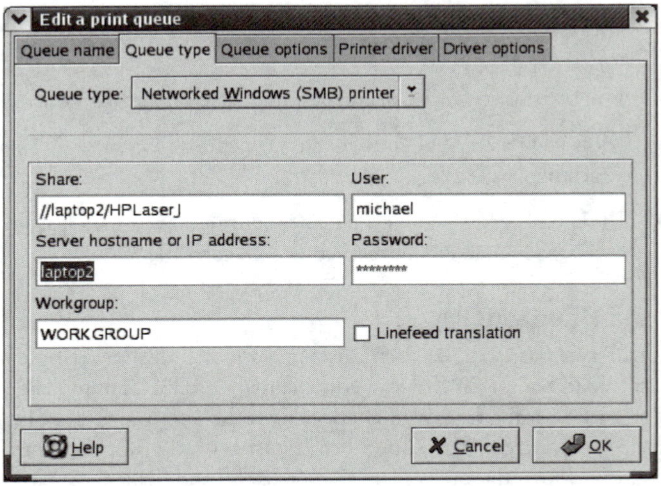

TABLE 29.3: INFORMATION FOR CONNECTING TO A SHARED SAMBA PRINTER

FIELD	DESCRIPTION
Share	The share name in the //*servername*/*printername* format.
Server Name Or IP Address	The name or IP address of the computer that's sharing the printer.
Workgroup	The Windows workgroup name; enter only if the Windows server is in a workgroup.
User	The Microsoft username of the authorized user.
Password	The Microsoft password associated with the user.

The Samba Configuration Files

There are three default Samba configuration files, all located in the /etc/samba directory. Two of them, lmhosts and smbusers, are fairly simple. The third, smb.conf, is the main Samba configuration file and the one we'll focus on in this section.

NOTE *You may also find a* secrets.tdb *file in this directory, which normally includes the security identifier (SID) used on a Microsoft Windows network.*

If you're going to follow along with this book, we suggest that you back up these files in another directory. That way, if you lose track of your changes, you can restore these files without reinstalling the applicable packages.

The smb.conf file especially includes a substantial number of useful comments that help you learn to configure Samba. If you're just learning Samba, you should back up smb.conf for three reasons:

◆ The comments in the original smb.conf can help you learn more about Samba.

◆ Tools such as SWAT and redhat-config-samba may eliminate some comments when they write changes to smb.conf.

◆ Tools such as SWAT and redhat-config-samba may leave out default settings such as workgroup=WORKGROUP from your smb.conf file.

Samba Daemons

There are two basic Samba daemons: smbd and nmbd. After changing any configuration file, you should at least reload Samba. When you edit the main Samba configuration file, /etc/samba/smb.conf, you need to make Samba read your changes with the service smb reload command. However, if you've made any major changes, it's useful to restart both daemons. Restarting the smbd daemon with the following command stops and starts both smbd and nmbd automatically:

```
# service smb restart
```

Other Samba Configuration Files

The other files in the /etc/samba directory are lmhosts and smbusers. As we mentioned earlier, they are fairly simple files. Other files may be added during the Samba configuration process.

LMHOSTS

Similar to /etc/hosts, the lmhosts file is a database of IP addresses and NetBIOS names. A NetBIOS name is a name of a Microsoft Windows computer, typically limited to 15 alphanumeric characters. The default lmhosts file includes one line; Microsoft operating systems also use the localhost name to refer to the local computer:

```
127.0.0.1 localhost
```

SMBUSERS

The smbusers file is a database of Linux and Microsoft Windows usernames. By default, it includes two lines:

```
root = administrator admin
nobody = guest pcguest smbguest
```

In other words, the Linux root user is mapped to the Microsoft accounts administrator and admin; the Linux nobody user is mapped to the Microsoft accounts guest, pcguest, and smbguest.

You can add to this file by using the smbadduser command. For example, say you have a Linux user jp and a Windows user Jean-Paul on your network. The commands shown in Figure 29.5 allow your Linux user jp to access user Jean-Paul's files on a Microsoft computer on your LAN.

FIGURE 29.5

Adding a Samba user

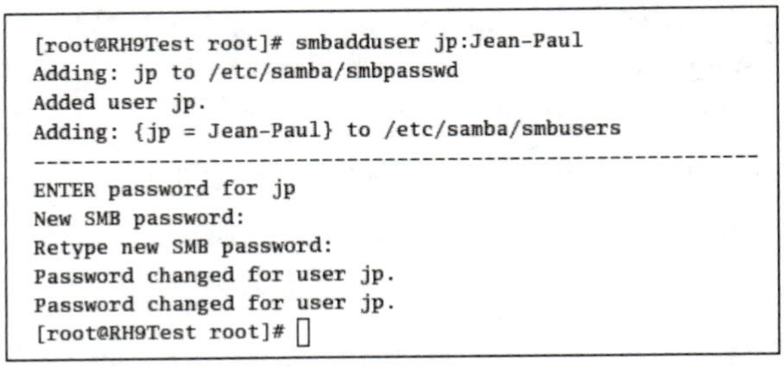

```
[root@RH9Test root]# smbadduser jp:Jean-Paul
Adding: jp to /etc/samba/smbpasswd
Added user jp.
Adding: {jp = Jean-Paul} to /etc/samba/smbusers
------------------------------------------------------------
ENTER password for jp
New SMB password:
Retype new SMB password:
Password changed for user jp.
Password changed for user jp.
[root@RH9Test root]# []
```

The commands shown in Figure 29.5 add a simple line to /etc/samba/smbusers:

```
jp = Jean-Paul
```

This database won't work until you activate the following line in smb.conf:

```
; username map = /etc/samba/smbusers
```

In Samba configuration, the hash mark (#) and the semicolon (;) are both used to start comment lines. To activate this line, open /etc/samba/smb.conf in a text editor and delete the semicolon from the front of this line. A number of other lines in smb.conf include the semicolon; the rest of this chapter explains what happens if you delete various semicolons to activate specific commands.

Once you begin adding Samba users, Linux adds an `smbpasswd` file to the `/etc/samba` directory. It includes the Microsoft Windows passwords that you've added, in encrypted format.

The Main Samba File: *smb.conf*

The default Samba configuration file, `/etc/samba/smb.conf`, includes a number of comments that make it a rich source of information. However, the comments may be cryptic to those of you who are less familiar with the Samba service. If you haven't already done so, save a copy of this file in another directory.

NOTE   If you've already configured Samba, you may not have the original `smb.conf` file with comments. You can get another copy by backing up and then removing your current Samba configuration files from `/etc/samba`, then reinstalling the `samba-common-*` package with the `rpm -Uvh --force samba-common-*` command. Don't forget to restore your original Samba configuration files when you're done.

The `smb.conf` file includes *global* settings for connecting to a desired Microsoft Windows–based network. It also includes *share* definitions for any directories and printers that you might want to share with other computers on your LAN. Different groups of settings help you work in a LAN that's configured as a Microsoft *workgroup*, as a member server, or even as a primary or backup domain controller.

The following sections include a basic analysis of the standard settings in `/etc/samba/smb.conf`, in order. Later in this chapter, you'll use SWAT and `redhat-config-samba` to configure `smb.conf`.

The following section analyzes the `smb.conf` file from the Red Hat `samba-*` RPM package. Many of the settings in this version of `smb.conf` vary from the Samba defaults.

SAMBA GLOBAL SETTINGS

The `smb.conf` file contains a substantial number of `[global]` variables. If you don't use a variable, Samba will assume the default for that variable.

With different global variables, you can:

◆ Limit the IP addresses allowed to access your server.

◆ Set printers as a part of the Samba browse list.

◆ Configure guest accounts and log files.

◆ Configure Samba to match the predominant Windows security mode on your network.

◆ Take advantage of the many password settings available.

◆ Map Linux usernames to Windows usernames.

◆ Customize configuration files for different computers.

◆ Limit Samba authentication by using Pluggable Authentication Modules (PAM), as described in Chapter 22.

◆ Configure Samba to send data in different-sized data chunks, and through different interfaces.

◆ Set the browse list, where shared information is advertised, possibly based on different master computers on a network.

◆ Make Samba conform to the logon parameters on a Microsoft network.

◆ Store profiles on a Linux computer.

◆ Set up Samba to work with WINS and DNS.

Linux is case sensitive and Windows is not; Samba helps you bridge the difference.

Basic Network Type

The first global variable describes the type of network that you're trying to join. While the name of the variable is `workgroup`, you can set it to the name of your Microsoft network's workgroup or domain. For example, if your network's domain is named bignet, substitute the following line in `smb.conf`:

```
workgroup=BIGNET
```

Samba also can include a description of your computer; Figure 29.6 reflects the following command for the computer named RH9test:

```
server string = Mike's Samba Server
```

FIGURE 29.6

A Microsoft Windows view of a shared Samba server

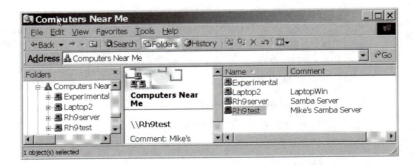

IP Address Limits

You can limit access to Samba through the `iptables` commands described in Chapter 22. You can further limit access with the `hosts allow` command. For example, either of the following commands limits access to the local computer and the 10.122.33.0 network:

```
hosts allow = 10.122.33. 127.
hosts allow = 10.122.33.0/255.255.255.0 127.
```

Samba and Printers

By default, printers are included in the list of shared, browsable items. The following commands load the list of printers from `/etc/printcap` for a standard CUPS-based system:

```
printcap name = /etc/printcap
load printers = yes
printing = cups
```

NOTE   *There are a number of parameters in Samba that look like they are misspelled. They may still be good. For example,* browsable *works as well as* browseable *and* writable *works as well as* writeable.

Alternatively, if you're using LPD (see Chapter 25), substitute the following values:

```
printcap name = /etc/printcap
load printers = yes
printing = lprng
```

Guest Accounts

Samba lets you create a standard guest account. For example, if you're setting up a workstation for people in a lobby, you may want them to access your advertising but nothing else. If you activate the standard below, make sure that pcguest is a real user on your Linux system:

```
; guest account = pcguest
```

Log Files

The following option configures different log files for each computer that connects to your Samba server. For example, if you have a Windows computer named Havel, the following line means that you can find debugging information in havel.log in the noted directory. A max log size of 0 means that there is no limit on the size of these log files; other limits are in kilobytes.

```
log file = /var/log/samba/%m.log
max log size = 0
```

NOTE   *Any expression in* smb.conf *that starts with a % can vary. For example,* %m *represents the name of the client computer, and thus changes depending on the client.*

Security Modes

There are several basic security modes on Microsoft Windows networks. Generally, what you select is based on the conditions for the shared directory and the type of shared network. The options are described in Table 29.4.

```
security = share
security = user
security = server
security = domain
```

TABLE 29.4: SAMBA SECURITY MODES

MODE	DESCRIPTION
share	For systems where shared directories do not require anything more than a password for access; most common for workgroups of peer-to-peer computers without any dedicated servers.

Continued on next page

TABLE 29.4: SAMBA SECURITY MODES *(continued)*

MODE	DESCRIPTION
user	For systems where shared directories are limited by usernames and passwords; common to server-level computers such as Windows 2000, Windows XP, and yes, Linux, on a peer-to-peer workgroup network.
server	For systems where usernames and passwords prefer a centralized database; if such a database cannot be found, this reverts to `security = user`.
domain	For systems that are connecting to a Windows-style domain; requires `smbuser` and `smbpasswd` database files in `/etc/samba`.

Password Settings

Several password settings are available in Samba. If you're configuring a central server for Microsoft Windows usernames and passwords, you can specify it here. The PDC can even be located on a Samba-enabled Linux computer.

If you have set `security = share` or `security = domain`, you should also specify the password servers for the network. For example, if you know that the names of your PDC and BDC are ntserv1 and ntserv2, you could insert the following command:

```
password server = ntserv1 ntserv2
```

Or, if you don't know the names of your PDC or BDC, the following command sets your Samba server on a search for domain controllers:

```
password server = *
```

Several Microsoft Windows operating systems don't work very well on passwords with mixed upper- and lowercase characters. The commands, if active, try all combinations of upper- and lowercase characters on an eight-character password and username:

```
; password level = 8
; username level = 8
```

Normally, Samba is configured to send encrypted passwords from the standard Samba passwords file. Remember, this password file includes Microsoft Windows usernames and passwords that you added with the `smbadduser` command. However, not all Microsoft Windows computers can handle encrypted passwords.

```
encrypt passwords = yes
smb passwd file = /etc/samba/smbpasswd
```

Without these commands, Samba would revert to the default, sending passwords over the network in clear text. That's still required for the first versions of Microsoft Windows 95 and earlier Microsoft operating systems.

If you've configured Samba with Secure Socket Layer (SSL) libraries, activate the following command:

```
; ssl CA certFile = /usr/share/ssl/certs/ca-bundle.crt
```

If users change their passwords on a Microsoft Windows computer, the following commands synchronize the corresponding Linux password:

```
unix password sync = Yes
passwd program = /usr/bin/passwd %u
passwd chat = *New*password* %n\n *Retype*new*password* %n\n *passwd:
```

➥ *all*authentication*tokens*updated*successfully*

Finally, you can use Pluggable Authentication Modules (PAM) to help secure your passwords (see Chapter 22); a PAM command supersedes the `password program` variable:

```
pam password change = yes
```

There's one more PAM command a few lines away. If you do set up clear-text passwords, the following command uses PAM to control access to your system:

```
obey pam restrictions = yes
```

Mapping Linux and Windows Users

As described earlier, you can match your Linux and Windows users with different usernames. When you use the `smbadduser` command, the result is stored in a database in `/etc/samba/smbusers`. You can also edit this file directly. If you plan to use this database, activate the following command:

```
; username map = /etc/samba/smbusers
```

Customizing Samba by Computer

You can configure Samba servers on remote computers. If you activate the following command, each computer will look for a specific configuration file. For example, if your Windows computer name is Chirac, the `%m` variable makes it look for the `/etc/samba/smb.conf.Chirac` configuration file when it connects.

```
; include = /etc/samba/smb.conf.%m
```

Performance Management

When you're more comfortable with Samba, you'll learn to optimize network performance. What you do depends on the size and traffic on your network. In the following command, `TCP_NODELAY` often doubles Samba performance. The `SO_RCVBUF` and `SO_SNDBUF` variables are buffers for data coming in and out of Samba. Optimal settings vary with the load on your Samba server. If you want to experiment, adjust each by 1KB (e.g., `SO_RCVBUF=7168` or `SO_RCVBUF=9216`):

```
socket options = TCP_NODELAY SO_RCVBUF=8192 SO_SNDBUF=8192
```

Network Interfaces

Servers can be configured with multiple network interface cards. You can limit Samba access to one network card, or you can set a Samba server to work with a specific remote network. For example, the following line sets Samba to work with the `eth1` network interface card and the 172.168.33.0 IP network address:

```
interfaces eth1 172.168.33.0/24
```

Browsing

On a Microsoft Windows–based network, *browsing* is the ability of computers to see available shared directories and printers. One computer is selected as a browse master; other computers with shares send their information to that computer.

You can even set your Samba server to send its shares to a remote network. If you don't know the IP address of the master browser on that network, just use the broadcast address. For example, the following command synchronizes browse lists between your LAN and the 192.168.1.0 network:

```
remote browse sync =  192.168.1.255
```

This command just sends your Samba server's browse information to that network (alternatively, you can specify the IP address of the browse master computer):

```
remote announce = 192.168.1.255
```

One computer on a Microsoft network keeps the browse list. An "election" is held to determine that computer; even a Samba server can be elected to maintain the browse list. However, the following command keeps the Samba server out of the election:

```
; local master = no
```

If you want your Samba server to participate in a browse election, you can fix its chances with the following command. At this level, Samba will normally win a browse election against any computer but a domain controller or a Microsoft Windows NT server:

```
; os level = 33
```

If you don't want to leave anything to chance, you can set Samba to be the master browser for your domain:

```
; domain master = yes
```

If your Samba server is underworked, you may want to set it to be the preferred master browser with the following command:

```
; preferred master = yes
```

Logon Management

If you have a Linux computer and Microsoft Windows computers on your network, you can set Samba to control the username and password database as a PDC for that network by activating the following command:

```
; domain logons = yes
```

NOTE *This also requires user level security and a* [netlogon] *directory, which are described in other parts of this file.*

A Microsoft network lets you configure logons by user or by computer. Each is configured by a logon script, which you can store on your Samba server. %m corresponds to each computer (machine) and %U corresponds to each user:

```
;  logon script = %m.bat
;  logon script = %U.bat
```

With a centralized profile, logons by user can provide a consistent look and feel for that user on any Microsoft computer on that network. You can store the profiles on your Samba server, in the logon path. %L represents the name of the server; while %U is the username:

```
;  logon path = \\%L\Profiles\%U
```

WINS and DNS

The Windows Internet Name Service (WINS) is similar to DNS, except that it is a database of NetBIOS names and IP addresses. If Samba isn't able to find the name of a computer in /etc/hosts, WINS and DNS provide two alternative databases.

The following command sets up WINS on the local Samba server:

```
;  wins support = yes
```

Alternatively, you can look to a different WINS server on a specific IP address (the address shown is arbitrary; substitute appropriately). In this case, your Samba server becomes a WINS client:

```
;  wins server = 192.168.0.22
```

If your Microsoft-based network includes older computers, you may want to activate this command to allow all computers access to the WINS database:

```
;  wins proxy = yes
```

Or, if the computer is not in the WINS database, you can set up your DNS server as an alternate database by activating this command:

```
;  dns proxy = yes
```

Case Management

Linux is a case-sensitive operating system; Microsoft operating systems are not. Normally, Samba preserves the case of transferred files. You can force everything into lower case; the following commands affect long filenames and filenames that follow the old Microsoft 8.3 filename format (e.g., abcdefgh.123):

```
;  preserve case = no
;  short preserve case = no
```

In contrast, you can set all files to default to uppercase with the following command:

```
;  default case = upper
```

If all of your users are disciplined about case-sensitive filenames on all computers on your network, you may be able to make your Samba server case-sensitive too with this command:

```
; case sensitive = yes
```

Remember, Microsoft Windows is not a case-sensitive operating system; if you activate case-sensitivity, any mistakes in the case of various filenames can cause problems.

NOTE Configuring Samba as a PDC is a rich and complex topic, which itself could fill a book this size. For more information, review the latest Samba HOWTO, available online at `us1.samba.org/samba/docs/Samba-HOWTO-Collection.html`.

DEFAULT GLOBAL SETTINGS

Default settings for global variables are listed in Table 29.5. Remember, if you use a default parameter, you don't even need to include it in `smb.conf`; tools such as SWAT and `redhat-config-samba` will delete it when you use them to update `smb.conf`.

TABLE 29.5: DEFAULT *SMB.CONF* GLOBAL SETTINGS

VARIABLE	DEFAULT
case sensitive	no
default case	lower
dns proxy	yes
domain logons	no
encrypt passwords	no
guest account	nobody
hosts allow	All hosts allowed access
include	No default
interfaces	All active interfaces except 127.0.0.1 (if you can send a broadcast message to that address)
load printers	yes
local master	yes
log file	No default
logon path	\\%N\%U\profile, where %N is the NIS server and %U is the username
logon script	No default
max log size	5000 (KB)
obey pam restrictions	no

Continued on next page

TABLE 29.5: DEFAULT *SMB.CONF* GLOBAL SETTINGS

VARIABLE	DEFAULT
pam password change	no
passwd chat	*new*password* %n\n *new*password* %n\n* changed
passwd program	/bin/passwd
passwd server	No default
password level	0
preferred master	auto
preserve case	yes
printcap name	/etc/printcap
printing	No default
remote announce	No default
remote browse sync	No default
security	user
server string	Samba %v, where %v = version number
short preserve case	yes
smb password file	No default
socket options	TCP_NODELAY
ssl CA certFile	/usr/local/ssl/certs/trustedCAs.pem
unix password sync	no
username level	0
username map	No default
wins proxy	no
wins server	Not enabled
wins support	no
workgroup	WORKGROUP

CONFIGURING A SHARE

Now it's time to analyze the way directories are shared from the packaged `smb.conf` configuration file. There are seven examples of shared directories in the standard `smb.conf` file; once we examine each of these examples, you'll have a much better idea of how to configure your own shared directories.

The [homes] Share

Microsoft Windows users with accounts on your Linux computer can get read and write access to their own home directories. All you need is the following standard commands in `smb.conf`:

```
[homes]
    comment = Home Directories
    browseable = no
    writeable = yes
    valid users = %S
    create mode = 0664
    directory mode = 0775
```

These commands are explained in Table 29.6.

TABLE 29.6: Typical Samba Home Directory Share Commands

COMMAND	DESCRIPTION
`[homes]`	This is a standard "special" section in `smb.conf`.
`comment = Home Directories`	This command describes the share for Windows Network Neighborhood, My Network Places, or `smbclient -L \\hostname`.
`browseable = no`	Normally, `browseable=no` keeps the shared directory from being shown in Network Neighborhood or My Network Places; this does not apply for users' own home directories.
`writeable = yes`	This command allows users to write to that directory; you can also use `read only=no`.
`valid users = %S`	The %S is the name of the service, which in this case is associated with the user\.
`create mode = 0644`	This command sets `rw-r--r--` permissions on new files. It does not override permissions set on Windows NT/2000/XP computers. It's also known as `create mask`.
`directory mode = 0775`	This command sets `rwxr-xr-x` permissions on new directories. It does not override permissions set on Windows NT/2000/XP computers. It's also known as `directory mask`.

To get to their directory from a Microsoft Windows computer, users simply must enter their Linux username and password in the Connect To *Computername* window, shown in Figure 29.7.

FIGURE 29.7
Connecting to a
shared Samba home
directory

The [tmp] share

You can set up the /tmp directory as a common place for users on your network to share files. The following commands set it up as accessible for any user:

```
[tmp]
    comment = Temporary file space
    path = /tmp
    read only = no
    public = yes
```

These commands are straightforward; the comment is added to the Windows Network Neighborhood or My Network Places view of /tmp; any valid user can write to this directory. The public = yes command is new and is synonymous with guest ok = yes. In other words, a password is not even required.

The [public] Share

You don't need to share directories with everyone. Similar to the User Private Group scheme described in Chapter 9, you can set up a directory that's readable to all, but writeable only by users in the group named staff:

```
[public]
    comment = Public Stuff
    path = /home/samba
    public = yes
    writable = yes
    printable = no
    write list = @staff
```

Before you set up this particular share, you need to make sure there is a /home/samba directory, as well as a staff group, in /etc/groups.

Another [public] Share

One variation may be useful for more public situations; the commands that follow configure a directory where all files are readable and writeable by all users. However, the `only guest = yes` command means that any user who connects to this directory has only the privileges of the guest user. Of course, you need to make sure that the `path` directory—in this case, `/usr/somewhere/else/public`—actually exists.

```
[public]
    path = /usr/somewhere/else/public
    public = yes
    only guest = yes
    writable = yes
    printable = no
```

A Share for Two

One more variation configures a share with just two valid users—in this case, Mary and Fred. While it isn't a public share, you'll see later that `browseable = yes` by default. In other words, other users can see Mary and Fred's share, but they can't access their shared directory unless they have one of their usernames and passwords:

```
[myshare]
    comment = Mary's and Fred's stuff
    path = /usr/somewhere/shared
    valid users = mary fred
    public = no
    writable = yes
    printable = no
    create mask = 0765
```

Remember, the items noted have to exist on the Samba server. In this case, that includes the `/usr/somewhere/shared` directory and the users named mary and fred.

A Private Directory

You can configure a private directory other than their home directory for individual users. For example, the following commands sets up a private directory, `/usr/somewhere/private`, for the Linux user named fred. Since `public = no`, guest users are not allowed to access this directory.

```
[fredsdir]
    comment = Fred's Service
    path = /usr/somewhere/private
    valid users = fred
    public = no
    writable = yes
    printable = no
```

A Shared Directory for a Computer

You can configure a directory just for a specific computer. This can be quite useful for different users on the same computer. For example, it's a good place for someone in a factory to leave information for his or her counterpart on a different shift:

```
[pchome]
    comment = PC Directories
    path = /usr/local/pc/%m
    public = no
    writable = yes
```

You just need to create the directory listed as the `path`. Remember, `%m` represents the name of the computer. For example, if a computer named factory1 is trying to connect, the previous `path` command means that you need to create a `/usr/local/pc/factory1` directory.

SHARING A PRINTER

If you've configured CUPS printers, you still need to configure the basic share. Even though the standard `smb.conf` file suggests the BSD-style print system, the following commands work with CUPS printers as well:

```
[printers]
    comment = All Printers
    path = /var/spool/samba
    browseable = no
    guest ok = no
    writable = no
    printable = yes
```

If you have a single LPD printer you want to share, a different preconfigured share is available in the standard `smb.conf` file to provide exclusive use—in this case, to the user named fred:

```
[fredsprn]
    comment = Fred's Printer
    valid users = fred
    path = /home/fred
    printer = freds_printer
    public = no
    writable = no
    printable = yes
```

The limit implied by `writable = no` does not affect print spool directories; your computer can still send print spool files to the print server.

CONFIGURING LOGON DIRECTORIES

When you use Samba to configure your Linux computer as a domain controller (PDC or BDC) on a Microsoft network, you need to configure logon and profile paths for each user. As before, the directories shown must already exist.

The following commands can configure logons to a Microsoft Windows–style domain, based on the directory specified by `path`:

```
[netlogon]
    comment = Network Logon Service
    path = /usr/local/samba/lib/netlogon
    guest ok = yes
    writable = no
    share modes = no
```

This is one directory where you want `share modes = no`; otherwise, a cracker might figure out how to get every user's logon information.

The following commands can configure profiles locally for users who log in to your Samba server as if it were a Microsoft Windows server:

```
[Profiles]
    path = /usr/local/samba/profiles
    browseable = no
    guest ok = yes
```

DEFAULT SHARE SETTINGS

Default settings for shared directories and printers are listed in Table 29.7. Remember, if you use a default parameter, you don't even need to include it in `smb.conf`; tools such as SWAT and `redhat-config-samba` delete default settings in `smb.conf`.

TABLE 29.7: DEFAULT *SMB.CONF* SHARE SETTINGS

VARIABLE	DEFAULT
browseable	yes
comment	No default
create mode	a.k.a. `create mask = 0744`
directory mode	a.k.a. `directory mask = 0755`
guest ok	no
path	No default
printable	no
public	a.k.a. `guest ok = no`
read only	yes
writable	no (the true default is `read only = yes`)
write list	No default
valid users	No default (any standard user can log in)

A Samba Troubleshooting Checklist

Samba configuration files, especially smb.conf, can be quite large. Small errors can throw a monkey wrench into your service. It's easy to spend a few hours revising your configuration when the problem is as simple as an extra firewall.

When troubleshooting, the first thing you should do is check the syntax of the smb.conf file. Pay particular attention to comments; it's common to accidentally delete a comment code such as ; or #. Next, you should check the browse list from the local Samba server. If the local browse list is good, take a careful look at your network. And there are a number of valid smb.conf settings that can cause problems.

TESTING *SMB.CONF*

Once you've configured smb.conf, it's easy to test. The testparm command acts as a syntax checker for your Samba configuration file. If you don't specify the location, testparm automatically checks the smb.conf file in the /etc/samba directory.

Before restarting or reloading the smb daemon, run testparm. If you've made a small mistake in editing, it can point you right to the source of the problem smb.conf, which can save you a lot of grief.

CHECKING THE LOCAL SAMBA BROWSE LIST

Once you've restarted Samba, check the list of what you're sharing by using the smbclient command. If you see the right list on the Samba server, you should be able to see the same list on Microsoft Windows computers on your network, barring a network- or firewall-related problem. For example, the following command checks the list on the computer named RH9test; mj is a user on that computer:

```
# smbclient -L \\RH9test -U mj
```

You're prompted for mj's password, then you should see the browse list for the RH9test computer. In the example shown in Figure 29.8, you can also see the members of the workgroup's named WORKGROUP and MYGROP.

NOTE   *Don't forget that the samba user should be in the* /etc/samba/smbusers *file; we did this earlier with the* smbadduser *command.*

CHECKING YOUR NETWORK

As discussed in Chapter 21, most network problems are physical; you may have a problem with a loose cable, no power on a hub, or a similar issue. We examined a number of commands in Chapter 21, such as ping and netstat, that help you check the status of a network.

One problem I often run into is firewalls. If there's a firewall on the Samba server, it can block communication with clients. If your Samba server can't see clients, you won't be able to log onto a shared Samba directory or printer.

OTHER SAMBA ISSUES

I've encountered other problems with Samba, mostly related to mistakes that I've made in the smb.conf configuration file. Some mistakes are valid options, as they'll pass a testparm syntax check, but they won't represent your Samba server properly on your LAN. Sometimes you can get clues from the applicable log file. As described earlier, there are default log files specific to each Samba client. For example, Figure 29.9 lists connections from the computer named laptop2.

FIGURE 29.8

Checking a local
Samba server

```
[root@RH9Desk root]# smbclient -L \\RH9Test -U mj
added interface ip=10.252.113.211 bcast=10.252.113.255 nmask=255.255.255.0
Password:
Domain=[WORKGROUP] OS=[Unix] Server=[Samba 2.2.7a]

        Sharename       Type     Comment
        ---------       ----     -------
        mao             Disk     Mao's Home Directory
        var             Disk     Logs and More
        IPC$            IPC      IPC Service (the samba server)
        ADMIN$          Disk     IPC Service (the samba server)
        MyLaserJet      Printer
        HPLasers        Printer
        printer         Printer
        SecondLaserJe   Printer
        mj              Disk         Home Directories

        Server                  Comment
        ---------               -------
        LAPTOP2                 LaptopWin
        RH9DESK                 samba server
        RH9SERVER
        RH9TEST                 the samba server

        Workgroup               Master
        ---------               -------
        MYGROUP                 RH9DESK
        WORKGROUP               RH9TEST
[root@RH9Desk root]# █
```

FIGURE 29.9

Samba log file
problems for a
specific client

```
[2002/12/09 13:35:42, 0] client/smbmount.c:send_fs_socket(383)
  mount.smbfs: entering daemon mode for service \\laptop2\redhatbeta, pid=12182
[2002/12/09 13:36:13, 0] client/smbmount.c:send_fs_socket(383)
  mount.smbfs: entering daemon mode for service \\laptop2\redhat, pid=12188
[2002/12/09 15:38:45, 0] client/smbmount.c:send_fs_socket(383)
  mount.smbfs: entering daemon mode for service \\laptop2\redhatbeta, pid=3738
[2002/12/09 15:41:05, 0] client/smbmount.c:send_fs_socket(383)
  mount.smbfs: entering daemon mode for service \\laptop2\redhat, pid=3801
[2002/12/09 19:26:34, 0] client/smbmount.c:send_fs_socket(383)
  mount.smbfs: entering daemon mode for service \\laptop2\redhatbeta, pid=2017
[2002/12/10 09:18:42, 0] client/smbmount.c:send_fs_socket(383)
  mount.smbfs: entering daemon mode for service \\laptop2\redhatbeta, pid=2003
[2002/12/10 11:15:38, 0] client/smbmount.c:send_fs_socket(383)
  mount.smbfs: entering daemon mode for service \\laptop2\downloads, pid=3489
[2002/12/10 11:16:54, 0] client/smbmount.c:send_fs_socket(383)
  mount.smbfs: entering daemon mode for service \\laptop2\downloads, pid=3526
[2002/12/10 11:18:44, 0] client/smbmount.c:send_fs_socket(383)
  mount.smbfs: entering daemon mode for service \\laptop2\downloads, pid=3535
[2002/12/10 11:23:42, 0] client/smbmount.c:send_fs_socket(383)
  mount.smbfs: entering daemon mode for service \\laptop2\downloads, pid=3543
[2002/12/11 14:19:40, 0] client/smbmount.c:send_fs_socket(383)
  mount.smbfs: entering daemon mode for service \\laptop2\redhatbeta, pid=2301
~

~

~

~
"smbmount.log" 22L, 1552C
```

Common mistakes you can make in `smb.conf` fall into the following areas:

The wrong workgroup   The Samba `workgroup` specified in the default `smb.conf` file is MYGROUP. This differs from the default value of `workgroup`, which is WORKGROUP. The problems get worse if you're setting up this computer on a domain and don't enter the right domain name for this variable.

`browsable = no`   If you set `browsable = no`, users normally will not be able to see your shared directory or printer in their Windows Network Neighborhood or My Network Places.

Improperly configured sharing   As you've seen in previous sections, there are a number of ways to share—with users, guests, groups, or everyone. If sharing is not properly configured, your users may not be able to get to the directories or printers that they need.

`writable = no`   Samba shared directories are read-only by default. If you don't specify otherwise, your users won't be able to write to appropriate shared directories.

Improperly configured firewalls   Standard Red Hat Linux firewalls block Samba communication. If you have a `hosts allow` variable, computers not on the list can't get to your Samba server.

The Samba Web Administration Tool (SWAT)

Current Samba packages include an all-in-one GUI configuration utility, the Samba Web Administration Tool (SWAT). As we mentioned earlier, it's included in the `samba-swat-*` RPM package. Before you can run SWAT, you must activate the corresponding `xinetd` daemon with the following command:

```
# chkconfig swat on
```

SWAT includes several menus, which we'll look at in the following sections. Briefly, once you make your desired configuration changes in each menu, you'll click the Commit Changes button to write the changes to file.

Once you've completed the changes, you must restart the `smbd` and `nmbd` daemons, either through the SWAT Service menu or with the `service smb restart` command.

The Home Menu

To start SWAT, open the browser of your choice and navigate to `localhost:901`. Even if you're logged in as the root user, SWAT prompts you for an authorized username and password. Once you enter that information, SWAT starts with the Home menu, shown in Figure 29.10.

As you can see, the SWAT Home menu includes links to other SWAT menus on the top row. We'll examine each menu in the following sections. The Home menu also includes access to a number of Samba documents. Some are man pages associated with specific commands or files. Toward the bottom of the document list are Samba HOWTOs and a copy of the first edition of *Using Samba*, in e-book format.

FIGURE 29.10

The SWAT
Home menu

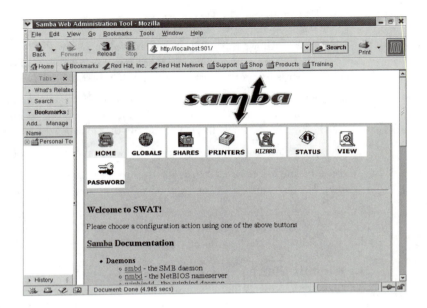

Samba Configuration Wizard

SWAT's Samba Configuration Wizard provides a way to address three basic settings for your Samba server. Click the Wizard link and scroll down to see the options shown in Figure 29.11.

FIGURE 29.11

The Samba
Configuration
Wizard

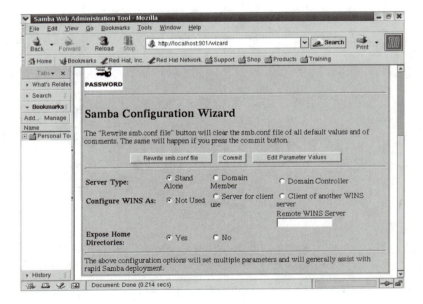

Let's take a look at each of these options:

Server Type   Allows you to select from one of three types of servers on a Microsoft-based network: Stand Alone, Domain Member, or Domain Controller (PDC or BDC). If you're connecting to a Microsoft peer-to-peer workgroup, stand-alone servers are your only valid option.

Configure WINS As   Lets you specify the role of WINS on your network. There are three choices: you can configure your Samba server as a WINS server; you can configure it as a client of a different WINS server, if you know its IP address; or you can avoid the use of WINS on your network.

This is associated with the `wins server` and `wins support` variables.

Expose Home Directories   Permits users to see the directories associated with their Linux usernames. This option is associated with the `[homes]` share we described earlier in this chapter.

Once you've made your selections, click the Commit button. This may not be the "Configuration Wizard" that you expect; you have a lot more work to do before you can start your Samba server. Click the Globals link at the top of the menu and continue on to the next section.

The Globals Menu

You can configure the `[global]` settings in your `smb.conf` file through the Globals menu. Click the link, and you should see a menu similar to the one shown in Figure 29.12.

FIGURE 29.12

SWAT global
variables

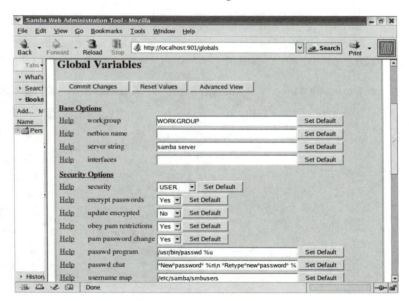

As you can see, a Help option is associated with each variable. Clicking Help opens the `smb.conf` man page in a new browser window, at the section with the desired variable.

In this and each of the other menus, you'll have access to the following three buttons: Commit Changes, Reset Values, and Advanced View. With individual settings, you'll also see a Set Default button. Their functions are summarized in Table 29.8.

TABLE 29.8: BASIC SWAT OPTION BUTTONS

BUTTON	DESCRIPTION
Commit Changes	Writes the changes you make to `smb.conf`
Reset Values	Restores the current values in `smb.conf` to the menu
Advanced View	Provides additional settings
Set Default	Activates the default setting associated with the variable

If you've read the "Samba Global Settings" section earlier in this chapter, several of the settings should look familiar to you. While I won't repeat the discussion of each variable, the way the variables are organized can help you understand how global settings work. These categories are listed in Table 29.9. Some of these categories appear only after you click the Advanced View button.

TABLE 29.9: GLOBAL VARIABLE CATEGORIES

CATEGORY	DESCRIPTION
Base	Specifies the basic options for the Samba server.
Security	Allows you to configure passwords, user accounts, and computers that are allowed to connect.
Logging	Lets you customize how and where information is logged.
Protocol	Customizes interaction with different Windows protocols.
Tuning	Permits you to optimize the performance of the Samba server.
Printing	Sets the basic print protocol; the standard Linux options are `cups` and `lprng`.
Filename Handing	Allows you to set how short and regular filenames are transferred between computers.
Domain	If you're configuring this computer as a domain controller (PDC or BDC), this allows you to set administrative and guest groups.
Logon	If you're setting up this Samba server as a logon controller, this allows you to configure logon and script file locations.
Browse	Configures the priority of this computer for the Microsoft browse list of shared directories and printers.
WINS	Sets basic options for using WINS and DNS servers.
Locking	Files are locked to prevent multiple users from writing to the same file simultaneously.
MSDfs	Allows the use of the Microsoft Distributed Filesystem tree.
Winbind	Works with the `/etc/nsswitch.conf` file for resolving computer hostnames.

When you've completed your changes, don't forget to click the Commit Changes button to record them in `smb.conf`. Click the Shares link at the top of the menu and continue to the next section.

TIP   Each SWAT variable includes a Help hyperlink. Click this hyperlink to open up a new browser window with more information on that variable.

The Shares Menu

In the SWAT Shares menu, you can configure existing shares or create new ones. The initial Shares menu is shown in Figure 29.13; you need to select a share before you can customize it.

FIGURE 29.13

The SWAT
Shares menu

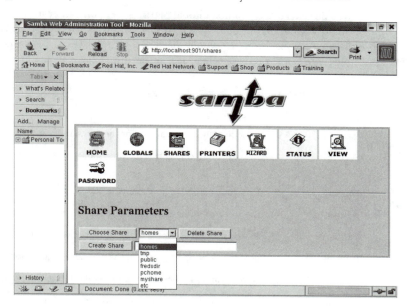

Existing shares are taken from the names listed in the `smb.conf` file; typical shares from the packaged `smb.conf` file include [homes] and [tmp]. Select an existing share and then click Choose Share.

Alternatively, you can configure a new shared directory. Enter the name of your choice in the Create Share text box, and then click Create Share to get to the full Shares menu, shown in Figure 29.14.

This illustrates the share parameters associated with the [homes] shared directory. We described all of these variables earlier in this chapter. If you prefer, click the Advanced View button for more configuration options.

When you've completed your changes, don't forget to click the Commit Changes button to record them in `smb.conf`. Now click the Printers link at the top of the menu and continue to the next section.

FIGURE 29.14

Configuring share
parameters

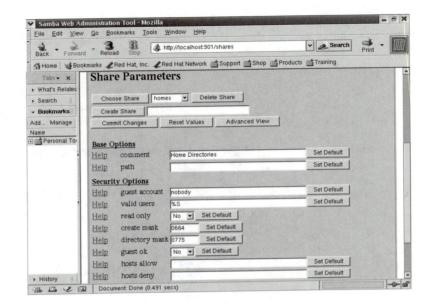

The Printers Menu

The SWAT Printers menu is similar to the Shares menu. You can choose to configure an existing
printer, or you can create a new printer. Once you've made your selection, click the Choose Printer or
Create Printer link. Individual options under the Choose Printer drop-down text box are read from
/etc/printcap. Remember, both CUPS and LPD list their printers in this file. Once you've made
your selection, you can customize different printer variables, as shown in Figure 29.15.

FIGURE 29.15

SWAT Printer
Parameters

When you've completed your changes, click the Commit Changes button to record them in `smb.conf`. Now click the View link at the top of the menu and continue to the next section.

The View Menu

The SWAT View menu gives you a look at your `smb.conf` configuration file. You'll note that all of the comments and most of the settings from the original `smb.conf` file are deleted. If a variable is set to its default value, it isn't included in the normal view, similar to what's shown in Figure 29.16.

FIGURE 29.16

The saved `smb.conf` file

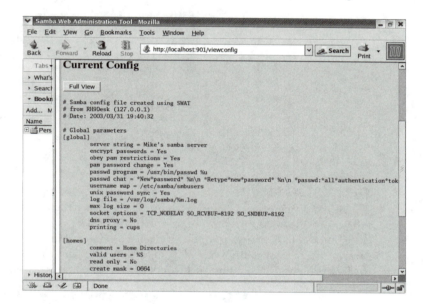

However, if you click the Full View button, you'll see an `smb.conf` file in full glory, with all available variables. You can then click the Normal View button to return to the current file. At this point, click the Password link at the top of the menu and continue to the next section.

The Password Menu

The SWAT Password menu lets you manage the Samba passwords stored on the local Samba server, as well as manage passwords on remote computers. As you can see in Figure 29.17, this menu consists of two sections.

SERVER PASSWORD MANAGEMENT

The Server Password Management section allows you to manage your Samba passwords, which are sent when you try to connect to a remote Samba or Microsoft Windows server. The buttons shown in Figure 29.17 are fairly self-explanatory; they are listed in Table 29.10.

FIGURE 29.17

Managing passwords

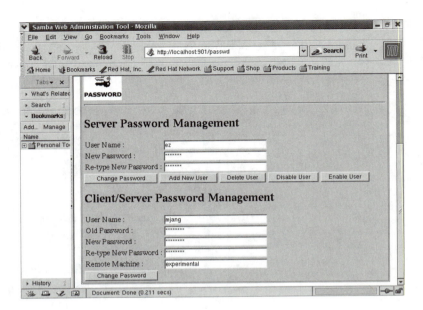

TABLE 29.10: SERVER PASSWORD MANAGEMENT FUNCTIONS

FUNCTION	DESCRIPTION
Change Password	Allows you to change the Samba password for Samba users; each user must already exist in /etc/passwd.
Add New User	Adds a new user to /etc/samba/smbpasswd; the user must already exist in /etc/passwd; however, this is not as flexible as the smbadduser command described earlier.
Delete User	Deletes the user from /etc/samba/smbpasswd.
Disable User	Prevents the user from connecting to remote Samba or Microsoft Windows servers.
Enable User	Allows the user to connect to remote Samba or Microsoft Windows servers.

CLIENT/SERVER PASSWORD MANAGEMENT

This section actually allows you to change your password on a remote Microsoft Windows or Samba server. In the example shown back in Figure 29.17, I changed the password for user mjang on a computer named experimental running Microsoft Windows 2000 .

This won't work if Samba can't find the name of your computer in /etc/hosts, DNS, or possibly WINS. It also won't work if the username does not exist on the remote computer. Now click the Status link at the top of the menu and continue to the next section.

The Server Status Menu

Once users start to connect from other computers to your Samba computer, you'll want to check your server status. As an example, Figure 29.18 shows a Samba server with connections from other computers named rh9server and laptop2, with private IP addresses.

FIGURE 29.18

Server Status

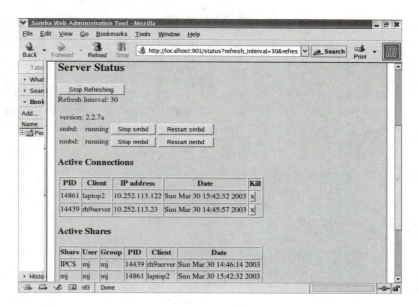

This is where SWAT is an active administration tool. At the top of the screen, you can see that the status of each connection is refreshed every 30 seconds. You can stop or restart the smbd and nmbd daemons. Under Active Connections, you can review the status of connections from different computers. You can also disconnect remote users by clicking the appropriate X button in the Kill column.

Whenever you make changes to smb.conf, you should reload or restart the smbd daemon. When you restart smbd, nmbd is restarted automatically.

The *redhat-config-samba* Alternative

SWAT can seem overwhelming. There is a simpler, though less flexible, way to configure your computer as a Samba server: redhat-config-samba. Install the redhat-config-samba RPM if required, and then run the program with the same name. You should see a tool similar to Figure 29.19.

This tool reads its initial settings from your current smb.conf file. The settings you see in Figure 29.19 reflect some of the shared directories from the packaged smb.conf file.

NOTE *The redhat-config-samba tool is fairly new, and its features are still subject to significant changes. Use it carefully. SWAT is a more mature tool and is at least my preferred choice.*

FIGURE 29.19
redhat-config-
samba

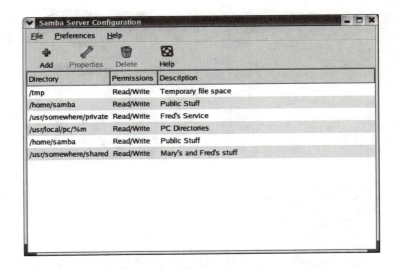

In the following sections, we'll look at configuring basic server settings, managing Samba users, and creating a new share.

Server Settings

In `redhat-config-samba`, click Preferences ➤ Server Settings to get to the Server Settings dialog box shown in Figure 29.20. As you can see, the basic server settings are simple, and the options should be familiar from previous sections. Since the Workgroup textbox is blank, the `workgroup` variable is set to the default, which is WORKGROUP; the server comment is "Mike's Samba Server."

FIGURE 29.20

The Basic tab of
the Server Settings
dialog box

Click the Security tab to see several key security variables. Remember, you can select between SHARE, USER, SERVER, or DOMAIN authentication modes. If you've selected SERVER or DOMAIN, you'll get to specify the name of the authentication server. Most current Windows servers use encrypted passwords. The Guest Account is an account you can designate in `/etc/passwd`, such as guest or ftp. These options are illustrated in Figure 29.21.

FIGURE 29.21

The Security tab of the Server Settings dialog box

User Management

You can manage users in `redhat-config-samba`. In this tool, click Preferences ➢ Samba Users to get to the Samba Users dialog box shown in Figure 29.22.

FIGURE 29.22

Managing Samba users

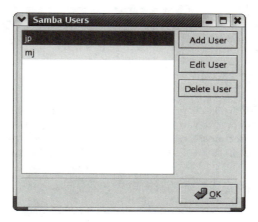

The options are fairly self-explanatory; you can add, edit, or delete users from the /etc/samba/ smbusers database. Click Add User to see the Create New Samba User dialog box. If you remember the discussion on the `smbadduser` command earlier in this chapter, you'll recognize the text boxes shown in Figure 29.23; the information that you need is identical.

FIGURE 29.23

The Create New Samba User dialog box

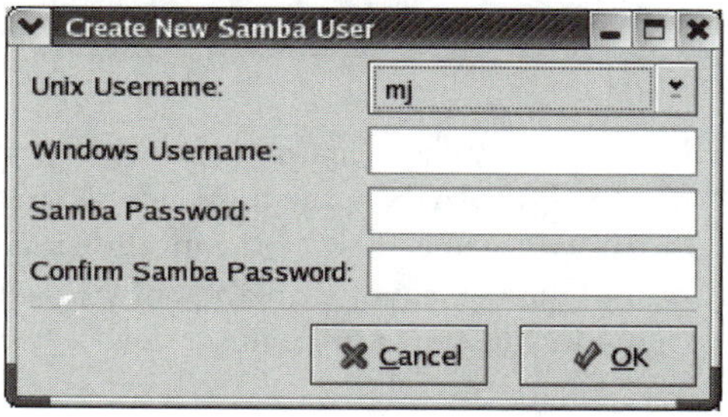

Creating a New Share

You can add a new directory share with `redhat-config-samba`. In this tool, click the Add button to reveal the Create Samba Share dialog box. There are several options shown in Figure 29.24.

FIGURE 29.24

The Create Samba Share dialog box

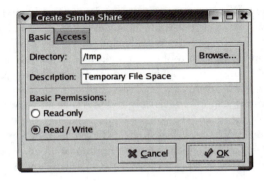

The options are fairly straightforward, but since they don't directly match the variables described earlier, we've summarized each option under the Basic tab in Table 29.11.

TABLE 29.11: CREATING A SAMBA SHARE

OPTION	DESCRIPTION
Directory	Specifies the directory that you want to share.
Browse	Calls a Select Directory dialog box to help you find the directory that you want to share.
Description	Corresponds to an `smb.conf` comment.
Read-Only	Remote users aren't permitted to write to this directory.
Read/Write	Remote users are allowed to write to this directory.

Under the Access tab, you can allow access to specified users from what you've added to the `/etc/samba/smbusers` file, or allow access to all users.

Summary

Samba is a heterogeneous service that bridges the gap between Linux and Microsoft Windows. Once you've configured Samba, you have a Linux computer that looks just like a Microsoft Windows member server on a workgroup or domain. You can even configure Samba to act just like a Microsoft PDC.

You can configure Linux as a Samba client. With the right packages, you can even use the `mount` command to connect to a shared directory from another Samba server or any Microsoft Windows server. You can even connect to a shared directory in terminal mode similar to an FTP connection.

The Samba configuration files are located in `/etc/samba`; the key file is `smb.conf`. The original `smb.conf` from the `samba-*` RPMs includes several comments that help you learn more.

The `smb.conf` file includes global settings that determine how your server connects to a Microsoft network. You can configure security, printer lists, log files, customized logon directories, browse priorities, and more. It also includes share settings, which let you configure different directories and printers. You can limit your share by user, determine how files are accessed and written, and more. Once you've configured `smb.conf`, the `testparm` command helps you check its syntax.

SWAT is a web browser–based tool for configuring `smb.conf`. Remember to activate the `swat` service in the `xinetd` daemon. It is highly customizable, with Home, Globals, Shares, Printers, View, Password, and Server Status menus.

Red Hat is developing a simpler alternative to SWAT: `redhat-config-samba`. Since it is fairly new, use it with caution. While it can help you configure basic shares, it does not have the flexibility of SWAT. In my opinion, SWAT is still the preferred GUI tool for Samba.

In the next chapter, we'll examine the most important web server on the Internet, Apache. You'll learn to configure it to serve web pages on your local network and more.

Chapter 30

Web Services

THE DEVELOPMENT OF LINUX closely parallels the growth of the World Wide Web. As described in Chapter 1, Linux is based on software developed by a community of volunteers. Apache, the most popular web server in use today, was also developed by a community of many of the same volunteers. So it should not be surprising that the success of Linux is closely tied to Apache and the World Wide Web.

In 1995, the most popular web server was the HTTP daemon from the National Center for Supercomputing Applications (NCSA) at the University of Illinois. When the developers of this web server left NCSA, several webmasters from around the world started updating and maintaining changes through patches, which led to its description as "a patchy" server. Thus, their web server software is known as *Apache*.

Because Apache and Linux developed in a similar way, their fortunes are closely aligned. However, Apache is also used on other Unix-style operating systems and Microsoft Windows. According to a Netcraft survey (`www.netcraft.com/survey`), Apache is by far the most popular web server on the Internet, and has been since early 1996.

This chapter covers the version of Apache included with Red Hat Linux 9: version 2.0.40. Later versions are available from the Apache project website, `httpd.apache.org`. As part of its Advanced Server offering, Red Hat also offers the Stronghold Enterprise web server, which is also based on Apache.

In addition, this chapter covers Red Hat's Content Accelerator, formerly known as Tux, which is a kernel-based web server designed to speed delivery of static information (such as pictures) and can be configured to work closely with Apache. This chapter covers the following topics:

- Exploring web server options
- Learning Apache basics
- Configuring Apache
- Incorporating the Red Hat Content Accelerator

Exploring Web Server Options

Apache is not the only web server available; there are actually some proprietary web servers that you can buy. Table 30.1 briefly describes several of the important ones. According to the Netcraft survey, four web servers are currently run by more than one percent of the websites on the Internet: Apache, Microsoft's Internet Information Server, Zeus, and Sun Microsystems's Sun One.

TABLE 30.1: WEB SERVERS

NAME	DESCRIPTION
AOLServer	Used by America Online; this is an open source web server. More information is available from www.aolserver.com.
Apache	The most popular web server on the Internet; more information is available from httpd.apache.org.
Boa	A high-performance, open source web server that, unlike other web servers, runs most connections as a single process. More information is available from www.boa.org.
Caudium	A modular open source web server. Like Boa, it runs most standard connections as a single process. More information is available from www.caudium.net.
Jigsaw	A web server developed by the World Wide Web Consortium (W3C). See www.w3.org/Jigsaw for more information. All software from this consortium conforms to their open source license.
Red Hat Content Accelerator	A kernel-based high-performance web server, formerly known as TUX. For more information, see www.redhat.com/docs/manuals/tux.
Resin	A server based on JavaServer Pages (JSP); more information is available from www.caucho.com/resin. This is a proprietary server available for purchase.
Roxin	A secure web server licensed under the GPL. For more information, see www.roxin.com.
Servertec	An application web server written in the Java programming language. See www.servertec.com for more information.
Stronghold	A secure web server based on Apache, owned by Red Hat; part of Red Hat's Advanced Server. For more information, see www.redhat.com/software/stronghold.
Sun One	A web server from Sun Microsystems; formerly known as iPlanet, it is now part of the Sun One series of application servers. More information is available from wwws.sun.com/software.
WN	A small, secure web server, licensed under the GPL. The U.S. website is available at hopf.math.nwu.edu.
Zeus	A commercial high-capacity web server. More information is available from www.zeus.co.uk.

Learning Apache Basics

Apache is a web server. In other words, it is a service that runs on an operating system such as Linux, and it responds to requests. When users enter the address of a desired web page into a browser, their computers look to DNS servers to find the IP address of the desired web server. Once contact is made, the browser asks for the web page, usually on TCP/IP port 80. Apache responds to such requests by sending a web page to the requesting computer.

If you're currently running a web server based on Apache 1.3.*x*, you have some decisions to make. Red Hat Linux 9 includes Apache version 2.0.40. If you install these Apache packages, you may need to make several configuration changes. You should not upgrade your Apache server until you understand and have tested your websites on the new system.

Apache 2.0

Red Hat incorporated Apache version 2.0.*x* for the first time in Red Hat Linux 8.0. Apache version 1.3.*x* is still in common use. Many of you experienced with Apache may not be familiar with the changes in version 2.0.*x*, which include the following:

- The Virtual Hosts features allow you to configure completely different websites using the same IP address.

- Directives have been changed. Those related to Perl, PHP (PHP Hypertext Processor), Python, Structured Query Language (SQL), and the Secure Sockets Layer (SSL) now have their own configuration files in the `/etc/httpd/conf.d` directory.

- Variables have changed. For example, you'll learn how to change the TCP/IP port associated with Apache using the `Listen` variable later in this chapter.

- Packages are more modular. We'll look at the different packages associated with Apache in the next section.

- Threads are used efficiently. Threads can share common data; in Apache 2.0, threads are normally processed-based, which prevents server crashes. Multi-Processing Modules (MPM) support customization in this area, which helps you optimize Apache for the host operating system.

- IPv6 addresses can be used. While there's a patch that allows the use of IPv6 addresses in Apache 1.3.*x*, it is no longer recommended.

While some of these features have been "back-ported" to Apache 1.3.*x* (one reason why I think these "older" Apache servers will be around for some time), they were developed for Apache 2.0.

Packages

Apache is a modular server. As described in Web Chapter 5, the only required Apache RPM package is `httpd-*`. There are a number of other Apache packages that you can install, as shown in Table 30.2.

TABLE 30.2: APACHE PACKAGES

NAME	DESCRIPTION
httpd	Installs the main Apache server
httpd-manual	Includes a complete manual for Apache
hwcrypto	Allows interfaces with Linux hardware cryptographic accelerators
mod_auth_pgsql	Allows access limits to PostgreSQL databases
mod_auth_mysql	Supports access limits to MySQL-based databases
mod_python	Adds a Python language interpreter to Apache
mod_perl	Adds a Perl language interpreter to Apache
mod_ssl	Includes SSL security in Apache
php	Installs PHP for dynamic scripts (PHP stands for PHP: Hypertext Preprocessor)
php-imap	Provides IMAP mail server support to Apache
php-ldap	Allows LDAP support for Apache
php-mysql	Implements PHP support of MySQL-based databases
php-odbc	Allows PHP interaction with Open Data Base Connectivity (ODBC)-based databases
php-pgsql	Installs a PHP interface with PostgreSQL-based databases
squid	Installs a proxy server
tux	Adds a kernel-based web server
webalizer	Includes a log analysis program for your web server

Configuring Apache

Once you've installed the desired Apache packages, your server should be ready to serve web pages to the local computer. All you need to do is start the **httpd** service and direct your web browser to the *localhost* address.

But a web server doesn't do you much good unless you can call its web pages from other computers. In this chapter, we'll analyze the main Apache configuration file, **httpd.conf**, in some detail.

These settings are based on the specifications of the Hypertext Transfer Protocol (HTTP) standards version 1.1. We provide only a brief overview of Apache 2.0; for more information, see *Linux Apache Web Server Administration*, Second Edition (Sybex, 2002).

TIP *If you install the* **httpd-manual-*** *RPM, you'll get a full Apache manual in HTML format in the* /var/www/manual *directory.*

Starting Apache

Once you've installed the Apache packages that you need, starting Apache is easy. As with other services described throughout this book, all you need to do is start the applicable script from the `/etc/rc.d/init.d` directory. In this case, the following command should work nicely:

```
# service httpd start
```

If you still have the default Apache configuration file, you'll probably see the following message:

```
Starting httpd: httpd: Could not determine the server's fully qualified domain
➥ name, using 127.0.0.1 for ServerName
```

Now you can open the browser of your choice to the localhost address. This is also known as the loopback IP address, which as defined in Chapter 20 is 127.0.0.1. Figure 30.1 shows the result in the Mozilla web browser.

FIGURE 30.1

Apache is properly installed.

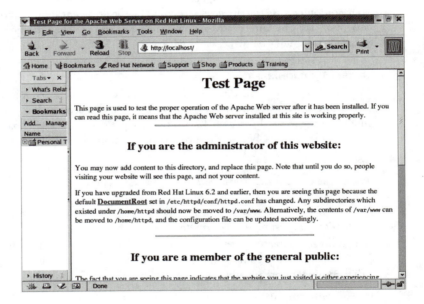

You'll also want to use a command such as `chkconfig`, as described in Chapter 13, to make sure Apache starts the next time you start Linux at an appropriate runlevel. For example, the following command starts the Apache daemon, `httpd`, whenever you start Linux in runlevel 2, 3, or 5:

```
# chkconfig --level 235 httpd on
```

Now you're ready to start customizing the Apache configuration.

Customizing Apache

The main Apache configuration file, `httpd.conf`, is located in the `/etc/httpd/conf` directory. It is split into three sections. In the global environment section, you can configure the basic settings for this web server. In the main server configuration section, you'll set up the basic defaults for any websites on your server. The Virtual Hosts section allows you to set up several different websites on your Apache server, even if you have only one IP address.

NOTE *There were originally three main configuration files for Apache:* access.conf, srm.conf, *and* httpd.conf, *all located in the same directory. While later versions of Apache 1.3.x incorporated the information from* access.conf *and* srm.conf *in* httpd.conf, *at least blank versions of* access.conf *and* srm.conf *were still required by the server. Apache 2.0.x no longer needs these extra configuration files.*

Commands in the Apache configuration file are known as *directives*. In the following sections, we'll analyze the directives from the default Apache httpd.conf installed with Red Hat Linux 9 in some detail. You can read the file for yourself; it includes many other useful comments.

Commands with a pound sign (#) in front are commented out in the default Apache configuration file. If you're learning about Apache for the first time, experiment a bit. Set up some website files on your computer. Use the directory specified by the DocumentRoot directive, which is by default /var/www/html. Try out some of these commands, restart the httpd daemon, and examine the changes for yourself. You might be surprised at what you can do.

GLOBAL ENVIRONMENT

We'll look at each of the directives in the global environment section of the default version of the Apache httpd.conf configuration file. Variables in this section apply to all Virtual Hosts that you might configure on this server. There are basic parameters, detailed parameters related to different clients, port settings, pointers to other configuration files, and module locations.

NOTE *If a directive is set to 0, it normally means you're setting no limit on that directive. For example, if you set* Timeout *to 0, connections from a client browser are kept open indefinitely.*

Basic Global Environment Parameters

The following directive gives users of your website some basic information about your software. While the following command tells users that your web server is Apache on a Unix-style system, other commands are possible, as described in Table 30.3:

```
ServerTokens OS
```

TABLE 30.3: *SERVERTOKENS* DIRECTIVE OPTIONS

DIRECTIVE	DESCRIPTION
ServerTokens Prod	Identifies the web server as Apache
ServerTokens Min	Identifies Apache and its version number
ServerTokens OS	Identifies Apache, its version number, and the type of operating system
ServerTokens Full	Identifies Apache, its version number, the type of operating system, and compiled modules

The `ServerRoot` directive identifies the directory with configuration, error, and log files:

```
ServerRoot "/etc/httpd"
```

If you run `ls -l /etc/httpd`, you'll see links to the real location of certain directories; for example, `/etc/httpd/logs` is linked to the `/var/log/httpd` directory.

Apache includes parent and child processes for different connections. The `ScoreBoardFile` parameter helps these processes communicate with each other. Otherwise, the communication is through active memory.

```
#ScoreBoardFile run/httpd.scoreboard
```

TIP   I normally avoid activating the `ScoreBoardFile` parameter; it's required only for certain architectures, which does not include Red Hat Linux 9.

You might note that `run` is a relative subdirectory. The full directory name is based on the `ServerRoot` directive—in other words, `/etc/httpd/run`.

The `PidFile` specifies the file where Apache records the process identifier (PID):

```
PidFile run/httpd.pid
```

If computers are having trouble communicating on your network, you need a `Timeout` value to keep Apache from hanging. The `Timeout` directive specifies a stop value in seconds.

```
Timeout 300
```

Normally, multiple requests are allowed through each connection. The following command disables this behavior:

```
KeepAlive Off
```

If the `KeepAlive` directive is on, you can regulate the number of requests per connection with the `MaxKeepAliveRequests` directive:

```
MaxKeepAliveRequests 100
```

Once a connection is made between Apache and someone's web browser, the `KeepAliveTimeout` directive specifies the number of seconds to wait for the next client request:

```
KeepAliveTimeout 15
```

Detailed Client Parameters

Apache includes a number of Multi-Processing Modules (MPM). These MPMs fall into three categories:

- Prefork MPMs are suited to process-based web servers; they are appropriate to use if you have Apache modules that do not require separate threads, which imitates the behavior of Apache 1.3.x.

- Worker MPMs support both types of modules; however, they should not be used if you're using Apache 1.3 modules, since threads can cause problems.

- Per-child MPMs support websites for clients that need different user IDs.

NOTE   *MPMs flexible; specific modules are available for Windows NT (*mpm_winnt*) and Novell Netware (*mpm_netware*) networks.*

There are a number of common directives that you can specify in each of these MPM categories. When Apache is started, the StartServers directive sets the number of available child server processes ready for users who want your web pages:

StartServers 8

Once Apache is started, requests from other users may come in. If the number of unused server processes falls below the MinSpareServers directive, additional httpd processes are started automatically:

MinSpareServers 5

When traffic goes down, the MaxSpareServers directive determines the maximum number of httpd processes that are allowed to run idle:

MaxSpareServers 20

You can regulate the number of clients requesting information from your web server with the MaxClients directive:

MaxClients 150

You can also regulate the number of requests for information from each client with the MaxRequests-PerChild directive:

MaxRequestsPerChild 1000

Apache 2.0 servers can start new threads for each request. The MinSpareThreads directive is similar to MinSpareServers; it allows Apache to handle a surge of additional requests:

MinSpareThreads 25

When the number of requests goes down, Apache monitors the number of spare threads; if they exceed the MaxSpareThreads directive, some are killed:

MaxSpareThreads 75

Every child process can create several threads to handle requests from each user of your website. The ThreadsPerChild directive is created when each child process starts:

ThreadsPerChild 25

You can limit the number of threads allowed for each child process with the MaxRequestsPerChild directive (there is no limit in the default httpd.conf file):

MaxRequestsPerChild 0

You can also limit the number of threads allowed for each child process with the MaxThreadsPer-Child directive:

MaxThreadsPerChild 20

Port Settings

You can set Apache to `Listen` to requests from only certain IP addresses and or TCP/IP ports. The default `httpd.conf` file includes the following directives:

```
#Listen 12.34.56.78:80
Listen 80
```

If you have more than one network adapter, you can also limit Apache to certain networks; for example, the following directive only listens to the network adapter with an IP address of 192.168.13.64 on TCP/IP port 80:

```
Listen 192.168.13.64:80
```

NOTE *The* `Listen` *directive supersedes the* `BindAddress` *and* `Port` *directives from Apache version* *1.3.x.*

Pointers to Other Configuration Files

As we noted earlier, there are other configuration files associated with the Apache 2.0.x server. By default, they're in the `/etc/httpd/conf.d` directory. Normally, file locations are determined by the `ServerRoot` directive, which is set to `/etc/httpd`, and the `Include` directive shown here:

```
Include conf.d/*.conf
```

Module Locations

When you need a module in Apache, it should be loaded in the `httpd.conf` configuration file. Normally, modules are listed in the following format:

```
LoadModule module_type location
```

For example, the following directive loads the module named `access_module` from the `ServerRoot` modules subdirectory, `/etc/httpd/modules`. You will find that this is linked to the actual directory with Apache modules: `/usr/lib/httpd/modules`.

```
LoadModule access_module modules/mod_access.so
```

Several modules are listed in the default `httpd.conf` file; Table 30.4 offers a brief description. The modules are listed in the same order as they appear in the file.

TABLE 30.4: STANDARD APACHE MODULES

MODULE	DESCRIPTION
`access_module`	Supports access control based on an identifier, such as a computer name or IP address.
`auth_module`	Allows authentication (usernames and passwords) with text files.
`auth_anon_module`	Lets users have anonymous access to areas that require authentication.
`auth_dbm_module`	Supports authentication with DBM (database management) files.

Continued on next page

TABLE 30.4: STANDARD APACHE MODULES *(continued)*

MODULE	DESCRIPTION
auth_digest_module	Sets authentication with MD5 digests.
include_module	Includes SSI (server-side includes) data for dynamic web pages.
log_config_module	Sets logging of requests to the server.
env_module	Allows control of the environment that is passed to CGI (Common Gateway Interface) scripts and SSI pages.
mime_magic_module	Sets Apache to define the file type from a look at the first few bytes of the contents.
cern_meta_module	Supports additional meta-information with a web page, per the standards of the W3C, which is housed at CERN (the French acronym for the European Laboratory for Particle Physics).
expires_module	Lets Apache set an expiration date for the page, to support a web browser refresh request.
headers_module	Allows control of HTTP request and response headers.
usertrack_module	Supports user tracking with cookies.
unique_id_module	Sets a unique identifier for each request
setenvif_module	Allows Apache to set environment variables based on request characteristics, such as the type of web browser.
mime_module	Associates the filename extension, such as .txt, with specific applications.
dav_module	Supports web-based distributed authoring and versioning functionality.
status_module	Gives information on server performance and activity.
autoindex_module	Allows the listing of files in a web directory.
asis_module	Sends files without adding extra headers.
info_module	Supports user access to server configuration information.
dav_fs_module	Supports the dav_module.
vhost_alias_module	Allows dynamically configured Virtual Hosts.
negotiation_module	Sets Apache to match content, such as language, to the settings from the browser.
dir_module	Supports viewing of files in Apache directories.
imap_module	Configures imagemap file directives (not related to e-mail).
actions_module	Lets you run CGS scripts.
speling_module	Allows for small mistakes in requested document names (ironically, the module name is misspelled).

Continued on next page

TABLE 30.4: STANDARD APACHE MODULES *(continued)*

MODULE	DESCRIPTION
userdir_module	Supports access to user-specific directories.
alias_module	Sets up redirected URLs.
rewrite_module	Supports rewriting of URLs.
proxy_module	Sets up a proxy server for Apache.
proxy_ftp_module	Allows proxy server support for FTP data.
proxy_http_module	Allows proxy server support for HTTP data.
proxy_connect_module	Required for proxy server connect requests.
cgi_module	Configures running of CGI scripts.
cgid_module	Supports running of CGI scripts with an external daemon.

One of the more interesting modules is the `info_module`; as you'll see toward the end of the next section, it supports a detailed view of your Apache server configuration in your browser at `localhost/server-info`.

MAIN SERVER CONFIGURATION

Before we move on to configuring Virtual Hosts, let's take a look at the next section in the `httpd.conf` configuration file, which includes the default directives for Apache. While you can set different settings for many of these directives, you do need to know the defaults in this section. We analyze the basic settings in this part of the `httpd.conf` file in order.

NOTE   This is a very long section; you may want to take a break if you're in the habit of reading through a complete section at a time.

System User

As determined by the User and Group directives, the Apache daemon, `httpd`, is assigned a specific user and group name here and in `/etc/passwd` and `/etc/group`:

```
User apache
Group apache
```

Administrative Contact

With web pages generated by Apache, there is a listing for an administrative contact, as determined by the `ServerAdmin` directive:

```
ServerAdmin root@localhost
```

Web Server Name

If you have an administrative website for your web server, you'll want to set it with the `ServerName` directive. If you don't have a fully qualified domain name in a DNS server, use the IP address.

```
#ServerName new.host.name:80
```

If you activate this directive, it will normally be superseded by the name you set for each Virtual Host.

Canonical Name

Technically, every URL, such as `http://www.Sybex.com/`, is supposed to have a trailing slash. But I never remember to put it in. Without the following directive, an attempt to navigate to `www.Sybex.com` would end up at the address specified by the `ServerName` directive. The standard `httpd.conf` file includes the `UseCanonicalName` directive to add the trailing slash automatically.

```
UseCanonicalName Off
```

Document Root

The root directory for your web server is specified by the `DocumentRoot` directive:

```
DocumentRoot "/var/www/html"
```

Web Directory Permissions

Next, we look at the default permissions for users within directories accessible through your server's websites. It's set up by the `<Directory />` container, which defines the permissions associated with the `DocumentRoot`:

```
<Directory />
    Options FollowSymLinks
    AllowOverride None
</Directory>
```

The `Options` directive determines where you can go for files from that directory. It can be set to several different values, as described in Table 30.5. The `AllowOverride` directive can go to the `.htaccess` file for a list of users or computers allowed to see certain files; the `AllowOverride None` setting doesn't even look at the `.htaccess` file.

TABLE 30.5: *OPTIONS* DIRECTIVE VALUES

VALUE	DESCRIPTION
All	Supports all settings except `MultiViews`.
ExecCGI	Allows the running of CGI scripts.
FollowSymLinks	Lets requests follow symbolically linked files or directories.
Includes	Allows the use of server-side includes (SSI).
IncludesNOEXEC	Allows SSIs, but no CGIs.

Continued on next page

TABLE 30.5: *OPTIONS* DIRECTIVE VALUES *(continued)*

VALUE	DESCRIPTION
Indexes	If there is no `index.html` type file, sets up Apache to return a list of files in that directory. Options for this file are specified by the `DirectoryIndex` directive.
MultiViews	Supports content negotiation, such as between web pages in different languages.
SymLinksIfOwnerMatch	Follows symbolic links if the target file or directory is owned by the same user.

.HTACCESS FILES

An `.htaccess` file is a distributed configuration file that you can use to configure individual directories on a website. It is a common way to implement restricted access to a specific directory.

An `.htaccess` file isn't necessary in most cases; you can configure access on a per-directory basis in the main Apache configuration file, `httpd.conf`. In the default version of the main Apache configuration file, look for `<Directory>` containers. Observe how the restrictions vary for different directories.

However, if you have a large number of websites on your server, such as the personal web pages associated with many ISPs, you may want to use `.htaccess` files to let individual users regulate access to web pages in their home directories. You can set up a standard scheme to read `.htaccess` files, as described later in the "User Directory Permissions" section.

If you want to implement distributed configuration files, you can do something to make it more secure. Look for the `AccessFileName` directive in `httpd.conf`. Assign a hidden file name other than `.htaccess`. Also see the "Access Control" section later in this chapter.

Specific Directory Permissions

Next, we'll look at the default permissions in `httpd.conf` for the /var/www/html directory, as specified by the following container:

```
<Directory "/var/www/html">
```

The following `Options` directive supports redirection via symbolic links and the listing of files in the current directory if there is no `index.html` type file (look ahead to Figure 30.2 for an example):

```
Options Indexes FollowSymLinks
```

As we mentioned in the previous section, the `AllowOverride` directive specifies the types of directives in the `.htaccess` file; the following option doesn't even look at `.htaccess`:

```
AllowOverride None
```

Finally, there are access control directives; the following looks for an `Allow` and then a `Deny` directive for this directory, in order:

```
Order allow,deny
Allow from all
```

Root Directory Permissions

Now the `httpd.conf` file adds a couple more directives for users that access the top directory of your website, also known as `DocumentRoot`:

```
<LocationMatch "^/$">
    Options -Indexes
    ErrorDocument 403 /error/noindex.html
</LocationMatch>
```

The `<LocationMatch "^/$">` container looks a little strange; this specific directive applies the commands therein (`Options` and `ErrorDocument`) to the root (/) directory.

The `Options -Indexes` directive prohibits the listing of files, courtesy of the - in front of the `Indexes` setting. If no `index.html` page is available, the `ErrorDocument` directive returns the noted error web page to the user. This location is based on the `ServerRoot` directive; thus, `noindex.html` is located in the `/etc/httpd/error` directory.

Oddly enough, the `noindex.html` file is the "Test Page" that is shown when Apache starts without the pages associated with a real website. It's shown back in Figure 30.1.

User Directory Permissions

You can set up web pages in your users' home directories. They are disabled by default with the following command:

```
UserDir disable
```

You can replace that command with the following:

```
UserDir public_html
```

Assume you have a user named ez, and she has a set of web page files in the `/home/ez/public_html` directory. Also, assume that your website is named **www.example.abc**. You need to set appropriate permissions:

```
# chmod 711 /home/ez
# chmod 755 /home/ez/public_html
# chmod 744 /home/ez/public_html/*
```

Then when you direct your browser to **www.example.abc/~ez**, you will be able to see any index.html web page that you might have stored in the `/home/ez/public_html` directory.

You can further regulate access to web pages and files in users' home directories. Look at the following sample commands from the default `httpd.conf` file:

```
#<Directory /home/*/public_html>
#    AllowOverride FileInfo AuthConfig Limit
```

```
#     Options MultiViews Indexes SymLinksIfOwnerMatch IncludesNoExec
#     <Limit GET POST OPTIONS>
#        Order allow,deny
#        Allow from all
#     </Limit>
#     <LimitExcept GET POST OPTIONS>
#        Order deny,allow
#        Deny from all
#     </LimitExcept>
#</Directory>
```

If you activate these commands, Apache allows you to browse the files in the `public_html` subdirectory, as described later in the "Directory Listings" section.

As described earlier, the `AllowOverride` directive relates to the access information that Apache reads from an individual `.htaccess` file. The different parameters associated with this directive are shown in Table 30.6. All descriptions refer to the commands that you can use in an `.htaccess` file on a per-directory basis.

TABLE 30.6: *ALLOWOVERRIDE* DIRECTIVE PARAMETERS

PARAMETER	DESCRIPTION
AuthConfig	Supports the use of authorization directives
FileInfo	Lets you configure various document types
Indexes	Permits you to configure indexing of the directory
Limit	Supports access control restrictions, such as deny and allow

The `Options` directive described in Table 30.5 supports content negotiation, file indexing, following symbolic links, and support for SSIs but not CGIs.

The `Limit` directive sets options for users who want to send (`POST`) and receive (`GET`) files from the user home directory; the `LimitExcept` directive denies the use of all other access commands.

Directory Index

When users navigate to your website, they're actually looking in a directory. The `DirectoryIndex` directive tells Apache the types of web pages to send back to the website user:

```
DirectoryIndex index.html index.html.var
```

The `index.html` document is a standard home page file used by many websites; `index.html.var` is one way to set up a dynamic home page. You can look at an example of `.var` files in the `/var/www/error` directory. Open those files in the text editor of your choice. You'll see standard error messages.

Access Control

As described in the sidebar ".htaccess Files," you can configure access control files on individual directories. By default, it's the hidden file .htaccess; you can set a different filename with the AccessFileName directive:

```
AccessFileName .htaccess
```

The following Files directive ensures that any file that starts with .ht is not viewable by users who are browsing your website:

```
<Files ~ "^\.ht">
    Order allow,deny
    Deny from all
</Files>
```

MIME Types

While the MIME (Multipurpose Internet Mail Extensions) standard was originally created for sending binary files over e-mail, it works for web pages as well. For example, you can configure your browser to open the PDF reader of your choice if you navigate to a PDF file on the Internet. The standard translation between MIME types and file extensions is listed through the TypesConfig directive:

```
TypesConfig /etc/mime.types
```

Many files do not have extensions such as .pdf or .doc. You can set the DefaultType directive to specify display options on a browser. If you use text files, the following standard should work well:

```
DefaultType text/plain
```

Alternatively, if most of your files are in binary format, you could end up sending dozens of pages of gibberish to your users unless you changed this directive to something like:

```
DefaultType application/octet-stream
```

If the extension doesn't provide a clue, you can use the MIMEMagicFile directive, which uses the mod_mime_magic module defined in Table 30.4:

```
<IfModule mod_mime_magic.c>
#   MIMEMagicFile /usr/share/magic.mime
    MIMEMagicFile conf/magic
</IfModule>
```

Remember, the location of a "relative" path such as conf/magic is based on the ServerRoot directive. In other words, this section points to the MIMEMagicFile at /etc/httpd/conf/magic.

There is one more related directive, toward the end of the httpd.conf file. The AddType directive allows you to override the configuration as defined by TypesConfig in /etc/mime.types:

```
AddType application/x-tar .tgz
```

Log Data

Apache logs can be very large. If you're running a large commercial website, you could easily collect hundreds of megabytes of log data every day. The choices you make for log data could easily overload your system.

Normally, `HostnameLookups` are set to `Off`; otherwise, Apache will look for the fully qualified domain name of every requesting user. Don't do this unless you have reliable access to a DNS server and the network capacity to handle that volume of information.

```
HostnameLookups Off
```

You can set the locations of different log files. The `ErrorLog` directive, as you'd expect, sets the location of the `error_log` file. With the given value of `ServerRoot`, the following log file is located in the `/etc/httpd/logs` directory:

```
ErrorLog logs/error_log
```

You can control the types of messages sent to the `ErrorLog` file; available values for the `LogLevel` directive (`debug`, `info`, `notice`, `warn`, `error`, `crit`, `alert`, `emerg`) are similar to those shown in the standard error log file, `/etc/syslog.conf`, back in Chapter 13.

```
LogLevel warn
```

Log information is sent to the `error_log` in a specific format, as defined by the following `LogFormat` directives:

```
LogFormat "%h %l %u %t \"%r\" %>s %b \"%{Referer}i\" \"%{User-Agent}i\"" combined
LogFormat "%h %l %u %t \"%r\" %>s %b" common
LogFormat "%{Referer}i -> %U" referer
LogFormat "%{User-agent}i" agent
```

Each of these lines specifies a set of data collected in four different formats: `combined`, `common`, `referer`, and `agent`.

The variables associated with `LogFormat` are described in Table 30.7. A substantial number of additional variables are available, which you can review in the `mod_log_config.html` file in the `/var/www/manual/mod` directory. Other request fields are per the standards of the World Wide Web consortium, at www.w3.org/Protocols/HTTP/HTRQ_Headers.html.

TABLE 30.7: *LogFormat* Directive Variables

VARIABLE	DESCRIPTION
%a	Remote IP address.
%b	Bytes sent (not including HTTP headers).
%h	Remote host.
%l	Remote log name.
%r	First line of the client request.

Continued on next page

TABLE 30.7: *LOGFORMAT* DIRECTIVE VARIABLES *(continued)*

VARIABLE	DESCRIPTION
%s	Request status.
%t	Time.
%u	Remote user.
referer	Notes the page where someone clicked on a link. (Yes, in Apache, *referer* is not spelled correctly.)
user-agent	Notes the client program, such as Mozilla.

You can set the location of several other types of logs, as defined through the `CustomLog` variable. You can set this up within one of your Virtual Hosts, so the owners of individual websites on your server can get their own log files:

```
# CustomLog logs/access_log common
CustomLog logs/access_log combined
#CustomLog logs/referer_log referer
#CustomLog logs/agent_log agent
#CustomLog logs/access_log combined
```

These lines specify the location of your log files. Based on the default `ServerRoot`, that's `/etc/httpd/logs`. The actual information that's sent to each log file is based on the referenced `LogFormat`. For example, the active `CustomLog` directive refers to the `combined` format, which you might recall is:

```
LogFormat "%h %l %u %t \"%r\" %>s %b \"%{Referer}i\" \"%{User-Agent}i\"" combined
```

The Server Signs the Web Page

The `httpd.conf` file can add one element to dynamically generated web pages, depending on the `ServerSignature` directive. Normally it's set as follows:

```
ServerSignature On
```

When `ServerSignature` is set to `On`, you might see a message similar to the following at the bottom of dynamically generated web pages:

```
Apache/2.0.40 Server at localhost Port 80
```

Alternatively, if you substitute `Email` for `On`, you'll get a hyperlink from the name of the computer, in this case, `localhost`, to the server administrator, as defined by the `ServerAdmin` directive.

Aliases

You can use the `Alias` directive to set up a link between a directory in the URL to a directory on your computer. For example, the first `Alias` directive in the default `httpd.conf` file links the `/icons/` subdirectory from a URL:

```
Alias /icons/ "/var/www/icons/"
```

to the /var/www/icons/ directory on the web server. This is also a good place to specify the permissions associated with /var/www/icons/.

```
<Directory "/var/www/icons">
    Options Indexes MultiViews
    AllowOverride None
    Order allow,deny
    Allow from all
</Directory>
```

These permissions allow users to read the contents of the directory, unless there's a DirectoryIndex file such as index.html, and support content negotiation, such as different languages, via MultiViews.

If you've installed the httpd-manual-* RPM and want to include the Apache manual on your website, change the following default Alias directive from

```
Alias /manual "/var/www/manual"
```

to

```
Alias /etc/httpd/manual "/var/www/manual"
```

This assumes that your ServerRoot directive is set to /etc/httpd. The following lines set permissions for the noted directory, and include the Web-based Distributed Authoring and Versioning (WebDAV) database:

```
<Directory "/var/www/manual">
    Options Indexes FollowSymLinks MultiViews
    AllowOverride None
    Order allow,deny
    Allow from all
</Directory>

<IfModule mod_dav_fs.c>
    # Location of the WebDAV lock database.
    DAVLockDB /var/lib/dav/lockdb
</IfModule>
```

Scripts

Scripts in httpd.conf refer to programs that are run through the web server. Apache starts in the default httpd.conf file with a ScriptAlias directive, which is a specialized Alias for scripts:

```
ScriptAlias /cgi-bin/ "/var/www/cgi-bin/"
```

Some scripts require access to the CGI daemon, which is defined by the Scriptsock directive:

```
<IfModule mod_cgid.c>
    Scriptsock      run/httpd.cgid
</IfModule>
```

Once again, this is a good opportunity to define the permissions associated with the scripts associated with your websites:

```
<Directory "/var/www/cgi-bin">
    AllowOverride None
    Options None
    Order allow,deny
    Allow from all
</Directory>
```

Note how these permissions don't allow the use of `.htaccess` but support script execution by all users.

If you change website names, you'll want to redirect users. For example, the following default `Redirect` directive takes users who navigate to your `/bears` directory to www.mommabears.com:

```
# Redirect permanent /bears http://www.mommabears.com
```

Directory Listings

Sometimes you want to see the files in a directory. For example, Figure 30.2 illustrates the files in the `/home/mike/public_html` directory, based on the `UserDir` directives described earlier, in the User Directory Permissions section.

FIGURE 30.2

Viewing home directory files

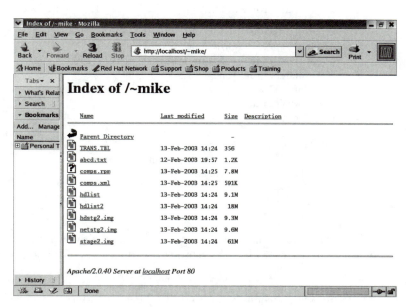

The `IndexOptions` directive determines how index files are shown in client web browsers. For example, the default `IndexOptions` line

```
IndexOptions FancyIndexing VersionSort NameWidth=*
```

configures `FancyIndexing`, for icons and file sizes; `VersionSort`, which sorts numbers such as RPM versions in a specific order; and a `NameWidth` as large as needed for the filenames in the directory.

Icons

Speaking of icons, a list of icons is available for different file types and extensions. These icons are shown with a file list, assuming you have set `IndexOptions FancyIndexing` as defined in the previous section. There are three basic `AddIcon*` directives:

```
AddIconByEncoding (CMP,/icons/compressed.gif)  x-compress x-gzip
```

The `AddIconByEncoding` directive shown here applies to compressed binary files. Several `AddIconBy-Type` directives are also included for four different file types:

```
AddIconByType (TXT,/icons/text.gif) text/*
AddIconByType (IMG,/icons/image2.gif) image/*
AddIconByType (SND,/icons/sound2.gif) audio/*
AddIconByType (VID,/icons/movie.gif) video/*
```

Finally, there are a series of `AddIcon` directives that associate a specific icon with different filename extensions:

```
AddIcon /icons/binary.gif .bin .exe
AddIcon /icons/binhex.gif .hqx
AddIcon /icons/tar.gif .tar
AddIcon /icons/world2.gif .wrl .wrl.gz .vrml .vrm .iv
AddIcon /icons/compressed.gif .Z .z .tgz .gz .zip
AddIcon /icons/a.gif .ps .ai .eps
AddIcon /icons/layout.gif .html .shtml .htm .pdf
AddIcon /icons/text.gif .txt
AddIcon /icons/c.gif .c
AddIcon /icons/p.gif .pl .py
AddIcon /icons/f.gif .for
AddIcon /icons/dvi.gif .dvi
AddIcon /icons/uuencoded.gif .uu
AddIcon /icons/script.gif .conf .sh .shar .csh .ksh .tcl
AddIcon /icons/tex.gif .tex
AddIcon /icons/bomb.gif core
AddIcon /icons/back.gif ..
AddIcon /icons/hand.right.gif README
AddIcon /icons/folder.gif ^^DIRECTORY^^
AddIcon /icons/blank.gif ^^BLANKICON^^
```

These `AddIcon` directives are straightforward. For example, if Apache sees a file with an **.exe** extension, it adds the `/icons/binary.gif` icon as a label for that particular file. But this list is not comprehensive; there is a `DefaultIcon` directive for files with unknown extensions:

```
DefaultIcon /icons/unknown.gif
```

If you like, you can activate the following `AddDescription` directives to give users a bit more information about files with specific extensions:

```
#AddDescription "GZIP compressed document" .gz
#AddDescription "tar archive" .tar
#AddDescription "GZIP compressed tar archive" .tgz
```

You can set up directories with various HTML files. For example, the `HeaderName` directive specifies a file to put before the file list; the `ReadmeName` directive specifies a file to put after the file list.

```
ReadmeName README.html
HeaderName HEADER.html
```

The `IndexIgnore` directive sets Apache to avoid listing the noted files in any directory list. Note how the default value includes the `HEADER.html` and `README.html` files.

```
IndexIgnore .??* *~ *# HEADER* README* RCS CVS *,v *,t
```

Decompression

Some browsers can read and automatically decompress certain files in your website directories. All you need to do is specify the encoding associated with certain filename extensions by using the `AddEncoding` directive:

```
AddEncoding x-compress Z
AddEncoding x-gzip gz tgz
```

Languages

Multilingual websites include web pages in multiple languages. The `DefaultLanguage` directive defines the language associated with all web pages that aren't already labeled. The following inactive directive specifies the Dutch language:

```
# DefaultLanguage nl
```

You can set up web pages in different languages, as defined by the `AddLanguage` directive. For example, `index.html.cz` is a web page associated with the Czech language:

```
AddLanguage cz .cz
```

Other language codes are listed in Table 30.8.

TABLE 30.8: *ADDLANGUAGE* CODES

CODE	LANGUAGE
ca	Catalan
cz	Czech
da	Danish
de	German

Continued on next page

TABLE 30.8: *ADDLANGUAGE CODES (continued)*

CODE	LANGUAGE
en	English
el	Modern Greek
es	Spanish
et	Estonian
fr	French
he	Hebrew
hr	Hungarian
it	Italian
ja	Japanese
kr	Korean
ltz	Luxembourgeois
nl	Dutch (Netherlands)
nn	Norwegian Nynorsk
no	Norwegian
pl	Polish
pt	Portuguese
pt-br	Brazilian Portuguese
ru	Russian
sv	Swedish
tw	Chinese *
zh-tw	Chinese

Anyone who follows the political situation in China in any depth will understand that the designation of tw *as Chinese has caused some controversy. As I understand it, the people behind Apache are in the process of converting all Chinese* AddLanguage *codes to* zh.

A web browser should tell the web server the preferred language. However, when this doesn't work, the LanguagePriority directive sets the preferred language:

```
LanguagePriority en da nl et fr de el it ja kr no pl pt  pt-br ltz ca es sv tw
```

This works hand in hand with the ForceLanguagePriority directive. As defined in the default httpd .conf file, it uses the LanguagePriority directive list to select from languages acceptable to the client web browser. If no acceptable language page is available, the first item on the LanguagePriority list (in this case, English) is used.

Many languages don't work too well unless you have the right set of characters. Most language characters have been organized into different ISO character sets. The default, which works for English and a number of similar languages, is ISO-8859-1. It's forced into the default websites for Apache with the following directive:

```
AddDefaultCharset ISO-8859-1
```

Several other character sets are available, as defined by the following `AddCharset` directives. For more information on these character sets, see www.iana.org/assignments/character-sets.

```
AddCharset ISO-8859-1  .iso8859-1  .latin1
AddCharset ISO-8859-2  .iso8859-2  .latin2 .cen
AddCharset ISO-8859-3  .iso8859-3  .latin3
AddCharset ISO-8859-4  .iso8859-4  .latin4
AddCharset ISO-8859-5  .iso8859-5  .latin5 .cyr .iso-ru
AddCharset ISO-8859-6  .iso8859-6  .latin6 .arb
AddCharset ISO-8859-7  .iso8859-7  .latin7 .grk
AddCharset ISO-8859-8  .iso8859-8  .latin8 .heb
AddCharset ISO-8859-9  .iso8859-9  .latin9 .trk
AddCharset ISO-2022-JP .iso2022-jp .jis
AddCharset ISO-2022-KR .iso2022-kr .kis
AddCharset ISO-2022-CN .iso2022-cn .cis
AddCharset Big5         .Big5       .big5
# For Russian, more than one charset is used (depends on client, mostly):
AddCharset WINDOWS-1251 .cp-1251    .win-1251
AddCharset CP866        .cp866
AddCharset KOI8-r       .koi8-r .koi8-ru
AddCharset KOI8-ru      .koi8-uk .ua
AddCharset ISO-10646-UCS-2 .ucs2
AddCharset ISO-10646-UCS-4 .ucs4
AddCharset UTF-8        .utf8
AddCharset GB2312       .gb2312 .gb
AddCharset utf-7        .utf7
AddCharset utf-8        .utf8
AddCharset big5         .big5 .b5
AddCharset EUC-TW       .euc-tw
AddCharset EUC-JP       .euc-jp
AddCharset EUC-KR       .euc-kr
AddCharset shift_jis    .sjis
```

Mapped Handlers

You can map filename extensions to a specific handler. For example, the following commented `AddHandler` directive activates CGI script handling for files with the `.cgi` extension, assuming you also have set the `Options ExecCGI` directive for the subject directory:

```
#AddHandler cgi-script .cgi
```

The following commented directive makes sure that files that already have HTTP headers don't get processed:

```
#AddHandler send-as-is asis
```

To activate commented directives, remove the comment mark (#) in `httpd.conf` in the text editor of your choice.

This directive processes image map files:

```
AddHandler imap-file map
```

Finally, this directive supports `.var` files, which are associated with finding the language specified by a web browser client:

```
AddHandler type-map var
```

Part of the process includes output filters. For example, the following `AddOutputFilter` directive looks in web pages with `.shtml` extensions for Server Side Includes.

Error Messages

On a web server, if you have an error, you get a message associated with a specific web page. Figure 30.3 illustrates the error message associated with the HTML 404 error code, also known as the "file not found" error.

FIGURE 30.3

An HTML 404 Error

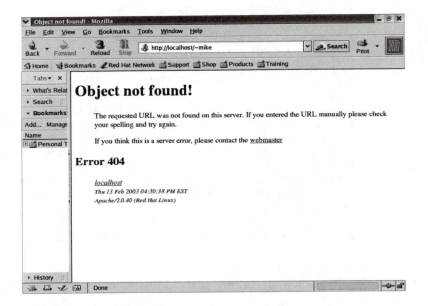

The default error directory is `/var/www/error`; the following `Alias` directive associates the `error` directory with those files:

```
Alias /error/ "/var/www/error/"
```

The following modules provide for content negotiation and SSIs in the web pages in the /var/www/error/ directory:

```
<IfModule mod_negotiation.c>
<IfModule mod_include.c>
```

The following permissions on the /var/www/error directory set the stage for error messages in English, Spanish, German, and French, in that order. You can read more about the other directives earlier in the "Directory Index" section earlier in this chapter.

```
<Directory "/var/www/error">
    AllowOverride None
    Options IncludesNoExec
    AddOutputFilter Includes html
    AddHandler type-map var
    Order allow,deny
    Allow from all
    LanguagePriority en es de fr
    ForceLanguagePriority Prefer Fallback
</Directory>
```

This works hand in hand with HTML error codes. The page a user sees depends on the error code and the web page defined by the following ErrorDocument directives:

```
ErrorDocument 400 /error/HTTP_BAD_REQUEST.html.var
ErrorDocument 401 /error/HTTP_UNAUTHORIZED.html.var
ErrorDocument 403 /error/HTTP_FORBIDDEN.html.var
ErrorDocument 404 /error/HTTP_NOT_FOUND.html.var
ErrorDocument 405 /error/HTTP_METHOD_NOT_ALLOWED.html.var
ErrorDocument 408 /error/HTTP_REQUEST_TIME_OUT.html.var
ErrorDocument 410 /error/HTTP_GONE.html.var
ErrorDocument 411 /error/HTTP_LENGTH_REQUIRED.html.var
ErrorDocument 412 /error/HTTP_PRECONDITION_FAILED.html.var
ErrorDocument 413/error/HTTP_REQUEST_ENTITY_TOO_LARGE.html.var
ErrorDocument 414 /error/HTTP_REQUEST_URI_TOO_LARGE.html.var
ErrorDocument 415 /error/HTTP_SERVICE_UNAVAILABLE.html.var
ErrorDocument 500 /error/HTTP_INTERNAL_SERVER_ERROR.html.var
ErrorDocument 501 /error/HTTP_NOT_IMPLEMENTED.html.var
ErrorDocument 502 /error/HTTP_BAD_GATEWAY.html.var
ErrorDocument 503 /error/HTTP_SERVICE_UNAVAILABLE.html.var
ErrorDocument 506 /error/HTTP_VARIANT_ALSO_VARIES.html.var
```

Browser Customization

When a web browser asks for a web page, it tells Apache what kind of browser it is. The BrowserMatch directive helps you customize the response to different web browsers:

```
BrowserMatch "Mozilla/2" nokeepalive
BrowserMatch "MSIE 4\.0b2;" nokeepalive downgrade-1.0 force-response-1.0
BrowserMatch "RealPlayer 4\.0" force-response-1.0
```

```
BrowserMatch "Java/1\.0" force-response-1.0
BrowserMatch "JDK/1\.0" force-response-1.0
```

The first two commands create special responses for older browsers; `Mozilla/2` corresponds to Netscape 2.*x*, and `MSIE 4\.0b2` corresponds to Microsoft Internet Explorer 4.*x*. These browsers do not conform to the current HTTP 1.1 standard. The last three commands force HTTP 1.0–level responses to the specified web browsers.

There is a special issue with Microsoft WebFolders, which does not properly handle WebDAV databases. This issue is addressed with the following `BrowserMatch` directives:

```
BrowserMatch "Microsoft Data Access Internet PublishingProvider"
➡ redirect-carefully
BrowserMatch "^WebDrive" redirect-carefully
```

Server Reports

You can send out reports on the status and configuration information on your Apache server with various server reports. For example, the following command stanza, when activated, can give you the current status of Apache:

```
#<Location /server-status>
#     SetHandler server-status
#     Order deny,allow
#     Deny from all
#     Allow from .your-domain.com
#</Location>
```

I would activate it with the following commands; otherwise, the `Deny from all` command would stop all traffic to the `http://servername/server-status` address. In this case, my LAN is on the 192.168.13.0/24 network:

```
<Location /server-status>
    SetHandler server-status
    Order deny,allow
    Deny from all
    Allow from 192.168.13.0/24
</Location>
```

You can see the result from another computer on my LAN through a different web browser in Figure 30.4.

You can get similar reports on your Apache configuration when you properly activate the following commands:

```
#<Location /server-info>
#     SetHandler server-info
#     Order deny,allow
#     Deny from all
#     Allow from .your-domain.com
#</Location>
```

FIGURE 30.4
Checking server
status remotely

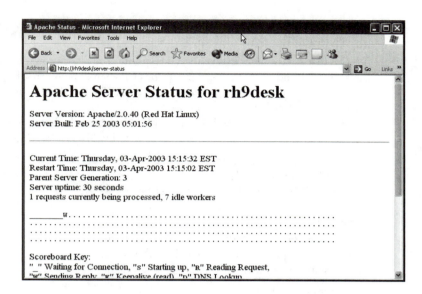

These commands are direct from the default `httpd.conf` file; remember to set `Allow from` *your_network_address*, similar to what I did in the previous stanza. When you do, you can see the results remotely, as shown in Figure 30.5.

FIGURE 30.5
Checking server
configuration
remotely

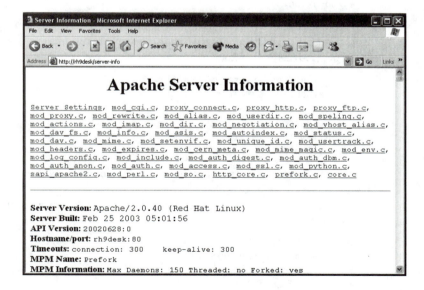

Proxy Server

Apache includes its own proxy server. You can set Apache to cache and serve requested web pages on local networks or all users. The basic commands are shown here; I've changed them a bit to apply the proxy server to my LAN with a network address of 192.168.13.0/24:

```
#<IfModule mod_proxy.c>
#ProxyRequests On
#
#<Proxy *>
#    Order deny,allow
#    Deny from all
#    Allow from 192.168.13.0/24
#</Proxy>
```

If you have multiple proxy servers, you should activate the following ProxyVia directive, which supports searches through a chain of proxy servers using HTTP 1.1:

```
#ProxyVia On
```

A proxy server has no purpose unless you configure a cache. Table 30.9 describes the series of special directives associated with caches. If you set up a proxy server, you may want to change some of these settings; for example, you may want a CacheSize larger than 5KB:

```
#CacheRoot "/etc/httpd/proxy"
#CacheSize 5
#CacheGcInterval 4
#CacheMaxExpire 24
#CacheLastModifiedFactor 0.1
#CacheDefaultExpire 1
#NoCache a-domain.com another-domain.edu joes.garage-sale.com
```

TABLE 30.9: APACHE CACHE DIRECTIVES

DIRECTIVE	DESCRIPTION
CacheDefaultExpire	Sets the time to cache a document, in seconds.
CacheGcInterval	Configures the time between attempts to clear old data from a cache, in hours.
CacheLastModifiedFactor	Sets the expiration time for files in the cache. If there is no expiration date and time associated with a web page, Apache sets it relative to the amount of time since the last known change to that page.
CacheMaxExpire	Selects the maximum time in seconds to cache a document.
CacheRoot	Configures the default directory with the proxy server cache.
CacheSize	Sets the size of the cache, in kilobytes.

VIRTUAL HOSTS

One of the strengths of Apache 2.0.*x* is its ability to set up multiple websites on a single IP address. This is possible with the concept of *Virtual Hosts.*

Older versions of Apache supported only IP-based Virtual Hosts, which required separate IP addresses for each website configured through your Apache server. Apache 2.0.*x* supports name-based Virtual Hosts.

In this scheme, DNS servers map multiple domain names, such as www.mommabears.com and www.sybex.com, to the same IP address, such as 10.111.123.45. You can set up httpd.conf to recognize the different domain names and serve the appropriate website.

NOTE   *You can't always use the name-based scheme; it doesn't work if you need a secure (SSL) part of your website, such as to support e-commerce. It also has problems with older clients, such as Netscape 2.0 and Internet Explorer 4.0 browsers. These browsers cannot handle a lot of information associated with the current HTTP 1.1 standard.*

The following code is an example of how to configure two Virtual Hosts, in this case for www.sybex.com and www.mommabears.com:

```
NameVirtualHost *
```

This NameVirtualHost directive listens to requests to all IP addresses on the local computer. Alternatively, you can substitute the actual IP address for the * in this section:

```
<VirtualHost *>
    ServerAdmin webmaster@sybex.com
    DocumentRoot /www/site1/sybex.com
    ServerName sybex.com
    ErrorLog logs/sybex.com-error_log
    CustomLog logs/sybex.com-access_log common
</VirtualHost>
```

The directives in the www.sybex.com <Virtual Host *> container supersede any settings made earlier in the httpd.conf file. You can customize each Virtual Host by adding the directives of your choice:

```
<VirtualHost *>
    ServerAdmin webmaster@mommabears.com
    DocumentRoot /www/site2/mommabears.com
    ServerName mommabears.com
    ErrorLog logs/mommabears.com-error_log
    CustomLog logs/mommabears.com-access_log common
</VirtualHost>
```

As you can see, the settings for the mommabears.com website are similar; remember, relative directories depend on the ServerRoot directive.

Customizing Apache Modules

There are a number of Apache module-specific configuration files in the /etc/httpd/conf.d directory, installed through some of the module RPMs described earlier in the "Packages" section. They are included in the basic Apache configuration courtesy of the `Include conf.d/*.conf` directive in the main `httpd.conf` file. These module files are summarized in Table 30.10.

TABLE 30.10: Apache Module Configuration Files

FILE	DESCRIPTION
`auth_mysql.conf`	Supports access to a MySQL database; the default version of this file includes various authentication commands.
`auth_pgsql.conf`	Supports access to a PostgreSQL database; the default version of this file includes various authentication commands.
`perl.conf`	Incorporates a Perl interpreter; supports the use of Perl commands and scripts.
`php.conf`	Incorporates a PHP scripting language interpreter.
`python.conf`	Configures a Python interpreter; allows the use of Python commands and scripts.
`ssl.conf`	Adds Secure Socket Layer (SSL) support; uses TCP/IP port 443 by default. Includes several directives for certificates and encryption methods.

Troubleshooting Apache

If you're unable to make a connection to a website configured on a Apache web server, you can check a number of things. Before you begin, check the network. The most common problem on any network is physical; for example, it's good to inspect connectors and cables. Then, check connectivity using commands such as `ping`; for more information, see Chapter 21.

CHECKING BASIC OPERATION

Once you're sure that your network is operational, the next step is to see if Apache is running. Start with the following command:

```
# service httpd status
```

You should see a message such as:

```
httpd (pid 3464 3463 3462 3461 3460 3459 3458) is running
```

This tells you that a number of Apache (`httpd`) daemons are running; the number depends on `httpd.conf` directives such as `StartServers`. If you're having a problem, there are three other fairly common messages:

```
httpd is stopped
```

This is fairly simple; try a `service httpd start` command. Rerun the `service httpd status` command. You might also see the following message:

```
httpd is dead but pid file exists
```

In this example, Apache can't start, in part because there is an `httpd.pid` file in the `/var/run` directory. This can happen after a power failure (assuming you don't have an uninterruptible power supply) where Linux never got a chance to erase the `httpd.pid` file. Try deleting the file and then run the `service httpd start` command. Rerun the `service httpd status` command. You might now see the following message:

```
httpd dead but subsys locked
```

That tells us something else is going wrong. It's time to inspect the log files.

CHECKING LOG FILES

The default location for your Apache log files as defined in `httpd.conf` is `/etc/httpd/logs`; however, you'll find this directory linked to a more standard location for log files, `/var/log/httpd`. Remember, you have the freedom to put log files in a different directory by using `CustomLog` directives in a Virtual Host container.

Read the log files in this directory for clues. The variety of errors that you might find is beyond the scope of this book; however, many of the log entries are self-explanatory.

CHECKING SYNTAX

The Apache web server includes its own syntax checker. The following command checks the syntax of the main configuration file, `httpd.conf`. If there is a problem, the command

```
# httpd -t
```

often identifies the line number with the problem, such as a misspelled directive. Alternatively, the following command starts Apache in debug mode, which can help you identify additional problems:

```
# httpd -X
```

CHECKING THE FIREWALL

Sometimes messages just aren't getting through to your web server. That may mean that you forgot to let in messages through the standard HTTP port (80) in the firewall. Run an `iptables -L` command to list current firewall rules. Refer to Chapter 22 for more information on this command.

As described with the various firewall utilities (Chapters 3, 4, and 19), you can set up firewalls that automatically allow data through the HTTP port. Remember, if you also serve secure web pages, you should also open up the associated port. In this case, for HTTPS, that is port 443. Standard TCP/IP port numbers are defined in `/etc/services`.

Configuring with the Red Hat GUI Apache Utility

Red Hat has developed a GUI tool for configuring Apache, which you can start with the `redhat-config-httpd` command. When you first start the tool in a GUI, you should see the Apache Configuration window, shown in Figure 30.6.

FIGURE 30.6

The graphical Apache configuration utility

As you can see, this utility includes four tabs, which we cover in the following sections. When you finish your changes and click OK, changes are written to your `httpd.conf` file, overwriting any changes that you may have made earlier in a text editor.

NOTE   As of this writing, `redhat-config-httpd` is still a work in progress. Before I use this utility, I first back up my current `httpd.conf` file. After I make changes, I make sure to test the syntax of `httpd.conf` with the `httpd -t` command. I open `httpd.conf` in a text editor to analyze the changes. Nevertheless, `redhat-config-httpd` is a great way to learn more about configuring Apache.

Setting Main Apache Parameters

The basic setup of Apache is straightforward. You're configuring three directives in the Apache Configuration window Main tab:

- The Server Name text box corresponds to the `ServerName` directive, which sets the name for the main website for the Apache server. This utility won't work unless you enter the name or IP address of your server in this text box. If you're configuring Virtual Hosts, don't enter any of those domain names in this text box. It is usually best to enter the IP address for your server, to avoid unnecessary traffic to any DNS servers connected to your network.

- The Webmaster Email Address text box corresponds to the `ServerAdmin` directive, which sets the default e-mail address listed by automatically generated web pages. You can see the default setting, `root@localhost`, in Figure 30.6.

- The Available Addresses box sets the TCP/IP ports where Apache listens for requests, using the `Listen` directive. Port 80 is the standard HTTP TCP/IP port, and Apache normally listens to requests from all addresses on the Internet, with the `Allow from all` command.

You can limit the range of computers allowed to view your website. Highlight All Available Addresses On Port 80 and click Edit. This opens the Edit An Address window, shown in Figure 30.7.

FIGURE 30.7

Limiting access to
your web server

For example, Figure 30.7 illustrates limiting access to the network adapter on your computer with an IP address of 192.168.13.64. This changes the `Listen` directive in `httpd.conf` to

```
Listen 192.168.13.64:80
```

If you need to configure other services, such as secure web pages (HTTPS), click the Add button. This opens the Add New Address window, which looks almost identical to Figure 30.7. You can then enter the IP address of the desired network adapter and the TCP/IP port associated with HTTPS, 443. When you've completed your desired changes, click the Virtual Hosts tab.

Configuring Virtual Hosts

Next, you can start configuring Virtual Hosts within Apache. If you haven't already done so, start the `redhat-config-httpd` utility and click the Virtual Hosts tab. The default view is shown in Figure 30.8.

FIGURE 30.8

The Virtual
Hosts tab

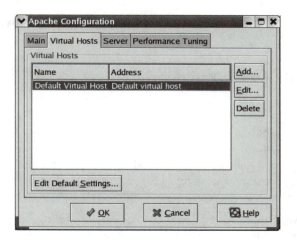

The Default Virtual Host settings associated with the default `httpd.conf` file are shown. If you want to know more about the default settings, click Edit or Edit Default Settings and analyze the properties window. However, we're focused on creating a Virtual Host for a real website, so click Add. This opens the Virtual Host Properties window, shown in Figure 30.9.

FIGURE 30.9

Configuring a
virtual host

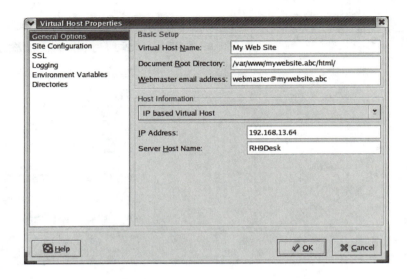

As you can see, there are six sections in this window: General Options, Site Configuration, SSL, Logging, Environment Variables, and Directories.

GENERAL OPTIONS

Every Virtual Host includes General Options, similar to those shown in Figure 30.9. In that figure, we've filled in some basic parameters for a website named `mywebsite.abc`.

As described earlier, you can set up multiple Virtual Hosts on a single IP address using the IP-based Virtual Host setting. The alternative, name-based Virtual Hosts, requires an IP address for each website configured through your Apache server.

SITE CONFIGURATION

Next, select the Site Configuration option on the left side of the window. This opens a list of directory pages and error file settings, as shown in Figure 30.10.

When users look for your website, they're taken to the directory associated with the `DocumentRoot` directive. As you can tell in Figure 30.9, that's the `/var/www/mywebsite.abc/html` directory. It looks for one of the filenames shown in the Directory Page Search List box: `index.php`, `index.html`, `index.htm`, or `index.shtml`.

The Error Pages shown at the bottom of the window display Apache's response to various HTTP errors. For example, the highlighted error, *file not found*, is associated with HTTP error code 404. The default behavior refers to `ErrorDocument` directives in `httpd.conf`. If you want special error pages, you can create special `ErrorDocument` directives for this particular Virtual Host. To do so, highlight the error code of your choice and click Edit. This opens the ApacheConf.py window, shown in Figure 30.11.

FIGURE 30.10

Site configuration settings

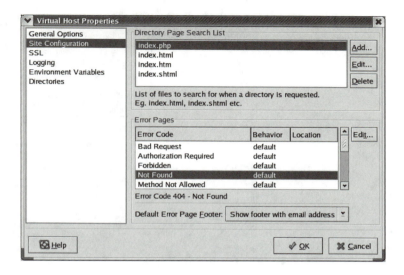

FIGURE 30.11

Changing error code behavior

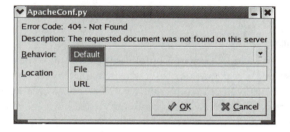

As you can see in the figure, you can point the user in three directions for Error Code 404: Default points to the standard `ErrorDocument` directive in `httpd.conf`; File allows you to specify the web page of your choice; and URL lets you set the location of the desired error message online.

Finally, the Default Error Page Footer specifies the information associated with each error page. The standard footer is based on the `bottom.html` file in the `/var/www/error/include` directory. You can choose to not show the footer at all, or you can show it with or without an e-mail address.

SSL

Next, select the SSL option on the left side of the window. This opens a series of options associated with the Secure Socket Layer, as shown in Figure 30.12. When you install the Apache `mod_ss1-*` RPM, you get a series of fake keys in the `/etc/httpd/conf` directory, which are shown in the figure.

FIGURE 30.12

Secure Socket Layer settings

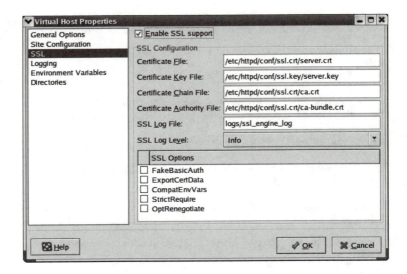

If you're actually planning to run a secure web server, you'll need a real set of certificate data from a Certificate Authority (CA) such as VeriSign (`www.verisign.com`) or Thawte (`www.thawte.com`). While we provide general instructions for setting up a secure server in the sidebar "Generating Security Keys," details are extensive and beyond the scope of this book. Refer to `httpd.apache.org`, `www.apache-ssl .org`, and *Linux Apache Web Server Administration*, Second Edition (Sybex, 2002) for more information.

Changes that you make here are written to the `ssl.conf` file in `/etc/httpd/conf.d` directory.

GENERATING SECURITY KEYS

This sidebar gives basic instructions on generating a real set of security keys for Apache. Assuming you have the appropriate RPM packages installed, follow these steps:

1. Delete the basic server keys with the following commands:

   ```
   # rm /etc/httpd/conf/ssl.key/server.key
   # rm /etc/httpd/conf/ssl.crt/server.crt
   ```

2. Navigate to the `/usr/share/ssl/certs` directory:

   ```
   # cd /usr/share/ssl/certs
   ```

3. Next, generate a new server key:

   ```
   # make genkey
   ```

   You're prompted twice for a special password known as a *passphrase*. Be careful—this case-sensitive password holds the key to the secure information on your web server.

Continued on next page

4. You can now set up a request to a CA with the following command:

```
# make certreq
```

You're prompted for your passphrase and administrative information for your server. Once complete, this command creates the following file, which you can send as part of your request to the CA:

```
/etc/httpd/conf/ssl.csr/server.csr
```

5. The CA should respond to you with a file that you can save as `server.crt` in the `/etc/httpd/conf/ssl.crt` directory.

You can make your own unofficial certificate for test purposes by running the `make testcert` command in step 4.

The next time you start Apache, it prompts you for the passphrase. If you don't get it right, Apache does not start.

LOGGING

Next, select the Logging option on the left side of the window. This opens a series of options associated with logging and log files, as shown in Figure 30.13.

FIGURE 30.13

Virtual Host logging

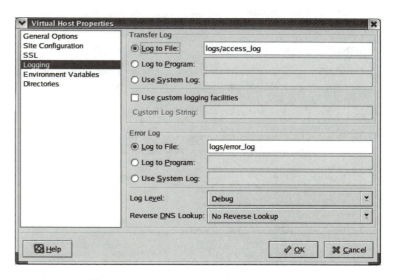

The default log files are shown in the figure; the path is relative to the `ServerRoot` directive, normally `/etc/httpd`. Naturally, you may want to specify log files in special directories associated with the Virtual Host, such as `mywebsite.abc/logs/access_log`.

You can specify the information that goes into this log file in the Custom Log String text box. The information here is associated with the `LogFormat` directive described earlier in this chapter.

The options available in the Log Level drop-down list match those described earlier for the `LogLevel` directive: Emergency, Alert, Critical, Error, Warn, Notice, Info, and Debug.

You may want to make sure the Reverse DNS Lookup setting is set to No Reverse Lookup. Unless you have a reliable and speedy connection to a DNS server, finding the fully qualified domain names associated with an IP address could hurt your web server's performance.

ENVIRONMENT VARIABLES

Next, select the Environment Variables option on the left side of the window. This opens a group of settings where you can set environment variables associated with CGI or SSI scripts, as shown in Figure 30.14.

FIGURE 30.14

Environment variables

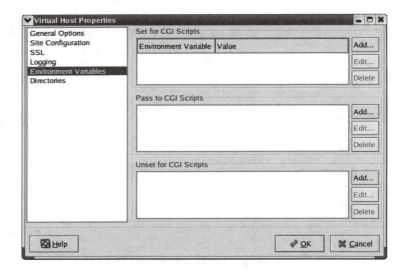

While the principle is the same as regular environment variables in the shell, what you set here applies only to CGI and or SSI scripts.

DIRECTORY OPTIONS

Finally, select the Directories option on the left side of the window. This opens a group of settings where you can set the `Options` directive for various directories, as shown in Figure 30.15.

The `Options` for the default directory are shown in Figure 30.15: `ExecCGI`, `FollowSymLinks`, `Includes`, `IncludesNOEXEC`, `Indexes`, and `SymLinuxIfOwnerMatch` (they are explained back in Table 30.5). You can edit the default settings by clicking the Edit button in the upper-right corner of the window.

You can specify `Options` for other directories. Click Add to open the Directory Options window shown in Figure 30.16. The options in this window are explained in Table 30.11.

Directory options

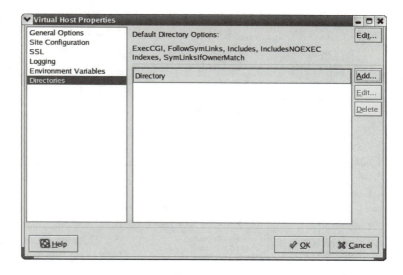

FIGURE 30.16

Setting `Options` on a new directory

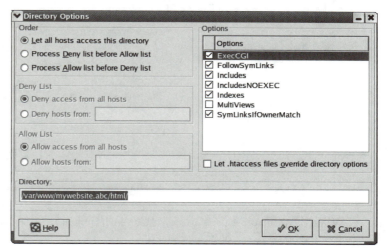

TABLE 30.11: SELECTIONS IN THE DIRECTORY OPTIONS WINDOW

SELECTION	DESCRIPTION
Order	Sets the order of directives; the options are `Allow from all`; `Order deny,allow`; or `Order allow,deny`.
Deny List	If you're not allowing in all hosts, you can deny access to this directory to some or all hosts, by domain name or IP address.

Continued on next page

TABLE 30.11: SELECTIONS IN THE DIRECTORY OPTIONS WINDOW *(continued)*

SELECTION	DESCRIPTION
Allow List	If you're not allowing in all hosts, you can allow access to this directory to some or all hosts, by domain name or IP address.
Directory	Specifies the directory to which the Options directive is to be applied.
Options	The settings associated with the Options directive.
.htaccess	If you activate this setting, the AllowOverride directive is added to this directory.

Configuring the Server

There are some basic settings associated with each Apache server. Return to the Apache Configuration window and click the Server tab. The information should look similar to Figure 30.17. These settings are summarized in Table 30.12.

FIGURE 30.17

Apache configuration server settings

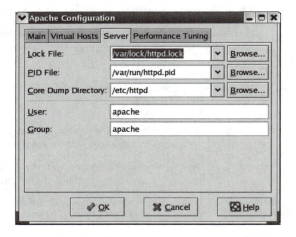

TABLE 30.12: APACHE CONFIGURATION SERVER SETTINGS

SETTING	DESCRIPTION
Lock File	The file opened by Apache when it starts.
PID File	Another file opened by the Apache when it starts. Includes the PIDs associated with open httpd daemons.
Core Dump Directory	Specifies the directory for core dumps, which are used for debugging. Must be writeable by the user associated with the Apache server, normally apache.
User	The username associated with the Apache server.
Group	The group name associated with the Apache server.

Performance Tuning

Several basic performance settings are associated with each Apache server. In the Apache Configuration window, click the Performance Tuning tab. The information should look similar to Figure 30.18. These settings are summarized in Table 30.13.

FIGURE 30.18

The Performance Tuning tab

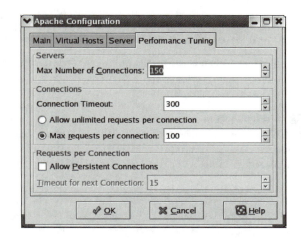

TABLE 30.13: APACHE CONFIGURATION PERFORMANCE SETTINGS

SETTING	DESCRIPTION
Max Number Of Connections	Corresponds to the maximum number of clients who can connect to your web server simultaneously; sets the MaxClients directive.
Connection Timeout	Sets the time the web server waits for further communication from a client browser, in seconds; sets the TimeOut directive.
Requests Per Connection	Limits the number of requested items per connected browser; sets the MaxRequestsPerChild directive.
Allow Persistent Connections	Keeps connections open to a browser, independent of TimeOut; if selected, the KeepAlive directive is set to true.
Timeout For Next Connection	Sets the time which Apache waits for the next request from a client, if KeepAlive is true; sets the KeepAliveTimeout directive.

Incorporating the Red Hat Content Accelerator

The Red Hat Content Accelerator is an alternative web server. Formerly known as TUX, this web server is designed to manage static web content quickly, because its settings reside directly in the Linux kernel. While this tool can also manage dynamic web pages, Red Hat recommends using the Content Accelerator for static pages in concert with Apache for dynamic pages.

This tool is still a work in progress, since TUX can work with Apache only if they're both loaded on the same computer. That's a less than convenient situation for larger websites, which often require several servers, often in different geographic locations. Since the package name for the Red Hat Content Accelerator is still TUX, we'll use the terms interchangeably in this section.

NOTE   *TUX stands for a Threaded Linux web server. Incidentally, it is also the name for the Linux mascot penguin.*

Installing and Starting TUX

Normally, the Red Hat Content Accelerator (TUX) and Apache can't run simultaneously. Therefore, to see if TUX works on your computer, we'll install and start it after stopping Apache, using the following steps:

1. Install the `tux-*` RPM on your computer.

2. Set up an `index.html` file in the default `DOCROOT` directory, `/var/www/html`. For the purpose of this exercise, I've modified and copied `/var/www/error/noindex.html`, which you should recognize from Figure 30.1.

3. Stop the Apache server with the `service httpd stop` command.

4. Start the TUX server with the `service tux start` command.

5. Navigate to the localhost in the browser of your choice.

You can review the result in Figure 30.19.

FIGURE 30.19

TUX at work

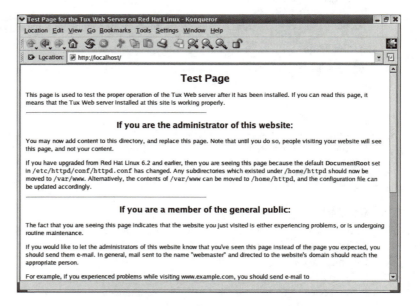

In the figure, we see TUX serving a standard `index.html` page from `/var/www/html`. So, TUX works in Linux. We'll take a brief look at the mechanics in the following sections.

NOTE   *Red Hat recommends that you configure the* DOCROOT *associated with TUX in a separate RAID partition. This corresponds to the Apache* DocumentRoot *directive. For more information on RAID, see Chapter 14.*

Deciphering the Content Accelerator Configuration

Since the Content Accelerator configuration is part of the kernel, the default settings aren't in a standard configuration file; they're located in /etc/sysconfig/tux. This file includes several parameters, which are listed in Table 30.14.

TABLE 30.14: TUX CONFIGURATION PARAMETERS

PARAMETER	DESCRIPTION
TUXTHREADS	Defines the allowed number of kernel threads; do *not* set this higher than the number of CPUs on your computer.
DOCROOT	Sets the top-level directory for requests to the web server; corresponds to the Apache DocumentRoot directive. Browsers expect to find a home page file such as index.html in this directory. The standard location is /var/www/html.
LOGFILE	Assigns a location for the TUX log file, normally /var/log/tux.
DAEMON_UID	Associates a user ID with TUX. The default is nobody.
DAEMON_GID	Associates a group ID with TUX. The default is nobody.
CGIROOT	Defines the directory for CGI scripts, if required.
MAX_KEEPALIVE_TIMEOUT	Sets a timeout value for connections, in case of network problems.
TUXMODULES	Defines modules for dynamic TUX data.
MODULEPATH	Sets the directory with Content Accelerator application program interface modules.

TUX also includes a series of log files; they're located in a file named /var/log/tux. However, these log files are compressed in binary format. To read them, you need the tux2w3c command. One result is shown in Figure 30.20, which illustrates a couple of connections within my network: one from the local computer (127.0.0.1), another from a computer with an IP address of 10.252.113.122.

Combining TUX and Apache

You can set both TUX and Apache to run simultaneously, as long as they're listening on different TCP/IP ports. The changes you need to make to the Apache httpd.conf file are simple; they involve two directives.

The Listen directive tells Apache about the computers and ports to check for input. Normally, it's set to listen to the standard HTTP port, with a Listen 80 command. If you're using TUX on the same computer, make it listen locally with this command:

```
Listen 127.0.0.1:8080
```

This corresponds to the way TUX looks for help with the `clientport` setting in the TUX kernel settings directory: `/proc/sys/net/tux`. The value in this file should already be set to port 8080.

Now, assuming you're using Apache Virtual Hosts, you'll want to specify the IP address associated with your web server through the `NameVirtualHost` directive:

```
NameVirtualHost 192.168.13.64:80
```

This corresponds to the standard TUX server port, which is located in the `/proc/net/tux/0/listen/0` file. This value in this file should already be set to:

```
http://0.0.0.0:80
```

which listens to requests from all IP addresses on TCP/IP port 80.

Once you've made these small changes, you're ready to set TUX and Apache working together; if you had stopped Apache per the earlier instructions, you should now be able to start it with the following command:

```
service httpd start
```

FIGURE 30.20

An interpreted TUX log file

```
[root@RH9Desk root]# tux2w3c /var/log/tux
127.0.0.1 - - [03/Apr/2003:16:08:08 -0500] "GET / HTTP/1.0" 200 2898 "-" ""
10.252.113.122 - - [03/Apr/2003:16:09:48 -0500] "GET / HTTP/1.1" 200 2898 "-" ""
10.252.113.122 - - [03/Apr/2003:16:09:48 -0500] "GET /icons/apache_pb.gif HTTP/1
.1" 404 0 "-" ""
10.252.113.122 - - [03/Apr/2003:16:09:48 -0500] "GET /icons/powered_by.gif HTTP/
1.1" 404 0 "-" ""
10.252.113.122 - - [03/Apr/2003:16:09:55 -0500] "GET / HTTP/1.1" 304 0 "-" ""
10.252.113.122 - - [03/Apr/2003:16:09:55 -0500] "GET /icons/apache_pb.gif HTTP/1
.1" 404 0 "-" ""
10.252.113.122 - - [03/Apr/2003:16:09:55 -0500] "GET /icons/powered_by.gif HTTP/
1.1" 404 0 "-" ""
10.252.113.122 - - [03/Apr/2003:16:09:55 -0500] "GET / HTTP/1.1" 304 0 "-" ""
10.252.113.122 - - [03/Apr/2003:16:09:56 -0500] "GET /icons/apache_pb.gif HTTP/1
.1" 404 0 "-" ""
10.252.113.122 - - [03/Apr/2003:16:09:56 -0500] "GET /icons/powered_by.gif HTTP/
1.1" 404 0 "-" ""
[root@RH9Desk root]# █
```

Summary

Linux is built for networking. In this age of the Internet, that means that Linux is built as an operating system that works with web servers. You can set up a number of different web servers on Linux, including Apache, TUX, AOLServer, BOA, Zeus, and more.

Apache is the most popular web server on the Internet. With Apache version 2.0.x, you can now set up multiple Virtual Hosts on the same web server, using a single IP address.

The main Apache configuration file, `httpd.conf`, is long but not that complex. We've analyzed it in three different sections: the global environment, which governs the operation of the server as a whole; parameters for the main server, which serve as defaults, and Virtual Hosts, where you can configure as many websites as your hardware can handle.

Red Hat recommends an alternative to Apache for static web pages, known as the Red Hat Content Accelerator. Formerly known as TUX, this web service is in many ways faster, because it resides directly in the Linux kernel. It's fairly easy to make these two web services work together. Red Hat recommends using TUX as the primary web server, referring to Apache for dynamic content.

This completes the main portion of this book. But the book doesn't end here—one appendix follows. It is a reference for many basic Linux commands.

Also, we've included five bonus chapters on the Sybex website. Web Chapter 1 takes a look at some of the major Linux certification programs. There are a broad range of Linux certifications available. CompTIA's Linux+ exam is targeted at near-entry-level Linux users with about six months of experience. The SAIR and LPI programs are targeted at junior- and mid-level systems administrators with two or more years of experience. Web Chapter 2 takes a look at the Red Hat "hands-on" certifications, which are among the most challenging and practical exams in the computer industry. Web Chapter 3 is a handy list of online resources and Web Chapter 4 contains a copy of the GNU/Linux General Public License. Lastly, Web Chapter 5 lists Red Hat Linux packages, by group, which can help you configure Kickstart installations. All of these can be found by navigating to www.sybex.com and doing a quick search for Mastering Red Hat Linux 9.

Appendix

Linux Command Reference

This appendix serves as a reference for many of the commands that you can type at the command-line interface.

Most Linux commands already have a manual; if you want to check them out, just refer to their man pages. It's easy to do; for a command such as `ls`, all you need to do is type the `man ls` command to open the standard Linux manual for that command.

However, man pages are written in a format that is less than comfortable to newer Linux users. A Linux guru might say that it's good for you to learn the "beauty" of the Linux man pages. That doesn't make man pages any easier to read. In this appendix, I've organized a few important commands functionally; for the most part, these groupings correspond to the different parts of this book.

There is no way I can provide a comprehensive list in a single appendix; one good book for this purpose is Bryan Pfaffenberger's *Linux Command Instant Reference*.

For example, for Part I, "Installing Red Hat Linux," there are only a few important commands. Functionally, they help you organize partitions, create boot disks, and set up network installations. The sections in this appendix are organized by different parts of this book. Subsections help you find commands based on what you want to do.

In addition, several commands are described in the bonus Web Chapters, 1 and 2, that are not detailed anywhere else. This appendix covers the command-line commands you need for the following topics:

◆ Installing Red Hat Linux

◆ Linux fundamentals

◆ Basic Linux administration

◆ X Window management

◆ Basic Linux networking

◆ Linux network services

◆ Linux file-sharing services

◆ Other commands

Installing Red Hat Linux

The command-line interface commands available to help you install Red Hat Linux are fairly straight-forward. Since Red Hat Linux is installed through a graphical interface, you don't need a lot of text commands. As you probably know, you can install Red Hat Linux without using any text commands. However, if you need a text command, it's probably critical to your installation.

Installation commands fall into four categories: preparing your hard disk, preparing a boot disk, setting up a network server, and setting up a Kickstart installation.

Preparing Your Hard Disk

You could rely on Disk Druid, as illustrated in Chapter 3, to configure partitions on your hard disk(s). However, Disk Druid can't split existing partitions like `fips` can. You don't have access to Disk Druid once Linux installation is complete. And it doesn't have the same degree of control over new partitions as `fdisk`. Also, while `parted` is dangerous (changes are immediate), it does resize partitions.

SPLITTING PARTITIONS

The Linux partition splitter is `fips`. This tool can only run from the MS-DOS command-line interface. As discussed in Chapter 2, if you have a Microsoft Windows operating system before XP, you can run it by restarting Microsoft Windows in MS-DOS mode. Otherwise, you need an MS-DOS boot disk, or something like the Microsoft Windows 98 startup disk.

When you run `fips`, follow these steps:

1. Copy `fips.exe` to a bootable floppy disk.

2. Restart your computer in MS-DOS mode; an MS-DOS or Microsoft Windows 98 boot disk is good for this purpose.

3. Run the `fips.exe` command from a DOS prompt. It is better if you run it from a different physical drive, such as a floppy, or the Red Hat Installation CD.

4. The `fips` command should read the partitions on your hard disk. Select the partition you want to split from the partition table that appears.

5. Specify a cylinder where you want the partition to be split.

6. Examine and confirm or change the new partition table.

CREATING NEW PARTITIONS

A split partition still needs to be assigned and formatted. You can do this with Disk Druid during Red Hat Linux installation or with `fdisk` at any time in Linux. If you have more than one hard disk, you'll need to specify the hard disk device. The syntax is:

```
# fdisk [-1] [-s partition] [device]
```

Here are several examples:

fdisk -l   Lists the partitions on all hard disks.

fdisk -s /dev/sda1   Returns the size of the first partition on the first SCSI hard drive.

fdisk /dev/hda   Starts the fdisk utility on the first IDE hard drive.

Once at the fdisk prompt, you can run the commands shown in Table A.1.

TABLE A.1: COMMANDS AT THE *FDISK* PROMPT

COMMAND	RESULT
a	Sets or unsets the bootable flag. You need to make at least one primary partition on one of your first two hard disks bootable.
b	Edits the label (if you have a Berkeley Standard Distribution partition).
c	Toggles the DOS compatibility flag. If you have a problem reading partitions, turn this off; it sometimes causes problems with the borders of a partition.
d	Deletes a partition. Before a partition is actually deleted, you need to select the partition number.
l	Lists known partition types. Over 100 different partition types are available.
m	Shows available fdisk commands.
n	Configures a new partition.
p	Lists the current partition table.
q	Exits fdisk without saving changes.
t	Allows you to change the partition system ID. You'll also need the partition number and the ID of the partition type you want, based on the known partition types (which you can find with the l command).
u	Toggles the display size of partitions between sectors and cylinders.
v	Verifies the current partition table.
w	Writes your changes and exits from fdisk. No changes are written to the partition table until you execute this command.

CREATING OR RESIZING PARTITIONS

There's a more flexible but in my opinion *dangerous* GNU tool known as **parted**. It works in a similar fashion to fdisk but can do more. The syntax is simple; the following command opens the second IDE hard disk for editing. If you don't specify a hard disk, **parted** opens the first available hard disk by default.

```
# parted /dev/hdb
```

It is worth restating that this is a dangerous command; once you run some of the options, you may erase all of the data on a partition or an entire hard disk. In addition, while you can format a hard disk partition with parted, you can only format to ext2; parted ext3 formatting is not available as of this writing.

Once at the (parted) prompt, you can run the commands shown in Table A.2.

TABLE A.2: COMMANDS AT THE *PARTED* PROMPT

COMMAND	RESULT
check *number*	Runs a basic filesystem check on the specified partition *number*. For a list of partition numbers, run the print command.
cp device *fr-number to-number*	Copies a filesystem on a specified device such as /dev/sda from a partition number (*fr-number*) to a different partition (*to-number*). Not yet an active option (as of this writing).
help	Prints a list of available commands.
mklabel *label*	Overwrites an entire hard disk with a label type such as bsd, loop, mac, or msdos. A dangerous command.
mkfs *number format*	Formats the specified partition; ext3 formats are not yet supported.
mkpart *type format start end*	Creates a new partition, of *type* primary, logical, or extended, of a specified *format*, with a *start* and *end* in MB. The *format* option does not work as of this writing.
mkpart *type format start end*	Creates a new partition, of *type* primary, logical, or extended, of a specified *format*, with a *start* and *end* in MB.
move *number start end*	Moves the specified partition to a new location on the drive, with a *start* and *end* in MB.
print	Displays the current partition table.
quit	Exits parted.
resize *number start end*	Resizes the specified partition with a *start* and *end* in MB.
rm *number*	Removes the specified partition.
select *device*	Points parted at a different device, such as /dev/sda.

Preparing a Boot Disk

Three basic commands are available that let you copy the contents of a Red Hat Linux image file onto a floppy disk. Two are usable in Linux; the other is designed for Microsoft operating systems.

CREATING A BOOT DISK IN A MICROSOFT OS

The `rawrite` command copies the contents of an image file, such as `boot.img`, to a floppy disk. The standard approach is to go into MS-DOS mode and run the `rawrite` command. Assuming `rawrite` is on the `dosutils` subdirectory of your D: drive, you're prompted with the following commands:

```
D:\> \dosutils\rawrite
Enter disk image source file name: d:\images\boot.img
Enter target diskette drive: a
Please insert a formatted diskette into drive A: and press -ENTER-:
```

Alternatively, on the first Red Hat Linux installation CD, there is a `\dosutils\rawritewin\` `rawwritewin.exe` command that provides a GUI for the same purpose. It opens the RawWrite window shown in Figure A.1.

FIGURE A.1

RawWrite for Windows

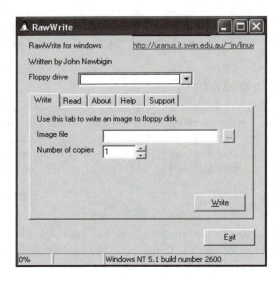

In Linux, it's common to use the `dd` command to convert an image file like `boot.img` to a floppy disk. For example, the following command copies the files from `boot.img` to the first floppy drive device on your system:

```
# dd if=/mnt/cdrom/images/bootdisk.img of=/dev/fd0
```

However, Linux understands the format of an image file. So you can just read it directly to the floppy drive device with a command like the following:

```
# cat /mnt/cdrom/images/bootdisk.img > /dev/fd0
```

Setting Up a Network Server

It's possible to set up an FTP, NFS, or HTTP network server with the Red Hat Linux installation files and packages. For details of this process, read Chapter 4. But in any of these cases, you'll want to copy the files from all Red Hat Linux installation CDs to a shared directory, such as /mnt/source. Once a Red Hat Linux installation CD is mounted, copy its files with the following command:

```
# cp -ar /mnt/cdrom/RedHat /mnt/source
```

Setting Up a Kickstart Installation

The details of setting up a Kickstart installation are covered in Chapter 5. To summarize, there's already a Kickstart file available; the settings that correspond to how you installed Red Hat Linux are stored in the /root directory in anaconda-ks.cfg. You can modify this file to meet your needs on another computer; remember to activate the partition commands, which are commented out by default.

The easiest way to set up a Kickstart installation is to copy the desired file as ks.cfg on a boot floppy. At the Red Hat Linux installation prompt, enter this command:

```
boot: linux ks=floppy
```

Linux Fundamentals

We cover several basic commands in Chapters 6, 7, and 8 that are fundamental to the way you navigate around Linux. Some commands allow you to manage files and directories, look through different files, or manipulate files. Other critical commands help you manage your partitions. Because the vi text editor may be all that you have available on a rescue floppy, understanding vi commands is also critical.

The format of this section is somewhat different, since the commands are well explained in their respective chapters.

Navigation

Basic navigational commands are briefly described in Table A.3. These commands are essential for anyone who wants to get around the Linux command-line interface. For more information on these commands, refer to Chapter 6.

TABLE A.3: NAVIGATIONAL COMMANDS

COMMAND	DESCRIPTION
cd *name*	Changes the directory; the directory name can be in absolute format, such as /etc/xinetd.d, or relative format, such as usr/source.
dir	Lists files in the current directory in a specialized manner; a special version of ls; some Linux distributions set alias dir=ls -l.
ls	Lists the files in the current directory; many switches are available.
pwd	Lists the present working directory, so you know where you are.

Managing Files and Directories

Basic commands for managing files and directories are briefly described in Table A.4. Managing files and directories is another essential skill at the command-line interface. For more information on these commands, refer to Chapter 6.

TABLE A.4: FILE MANAGEMENT COMMANDS

COMMAND	DESCRIPTION
cp *file1 file2*	Copies a file; with appropriate switches, this command can be used to copy the contents of a directory and its subdirectories.
file *filename*	Determines the file type of the file; options include text, image data, gzip compressed file, cpio archive, mail text, and more.
ln *file1 file2*	Links two different files. A hard link creates a full copy of the same file; a soft link creates a pointer.
mkdir *name*	Creates a new directory. The name can be in an absolute or relative path format; using the proper switches, you can even create multiple levels of subdirectories with one command.
mv *file1 file2*	Deletes and copies a file.
rm *filename*	Deletes a file; using the right switches, you can delete entire directories and subdirectories. This can be a very dangerous command, especially for the root user.
rmdir *dirname*	Deletes a directory; using the right switches, you can delete entire directories and subdirectories. By default, the directory must be empty.
touch *filename*	Creates an empty file with *filename*.
umask *abcd*	Sets default permissions for newly created files by that user.

Reading through Different Files

Table A.5 describes basic commands for searching through files. You need to be able to look through various files to manage your Linux operating system. For more information on these commands, see Chapter 6.

TABLE A.5: FILE-READING COMMANDS

COMMAND	DESCRIPTION
cat *filename*	Reads the contents of a file; also scrolls one or more text files to a screen. This command can also be used to redirect (>) the contents of an image file, such as the Red Hat installation bootdisk.img, to a floppy device.
head *filename*	Sends the first few lines of a file to the screen; the default is 10 lines.

Continued on next page

TABLE A.5: FILE-READING COMMANDS *(continued)*

COMMAND	DESCRIPTION
less *filename*	Opens a file in a text-style reader; allows up and down scrolling one screen at a time. vi search commands are allowed.
more *filename*	Opens a file in a text-style reader; allows scrolling one screen at a time. vi search commands are allowed.

Manipulating Files

Basic commands for manipulating files are briefly described in Table A.6. You need to be able to examine the contents in order to manipulate files on your Linux operating system. For more information on these commands, refer to Chapter 6.

TABLE A.6: FILE-MANIPULATION COMMANDS

COMMAND	DESCRIPTION
find / -name *file* -print	Finds the location of the file, starting the search in the root (/) directory. You can use wildcards, and start in other directories.
grep *string file*	Searches for a text string in the specified file. You can use wildcards to extend the search to a series of files.
locate *file*	Searches through the slocate database for the location of a specified file. Wildcards are assumed; for example, the locate abc command will also find the location of a file named abcd. The slocate database is refreshed as a default cron job every night.
wc *file*	Displays the number of lines, words, and characters in a text file.

Managing Partitions

Commands are available to help you manage partitions. Several of these commands are also related to the way you configure partitions (fdisk, fips, parted), and are covered earlier in this appendix. The commands shown in Table A.7 are addressed in more detail in Chapter 7.

TABLE A.7: PARTITION-MANAGEMENT COMMANDS

COMMAND	DESCRIPTION
df	Reports partitions on the current hard disk.
du	Notes file-space usage of each file; includes files in subdirectories.
dumpe2fs *device*	Lists all information related to the device (e.g., /dev/sdb2).

Continued on next page

TABLE A.7: PARTITION-MANAGEMENT COMMANDS *(continued)*

COMMAND	DESCRIPTION
e2label *device label*	If you just specify the *device* (e.g. /dev/hda1), this command returns the current label. Otherwise, it assigns a new label; this should correspond to an entry in /etc/fstab.
fsck *device*	Checks and repairs a Linux filesystem; you should specify the device associated with an *unmounted* partition. This command normally detects the filesystem and uses the correct format; otherwise, you can use a command such as fsck.minix *device*, fsck.ext2 *device*, or e2fsck *device*. The last two commands work for both the ext2 and ext3 formats.
mount *filesystem device*	Mounts a filesystem such as /home on a device such as /dev/hda2.
tune2fs *device*	Converts a partition from ext2 to ext3.
umount *filesystem*	Unmounts the specified filesystem, such as /home.

The *vi* Editor

As discussed in Chapter 6, three modes are available in vi: *command* mode, *insert* mode, and *execute* mode. For more information about the available commands, see the *Linux Instant Command Reference*.

COMMAND MODE

In vi command mode, you can manipulate existing text in a file. Table A.8 shows some of the available commands. These commands affect the text file based on the current location of the cursor.

TABLE A.8: *VI* COMMAND MODE COMMANDS

COMMAND	FUNCTION
cc	Deletes the current line and moves to insert mode so you can type in a replacement.
cw	Deletes the current word and moves to insert mode so you can type in a replacement.
dd	Deletes the current line.
dw	Deletes the current word.
D	Deletes the remainder of the line, starting with the current position of the cursor.
p	Copies the *register*, the current contents of the buffer, to the line after the cursor.
:reg	Shows the contents of the register.
u	Undoes the last change.
U	Restores the current line.
nY	Copies *n* lines into the register. See the p command.

INSERT MODE

There are several ways to start insert mode in vi. Once in this mode, you can enter the desired text. Some vi command mode commands, such as cw, also automatically start insert mode. See Table A.9 for some of the available commands. These commands are based on the current location of the cursor.

TABLE A.9: *VI* INSERT MODE COMMANDS

COMMAND	FUNCTION
a	Inserts new text after the current location of the cursor.
A	Inserts new text at the end of the current line.
Esc	Returns to command mode.
i	Inserts new text at the current cursor location.
I	Inserts new text at the beginning of the line.
o	Starts a new line after the current line.
O	Starts a new line before the current line.

EXECUTE MODE

You can run standard shell commands from inside the vi editor; just start the command with an :!, followed by the shell command. A couple of special execute mode commands allow you to write and exit the file (see Table A.10). You can combine these commands; for example, :wq writes the file and exits the vi editor.

TABLE A.10: EXECUTE COMMANDS

COMMAND	FUNCTION
:!*command*	Runs the specified shell *command*. Starts in the directory where you started the vi text editor.
q	Exits the file. If you've made changes, you can leave vi without writing those changes with the q! command.
w	Writes the current file.

Basic Linux Administration

In Chapters 9 through 14, we covered a number of administrative commands. These commands help you manage your Linux system. Some enable you to manage users and groups. Others allow you to work with packages like those you might find in an RPM or a tarball. Some of these packages have to be compiled before they can be installed.

Other important administrative commands help you run through the boot process or set up jobs, such as backups, that can be run in the middle of the night.

User and Group Commands

Commands that help you administer users and groups are briefly described in Table A.11. Some allow you to create users and groups; others let you configure them for the Shadow Password Suite. For more information on these commands, refer to Chapter 9.

TABLE A.11: USER AND GROUP ADMINISTRATIVE COMMANDS

COMMAND	FUNCTION
chage *option user*	Depending on the option, sets the life of a user's password or account.
grpconv	Converts passwords in /etc/group and stores them in /etc/gshadow.
grpunconv	Reverses the grpconv process, restoring passwords to /etc/group.
newusers *file*	Adds new users from a list in *file*.
pwconv	Converts passwords in /etc/passwd and stores them in /etc/shadow.
pwunconv	Reverses the pwconv process, restoring passwords to /etc/group.
useradd *name*	Adds a new user with *name*.
userdel *name*	Deletes a user with *name*; use the -r option if you also want to delete that user's home directory.

Modifying User and Group Access

Users and group access can be limited by quotas. A quota limits the number or size of available files. You can organize group access in a specific directory by using the User Private Group scheme. We've listed the relevant commands in Table A.12. For more information on these commands, refer to Chapter 9.

TABLE A.12: USER AND GROUP ACCESS COMMANDS

COMMAND	FUNCTION
edquota *user*	Opens a quota configuration file for the *user*.
grpquota *group*	Opens a quota configuration file for the *group*.
quotacheck	Creates base quota configuration files; usually run with the -avum options.
quotaon *filesystem*	Activates quotas for a specific filesystem, such as /home.

Package Management

Red Hat Linux lets you install packages from RPMs or tarballs. You can install RPM packages with the appropriate `rpm` command; we covered this command in detail in Chapter 10. Tarballs are a little more problematic; they must first be uncompressed and unpackaged. A good example of this process is shown in Chapter 12, using the Linux kernel.

Generally, once you've installed an RPM package, it's ready for use. You might have to activate it with a command such as `chkconfig`, but all the components are there in the correct locations.

However, uncompressing and unpacking a tarball is not enough. For example, if you were to download a `newprogram.tar.gz` package from the Internet, you could uncompress and unpack it with a command like the following:

```
# tar xzvf newprogram.tar.gz
```

This command sets up a series of files in some directory, probably something like *newprogram*. There is generally a README file in this directory containing installation instructions. Sometimes there's a script, such as `install.pl`, that's ready for use. Alternatively, you might have to edit settings and then compile the program.

To compile a program, first navigate to the program directory. Sometimes it's enough to edit the appropriate configuration file, navigate to the right directory, and then run the `make` command. However, the situation could be more complex, and you might have to use commands like `make mrproper`, `make modules`, and `make modules_install` for the kernel, as described in Chapter 12.

Boot Process Commands

Commands that manage the boot process are briefly described in Table A.13. These commands are hard to classify. Some check boot messages; others use parts of the boot process. For more information on these commands, refer to Chapter 11.

TABLE A.13: BOOT PROCESS COMMANDS

COMMAND	DESCRIPTION
dmesg	Lists the boot messages, normally stored in the kernel ring buffer; alternatively, you can check the end of /var/log/messages for the same information.
grub-install	Installs GRUB as the bootloader; designed to convert your system from another bootloader, such as LILO.
init *runlevel*	Specifies a new runlevel; helps you test a new configuration or enter single-user mode for troubleshooting.
initdefault	Specifies the default runlevel in /etc/inittab.
kudzu	Starts the Red Hat Linux hardware configuration utility, which normally runs automatically when you install or remove hardware.
mkbootdisk *version*	Creates a customized boot disk based on the specified kernel version from the /boot directory.

Administrative Commands

Table A.14 explains some important administrative commands that help you manage your system conveniently. For example, the `cron` and `at` daemons allow you to schedule operations when they won't interfere with user activity, such as during the middle of the night. For more information on these commands, refer to Chapter 13.

TABLE A.14: ADMINISTRATIVE COMMANDS

COMMAND	DESCRIPTION
`at file time`	A onetime command for executing a job or program; closely related to `atq`, `atrm`, and `batch`.
`atq`	A query to the current list of `at` jobs.
`atrm job`	A command that removes a job from the queue.
`batch file`	A specialized `at` job that normally runs when the demand on the CPU is below 80% of capacity.
`crontab`	A command that opens a file where you can configure jobs to be run at regular intervals.
`kill PID`	A command that stops the process with the given PID.
`logrotate`	A `cron` job that rotates log files on a regular basis; by default, it's in the `/etc/cron.daily` directory.
`nice -n number command`	A command that starts another command with a lower priority.
`ps`	A command that lists running processes. The x option lists processes for all users; many other options are available.
`renice PID`	A command that raises the priority of a process with the given PID.
`tmpwatch`	A `cron` job that erases `/tmp` and `/var/tmp` files on a regular basis; by default, it's in the `/etc/cron.daily` directory.
`top`	A utility that dynamically displays processes that require the most CPU resources.
`who`	A command that lists logged-on users.

Backup Commands

Other important commands (shown in Table A.15) are related to backing up the data on your system. Some allow you to back up and restore data directly, or you can set up a RAID array that provides data redundancy. For more information on these commands, see Chapter 14.

TABLE A.15: BACKUP COMMANDS

COMMAND	DESCRIPTION
cdrecord *options file*	Copies a file, often an .iso file, to a recordable CD on an appropriate drive.
dump *type device directory*	Backs up a directory to a *device* using a certain *type* of backup.
dvdrecord *options file*	Copies a file, often an .iso file, to a recordable DVD on an appropriate drive.
cpio	Takes input from a list (such as from a find command) and copies it to standard output, which can be directed to a file such as backedup.cpio.
mkisofs *options new.iso directory*	Creates a *new.iso* file from the files in a *directory* based on *options*.
mkraid	Creates a RAID device based on criteria defined in /etc/raidtab.
restore	Restores from a backup created with dump.
tar	Archives from a group of files into one tape archive file.

X Window Management

Because this appendix is a Linux text command reference, this section addresses only tools that you can call from a command-line interface. However, many of the tools in this section require a GUI such as GNOME or KDE. Several important tools are available to help you configure the GUI, as well as the GNOME and KDE desktop environments. Red Hat is also creating a series of GUI tools that enable you to administer just about every part of Linux.

X Window Configuration

There are two basic tools for configuring the Linux GUI: xf86config and redhat-config-xfree86. You can run either tool from the regular command-line interface. Both tools are designed to help you edit the main X Window configuration file, /etc/X11/XF86Config. Alternatively, you can always edit this file directly in a text editor such as vi. You'll find more information on each of these options in Chapter 15.

XF86CONFIG

While xf86config is not included in Red Hat Linux 9, it is a standard tool that you can use if you download another version of the XFree86 server from www.xfree86.org. When you run xf86config, you can configure serveral different components, as described in Table A.16. Note that you don't have to have every possible bit of information.

TABLE A.16: INFORMATION FOR *XF86CONFIG*

DATA	OPTIONS	REQUIREMENT/DEFAULT
Mouse	Nine different protocol types available	Microsoft protocol
Third Button	Chord Middle (for a Logitech mouse with three buttons or a mouse with a clickable scroll wheel)	No
Simulate Middle Button	Eumlate3Buttons (when you click both the right and left buttons simultaneously, this simulates a middle button command in the GUI)	No
Mouse Device	Device name	/dev/mouse
Keyboard	25 options	Generic 101-key PC (choice 1)
National Layout	By country	Must make a selection; U.S. English is most standard
Variant Name	Create your own label	Default label = us
XKB Options	If you want special keys, type **y**	No
Monitor Horizontal Sync	You can select or type in a special rate	31.5MHz
Monitor Vertical Refresh	You can select or type in a special rate	50–70KHz
Identifier	Monitor label	"My Monitor"
Video Card Database	Type **y** for preconfigured cards	No
Video Card Memory	Memory in KB	256KB
Identifier	Video card label	"My Video Card"
Color Depth	1–24 bits	Configured for 8, 16, and 24 bits

REDHAT-CONFIG-XFREE86

One of the advantages of `redhat-config-xfree86` is that you can start it from the command-line interface. It's functionally similar to the older `XF86Setup` tool; it probes your system and opens menus in a minimal GUI configuration. And you don't have to make so many choices with `redhat-config-xfree86`; unlike with `xf86config`, you don't need to make decisions on input devices (a mouse and a keyboard). Based on what you know about your video card and monitor, you can configure a number of items, as described in Table A.17.

TABLE A.17: INFORMATION FOR *REDHAT-CONFIG-XFREE86*

DATA	OPTIONS
Resolution	640×480 through 1920×1440.
Color Depth	8 bit (256 Colors), 15 bit or 16 bit (Thousands of Colors), and 24 bit (Millions of Colors).
Monitor Type	Configurable by make/model; generic versions available. Can also set Horizontal Sync and Vertical Refresh Rate; in some cases, probing is allowed.
DPI	Click the Set DPI button and you can enter the height and width of your monitor.
Video Card	Configurable by make/model. You can set memory; some cards can be probed. You can select a different driver. If your card was detected, special options may be added; you can add other options for XF86Config.
	In some cases, it's also possible to enable 3D acceleration; however, Linux support for 3D often lags the hardware release from the video card manufacturer.

GUI Administration Tools

Linux provides several other GUI-based administrative tools. Many are in the `redhat-config-*` series; they're available only if you've installed the corresponding RPM packages. Most of the tools listed in Table A.18 are discussed in more detail in Chapters 15 and 19. Most won't work unless you're already in a GUI such as GNOME or KDE. However, you can start them from a terminal window in a GUI using the tool name shown in the table.

TABLE A.18: GRAPHICAL ADMINISTRATION TOOLS

TOOL	DESCRIPTION
`ethereal`	A network traffic analyzer; see Chapter 22.
`gfloppy`	A tool for formatting 3.5- or 5.25-inch floppy disks.
`hwbrowser`	A tool that reads detected hardware on your computer.
`nautilus`	A GNOME file manager.
`redhat-config-bind`	A DNS Server configuration tool; closely related to `redhat-config-bind-gui`.
`redhat-config-date`	A date/time zone configurator; can synchronize with an available NTP server (both commands start the same tool).
`redhat-config-time`	
`redhat-config-httpd`	A tool for configuring the Apache Web server via `/etc/httpd/conf/httpd.conf`.
`redhat-config-keyboard`	A basic keyboard configurator.

Continued on next page

TABLE A.18: GRAPHICAL ADMINISTRATION TOOLS *(continued)*

TOOL	DESCRIPTION
`redhat-config-kickstart`	A tool for configuring a Kickstart file; see Chapter 5.
`redhat-config-language`	A tool that allows you to select the default from the languages you've installed.
`redhat-config-mouse`	A tool for configuring Linux for your mouse or pointing device; if you have a serial mouse, you can set the port. It's the GUI version of `mouseconfig`.
`redhat-config-network`	A tool that allows you to configure existing network devices, `/etc/hosts`, `/etc/resolv.conf`; different profiles allow for different configurations, such as docking ports. The text version is `redhat-config-network-tui`.
`redhat-config-network-druid`	A tool for configuring new network adapters, including telephone modems; a.k.a. the Internet Configuration Wizard.
`redhat-config-nfs`	An NFS server configuration tool.
`redhat-config-packages`	A basic RPM package management tool; you can install or remove packages by groups, or individual RPMs. Successor to gnorpm.
`redhat-config-printer`	A printer configuration tool, equivalent to `printconf`; see Chapter 25 for more information; closely related to `redhat-config-printer-gui`; the text mode version is `redhat-config-printer-tui`.
`redhat-config-proc`	A kernel tuner; changes are written to `/etc/sysctl.conf`, and used in `/proc` files.
`redhat-config-rootpassword`	A tool that allows changes to the root password.
`redhat-config-samba`	A tool to configure shared directories on a Samba server.
`redhat-config-securitylevel`	An `iptables` firewall configurator; it's the GUI version of `lokkit`.
`redhat-config-services`	A graphical front end for `chkconfig`; controls active services in different runlevels.
`redhat-config-soundcard`	A tool that probes for and lists detectable sound cards; if you need to customize settings, use `sndconfig` or edit `/etc/modules.conf` directly.
`redhat-config-users`	A user and group management tool; frond end for editing the main user and group files in `/etc`: `passwd`, `group`, `shadow`, `gshadow`.
`redhat-config-xfree86`	Previously discussed; successor to `Xconfigurator`.
`redhat-logviewer`	A tool that opens log files from `/var/log`.
`switchdesk`	A tool that allows you to switch between available GUIs; normally GNOME, KDE, and twm.

Basic Linux Networking

The next category of commands we'll examine is designed to help you configure and control networking on your Linux computer. Some commands provide fundamental information to your network card(s). Others set up where your network looks for domains, network settings, and similar information.

Commands for troubleshooting your network and for protecting your system with an `iptables` firewall also fall into this category. For more information on the commands in this section, see Chapters 21 and 22.

Network Card Commands

The two key commands for setting up a network card are `ifconfig` and `arp`. Related commands let you activate and deactivate the network card of your choice. These commands are listed in Table A.19.

TABLE A.19: NETWORK CARD COMMANDS

COMMAND	DESCRIPTION
arp	Controls a database of hardware and IP addresses.
ifconfig	Returns active network adapters. You can specify TCP/IP information such as IP address, network mask, hardware address, etc.; you can also specify special IRQ or I/O ports for a card.
ifdown *device*	A command that deactivates a network device.
ifdown-*	A command that starts a script in /etc/sysconfig/network-scripts for deactivating a specific device.
ifup *device*	Activates a network device.
ifup-*	Starts a script in /etc/sysconfig/network-scripts for activating a specific device.

Network Domain Management

Commands are available that help you identify your Linux computer on different kinds of networks. When you run a command such as `hostname` by itself, the shell returns the current domain name. Alternatively, you can assign a new name with the command, such as `hostname` *newname*. Table A.20 describes the network domain management commands.

TABLE A.20: NETWORK DOMAIN COMMANDS

COMMAND	DESCRIPTION
domainname	Lists or assigns an NIS domain name to the current computer; permanent changes should be in /etc/sysconfig/network in NISDOMAIN=*domainname* format.
hostname	Lists or assigns a hostname to the current computer; permanent changes should be in /etc/sysconfig/network in HOSTNAME=*hostname* format.

Continued on next page

TABLE A.20: NETWORK DOMAIN COMMANDS *(continued)*

COMMAND	DESCRIPTION
nisdomainname	See domainname.
ypdomainname	See domainname.

Network Troubleshooting Commands

Linux provides three basic network troubleshooting commands: netstat, ping, and traceroute. See Chapter 22 for examples of these commands in action.

The netstat command shows information about your current network connections. Some netstat options are shown in Table A.21.

TABLE A.21: *NETSTAT* COMMANDS

COMMAND	RESULT
netstat	Lists all open TCP/IP network connections on different ports.
netstat -a	Lists activity on all available network ports.
netstat -c	Like netstat -a, but the command is rerun every second, and the results are continuously sent to the screen.
netstat -e	Provides extra information on each connection.
netstat -l	Limits the list to services such as Telnet and Apache (httpd) that are listening for requests.
netstat -n	Specifies that IP addresses are OK; a good alternative if there's a problem finding the hostname, such as a problem with a reverse DNS zone.
netstat -p	Includes the name and PID of the process for each open port.

The ping command sends a packet of data to test connectivity to a specified host computer. Chapter 21 describes the standard ping troubleshooting commands. Other options for this command are shown in Table A.22.

TABLE A.22: *PING* COMMANDS

COMMAND	RESULT
ping *hostname*	Tests connectivity between your computer and *hostname*.
ping -c *n hostname*	Limits the connectivity test to *n* packets; you don't need to press Ctrl+C to stop the process.
ping -i *n hostname*	Waits *n* seconds between pings; the default is one second.

Continued on next page

TABLE A.22: *PING* COMMANDS *(continued)*

COMMAND	RESULT
ping -n *hostname*	Uses IP addresses in the output; useful if you're having trouble finding a DNS server.
ping -s *data*	Sends a packet of *data* bytes in a ping; the source of some "ping of death" commands.

NOTE   *This book does not endorse the use of "ping of death" commands, unless you're using them to test your own system's resistance to attack. Chapter 22 describes an* iptables *command that can stop the "ping of death."*

The traceroute command helps you isolate problems on a large network. As it travels from router to router, it listens for ICMP "time exceeded" messages, and returns them to your computer. In that way, it lets you track the path of a message. If you're tracking a message on the Internet, the default 30 hops may not be sufficient; the following command allows you to trace that message for 40 hops:

```
# traceroute -m 40 www.example.com
```

Alternatively, if the Internet is responding slowly, you can give it additional time to send the ICMP messages back to your computer; for example, the following waits up to 10 seconds:

```
# traceroute -w 10 www.example.com
```

Firewalls with *iptables*

The iptables command is complex; Chapter 22 provides a basic explanation. For your reference, iptables commands are built to a very specific format:

```
# iptables -t table option pattern -j target
```

Table A.23 describes each of these items.

TABLE A.23: *IPTABLES* COMMAND FORMAT

ITEM	DESCRIPTION
-t *table*	This item specifies the type of table. The options are filter and nat; filter is the default.
option	You can add a rule to (-A), delete from (-D), or insert into an iptables chain; the three standard chains are INPUT, OUTPUT, and FORWARD. You can create your own chain; for example, Red Hat's lokkit creates the RH-Lokkit-0-50-INPUT chain.
pattern	You can set iptables to look for a pattern in each packet; the pattern can match IP address, TCP/IP port number, or type of protocol.
-j *target*	If there is a pattern match, this tells iptables what to do; target options are to ACCEPT, DROP, REJECT, or LOG.

Linux Network Services

You can activate many basic networks services on a Linux computer. Several are controlled by the xinetd daemon. Many administrators set up their own DNS servers so they don't have to maintain /etc/hosts on every computer on their networks. Others set up their own DHCP servers; this frees them from having to maintain IP address information on every computer on their networks. Commands are also available to help you set up and configure printers, as well as configure the sendmail server.

This section addresses just the commands that you might run at the command-line interface; no GUI tools are discussed. For more information on the services in this section, refer to Chapters 23–26.

Commands for *xinetd* Services

As we mentioned, many services, including the Remote Shell and Telnet, are controlled through the Extended Internet Services Daemon, xinetd. This daemon listens for requests and starts network services on demand.

You can start the Remote Shell from a client using a number of different commands, which appear in Table A.24.

TABLE A.24: REMOTE SHELL COMMANDS

COMMAND	DESCRIPTION
rlogin *hostname*	Logs into a remote computer with a Remote Shell server; uses the current username.
rlogin -l *username hostname*	Logs into the remote *hostname* computer with a different *username*.
rsh *hostname*	Logs into a remote computer with a Remote Shell server; uses the current username.
rsh -l *username hostname*	Logs into the remote *hostname* computer with a different *username*.
rexec *hostname command*	Logs into the remote computer *hostname* and executes the *command*.

Variations on the telnet command are quite rich, but many cover very special situations. Since telnet provides a straightforward remote login interface, not many variations are required. A few useful options are shown in Table A.25.

TABLE A.25: *TELNET* COMMANDS

COMMAND	DESCRIPTION
telnet *hostname*	Opens a console login interface on *hostname*.
telnet -a *hostname*	Sends the current USER as the username for the telnet login process.
telnet -f *hostname*	Supports the use of Kerberos on the Telnet server.
telnet -l *username hostname*	Attempts to log into the *hostname* computer as *username*.

DNS and DHCP

There aren't a lot of commands related to the DNS or DHCP servers or clients. Chapter 24 explains the configuration of these systems; the commands in their main configuration files, /etc/named.conf and /etc/dhcpd.conf, are addressed in detail in that chapter. Table A.26 describes a few basic commands.

TABLE A.26: DNS AND DHCP COMMANDS

COMMAND	DESCRIPTION
named	DNS server daemon.
dhcpd	DHCP server daemon.
dhclient	DHCP client daemon; can also be used as a command to refresh IP address data. In previous Red Hat distributions, this command was called dhcpcd or pump.

Printer Commands

Associated with the CUPS and LPD print systems are several basic commands, some of which apply to both systems. For example, with the cups-1pd service, which is part of xinetd, LPD commands are automatically translated for a CUPS system. Basic print commands are described in Table A.27.

TABLE A.27: BASIC PRINT COMMANDS

COMMAND	DESCRIPTION
lpr *file*	Prints the *file*; this is the basic LPD print command.
lpc	Manages LPD print queues and active printers.
lpq	Examines the print spool; you can specify the printer with the -P switch.
lprm *job*	Removes a print job with *job* number.
cupsaddsmb	Allows you to share a CUPS printer via Samba.
cupsconfig	Opens the CUPS configuration utility in the Lynx text browser.
cups-1pd	Starts the CUPS LPD xinetd service that allows CUPS to read LPD commands.
filter	Adds a new CUPS filter.
lp *file*	Prints the *file* using CUPS.
lppasswd	Controls access to the CUPS configuration.
lpoptions	Sets CUPS printer options/defaults.
lpstatus	Prints CUPS status (queue) information.

Mail Management Commands

Linux offers commands that help you manage the sendmail mail server. The most important of these commands, the m4 macro processor, just processes the sendmail configuration file. Other commands allow you to manage aliases, databases, and more. These commands are described in Table A.28. For more information on sendmail, read Chapter 26.

TABLE A.28: SENDMAIL COMMANDS

COMMAND	DESCRIPTION
m4	Processes the sendmail macro file, normally `/etc/mail/sendmail.mc`, into a format suitable for the sendmail configuration file, normally `/etc/mail/sendmail.cf`.
mailq	Sends a summary of queued mail message headers to the printer; `sendmail -bp` performs the same task.
makemap	Creates sendmail database maps from `/etc/mail` configuration files.
mailstats	Returns mail statistics—numbers of messages, total sizes, and more.
newaliases	When you change `/etc/aliases`, this command updates the sendmail database.
praliases	Shows current aliases from the database.
rmail	Reads UUCP-based mail.
smrsh	Enters the sendmail shell.

Linux File-Sharing Services

You can share files from a Linux computer in many ways. Generally, you configure a server and then share files through a directory. The four major types of Linux sharing servers are FTP, NFS, Samba, and Apache. If you've enabled NIS, it also shares configuration files. While there are graphical configuration tools available for each of these services, they all can be set up from the command-line interface as well, and they each include regular text commands for the client and server. For detailed information on these services, see Chapters 27–30.

FTP Servers

The basic FTP commands are covered in detail in Chapter 27. This section summarizes associated commands and configuration files.. While the Red Hat Linux 9 Installation CD now includes only vsFTP, WU-FTP is a popular option also available in RPM format. The vsFTP server comes highly recommended; Red Hat uses it on its own FTP servers.

vsFTP COMMANDS AND CONFIGURATION FILES

The vsFTP package includes its own set of configuration files. It is simpler than alternative servers such as WU-FTP; the only command you need is the **vsftpd** daemon. The vsFTP server is now a regular service in the `/etc/rc.d/init.d` directory; it is no longer an `xinetd` service. If both servers are installed, be sure to activate only one at a time. The vsFTP configuration files are shown in Table A.29.

TABLE A.29: vsFTP CONFIGURATION FILES

FILE	DESCRIPTION
`/etc/vsftpd.conf`	The primary configuration file.
`/etc/vsftpd.ftpusers`	A list of users not allowed to log in; should include service-level users such as news, bin, and mail, as well as root.
`/etc/vsftpd.user_list`	A list of allowed or denied users, depending on the `userlist_deny` variable in `/etc/vsftpd.conf`.

WU-FTP COMMANDS AND CONFIGURATION FILES

One major alternative to vsFTP is WU-FTP, which you can download through the home page of their development group at `www.wu-ftpd.org` or the resource center at `www.landfield.com/wu-ftpd/`. The commands shown in Table A.30 are available to help you manage a WU-FTP server. Remember, WU-FTP is an `xinetd` service that you also need to activate through the `wu-ftpd` file in the `/etc/xinted.d` directory. Alternatively, you can use `chkconfig` to activate this service.

TABLE A.30: WU-FTP COMMANDS

COMMAND	DESCRIPTION
`ckconfig`	Checks the integrity of the configuration files.
`ftpcount`	Lists the number of connections.
`ftpwho`	Lists connected users and origin IP addresses.
`ftprestart`	Stops and restarts an FTP server.
`ftpshut`	Allows you to shut down an FTP server now or at a specified time.
`in.ftpd`	Starts the FTP server daemon.
`in.wuftpd`	Starts the WU-FTP server.
`privatepw`	Adds and deletes FTP groups from `/etc/ftpgroups`; these groups need to correspond to a real group in `/etc/group`.

The WU-FTP server also has a group of configuration files, as shown in Table A.31. You might recall from Chapter 27 that the functionality of some of these files is now part of `/etc/ftpaccess`.

TABLE A.31: WU-FTP CONFIGURATION FILES

FILE	FUNCTIONALITY
/etc/ftpaccess	Opens the basic WU-FTP configuration file.
/etc/ftpconversions	Lists commands that are run automatically during FTP uploads or downloads.
/etc/ftpgroups	Defines special groups with a specific password, defined through the privatepw command.
/etc/ftphosts	Allows or denies access to a specific user account.
/etc/ftpusers	Allows or denies access to specific users.

FTP Client

There are a number of FTP clients available; all that I've seen are front-ends to the FTP text client. The list of available FTP client commands is quite varied. The more important commands were addressed in Chapter 27. A fuller list follows in Table A.32. This is just a basic list, without options. You can get more information from the ftp> prompt by entering help *command*.

TABLE A.32: FTP CLIENT COMMANDS

COMMAND	DESCRIPTION
!	Escapes to the shell; the !ls -l command gives you a full list of files in the current local directory.
$	Executes a macro.
append	Appends a file to another file; e.g., the append *local remote* command adds the contents of the *local* file to the *remote* file.
ascii	Sets file transfer to ASCII mode.
bell	Toggles a beep when a command, such as a file transfer, is complete.
binary	Sets file transfer to binary mode.
bye	Exits the current FTP session.
cd	Changes the directory.
cdup	Moves up one directory level.
close	Closes the connection without exiting FTP.
delete	Deletes the specified file on a remote directory.
dir	Equivalent to ls -l.
exit	Closes connection and exits FTP.

Continued on next page

TABLE A.32: FTP CLIENT COMMANDS *(continued)*

COMMAND	DESCRIPTION
get	Copies a file from the FTP server.
hash	Toggles the use of hash marks, so you can monitor the progress of a file transfer.
lcd	Changes the working directory on the local computer.
ls	Equivalent to ls -l in the bash shell.
mdelete	Deletes multiple files.
mdir	Takes the contents of a remote directory and outputs them to a local file.
mget	Copies multiple files from the FTP server.
mkdir	Creates a new directory on the FTP server.
mput	Sends multiple files to the FTP server.
newer	Uses the get command if the remote file is newer.
open	From the FTP prompt, connects to a remote FTP server.
put	Copies a file to the FTP server.
pwd	Lists the working directory on the FTP server.
quit	Exits the FTP shell.
rename	Renames a file on the FTP server.
rmdir	Removes a remote directory.
status	Checks the status of the connection.
system	Shows the basic system type, usually Unix.
user	Logs in as a user.

NFS Commands

The Network File System (NFS) is used to share directories between Linux and Unix computers. The basic configuration process is described in detail in Chapter 28; Table A.33 summarizes some important commands.

TABLE A.33: NFS COMMANDS

COMMAND	DESCRIPTION
exportfs	Exports and maintains the list of available NFS directories, based on /etc/exports.
nfsstat	Returns information on shared NFS directories; the output from this command is a good place to look for connection problems.

Continued on next page

TABLE A.33: NFS COMMANDS *(continued)*

COMMAND	DESCRIPTION
nhfsstone	Tests the load on an NFS server.
rpc.mountd	Starts the NFS mount daemon, the service that actually checks mount requests against what's allowed in /etc/exports.
nhfsrun	Tests program; runs nhfsstone with a range of demands on the server.
showmount	Shows available directories from an NFS server.

NIS Commands

The Network Information System (NIS) allows you to set up a single database of key configuration files such as /etc/passwd in a LAN of Linux and Unix computers. The basic configuration process is described in detail in Chapter 28; the important commands are summarized in Table A.34. Many key NIS commands are in an unusual directory, /usr/lib/yp. If you use NIS, you might consider adding that directory to your PATH with the PATH=$PATH:/usr/lib/yp command.

TABLE A.34: NIS COMMANDS

COMMAND	DESCRIPTION
create_printcap	Processes an LPD file such as /etc/printcap to an NIS database map; does not process a CUPS printer configuration file.
makedbm	Creates an NIS database file.
match_printcap	Works with the printcap_path in /etc/lpd.conf; does not process a CUPS printer configuration file.
mknetid	Generates an NIS database map from key configuration files: /etc/passwd, /etc/group, and /etc/hosts.
pwupdate	Updates the NIS database map for regular and shadow passwords.
revnetgroup	Generates reverse NIS netgroup data.
ypcat	Reads files from an NIS server database.
ypchfn	Changes a user's finger information in the NIS database.
ypchsh	Changes a user's default shell in the NIS database.
ypinit	Builds a database for a master or slave NIS server.
ypmatch	Searches for a user in the NIS database.
yppasswd	Changes a password in the NIS database.
yppush	Replicates an NIS master database to an NIS slave server.
ypxfr	Copies an NIS database; common for NIS slave servers.

Samba Commands

Samba lets you configure Linux to connect and share directories with Microsoft Windows computers. Linux and Unix computers can also use Samba to share directories with each other.

As discussed in Chapter 29, you could use the SWAT utility to configure Samba. SWAT is certainly a rich and detailed tool. But remember, like other GUI tools, it is just a front end to a group of commands. There are a substantial number of Samba commands—some related to the server, others used commonly by Samba clients.

SAMBA SERVER COMMANDS

When you configure a Samba server, you're sharing directories and printers in a format compatible with Microsoft Windows. Important Samba server commands are shown in Table A.35.

TABLE A.35: SAMBA SERVER COMMANDS

COMMAND	DESCRIPTION
make_unicodemap	Specifies a translation—from DOS or Unix text to 16-bit Unicode.
mksmbpasswd.sh	Starts a script that directly edits the SMB password file, /etc/samba/smbpasswd.
smbadduser	Sets up a database entry between a Linux user and a Microsoft Windows user; prompts for a password and enters the result in /etc/smbusers and /etc/smbpasswd.
smbcontrol	Allows you to send messages to an SMB server, such as debug, elections, and ping messages.
smbpasswd	Changes a user's Samba password; can apply to local or remote Samba servers.
smbstatus	Displays the status of connections to the local SMB server.
testparm	Checks the syntax of smb.conf.
testprns	Checks a proposed Samba share name for a printer.
winbindd	Starts the name service daemon for Microsoft Windows–style server names.

SAMBA CLIENT COMMANDS

When you configure a Samba client, you're using commands on a Linux or Unix computer to connect to a shared Samba or Microsoft Windows directory. Important Samba client commands are shown in Table A.36.

TABLE A.36: SAMBA CLIENT COMMANDS

COMMAND	DESCRIPTION
mount.smb	Allows you to use the mount command as a front end to connect to a shared Samba directory.
nmblookup	Searches for the IP address associated with a NetBIOS name.

Continued on next page

TABLE A.36: SAMBA CLIENT COMMANDS *(continued)*

COMMAND	DESCRIPTION
rpcclient	Permits connections to remote procedure calls on a Microsoft Windows server.
smbcacls	Allows you to view and set the Access Control List on a Microsoft Windows server.
smbclient	Lets you connect directly to a Samba server, with an FTP-style interface.
smbmount	Mounts a Samba filesystem; you can use the mount command as a front end to this command.
smbprint	Sends a print job to a shared printer on a Samba server.
smbumount	Unmounts a shared Samba directory.

Apache Commands

Apache is the most popular web server on the Internet, as well as the default web server for Red Hat Linux. As discussed in Chapter 30, the standard way to configure Apache is by editing the /etc/httpd/conf/httpd.conf configuration file. Commands are available to help you work with whatever Apache configuration you use. Some of the more important ones are listed in Table A.37.

TABLE A.37: APACHE COMMANDS

COMMAND	DESCRIPTION
ab	A tool for testing the performance of your Apache server.
apachectl	A control script for your Apache server.
htdbm	A new Apache 2.0 tool for managing authorized user/password databases.
htdigest	A tool that creates an authentication database of users and passwords.
htpasswd	A tool that allows you to set up individual users and passwords for your web server.
httpd	The Apache daemon; httpd -t tests the syntax of your httpd.conf configuration file.
logresolve	A tool that performs a reverse name lookup for Apache log files, so you know the computers or domains that are connecting to your server.
rotatelogs	A tool that rotates Apache log files automatically; otherwise, to use the standard logrotate job, which is governed by cron, you'd have to stop the Apache server.

Other Commands

Web Chapter 1 describes commands related to basic Linux certification. These commands are explained in more detail in Table A.38.

TABLE A.38: OTHER LINUX COMMANDS

COMMAND	DESCRIPTION
dhcpcd	Starts the DHCP client for Red Hat Linux 7.2 (now obsolete).
ifport	Associates a network type such as 10baseT (Ethernet) or 100baseT (Fast Ethernet) with a network interface; it works only with a limited group of fairly generic network drivers.
ifuser	Confirms a connection to a host or an IP address via a specific network device; commonly used in a script.
innd	Starts the Internet Network News Daemon; you can use this daemon to configure newsgroups. Key configuration files are in the /etc/news directory, including inn.conf. There's also a configuration file syntax checker, /usr/lib/news/bin/inncheck.
ncpmount	Mounts a shared Novell directory; requires the ipxutils-* and ncpfs-* RPM packages.
pump	Starts the DHCP client for Red Hat Linux 7.1 (now obsolete).
route	Lists the routing table; e.g., the route -n command lists the routing table for the local computer. Associates different IP addresses with network devices and IP gateway addresses.
slattach	Associates a network device (such as eth0) to a serial port (such as /dev/ttyS0); prepares a device for a PPP or SLIP connection.
stunnel	Incorporates SSL encryption in a direct connection between two computers over a public network such as the Internet; one way to implement virtual private networking.
su	The superuser command; a regular user who wants to assume root user privileges, and who has the root password, can use this command to log in as root. Alternatively, su -c 'command' can work for the single command.
sudo	The "superuser do" command; refers to /etc/sudoers for authorized users. By default, once the root password is given, the authorization is good for 5 minutes.
talkd	Starts the talk daemon, part of the talk-server-* RPM package, which can help one user initiate a conversation with another.
whois	Queries the Internet registry database; for example, administrative information for the Sybex website is available through the whois Sybex.com command.

Summary

This appendix summarizes some of the more important commands that you may use at the command-line interface. It is taken from the basic commands used in this book, but keep in mind that it is far from a comprehensive list.

Index